SCOTTISH PLANNING LAW AND PROCEDURE

by
ERIC YOUNG

M.A., LL.B., Hon. M.R.T.P.I., Solicitor,
Senior Lecturer in Law,
University of Strathclyde

and

JEREMY ROWAN-ROBINSON

M.A., LL.M., Legal Associate of the
Royal Town Planning Institute,
Solicitor (England and Wales),
Senior Lecturer in Law,
University of Aberdeen

with a contribution by
C. M. G. HIMSWORTH

B.A., LL.B., Solicitor (England and Wales),
Lecturer in Law, University of Edinburgh

WILLIAM HODGE & COMPANY LIMITED
GLASGOW
1985

Printed in Great Britain by
William Hodge & Co Ltd, Glasgow
ISBN 0 85279 122 4

PREFACE

When we started work on this book it was our intention simply to update Eric Young's *The Law of Planning in Scotland,* published in 1978. However, in the period since that book appeared the legislature, the executive and the courts have all been very active in the field of town and country planning. Although the government stated in 1979 that it intended to avoid constant interference with local authorities in matters of detail and to reduce the volume of circulars and other guidance being issued (see Cmnd. 7634), the period since then has been characterised by a continuous stream of primary and secondary legislation, circulars, advice and reports on planning matters. Indeed, so numerous have the changes been of late that a research report, *Development Control Performance in Scotland* (S.D.D., 1985), made a plea for a period of stability.

The numerous changes in planning law and procedures have had consequences for this book. Although it is to some extent based on, and incorporates parts of, *The Law of Planning in Scotland,* a great deal of it is new. In an attempt to set the subject-matter of the book more firmly in its administrative law context, we have also dealt with a number of topics not covered in the earlier work and have expanded the treatment of other matters. The resulting changes are such that instead of describing this book as a second edition we have thought it right to give it a new title. Nonetheless, although this book is in many respects more detailed and is wider in its scope than *The Law of Planning in Scotland,* our objective remains the same as that of the earlier work—to provide a reasonably straightforward guide to those who have to find a path through the jungle of Acts, regulations, orders, directions, decisions and ministerial guidance relating to Scottish planning law and procedures.

A further consequence of the continuing high level of activity in the legislative, executive and judicial fields has been the difficulty of producing a work which may fairly be described as up to date. We have attempted to state the law as at 1st January 1985. However, our publishers have kindly allowed us, while the book was being printed, to make reference to a number of important developments subsequent to that date. Certain other developments and proposals for change which could not be incorporated in the text of the book are mentioned in a note which follows the table of contents.

In the writing of the book we have incurred substantial debts to a number of people. Chris Himsworth gave us a great deal of assistance, re-working our initial ideas for chapter 2 and writing parts of chapters 3 and 20. Responsibility for the final version is, of course, ours. We are very grateful to our publishers for their encouragement and their willingness to accept for publication a book substantially larger that was originally envisaged; to Ruth Anderson, Helen Dignan, Elizabeth McCallum and Maureen Reid for typing (and re-typing) the manuscript; and to Edna Young for undertaking the labour of preparing the tables of cases, statutes and statutory instruments and for assisting with proof-reading. Last but not least, we owe a large debt to our families for their forbearance while we worked on the book.

ERIC YOUNG
JEREMY ROWAN-ROBINSON

'At 1.00 p.m. Winston Churchill closed his Cabinet folder and lit another cigar. Sir Edward Bridges drew his attention to the fact that there was still one remaining item.

'It was town and country planning. The determination of those days that we would not go back to the 1930s had inspired Beveridge, the Cabinet White Paper on full employment, and also the three basic reports on town and country planning by Uthwatt, Barlow and Scott . . .

'W. S. Morrison had assessed these reports and was presenting his conclusions. Winston was not amused. "Ah, yes", said he. "All this stuff about planning and compensation and betterment. Broad vistas and all that. But give to me the eighteenth century alley, where foot-pads lurk, and the harlot plies her trade, and none of this new-fangled planning doctrine."'

—Harold Wilson, *The Governance of Britain,* (Weidenfield and Nicolson, 1976)

CONTENTS

PREFACE   iii

NOTE ON RECENT DEVELOPMENTS AND PROPOSALS

  FOR CHANGE   viii

TABLE OF CASES   xi

TABLE OF STATUTES   xxviii

TABLE OF STATUTORY INSTRUMENTS..   xxxvi

ABBREVIATIONS..   xliii

CHAPTER 1

Introduction   1

CHAPTER 2

Planning, decision-making and the
  courts   20

CHAPTER 3

The administration of town and
  country planning   43

CHAPTER 4

National planning policy   58

CHAPTER 5

Local planning policy   72
A. Introduction   72
B. 'Old style' development plans and
  transition to the new system   ..   76

C. The new system   79
D. Regional reports   109
E. Non-statutory policy statements ..   112

CHAPTER 6

Development   116
A. Operations..   118
B. Material change of use   125
C. Uses specifically declared not to
  involve development   152
D. Uses specifically declared to
  involve development   161
E. Application to determine whether
  planning permission required ..   163

CHAPTER 7

Development not requiring submission
  of a planning application   167
A. Development not requiring
  planning permission   167
B. Planning permission deemed to be
  granted   171
C. Permission granted by development order   171

D. Designation of enterprise zones .. 184

CHAPTER 8

Control of development 1:
  Planning applications 185

CHAPTER 9

Control of development 2:
  The development plan and other
  material considerations 207

CHAPTER 10

Control of development 3:
  Conditions 231

CHAPTER 11

Control of development 4:
  Planning authority's decision and
  other matters 251

CHAPTER 12

Planning agreements 276

CHAPTER 13

The enforcement of planning control 289
A. Taking enforcement action .. 290
B. Immunity from enforcement
    action 310
C. Challenging enforcement notices 321
D. Consequences of enforcement
    notice 339
E. Stop notices and interdict .. 344

CHAPTER 14

Adverse planning decisions:
  compensation 353

CHAPTER 15

Adverse planning decisions:
  purchase notices 365

CHAPTER 16

Control of the existing use of land .. 374
A. Introduction 374
B. Control of existing uses, buildings
    and works 376
C. Restrictions on development
    which has been granted
    planning permission but which
    has yet to be implemented .. 380
D. Existing use development .. 388

CHAPTER 17

Positive planning 394

CHAPTER 18

Planning blight and injurious
  affection 404
A. Introduction 404
B. Planning blight 407
C. Injurious affection 418
D. Conclusion.. 427

CHAPTER 19

Special controls 429
A. Introduction 429
B. Buildings of special architectural
    or historic interest 430
C. Conservation areas 447
D. Control of advertisements .. 452
E Tree preservation 460
F. Waste land 468
G. Minerals 469
H. Industrial development certi-
    ficates 477
I. Office development permits .. 478

CHAPTER 20

Appeal and objection procedures . . 479
A. General 479
B. Written submissions 487
C. Public inquiries 490
D. Major inquiries 516

CHAPTER 21

**Challenge of plans, orders and
planning decisions in the Court of
Session** 519
A. Statutory applications to quash . . 519
B. Questioning the validity of
    enforcement notices 536

C. Appeals against s.51 determina-
    tions 536
D. Non-statutory challenge 537

Appendices
1. Planning authorities in Scotland . . 543
2. Scale of fees for planning applications 544
3. Planning circulars 546
4. Directions 551

Index 596

NOTE ON RECENT DEVELOPMENTS
AND PROPOSALS FOR CHANGE

Among the recent developments which it has not been possible to take into account in the text of this book, mention may be made of the following changes and proposals for change.

Legislation, etc.

1. The Town and Country Planning (Compensation) Act 1985 (see pp. 387 and 392 below) received the Royal Assent on 9th May 1985. S.D.D. Circular 19/1985, 'Town and Country Planning (Compensation) Act 1985' (16th July 1985), states that the government will be reviewing certain aspects of the planning compensation provisions and that a consultation paper will be issued in due course.

2. The proposals, mentioned at p. 28 below, for an accelerated procedure for judicial review, were given effect by the Act of Sederunt (Rules of Court Amendment No. 2) (Judicial Review) 1985 which came into operation on 30th April 1985. The new procedure does not, however, apply to applications to the Court of Session under s.232 or s.233 of the Town and Country Planning (Scotland) Act 1972 (see chapter 21).

3. The Council of the European Communities has agreed a directive which will make an environmental impact assessment mandatory for certain types of development (see p. 52 below and 1985 S.P.L.P. 47).

4. The Town and Country Planning (Compensation for Restrictions on Mineral Working) Regulations 1985 came into operation on 1st June 1985. These regulations apply only to England and Wales but provide an indication of the likely form of the corresponding regulations which will be introduced for Scotland. They provide that where 'mineral compensation requirements' (see pp. 472-475 below) are satisfied in relation to a revocation or discontinuance order, compensation is to be calculated in the normal way but there is to be deducted from the total figure either the sum of £2,500 or 10 per cent of a sum calculated in accordance with a formula prescribed in the regulations, whichever is the greater. The deduction is not in any case to exceed £100,000. Where 'mineral compensation requirements' are satisfied in relation to a suspension order or an order prohibiting the resumption of operations, compensation is to be calculated as for a normal discontinuance order but there is to be deducted from the total figure the sum of £5,000. In assessing compensation for a prohibition order, no account is to be taken of the value of any minerals which cannot be won or worked in consequence of the order.

5. The Town and Country Planning (General Development) (Scotland) Amendment Order 1985 introduces two new classes of permitted development associated with telecommunications, and replaces the class of development related to the Post Office (Class XV.I) in Schedule 1 to the G.D.O. with a new version which no longer deals with telecommunications. The provisions of the new order, which comes into operation on 1st November 1985, are described in S.D.D. Circular 25/1985.

6. With effect from 22nd September 1985, the Town and Country Planning (Amendment) Act 1985 extends s.60 of the Town and Country Planning (Scotland) Act 1972 (relating to the replacement of trees subject to a tree preservation order—see pp. 465 and 466 below) to trees in woodlands.

7. As from 22nd August 1985 the Town and Country Planning (Fees for Applications and Deemed Applications) (Scotland) Regulations 1983 (see p. 199 and Appendix 2 below) must be read in conjunction with the Town and Country Planning (Fees for Applications and Deemed Applications) (Scotland) Amendment Regulations 1985. The 1985 regulations increase the rates of fees for planning applications by approximately 12½ per cent and make several other relatively minor changes to the fees scheme. The changes are described in detail in S.D.D. Circular 26/1985 (cancelling S.D.D. Circular 33/1983).

Circulars, other policy guidance and proposals

1. S.D.D. Circular 9/1985 (29th May 1985) introduced national planning guidelines (see p. 64 below) on 'High Technology: Individual High Amenity Sites'. The aim of the guidelines is to ensure that a limited number of sites suitable for single-user high technology are identified and safeguarded in development plans. Planning authorities are required to notify the Secretary of State when they propose to grant planning permission to develop such a site or land adjacent to such a site (Town and Country Planning (Notification of Applications) (Scotland) Amendment Direction 1985).

2. S.D.D. Circular 17/1985, 'Development Control—Priorities and Procedures' (16th July 1985), reaffirms that planning permission should always be granted unless there are sound and clear-cut reasons for refusal. Authorities are encouraged to give special priority to planning applications for manufacturing and service industries and to deal sympathetically with proposals for the formation and expansion of small businesses. The circular also takes up a number of the recommendations in a research report *Development Control Performance in Scotland* (S.D.D., 1985).

3. S.D.D. Circular 18/1985, 'Development by Statutory Undertakers— Consultation with Planning Authorities' (16th July 1985), provides guidance on the circumstances in which proposals by statutory undertakers to carry out development which is permitted under the general development order should be the subject of prior consultation with planning authorities.

4. The Scottish Development Department has issued a revised list of 'Current Scottish Development Department and Scottish Office Finance Division Circulars and Memoranda, Acts and Statutory Instruments', current as at 30th September 1984.

5. Proposals 'to simplify the planning system and reduce the burden of control' are contained in a White Paper, *Lifting the Burden* (Cmnd. 9571), published on 16th July 1985. The package of proposals in the White Paper (many of which have already been the subject of consultation papers mentioned at various points in the text of this book) includes a commitment to introduce legislation to permit the setting up of simplified planning zones (see pp. 6, 61 and 63 below). The White Paper proposes some enlargement of the categories of development accorded 'permitted development' status by the general development order and states that the use classes order and the advertisement control regulations are to be reviewed. It is also proposed that steps be taken to improve the pre-inquiry stages of major public inquires and that the Secretary of State should have power to make an award of expenses in connection with appeals dealt with by written representations (see p. 489 below).

6. S.D.D. Circular 24/1985, 'Development in the Countryside and Green Belts' (2nd September 1985), contains a restatement and updating of policy and guidance in respect of development in the countryside and in green belts. D.H.S. Circular 40/1960 is cancelled.

Recent court cases

So far as recent decisions of the English courts are concerned, mention may be made of the following:

1. In *R.* v *London Borough of Greenwich, ex parte Patel, The Times,* 5th July 1985 the Court of Appeal refused to follow the important decision of the First Division of the Court of Session in *McDaid* v *Clydebank District Council* 1984 S.L.T. 162 (concerning challenge of the validity of enforcement notices—see pp. 294, 335 and 535 below).

2. The decision in *Purbeck District Council* v *Secretary of State for the Environment* (1982) 80 L.G.R. 545 (see pp. 366 and 368 below) was distinguished by the Court of Appeal in *Balco Transport Services Ltd.* v *Secretary of State for the Environment, The Times,* 8th August 1985 in which it was held that where land has become incapable of reasonably beneficial use in its existing state, and that state results from a breach of planning control now immune from enforcement action, the landowner can take advantage of the statutory provisions on purchase notices.

3. In *Wivenhoe Port Ltd.* v *Colchester Borough Council* [1985] J.P.L. 396 the Court of Appeal accepted that in some circumstances it is permissible to make reference to a planning application as an aid to construction of a planning permission (see p. 271 below).

TABLE OF CASES

A

A. I. & P. (Stratford) Ltd. v London Borough of Tower Hamlets   236

Accountancy Tuition Centre v Secretary of State for the Environment   498, 511

Ackerman v Secretary of State for the Environment   483, 497

Adams & Wade Ltd. v Minister of Housing and Local Government   367, 371

Ahmed v Birmingham Corporation   150

Albyn Properties Ltd. v Knox   511

Alderson v Secretary of State for the Environment   235, 246

Alexandra Transport Co. Ltd. v Secretary of State for Scotland (1972)   117

Alexandra Transport Co. Ltd. v Secretary of State for Scotland (1974)   125, 162, 271

Allen v Gulf Oil Refining Co.   406

Allen and Allen v Marple U.D.C.   409

Allnatt (London) Properties Ltd. v Middlesex County Council   229, 242, 243, 248

Amalgamated Investment and Property Co. Ltd. v John Walker and Sons   431

Anglia Building Society v Secretary of State for the Environment   217

Anisminic Ltd. v Foreign Compensation Commission   25, 534, 535, 536

Anns v Merton London Borough Council   21

Arcam Demolition and Construction Co. Ltd. v Worcestershire County Council   343

Argyll and Bute District Council v Secretary of State for Scotland   47, 116, 537

Arrondelle v Government of the United Kingdom   427

Arsenal Football Club Ltd. v Ende   529

Ashbridge Investments v Minister of Housing and Local Government   26, 524 525, 526, 532

Ashby v Secretary of State for the Environment   274

Ashley v Magistrates of Rothesay   29

Associated Provincial Picture Houses Ltd. v Wednesbury Corporation   24, 29, 30, 98, 212, 238, 252, 253, 526

Aston v Secretary of State for the Environment   146

Atkinson v Secretary of State for the Environment   240

Attorney-General v Ashborne Recreation Ground Co.   350

Attorney-General v Barnes Corporation and Ranelagh Club   280

Attorney-General v Bastow   350

Attorney-General v Calderdale Borough Council   152, 433

Attorney-General v Melville Construction Co. Ltd.   466

Attorney-General v Sharp   350

Attorney-General v Smith   350

Attorney-General, ex rel. Bedfordshire C.C. v Trustees of the Howard United Reformed Church, Bedford   436

Attorney-General, ex rel. Co-operative Retail Services Ltd. v Taff-Ely Borough Council   49, 194, 209, 259, 272

Attorney-General of the Gambia v N'Jie   529

Augier v Secretary of State for the Environment   226, 241, 280

Avis v Minister of Housing and Local Government   358

Avon County Council v Millard   276

Ayr Harbour Trustees v Oswald   31

B

Backer v Secretary of State for the Environment (1980)   314

Backer v Secretary of State for the Environment (1982)   141, 313

Balco Transport Services v Secretary of State
  for the Environment   143, 168
Bambury v London Borough of Hounslow
                                   293, 306
Banks Horticultural Products v Secretary of
  State for the Environment 224, 506, 512
Barling (David W.) v Secretary of State for
  the Environment   130, 131
Barnet London Borough Council v Eastern
  Electricity Board   466
Barratt Developments (Eastern) Ltd. v
  Secretary of State for the Environment
                                        216
Barratt Developments (Scotland) Ltd. v
  Secretary of State for Scotland
                              507, 514, 532
Barrie (James) (Sand and Gravel) Ltd. v
  Lanark District Council   335, 346
Barvis Ltd. v Secretary of State for the
  Environment   118, 119
Bath City Council v Secretary of State for
  the Environment   297, 303, 331, 442
Battelley v Finsbury Borough Council   49
Bearsden Town Council v Glasgow
  Corporation   226, 528
Beecham Group Ltd.'s Application(Re)   287
Behrman v Secretary of State for the
  Environment   500
Belfast Corporation v O. D. Cars Ltd.   354
Bell (R.) & Co. (Estates) Ltd. v Department
  of the Environment for Northern Ireland
                                        239
Bell and Colvill Ltd. v Secretary of State for
  the Environment   208, 212, 253, 514
Bellway Ltd. v Strathclyde Regional Council
                         204, 538, 539, 541, 542
Belmont Farm Ltd. v Minister of Housing
  and Local Government   155, 180
Ben Jay Auto Sales v Minister of Housing
  and Local Government   150
Bendles Motors Ltd. v Bristol Corporation
                                   127, 134
Bevan v Secretary of State for Wales   331
Bilboe (J. F.) v Secretary of State for the
  Environment   162, 192, 314
Binney and Anscomb v Secretaries of State
  for Environment and Transport   480
Birkdale District Electricity Supply Company
  v Southport Corporation   277
Birmingham Corporation v Minister of
  Housing and Local Government
                         134, 136, 162, 225, 330

Birnie v Banff County Council   240, 250
Bizony v Secretary of State for the
  Environment   239, 529
Black v. Tennent   541, 542
Blackpool Borough Council v Secretary of
  State for the Environment 134, 136, 137
Blackpool Corporation v Locker   68
Blantyre (Lord) v Clyde Navigation
  Trustees   406
Blow v Norfolk County Council   378
Bolivian and General Tin Trust v Secretary
  of State for the Environment   317
Bollans v Surrey County Council   467
Bolton Corporation v Owen   409
Bond v Nottingham Corporation   353
Bone v Staines U.D.C.   409
Borg v Khan   136
Bovis Homes (Scotland) Ltd. v Inverclyde
  District Council   31, 34, 260, 538, 539
Bovis Homes Southern Ltd.'s Application
  (Re)   287
Bowling v Leeds County Borough Council
                              409, 412, 413
Boyer (William) & Sons Ltd. v Minister of
  Housing and Local Government   506
Braddon v Secretary of State for the
  Environment   134
Bradford Metropolitan District Council v
  Secretary of State for the Environment
                                        176
Bradley (Edwin H.) & Sons Ltd. v Secretary
  of State for the Environment
                     83, 91, 92, 93, 526, 530
Bradwell Industrial Aggregates v Secretary of
  State for the Environment   212, 224
Brain v London County Council   158
Brayhead (Ascot) Ltd. v Berkshire County
  Council   34, 261
Brazil (Concrete) Ltd. v Amersham R.D.C.
                     125, 127, 147, 156, 160
Breachberry Ltd. v Secertary of State for the
  Environment   137, 138
Bremer v Haringey London Borough Council
                                        373
Brighton Borough Council v Secretary of
  State for the Environment   219
Bristol Stadium Ltd. v Brown   345, 347
Britannia (Cheltenham) Ltd. v Secretary of
  State for the Environment
                         187, 245, 246, 255

British Airports Authority v Secretary of State for Scotland
26, 27, 173, 229, 231, 232, 233, 236, 237, 238, 239, 243, 247, 248, 249, 274, 375, 526, 532

British Dredging (Services) Ltd. v Secretary of State for Wales 525

Britt v Buckinghamshire County Council
5, 119, 301, 315, 326, 468

Broderick v Erewash Borough Council 409

Bromley (London Borough of) v George Haeltschi & Son Ltd. 150

Bromley London Borough Council v Greater London Council 28

Bromsgrove District Council v Carthy 342

Bromsgrove District Council v Secretary of State for the Environment 130, 151

Brookdene Investments Ltd. v Minister of Housing and Local Government 369

Brookes v Flintshire C.C. 131

Brooks v Gloucestershire County Council
127, 129, 139, 151

Brooks and Burton v Secretary of State for the Environment
5, 37, 140, 158, 160, 182, 302

Brown v Hamilton District Council 22, 28

Brown v Hayes and Harlington U.D.C. 179

Brown v Secretary of State for the Environment 214, 224

Broxbourne Borough Council v Secretary of State for the Environment 316, 319

Broxbourne Borough Council v Small 340

Bryant & Bryant v City of Bristol 414

Buccleuch (Duke of) v Cowan 406

Buccleuch (Duke of) v Metropolitan Board of Works 419, 422

Buckhaven and Methil (Magistrates of) v Wemyss Coal Co. 349, 351

Buckinghamshire County Council v Callingham 119

Bullock v Secretary of State for the Environment 461

Burdle v Secretary of State for the Environment 127, 129, 131, 308

Burgess v Jarvis 307

Burkmar v Secretary of State for the Environment 137, 138

Burlin v Manchester City Council 383, 384

Burmah Oil Company (Burma Trading) Ltd. v Lord Advocate 353

Burn v Secretary of State for the Environment 141, 313

Burner v Secretary of State for the Environment 332

Bushell v Secretary of State for the Environment
480, 481, 483, 498, 499, 509, 510

Button v Jenkins 332

Buxton v Minister of Housing and Local Government 216, 529

C

Calcaria Construction Co. (York) Ltd. v Secretary of State for the Environment 258

Caledonian Railway Co. v Glasgow Corporation 538

Caledonian Railway Co. v Ogilvy
406, 419, 422

Caledonian Railway Co. v Walker's Trustees
406, 419, 422, 423

Caledonian Terminal Investments Ltd. v Edinburgh Corporation
140, 141, 161, 246, 378, 381, 382

Calflane Ltd. v Secretary of State for the Environment 219, 507

Camden (London Borough of) v Backer and Aird 300, 314

Camden London Borough Council v Secretary of State for the Environment (1975) 508, 509, 527

Camden (London Borough of) v Secretary of State for the Environment (1978)
129, 130, 332

Camden (London Borough of) v Secretary of State for the Environment (1980) 512

Campbell (Malcolm) v Glasgow Corporation
412, 415

Cannon Brewery Co. Ltd. v Gas, Light and Coke Co. 353

Caravans and Automobiles Ltd. v Southall Borough Council 294

Cardiff Corporation v Secretary of State for Wales 189, 191, 252, 259, 263

Cardiff Rating Authority v Guest Keen Baldwin's Iron & Steel Co. Ltd. 118

Cardigan Timber Co. v Cardiganshire C.C. 467

Carpet Decor (Guildford) Ltd. v Secretary of State for the Environment
160, 173, 242, 256, 270

Cater v Essex County Council 296

Cawoods Aggregates (South Eastern) Ltd. v Southwark London Borough 383

Cedar Holdings Ltd. v Walsall Metropolitan Borough Council 415

Central Regional Council v Clackmannan District Council 335, 346

Centre Hotels (Cranston) Ltd. v Secretary of State for the Environment 187, 271

Chadburn (Walter) & Son v Leeds Corporation 158

Chalgray Ltd. v Secretary of State for the Environment 258, 272, 332, 522

Charlton Sand & Ballast Co. v Minister of Housing and Local Government 506

Chelmsford Corporation v Secretary of State for the Environment 212, 258, 259

Chelmsford R.D.C. v Powell 33

Cheshire County Council v Woodward 116, 119

Chichester District Council v Secretary of State for the Environment 531

Choudry v Secretary of State for the Environment 304, 330

Chris Fashionware (West End) Ltd. v Secretary of State for the Environment 223, 513

Chrysanthou (Costas) v Secretary of State for the Environment 138, 139, 148, 149

Church of Scotland General Trustees v Helensburgh Town Council 416

Clarke v Minister of Housing and Local Government 137, 302

Cleaver v Secretary of State for the Environment 303, 332

Clwyd County Council v Secretary of State for Wales 264, 300, 345

Clyde & Co. v Secretary of State for the Environment 112, 210, 213, 214, 215, 217, 219, 223, 224, 228, 235

Cohen (George) 600 Group Ltd. v Minister of Housing and Local Government 158

Cole v Somerset County Council 387

Coleen Properties Ltd. v Minister of Housing and Local Government 26, 398, 502, 505, 509, 525

Coleshill and District Investment Co. Ltd. v Minister of Housing and Local Government 68, 116, 117, 118, 121, 123, 124, 125

Collis Radio Ltd. v Secretary of State for the Environment 214, 215, 217, 235, 501

Colonial Sugar Refining Co. Ltd. v Melbourne Harbour Trust Commissioners 353

Comley and Comley v Kent County Council 409

Commercial and Residential Property Development Co. Ltd. v Secretary of State for the Environment 135, 137, 138, 159, 224, 239

Company Developments (Property Ltd. v Secretary of State for the Environment 398

Continental Sprays Ltd. v Minister of Housing and Local Government 506

Cook v Secretary of State for the Environment 151

Cook v Secretary of State for Wales 151

Cooper v Bailey 121, 454

Co-operative Retail Services Ltd. v Secretary of State for the Environment 332, 494, 500, 522, 537

Co-operative Retail Services Ltd. v Taff-Ely Borough Council (1979) 49, 194, 209, 259, 272

Co-operative Retail Services Ltd. v Taff-Ely Borough Council (1983) 22

Copeland Borough Council v Secretary of State for the Environment 215, 301, 302, 311, 330

Cord v Secretary of State for the Environment 305

Costello v Dacorum District Council 291

Cottrell v Secretary of State for the Environment 319, 320

Covent Garden Community Association Ltd. v Greater London Council 114, 542

Cowper Essex v Acton Local Board 419

Crabtree (A) and Co. v Minister of Housing and Local Government 402

Crisp from the Fens Ltd. v Rutland C.C. 271, 272

Crowborough Parish Council v Secretary of State for the Environment 155

Curtiss v David O'Morgan 296

D

D.F.P. (Midlands) v Secretary of State for the Environment 514

Darlassis v Minister of Education 481, 484, 509, 510, 527

David (Thomas) (Porthcawl) Ltd. v
  Penybont R.D.C. 123, 126, 308, 311, 470
Davies v Mid-Glamorgan County Council 425
Davies v London Borough of Hammersmith
  and Fulham 211
Davies v Secretary of State for Wales
  494, 522, 528
Davis v Miller 292
Davy v Spelthorne Borough Council
  221, 290, 334, 338, 339, 538
Dawson v Secretary of State for the
  Environment 173, 177
Day and Mid-Warwickshire Motors Ltd. v
  Secretary of State for the Environment
  304, 332
de Mulder v Secretary of State for the
  Environment 130, 139, 304, 308
Denham Developments Ltd. v Secretary of
  State for the Environment 168, 304
Devonshire County Council v Allens
  Caravans (Estates) Ltd. 136, 138
Devonshire C.C. v Horton 135, 136
Dominant Sites Ltd. v Berkshire C.C. 454
Dover District Council v McKeen 322
Draco v Oxfordshire C.C. 142
Duffy v Pilling 137
Duffy v Secretary of State for the
  Environment 127, 128, 514
Duke of Wellington Social Club v Blyth
  Borough Council 416
Dundee (City of) District Council v Peddie
  351
Dunton Park Caravan Site Ltd. v Secretary
  of State for the Environment 308, 332
Dutton v Bognor Regis Urban District
  Council 21
Dyble v Minister of Housing and Local
  Government 140

E

Ealing Borough Council v Minister of
  Housing and Local Government 370
Ealing Borough Council v Ryan 161, 162
Ealing Corporation v Jones 530
Earl Car Sales (Edinburgh) Ltd. v City of
  Edinburgh District Council 335, 346
East Barnet U.D.C. v British Transport
  Commission 131, 134, 135, 136, 138,
  139, 173, 212, 270, 323
East Hampshire District Council v Secretary
  of State for the Environment 506

East Riding County Council v Park Estates
  (Bridlington) Ltd. 298
East Suffolk County Council v Secretary of
  State for the Environment 256, 270
Easter Ross Land Use Committee v Secretary
  of State for Scotland 81, 523, 528
Eckersley v Secretary of State for the
  Environment 525
Edgwarebury Park Investments v Minister
  of Housing and Local Government
  164, 538
Edmunds v Secretary of State for Wales 272
Edwards v Minister of Transport 419
Edwick v Sunbury-on-Thames U.D.C.
  (No. 2) 295
Eldon Garages Ltd. v Kingston-Upon-Hull
  County Borough Council
  289, 297, 298, 299
Ellick v Sedgemoor District Council 409
Ellinas v Secretary of State for the
  Environment 489
Ellis v Secretary of State for the
  Environment 514
Ellis v Worcestershire C.C. 269
Elmbridge B.C. v Secretary of State for the
  Environment 34
Emma Hotels Ltd. v Secretary of State for
  the Environment (1979) 149, 151
Emma Hotels Ltd. v Secretary of State for
  the Environment (1980) 134, 149
Empire Motors (Swansea) Ltd. v Swansea
  City Council 411
Enfield London Borough Council v Secretary
  of State for the Environment 207
English Clays Lovering Pochin & Co. Ltd. v
  Plymouth Corporation 182
English-Speaking Union of the Common-
  wealth v City of Westminster London
  Borough Council 165, 166
Enticott and Fullite Ltd. v Secretary of
  State for the Environment 318, 514
Errington v Metropolitan District Railway
  Co. Ltd. 398
Errington v Minister of Health 483, 524
Esdell Caravan Parks Ltd. v Hemel
  Hempstead R.D.C. 140, 220, 228, 229
Essex C.C. v Essex Incorporated Congrega-
  tional Church Union 416
Essex County Council v Minister of Housing
  and Local Government 184, 481
Essex County Council v Secretary of State
  for the Environment 158

Etheridge v Secretary of State for the
    Environment   191, 264
Evans v Dorset County Council   378
Ewen Developments Ltd. v Secretary of State
    for the Environment   173, 178, 306, 311

F

Fairmount Investments Ltd. v Secretary of
    State for the Environment
                483, 484, 502, 507, 509, 524
Farm Facilities Ltd. v Secretary of State for
    the Environment   156
Farrington (Philip) Properties Ltd. v
    Secretary of State for the Environment
                                    136
Fawcett Properties Ltd. v Buckingham
    County Council 212, 225, 232, 233, 234,
                    246, 248, 271, 538
Fayrewood Fish Farms Ltd. v Secretary of
    State for the Environment   121, 180
Federated Estates Ltd. v Secretary of State
    for the Environment   208
Finlay (Marie) v Secretary of State for the
    Environment   226, 513
Finn (L.O.) & Co. v Secretary of State
    for the Environment   217
Fitzpatrick Developments Ltd. v Minister of
    Housing and Local Government 215, 228
Flanagan v Long Eaton U.D.C.   408
Flashman v London Borough of Camden 339
Fogg v Birkenhead County Borough Council
                                    408
Forkhurst v Secretary of State for the
    Environment   156, 158, 506
Fourth Investments Ltd. v Bury Metropolitan
    Borough Council   106
France Fenwick & Co. v The King   354
Francis v Yiewsley and West Drayton U.D.C.
                                296, 298
French Kier Developments Ltd. v Secretary
    of State for the Environment
                    501, 509, 511, 512
French Kier Developments Ltd. v Secretary
    of State for the Environment (No. 2) 512
Frith v Minister of Housing and Local
    Government   148
Fry v Essex County Council   387
Furmston v Secretary of State for the
    Environment   483
Fyson v Buckinghamshire County Council
                                    143

G

Gaiman v National Association for Mental
    Health   39
Garland v Minister of Housing and Local
    Government 173, 298, 302, 311, 322, 330
Gee v National Trust   287
General Estates Co. Ltd. v Minister of
    Housing and Local Government   367
General Poster and Publicity Co. Ltd. v
    Secretary of State for Scotland 480, 481
George v Secretary of State for the
    Environment   484, 524, 528
Gill & Co. (London) Ltd. v Secretary of
    State for the Environment   500
Givaudan v Minister of Housing and Local
    Government   511
Glacier Metal Co. Ltd. v London Borough
    of Hillingdon   188, 254
Glamorgan County Council v Carter   317
Glasgow Corporation v Arbuckle Smith and
    Co.   402
Glasgow (City of) District Council v
    Secretary of State for Scotland (1980)
    121, 123, 124, 125, 165, 229, 447, 526, 531
Glasgow (City of) District Council v
    Secretary of State for Scotland (1985)
                            26, 138, 157
Glasgow (City of) Union Railway v Hunter
                            406, 419, 421
Glodwick Mutual Institute and Social Club v
    Oldham Metropolitan Borough Council
                                    413
Godstone R.D.C. v Brazil   307
Gordondale Investments Ltd. v Secretary of
    State for the Environment 523, 525, 527
Gorrie & Banks Ltd. v Musselburgh Town
    Council   227
Gosling v Secretary of State for the
    Environment   513, 531
Graham v Glasgow Corporation   29
Grampian Regional Council v City of
    Aberdeen District Council   239, 526
Grampian Regional Council v Secretary of
    State for Scotland 26, 190, 239, 267, 526
Granada Theatres Ltd. v Secretary of State
    for the Environment (1976)   489
Granada Theatres Ltd. v Secretary of State
    for the Environment (1980) 217, 253
Gravesham Borough Council v Secretary of
    State for the Environment   153, 175
Gray v Oxfordshire County Council
                            134, 137, 138

Gredley (Investment Developments) Co. Ltd.
v London Borough of Newham 142
Green v Secretaries of State for Environment
and Transport 219
Greenwich (London Borough of) v Secretary
of State for the Environment
501, 512, 514, 527
Gregory v Camden London Borough Council
216, 541
Griffiths v Secretary of State for the
Environment 521, 533
Grillo v Minister of Housing and Local
Government 143
Grover's Executors v Rickmansworth
U.D.C. 143
Growngrand Ltd. v Kensington and Chelsea
Royal Borough 389
Guildford R.D.C. v Penny 119, 138, 139

H

Haigh v Secretary of State for the
Environment 150, 304
Halford v Oxfordshire County Council 383
Halifax Building Society v Secretary of
State for the Environment 483
Hall & Co. Ltd. v Shoreham-by-Sea Urban
District Council 231, 235, 244, 246,
248, 254, 354, 396
Hallett v Nicholson 21
Hambledon and Chiddingfold Parish
Councils v Secretary of State for the
Environment 218, 510
Hamilton v Roxburgh County Council
333, 503, 509, 524, 533
Hamilton v Secretary of State for Scotland
25, 484, 524, 533, 534, 535, 536
Hamilton v West Sussex C.C. 261
Hamilton District Council v Alexander
Moffat & Son (Demolition) Ltd.
121, 125, 351, 539
Hammersmith and City Railway Co. v Brand
406, 421, 422
Hammersmith London Borough Council v
Secretary of State for the Environment
323, 330
Hammersmith London Borough Council v
Winner Investments 293
Hanily v Minister of Housing and Local
Government 193
Hanks v Minister of Housing and Local
Government 531

Hanks v Secretary of State for the
Environment 212, 228
Hansford v Minister of Housing and Local
Government 327
Harding v Secretary of State for the
Environment 181, 301
Harris v Secretary of State for Scotland
246, 498, 510, 526, 528
Harrison v Gloucester County Council 379
Hartley v Minister of Housing and Local
Government 141, 142, 151
Hartnell v Minister of Housing and Local
Government 242, 243, 532
Harwich Harbour Conservancy Board v
Secretary of State for the Environment
227
Hatfield Construction Ltd. v Secretary of
State for the Environment 221
Havering (London Borough of) v Secretary
of State for the Environment 340
Hawes v Thornton Cleveleys U.D.C. 143
Hawkey v Secretary of State for the
Environment 307
Hayns v Secretary of State for the
Environment 241
Hermanns (Walter) & Sons Ltd. v Secretary
of State for the Environment 217
Heron Corporation Ltd. v Manchester City
Council 190, 191, 258
Heron Service Stations Ltd. v Coupe 454
Hewitt v Leicester Corporation 293
Hewlett v Secretary of State for the
Environment 120, 506, 514
Hibernian Property Co. Ltd. v Secretary of
State for the Environment
484, 502, 524, 527
Hickmott v Dorset County Council 424
Hidderley v Warwickshire County Council
137, 155
High Peak Borough Council v Secretary of
State for the Environment 264
Hildenborough Village Preservation Associa-
tion v Secretary of State for the
Environment 280
Hill v Department of the Environment
409, 417
Hillhead Housing Association v Stewart 120
Hilliard v Secretary of State for the
Environment 129, 130, 147, 300
Hipsey v Secretary of State for the
Environment 140, 318

Hitchins (Robert) Builders Ltd. v Secretary of State for the Environment   245, 513
Hobbs (Quarries) Ltd. v Somerset County Council   383
Hoddesdon U.D.C. v Secretary of State for the Environment   367
Hodgetts v Chiltern District Council   341
Hollis v Secretary of State for the Environment   506, 513, 529, 532
Holmes v Bradfield R.D.C.   383
Holmes v Knowsley Borough Council   411
Holmes v Secretary of State for the Environment   208
Holmes (Peter) and Son v Secretary of State for Scotland   481, 524, 540
Hooper v Slater   178
Hope v Secretary of State for the Environment (1975)   514
Hope v Secretary of State for the Environment (1979)   513
Horwitz v Rowson   157
Hounslow (London Borough of) v Secretary of State for the Environment   296, 303, 322, 331
Hoveringham Gravels Ltd. v Chiltern District Council   269
Hoveringham Gravels v Secretary of State for the Environment   229, 355
Howard v Secretary of State for the Environment   31, 33, 325
Howell v Sunbury-on-Thames U.D.C.   124, 134
Howes v Secretary of State for the Environment   311
Hudson (D.E.) v Secretary of State for the Environment   506
Hurley v Cheshire County Council   417
Hussain v Secretary of State for the Environment   150, 160
Hutchison v Firetto   336

I

Ibbotson v Tayside Regional Council   416
Iddenden v Secretary of State for the Environment   125, 302
Impey v Secretary of State for the Environment   141, 313
Inglis v British Airports Authority   68, 425, 426
Inglis v British Airports Authority (No. 2)   426

Innes v Royal Burgh of Kirkcaldy   30, 252
Institute of Patent Agents v Lockwood   349, 351
Inverclyde District Council v Inverkip Building Co. Ltd.   25, 27, 34, 39, 189, 190, 246, 249, 250, 256, 257, 539
Inverclyde District Council v Secretary of State for Scotland 33, 189, 190, 191, 257, 258, 266, 267
Irlam Brick Company v Warrington Borough Council   271
Islington (London Borough of) v Secretary of State for the Environment   521
Iveagh v Minister of Housing and Local Government   382, 513

J

James v Brecon County Council   119
James v Minister of Housing and Local Government   260
James v Secretary of State for Wales   33, 139
Jeary v Chailey Rural District Council   290, 323, 334, 338, 339, 534
Jennings Motors Ltd. v Secretary of State for the Environment   127, 144, 145, 146, 147
Jillings (L.R.) v Secretary of State for the Environment   125, 148, 160, 513
John v Reveille Newspapers Ltd.   459
Johnston v Secretary of State for the Environment   128, 129, 132, 342
Jones v Merioneth C.C.   454
Jones v Secretary of State for the Environment   136, 139, 148, 305
Jones v Secretary of State for Wales   280
Jones v Stockport Metropolitan Borough   179, 180, 181, 390
Johnson (B.) and Co. (Builders) Ltd. v Minister of Health   481, 495
Joyce Shopfitters Ltd. v Secretary of State for the Environment   147

K

K. & B. Metals Ltd. v Birmingham City Council   378, 382
Kember v Secretary of State for the Environment   236
Kensington and Chelsea Royal London Borough Council v C.G. Hotels   120
Kensington and Chelsea (Royal Borough of) v Elmton Ltd.   459

Kensington and Chelsea (Royal Borough of) v Secretary of State for the Environment 139, 330

Kent County Council v Batchelor 461

Kent County Council v Batchelor (No. 2) 466

Kent County Council v Kingsway Investments (Kent) Ltd. 238, 348, 249, 262

Kent County Council v Secretary of State for the Environment 31, 255, 495, 499, 509, 527, 531

Kent Messenger Ltd. v Secretary of State for the Environment 219, 439, 512

Kentucky Fried Chicken (G.B.) Ltd. v Secretary of State for the Environment 507

Kerrier District Council v Secretary of State for the Environment 193, 270, 298, 299, 330

Kilmarnock (Magistrates of) v Secretary of State for Scotland 30

Kilsyth (Magistrates of) v Stirling County Council 528

King and King v Secretary of State for the Environment 306, 307

Kingston-Upon-Thames Royal London Borough Council v Secretary of State for the Environment 173, 236, 242

Kingsway Investments (Kent) Ltd. v Kent County Council 263

Kirkpatrick (J. & A.) v Lord Advocate 504, 506, 526

Knights Motors v Secretary of State for the Environment 501, 512

Kwik Save Discount Group v Secretary of State for the Environment 133, 156, 272

Kwik Save Discount Group v Secretary of State for Wales 128, 132, 133, 256, 270

L

LTSS Print and Supply Services Ltd. v Hackney London Borough Council 168

L.W.T. Contractors Ltd. v Secretary of State for the Environment 326

Ladbroke Rentals Ltd. v Secretary of State for the Environment 229, 241, 506

Lade and Lade v Brighton Corporation 413

Lake v Cheshire County Council 417

Lake District Special Planning Board v Secretary of State for the Environment 484, 507

Lamb (W.T.) Properties Ltd. v Secretary of State for the Environment 158

Lamplugh (Re) 377, 525

Larkin (C.W.) v Basildon District Council 176

Lavender (H.) & Son Ltd. v Minister of Housing and Local Government 31, 207, 480, 495, 509

Lawrie v Edinburgh Corporation 469

Lee (Isaac) v London Borough of Bromley 304

Leighton and Newman Car Sales Ltd. v Secretary of State for the Environment 145, 146, 242

Lenlyn Ltd. v Secretary of State for the Environment 325, 522

Lever Finance Ltd. v Westminister (City) London Borough Council 36, 37, 38, 193

Lewis v Secretary of State for the Environment 134, 136, 139

Lewisham Borough Council v Roberts 68

Lewisham Borough Council v South Eastern Ry. 178

Lewstar Ltd. v Secretary of State for the Environment 223

Ley and Ley v Kent County Council 410

Link Homes Ltd. v Secretary of State for the Environment 30, 207, 211

Lipson v Secretary of State for the Environment 137

Lithgow v Secretary of State for Scotland 483, 484, 510, 524, 526, 533, 534

Lobb v Secretary of State for the Environment 190, 269

Lockers Estates (Holdings) Ltd. v Oadby U.D.C. 416

London and Clydeside Estates Ltd. v Aberdeen District Council 27, 28, 32, 33, 34, 194, 260, 261, 333, 338, 339, 539

London and Clydeside Properties Ltd. v City of Aberdeen District Council 492, 504, 505, 506, 509, 531

London Ballast Co. v Buckinghamshire C.C. 33, 260

London (City of) Corporation v Secretary of State for the Environment 160, 173, 242

London County Council v Marks & Spencer Ltd. 125

London Welsh Association v Secretary of State for the Environment 512

Loromah Estates Ltd. v London Borough of Haringey 384
Louisville Investments Ltd. v Basingstoke District Council 413, 415, 416
Lovelock v Secretary of State for Transport 497
Lovelock v Minister of Transport 333
Lowe (David) & Sons Ltd. v Musselburgh Town Council 223, 225, 233, 234, 246, 284
Lucas (F.) & Sons Ltd. v Dorking and Horley R.D.C. 269, 311
Luke (Lord) of Pavenham v Minister of Housing and Local Government 505, 508, 509
Lydcare Ltd. v Secretary of State for the Environment 149, 150, 157, 160
Lyons v F. W. Booth (Contractors) Ltd. and Maidstone Borough Council 21

MAC

McCowan v Secretary of State for Scotland (1972) 523, 527
McCowan v Secretary of State for Scotland (1973) 527
McDaid v Clydebank District Council 4, 292, 294, 295, 329, 333, 334, 335, 336, 338, 535, 536, 538, 539
McDermott v Department of Transport 414
Macdonald v Glasgow Corporation 163, 343
McDonald v Howard Cook Advertising Ltd. 455
McKinnon Campbell v Greater Manchester Council 416
McLaren v Secretary of State for the Environment 226, 243, 285
McMeechan v Secretary of State for the Environment 527
McMillan v Inverness-shire County Council 527
McMillan v Strathclyde Regional Council 421
McNaughton v Peter McIntyre (Clyde) Ltd. 297, 298, 329, 334, 343
MacPherson v Secretary of State for Scotland 179, 180

M

Maddern v Secretary of State for the Environment 143
Maiden (Arthur) Ltd. v Lanark County Council (No. 1) 454, 455
Maiden (Arthur) Ltd. v Lanark County Council (No. 2) 455
Maiden (Arthur) Ltd. v Royal Burgh of Kirkcaldy 455
Maidstone Borough Council v Mortimer 342, 466
Main v Lord Doune 271
Main v Swansea City Council 194
Malvern Hills District Council v Secretary of State for the Environment 264, 347
Mancini v Coventry City Council 413, 415, 416
Manning v Secretary of State for the Environment 272
Mansi v Elstree R.D.C. 304, 305, 306, 324, 332
Marine Associates Ltd. v City of Aberdeen District Council 346
Maritime Electric Company v General Dairies Ltd. 35
Marshall v Nottingham City Corporation 134, 136, 138, 139
Mason v Secretary of State for the Environment 507
Maurice v London County Council 229, 529
Mayflower Cambridge Ltd. v Secretary of State for the Environment 137
Mead v Chelmsford R.D.C. 307
Meek v Lothian Regional Council 30
Mercer v Manchester Corporation 409
Mercer v Uckfield Rural District Council 324
Metallic Protectives Ltd. v Secretary of State for the Environment 303, 322, 329
Methuen-Campbell v Walters 152
Metropolitan Board of Works v McCarthy 422
Midlothian District Council v Secretary of State for Scotland 528
Millard v Secretary of State for the Environment 222
Miller v Weymouth and Melcombe Regis Corporation 34, 377, 513, 527, 531
Miller (James) & Partners (Guildford) Ltd. v Secretary of State for the Environment 219

Miller (T.A.) v Minister of Housing and Local Government   137, 142, 498, 501

Miller-Mead v Minister of Housing and Local Government   142, 179, 271, 272, 289, 290, 296, 297, 298, 328, 329, 333, 338, 339

Mills and Allen v City of Glasgow District Council   455

Minister of Agriculture, Fisheries and Food v Appleton   155

Minister of Transport v Holland   411

Ministry of Agriculture, Fisheries and Food v Jenkins   168

Mixnam's Properties Ltd. v Chertsey U.D.C.   233, 238

Moldene Ltd. v Secretary of State for the Environment   208

Monomart (Warehouses) Ltd. v Secretary of State for the Environment   305

Moody v Godstone R.D.C.   293

Morelli v Department of the Environment   197

Mornford Investments v Minister of Housing and Local Government   137, 156, 159

Morris v Secretary of State for the Environment   308, 331, 332

Moss' Empires Ltd. v Assessor for Glagow   25, 333

Mounsdon v Weymouth & Melcombe Regis Borough Council   270

Moxey v Hertford Rural District Council   390

Muir v Caledonian Railway Co.   406

Munnich v Godstone R.D.C.   293, 296

Murfitt v Secretary of State for the Environment   117, 312, 313

Murphy (J.) & Sons Ltd. v Secretary of State for the Environment   218

Myton Ltd. v Minister of Housing and Local Government   73, 112, 210, 211

Nisbet Hamilton v Northern Lighthouses Commissioners   406, 419

Norfolk County Council v Secretary of State for the Environment   37, 259, 272

North Sea Land Equipment v Secretary of State for the Environment   160, 305

North Surrey Water Company v Secretary of State for the Environment   222

North Warwickshire Borough Council v Secretary of State for the Environment   154

North West Leicestershire District Council v Secretary of State for the Environment   176

Northavon District Council v Secretary of State for the Environment   122, 155, 162, 180

Nowell (Executor) v Kirkburton U.D.C.   407

Newbury District Council v Secretary of State for the Environment (1981)   26, 68, 144, 145, 147, 178, 212, 233, 236, 237, 246, 249, 250, 270

Newbury District Council v Secretary of State for the Environment (1983)   223, 507

Newport v Secretary of State for the Environment   304, 332

Niarchos (London) Ltd. v Secretary of State for the Environment   208, 214, 219, 253, 511

Niarchos (London) Ltd. v Secretary of State for the Environment (No. 2)   254

Nicholls v Secretary of State for the Environment   142

Nicholson v Secretary of State for Energy   498

Nicol (D. & J.) v Dundee Harbour Trustees   540

N

National Provincial Bank Ltd. v Portsmouth Corporation   389

Nelsovil v Minister of Housing and Local Government   326

New Forest District Council v Secretary of State for the Environment   221, 225

O

Ormston v Horsham R.D.C.   296

Ostreicher v Secretary of State for the Environment   494, 497

Overland v Minister of Housing and Local Government   360

P

P.A.D. Entertainments Ltd. v Secretary of State for the Environment   33, 325

Page v Borough of Gillingham   408

Parkes v Secretary of State for the
    Environment   116, 117, 376
Patchett v Leatham   68
Patel v Betts   339
Paterson v Secretary of State for Scotland
            503, 504, 506, 526, 527, 528
Paul v Ayrshire County Council
            133, 141, 153, 254, 303
Peacock Homes Ltd. v Secretary of State
    for the Environment   223, 301, 313
Peak Park Joint Planning Board v
    Secretary of State for the Environment
            239, 241, 242, 531
Peak Park Joint Planning Board v Secretary
    of State for the Environment and Cyril
    Kay   221, 222
Peake v Secretary of State for Wales 140, 257
Peaktop Properties (Hampstead) Ltd. v
    Camden London Borough Council
            162, 389, 391, 392
Pennine   Raceway   Ltd.   v   Kirklees
    Metropolitan Borough Council (1983)
                             280, 383
Pennine   Raceway   Ltd.   v   Kirklees
    Metropolitan Borough Council (1984)
                             383, 384, 387
Penny and South Eastern Railway Co. (Re)
                             406, 419
Penwith District Council v Secretary of
    State for the Environment   242
Performance Cars Ltd. v Secretary of
    State for the Environment 495, 500, 522
Perkins v Secretary of State for the
    Environment   312, 313, 332
Perkins v West Wiltshire District Council
                                      413
Perry v Stanborough (Developments) Ltd.
                                      290
Petticoat Lane Rentals Ltd. v Secretary of
    State for the Environment 144, 145, 146
Philglow Ltd. v Secretary of State for the
    Environment   115, 142, 211, 223
Pilkington v Secretary of State for the
    Environment   268, 269, 298
Pioneer Aggregates (U.K.) Ltd. v Secretary
    of State for the Environment
            142, 144, 269, 270
Pirie v Bauld   334, 342, 343, 345
Plymouth City Corporation v Secretary of
    State for the Environment   372
Pointe Gourde Quarrying and Transport
    Co. v Sub-Intendent of Crown Lands
                                      384

Pollock v Secretary of State for the
    Environment   148, 509
Pople v Secretary of State for Scotland   510
Poyser and Mills' Arbitration (Re)
            92, 104, 511
Prengate Properties Ltd. v Secretary of
    State for the Environment 178, 306, 323
Prest v Secretary of State for Wales
            212, 219, 224, 513
Preston Borough Council v Secretary of
    State for the Environment
            34, 507, 513, 531
Price   Brothers   (Rode   Heath)   Ltd.   v
    Secretary of State for the Environment
            212, 532
Property   Investment   Holdings   Ltd.   v
    Secretary of State for the Environment
            165, 531
Prossor v Minister of Housing and Local
    Government   144, 145, 146, 242
Purbeck District Council v Secretary of
    State for the Environment   366, 368
Pye (J.A.) (Oxford) Estates Ltd. v
    Secretary of State for the Environment
            208, 211
Pye (J.A.) (Oxford) Estates Ltd. v West
    Oxfordshire District Council   212, 222
Pye (J.A.) (Oxford) Estates Ltd. v
    Wychavon District Council   221
Pyrford Properties Ltd. v Secretary of
    State for the Environment 208, 509, 525
Pyx Granite Co. Ltd. v Minister of
    Housing and Local Government
            166, 233, 236, 242, 248, 539

R

R. v Amber Valley District Council,
    ex parte Jackson   252
R. v Axbridge R.D.C.   131
R. v Berkshire County Council, ex parte
    Mangnall   224
R. v Bowman   244
R. v Bradford-on-Avon Urban District
    Council, ex parte Boulton   189, 194
R. v Bromley London Borough Council,
    ex parte Sievers   263
R. v Camden London Borough Council,
    ex parte Comyn Ching and Co.
    (London) Ltd.   444, 539
R. v Chertsey Justices, ex parte Franks   342
R. v City of London Corporation, ex
    parte Allan   114, 211

R. v Derbyshire County Council, ex parte North East Derbyshire District Council 162

R. v East Yorkshire Borough of Beverley Council, ex parte Wilson 219, 270

R. v Hammersmith and Fulham London Borough Council, ex parte People Before Profit Ltd. 104, 207, 211, 251

R. v Haringey London Borough Council, ex parte Barrs 251, 253

R. v Hillingdon London Borough Council, ex parte Royco Homes Ltd. 223, 225, 226, 235, 248, 254, 354, 396, 539

R. v Jenner 347

R. v Lambeth London Borough Council, ex parte Sharp 33, 273

R. v Liverpool Taxi Operators' Association 39

R. v Local Commissioner for Administration, ex parte Bradford Metropolitan City Council 57

R. v Melton and Belvoir Justices, ex parte Tynan 325

R. v Minister of Housing and Local Government, ex parte Chichester R.D.C. 367

R. v North Hertfordshire District Council, ex parte Sullivan 439

R. v St. Edmondsbury Borough Council, ex parte Investors in Industry Commercial Properties Ltd. 252

R. v Secretary of State for the Environment, ex parte Bilton (Percy) Industrial Properties 31, 190, 263, 537

R. v Secretary of State for the Environment, ex parte Hampshire County Council 444, 537

R. v Secretary of State for the Environment, ex parte Mistral Investments 494

R. v Secretary of State for the Environment, ex parte Newprop 202

R. v Secretary of State for the Environment, ex parte Ostler 25, 525, 534, 535

R. v Secretary of State for the Environment, ex parte Powis 180, 532

R. v Secretary of State for the Environment, ex parte Reinisch 30, 207, 271, 480, 515, 537

R. v Secretary of State for the Environment, ex parte Three Rivers District Council 340, 537

R. v Sevenoaks District Council, ex parte W. J. Terry 208, 285

R. v Sheffield City Council, ex parte Mansfield 206

R. v Smith 334

R. v Stroud District Council, ex parte Goodenough 32, 290, 444, 447, 542

R. v Worthing Borough Council 68, 191, 251

R. v Yeovil Borough Council, ex parte Trustees of Elim Pentecostal Church 259

R. (Bryson) v Ministry of Development for Northern Ireland 542

R. (Thallon) v Department of the Environment 222

R. (Nicholl) v Recorder of Belfast 528

R.K.T. Investments Ltd. v Hackney L.B.C. 34, 261

R.M.C. Management Services Ltd. v Secretary of State for the Environment 215

Rael-Brook Ltd. v Minister of Housing and Local Government 139, 158

Ragsdale v Creswick 342

Rann v Secretary of State for the Environment 159, 161

Ramson & Luck v Surbiton Borough Council 278

Ratcliffe v Secretary of State for the Environment 142, 163

Ravenseft Properties Ltd. v British Gas Corporation 22, 218

Rawson v Ministry of Health 416

Rea v Minister of Transport 509

Redbridge London Borough Council v Perry 336, 342

Reid v Mini-Cabs 349

Restormel (Borough of) v Secretary of State for the Environment 148

Rhodes v Minister of Housing and Local Government 224, 501

Richmond-upon-Thames London Borough Council v Secretary of State for the Environment (1972) 327

Richmond-upon-Thames London Borough Council v Secretary of State for the Environment (1978) 219, 449

Richmond-upon-Thames London Borough
  Council v Secretary of State for the
  Environment (1984)
              208, 221, 222, 278, 285, 531
Ricket v Metropolitan Railway Co.   422
Ridge v Baldwin   322
Roberts v Vale Royal District Council
                                  162, 192
Rochdale Metropolitan Borough Council
  v Simmonds
          173, 298, 299, 301, 302, 306, 337
Rodger (Builders) Ltd. v Fawdry   281
Rogelan Building Group v Secretary of
  State for the Environment   532
Ross v Aberdeen County Council
                        123, 138, 302, 326
Rossi v Edinburgh Corporation   29
Routh v Reading Corporation   534
Rugby School (Governors of) v Secretary
  State for the Environment   211
Russell (Alexander) Ltd. v Secretary of
  State for Scotland   187, 263

S

S.J.D. Properties Ltd. v Secretary of
  State for the Environment   150
Sabey and Sabey v Hartlepool County
  Borough Council   415
Sabey (H.) & Co. Ltd. v Secretary of
  State for the Environment   506
Sainsbury (J.) Ltd. v Secretary of State
  for the Environment   220
St. Albans District Council v Norman
  Harper Autosales Ltd.   342
St. John's Church, Bishop's Hatfield
  (Re)   152
St. John's Church, Galashiels (Trustees
  of) v Borders Regional Council
                        413, 414, 415, 416
St. Winifred's, Kenley (Re)   152, 156, 157
Sainty v Minister of Housing and Local
  Government   174, 176
Salisbury (A.L.) Ltd. v York Corporation
                                      391
Salisbury District Council v Secretary of
  State for the Environment   264, 269
Sample (Warkworth) Ltd. v Alnwick
  District Council   348
Sampson's Executors v Nottingham
  County Council   153

Sand and Gravel Association Ltd. v
  Buckinghamshire County Council
              98, 103, 106, 253, 520, 530
Sanders v Secretary of State for the
  Environment   331
Scarborough Borough Council v Adams
                        293, 294, 339, 341
Schleider v Secretary of State for the
  Environment   527
Scott v Secretary of State for the
  Environment   302
Scott Markets Ltd. v London Borough
  of Waltham Forest   346
Scrivener v Minister of Housing and Local
  Government   158, 160
Scurlock v Secretary of State for Wales
                                  153, 174
Secretary of State for Education and
  Science v Tameside Metropolitan
  Borough Council   540
Seddon Properties Ltd. v Secretary of
  State for the Environment   512, 525
Segal v Manchester Corporation   411
Shanley (M.J.) Ltd. (In liquidation) v
  Secretary of State for the Environment
                             245, 246, 396
Sheffield City Council v Secretary of
  State for the Environment   512
Shemara Ltd. v Luton Corporation   258
Shephard v Buckinghamshire County
  Council   125, 139, 157, 160
Shepherd and Shepherd v Lancashire
  County Council   424, 425
Sheppard v Secretary of State for the
  Environment   269, 270, 371, 372
Sievers v London Borough of Bromley   33
Simmonds v Secretary of State for the
  Environment   178
Simpson v Edinburgh Corporation
          25, 73, 207, 209, 216, 529, 541, 542
Sinclair-Lockhart's Trustees v Central
  Land Board   152
Skinner and King v Secretary of State for
  the Environment   293, 295
Slough Estates Ltd. v Slough Borough
  Council (No. 2) 259, 270, 271, 272, 538
Smart & Courtney Dale Ltd. v Dover
  R.D.C.   366, 368
Smart (J.) & Co. (Contractors) Ltd. v
  Secretary of State for Scotland
                             506, 507, 508

Smith v East Elloe R.D.C.
25, 523, 524, 533, 534, 535, 536
Smith v King 324, 336, 337, 338
Smith v Secretary of State for the Environment 167
Smith v Somerset County Council 409
Smyth v Minister of Housing and Local Government 167
Snook v Secretary of State for the Environment 134, 136, 138, 139, 148
Snow v Secretary of State for the Environment 501
Snowden v City of Bradford Metropolitan Council 223
Sorrell v Maidstone R.D.C. 393
Sosmo Trust Ltd. v Secretary of State for the Environment 219, 220
South Cambridge District Council v L.F.W. Stokes 342
South Glamorgan County Council v Hobbs (Quarries) Ltd. 182
South Oxfordshire District Council v Secretary of State for the Environment 214, 217, 222, 254, 264
Southend-on-Sea Corporation v Hodgson (Wickford) Ltd. 30, 36, 37, 38
Southern Olympia (Syndicate) Ltd. v West Sussex County Council 383
Sovmots Investments Ltd. v Secretary of State for the Environment 214, 219, 220, 399
Spackman v Secretary of State for the Environment 222, 264
Sparkes v Secretary of State for Wales 411
Spedeworth v Secretary of State for the Environment 387
Square Meals Frozen Foods Ltd. v Dunstable Corporation 335, 339
Stafford v Minister of Health 483
Steele v Minister of Housing and Local Government 527
Steeples (J.J.) v Derbyshire County Council 33, 252, 261, 285
Stevens v London Borough of Bromley 292, 293, 342
Stevenson v Midlothian District Council 469
Stodart v Dalzell 281
Stoke-on-Trent City Council v B. & Q. (Retail) Ltd. 350
Strable v Borough Council of Dartford 21
Street v Essex County Council 120

Stringer v Minister of Housing and Local Government 2, 31, 73, 207, 212, 213, 215, 216 218, 224, 267, 284, 285, 286, 355, 480
Stuart v British Airports Authority 426
Stubbs v West Hartlepool Corporation 412, 413
Sunbell Properties Ltd. v Dorset County Council 273
Sunbury-on-Thames U.D.C. v Mann 117, 179
Sutton London Borough Council v Secretary of State for the Environment 188, 192, 226, 270
Swallow and Pearson v Middlesex County Council 307
Sykes v Secretary of State for the Environment 155, 303

T

T.L.G. Building Materials v Secretary of State for the Environment 128, 131, 308, 331
Tameside Metropolitan Borough Council v Secretary of State for the Environment 221, 225, 527
Tandridge District Council v Powers 342
Tandridge District Council v Secretary of State for the Environment 157
Tarmac Properties v Secretary of State for Wales 285
Tempo Discount Warehouses Ltd. v London Borough of Enfield 217, 512
Tessier v Secretary of State for the Environment 156, 157, 158
Test Valley Investments Ltd. v Tanner 342
Thirkwell (Lewis) Ltd. v Secretary of State for the Environment 258, 514
Thornville Properties v Secretary of State for the Environment 211, 512
Thrasyvoulou v Secretary of State for the Environment 326
Tidswell v Secretary of State for the Environment 179, 290
Tierney (Francis Joseph) v Secretary of State for the Environment 212, 513
Toogood v Bristol Corporation 373
Tiverton and North Devon Railway Co. v Loosemore 353

Tower Hamlets (London Borough of) v Secretary of State for the Environment 223

Trentham (G. Percy) Ltd v Gloucestershire County Council 125, 127, 129, 131, 133, 160

Trevors Warehouses Ltd. v Secretary of State for the Environment 304, 332

Tromans v Secretary of State for the Environment 208

Toomey (J.) Motors Ltd. v Basildon District Council 145, 147, 270

Toomey (J.) Motors Ltd. v Secretary of State for the Environment 300

Tulk v Moxhay 281

Turner v Secretary of State for the Environment 529, 530

U

United Refineries v Essex County Council 118, 264

V

Vale Estates (Acton) Ltd. v Secretary of State for the Environment 509

Vale of Glamorgan Borough Council v Palmer and Bowles 33, 463, 466

Vickers-Armstrong v Central Land Board 128, 147

Vyner v Secretary of State for the Environment 130, 149

W

W. & S. (Long Eaton) Ltd. v Derbyshire C.C. 373

Wain v Secretary of State for the Environment (1978) 332

Wain v Secretary of State for the Environment (1981) 368

Wakelin v Secretary of State for the Environment 129, 132, 161

Wallace v Simmers 281

Walters v Secretary of State for the Environment 218, 220

Walton-on-Thames Charities (Trustees of) v Walton and Weybridge U.D.C. 270, 393

Warnock v Secretary of State for the Environment 130, 150, 155

Watch House, Boswinger (Re) 377

Watford Borough Council v Secretary of State for the Environment 296

Watt v Jamieson 405

Watt v Lord Advocate 26, 526, 539

Waverley District Council v Secretary of State for the Environment 256

Wealden District Council v Secretary of State for the Environment 119, 302, 331

Webb v Minister of Housing and Local Government 524

Webber v Minister of Housing and Local Government 144

Wednesbury Corporation v Minister of Housing and Local Government (No. 2) 498

Wells v Minister of Housing and Local Government 37, 38, 165, 166, 222

Welsh Aggregates Ltd. v Secretary of State for the Environment 126, 181, 264, 271

Wessex Regional Health Authority v Salisbury District Council 253, 255

Western Fish Products Ltd. v Penwith District Council (1977) 276

Western Fish Products Ltd. v Penwith District Council (1981) 36, 38, 39, 49, 117, 165, 223

Westminster Bank Ltd. v Beverley Borough Council 238

Westminster Bank Ltd. v Minister of Housing and Local Government 27, 228, 229, 238, 353, 354, 355, 460, 510

Westminster City Council v British Waterways Board 217, 225, 234, 254

Westminster City Council v Great Portland Estates plc. 2, 84, 85, 92, 97, 99, 104, 106, 112, 114, 211, 212, 217, 225, 234, 254, 284

Westminster City Council v Jones 350

Westminster (City of) v Secretary of State for the Environment 302

Westminster City Council v Secretary of State for the Environment 99, 106, 208, 222, 278, 533, 535

Westminster City Council v Secretary of State for the Environment (No. 2) 449

Westminster Renslade Ltd. v Secretary of State for the Environment 208, 221, 235, 254, 396, 507

Wheatcroft (Bernard) Ltd. v Secretary of State for the Environment 188, 238, 255

Wheatfield Inns (Belfast) Ltd. v Croft Inns Ltd. 142

Whistlecraft (George A.) v Secretary of State for the Environment 223

Whiteacre Estates U.K. Ltd. v Secretary of State for the Environment 532

Wholesale Mail Order Supplies Ltd. v Secretary of State for the Environment 507

Wild v Secretary of State for the Environment 326

Williams v Cheadle and Gatley U.D.C. 409

Williams v Minister of Housing and Local Government 125, 126, 127, 138, 139

Williams-Denton v Watford R.D.C. 131

Williamson v Stevens 256

Wilson v Independent Broadcasting Authority 542

Wilson v Secretary of State for the Environment 527

Wilson v Secretary of State for Scotland 506

Wilson v West Sussex C.C. 138, 256, 257, 272, 301

Wimpey (George) & Co. Ltd. v New Forest District Council 241, 267

Winchester City Council v Secretary of State for the Environment 502, 507

Windsor and Maidenhead Royal Borough Council v Brandrose Investments Ltd. 286, 291

Winmill v Secretary of State for the Environment 134, 137, 138, 139

Winton v Secretary of State for the Environment 132, 156

Wipperman v Barking London Borough Council 142, 151

Wontner Smith and Co. v Secretary of State for the Environment 489, 502

Wood v Secretary of State for the Environment 129, 173, 257

Wordie Property Company Ltd. v Secretary of State for Scotland 214, 219, 238, 499, 504, 505, 506, 508, 509, 511, 522, 525, 526, 527

Worthy Fuel Injection Ltd. v Secretary of State for the Environment 311

Wyse v Newcastle-under-Lyme Borough Council 409

Y

Ynys Mon-Isle of Anglesey Borough Council v Secretary of State for Wales 226

Ynystawe, Ynyforgan and Glais Gipsy Site Action Group v Secretary of State for Wales 224, 235, 512

Young v Neilson 174

Young v Secretary of State for the Environment 143, 168

TABLE OF STATUTES

1845

Lands Clauses Consolidation (Scotland) Act (8 & 9 Vict., c.19) - - 422
    s.61   401, 418, 419, 420, 421, 423, 424
    s.114 - - - - - 418

Railways Clauses Consolidation (Scotland) Act (8 & 9 Vict., c.33)
    s.6 - - 401, 421, 422, 423, 424
    s.16 - - - - - 421, 422

1868

Court of Session Act (31 & 32 Vict., c.100)
    s.91 - - - - - - 28

1892

Burgh Police (Scotland) Act (55 & 56 Vict., c.55)
    s.381 - - - - - - 349

1909

Electric Lighting Act (9 Edw. 7, c.34) - - - - - 171, 487

Housing, Town Planning, Etc. Act (9 Edw. 7, c.44)   - - - 5, 8, 11

1919

Housing, Town Planning, Etc. (Scotland) Act (9 & 10 Geo. 5, c.60) - 8, 10

1925

Town Planning (Scotland) Act (15 & 16 Geo. 5, c.17) - - - - 8

Law of Property Act (15 & 16 Geo. 5, c.20)
    s.54 - - - - - - 287

1932

Town and Country Planning (Scotland) Act (22 & 23 Geo. 5, c.50) - 8, 10, 11, 278

Sunday Entertainments Act (22 & 23 Geo. 5, c.51)   - - - - 29

1943

Town and Country Planning (Interim Development) (Scotland) Act (6 & 7 Geo. 6, c.43) - - - - 10

1945

Town and Country Planning (Scotland) Act (8 & 9 Geo. 6, c.33) - 397

1946

Statutory Instruments Act (9 & 10 Geo. 6, c.36)
    s.2 - - - - - - 62

1947

Acquisition of Land (Authorisation Procedure) (Scotland) Act (10 & 11 Geo. 6, c.42) - - - 399, 422
    s.1 - - - - - - 420
    Sched. 2 - - - - - 421
    Sched. 2, para 4 - - - 420, 421

Town and Country Planning Act (10 & 11 Geo. 6, c.51) - - - 9, 296, 354

Town and Country Planning (Scotland) Act (10 & 11 Geo. 6, c.53) 9, 10, 11, 12, 14, 15, 17, 72, 74, 77, 123, 141, 162, 163, 228, 278, 356-359, 391, 430, 541
    Part II - - - - 167, 168
    Part III - - - - 397
    Part V - - - 357, 359
    Sched. 3 - - 357, 388, 390

1948

Agriculture (Scotland) Act (11 & 12 Geo. 6, c.45) - - - - 179

1949

Agricultural Holdings (Scotland) Act (12, 13 & 14 Geo. 6, c.75) - - 193

1953

Town and Country Planning Act (1 & 2 Eliz. 2, c.16) - - - 12, 357

Historic Buildings and Ancient Monuments Act (1 & 2 Eliz. 2, c.49) - - - - - - 445
    Part I - - - - 448

1954

Town and Country Planning (Scotland) Act (2 & 3 Eliz. 2, c.73) 12, 357, 358

1957

Electricity Act (5 & 6 Eliz. 2, c.48) 171, 487

Housing Act (5 & 6 Eliz. 2, c.56)   -   525

1958

Tribunals and Inquiries Act (6 & 7
Eliz. 2, c.66) -   -   -   -   -   482

1959

Building (Scotland) Act (7 & 8 Eliz.
2, c.24) -   -   -   -   -   -   429
   s.17   -   -   -   -   -   -   446

Town and Country Planning (Scotland) Act (7 & 8 Eliz. 2, c.70)   -   12
   s.24   -   -   -   -   -   -   400
   s.38   -   -   -   -   -   -   408

1960

Caravan Sites and Control of
Development Act (8 & 9 Eliz. 2,
c.62)   -   -   182, 183, 296, 334, 429

1962

Local Authorities (Historic Buildings)
Act (10 & 11 Eliz. 2, c.36)   -   445, 448

Town and Country Planning Act (10
& 11 Eliz. 2, c.38) -   -   -   329, 334

Pipe-lines Act (10 & 11 Eliz. 2, c.58) -   171

1963

Town and Country Planning Act
(c.17)   -   -   -   -   -   -   390
   s.2   -   -   -   -   -   -   393

Land Compensation (Scotland) Act
(c.51)   -   -   -   -   78, 260, 373
   s.12   -   -   -   -   362, 404, 426
   s.16   -   -   -   -   -   404, 418
   s.23   -   -   -   -   -   -   388
   s.39   -   -   -   -   370, 371, 417

1964

Local Government (Development
and Finance) (Scotland) Act (c.67)
   s.1   -   -   -   -   -   -   400
   s.7   -   -   -   -   -   -   401

1966

Housing (Scotland) Act (c.49)
   Part II   -   -   -   -   -   450
   Part III   -   -   -   -   -   450

1967

Land Commission Act (c.1)   -   -   12

Forestry Act (c.10)   -   -   -   -   465
   s.4   -   -   -   -   -   -   467
   s.9   -   -   -   -   -   -   465
   s.15   -   -   -   -   -   -   465

Parliamentary Commissioner Act
(c.13)   -   -   -   -   -   53, 54
   s.5   -   -   -   -   -   53, 54
   s.12   -   -   -   -   -   -   54
   Sched. 3   -   -   -   -   -   54

Civic Amenities Act (c.69)
   s.4   -   -   -   -   -   -   445
   s.5   -   -   -   -   -   -   445

Countryside (Scotland) Act (c.86)
   s.13   -   -   -   -   -   -   283
   s.49A   -   -   -   -   -   283

1968

New Towns (Scotland) Act (c.16)
   s.6   -   -   -   -   -   62, 184

1969

Commissioner for Complaints Act
(N.I.) (c.25)   -   -   -   -   55

Town and Country Planning (Scot-
land) Act (c.30)   -   20, 75, 77, 79, 91,
                    262, 278, 296, 339, 431
   Part IV   -   -   -   -   -   397
   s.58   -   -   -   -   -   -   445
   s.65   -   -   -   -   -   -   49

Housing (Scotland) Act (c.34)
   Part I   -   -   -   -   -   450
   s.4   -   -   -   -   -   -   450

1970

Conveyancing and Feudal Reform
(Scotland) Act (c.35)   -   -   -   271
   s.1   -   -   -   -   -   -   288

Building (Scotland) Act (c.38)   -   -   429

Chronically Sick and Disabled
Persons Act (c.44) -   -   -   -   257

1971

Tribunals and Inquiries Act (c.62)   -   102,
                    481, 482, 490, 521, 533
   s.1   -   -   -   -   -   90, 482
   s.11   -   -   -   -   -   -   482
   s.12   -   -   -   -   482, 489, 511

Town and Country Planning Act
(c.78)   -   -   -   -   84, 97, 341
   s.22   -   -   -   -   -   -   162
   s.33   -   -   -   -   -   -   146
   s.35   -   -   -   -   -   -   517
   s.52   -   -   -   -   276, 286, 287
   s.54   -   -   -   -   -   -   433
   s.59   -   -   -   -   -   -   461
   s.62   -   -   -   -   -   -   461

s.87 - - - - - - 312
s.89 - - - - - - 342
s.96 - - - - - - 442
s.169 - - - - - 392
s.180 - - - - - 366
s.243 - - 334, 335, 336, 337
s.284 - - - - - 292
Sched. 8, para 11 - - - 389
Sched. 18, para 1 - - - 392

1972

Town and Country Planning (Amendment) Act (c.42)
s.10 - - - - - - 451

Town and Country Planning (Scotland) Act (c.52) 10, 16, 47, 95, 98, 116,
121, 122, 125, 126, 152, 153, 161,
162, 163, 212, 213, 262, 268
s.3 - - - - - - 49
Part II - 58, 75, 76, 77, 79, 520
s.4 - - - - - 46, 80, 93
s.5 46, 80, 81, 83, 84, 85, 86, 87,
110, 213
s.6 - 46, 82, 83, 87, 88, 94, 530, 540
s.7 - - 46, 61, 88, 89, 90, 91, 92
s.8 - - - - - 46, 93, 94
s.9 47, 94, 95, 96, 97, 100, 102, 213
s.10 - - - 47, 101, 102, 107, 530
s.11 - - - - - 47, 102
s.12 - - - 47, 61, 102, 105, 481
s.13 - - - - 47, 106, 107
s.14 - - - - - - 89
s.16 - - - - - 93, 106
s.17 - - - - - - 79
s.18 - - - - - - 78
Part III 163, 164, 167, 168, 169, 320,
339, 341, 380, 381, 386, 387
s.19 116, 119, 122-124, 133, 151, 152,
153, 154, 155, 157, 161, 162, 163,
167, 176, 283, 323, 356, 358, 388,
452, 469, 476
s.20 167, 168, 171, 185, 290, 320, 341,
388
s.21 - - 62, 172, 184, 356, 380
s.23 - - - - - 195, 205
s.24 - 189, 193, 194, 198, 205, 477
s.25 - - 195, 198, 199, 205, 448
s.26 47, 69, 74, 160, 194, 205, 207, 208,
210, 212, 214, 231, 232, 244, 251,
257, 258, 284, 450, 460, 461, 493,
494, 495, 497, 498, 500, 508
s.27 47, 160, 231, 232, 240, 242, 243,
244, 247, 256, 258, 375, 461

s.27A - - 47, 232, 473, 475, 476
s.28 - - - 47, 192, 209
s.29 - - - 47, 187, 257, 262, 478
s.30 - - 47, 146, 256, 257, 268, 270
s.30A - - - - 47, 259
s.31 - - - 47, 164, 261, 380
s.31A - - - - 47, 192
s.32 - - 202, 203, 209, 273, 521
s.33 61, 166, 192, 266, 267, 268, 322,
476, 485, 487, 490, 501, 521
s.34 - 192, 260, 266, 485, 487, 490
s.35 - - - - - 361, 362
s.36 - - - - - - 362
s.37 - - - - - - 171
s.38 232, 240, 262, 263, 264, 265, 365,
386, 471
s.39 232, 240, 262, 263, 264, 265, 365,
386
s.40 - - - - 262, 264, 265
s.41 - - - - - 265, 266
s.41A - - - - 232, 471
s.42 46, 47, 376, 380-383, 385, 387,
472, 473, 475, 539
s.43 - - - - 380, 385, 386
s.44 - - - - - 268, 517
s.45 - - - - - - 517
s.46 - - - - - - 517
s.47 - - - - - - 517
s.49 46, 47, 241, 376-379, 381, 450,
472, 473, 475
s.49A - - 46, 47, 473, 474, 475
s.49B - - - 46, 47, 473, 474
s.49D - - - - - - 475
s.49E - - - - - - 475
s.49G - - - - - 46, 474
s.50 15, 16, 31, 46, 47, 68, 254,
276-288, 291, 440, 450
s.51 163, 164, 165, 166, 169, 485, 536,
537
Part IV - - - - 169, 386
s.52 - - - - 47, 432, 433, 434
s.53 47, 290, 435, 438, 440, 441, 442,
446, 447
s.54 - - 47, 433, 436, 438, 439, 440
s.54A - - - 47, 441, 449
s.54B - - - - - 441
s.54C - - - 47, 446, 449
s.55 - - - 47, 435, 436, 437
s.56 - - 47, 432, 437, 444, 449
s.57 - - - 47, 232, 461, 462
s.58 - - - 461, 462, 463, 464
s.59 - - - - - - 464

s.59A	-	-	-	-	467, 468
s.60	-	-	-	-	47, 465, 466
s.61	-	-	-	451, 452, 456, 460
s.62	-	-	-	-	163, 171, 452
s.63	-	-	-	443, 468, 469, 485
s.63A	-	-	-	-	- 469
s.64	-	-	-	-	274, 477, 478
s.65	-	-	-	-	477, 478
s.66	-	-	-	-	477, 478
s.67	-	-	-	-	477, 478
s.68	-	-	-	-	477, 478
s.69	-	-	-	-	477, 478
s.70	-	-	-	-	477, 478
s.76	-	-	-	-	- 478
s.77	-	-	-	-	- 478
s.78	-	-	-	-	- 478
s.79	-	-	-	-	- 478
s.80	-	-	-	-	- 478
s.81	-	-	-	-	- 478
s.82	-	-	-	-	- 478
s.83	-	-	-	-	- 478
Part V	-	-	-	-	47, 386
s.84	74, 239, 284, 290, 292-296, 298, 301-3, 306, 307, 309, 310-315, 323, 324, 340, 347, 450, 458, 469, 470
s.84A	-	-	-	-	- 290
s.85	294, 295, 306, 314, 321-329, 332-338, 342-344, 346, 347, 469, 535, 536, 537
s.86	-	297, 334, 336, 341-343, 470
s.87	-	-	-	-	344-347
s.87A	-	-	-	-	310, 469
s.88	-	340, 341, 343, 344, 469
s.89	-	-	-	-	339, 340
s.89A	-	-	-	-	- 340
s.90	-	-	-	-	315-320
s.91	-	-	-	319, 320, 485
s.92	-	-	-	47, 442, 450
s.93	-	-	-	-	47, 442
s.94	-	-	-	-	47, 442
s.95	-	-	-	-	47, 442
s.96	-	-	-	-	47, 442
s.97	-	-	47, 443, 444, 451
s.98	-	-	-	-	466, 467
s.99	-	-	-	47, 466, 467, 485
s.100	-	-	-	47, 379, 475
s.101	-	-	-	-	452, 459
Part VI	-	-	370, 396, 397, 403
s.102	-	46, 47, 74, 395, 397-399
s.103	-	-	-	-	- 399
s.104	-	-	-	403, 444, 445
s.105	-	-	-	-	403, 444
s.106	-	-	-	-	403, 445
s.107	-	-	-	-	403, 445
s.108	-	-	-	-	- 401
s.109	-	46, 47, 395, 399, 400, 403
s.110	-	-	-	-	46, 47
s.113	-	-	46, 47, 401, 402, 403
s.114	-	-	-	46, 47, 400
s.115	-	-	-	-	- 403
s.116	-	-	-	-	- 403
s.117	-	-	-	-	- 401
s.118	-	-	-	-	- 401
s.119	-	-	-	-	- 401
s.120	-	-	-	-	- 401
s.121	-	-	-	-	- 399
Part VII	-	-	358-364, 385, 388
s.124	-	-	-	-	- 359
s.125	-	-	-	-	- 359
s.126	-	-	-	-	- 359
s.127	-	-	-	-	- 359
s.128	-	-	-	-	- 359
s.129	-	-	-	-	- 359
s.130	-	-	-	-	- 359
s.131	-	-	-	-	- 359
s.132	-	-	-	-	- 359
s.133	-	-	-	-	- 359
s.134	-	-	-	-	- 359
s.135	-	-	-	-	- 359
s.136	-	-	-	265, 360, 361
s.137	-	-	-	-	- 361
s.138	-	-	-	-	- 361
s.139	-	-	-	-	- 360
s.141	-	-	-	-	- 362
s.142	-	-	-	-	- 362
s.143	-	-	-	-	- 362
s.144	-	-	-	-	- 362
s.146	-	-	-	-	- 363
s.147	-	-	-	-	- 363
s.148	-	-	-	-	363, 385
s.149	-	-	-	-	- 363
s.153	-	- 356, 383-385, 387, 472
s.153A	-	-	383, 387, 472, 473
s.154	-	-	-	-	356, 387
s.155	-	-	-	-	384, 385
s.156	-	-	-	-	359, 385
s.157	-	-	-	-	- 385
s.158	-	- 265, 356, 384, 390-393
s.159	-	-	-	378, 379, 475
s.159A	-	-	-	378, 473, 475
s.159B	-	-	-	378, 473, 475
s.160	-	-	-	-	- 443
s.161	-	-	-	-	- 443
s.162	-	-	-	432, 438, 443
s.163	-	-	-	-	462, 467
s.164	-	-	-	-	- 467

s.165	- - - -	452, 459
s.166	- - - -	347, 348
s.167A	- - -	472, 474, 475
s.167B	- - - -	473
s.167C	- - - -	473
Part IX	- - - -	354
s.169	- 265, 365, 366, 369-372	
s.170	- - - -	370
s.171	- - - -	371
s.172	- - -	369-371
s.173	- - -	371, 372
s.175	- - - -	371
s.176	- - -	373, 385
s.177	- - -	373, 385
s.178	- - -	373, 379
s.179	- - -	373, 443
s.180	- - -	373, 462
s.181	- 407-409, 411, 414, 415	
s.182	- - 410, 412-414	
s.183	- - -	414, 415
s.184	- - - -	415
s.185	- - - -	417
s.186	- - - -	418
s.187	- - -	414, 417
s.188	- - - -	415
s.189	- - - -	411
s.190	- - - -	411
s.191	- - - -	417
s.192	- - - -	411
s.193	- - - -	411
s.194	- - -	413, 416
s.195	- - - -	417
s.196	- - 408, 410, 411, 414	
s.197	- - 370, 371, 417	
Part X	- - - -	274
s.198	- - -	240, 274
s.198A	- - - -	275
s.199	- - - -	275
s.203	- - - -	275
s.204	- - -	274, 275
s.205	- - - -	275
s.205A	- - - -	275
s.206	- - - -	275
s.210A	- - - -	275
Part XI	- - - -	274
s.211	- - - -	274
s.212	- - - -	274
s.214	- - - -	274
s.224	- - - -	520
s.226	- - - -	265
s.231	18, 22, 23, 93, 106, 320, 322, 332, 336, 371, 378, 382, 519, 520, 521, 522, 533, 535, 536, 537	
s.232	18, 22, 23, 93, 106, 519, 520, 522, 526, 527, 528, 530, 531, 532, 533, 535, 536, 537	
s.233	18, 22, 23, 34, 202, 248, 268, 320, 322, 332, 336, 371, 378, 382, 482, 519, 520, 521, 522, 526, 527, 528, 530, 531, 532, 533, 535, 536, 537	
s.234	- - -	166, 519, 537
s.235	- - - -	274
s.236	- - - -	274
s.237	- - - -	396
s.243	- - - -	415
s.251	- - -	469, 470, 476
s.251A	- - - -	472
s.253	- - 168, 169, 436, 463	
s.254	- - - -	168
s.255	- - - -	168
s.257	- - - -	441
s.260	- - -	290, 382
s.262	- - -	47, 447, 448
s.262A	- - -	47, 449, 450
s.262B	- - -	47, 448
s.263	- - 384, 388, 391, 393	
s.265	- - -	292, 345
s.266	- - -	292, 345
s.267	481, 482, 494, 497, 500, 514	
s.269	- - - -	293
s.270	- - -	292, 348
s.273	- - -	62, 387, 452
s.274	- - -	228, 446
s.275	116, 117, 118, 122, 141, 152, 154, 155, 179, 274, 399, 401, 433, 438, 449, 452, 469	
s.278	- - -	398, 420, 421
s.279	- - - -	485
Sched. 3	- - -	74, 77, 78
Para. 1	- - -	76, 77
Para. 3	- - - -	77
Para. 5	- - - -	77
Sched. 4	- - - -	78
Sched. 5		
Para. 1	- - - -	77
Para. 2	- - - -	78
Para. 3	- - - -	78
Para. 5	- - - -	78
Para. 5A	- - - -	79
Para. 6	- - - -	79
Para. 7	- - - -	79
Sched. 6	369, 375, 384, 388-393, 426, 445	

Part I - - - 356, 358, 388	s.20 - - - - - - 427
Para. 1 - - - - 389, 393	s.21 - - - - - - 427
Part II - - -356, 358, 390-392	s.22 - - - - - - 427
Para. 3 - - - - - 392	s.24 - - - - - - 427
Para. 7 - - - - - 393	s.25 - - - - - - 427
Para. 8 - - - - - 393	s.26 - - - - - - 427
Para. 10 - - - - 389	s.27 - - - - - - 418
Para. 12 - - - - 389	s.31 - - - - - - 418
Para. 13 - - - - - 390	s.41 - - - - - - 419
Sched. 7 - - - - 485, 486	s.49 - - - - - 289, 370, 420
Para. 2 - - 326, 327, 486, 522	s.50 - - - - - 370, 420
Para. 3 - - - - - 486	s.51 - - - - - - 420
Para. 5 - - - - 500, 514	s.52 - - - - - - 420
Para. 7 - - - - - 489	s.53 - - - - - - 420
Sched. 10 - - - - 438	s.54 - - - - - - 421
Para. 5 - - - - - 440	s.61 - - - - - - 424
Para. 7 - - - - - 441	Part V - - - - 289, 417
Para. 8 - - - - - 441	s.64 - - - - - 408, 416
Part II - - - - - 442	s.65 - - - - - 408, 416
Sched. 12 - - - - 318, 319	s.66 - - - - - 408, 409
Para. 4 - - - - - 320	s.67 - - - - - - 409
Para. 6 - - - - - 320	s.68 - - - - - 409, 413
Sched. 16 - - - 369, 388, 391	s.69 - - - - - 409, 415
Sched. 17 - - - - 373, 443	s.70 - - - - - 408, 409
Sched. 18 - - - - - 275	s.71 - - - - - 409, 414
Sched. 22 - - - - - 232	s.72 - - - - - - 412
Para. 14 - - - - - 262	s.73 - - - - - - 411
Para. 15 - - - - 263, 265	s.74 - - - - - - 417
Para. 16 - - - - 263, 265	s.75 - - - - - - 417
Para. 49 - - - - - 408	s.76 - - - - - - 417
Sched. 24 - - - 398, 420, 421	Local Government (Scotland) Act
Local Government Act (c.70) - - 48	(c.65) 10, 18, 19, 43, 44, 48, 75, 79, 95,
s.222 - - - - 350, 351	100, 109, 204, 396
1973	Part IV - - - - - 48
Land Compensation Act (c.26) - - 412	s.56 - - - - - - 49
Land Compensation (Scotland) Act	s.69 - - - - 29, 276, 280
(c.56) - - - - 10, 68, 407, 410	s.70 - - - - - 396, 400
Part I - - - - 424, 425	s.71 - - - - - - 396
s.1 - - - - - 424, 425	s.73 - - - - - - 400
s.2 - - - - - - 425	s.74 - - - - - - 402
s.3 - - - - - - 426	Part IX - - - - 45, 46
s.4 - - - - - - 426	s.172 - - - 45, 46, 47, 279
s.5 - - - - - - 426	s.173 - 19, 46, 101, 109, 110, 205
s.6 - - - - - - 426	s.174 - - - - - 81
s.9 - - - - - - 425	s.175 - 61, 88, 89, 90, 91, 92, 105
s.10 - - - - - - 425	s.176 - - - 95, 96, 100, 101
s.11 - - - - - - 425	s.177 - - - - 46, 95
s.14 - - - - - - 426	s.179 46, 203, 204, 209, 365, 485, 490,
s.16 - - - - - - 426	540
Part II - - - - 424, 426	s.181 - - 46, 377, 378, 382
s.18 - - - - - - 426	s.189 - - - - - 351
	Sched. 22 - - - 45, 46, 279

Sched. 23, para 18   -   -   -   385

Sched. 29 -   -   -   -   -   382

1974

Local Government Act (c.7)   -   -   55

Finance Act (c.30)   -   -   -   -   12

Town and Country Amenities Act
(c.32) -   -   -   -   10, 198, 467

s.2   -   -   -   -   447, 448, 449

s.3   -   -   -   -   -   451, 460

s.5   -   -   -   -   -   443, 451

s.6   -   -   -   -   -   -   445

s.7   -   -   -   -   -   -   441

s.11   -   -   462, 463, 465, 466, 467

Housing Act (c.44)
s.126   -   -   -   -   -   282

Housing (Scotland) Act (c.45) -   -   409

Part II   -   -   -   -   -   450

s.20 -   -   -   -   -   -   450

1975

Offshore Petroleum Development
(Scotland) Act (c.8)
s.9   -   -   -   -   -   -   244

Criminal Procedure (Scotland) Act
(c.21)

s.289F   -   -   -   -   459, 466

s.289G   -   -   -   -   459, 466

s.331   -   -   -   -   -   -   342

Local Government (Scotland) Act
(c.30)

Part II   -   -   -   -   -   55

Sched. 4 -   -   -   -   -   55

Sched. 5 -   -   -   -   -   55

Petroleum and Submarine Pipe-lines
Act (c.74)

s.36 -   -   -   -   -   -   429

Community Land Act (c.77) 13, 17, 396, 401

s.22 -   -   -   -   -   -   407

s.23 -   -   -   -   -   -   407

s.58 -   -   -   -   -   -   414

Sched. 10, para. 7   -   -   -   414

1976

Crofting Reform (Scotland) Act
(c.21)

s.11 -   -   -   -   -   -   411

Sched. 1 -   -   -   -   -   411

Development Land Tax Act (c.24)   -   13

Licensing (Scotland) Act (c.66)
s.16 -   -   -   -   -   -   48

s.23 -   -   -   -   -   -   429

Health Services Act (c.83)   -   -   429

1977

Town and Country Planning (Scotland) Act (c.10)   -   10, 75, 79, 105, 289

s.2   -   -   79, 94, 100, 101, 102, 105

s.5   -   -   78, 79, 292, 345, 347, 348

Town and Country Planning (Amendment) Act (c.29)

s.3   -   -   -   -   -   -   292

Housing (Homeless Persons) Act
(c.48)   -   -   -   -   -   -   22

1978

Inner Urban Areas Act (c.50)   -   -   401

1979

Ancient Monuments and Archaeological Areas Act (c.46)

s.1   -   -   -   -   -   -   436

1980

Local Government, Planning and
Land Act (c.65)   -   -   10, 13, 193, 272

s.87 -   -   -   -   -   -   199

s.90 -   -   -   -   -   -   431

s.92 -   -   74, 193, 396, 397, 414

Part X   -   -   -   -   -   403

s.101   -   -   -   -   -   407

s.112   -   -   -   -   -   426

s.113   -   -   -   -   -   426

s.147   -   -   -   -   -   409

s.179   -   -   -   -   62, 272

Sched. 15, para. 5   -   -   -   431

Sched. 17, para. 2   -   -   -   407

Sched. 32 -   -   -   -   62, 272

Para. 19   -   -   -   -   164

1981

Local Government (Miscellaneous
Provisions) (Scotland) Act (c.23)   -

10, 75, 79

s.25 -   -   -   -   60, 400, 464

s.36 -   -   -   -   -   257

s.41 -   -   -   -   -   101, 102

Sched. 2 -   -   -   -   -   60

Para. 9   -   -   -   -   -   400

Para. 22   -   -   -   -   -   464

Para. 23   -   -   -   -   -   464

Para. 25   -   -   -   -   -   275

Para. 28   -   -   -   -   -   275

Sched. 3, para. 16   -   -   -   275

Sched. 4   -   -   -   -   101, 102

Town and Country Planning
  (Minerals) Act (c.36)   10, 18, 122, 375,
                           470-477, 521
    s.19 - - - - - 123, 476
    s.20 - - - - - - 472
    s.21 - - - - - - 477
    s.22 - - - - 232, 475, 476
    s.23 - - - - - - 471
    s.24 - - - - - 232, 471
    s.25 - - - - - - 381
    s.27 - - - - 46, 474, 475
    s.28 - - - - - 379, 475
    s.29 - - - - 383, 472, 473
    s.30 - - - - 378, 473, 475
    s.31 - - - 472, 473, 474, 475
    s.35 - - - - - 46, 476
    Sched. 2, para. 2 - - - 202

1982
Planning Inquiries (Attendance of
  Public) Act (c.21) - - - - 497

Local Government (Miscellaneous
  Provisions) Act (c.30)
    s.33 - - - - - - 282

Local Government and Planning
  (Scotland) Act (c.43)   10, 44, 67, 75, 79,
                          94, 107, 289, 322, 346
    s.15 - - - - - - 283
    s.36 - - - - - 60, 88, 89
    s.37 - - - - - 60, 93, 94
    s.38 - - - - - 60, 102
    s.39 - - - - - - 60
    s.40 - - - - 60, 106, 107
    s.41 - - - - - - 195
    s.42 - - - - - - 446
    s.43 - - - - - - 290
    s.44 - - - - - - 469
    s.45 - - - - - - 275
    s.46 - - - - 60, 192, 380
    s.47 - - - 322, 332, 336, 521
    s.48   60, 279, 293, 296, 302, 306, 307,
           309, 323-327, 340, 343, 344, 365,
           433, 439, 440, 441, 442, 449, 468,
                                    469, 476
    s.66 - - - - 438, 442, 449
    s.69 - - - - - - 490
    Sched. 2 - - - - 60, 279
      Para. 3 - - - - - 193
      Para. 4 - - - - - 202
      Para. 5 - - - - - 205
      Para. 6 - - - - - 192
      Para. 7 - - - - 187, 257

      Para. 8 - - - - - 259
      Para. 9 - - - - - 261
      Para. 10 - - - - 202, 203
      Para. 11 - - 192, 266, 476
      Para. 12 - - - 192, 266
      Para. 13 - - - - - 263
      Para. 14 - - - - - 46
      Para. 15 - - 433, 439, 440
      Para. 16 - - - - - 441
      Para. 17 - - - - - 468
      Para. 19   293, 296, 302, 306, 307,
                 309, 312, 314, 340
      Para. 20 - - - 33, 323-327
      Para. 23 - - 343, 344, 469
      Para. 25 - - - - - 340
      Para. 26 - - - - - 442
      Para. 27 - - - - - 442
      Para. 29 - - - - - 466
      Para. 31 - - - - - 459
      Para. 32 - - - - - 361
      Para. 33 - - - - - 365
      Para. 35 - - - - - 521
      Para. 36 - - - - - 520
      Para. 38 - - - - - 449
    Sched. 3 - - 46, 203, 209, 490
    Sched. 4 - - - - 171, 449
    Part I - - 438, 442, 521, 533

Civic Government (Scotland) Act
  (c.45)
    s.87 - - - - - 443, 444

Criminal Justice Act (c.48)
    s.54 - - - - - 459, 466

1984
Town and Country Planning Act
  (c.10) - - - 10, 168, 169, 191, 192
    s.1 - - - 164, 192, 436, 451
    s.2 - - - - - - 463
    s.3 - - - - - - 310
    s.4 - - - - - 169, 309
    s.5 - - - - - - 170

Telecommunications Act (c.12)
    Sched. 2 - - - - - 172

Roads (Scotland) Act (c.54)   122, 174, 487
    s.5 - - - - - - 89
    s.7 - - - - - - 89
    s.9 - - - - - - 89
    s.12 - - - - - - 89
    s.156 - - - - - 89, 408
    Sched. 9 - - - - 89, 408
      Para. 70 - - - - - 274
    Sched. 11 - - - - 274, 520

TABLE OF STATUTORY INSTRUMENTS

1948

965 Town and Country Planning (Use Classes for Third Schedule Purposes) (Scotland) Order 1948 - - - - - - - - - - 390

1950

942 Town and Country Planning (General Development) (Scotland) Order 1950 - - - - - - - - - - - - - 189

1954

1679 Town and Country Planning (Compensation) (Scotland) Regulations 1954

Reg. 3 - - - - - - - - - - -	362
Reg. 4 - - - - - - - - - - -	362
Reg. 6 - - - - - - - - - -	362, 363
Reg. 7 - - - - - - - - - - -	363
Reg. 9 - - - - - - - - - - -	385
Reg. 10 - - - - - - - - - - -	385

1955

652 Town and Country Planning (Diversion of Payments) (Scotland) Regulations 1955 - - - - - - - - - - - - 363

1961

195 Town and Country Planning (Control of Advertisements) (Scotland) Regulations 1961 - - - - - - - - - 455, 459

1966

1033 Town and Country Planning (Erection of Industrial Buildings) (Scotland) Regulations 1966 - - - - - - - - - - 478

1385 Town and Country Planning (Development Plans) (Scotland) Regulations 1966 - - - - - - - - - - - - - 77

Reg. 6 - - - - - - - - - - -	77
Reg. 7 - - - - - - - - - - -	77
Reg. 8 - - - - - - - - - - -	77
Reg. 9 - - - - - - - - - - -	77
Reg. 10 - - - - - - - - - - -	77
Sched. 1 - - - - - - - - - - -	77

1968

392 Town and Country Planning (Grants) (Scotland) Regulations 1968 - - - 396

1971

778   Town and Country Planning (Minerals) (Scotland) Regulations 1971   -   364, 470, 471
        Reg. 4   -   -   -   -   -   -   -   -   -   -   -   - 308, 470
        Reg. 5   -   -   -   -   -   -   *-   -   -   -   -   - 313, 471
        Reg. 7   -   -   -   -   -   -   -   -   -   -   -   -   - 471

1972

2002   Transfer of Functions (Secretary of State and Lord Advocate) Order
        1972   -   -   -   -   -   -   -   -   -   -   -   -   - 482

1973

1165   Town and Country Planning (Use Classes) (Scotland) Order 1973   -   60, 140, 147,
                                                                    155-161, 166, 178, 242
        Art. 2   -   -   -   -   -   -   -   -   - 156, 157, 158, 160
        Art. 3   -   -   -   -   -   -   -   -   -   - 156, 159, 160
        Sched.   -   -   -   -   -   -   -   -   -   - 156, 160, 178

1975

379   Town and Country Planning (Scotland) Act 1972 (Commencement No. 1)
        (Orkney Islands Area) Order 1975 -   -   -   -   -   -   -   -   - 76

380   Town and Country Planning (Scotland) Act 1972 (Commencement No. 2)
        Order 1975   -   -   -   -   -   -   -   -   -   -   - 76

460   The Noise Insulation (Scotland) Regulations 1975   -   -   -   -   - 426

679   Town and Country Planning (General Development) (Scotland) Order
        1975   -   -   -   -   -   -   -   -   -   -   -   - 260

1204   Town and Country Planning (Tree Preservation Order and Trees in
        Conservation Areas) (Scotland) Regulations 1975   -   -   -   -   - 463-467
        Reg. 4   -   -   -   -   -   -   -   -   -   -   -   - 463
        Reg. 5   -   -   -   -   -   -   -   -   -   -   - 464
        Reg. 7   -   -   -   -   -   -   -   -   -   -   - 464
        Reg. 8   -   -   -   -   -   -   -   -   -   -   - 464
        Reg. 11   -   -   -   -   -   -   -   -   -   - 461, 467
        Sched.   -   -   -   -   -   -   -   -   -   -   - 463

1379   Tribunals and Inquiries (Discretionary Inquiries) Order 1975   -   -   - 482

2069   Town and Country Planning (Listed Buildings and Buildings in Conserva-
        tion Areas) (Scotland) Regulations 1975 -   -   -   -   -   -   - 431
        Reg. 4   -   -   -   -   -   -   -   -   -   -   -   - 438
        Reg. 5   -   -   -   -   -   -   -   -   -   -   - 438, 439
        Reg. 6   -   -   -   -   -   -   -   -   -   - 438, 439, 441
        Reg. 7   -   -   -   -   -   -   -   -   -   -   - 441
        Reg. 8   -   -   -   -   -   -   -   -   -   - 438, 443
        Reg. 11   -   -   -   -   -   -   -   -   -   -   - 441
        Reg. 12   -   -   -   -   -   -   -   -   -   -   - 434
        Reg. 13   -   -   -   -   -   -   -   -   -   -   - 449
        Sched. 6   -   -   -   -   -   -   -   -   -   -   - 449

1976

210   Town and Country Planning (Determination of Appeals by Appointed
        Persons) (Prescribed Classes) (Scotland) Regulations 1976   -   -   -   - 485

1419 Town and Country Planning General Regulations 1976 - - - - - 273

1559 Compulsory Purchase by Public Authorities (Inquiries Procedure) (Scotland) Rules 1976 - - - - - - - - - 481, 482, 491

2022 Town and Country Planning (General) (Scotland) Regulations 1976
      Reg. 3 - - - - - - - - - - - - 413
      Reg. 4 - - - - - - - - 347, 370, 379, 384, 391
      Reg. 7 - - - - - - - - - - - 385
      Sched. 1 - - - - - - - - - - - 414

1977

255 Town and Country Planning (Listed Building and Buildings in Conservation Areas) (Scotland) Amendment Regulations 1977 - - - - - 431, 438

794 Town and Country Planning (Development Plans) (Scotland) Order 1977 - - - - - - - - - - - - - 78

1978

892 Town and Country Planning (Determination of Appeals by Appointed Persons) (Prescribed Classes) (Scotland) Regulations 1978 - - - 485

1979

791 Forestry (Felling of Trees) Regulations 1979 - - - - - - 465

792 Forestry (Exceptions from Restriction of Felling) Regulations 1979 - - 465

838 Town and Country Planning (Industrial Development Certificate) Regulations 1979 - - - - - - - - - - - 478

839 Town and Country Planning (Industrial Development Certificates: Exemption) Order 1979 - - - - - - - - - - 478

1980

1675 Town and Country Planning (Determination of Appeals by Appointed Persons) (Prescribed Classes) (Scotland) Regulations 1980 - 60, 326, 485, 490

1676 Town and Country Planning (Inquiries Procedure) (Scotland) Rules 1980 - - - - - - - 319, 326, 441, 481, 482, 490-513
      Rule 2 - - - - - - - - - - 490, 491
      Rule 3 - - - - - - - - - - - 493
      Rule 4 - - - - - - - - - - - 493
      Rule 5 - - - - - - - - - - - 494
      Rule 6 - - - - - - - - - - 494, 495
      Rule 7 - - - - - - - - - - - 497
      Rule 8 - - - - - - - - - - 495, 499
      Rule 9 - - - - - - - - - - - 495
      Rule 10 - - - - - - - - 497, 498, 499, 500, 515
      Rule 11 - - - - - - - - - - - 502
      Rule 12 - - - - - - - - - 503-510, 514
      Rule 13 - - - - - - - - - - - 511

1677 Town and Country Planning Appeals (Determination by Appointed Person) (Inquiries Procedure) (Scotland) Rules 1980   319, 326, 481, 482, 490-502, 513-514
      Rule 2 - - - - - - - - - - 490, 491
      Rule 3 - - - - - - - - - - - 493

Rule 4 - - - - - - - - - - - - 493
Rule 6 - - - - - - - - - - - - 494
Rule 7 - - - - - - - - - - - 494, 495
Rule 8 - - - - - - - - - - - - 497
Rule 9 - - - - - - - - - - - 495, 499
Rule 10 - - - - - - - - - - - - 495
Rule 11 - - - - - - - - - 497, 498, 499, 500, 515
Rule 12 - - - - - - - - - - - - 502
Rule 13 - - - - - - - - - - - - 513
Rule 14 - - - - - - - - - - - - 513
Sched. - - - - - - - - - - - - 490

1981

829 Town and Country Planning (Development by Planning Authorities)
(Scotland) Regulations 1981 - - - - - - - - - 171, 273

830 Town and Country Planning (General Development) (Scotland) Order
1981   60, 157, 159, 162, 163, 171, 172-183, 188, 189, 205, 218, 242, 258, 260,
                                                                274, 302, 366, 386-388
Art. 1 - - - - - - - - - - - 172
Art. 2 - - - - 173, 174, 175, 178, 179, 181, 182, 188, 189, 196, 198
Art. 3 - - - - - - 63, 172, 173, 183, 356, 380, 387, 450
Art. 4 - - - - - - - 63, 99, 183, 199, 380, 386, 387
Art. 6 - - - - - - - - - - - 194
Art. 7 - - - - - - - 195, 196, 197, 198, 205
Art. 8 - - - - - - - - - 187, 188, 189, 265
Art. 9 - - - - - - - - - - 164, 190, 201
Art. 10 - - - - - - - 195, 200, 201, 259, 260, 261
Art. 11 - - - - - - - - - - 209, 254
Art. 12 - - - - - - - - - - - 209
Art. 13 - - - - - - - - - 204, 205, 218, 273
Art. 14 - - - - - - - - - - - 440
Art. 15 - - - - - - - - - - 202, 203
Art. 16 - - - - - - - - 202, 266, 267, 487, 488
Art. 17 - - - - - - - - - - - 164, 261
Art. 18 - - - - - - - - - 318, 319, 320
Sched. 1 - - - - - 63, 172, 173-183, 356, 380, 386, 387, 450
Sched. 1, Part II - - - - - - - - - - 173
Sched. 2 - - - - - - - - - - - - 197
Sched. 3 - - - - - - - - - - - - 194
Sched. 3, Part IV - - - - - - - - - - 196
Sched. 3, Part V - - - - - - - - - - 196
Sched. 3, Part VI - - - - - - - - - - 198
Sched. 4 - - - - - - - - - - - - 200
Sched. 4, Part II - - - - - - - - - - 261
Sched. 5 - - - - - - - - - - - - 318
Sched. 6 - - - - - - - - - - - 318, 320

975 Clydebank District Enterprise Zone Designation Order 1981 - - - - 60

1069 City of Glasgow District Enterprise Zone Designation Order 1981 - - - 60

1385 Town and Country Planning (Tree Preservation Order and Trees in
Conservation Areas) (Scotland) Amendment Regulations 1981 - - 463, 464

1476 Forestry (Exceptions from Restriction of Felling) (Amendment) Regulations 1981 - - - - - - - - - - - - - 465

1826 Town and Country Planning (Industrial Development Certificates) (Prescribed Classes of Building) Regulations 1981 - - - - - - 478

1982

86 Town and Country Planning (Minerals) Act 1981 (Commencement No. 1) Order 1982 - - - - - - - - - - 472, 473, 475, 477

973 Town and Country Planning (Minerals) (Scotland) Regulations 1982 - - - 470

1397 Local Government and Planning (Scotland) Act 1982 (Commencement No. 2) Order 1982 - - - - - - - - - - - - 441

1983

108 Town and Country Planning (Grants) (Scotland) Amendment Regulations 1983 - - - - - - - - - - - - - - 396

673 Community Land Act 1975 (Appointed Day for Repeal) Order 1983 - - - 13

1590 Town and Country Planning (Structure and Local Plans) (Scotland) Regulations 1983 - - - - - - - 60, 79, 84, 86, 96, 223
    Reg. 2 - - - - - - - - - - - - - 87
    Reg. 3 - - - - - - - - - - - 82, 101
    Reg. 4 - - - - - - - - - - 81, 101, 102
    Reg. 6 - - - - - - - - - - - - 86
    Reg. 7 - - - - - - - - - - - - 84
    Reg. 8 - - - - - - - - - - - - 86
    Reg. 9 - - - - - - - - - - - - 86
    Reg. 10 - - - - - - - - - - - - 86
    Reg. 11 - - - - - - - - - - - - 81
    Reg. 12 - - - - - - - - - - - - 87
    Reg. 13 - - - - - - - - - - - - 87
    Reg. 14 - - - - - - - - - - - - 88
    Reg. 15 - - - - - - - - - - - - 88
    Reg. 16 - - - - - - - - - - - - 87
    Reg. 17 - - - - - - - - - - - - 89
    Reg. 18 - - - - - - - - - - - - 92
    Reg. 19 - - - - - - - - - - - - 93
    Reg. 23 - - - - - - - - - - - - 96
    Reg. 24 - - - - - - - - - - - - 99
    Reg. 25 - - - - - - - - - - - 98, 99
    Reg. 26 - - - - - - - - - - - - 100
    Reg. 27 - - - - - - - - - - - - 100
    Reg. 29 - - - - - - - - - - - 97, 102
    Reg. 30 - - - - - - - - - - - - 102
    Reg. 31 - - - - - - - - - - - - 102
    Reg. 32 - - - - - - - - - - - 103, 105
    Reg. 33 - - - - - - - - - - - - 103
    Reg. 34 - - - - - - - - - - - - 103
    Reg. 35 - - - - - - - - - - - - 104
    Reg. 37 - - - - - - - - - - - - 104
    Reg. 38 - - - - - - - - - - - - 105
    Reg. 39 - - - - - - - - - - - - 105

Reg. 40 - - - - - - - - - - - - - 105
Reg. 41 - - - - - - - - - - - - - 107
Reg. 42 - - - - - - - - - - - 87, 102, 106
Reg. 43 - - - - - - - - - - - - 93, 106
Reg. 44 - - - - - - - - - - - 87, 93, 106
Reg. 45 - - - - - - - - - - - 79, 94, 107
Sched. - - - - - - - - - - - - 87, 102

1619 Town and Country Planning (Use Classes) (Scotland) Amendment Order
1983 - - - - - - - - - - - - - 60, 156

1620 Town and Country Planning (General Development) (Scotland) Amendment Order 1983 - - - - - - - - - 60, 172, 173, 387

1697 Town and Country Planning (Fees for Applications and Deemed
Applications) (Scotland) Regulations 1983 - - - - - - 199, 320
Reg. 4 - - - - - - - - - - - - - 200
Reg. 5 - - - - - - - - - - - - - 200
Reg. 6 - - - - - - - - - - - - - 200
Reg. 7 - - - - - - - - - - - - - 200
Reg. 8 - - - - - - - - - - - - - 325
Reg. 9 - - - - - - - - - - - - - 456

1984

236 Town and Country Planning (Enforcement of Control) (Scotland) Regulations 1984 - - - - - - - - 296, 307, 309, 310, 325
Reg. 7 - - - - - - - - - - - - - 464

237 Town and Country Planning (General Development) (Scotland) Amendment Order 1984 - - - - - - - - 172, 195, 197, 200

238 Town and Country Planning (Development by Planning Authorities)
(Scotland) Amendment Regulations 1984 - - - - - - 171, 273

329 Town and Country Planning (Tree Preservation Order and Trees in
Conservation Areas) (Scotland) Amendment Regulations 1984 - - - 463

467 Town and Country Planning (Control of Advertisements) (Scotland)
Regulations 1984 - - - - - - - - 163, 171, 452-460
Reg. 2 - - - - - - - - - 452, 453, 454, 458
Reg. 3 - - - - - - - - - - 452, 453, 454
Reg. 4 - - - - - - - - - - - 452, 456
Reg. 5 - - - - - - - - - - - - - 452
Reg. 6 - - - - - - - - - - - 455, 458
Reg. 7 - - - - - - - - - - - - - 459
Reg. 8 - - - - - - - - - - - - - 460
Reg. 9 - - - - - - - - - - - - - 460
Reg. 10 - - - - - - - - - - - - - 454
Reg. 11 - - - - - - - - - - - - - 455
Reg. 12 - - - - - - - - - - - - - 455
Reg. 13 - - - - - - - - - - - - - 455
Reg. 14 - - - - - - - - - - 455, 456, 457
Reg. 15 - - - - - - - - - - - - - 456
Reg. 16 - - - - - - - - - - - - - 456
Reg. 17 - - - - - - - - - - - - - 456
Reg. 18 - - - - - - - - - - - - - 457

Reg. 19 - - - - - - - - - - - - 455, 457
Reg. 21 - - - - - - - - - - - - - 457
Reg. 22 - - - - - - - - - - - 456, 457, 459
Reg. 23 - - - - - - - - - - - 456, 457, 459
Reg. 24 - - - - - - - - - - - - 458, 459
Reg. 25 - - - - - - - - - - - - - 459
Reg. 26 - - - - - - - - - - - - - 459
Reg. 27 - - - - - - - - - - - - - 458
Reg. 30 - - - - - - - - - - - - - 459
Reg. 33 - - - - - - - - - - - - - 452
Reg. 34 - - - - - - - - - - - - - 446
Sched. 1, Part I - - - - - - - - - 455, 456, 458
Sched. 1, Part II - - - - - - - - - - 455, 458
Sched. 2 - - - - - - - - - - - - 460
Sched. 4 - - - - - - - - - - - 454, 455

474 Civil Aviation (Aerial Advertising) (Captive Balloons) Regulations 1984 - - 453

526 Increase of Criminal Penalties, etc. (Scotland) Order 1984 - - - - 341, 346

995 Town and Country Planning (Special Enforcement Notices) (Scotland)
      Regulations 1984 - - - - - - - - - - - 310

996 Town and Country Planning (Crown Land Applications) (Scotland)
      Regulations 1984 - - - - - - - - 164, 192, 436, 451

1832 Petroleum (Production) (Landward Areas) Regulations 1984 - - - - 429

1985

291 Town and Country Planning (Limit of Annual Value) (Scotland) Order
      1985 - - - - - - - - - - - - 411, 425

ABBREVIATIONS

1947 Act	The Town and Country Planning (Scotland) Act 1947
1972 Act	The Town and Country Planning (Scotland) Act 1972
1973 Act	The Local Government (Scotland) Act 1973
L.C.(S.)A. 1973	The Land Compensation (Scotland) Act 1973
1977 Act	The Town and Country Planning (Scotland) Act 1977
1981 Act	The Town and Country Planning (Minerals) Act 1981
1982 Act	The Local Government and Planning (Scotland) Act 1982
1984 Act	The Town and Country Planning Act 1984
C.A.	Court of Appeal
D.A.F.S.	Department of Agriculture and Fisheries for Scotland
D.H.S.	Department of Health for Scotland
D.o.E.	Department of the Environment
Delegated Appeals Rules / D.A.R.	The Town and Country Planning Appeals (Determination by Appointed Person) (Inquiries Procedure) (Scotland) Rules 1980
General Development Order / G.D.O.	The Town and Country Planning (General Development) (Scotland) Order 1981, as amended
H.L.	House of Lords
Inquiries Procedure Rules / I.P.R.	The Town and Country Planning (Inquiries Procedure) (Scotland) Rules 1980
L.B.C.	London Borough Council
L.T.	Lands Tribunal
Listed Buildings Regulations	The Town and Country Planning (Listed Buildings and Buildings in Conservation Areas) (Scotland) Regulations 1975, as amended
M.H.L.G.	Ministry of Housing and Local Government
PAN	Planning Advice Note
S.D.D.	Scottish Development Department
S.E.P.D.	Scottish Economic Planning Department
Use Classes Order / U.C.O.	The Town and Country Planning (Use Classes) (Scotland) Order 1973, as amended

References to *Bulletins of Selected Appeal Decisions* and to *Scottish Bulletins of Selected Appeal Decisions* are references to the Bulletins issued by the Ministry of Housing and Local Government and the Department of Health for Scotland respectively. References to *Scottish Planning Appeal Decisions (SPADS)* are references to the summaries of appeal decisions published by the Planning Exchange, Glasgow. The booklet *Selected Enforcement and Allied Appeals* was published by H.M.S.O. in 1974.

Law reports, journals, etc.

A.C. or App. Cas	Appeal Cases (Law Reports)
All E.R.	All England Law Reports

C.L.P.	Current Legal Problems
C.L.Y.	Current Law Year Book
Ch. or Ch. D	Chancery (Law Reports)
Conv.	Conveyancer and Property Lawyer
E. & B.	Ellis and Blackburn's Reports (Queen's Bench 1858-1861)
E.G.	Estates Gazette
F.	Fraser (Court of Session, etc. reports 1898-1906)
J.P.L.	Journal of Planning and Environment Law
J.L.S.S.	Journal of the Law Society of Scotland
K.B.	King's Bench (Law Reports)
L.G.R.	Knight's Local Government Reports
L.Q.R.	Law Quarterly Review
L.R.	Law Reports
Lloyds Rep.	Lloyds Law Reports
M.	Macpherson (Court of Session, etc. reports 1862-1873)
M.L.R.	Modern Law Review
Macq.	Macqueen's Reports (1851-1865)
N.I.	Northern Ireland Reports
New L.J.	New Law Journal
P.	Probate, Divorce and Admiralty (Law Reports)
P.L.	Public Law
P.&C.R.	Property and Compensation Reports
Ph.	Phillips' Reports (Chancery 1841-1849)
Q.B.	Queen's Bench (Law Reports)
R.	Rettie (Court of Session, etc. reports 1873-1898)
R.V.R.	Rating and Valuation Reporter
S.C.	Session Cases (Court of Session, etc. reports)
S.J.	Solicitors' Journal
S.L.T.	Scots Law Times
S.L.T. (Lands Tr.)	Scots Law Times Lands Tribunal reports
S.L.T. (Notes)	Scots Law Times Notes of Recent Decisions
S.L.T. (Sh. Ct.)	Scots Law Times Sheriff Court reports
S.P.L.P.	Scottish Planning Law and Practice
SCOLAG	Bulletin of the Scottish Legal Action Group
T.L.R.	Times Law Reports
W.L.R.	Weekly Law Reports

CHAPTER 1
INTRODUCTION

In a lecture delivered in 1976 Professor Jeffrey Jowell said:[1]

'The enterprise of law and the enterprise of planning are remarkably similar. They are both concerned with the control and guidance of change. They are both concerned with the resolution of conflict, in the interest of social justice and stability. They both interact with the legislative process, and are concerned with the identification of social values. They are both involved, therefore, in assessing and recognising the role of power in society, yet moderating this power, and balancing it in the light of minority interests and other enduring values.'

One might add that although those engaged in town and country planning generally appear more ready than are lawyers to question the purposes of, and the values inherent in, the enterprise in which they are engaged, both town and country planning and the law relating thereto appear to be in a state of almost continual flux.

While the focus of this book is almost entirely legal, it may be appropriate to begin by attempting to indicate the objectives of town and country planning, an enterprise which, as Blowers points out,[2] is regarded by some as an 'esoteric, impenetrable activity'.

Planning and its objectives

No explicit statements as to the general objectives which town and country planning should serve are to be found in the planning legislation. A consultative paper, *Review of the Management of Planning,* issued by the Scottish Development Department in 1977, stated that town and country planning 'was initially, and is still mainly, a means of controlling and guiding the use of land and the processes of change in the environment', its main feature being that it provides a means whereby alternative or competing choices for the use of land can be discussed and informed decisions made.

It is difficult to be much more specific as to the aims of town and country

---

[1] 'The Limits of Law in Urban Planning' 1977 *Current Legal Problems* 63.
[2] A. Blowers, *The Limits of Power: The Politics of Local Planning Policy* (Pergamon Press, 1980).

planning, primarily because planning is not an end in itself. This would seem to have been recognised by the courts. The absence of any explicit statement of objectives has inevitably resulted in a good deal of litigation over the years concerning the proper scope of planning. The courts have tended to determine such questions on the basis of the particular circumstances of each case; for the most part they have avoided specific statements about the scope of planning and have contented themselves with generalisations. '[A] planning purpose', said Lord Scarman in *Westminster City Council* v *Great Portland Estates plc*[3] 'is one which relates to the character of the use of land'; and in *Stringer* v *Minister of Housing and Local Government*,[4] Cooke J. observed that 'any consideration which relates to the use and development of land is capable of being a planning consideration'.

The range of purposes for which statutory planning powers can be employed is, therefore, very wide. Presenting perhaps a somewhat idealised picture, Cherry states[5] that town planning has

'come to represent a means of public control over the development of towns, cities, their hinterlands and regions, and the adaptations of these to the changing conditions of modern life. Negatively it is concerned with the control of abuse and the regulation of those things considered harmful to the community; positively it represents social, economic and environmental policy to achieve certain aims unattainable through the unfettered operation of the private sector. It deals with the problems of urbanisation, not only remedying malfunction, but also creating the conditions for harmonious living . . . It deals with the allocation of land for stated purposes; it seeks to relate economic policy to the physical structuring of cities and it aims to enhance living conditions for the community as a whole.'

The role of planning and the range of purposes it ought to serve are, however, matters of almost continual debate. As planning is concerned with means rather than ends this is, perhaps, not surprising. It must, inevitably, change with the times. As Cherry says:[6] 'The activity of town planning, mediated through political processes and operated through a variety of institutional arrangements, responds and adapts to different expressions of political values and social preferences which change over time.' By its very nature, therefore, town and country planning cannot stand still; it has to adapt to changing circumstances and its scope has changed very considerably over the years. Planning must, in the words of the Uthwatt Committee,[7] 'advance with the condition of the society which it is designed to serve'.

3   [1984] 3 W.L.R. 1035.
4   [1970] 1 W.L.R. 1281.
5   Gordon E. Cherry, *The Politics of Town Planning* (Longman, 1982). For an early statement of the aims and advantages of statutory town planning see T. M. Cooper and W. E. Whyte, *The Law of Housing and Town Planning in Scotland* (William Hodge & Co., 1920).
6   *The Politics of Town Planning.*
7   *Final Report of the Expert Committee on Compensation and Betterment* (Cmd. 6386, 1942).

Though there are probably many who would wish to see planning confined to what has been described as its 'mechanistic land allocation function',[8] there are others who see planning (or at least did so when confidence in planning's role was perhaps higher than it now is) as 'the key discipline in the integrated science of urban governance'[9] and the plannner as 'the helmsman steering the city'.[10]. In recent times the role, objectives, methods, performance and institutional framework of town and country planning have all come under attack from within and without the planning profession. Central government's apparent concern to confine planning to its land use base[11] and thus to compel it to operate in what is seen by some as a socio-economic vacuum has been a continuing source of frustration in some quarters.

Allegations of planning's shortcomings have been many and have been made from very different viewpoints; town planning has, for example, been criticised for its ineffectiveness and the slowness of its procedures, for its failure to seek redistributive goals or social change and its 'pre-dominantly upper class and paternalistic ideology',[12] for the weakness of the development planning system, for the limited provision made for public involvement in the process and for the inadequacies of the public inquiry system. Denman goes as far as to suggest that 'land use planning in the U.K. has become a process without a purpose'.[13]

Not all such criticisms can properly be laid at the door of town and country planning; some of them are criticisms of the political or governmental system through which planning has to work. Although town and country planning can, as was said in the S.D.D. consultative paper mentioned above, 'contribute to the solution of a wide range of social problems, it cannot either cause or cure them on its own'. As that paper also said: 'It is arguable indeed that society expects planning to achieve too much.'

Planning law and procedures

Concerned as it is with regulating relationships between private property and public powers, and because of the significant effects it can have on the property and lives of large numbers of people, the law relating to town and

---

[8]   J. P. W. B. McAuslan, 'The Plan, the Planners and the Lawyers' [1971] *Public Law* 247.
[9]   See Patrick McAuslan, *Land, Law and Planning* (Weidenfeld & Nicolson, 1975), p. 40.
[10] See J. B. McLoughlin, *Urban and Regional Planning: A Systems Approach* (Faber, 1969).
[11] It is, however, arguable that this is consistent with the legislative framework within which town planning operates.
[12] See J. F. Simmie, 'Physical Planning and Social Policy' 1971 Jo. R.T.P.I. 450. See too D. L. Foley, 'British Town Planning: One Ideology or Three?' (1960) 11 *British Journal of Sociology* 211.
[13] D. Denman, *Land in a Free Society* (Centre for Policy Studies, 1980).

country planning is, as Sir Desmond Heap said in 1948,[14] 'invested with a general importance quite beyond that normally accorded to a specialised subject'.

Though the directions taken by town and country planning may alter in response to different political pressures at different times, planning objectives (whatever they may be at any particular time) cannot generally be achieved without legislation. As society's demands and expectations have risen, so, since town planning first made its appearance on the statute book in 1909, has the volume of legislation on the subject increased very considerably. Over the last forty years in particular, fresh and amending legislation has been a frequent occurrence. To the great mass of primary legislation there must be added a large number of orders, regulations and directions, many of them of considerable practical importance. As Professor J. Bennett Miller aptly observed, 'almost any point connected with planning seems inexorably doomed to be drowned in verbiage'.[15]

In addition, account must be taken of the very important contribution which the courts (primarily in England but to an increasing extent in Scotland) have made to planning law. As Wade has pointed out:[16] 'Of all the administrative controls and services which multiply in the modern state, the one which generates most litigation in the courts is town and country planning.' The great body of case law which has been built upon the statutory foundations of planning is indicative not only of the practical importance of town planning but also of the many difficulties to which the legislation can give rise. Although this book is concerned with the law of planning in Scotland and although the Scottish legislation differs in a number of important respects and in many matters of detail from that operating in England and Wales (see below), in the main the legislation operating on both sides of the border is very similar, and at many points in the text we have made reference to decisions made by the English courts. Such decisions are not, of course, binding in Scotland and on a few occasions the Scottish courts have adopted an approach different from that taken by the English courts.[17] However, English decisions have generally been found to be of assistance by the Scottish courts in the interpretation of the Scottish legislation. The questions with which the courts have had to deal in this field are among the most difficult in the field of judicial review of administrative action. In ensuring that statutory duties and procedures are observed and that the many discretionary powers conferred by the planning legislation are exercised within certain limits, the courts play an important role in shaping the way in which the planning system operates. There are, however, important limitations on judicial control; it is necessarily unsystematic and sporadic and is essentially negative in nature in that it is primarily concerned with the detection and correction of error rather than with the effectiveness or adequacy of the planning process.

[14]   Preface to *An Outline of Planning Law* (Sweet and Maxwell, 1st edition, 1949).
[15]   (1969) 14 J.L.S.S. 146.
[16]   H. W. R. Wade, *Administrative Law* (Clarendon Press, 5th edition, 1982), p. 162.
[17]   See, for example, *McDaid* v *Clydebank District Council* 1984 S.L.T. 162.

A substantial body of principle has also been established through decisions of the ministers, reporters and inspectors on appeals raising matters of planning law and procedure. We have therefore felt it appropriate to make reference in the text to appeal decisions dealing with questions which have not yet come before the courts. The views on law and procedure expressed in such decisions are not, of course, authoritative but it can be useful, particularly to those considering appeal to the Secretary of State, to know what departmental views have been expressed on a particular point. Further, the general pattern of the law's development in several of the areas dealt with in this book has, in Grant's words,[18] 'been one of ministerial initiative, followed by judicial confirmation or occasional check or reformulation'.

The legislation and judicial decisions which go to make up the body of planning law have been subjected to a number of criticisms. At a 'technical' level the legislation has been criticised as over-complex and as an unsatisfactory amalgam of very general principles and minute detail, poorly integrated and lacking any overall coherence.[19] Grant points out[20] that comprehending and interpreting the law is a difficult enough task for the professional let alone the layman; the paradox is, as he also says, 'that this is an administrative system which is perhaps more than any other reliant on general public support, yet which in an era of public participation evinces every sign of slipping farther and farther away from popular intelligibility.' To somewhat similar effect, Sir Desmond Heap suggested in the Hamlyn Lectures delivered in 1975[21] that the quantity and complexity of planning law were putting in issue the credibility and acceptability of planning control. Though the courts might be accused of contributing to the technicality of planning law, judges too have commented critically on the degree of complexity into which the law has now come.[22] Comments of this kind are, however, no new phenomenon. As early as 1910, when the statutory provisions on planning law ran to a mere fourteen sections of the Housing, Town Planning, Etc. Act 1909 and one set of regulations, comprising altogether only eighteen pages of print, J. L. Jack expressed the view that if the procedures were to be effective they would have to be simplified![23]

Procedures relating to both development planning and development control have frequently been criticised as unnecessarily time-consuming with the result that investment is held up and the local, regional or national economy is damaged. In what has so far amounted to a change in emphasis rather than a radical change of direction or philosophy, government has in

---

[18] Malcolm Grant, *Urban Planning Law* (Sweet and Maxwell, 1982), p. 152.
[19] See, for example, Malcolm Grant, *Urban Planning Law*, p. 36.
[20] ibid.
[21] *The Land and the Development; or the Turmoil and the Torment* (Stevens, 1975).
[22] See, for example, *Britt* v *Buckinghamshire County Council* (1963) 14 P. & C.R. 318; and *Brooks and Burton* v *Secretary of State for the Environment* [1977] 1 W.L.R. 1294.
[23] J. L. Jack, *A Handbook of Town Planning as Applicable to Scotland* (W. Green & Son, 1910).

recent years sought in a number of ways to make planning procedures less time-consuming. Development planning procedures have, for example, been streamlined and efforts have been made to speed up the making of decisions on applications for planning permission and on planning appeals. Certain minor types of development have been removed from the ambit of planning control altogether.

The present government have also shown an interest in reducing the discretionary element in the planning process and moving towards what might be described as a zoning system for some areas, a system which combines greater certainty for developers with reduced procedural controls. They have introduced enterprise zones in a number of areas of physical and economic decline; the order made by the Secretary of State designating such an area, *inter alia,* grants planning permission for a particular development or development of any class specified. There has been considered (but not pursued) the wider use of special development orders as a means of granting planning permission for specified categories of development in particular areas; the sort of development the government appeared to have in mind included industrial and residential development in accord with local plans and the intensification or extension of development in areas already developed with uses acceptable to the planning authority. And the government are currently discussing the possibility of introducing simplified planning zones—defined areas in which planning authorities would be able to give general planning permission for specified categories of development. It is too early to say whether these initiatives will result in something more than a change in emphasis in the operation of the planning process.

However, so long as the community appears to wish the planning system to control as much as it now does, it is doubtful whether the complexities of the system and the time taken to reach decisions can be materially reduced. The form of many of the present procedures is dictated in large measure by a desire to ensure that individual rights and interests are protected, that those responsible for decision-making have all relevant information before them and that the activities of various bodies are satisfactorily co-ordinated. Abrogation of such safeguards would speed up the system but probably would not command general support and might well have an adverse effect on the quality of decisions. And at the same time as government has sought to meet criticisms relating to the over-detailed nature of some planning controls and the slowness of decision-making, it has also been faced with arguments that the system is not effective in protecting the environment and that inadequate provision is made for involving groups and individuals in planning. Legislative action has been taken to meet some such criticisms; new controls designed to safeguard the environment have been introduced—for example, in relation to mineral operations and development in areas of national scenic importance—and procedures have been introduced which give neighbours an opportunity to express their views on applications for permission to carry out development.

The vision commonly presented by the courts and by many lawyers is that the law provides an apolitical, neutral framework for the exercise of power and is not itself 'biased' in any way for or against a particular philosophy or ideology. That view has not gone unchallenged. It has been argued that the planning legislation and the courts' interpretation of that legislation embody beliefs and value judgments about power and society and that the values permeating the law have in practice contributed to the current disarray of planning and have had an adverse effect on attempts to find solutions to planning problems.[24]

The scope of this book

While this book does no more than mention those historical, administrative and political aspects of town and country planning which appear necessary to an understanding of the law, and contains little by way of criticism of the law or its ideological basis, this is not because we consider such matters unimportant or because we think that they should not concern lawyers. Such issues are, however, very well dealt with in other works[25] and we considered that there was a need for a book which sought to provide a reasonably straightforward account of planning law and procedure in Scotland. The book is concerned with what might be described as 'mainstream' planning law—primarily the law contained in the Town and Country Planning Acts, the subordinate legislation made under those Acts and the relevant judicial and ministerial decisions. It does not deal with other legislation affecting land use. There is a considerable volume of such other legislation and to deal with it in adequate fashion would require substantial enlargement of an already large and complex text. We do not, for example, discuss the operation of the Inner Urban Areas Act 1978 and other initiatives such as the urban programme for tackling urban deprivation. We do not attempt to explain the provisions of the Industrial Development Act 1982 and the government's policies for providing industrial development and employment opportunities in the regions; nor do we examine the promotional powers available to local authorities to undertake such activity—except in so far as these are contained in the Town and Country Planning Acts. The promotional activities of the Scottish Development Agency and the Highlands and Islands Development Board are beyond the scope of this book. The New Towns Act 1946 and the New Towns (Scotland) Act 1968, which provide for the establishment and development of the five new towns in Scotland, are not considered. Also omitted is the legislation dealing with nature conservation and the promotion of access to the countryside contained in

---

[24]   See, in particular, J.P.W.B. McAuslan, 'Planning Law's Contribution to the Problems of an Urban Society' (1974) 37 M.L.R. 134. See too McAuslan, 'The Plan, the Planners and the Lawyers' [1971] *Public Law* 247.

[25]   Books which deal with planning law in its political, administrative or ideological context include Patrick McAuslan, *Land, Law and Planning*; N. A. Roberts, *The Reform of Planning Law* (Macmillan, 1976); Patrick McAuslan, *The Ideologies of Planning Law* (Pergamon Press, 1980); and Malcolm Grant, *Urban Planning Law*.

the National Parks and Access to the Countryside Act 1949, the Countryside (Scotland) Acts of 1967 and 1981 and the Wildlife and Countryside Act 1981. Furthermore, there are numerous discrete codes of legislation concerned with the regulation of certain special land uses which are beyond the scope of this book. These include, for example, the Caravan Sites and Control of Development Act 1960 and the Ancient Monuments and Archaeological Areas Act 1979.

Even within the parameters of 'mainstream' planning the book does not deal in equal detail with all aspects of planning law and procedure; it concentrates on those matters which we think to be of practical significance and, in particular, on those areas of the law where litigation has shown that difficulties are liable to arise.

Planning legislation before 1947[26]

By way of an introduction to the present system of planning law and procedure we provide a brief summary of the way in which planning legislation has evolved over the years.

In *The Law of Housing and Town Planning in Scotland*[27] T. M. Cooper and W. E. Whyte declared that:

'It seems extraordinary that until the passing of the Housing and Town Planning Act of 1909, local authorities in this country did not possess any right or power to control or regulate the development of the towns and districts under their jurisdiction . . . [L]ocal authorities had no power to question the methods of estate development in their area, and as a consequence, each owner naturally applied himself exclusively to the laying-out of his land according to the opportunities afforded to him and in consonance with his own ideas and wishes.'

The 'dire results of neglect to apply town planning principles in the past' were, said Cooper and Whyte, 'amply evidenced everywhere'.

Under the powers conferred by the Housing, Town Planning, Etc. Act 1909[28] local authorities might make town planning schemes for defined areas which were in course of development or which appeared likely to be used for building purposes. The Town and Country Planning (Scotland) Act 1932 extended the scope for planning action by enabling local authorities to make planning schemes for almost any land.

The powers of local authorities under the planning legislation enacted prior to the second world war were, however, hedged about with such

[26]   On the history of the planning legislation, see G. E. Cherry, *The Evolution of British Town Planning* (Leonard Hill Books, 1974); J. B. Cullingworth, *Peacetime History of Environmental Planning, Vols. I-IV* (H.M.S.O., 1978-1980); and J. A. G. Griffith, 'The Law of Property (Land)', in M. Ginsberg (ed.), *Law and Opinion in England in the 20th Century* (Stevens, 1959).

[27]   William Hodge & Co., 1920.

[28]   The 1909 Act was amended by the Housing, Town Planning, Etc. (Scotland) Act 1919 and the provisions of both Acts were, with some minor amendments, consolidated in the Town Planning (Scotland) Act 1925.

restrictions that it proved extremely difficult, even for those authorities who wished to exercise their planning powers, to take any effective planning action. Planning schemes were only a partial control over development, they were very inflexible and the prospect of having to pay heavy compensation to those who sustained loss in consequence of the making of a planning scheme deterred many authorities from taking action under the legislation.

In the 1930s major land use problems began to emerge. It was clear that the existing planning machinery was quite incapable of dealing satisfactorily with those problems or with the further town planning problems brought about by the second world war. In the words of Sir Desmond Heap: 'New thinking was called for and the hour produced the thinking',[29] in particular the great trilogy of reports—those of the Barlow Commission[30] and the Scott[31] and Uthwatt[32] Committees.[33] Taken together these reports recommended:

> 'that planning control should cover the whole country, that there should be a national policy for industrial location and population distribution; also that there should be a central planning authority concerned with: urban redevelopment; reduction of congestion; achieving industrial "balance" within and between regions; examining the potential of garden suburbs, satellite towns and trading estates; research and information about industry, resources and amenities; correlation of local planning schemes in the national interest.'[34]

The legislation which followed, and which sought to give effect to the recommendations contained in these reports, culminated in the legislation of 1947 (the Town and Country Planning Act 1947 and the Town and Country Planning (Scotland) Act 1947), which repealed most of the earlier planning legislation.

The 1947 Act and after

The town and country planning legislation of 1947 has been described as a 'daring experiment in social control of the environment'.[35] The coming into operation of the 1947 legislation on 1st July 1948 resulted in what Sir Desmond Heap aptly calls 'a brand new beginning in the matter of control over land and its development';[36] as he says: 'Nothing associated with the

---

[29] *The Land and the Development; or the Turmoil and the Torment.*
[30] *Report of the Royal Commission on the Distribution of the Industrial Population* (Cmd. 6153, 1940).
[31] *Report of the Committee on Land Utilisation in Rural Areas* (Cmd. 6378, 1942).
[32] *Interim and Final Reports of the Expert Committee on Compensation and Betterment* (Cmd. 6291, 1941; and Cmd. 6386, 1942).
[33] See too the White Paper, *Control of Land Use* (Cmd. 6537, 1944).
[34] J. B. McLoughlin, *Control and Urban Planning* (Faber, 1973).
[35] Charles Haar, *Land-Use Planning in a Free Society* (Harvard University Press, 1951).
[36] *The Land and the Development; or the Turmoil and the Torment.*

land was ever to be the same again.' It should perhaps be said, however, that although the legislation of 1947 can properly be regarded as the starting point of modern land use planning in Britain, certain of the procedures to be found in the Town and Country Planning (Scotland) Act 1947 (and in the legislation currently in force) may be seen as logical extensions of procedures originally introduced by earlier legislation.[37]

Although still based to a considerable extent on the foundations laid by the Town and Country Planning (Scotland) Act 1947—in particular, the concept of development control within the framework of a development plan is still central to the town planning system—planning legislation has been subject to almost constant amendment in the years since 1947. Some of the recent legislative changes have been mentioned above and the changes of direction which have taken place over the years in the law on compensation and betterment are outlined below. Other important changes made in recent times include the introduction of a new type of development plan, provision for increased public involvement in the making of development plans and in the exercise by planning authorities of development control powers, the devolving to planning authorities and to inquiry reporters of powers previously exercised by the Secretary of State, the strengthening of controls over buildings of special architectural or historic interest, amendments intended to increase the effectiveness of that part of the legislation concerned with controlling breaches of planning control, and the introduction of fees for planning applications. Thus, although almost all of the Scottish legislation on town and country planning was consolidated[38] in the Town and Country Planning (Scotland) Act 1972, that Act has been the subject of numerous amendments.[39]

Further legislative changes are under consideration. Consultation papers were issued in 1984 on simplified planning zones (see p.6 above) and on planning control over hazardous development. So far as the latter is concerned, the present law does not ensure that the introduction of hazardous substances on premises is always subject to planning control; the solution proposed is that the consent of the planning authority should be required before premises are used for the manufacture, storage or processing of hazardous substances. A further consultation paper issued on 31st July 1984 proposed a large number of (mainly minor) amendments to

[37]   The present statutory provisions on planning permission can, for example, be seen to have developed out of the provisions relating to interim development permission introduced by the 1919 Act and extended by the 1932 Act and by the Town and Country Planning (Interim Development) (Scotland) Act 1943.

[38]   With a few very minor amendments derived from recommendations made by the Scottish Law Commission (see Cmnd. 4949).

[39]   See, in particular, the Land Compensation (Scotland) Act 1973, the Local Government (Scotland) Act 1973, the Town and Country Amenities Act 1974, the Town and Country Planning (Scotland) Act 1977, the Local Government, Planning and Land Act 1980, the Local Government (Miscellaneous Provisions) (Scotland) Act 1981, the Town and Country Planning (Minerals) Act 1981, the Local Government and Planning (Scotland) Act 1982 and the Town and Country Planning Act 1984.

the legislation. These include giving high technology industries freedom to change from one use to an alternative use encompassed by the same planning permission without need for a further grant of permission. The more important of the other proposals contained in the consultation paper are mentioned at appropriate points in the text of this book.

Planning and land values

Mention was made in the previous section of the legislative changes over the years in the law on compensation and betterment. Any summary of the evolution of town and country planning would be incomplete without some mention of the development of the law on compensation and betterment with which it is inter-connected.

The exercise of planning powers can have a very great effect on the open-market value of particular parcels of land. This inevitably raises questions as to how such increases and decreases in land values should be apportioned between the community and individual landowners. For example, ought the community to compensate the owner who is refused planning permission and who is therefore unable to carry out development and cannot realise the development value of his land? When development value is released by a grant of planning permission, ought the community to take some share in the increased value which the community itself has helped to create?

The attempt which was made by the Acts of 1909 and 1932 to deal with these problems was markedly unsuccessful. Under those Acts local authorities were required to pay compensation to landowners who suffered loss as a result of a planning scheme, but in the words of the White Paper *Land*,[40] 'provisions designed to enable these authorities to receive a share of "betterment"—the increases in value which accrued to landowners from public expenditure and planning control—were largely ineffective.' The result was, as the White Paper said, that 'effective planning was financially impossible'.

The Expert Committee on Compensation and Betterment (the Uthwatt Committee), which reported in 1942,[41] concluded that any attempt to deal with gains and losses of development value as they arose was doomed to failure and that the financial problems inseparable from planning action could only be solved by thoroughgoing reform of the system. Though the planning legislation of 1947 did not implement the detailed recommendations of the Uthwatt Committee, it drew heavily on the Committee's work and attempted to provide a comprehensive solution to the related problems of planning, compensation and betterment. The 1947 Act attempted, in effect, to transfer to the state the development value in all land. This the Act sought to achieve by providing:

---

[40] Cmnd. 5730, 1974.
[41] See Cmd. 6386.

(a) that if planning permission was granted for the development of land, a development charge (equal in amount to the increase in the value of the land arising from the grant of permission) was to be paid;

(b) that where planning permission was refused or was granted subject to conditions, compensation would not normally be paid; and

(c) that where land was acquired compulsorily, compensation was to be restricted to 'existing use' value.

Owners of land were to be compensated on a 'once and for all' basis for lost development value.

This complex scheme for the control of land values was designed not only to provide an equitable means of recouping betterment but also to enable planning authorities to exercise their increased planning powers on the basis of the suitability of land for a particular purpose irrespective of the value which the land might have been able to command in a free market. In particular, since land was to be available to planning authorities at existing use value rather than market value, authorities would, it was thought, be better able to make use of the powers conferred upon them by the 1947 Act[42] to take positive action to secure the implementation of their plans.

Whether or not the financial scheme of the 1947 Act could ever have worked satisfactorily is still a matter of dispute but following a change of government in 1951 the scheme was largely dismantled. The effects of the Town and Country Planning Act 1953 and the Town and Country Planning (Scotland) Act 1954 were to abolish the development charge and thus to restore to landowners the development value in land, and to make very limited provision for the payment of compensation to landowners who suffer loss as a result of adverse planning decisions.[43] Under the Town and Country Planning (Scotland) Act 1959 there was a return to market value as the basis of compensation for land acquired by public bodies.

A second attempt by a Labour government to deal with the problems of land values and positive planning was made in 1967 with the establishment of the Land Commission, a body charged with the twin functions of collecting betterment levy and acquiring land required for the implementation of national, regional and local plans. The Land Commission Act 1967 was repealed following a change of government in 1970 and development gains were left to be dealt with under the general taxation system. There was, however, continuing public concern about high land prices and the large unearned profits being made from land, and in 1973 the Chancellor of the Exchequer announced that the (Conservative) government intended to introduce a new tax on development gains. These proposals were adopted by the Labour government which took office in 1974 and were enacted in the Finance Act 1974.

---

[42]   Under the 1947 Act planning authorities were given very wide powers of compulsory acquisition.

[43]   See chapters 14 and 16.

This rare example of a bi-partisan approach proved short-lived. The White Paper *Land,* published in September 1974, made clear that the Labour government was not merely concerned with recouping betterment but also wished to place in the hands of the community greatly increased power 'to plan positively, to decide where and when particular developments should take place'. The White Paper declared that 'the key to positive planning, and to a successful attack on betterment problems', was acquisition by the community of development land 'at the value of its current use rather than at a value based on speculation as to its possible development'. At the heart, therefore, of the Community Land Act 1975, which implemented most of the White Paper's proposals, were provisions designed (a) to ensure that major development took place only on land which was either in, or had passed through, public ownership and (b) to ensure that the price paid by a public authority for land they purchased did not exceed the land's current use value. That position was, however, to be reached by stages, and before the community land scheme came into full effect the 1975 Act was repealed[44] by a Conservative government.

Complementing the community land scheme were provisions contained in the Development Land Tax Act 1976 for a new tax payable on the development value of land realised on disposal of the land or on the commencement of a project of material development. In his budget speech on 19th March 1985, the Chancellor of the Exchequer announced the abolition of development land tax with respect to disposals or deemed disposals of land on or after 19th March 1985.[45]

The present law

The remainder of this introducton is given over to an outline of the main features of planning law as dealt with in this book and to a brief comment on the principal differences between the Scottish and English legislation.

The role of the courts. In town and country planning, as in all areas of administrative decision-making it is, as Grant says,[46] 'the judges who ultimately hold the balance between private right and public power, albeit within the framework both of the relevant legislation and of a developing body of principles of judicial review applicable across a broad range of administrative activity'.

Alder declares[47] that town planning, and development control in particular, 'is one of the most intensively-litigated areas of administrative law and provides a focus for the analysis of several difficult and controversial questions in the field of judicial review of administrative

---

[44]   See the Local Government, Planning and Land Act 1980 and the Community Land Act 1975 (Appointed Day for Repeal) Order 1983.
[45]   Development gains will in future be liable to income tax, capital gains tax or corporation tax.
[46]   Malcolm Grant, 'Planning, Politics and the Judges' [1978] J.P.L. 512.
[47]   John Alder, *Development Control* (Sweet and Maxwell, 1979).

action.' In the absence of a Scottish textbook on administrative law and in order to draw together certain of the strands which run through this book, chapter 2 seeks to outline the principles on which the courts exercise their supervisory powers over the many and disparate activities of the authorities concerned with planning.

The administrative framework. Chapter 3 contains a brief discussion of the public authorities involved in town and country planning (primarily the Secretary of State for Scotland and regional, general and district planning authorities), the allocation of functions between those authorities and aspects of the internal functioning of such authorities. The administration of town and country planning is largely a matter for the appropriate local authorities. However, the duties imposed upon those authorities and their wide discretionary powers are subject to a number of administrative checks; in particular, the Secretary of State possesses important supervisory powers over the activities of planning authorities and there is a right of appeal to him against planning authorities' development control decisions. Allegations of maladministration can, in appropriate circumstances, be made to the Parliamentary Commissioner for Administration or to the Commissioner for Local Administration,.

National planning policy. There is no obligation upon the Secretary of State to prepare national policy statements on town and country planning. Nonetheless, policy 'guidance' is widely employed by the minister to secure the implementation of national objectives, to ensure some consistency and co-ordination in planning policy and practice and to assist those concerned with the development of land. In chapter 4 we consider the main sources of national policy: legislation, both primary and delegated, national planning guidelines, circulars and planning advice notes.

Local planning policies. The most formal source of planning policy is the development plan. Under the 1947 Act each local planning authority was under a duty to prepare and submit for the approval of the Secretary of State a development plan setting out the authority's main planning proposals. Development plans drawn up under the 1947 Act were made in respect of almost the whole of Scotland but are now being steadily superseded by development plans of a very different type. Under the new system broad planning strategy is dealt with in structure plans, while detailed planning policies are set out in local plans. Structure plans require the approval of the Secretary of State but local plans do not normally require ministerial approval. Under the new system members of the public have an opportunity to put forward their views at an early stage in the preparation of both structure and local plans.

The development plan is intended to provide the policy framework within which planning authorities consider the exercise of their planning powers. The plan also serves as a guide to landowners, developers and members of the public as to planning authorities' main policies and proposals for the future use and development of land in their areas. The making and approval of structure and local plans, the preparation of regional reports and the effect of non-statutory policies are considered in chapter 5.

Control of development. Although many modificatons have been made by subsequent legislation, the basic framework for the control of development established by the 1947 Act remains largely intact.

Central to development control are statutory provisions defining 'development' and laying down that the carrying out of development will normally require planning permission. 'Development' means the carrying out of building, engineering, mining or other operations, or the making of any material change in the use of land. The meaning of 'development' and the large body of case law that has accumulated around the statutory definition are considered in chapter 6.

If particular proposals fall within the statutory definition of development then, subject to certain exceptions (outlined in chapter 7), planning permission will be required. Planning permission may be granted by a development order made by the Secretary of State; under the general development order currently in force planning permission is automatically granted for a fairly wide range of developments (see chapter 7). In most other cases in which planning permission is required application must be made to the appropriate planning authority. The need to consider each individual application on its own merits gives the development control system a good deal of flexibility.

The procedures relating to the making of applications for planning permission and related types of application are considered in chapter 8; that chapter also deals with the powers of the Secretary of State and of regional planning authorities to 'call in' planning applications and outlines the matters to be taken into account by a planning authority in determining an application. Of particular importance among the matters to which regard must be had in the determination of an application are the provisions of the development plan and 'any other material considerations'; the law on these matters is considered in chapter 9. Planning authorities are empowered to grant planning permission subject to 'such conditions as they think fit'; this is a wide power but it is not unlimited and the limits which the courts have placed on the discretion of planning authorities are considered in chapter 10. Aspects of the law relating to planning authorities' decisions on applications, including the right of an aggrieved applicant to appeal to the Secretary of State, the effect of planning permission, interpretation of planning permissions and the time limits upon planning permissions are considered, together with other statutory provisions concerned with development control, in chapter 11.

Planning agreements. Planning authorities are empowered by s.50 of the 1972 Act to enter into agreements with persons having an interest in land for the purpose of restricting or regulating the development or use of the land. Such agreements can in some circumstances offer advantages to both parties and the use being made of s.50 agreements is increasing. Difficult questions arise, however, over the interpretation of s.50; the principal difficulties are considered in chapter 12.

Enforcement of planning control. An essential element in the control of development is the power to take action in respect of unauthorised development—whether carried out without the grant of permission required by the legislation or carried out in breach of a condition attached to a grant of planning permission. Despite a number of legislative changes designed to overcome some of the perceived weaknesses in the enforcement machinery, the law on enforcement remains an area of great complexity. A breach of 'ordinary' planning control does not in itself involve a criminal offence. The 1972 Act confers upon planning authorities a discretion to serve an enforcement notice requiring a breach of planning control to be remedied. Contravention of the terms of an effective enforcement notice may result in sanctions, including, in some cases, prosecution. Chapter 13 deals with the taking of enforcement action, the time limits within which such action must be taken, the right to appeal against an enforcement notice to the Secretary of State, the opportunities for challenging enforcement notices in the courts, the effects of an enforcement notice and the possible use of interdict as a means of restraining a breach of planning control.

Adverse planning decisions: purchase notices and compensation. Chapters 14 and 15 are primarily concerned with the possible remedies (other than appeal or objection to the Secretary of State) where planning decisions have an adverse effect on the value of land. Compensation is not, in general, payable in respect of a refusal or conditional grant of planning permission. There are, however, exceptions to this general principle. One such exception, considered in chapter 14, is that where an adverse planning decision has been made on an application for the carrying out of 'new development' on land to which there is attached an unexpended balance of established development value, compensation may be payable; in practice very few cases qualify.

If the effect of a planning decision—for example, a refusal of planning permission—is to render the land in question incapable of reasonably beneficial use, the landowner may be able, by serving a purchase notice on the planning authority, to compel the authority to acquire the land. The law relating to purchase notices is considered in chapter 15.

Control of existing use. A right to compensation is quite likely to arise where planning action interferes in some way with existing rights. The general effect of the planning legislation introduced in 1947 was to leave to the landowner the right to continue the existing use of land and although the legislation makes provision for action such as the revocation of planning permission or the prohibition of an existing use of land, since such action derogates from existing rights compensation will normally be payable. The provision which statute makes for the control of the existing use of land is considered in chapter 16.

Positive planning. In its original form the 1947 Act envisaged, as did the Community Land Act 1975, that planning authorities would often take the initiative in ensuring that land was used in the manner desired by them. Although the 'positive planning' role of planning authorities is now much less significant than has at other times been envisaged, and the major function of planning authorities is now that of regulating private sector proposals, local authorities still possess wide powers to acquire land for planning purposes. Development plans are intended to have a promotional as well as a controlling influence on development; they also seek to co-ordinate the planning and provision of infrastructure required for the development of land. The co-ordinating function of development plans and planning authorities' powers to acquire, dispose of and secure the development of land are outlined in chapter 17.

Planning blight and injurious affection. Where the implementation of public authorities' proposals will necessitate acquisition of land at some time in the future, the marketability of that land is likely to be adversely affected. The planning legislation seeks to alleviate the hardship that can be caused by such planning 'blight'; an owner-occupier of such land can in some circumstances serve on the authority responsible for the proposals a blight notice compelling that authority to acquire the land at an 'unblighted' price. Chapter 18 deals not only with 'blight' in this narrow sense but also outlines the provision made by statute for the payment of compensation in respect of depreciation in the value of neighbouring land caused by the carrying out of schemes of public works.

Special controls. The protection and improvement of the physical environment are, of course, matters to which planning authorities will have regard in the exercise of their general planning powers, but over and above those general powers there are available to planning authorities certain additional powers, the object of which is, in the main, the protection and improvement of the environment.

Buildings listed by the Secretary of State as being of special architectural or historic interest are subject to stringent controls—unless the consent of the planning authority has first been obtained, it is an offence to demolish any such building or to alter it in any manner which would affect its character. Areas which authorities consider to be of special architectural or historic interest can be designated as conservation areas; special regard will be had to the preservation and enhancement of the character and appearance of a conservation area and the demolition of buildings within such an area is subject to control. Special provision is also made for the control of outdoor advertisements, for the making, on amenity grounds, of tree preservation orders and for the making of orders requiring remedial action to be taken in respect of waste land. Mineral operations can present special environmental problems and the Town and Country Planning (Minerals) Act 1981 makes provision for the exercise of additional controls over such operations. Each of these special controls is considered in chapter 19.

Appeal and objection procedures. Inevitably, those adversely affected by the exercise of planning powers, whether it be the refusal of a planning application, the service of an enforcement notice, the making of a discontinuance order or the promotion of a compulsory purchase order, will often feel aggrieved. Grievance procedures are an important component of the planning legislation. Generally they take the form of a right of appeal or objection to the Secretary of State. Appeal and objection procedures are discussed in chapter 20. Attention is focused in particular on the use of written submissions and on the public inquiry for processing appeals and objections and on the substantial body of case law which has grown up around these procedures.

Challenging the validity of plans and decisions. Challenge of the validity of structure and local plans and of many of the more important decisions and orders which can be made under the planning legislation is regulated by ss.231 to 233 of the 1972 Act. Those decisions not specified in those sections are subject to the ordinary supervisory powers of the Court of Session. The somewhat complex position regarding recourse to the Court of Session is considered in chapter 21.

Differences between Scottish and English planning law

As might be expected, Scottish planning law is similar to and in many respects identical to that which operates in England and Wales. To avoid confusion amongst those engaged in the development of land a measure of conformity would seem to be desirable. Nonetheless, as we indicated earlier, there are differences in law and procedure. These are too numerous to catalogue but it may be helpful to mention some of the more important areas of difference.

First of all, there are what might be termed structural differences. The Local Government (Scotland) Act 1973 introduced a two-tier structure of regions and districts throughout Scotland with the exception of the three islands areas—Orkney, Shetland and the Western Isles—which are all-purpose authorities (see chapter 3). In six of the nine regions, planning is split between the two tiers in much the same way as it is divided between the counties and districts in England and Wales. However, in the three rural regions—Highland, Dumfries and Galloway and Borders—the districts were not considered to have the resources necessary to provide a satisfactory local planning service and in these areas planning (both local and strategic) is a regional function carried out by the regional councils as 'general planning authorities'. The three islands councils are also 'general planning authorities'.

Secondly, there are differences inherent in the different legal systems within which the two planning systems operate. This has implications, for example, as regards the procedure for judicial review and the remedies available, and in relation to such matters as the interpretation of the scope of the power to enter into agreements under the planning legislation regulating the development and use of land (see chapter 12).

Thirdly, the Local Government (Scotland) Act 1973 (s.173) makes provision for the preparation by regional and general planning authorities of regional reports (see chapter 5). There is no corresponding provision for England and Wales. Such reports have been used to provide a basis for the preparation of the first round of structure plans in Scotland and have been used in some authorities to assist corporate planning.

Fourthly, unlike England and Wales, local plan coverage in Scotland is to be comprehensive. District and general planning authorities are obliged by the Local Government (Scotland) Act 1973 to prepare local plans for all parts of their area as soon as practicable. Regional planning authorities may only intervene to prepare local plans in prescribed circumstances. There is no provision for, and indeed no need for, development plan schemes in Scotland.

Fifthly, there are a number of notable differences in the development control process. Three examples may be given. First of all, although there is no equivalent in Scotland to 'county matters' (prescribed categories of planning applications which fall to be determined by county councils in England and Wales rather than district councils), regional planning authorities may direct districts to refer applications to them (the region) for determination where the development proposed does not conform to an approved structure plan or where it raises a major planning issue of general significance. County councils in England and Wales no longer have power to issue such directions. Secondly, Scotland has gone further than England and Wales as regards the categories of people to be notified of planning applications. In particular, neighbours must now be informed; and the types of development subject to publicity requirements as potential 'bad neighbours' are more extensive. Thirdly, in England and Wales it is an offence to fail to comply with an enforcement notice which has taken effect and which requires the taking of steps other than the discontinuance of a use of land. It is not an offence in Scotland; the only sanction available to planning authorities is to take direct action to secure compliance with the notice.

In addition to these matters, there are very many differences in the detail of the law, not only in the primary legislation but in delegated legislation too. There are also important differences in the nature and content of policy guidance issued to planning authorities by the respective Secretaries of State.[48]

---

[48] Contrast, for example, development control policy notes (England and Wales) with national planning guidelines (Scotland)—see chapter 4; contrast also the general tenor of D.o.E. Circular 22/1980 entitled 'Development Control—Policy and Practice' with that of S.D.D. Circular 24/1981 entitled 'Development Control'.

CHAPTER 2

PLANNING, DECISION-MAKING AND THE COURTS

Introduction

In a work devoted to the study of planning law it is hardly necessary to stress the significance of law in the planning process. Planning legislation is used as the primary instrument for the implementation of planning policy. It creates the planning authorities, allocates powers and duties between them, determines procedures and confers rights, benefits and disabilities upon individuals affected by planning decisions. As long as one's understanding of planning is confined to that within the public domain and not extended, for instance, to those powers of land-use control available to individuals by virtue of their ownership of land, the relevant law is almost exclusively statute-based and comprehensively covered by the Planning Acts themselves. The substance of this book immediately becomes a description and analysis of those Acts.

It is, however, an essential part of that analysis to take full account of the authoritative interpretative role of the courts in relation to the planning code. At practically every point, one would have only a very partial and unreliable account of the law if one were to read the words of a statute without regard to the treatment they have received at the hands of the courts. We know what the law means—and then only with uncertainty at some points—because the courts have said what it means. We know, for instance, what conditions planning authorities may lawfully attach to a planning permission because we have authoritative judicial interpretation of the phrase 'such conditions as they think fit'.[1]

Such authoritative pronouncements do not arise because courts are given a direct decision-making or appellate role within the planning structure. Sheriffs were at one time authorised to hear planning enforcement appeals from local authorities but that is not the case today.[2] On the other hand, the courts do have a general jurisdiction—in part expressly conferred by legislation and in part asserted by the courts to exist by implication—to consider challenges by individuals to the validity of most forms of administrative action. And it is this process of judicial review of the legal validity of administrative action that becomes very important in its production of a definitive commentary upon the planning code. The power,

---

[1]   See p. 231 below.
[2]   The former power of sheriffs to hear such appeals was removed by the Town and Country Planning (Scotland) Act 1969.

as we shall see, is one which in Scotland is exercisable by the Court of Session rather than in the sheriff courts. It is, therefore, to relevant decisions of that court to which we turn for authority in the first instance. However, the maintenance of legal authority on a coherent basis is achieved by a system of legal precedent operating in a hierarchy of courts. We have, therefore, to take account of the small number of House of Lords' decisions in Scottish planning cases which are regarded as binding the Court of Session. Within the Court of Session, decisions of the Inner House will take precedence over those in the Outer House. English decisions are also important because, in the first place, planning law is in most respects almost identical in the two jurisdictions and an issue raised and decided in one will have a direct counterpart in the other. Secondly, English decisions are so plentiful and therefore produce more substantial coverage of problem areas of the law. Thirdly, and perhaps most importantly in practice, English decisions are widely cited in argument in the Scottish courts and are frequently relied on in Scottish decisions. This will be evident at many points in this book.

One other preliminary point. Reference has already been made to the emphasis in this chapter upon the general judicial supervision over planning authorities exercised by the Court of Session. We should also bear in mind that local authorities and central departments can be made the subject of other forms of legal action. They are, in general, subject to the criminal law and occasional prosecutions are brought. They are capable of entering into contracts which can be enforced against them. Whilst the criminal law is probably only rarely invoked against a planning authority as such, questions of contractual capacity and liability can arise.[3]

Also of some potential significance to a planning authority is their liability in delict and, in particular, for the negligence of their servants. In areas outside planning, the law has developed substantially in recent years to enlarge the scope of negligence by local authorities. The distinction formerly maintained between the negligent exercise of a duty, which could attract liability, and the negligent exercise of a discretion, which could not, has collapsed. In the most famous recent case, *Anns v Merton London Borough Council*,[4] it was the failure of a building inspector to exercise a power to examine the foundations of a building which was held to be negligent in an action following the building's collapse. Liability depended upon establishing that the building control authority was in such a relationship to future occupants of the building as to create a duty of care owed to them. Following *Anns* there has been speculation as to which other local authority functions might also create such a duty of care. In *Lyons v F. W. Booth (Contractors) Ltd. and Maidstone Borough Council*,[5] Drake J. accepted that an authority's

---

[3]   See chapter 12 on planning agreements.

[4]   [1978] A.C. 728. See also the earlier English case which paved the way to *Anns—Dutton* v *Bognor Regis Urban District Council* [1972] 1 Q.B. 373. The reasoning in *Anns* was accepted as applicable to Scotland in *Hallett* v *Nicholson* 1979 S.C. 1. For discussion of that case and the position of planning authorities see M. A. Jones, 1983 S.P.L.P. 14.

[5]   (1982) 262 E.G. 981. Contrast, however, *Strable* v *Borough Council of Dartford* [1984] J.P.L. 329.

duty of care when approving a planning application was in principle the same as the duty imposed on a building control authority. Nor is it inconceivable that the grant of planning permission for a building with insufficient regard for the safety of future occupants or of others might be treated as negligent. This was a point taken in argument but not finally determined in *Ravenseft Properties Ltd.* v *British Gas Corporation*[6]—the case which arose out of the Clarkston disaster in which gas escaping into a void in the basement of a building exploded and wrecked a row of shops. It has also become clear that a planning authority may, in appropriate circumstances, be held liable for negligent mis-statements made by their officials. In *Co-operative Retail Services Ltd.* v *Taff-Ely Borough Council*,[7] it was held that, in principle, the clerk of the Council's mis-statement to the effect that planning permission had been granted when it had not could render the Council liable for the loss (reflecting the inflated price paid for the site) suffered by the intending developer.[8]

The supervisory role of the Court of Session

There is a simply stated principle that the Court of Session enjoys, subject to statutory intervention, an inherent power of review or supervision over the acts or omissions of administrative authorities. Among these authorities are those with planning responsibilities in central and local government. However simple to state in outline, this principle of judicial review is one of profound constitutional and political significance and one which has generated a wealth of decisions in its application to both Scotland and England. Some of this wealth will be explored shortly but, first, two important glosses upon the opening statement:

(*a*) Since *Brown* v *Hamilton District Council*[9] in 1982 we can now say with confidence that the general supervisory jurisdiction is exclusive to the Court of Session and is not shared with the sheriff court. As we have seen, the sheriff can be invested with statutory appellate powers but *Brown*, which was not itself a planning case but one concerning local authority powers under the Housing (Homeless Persons) Act 1977, established that he has no inherent powers of review. The hopes of some interested parties that a forum for local and relatively cheap review might be confirmed as an alternative to the Court of Session were frustrated. Local authorities were probably relieved.

(*b*) The other preliminary point is that there has been substantial statutory intervention into the general principles of review in the shape of ss. 231 to 233 of the 1972 Act. As we shall find in chapter 21, the effect of these sections

[6]   Court of Session, 31st January 1979 (unreported, but see 1981 S.P.L.P. 76).
[7]   (1983) 133 New L.J. 577.
[8]   But, for reasons specific to the complex facts of the case, no liability was established in *Taff-Ely*; see C. Crawford, '*Taff-Ely Revisited—the Negligence Aspect*' (1983) 267 E.G. 579.
[9]   1983 S.L.T. 397 (H.L.).

is, at the same time, both to narrow and to broaden the scope of judicial review. On the one hand, they exclude from general review (other than in the terms they specify) the important types of decision to which they apply. On the other hand, in relation to those decisions they arguably extend the grounds upon which they may be challenged. The jurisdictional tests of invalidity to be discussed in this chapter are not the sole heads of challenge under ss. 231 to 233 although they are relevant to it.

Returning to the Court of Session's inherent powers of review, our main concern at this point is with the principles underpinning that review—the approach adopted by the court—rather than with findings in specific cases before it. Many of these, together with decisions from the English courts, are incorporated at appropriate points in the chapters dealing with the substantive law.

At the core of judicial review are two assumptions made by the court. In the first place there is an assumption that those bodies which exercise powers conferred by Parliament (and, in the case of local authorities, are bodies created by Parliament) are entitled to act only within the limits, express or implied, of those powers. Planning authorities have no 'general competence'. It is not that they may do all those things not expressly prohibited by the law. They are instead forbidden to do anything which lacks positive statutory authority. They must act *intra vires*; they must not act *ultra vires*.

The second assumption is that, on the application of an appropriate individual, it is for the courts to decide upon the limits of an authority's powers; upon whether they have acted *ultra vires*. The courts must act as the guardians of Parliament's will; they must police the limits of administrative powers. In assuming this role, they do not, of course, act completely alone. When a local authority's decision is taken on appeal to the Secretary of State, the minister may certainly have regard as much to the legality of the decision as to its merits.[10] Ombudsmen may investigate procedural irregularity as maladministration which would also constitute unlawful behaviour.[11] Nor is it inevitable, of course, that the ordinary courts should exercise any substantial measure of supervision over planning powers at all. It would by no means be constitutionally inconceivable that this task be given instead to a specialist tribunal—largely displacing the powers of the Court of Session.

Given the present dispensation, however, the function of that court together with its counterparts in England (and the House of Lords in relation to both) attracts two lines of inquiry. The first is an explanation of the principles applied, an analysis of the rules expounded by the courts. The second, less important in this work but essential to a broader evaluation of the planning process, is an assessment of the impact upon that process of the insertion of judicial supervision.

[10] See for example p. 266 below.
[11] See p. 53 below.

The principles of judicial review[12]

Although the two processes bear some resemblance to each other the inherent power of judicial review is not the same as that of deciding statutorily prescribed appeals. In the latter case, Parliament may confer wide appellate powers. The court may be permitted to correct errors of law of all types, or errors of fact or to reach a different decision on the basis of a different evaluation of the facts in the matter before it. The court may be authorised to substitute its own decision for that made initially by the administrative body.

When we turn to judicial review, deriving not from statute but from the inherent powers of the court, we are looking at a process in which the role of the court is both less clearly defined and (notionally at least) more limited. Most important, for our purposes, are the grounds of challenge to administrative action most relevant to the planning function and these are discussed below. We should, however, look first at the surrounding principles. These are principles in no way confined to planning law but which are said to be of general application across the entire range of administrative activity. In one way the generality of the principles of judicial review is attractive. It can enable the development of the law in one field to benefit from principles established elsewhere—planning law is only one area in many to have felt the very substantial effects of an English Court of Appeal decision of 1947 concerning cinema licensing.[13] On the other hand, there are those who are rightly sceptical about the easy transferability of principles across functions which, on their face, have little to unite them. At the very least, we have to acknowledge that, however common the principles, their application should and does vary from one statutory context to another. But what are the general principles of judicial review? Severely compressed, they may perhaps be summarised in the following way.

The starting point is the assertion by the courts of the power referred to above to oversee the actions of administrative bodies in support of the constitutional principles of legislative supremacy and the rule of law. How they do this requires knowledge of who may challenge the *vires* of an administrative authority; the grounds upon which such a challenge may be founded; and the scope of the remedies available if a challenge is successful.

An administrative action or decision is not open to challenge by all and sundry. An individual wishing to commence proceedings must himself have

---

[12]   There is no Scottish text devoted to judicial review or to administrative law as a whole. J. D. B. Mitchell's *Constitutional Law* (W. Green & Son, 2nd ed., 1968) has a chapter on the subject. The standard English texts are Wade and Phillips, *Constitutional and Administrative Law* (Longman, 9th ed. by A. W. Bradley, 1977); H. W. R. Wade, *Administrative Law* (Clarendon Press, 5th ed., 1982); *de Smith's Judicial Review of Administrative Action* (Stevens, 4th ed. by J. M. Evans, 1980); D. Foulkes, *Administrative Law* (Butterworths, 5th ed., 1982); and P. Craig, *Administrative Law* (Sweet & Maxwell, 1983). On most of the central (substantive) principles of judicial review, these English works are a useful guide to the law in Scotland as well.

[13]   *Associated Provincial Picture Houses Ltd.* v *Wednesbury Corporation* [1948] 1 K.B. 223 (see below).

sufficient title and interest to sue. In a planning matter a person who, for instance, has himself been refused planning permission would have such an interest. A member of the public less closely related to a decision may not.[14] A planning authority on the other hand may be able to challenge the *vires* of one of their own decisions.[15] Undue delay in bringing proceedings may be a bar to success.[16]

More seriously, the court might be forced to conclude that its own general power to review has been excluded by specific statutory provision, although courts have been extremely reluctant to concede that a total exclusion of review has been achieved. They have managed to assert their jurisdiction despite statutory provisions declaring an administrative decision to be 'final'[17] although they have acknowledged that a provision 'ousting' the courts' jurisdiction after a specific period of time may be effective.[18] There has also been some recognition by the courts of a need to 'exhaust' suitable alternative remedies provided by legislation. Where, for example, provision is made for appeal to the Secretary of State against the decision of a planning authority, the court may treat its common law jurisdiction as excluded or at least suspended. Much will depend on the court's view of the particular statutory provision.[19] Rather different is the scope for effective exclusion of the court by the use of very broad language when discretionary administrative powers are conferred. It may be Parliament's clear intention that the role of the court should be reduced but just because a power or duty is expressed in subjective terms such as 'if the Secretary of State is satisfied' does not necessarily mean that the court will be prepared to allow the authority in question to be the final arbiter of its own powers. The court may still have to be satisfied that there is a proper basis for the action taken.[20]

Common to all the grounds of challenge discussed below is the concept of jurisdiction.[21] The court is not, in theory at least, concerned with the policy merits of an act or decision but with whether it lies within an authority's powers. The court's function is not to re-evaluate criteria relied on by the authority. Nor does a court normally become concerned with the reassessment or reinterpretation of the facts upon which an act or decision is based. A mere error of fact, therefore, will not necessarily vitiate a decision. Only if a 'fact' or a 'state of facts' is fundamental to the very existence of an

---

[14] See *Simpson* v *Edinburgh Corporation* 1960 S.C. 313; 1961 S.L.T. 17 (discussed at p. 541 below).

[15] See *Inverclyde District Council* v *Inverkip Building Co. Ltd.* 1981 S.C. 401; 1982 S.L.T. 401.

[16] See C. T. Reid, 'Mora and Administrative Law' 1981 S.L.T. (News) 253.

[17] See *Moss' Empires Ltd* v *Assessor for Glasgow* 1917 S.C. (H.L.) 1; and *Anisminic Ltd.* v *Foreign Compensation Commission* [1969] 2 A.C. 147.

[18] See *Smith* v *East Elloe R.D.C.* [1956] A.C. 736; *Hamilton* v *Secretary of State for Scotland* 1972 S.C. 72; 1972 S.L.T. 233; and *R.* v *Secretary of State for the Environment, ex p. Ostler* [1977] Q.B. 122 (discussed in chapter 21 below).

[19] See the cases discussed at p. 538–540 below.

[20] See 'Abuse of discretion' below.

[21] For discussion of this concept see, in addition to the works cited in note 12 above, A. W. Bradley, 'Jurisdictional Aspects of Judicial Review in Scotland' in *In Memoriam J.D.B. Mitchell* (Eds. Bates et al, Sweet & Maxwell, 1983).

authority's jurisdiction will it be appropriate for a reviewing court to investigate it.[22] The proof of relevant facts may also be relevant, however, in proceedings in which a discretionary decision is challenged on the grounds that there is no evidence upon which the particular conclusion could be based.[23]

Not even all errors of law are open to challenge in the process of judicial review. The courts (in Scotland at least) hold on to the distinction between an error of law which goes to an administrative authority's jurisdiction and one which does not. If the error is of such a nature that the authority has, in effect 'asked itself the wrong question', that is, it has wrongly defined the limits of its statutory powers, and has as a result done something not authorised by statute, the court may intervene.[24] The Court of Session has, however, no jurisdiction at common law to correct an *intra vires* error of law—where, for instance, an authority has 'asked itself the right question' but arrived at an erroneous conclusion. The distinction between *ultra vires* and *intra vires* error may be a very fine one.[25] What is clear, however, is that very many errors of law are capable of being categorised as going to an authority's jurisdiction, thus opening the door to judicial review.

Once it is embarked upon its reviewing function, the essence of the court's task is the process of statutory interpretation. It is both as simple and as difficult as ascertaining Parliament's will as expressed in legislation and applying this to the circumstances of the case before the court. Interpretation is never a merely mechanical, technical exercise. Merely to ascertain the meaning of individual words can be difficult;[26] determining the limits of widely expressed discretionary powers of the type found throughout the planning legislation can be infinitely more difficult. Choices of meaning have to be made by judges whose approach to the task will, therefore, greatly affect the outcome. Some examples of how the courts have dealt with specific aspects of interpretation are given below and, thereafter, throughout this book. Two particular issues should, however, be mentioned here.

One concerns the situation where an authority appear to have been given

[22] See, for example, *Ashbridge Investments Ltd.* v *Minister of Housing and Local Government* [1965] 1 W.L.R. 1320; and *Coleen Properties Ltd.* v *Minister of Housing and Local Government* [1971] 1 W.L.R. 433. On the problems in this area see, however, Wade, *Administrative Law* (5th ed.), pp. 287–295.

[23] See, for example, *British Airports Authority* v *Secretary of State for Scotland* 1979 S.C. 200; 1979 S.L.T. 197.

[24] See *Watt* v *Lord Advocate* 1979 S.C. 120; 1979 S.L.T. 137. In the town planning field see *City of Glasgow District Council* v *Secretary of State for Scotland* 1985 S.L.T. 19; and *Grampian Regional Council* v *Secretary of State for Scotland* 1983 S.L.T. 526.

[25] Contrast, for example, the views of Lord Dunpark in *Watt* (1977 S.L.T. 130) with those of the members of the First Division.

[26] A good example is *Newbury District Council* v *Secretary of State for the Environment* [1981] A.C. 578. In that case the Secretary of State, a unanimous Divisional Court and a unanimous Court of Appeal held that a particular building could not be described as a 'repository', Lord Denning saying that 'no one, conversant with the English language, would dream' of so describing the building and Lawton L.J. declaring that 'no literate person' would describe the building as a 'repository'. In the House of Lords, however, all five judges held the building to be a 'repository'.

in two different statutes the power to achieve the same policy objective. Are they obliged to avail themselves of the power under one Act rather than of that under another? It has been held that they are not. An authority cannot be faulted for choosing to rely on one Act rather than another even though the consequences for individuals affected by their action may be quite different.[27]

Another question arises in review proceedings where a part only of an administrative decision is challenged or eventually found to be *ultra vires*. If, for instance, a condition attached to a planning decision is found to be unlawful, the court will have to consider whether to strike down the whole permission or to sever the bad part of the decision—the defective condition—leaving the good part intact. Broadly speaking, it seems that the decision on severance will depend on the court's view of whether the effect of excising the bad part would be to leave standing a decision significantly different from the original; if it would, the whole decision will fall.[28] On a statutory application to quash, however, the court has no such choice; if part of the decision in question is bad it must either quash the decision as a whole or leave it standing.[29]

This leads us to the consequences generally of judicial review proceedings and the remedies available. There is a very compelling logic behind the argument that if an action or decision is held to be *ultra vires*, it must be totally without legal effect and must always have been so. It is a complete nullity. It is void and not merely voidable if that latter term be taken to imply the validity (other than merely an initial presumption of validity) of an *ultra vires* decision up to the time of the court's order.

The purity of this logic is not, however, always accepted. For one thing, it has been appreciated that voidness is best regarded not as an absolute but a relative quality. An action or decision may be void for some purposes but valid for others. More significantly in practice, the courts themselves have generally taken a pragmatic approach. By treating an *ultra vires* decision as effective until quashed, the courts escape what Wade calls 'the more inconvenient consequences of carrying their doctrine of nullity to its logical conclusions'.[30] Thus in *London and Clydeside Estates Ltd.* v *Aberdeen District Council*[31] the House of Lords held that an *ultra vires* decision was not a complete nullity in the sense that it had to be regarded for legal purposes as completely non-existent. To have held the decision in that case a complete nullity would have resulted in the victim of procedural error by the planning authority being left without a remedy. Lord Hailsham said that courts

[27] See *Westminster Bank Ltd.* v *Minister of Housing and Local Government* [1971] A.C. 508.
[28] See *London and Clydeside Estates Ltd.* v *Aberdeen District Council* 1980 S.C. (H.L.) 1; 1980 S.L.T. 81; *Inverclyde District Council* v *Inverkip Building Co. Ltd.* 1983 S.L.T. 563; and pp. 248–250 below.
[29] See *British Airports Authority* v *Secretary of State for Scotland* 1979 S.C. 200; 1979 S.L.T. 197.
[30] See *Administrative Law* (5th ed.), p. 310 and generally pp. 308–315.
[31] 1980 S.C. (H.L.) 1; 1980 S.L.T. 81.

should not consider themselves bound to fit the facts of a particular case into 'rigid legal categories or to stretch or cramp them on a bed of Procrustes invented by lawyers for the purposes of convenient exposition'.[32]

When we speak, in the context of judicial review, of the remedy to be awarded by the Court of Session if it does hold the act or decision of a public authority to be *ultra vires*, we are referring to the ordinary remedies available in that court.[33] A pursuer may be granted, as appropriate, reduction, declarator, interdict or an order under s.91 of the Court of Session Act 1868. Failing these, the *nobile officium* of the Court of Session may be invoked to provide a remedy in exceptional circumstances and where no other is available.[34] At present, no special procedural rules apply to actions where these remedies are sought in judicial review cases. Following criticism of this situation by Lord Fraser in *Brown* v *Hamilton District Council*[35] and the publication of the report of a working party chaired by Lord Dunpark in 1984,[36] it is now intended that a special accelerated procedure should be introduced. There would be a new 'application for the exercise of the supervisory jurisdiction of the Court of Session' which would leave to the Court the choice of an appropriate remedy to be awarded at the end of the proceedings.

The heads of challenge in judicial review

Whilst the numbers of cases of judicial review have risen considerably in recent years (in England more than in Scotland) and planning cases are particularly numerous, it is not a simple matter to categorise the different heads of challenge. It is, in any event, probably unhelpful to attempt precise classification. The courts do not do this themselves and have warned against imposing artificial limits upon the generality of the *ultra vires* principle.[37] Within the planning sphere, however, it may be useful to indicate three broad areas of judicial activity, illustrations of which recur throughout this book. The first concerns the abuse (including the non-use) of discretionary power—the central point being that statutory powers, however broadly expressed, are not without legal limits. The second is procedural irregularity—failure to comply with statutory procedural requirements may produce an *ultra vires* act. The third category is related and is breach of the rules of natural justice—procedural requirements presumed by the courts to apply in some administrative situations.

---

[32]   1980 S.C. (H.L.) 1, at p. 31.
[33]   For remedies generally see A. W. Bradley, *Remedies in Administrative Law* (Scottish Law Commission Memorandum No. 14, 1971).
[34]   See *London and Clydeside Estates* above.
[35]   1983 S.L.T. 397 (H.L.).
[36]   *Report by the Working Party on Procedure for Judicial Review of Administrative Action* (1984). See J. L. Murdoch, 'Reviewing Administrative Action' (1984) 98 SCOLAG 160; and A. C. Page, 'Just and Reasonable' 1984 S.L.T. (News) 290.
[37]   See, for example, the speech of Lord Scarman in *Bromley London Borough Council* v *Greater London Council* [1983] 1 A.C. 768.

Abuse of discretion. If an Act of Parliament empowers a local authority to do A and the authority do B, there is no disputing a court's duty to hold that the authority have exceeded their powers. B is an *ultra vires* act and of no legal effect. Only if B can be subsumed within A, (or regarded as calculated to facilitate or to be conducive or incidental to A[38]) can it be held to be valid.

Sometimes, however, Parliament quite deliberately goes out of its way to reduce the chances of successful judicial review by conferring a particularly broad decision-making power upon an authority. The authority is given wide policy choice and has a discretionary area within which it is free to act—a feature of many parts of town and country planning legislation. To take perhaps the best example, authorities are given a general power when granting planning permission to attach conditions. By way of re-confirmation of the generality of the power they may be 'such conditions as they think fit'. The power is broad and subjective but not broad enough to defeat all challenge in the courts.[39]

What the courts have done is, on the one hand, to proclaim their determination not to encroach upon those areas of decision-making entrusted by Parliament to administrative authorities but, on the other, to insist that there are implied legally-defined limits to discretionary power. Some of these judicially-created limits are unsurprising. So, for instance, the exercise of a power maliciously or vindictively would, if the bad faith could be established, plainly be contrary to Parliament's implied intent. The requirement that powers should not be used for a malicious purpose does not have to be spelled out. Quite quickly, however, this most obvious limit is joined by others. An improper purpose, however honest or well-meaning, will disqualify as will the failure to take into account considerations relevant to the decision in hand or the admission of irrelevant considerations.[40]

Although the authority for these judicially prescribed limits to discretionary power is scattered over a very wide range of decisions in both the Scottish and English courts, one source towers above the others and, indeed, its influence seems to grow with time. This is the judgment of Lord Greene M.R. in *Associated Provincial Picture Houses Ltd.* v *Wednesbury Corporation.*[41] This was the case in which the English Court of Appeal considered the validity of a condition attached by the local authority to a cinema licence issued under the Sunday Entertainments Act 1932. The case has no continuing significance in the field of cinema licensing but it is important for the manner in which Lord Greene circumscribed the powers of a court to interfere with the exercise of a discretionary administrative power conferred by Parliament. The law recognises certain principles within which a discretion must be exercised, but within the four corners of those

---

[38] See s.69 of the Local Government (Scotland) Act 1973 which provides statutory authority for a principle already adopted by the courts in, for example, *Graham* v *Glasgow Corporation* 1936 S.C. 108.

[39] See chapter 10 and p. 251 below.

[40] See, for example, *Ashley* v *Magistrates of Rothesay* (1873) 11 M. 708; and *Rossi* v *Edinburgh Corporation* (1904) 7 F. (H.L.) 85.

[41] [1948] 1 K.B. 223.

principles the discretion is absolute and cannot be questioned. The principles themselves add up to the requirement that a discretionary power be exercised 'reasonably'—which, for Lord Greene embraced all those requirements of good faith, relevance of considerations taken into account and the other qualities listed above. The judgment is also important; however, for its recognition that a discretionary decision, although unimpeachable under any of the heads mentioned, may be challenged as one 'so unreasonable that no reasonable authority could ever have come to it'. The *Wednesbury* principles (or sometimes simply 'principle') are now frequently invoked in cases involving discretionary decisions of all types. They are adopted as a convenient shorthand description of the basis of a reviewing court's powers and have the attraction (but also the attendant ambiguity) of both asserting the discretionary freedom of statutory bodies but at the same time providing for the courts a list of malleable controls over that freedom. For what is 'improper' or 'irrelevant', or, on the other hand, 'proper' or 'relevant' is a matter for judicial decision in the process of statutory interpretation—a task which is more than usually difficult in the town planning field in that the legislation gives very little explicit guidance as to its scope and objectives. This produces the wealth of decisions on the validity of conditions and indeed on the validity of planning permissions themselves.[42]

The examples of abuse of discretionary power given so far all imply some positive failure on the part of the authority but the courts have also looked critically upon situations where an authority have in effect neglected a duty to exercise the discretion conferred by Parliament. If an authority are statutorily obliged to build roads or to provide schools the duty is enforceable by the courts. The duty of a public body possessed of discretionary powers 'to exercise a free and unhindered discretion' is similarly enforceable.[43]

A planning authority must not, therefore, fetter their discretion by self-created rules or policies. Although policies (whether set out in the development plan or elsewhere) are, of course, central to town and country planning, policy must not be so rigid as to prevent an authority from fairly judging each individual case 'on its own merits and as the public interest requires at the time'.[44] Or, as was said in *Innes* v *Royal Burgh of Kirkcaldy*[45] and *Meek* v *Lothian Regional Council*[46] authorities must not exercise their powers with 'closed minds'.[47] A planning authority cannot, therefore, simply

---

[42] See chapters 10 and 11 below.
[43] See *Southend-on-Sea Corporation* v *Hodgson (Wickford) Ltd.* [1962] 1 Q.B. 416.
[44] Wade, *Administrative Law* (5th ed.), p. 331.
[45] 1963 S.L.T. 325—although that case has to be treated cautiously insofar as it has implications for politically 'closed minds'.
[46] 1980 S.L.T. (Notes) 61.
[47] See too *Magistrates of Kilmarnock* v *Secretary of State for Scotland* 1961 S.C. 350; 1961 S.L.T. 333; *R.* v *Secretary of State for the Environment, ex p. Reinisch* (1971) 22 P. & C.R. 1022; and *Link Homes Ltd.* v *Secretary of State for the Environment* [1976] J.P.L. 430. In Evans' words: 'a factor that may properly be taken into account in exercising a discretion may become an unlawful fetter upon discretion if it is elevated to the status of a general rule that results in the pursuit of consistency at the expense of the merits of individual cases' (*de Smith's Judicial Review of Administrative Action* (4th ed.), p. 312).

resolve to refuse all applications in a particular area as premature pending the making of a plan for the area.

Nor may a body entrusted with discretionary power act under the direction of another[48] or abdicate the exercise of its powers to another.[49] In *H. Lavender & Son Ltd.* v *Minister of Housing and Local Government*[50] the minister dismissed a planning appeal on the grounds (a) that it was his policy that high quality agricultural land should not be released for mineral working unless the Minister of Agriculture was not opposed to such a course of action and (b) that in the present case the agricultural objection had not been waived. The minister's decision was quashed, Willis J. stating: 'by applying and acting upon his stated policy I think that the Minister has fettered himself in such a way that in this case it was not he who made the decision for which Parliament made him responsible. It was the decision of the Minister of Agriculture not to waive his objection which was decisive in this case.' This does not mean, of course, that an authority is not entitled to consult with the Secretary of State and other persons and bodies and take their views into account. Nor does it mean that one minister may not consult with another.[51] In several situations the planning legislation actually requires planning authorities to consult with specified persons and authorities.[52]

Related to this general rule that discretionary powers should not be fettered is a somewhat ill-defined principle that a public body is not free to enter into a contractual or other undertaking where there is a real likelihood that the undertaking would seriously conflict with one of the authority's basic functions.[53] The contractual obligation might limit future freedom. However, the provisions of s.50 of the 1972 Act, empowering planning authorities to enter into agreements relating to the use or development of land, appear to be designed to enable authorities to fetter the future exercise of their statutory powers to a greater extent than would otherwise be possible. The extent of these powers is considered below.[54]

Discretionary powers may give rise to duties. Though authorities are not, and cannot be, obliged to exercise their discretion in any particular way, they are bound to determine matters entrusted to them by Parliament for decision. In *Bovis Homes (Scotland) Ltd.* v *Inverclyde District Council*[55] it

---

[48]   Statute specifically provides that in certain circumstances the Secretary of State may direct planning authorities as to how they are to act.

[49]   As to planning authorities' powers to delegate decision-making powers, see, however, p. 48 below.

[50]   [1970] 1 W.L.R. 1231.

[51]   See *Kent County Council* v *Secretary of State for the Environment* (1977) 75 L.G.R. 452. (One minister entitled to take account of the views of another minister.)

[52]   As to what is meant by 'consultation' see C. T. Reid 'A Planning Authority's Duty to Consult' 1982 S.P.L.P. 4.

[53]   See, for example, *Ayr Harbour Trustees* v *Oswald* (1885) 10 R. (H.L.) 85; and *Stringer* v *Minister of Housing and Local Government* [1970] 1 W.L.R. 1281.

[54]   See p. 285.

[55]   1982 S.L.T. 473. See too *Howard* v *Secretary of State for the Environment* [1975] Q.B. 235; and *R.* v *Secretary of State for the Environment, ex p. Percy Bilton Industrial Properties* (1975) 31 P. & C.R. 154.

was held that the planning authority were obliged to make a decision one way or another on an application for planning permission and the court ordered the authority to do so, even though the statutory period for making the decision had expired. In some circumstances at least, it seems that an authority are under a duty to consider whether they ought to exercise their discretionary powers.[56]

Procedural irregularity. When insisting that a discretionary power be not abused, the courts are not requiring any particular outcome. They are asserting the necessity that decisions be made under conditions assumed to be intended by Parliament—conditions untainted by, for instance, bad faith or irrelevance.

Sometimes Parliament itself makes further provision for desirable decision-making conditions by specifying the procedures according to which powers may be exercised. These may be procedures designed to ensure fairness to applicants for planning permission or to persons otherwise affected by planning powers. They may be rules to ensure that persons other than those most directly affected are at least informed or consulted about the issues. When such procedural requirements are laid down, the courts are bound to assume that they must be observed. As it was put by Lord Hailsham in *London and Clydeside Estates Ltd.* v *Aberdeen District Council*:[57] 'When Parliament lays down a statutory requirement for the exercise of legal authority it expects its authority to be obeyed down to the minutest detail.' Lord Hailsham went on to say, however, that 'what the courts have to decide in a particular case is the legal consequence of non-compliance on the rights of the subject viewed in the light of a concrete state of facts and a continuing chain of events'.

The reason for courts wishing to distinguish between different forms of procedural failing is clear enough. There would be little sense in making every planning decision vulnerable to the complaint of any aggrieved applicant who could point out a tiny deviation from the procedural straight and narrow. But deciding which errors are serious enough to produce invalidity is inevitably an imprecise art and one practised *post hoc*—after the alleged mistake has been made. Broadly speaking, however, what the court has to decide is whether a procedural requirement should be regarded as mandatory, in which case failure will invalidate the action taken, or whether the requirement is merely directory, in which case failure will not necessarily have such consequences. The law is, however, more flexible than is suggested by this distinction taken alone. In *London and Clydeside Estates*, Lord Hailsham spoke of the categories shading into one another and of there being a 'spectrum of possibilities'.

It can, therefore, be very difficult to forecast how the courts will treat a particular requirement. The decision as to whether a requirement is mandatory or directory may well depend on the court's view of such factors

---

[56]   *R.* v *Stroud District Council, ex p. Goodenough* (1980) 43 P. & C.R. 59.
[57]   1980 S.C. (H.L.) 1; 1980 S.L.T. 81.

as the importance of the particular requirement in the overall scheme of the legislation, its significance in relation to the protection of individual rights and whether the defect is merely technical or will result in a real risk of prejudice.

Thus procedures relating to a citizen's right of appeal are very likely to be regarded as mandatory[58] as are the statutory requirements as to the matters to be specified in an enforcement notice.[59] In the perhaps special circumstances of *Steeples* v *Derbyshire County Council*[60] a failure on the part of an authority to place a notice in the appropriate register was treated as mandatory and as invalidating the authority's resolution. In *Howard* v *Secretary of State for the Environment*[61] notice of appeal against an enforcement notice was given within the prescribed time limit but the notice did not, as the statute required, state the grounds of appeal. The Court of Appeal treated the former requirement as mandatory[62] but considered the requirement as to specification of the grounds of appeal to be merely directory—the Secretary of State could require such grounds to be submitted at a later date.[63] In *Inverclyde District Council* v *Secretary of State for Scotland*[64] the House of Lords held that the requirement in the General Development Order that an application for approval of reserved matters should provide certain particulars was merely directory, so that there was no reason why these particulars should not be proferred later.

The planning legislation states that a decision on a planning application is to be made within two months. That requirement is merely directory and a decision given outside that period will, therefore, be good—at least if the permission is acted upon or for the purposes of appeal to the Secretary of State.[65] The duty on a planning authority to issue a decision on a planning application does not, however, cease at the end of the specified period; it is a

[58] See, for example, *London and Clydeside Estates* (above); *Wilson* v *Secretary of State for the Environment* [1973] 1 W.L.R. 1083; and *R.* v *Lambeth London Borough Council, ex parte Sharp, The Times,* 28th December 1984.

[59] As is mentioned below (p. 328), the Secretary of State has power to correct certain types of defect in an enforcement notice.

[60] [1985] I.W.L.R. 256. See too *Vale of Glamorgan Borough Council* v *Palmer and Bowles* (1982) 81 L.G.R. 679.

[61] [1975] Q.B. 235. See too *Chelmsford R.D.C.* v *Powell* [1963] 1 W.L.R. 123.

[62] See, however, *Sievers* v *London Borough of Bromley* [1980] J.P.L. 520. In that case an application for approval of reserved matters was submitted two days after the due date. The application was held valid because the lateness, if any, was *de minimis* and in any case Saturday and Sunday should not be counted since there was no way an application could, on those days, be 'left' at the local authority's office as provided by the legislation.

[63] In *P.A.D. Entertainments Ltd.* v *Secretary of State for the Environment* [1982] J.P.L. 706 the minister was held entitled to dismiss an appeal without a hearing if no grounds were supplied. See now also Local Government and Planning (Scotland) Act 1982, Sched. 2, para. 20(b).

[64] 1982 S.L.T. 200.

[65] See *James* v *Secretary of State for Wales* [1966] 1 W.L.R. 135 (C.A.); [1968] A.C. 409 (H.L.); and *London Ballast Co.* v *Buckinghamshire C.C.* (1966) 18 P. & C.R. 446 (applied in *London and Clydeside Estates* above).

continuing obligation and the court will, if necessary, require the authority to issue a decision outside the time limit.[66]

In *Inverclyde District Council* v *Inverkip Building Co. Ltd.*,[67] the Second Division held (upholding the decision of Lord McDonald[68]) that although the planning authority mistakenly believed they were imposing certain conditions as 'reserved matters', this was no more than a technical irregularity; even if the form of the document granting planning permission was wrong, the permission was still valid.

In *London and Clydeside Estates* (above) the House of Lords appear to have considered that the courts should preserve a wide discretion to take whatever action they think appropriate to remedy the results of any particular defect in procedure. Lord Hailsham thought it was neither necessary nor desirable to try to divide cases into two mutually exclusive categories, one resulting in a decision being a nullity, the other not. In that case it was held that, although there had been a failure to comply with a mandatory procedural requirement in connection with the issue of a certificate of appropriate alternative development, that failure did not make the certificate a complete nullity in the sense of being the same thing as a failure to issue a certificate at all. The certificate had some legal effect until it was set aside; in particular, it might be the proper subject of an appeal to the Secretary of State.

Similarly in *Brayhead (Ascot) Ltd.* v *Berkshire County Council*[69] it was held that the duty to give reasons for a condition attached to a grant of planning permission was mandatory but that a failure to comply with that obligation did not make the condition a nullity.[70] Reasons could still be demanded and could, if necessary, be ordered by the court.

A mere clerical error or inaccuracy or an obvious mistake may well not affect a decision.[71] When a decision is challenged under s.233 of the 1972 Act on account of a procedural defect the decision will not be quashed by the court unless it has resulted in substantial prejudice to the applicant.[72]

Personal bar: a brief excursus.[73] Although the concept of *vires* is a useful if imprecise tool in the resolution of some types of procedural irregularity, it is

---

[66] See *London and Clydeside Estates* (above); and *Bovis Homes (Scotland) Ltd.* v *Inverclyde District Council* 1982 S.L.T. 473.

[67] 1983 S.L.T. 563.

[68] 1981 S.C. 401; 1982 S.L.T. 401.

[69] [1964] 2 Q.B. 303.

[70] However, in *R.K.T. Investments Ltd.* v *Hackney L.B.C.* (1978) 36 P. & C.R. 442 Sir Douglas Frank considered the duty to be directory.

[71] See, for example, *Miller* v *Weymouth and Melcombe Regis Corporation* (1974) 27 P. & C.R. 468; *Preston Borough Council* v *Secretary of State for the Environment* [1978] J.P.L. 547; and *Elmbridge B.C.* v *Secretary of State for the Environment* [1980] J.P.L. 463.

[72] See chapter 21 below.

[73] See generally A. W. Bradley, 'Administrative Justice and the Binding Effect of Official Acts' 1981 *Current Legal Problems* p. 1; and C. Crawford and C. T. Reid, *Planning Officers' Advice and Undertakings: Estoppel and Personal Bar in Public Law* (S.P.L.P. Occasional Paper, 1982).

not a complete panacea. One illustration of the limitations of the *ultra vires* doctrine taken alone in the solving of a practical difficulty occurs where a planning authority's officials have made representations to an individual—typically a potential developer—but the authority subsequently wish to avoid the consequences of those representations. The situation in which officials meet developers informally in advance of a formal application occurs daily in planning practice but it is only in a tiny number of cases that, for instance, an official assures a developer that planning permission is unnecessary, the developer proceeds in accordance with that assurance and the authority then decide that permission is necessary but refuse it. Enforcement action may ensue. If it can be shown that the power to decide was delegated by the authority to the official concerned, then a problem does not arise.[74] The official's decision is that of the authority and, without the consent of the applicant or the payment of compensation, they cannot undo it.

The problem does, however, arise where no delegation has taken place. In such a situation the planning authority may resent any suggestion that the unauthorised statement of their official can tie their hands. It is their view rather than his which should prevail and this is an approach to which the doctrine of *vires* strictly construed lends much support. If a power may be exercised only by the person or authority designated by statute, and even formal delegation is permitted only to the extent statutorily prescribed, then the unauthorised behaviour of an employee cannot, it is argued, produce a valid exercise of power. To the extent that this argument contains within it the proposition that an authority cannot either by their own act or that of their servant extend their powers, it has received judicial approval. If an officer acts outwith the powers conferred on his authority, this clearly cannot constitute a valid act.[75] It is, however, much less clear what the result should be where the decision imputed to the official was not outwith his council's powers and where a third party has relied upon it as an exercise of ostensible authority.

It is in these circumstances that justice seems to demand a solution which takes rather more account of the predicament of the developer. Why should he suffer when he is told one thing by an officer with apparent authority only to be told something else by a committee a short time later? A solution may lie in an appeal to the Secretary of State against enforcement action. Alternatively, the authority may themselves be persuaded to exercise their discretion not to start enforcement proceedings either on further consideration of the matter themselves or following investigation by the local ombudsman. There are clear signs that the issue of inconsistent guidance or decisions from different parts of a planning authority may amount to maladministration. But is there a remedy available also from the courts?

The answer is that in some circumstances there may be. In the cases discussed below we find that the courts have imported from private law the

---

[74] For powers of planning authorities to delegate see p. 48 below.
[75] *Maritime Electric Company* v *General Dairies Ltd.* [1937] A.C. 610.

doctrine of personal bar or, as it is called in England, estoppel. This involves denying to a party in the position of a planning authority the right to rely on their strict legal entitlement where it would be unfair to another party and where the unfairness arises out of earlier representations made to that other party. At one stage it seemed that the English courts from which the major decisions have come were becoming prepared not only to employ the doctrine of estoppel but to do so quite generously on behalf of aggrieved developers. Latterly, and since the *Western Fish Products*[76] case in particular, they have adopted a more restrictive approach. Views on the desirability of this shift have varied. What is clear, however, is that when 'fairness' is to determine the outcome, it is not only fairness to developers which should be taken into account but also fairness to the public whose interests are required by statute to be safeguarded by the planning authority. It may be 'fair' to a developer that he benefits from the mistaken advice of an official but 'unfair' to neighbours who may lose the chance to have their objections considered and perhaps sustained by the formally constituted committee.

   In *Southend-on-Sea Corporation* v *Hodgson (Wickford) Ltd.*[77] it was held that a planning authority were entitled to serve an enforcement notice notwithstanding that one of their officials had earlier written to the developer stating that planning permission was not required for the development in question. At the time of that decision there was, however, no statutory provision for the delegation to officials of the power to make planning decisions. By the time *Lever Finance Ltd.* v *Westminster (City) London Borough Council*[78] was decided, statute permitted the delegation of certain planning functions to officials and in *Lever*, which seems almost indistinguishable on its facts from the *Southend* case, the Court of Appeal held that where, in the course of a telephone conversation, a planning officer, acting within his ostensible authority, had informed a developer that proposed variations from approved plans were not material and did not require consent, the planning authority were bound by the officer's statement and could not take enforcement action in respect of development carried out on the strength of the official's assurance. Sachs L.J. considered that the continuance, after the coming into operation of the statutory provisions permitting delegation of certain functions to officials, of the practice of allowing a planning officer to decide whether an alteration to a detailed planning permission was material or not, resulted in an implied delegation to the officer of power to deal with an application as to whether any further permission was required; and that the formalities for such an application were sufficiently observed if the decision on the application was recorded by the respective parties. Lord Denning M.R., with whom Megaw L.J. concurred, also reached the conclusion that the planning authority were bound by the officer's statement but seems to have applied a wider principle.

[76] *Western Fish Products Ltd.* v *Penwith District Council* [1981] 2 All E.R. 204.
[77] [1962] 1 Q.B. 416.
[78] [1971] 1 Q.B. 222.

He said:[79]

'If the planning officer tells the developer that a proposed variation is not material, and the developer acts on it, then the planning authority cannot go back on it. I know that there are authorities which say that a public authority cannot be estopped by any representations made by its officers. It cannot be estopped from doing its public duty: see, for instance, the recent decision of the Divisional Court in *Southend-on-Sea Corporation* v *Hodgson (Wickford) Ltd.*[80] But those statements must now be taken with considerable reserve. There are many matters which public authorities can now delegate to their officers. If an officer, acting within the scope of his ostensible authority makes a representation on which another acts, then a public authority may be bound by it, just as much as a private concern would be. A good instance is the recent decision of this court in *Wells* v *Minister of Housing and Local Government.*[81] It was proved in that case that it was the practice of planning authorities, acting through their officers, to tell applicants whether or not planning permission was necessary. A letter was written by the council engineer telling the applicants that no permission was necessary. The applicants acted on it. It was held that the planning authority could not go back on it. I would like to quote what I then said:

"It has been their practice to tell applicants that no planning permission is necessary. Are they now to be allowed to say that this practice was all wrong and their letters were of no effect? I do not think so. I take the law to be that a defect in procedure can be cured, and an irregularity can be waived, even by a public authority, so as to render valid that which would otherwise be invalid.'''

The fact that a representation has been acted upon may not, however, be sufficient to make that representation binding on the planning authority; as was pointed out by Lord Widgery C.J. in *Norfolk County Council* v *Secretary of State for the Environment,*[82] 'the mere fact that my agent has made a representation within his ostensible authority on which you act is not enough to estop me from denying his actual authority unless you have acted to your detriment'. In this case it was held that since applicants for planning permission had not suffered any loss by acting upon a permission issued in error by an official, the planning authority were entitled to deny the validity of the permission.

In *Brooks and Burton* v *Secretary of State for the Environment,*[83] Lord Widgery warned against further extension of the doctrine expressed in *Lever*. In *Brooks and Burton* it was argued that the planning authority were

[79] [1971] 1 Q.B. 222, at p. 230.
[80] [1962] 1 Q.B. 416.
[81] [1967] 1 W.L.R. 1000.
[82] [1973] 1 W.L.R. 1400.
[83] [1977] 1 W.L.R. 1294.

barred from serving an enforcement notice because of earlier statements by officials to the effect that the activities in question would not require planning permission. The Divisional Court held that it had not been shown that the appellants gave the officials sufficient information for them to give a precise answer so as to bind the authority. Lord Widgery declared that 'any attempt to expand the doctrine of estoppel in *Lever* was to be deprecated' because it was extremely important that a planning authority's officers should feel free to help applicants 'without all the time having the shadow of estoppel hanging over them and the possibility of their immobilising the authority by some careless remark'.

Lord Widgery's concern was received with sympathy by the Court of Appeal in *Western Fish Products Ltd.* v *Penwith District Council.*[84] The decision in that case has virtually reinstated the *Southend* position and, whilst not overturning *Lever* in so many words, has cast much doubt upon the generous elaboration of the doctrine of estoppel in that case. The facts in *Western Fish Products* were complex but again concerned a situation in which a planning official had indicated by letter to a developer (in this case of a fish processing plant) that the proposed development could proceed without further planning permission on the basis of established use rights. The council subsequently requested applications for planning permission, refused them when submitted, and started enforcement proceedings.

The Court of Appeal upheld the council's action on several grounds. In particular, they held that, on the facts of this case, the letter sent by the officer was not to be regarded as a representation as to existing use rights nor could the developer be seen as having relied on it to his detriment. More significantly, however, the court propounded the general principle that 'an estoppel cannot be raised to prevent the exercise of a statutory discretion or to prevent or excuse the performance of a statutory duty'. To this principle they recognised only two kinds of exception. The first, which as the court admitted 'is akin to *res judicata* and, therefore, scarcely an example of estoppel at all', is where there is formal, statutory delegation to the officer, which was not the case in *Western Fish Products*. The other exception is that where the planning authority, as in *Wells* (above), 'waives a procedural requirement relating to any application made to it for the exercise of its statutory powers, it may be estopped from relying on lack of formality'.

The court recognised that it was defending the *Southend* principle against an erosion such as that produced by the *Lever* case which the court criticised. The decision in *Lever* may have had the effect of preventing an injustice to the developer but:

'it also may fairly be regarded as having caused an injustice to one or more members of the public, the owners of adjacent houses who would be adversely affected by this wrong and careless decision of the planning officer that the modifications were not material. Yet they were not, and it would seem could not, be heard. How, in their absence, could the court balance the respective injustices according as the court did or did not hold that there was an estoppel in favour of the plaintiffs? What "equity" is there in holding, if such be the effect of the decision, that the potential injustice to a third party, as a result of the granting of the estoppel is irrelevant? At least it can be said that the less frequently this situation arises the better for justice.'[85]

Thus it is clear that the English courts have substantially reinstated the test of *vires* as the principal determinant of decisions in this difficult area. It is Parliament's wish that discretion be exercised and decisions made by planning authorities in the absence of formal delegation to officers. That wish is sustained even if at the cost of 'fairness' to affected developers. But, as the court held in *Western Fish Products*, 'the creation of new rights and remedies is a matter for Parliament, not the judges'.

Unfortunately, there is a lack of modern authority on the application of the doctrine of personal bar (which is a parallel to the English estoppel) to planning issues in the Scottish courts.[86] For the time being, one may tend to assume that a similar form of reasoning would be applied.

Natural justice. In some situations the courts have insisted upon the observance of not only the procedural requirements explicit in legislation but also additional implied standards. These are the standards of procedural fairness contained in the principles of natural justice. Even if statute is silent the individual may be able to claim the protection afforded by these principles.

Although it is reasonably clear that the two central pillars of natural justice are the rule that the other side be heard (*audi alteram partem*) and that the 'judge' be unbiased (*nemo iudex in sua causa*), the precise content of those rules and the rules which govern whether they apply at all are much less clear. To take this last point first, however, it is certain that, while natural justice may have some application to planning practice, it does not affect the largest category of planning decisions—those where planning authorities decide, at first instance, the outcome of planning applications. In *Gaiman* v *National Association for Mental Health*,[87] Megarry J. pointed out that thousands of planning applications are refused every year without any hearing, yet he knew 'of no suggestion that local planning authorities are thereby universally acting in contravention of the principles of natural justice'. It would be difficult to imagine any substantial extension of the principles here and the grosser forms of procedural unfairness are, in any event, open to correction either on appeal to the Secretary of State or by judicial review on the principles relating to abuse of discretion already

---

[85] [1981] 2 All E.R. 204, at p. 221.
[86] For a review see Crawford and Reid (note 73 above). And see *Inverclyde District Council* v *Inverkip Building Co. Ltd.* 1981 S.C. 401; 1982 S.L.T. 401.
[87] [1971] Ch. 317. but see also the remarks of Lord Denning in *R.* v *Liverpool Taxi Operators' Association* [1972] 2 Q.B. 299.

discussed. Where the principles of natural justice clearly do have some application is at the stage of appeals to the Secretary of State (and the holding of the associated public inquiries) and in relation to development plan procedures. These are discussed in later chapters.[88]

The impact of judicial review

If those are the principles of judicial review, what can we say about the consequences of their application by courts upon the planning system as a whole? This is a subject of considerable significance and one addressed at length in other studies.[89] What follows owes much to those more substantial works.

An important characteristic of judicial review is the generality of the principles which apply. What constitutes a breach of the rules of natural justice cannot be precisely defined. Nor can the content of the procedural irregularity or abuse of administrative discretion which will justify a court's intervention. The tests of validity for a planning condition are, for instance, notoriously vague. It may be that this is an inevitable consequence of attempts to construe the meaning of statutory language (which cannot itself be unambiguous) in the light of principles of review notionally available across the whole range of administrative activity. Sceptics may, with some justification, claim that the principles of review are cast in such broad terms that they do not impose any serious constraint upon judicial decision-making. The courts have, at all events, arrogated to themselves a power to intervene in administration in a manner which allows considerable discretionary freedom.

One immediate consequence of this is that much of planning law is at many of its edges, some of them important, left quite uncertain. The chapters to follow on the rules governing the grant of planning permission and the imposition of conditions are witness to this. It is, of course, true that judicial interpretation of the planning code has contributed much to its clarification—the code means what the courts have said it means—but not all of its uncertainties have been resolved. Extrapolation from the decision of one court in one case, perhaps expressed in the opinions of several judges, is not an exact art. Because of the sporadic and selective operation of judicial review, dependent upon the initiative of pursuers challenging particular decisions, some parts of the code receive much greater attention than others. Decisions of planning authorities impinging directly and adversely upon land values, whether affecting, in turn, compensation or development potential, attract most judicial attention. Sections of the code further removed from the 'sharp end' of planning practice receive less of the benefit of judicial exegesis.

Although uncertainty in the law may be one consequence of the latitude in judicial decision-making and may be one of the lawyer's preoccupations, the

[88]   See chapters 5 and 21 below.
[89]   In particular the works of J.P.W.B. McAuslan. See his *Land, Law and Planning* (1975), and *The Ideologies of Planning Law* (1980).

more important general result is the transfer of the power to decide some of the most significant issues in planning from administrative authorities to the courts. 'Juger l'administration, c'est aussi administrer'.[90] The influence of this reallocation of power goes beyond any impact on individual cases. It affects the operation of the planning system as a whole. Planning as a process of implementation of social policy is one heavily affected by the law. Planners and planning committees are alert to (and often sit in awe of) the legal implications of their actions. Lawyers are frequently involved in all stages of the planning process.

What has exercised commentators in recent years has been the evaluation of the impact of the superimposition of lawyers and legal procedures, techniques and values upon planning. Is it simply an inevitable consequence of a need for the judicial resolution of disputes in areas where rules lack total precision? Or of the need for judicial protection from abuse of public powers capable of substantial invasion of private rights? Is legal influence benign or does it tend to frustrate major purposes in the planning enterprise?

There are those who argue that the power of courts to determine such central matters as the considerations legitimately taken into account when granting or refusing planning permission, the borderline between legitimate and illegitimate planning conditions, and the fairness or otherwise of inquiry and decision-making procedures is inappropriate. Judges and judicial processes, it is argued, do not integrate successfully into a system of planning which has different goals and a different orientation from their own. It is not necessary to suggest, although some do, that judges deliberately and crudely sabotage the planning process. Nor is it even necessary to imply that, by virtue of their birth, social origins and training, judges cannot help but react destructively to a system uncongenial to their own preferences and prejudices.[91] It is more that the institutional values and the procedures of the law impose themselves upon planning in such a way as to displace other values which ought arguably to be those to prevail. Certainly the most comprehensive and sophisticated study in this field is that of Professor Patrick McAuslan who has adopted the notion of three competing ideologies in the planning system. It is impossible to attempt to do justice to his argument here but it leads, in summary, to the conclusion that the ideology of private property and its protection (to which he sees the judicial system wedded) effectively overwhelms both the ideology of the public interest represented by planning professionals and, even more significantly for McAuslan, the ideology of public participation.[92] This last ideology, which is palely reflected in some aspects of planning practice, incorporates a commitment to substantial popular control over planning decisions.

[90] Portalis; quoted in the frontispiece to *The Politics of the Judiciary* (below).
[91] For a polemically critical view of the judicial role see J.A.G. Griffith, *The Politics of the Judiciary* (Fontana, 2nd ed., 1981). See also E. Young 'Developing a System of Administrative Law?' and others in P. Robson and P. Watchman (eds.), *Justice, Lord Denning and the Constitution* (Gower, 1981).
[92] See *The Ideologies of Planning Law* in the Introduction and then throughout.

There must be much truth in the conclusions McAuslan reaches. Whatever the utility of his ideologies and whatever his detailed findings about their interaction, there can be no doubt at all about the validity of his central theme that courts and lawyers, far from being neutral in their influence on planning, substantially affect its operation. Whether or not the subordination of public participation is good or bad is, of course, an issue for political philosophy. The same is true of the prior question of the desirability of judicial intervention in planning. As suggested earlier, it is, for some, an inevitable consequence of the extension of public planning powers. The rule of law demands that the judiciary protect individual rights from invasion and abuse by a powerful executive. The extent of individual rights and executive powers are matters which are constitutionally entirely appropriately decided by courts.

If, on the other hand, planning is viewed as the benevolent intervention of public authorities on behalf of the community as a whole, then the legitimate role of courts is narrower; their capacity to displace the decisions of democratically accountable bodies should be more restricted.[93] The choice between these two conceptions of the judicial role in planning cannot be made without recourse to considerations well beyond the compass of this book. It is, nevertheless, a choice to be borne in mind as the substance of planning law is considered.

---

[93]   The tension between these two approaches is not new. An interesting recent analysis is contained in C. Harlow and R. Rawlings, *Law and Administration* (Weidenfeld and Nicolson, 1984) and especially in their early chapters on 'red light' and 'green light' theories. See also their chapters 14 and 15 on planning.

CHAPTER 3

THE ADMINISTRATION OF TOWN AND COUNTRY PLANNING

Introduction

Land use planning is a function of government and it is a necessary part of the introduction to this work to provide an account of the public authorities involved in planning, the allocation of functions between them, and their inter-relationships. The focus in this chapter, however, is primarily legal and we can supply no more than a glimpse of the political and financial aspects which are important for an understanding of the planning process. In the main, we are concerned with those parts of central and local government which possess the principal planning powers.

Also considered in this chapter are the powers possessed by the Parliamentary and Local Commissioners for Administration in relation to complaints of maladministration on the part of central and local government in the exercise of planning powers.

A. THE PUBLIC AUTHORITIES INVOLVED IN PLANNING

1. *Local authorities*

The local government system and the allocation of functions within it. When the Royal Commission on Local Government in Scotland (the Wheatley Commission) reported in 1969 it favoured the replacement of the then-existing system of local government with a new two-tier system applying throughout the country. The pattern of counties of cities, counties and, within them, large and small burghs and districts was to give way to a more or less uniform arrangement of seven upper-tier regions and thirty-seven lower-tier districts.[1] It was substantially to this arrangement that the Local Government (Scotland) Act 1973 gave statutory effect from 16th May 1975. The only important modifications to Wheatley were the hiving off of the western and northern islands to give them separate islands councils of their own and increases in the total number of regions and districts to nine and fifty-three respectively. This continues to be the pattern of Scottish local government.

Although there were, of course, other factors to be taken into account, the main considerations determining the size of the areas and populations subject to the new councils were the differing requirements of the functions

---

[1]   Cmnd. 4150.

to be performed. Thus the police, fire, education and roads services, for instance, required large resources and, therefore, large authorities and were allocated to the regional and islands councils although, for the purposes of the police and fire services, all three islands authorities are joined with the Highland Region to form combined Northern authorities. Functions deemed to require smaller areas or populations are allocated to the district councils and, necessarily, to the islands councils. Thus parks, environmental health and building control functions operate at the district level and, perhaps more problematically, so does housing. The 1973 Act also allowed for the possibility of the concurrent exercise of some functions by both levels of authority on the mainland but it was the principal recommendation of the Stodart Committee reporting in 1981 that such concurrence should be abolished because it led to inefficiency, duplication of effort and resources, public confusion and a lack of accountability.[2] With effect from April 1983, the Local Government and Planning (Scotland) Act 1982 ended virtually all concurrence of function in Scottish local government.

The town and country planning function is inserted, as the Stodart Committee also found, rather uneasily into the reorganised pattern of local government. It has two difficult characteristics. In the first place, in the view of Wheatley (as confirmed by Stodart), planning refuses to be either a completely large-scale or a completely small-scale function.[3] Both the regional ideal itself and underlying planning theory insist that structure planning be a function for regions. On the other hand, the preparation of local plans and most aspects of development control are better fitted to smaller areas and authorities. Whereas most other functions could be allocated to one or other tier of authority without serious difficulties (apart from the splitting of related functions such as housing and social work), planning could not be treated in this way. '[A]nxious though we were', concluded Stodart, 'to remove wherever possible dual responsibility for a single function from the two tiers of local government, we were unable to do so in any way that we believed would be effective, so far as planning was concerned.'[4]

The other difficulty is that, in the normal way, the operation of a two-tier system of local government implies no formal hierarchy of authorities. Regional councils may have the benefit of larger populations and areas (although some districts are larger than some regions in other areas) and they may be better resourced generally but they cannot normally instruct district councils within their region on what to do. Each tier has its own responsibilities and discharges them largely independently of the other. There may be and, indeed, there are ways in which regions and districts may seek to co-ordinate their activities on an extra-statutory basis. Planning, however, requires at some points, a more hierarchical structure. There have to be procedural devices available to ensure, with recourse if necessary to

[2] Cmnd. 8115, para. 19.
[3] Cmnd. 4150, paras. 188-219; Cmnd. 8115, paras. 38-60.
[4] Cmnd. 8115, para. 49. See also M. Keating, 'The Stodart Committee and Planning in Scotland' *The Planner*, Vol. 68, p. 22.

the Secretary of State, that district planning powers are exercised in a manner consistent with regional action. These are discussed in detail as they arise elsewhere but the main examples occur in the approval of local plans and the handling of major planning applications.

Drawing these strands together, we may summarise the position on the allocation of planning functions by saying, firstly, that no problem arises in the islands areas where the Western Isles, Orkney and Shetland Islands Councils exercise all functions. In the planning legislation they are referred to as 'general planning authorities'. Also dubbed general planning authorities are the councils of the Highlands, Dumfries and Galloway and Borders Regions because in relation to planning (and also building control and libraries) the district councils in those regions possess no powers; they are regarded as too small (in resource terms) to warrant them. This is the only departure from an otherwise uniform allocation of powers on the mainland. In all other areas, planning functions are divided between the regional planning authorities and district planning authorities with devices for procedural co-ordination built in.[5] The detailed division of planning functions between regions and districts is to be found in Schedule 22 to the Local Government (Scotland) Act 1973. Regional planning functions are those described as such in Part I of the Schedule together with the functions conferred on regional or general planning authorities by Part IX of the 1973 Act (see 1973 Act, s.172(4)). The principal regional planning functions are set out in Table 1 below.

[5]   For a list of the planning authorities in Scotland see Appendix 1 (p. 543 below).

TABLE 1: REGIONAL PLANNING FUNCTIONS

Description of function	*Statutory provision*
(a) Survey and structure plans	1972 Act, ss.4 to 8 (see chapter 5 below)
(b) Regional reports	1973 Act, s.173 (see chapter 5 below)
(c) Acquisition, appropriation, disposal and development of land in connection with functions exercised by regional and general planning authorities	1972 Act, ss.102, 109, 110, 113 and 114
(d) Reserve powers regarding local plans	1973 Act, s.177 (see p.95 below)
(e) Powers to 'call in' planning applications	1973 Act, s.179 (see p.202 below)[6]
(f) Powers relating to orders under ss.42, 49, 49A and 49B of the 1972 Act	1973 Act, s.181[7]
(g) Powers relating to agreements regulating the development or use of land	1972 Act, s.50[8]

District planning functions are those described as such in Part II of Schedule 22 to the Local Government (Scotland) Act 1973, together with those functions conferred on general or district planning authorities by Part IX of the 1973 Act (see 1973 Act, s.172(4)). The principal district planning functions are set out in Table 2 below.

---

[6]   As amended by the Local Government and Planning (Scotland) Act 1982, Schedule 3, para. 24.

[7]   As applied by the 1972 Act s.49G (added by the Town and Country Planning (Minerals) Act 1981, ss.27 and 35).

[8]   As amended by the Local Government and Planning (Scotland) Act 1982, Schedule 2, para. 14.

TABLE 2: DISTRICT PLANNING FUNCTIONS

Description of function	Statutory provision
(a) Preparation of local plans	1972 Act, ss.9-13
(b) Determination of planning applications	1972 Act, ss.26-31A
(c) Enforcement of planning control	1972 Act, Part V
(d) Acquisition, appropriation, disposal and development of land in connection with functions exercised by district planning authorities	1972 Act, ss.102, 109, 110, 113 and 114
(e) Protection of buildings of special architectural or historic interest	1972 Act, ss.52-56 and 92-97
(f) Powers relating to conservation areas	1972 Act, ss.262-262B
(g) Powers relating to tree preservation	1972 Act, ss.57, 60 and 99
(h) Powers relating to orders under ss.42, 49, 49A and 49B of the 1972 Act	As specified; also 1972 Act, s.100
(i) Powers relating to agreements regulating the development or use of land	1972 Act, s.50

Whenever the term 'planning authority' appears in any statute it is, unless otherwise provided, to be construed as a reference to a general planning authority and to a district planning authority (see 1973 Act, s.172(3)). In the pages which follow the term 'planning authority' is used in the same sense unless the contrary is clear from the context.

The functions specified in Tables 1 and 2 above are normally to be exercised by an authority within their own area only and generally there is no difficulty in defining the geographical limits of an authority's jurisdiction. The question has arisen, however, as to the limits of that jurisdiction on the seashore. In *Argyll and Bute District Council* v *Secretary of State for Scotland*[9] the Second Division of the Court of Session held that there could be drawn from the Town and Country Planning (Scotland) Act 1972 the

---

[9] 1976 S.C. 248; 1977 S.L.T. 33. See C.M.G. Himsworth, 'The Limits of the Planning Realm' [1977] J.P.L. 21; and E. Young, 'Seaward Limits of Planning Jurisdiction in Scotland' (1977) 22 J.L.S.S.61.

inference that planning jurisdiction was restricted to the area above low-water mark of tidal waters and that a planning authority therefore had no control over activities carried out below that mark.[10]

Finally, we should mention community councils. These are not local authorities proper but were introduced on the recommendation of the Wheatley Commission by the 1973 Act. They are intended principally to improve communication between communities and local and other public authorities and have been set up in accordance with schemes drawn up by all district and islands councils and approved by the Secretary of State.[11] Rules about membership and procedures vary from scheme to scheme and the actual implementation of schemes and establishment of the councils has been uneven. In England and Wales parish councils and community councils set up under the Local Government Act 1972 have a formal role to play in the planning process. They do have local authority status and they enjoy the right to be consulted about some applications for planning permission. Although Scottish community councils have a statutory right to object to liquor licence applications under s.16 of the Licensing (Scotland) Act 1976, they have no equivalent right under the planning legislation. In many areas, however, there are informal consultative procedures which involve community councils in the making of planning decisions.

The internal functioning of local authorities. Turning to the way in which local authorities are organised to go about their business, planning is treated like other functions. The first principle of the internal structuring of British local authorities is that it is the full council that is the formal authority and it is in the full council that statutory powers are vested in the first instance. The council consists of the body of members elected en bloc on four year cycles (islands and regional councillors in 1982 and four-yearly thereafter, district councils in 1984). Only in exceptional cases are statutory functions vested in the first instance in persons other than the full council and planning is not such a function.

Although the primary allocation of powers to the full council accords with the principle that the major decisions of the authority should indeed be made in the authority's plenary forum, there would be little practical sense in attempting to compel all day to day decisions to be made there. It is obvious that there is a need for the substantial delegation of decision-making within the organisation and this has been the long-standing tradition. Local government is, in the main, government by committee.

But the power to delegate has to be expressly conferred. The normal presumption is that when Parliament confers powers upon a specific authority or type of authority then it does intend that the named authority should actually exercise the power themselves. If no delegation is authorised then an act or decision by someone claiming to act on the authority's behalf

---

[10]   Note, however, the non-statutory consultation procedures governing exploration for and development of hydrocarbon resources in estuaries (S.D.D. Planning Information Note C3 (1982); and D.o.E. Circular 2/85).
[11]   Cmnd. 4150, chapter 26; and 1973 Act, Part IV.

will be invalid and it would seem that such an act or decision may not subsequently be ratified by the authority.[12]

Happily, and not surprisingly, powers of delegation within local authorities are expressly conferred and these overcome most, but not all,[13] of the legal difficulties which might otherwise arise in the decision-making process. Section 56 of the 1973 Act permits a local authority to 'arrange for the discharge' of any of their functions by a committee, sub-committee or officer of the authority or, indeed by another local authority. The power to delegate to an officer was new.[14] There is still no power to delegate formally to a single member—even the convener of a committee or of the council itself.

The legal effect of an authority's arranging for the discharge of a function by a committee, sub-committee or officer, whether this is achieved in the council's standing orders or by an *ad hoc* decision,[15] is that the committee or individual is empowered to act in place of the authority as a whole. The decision of the committee or individual to whom power has been delegated will be effective when made. Such an arrangement can subsequently be revoked but not retrospectively.[16] Notwithstanding the delegation of functions, s.56(4) of the 1973 Act specifically reserves to the local authority or committee, as the case may be, the power to exercise the functions concurrently. Arranging for the discharge of their functions by several committees does not affect the continuing overall responsibility of the full council for the whole of their functions.[17]

The practical response of Scottish planning authorities to the power to delegate is a very widespread use of delegation to a planning committee or to a committee combining planning with other responsibilities. There is then routine sub-delegation to sub-committees of much of the committee's business. Less use seems to be made of the power to delegate functions to planning officers.[18]

Apart from the formal retention by the full council of overall responsibility for the authority's functions, there is also commonly a further reflection of the need for some routine coherence in a council's policies. Based upon the recommendations of the Paterson Committee,[19] most

[12] See *Attorney-General, ex rel. Co-operative Retail Services Ltd.* v *Taff-Ely B.C.* (1979) 39 P. & C.R. 233; affirmed (1981) 42 P. & C.R. 1.

[13] See, in particular, the discussion in chapter 2 on personal bar.

[14] New, that is, as a general power. There had been enacted, but never implemented, a limited power to delegate planning powers to officers—see the Town and Country Planning (Scotland) Act 1969, s.65 (re-enacted in the 1972 Act, s.3).

[15] According to Megaw L.J. in *Western Fish Products Ltd.* v *Penwith D.C.* [1981] 2 All E.R. 204, at p. 219, delegation 'has to be done formally by the authority acting as such'.

[16] *Battelley* v *Finsbury Borough Council* (1958) 56 L.G.R. 165.

[17] For discussion of the (English) authorities see H.W.R. Wade, *Administrative Law* (Clarendon Press, Oxford, 5th ed., 1982), chapter 11; and C. A. Cross, *Principles of Local Government Law* (Sweet and Maxwell, 6th ed., 1981), chapter 4.

[18] In S.D.D. Circular 24/1981 planning authorities are encouraged to delegate the power to make decisions to officials or small sub-committees in order to speed up the processing of planning applications.

[19] *The New Scottish Local Authorities* (H.M.S.O., 1973).

authorities have a policy and resources committee, or its equivalent, designed to ensure the co-ordination of plans and policies. And there may, on the officer side, be co-ordination through a management team.

One of the most difficult legal problems arising out of acts and decisions taken by others on an authority's behalf relates to the status of decisions made by officers not formally in possession of delegated powers but communicated to members of the public who assume the decisions to be authoritative. This is a matter discussed in chapter 2.

The general pattern of internal organisation of local authorities in planning matters is thus broadly the same as for other functions. In some respects, of course, planning has its own specialised procedures—its own required processes of consultation, its own timetables, its own ways for the making and communication of decisions and these are discussed in later chapters. But these operate in supplementation of the standard legal and non-legal rules of local government practice.

The main extra-statutory characteristic of local government is that, subject to the possibilities for delegation discussed above, it is government by elected members with the substantial assistance and advice of appointed officials in both decision making and implementation. The fact of their election means that, in modern times, the great majority of members and their councils and committees are party politically orientated. Members are elected because of their adherence to a party and most important policy decisions are taken on a party basis. Planning is no exception to this general position although the technical nature of many planning decisions tends to reduce their party political significance. The further result is that the professional expertise of officials becomes more important. It would be completely misleading in practice to view officials as performing a merely advisory role. Inevitably they acquire great power and influence over the decisions made in name by the elected members they serve.

2. The Secretary of State for Scotland and the Scottish Office

Any reader of Scottish planning legislation will be aware that the role of the Secretary of State for Scotland is one that cannot be ignored. Referred to simply as the 'Secretary of State' because, in law, all holders of that office, whatever their individual title, are deemed to constitute a single Secretary of State and, therefore, legally competent to perform the functions of any, the Secretary of State for Scotland is the central government minister responsible for planning. He is responsible to Parliament for his own actions and those of his department and, as a member of the government and Cabinet, he shares collective responsibility for the decisions of government as a whole. In contrast with his English counterpart, the Scottish Secretary's responsibilities extend far beyond the spheres of planning and the environment. He is also, for Scotland, the minister with responsibilities including roads and transport; education (except universities); economic planning; and police and prisons. His department is the Scottish Office which is based primarily in Edinburgh but with outposts in London and Glasgow. Specialisation within the Secretary of State's total range of interests is achieved through the appointment of junior ministers with formally designated sub-divisions of responsibility. Currently there is a minister of state (in the Lords) and three parliamentary under-secretaries, one of whom has responsibility for planning. The Scottish Office is similarly divided to produce five sub-departments—the Scottish Education Department, the Scottish Home and Health Department, the Department of Agriculture and Fisheries for Scotland, the Industry Department for Scotland and the Scottish Development Department (S.D.D.) which has responsibility for housing, roads and, importantly for our purposes, planning. Thus, when we speak of planning at the central government level in Scotland we are talking about an organisation headed politically by the Secretary of State and a junior minister responsible for the planning division of the Scottish Development Department. The Department's staff necessarily includes both administrators and professional planners. A central government planning element 'hived off' from the S.D.D. is the Inquiry Reporters' Unit.[20]

Although it is true to say that the Secretary of State enjoys central government responsibility for the planning process in Scotland, planning joins many other areas of domestic policy as one in which central purposes are achieved principally through the efforts of local authorities acting under the various forms of central supervision. The Secretary of State's statutory powers amount, therefore, to those felt necessary by successive holders of the office to control the activities, in both their substance and procedure, of local authorities. To talk of supervision and control in this context is to risk entering a debate about the relationship (both actual and desirable) between central government and local authorities which extends much more widely than the planning process and certainly more widely than can be appropriately handled here. We are confined principally to questions of law and our concern at this point is with the formal statutory relationship between the Secretary of State and local authorities. In accepting these limitations, it is important to acknowledge nevertheless that the statutory position for the time being does not tell the whole story. It does not, for instance, tell us much about the political considerations that brought about or now sustain that position; it does not tell us about the extent of use or non-use of available powers; nor about the informal processes of communication and pressure operating in both directions between levels of government. We touch on some of these matters in later chapters.[21]

The law is, however, a necessary starting point and we shall find that various forms of statutory intervention by the Secretary of State are of great significance. He has, in the first place, wide powers to promulgate delegated legislation and, amongst these, the power to adjust, through the medium of use class orders, the meaning of development and thus the types of activity requiring planning permission, to provide for the granting of planning permission by development orders for specified categories of development,

[20] See chapter 20.
[21] See especially chapter 4.

and to determine the detailed procedure according to which planning
applications are processed, development plans are drawn up and public
inquiries conducted. The Secretary of State's general powers in determining
appeals against adverse planning decisions, his powers to 'call-in' applications from planning authorities for determination by himself, his powers of
direction, of approving or disapproving development plans and his powers
of mediation between authorities represent very substantial formal control
over the planning process as a whole. In his broader relationship with
Scottish local authorities, it is usually said that the Secretary of State's single
power of control that dominates all others is the financial power—that of
determining the limits of local capital expenditure and, through his fixing of
the annual rate support grant, imposing fairly close limits on revenue
expenditure also. During a period in which the official central government
approach has been one of relaxing needlessly detailed administrative
controls to give local authorities greater 'freedom' but, at the same time,
seeking to retain the power to safeguard both national economic and
financial policy and national social policies implemented through local
government, overall spending limits tied in some cases to a degree of
programme approval have provided a useful framework of control. This
strategy based on financial controls has less immediate relevance to the
planning process as such. Of course, financial factors will frequently
determine the rate of progress ultimately made towards the implementation
of planning goals—financial constraints, for example, clearly affect an
authority's freedom to purchase or develop land. But, since the local
authority role in planning has less to do with implementation and much more
to do with the co-ordination and licensing of development, it is not
surprising that in this area the Secretary of State has to place much greater
reliance upon the control achieved through detailed legislative and administrative regulation.

3. *The European Economic Community*

Discussion of the public authorities involved in planning would be
incomplete without some mention of the role played by the European
Economic Community. Although the Treaty of Rome makes no specific
mention of the pursuit of environmental objectives, the Community has,
nonetheless, involved itself with the promotion of social and environmental
policies. Whilst the principal concern of the Treaty is with such matters as
economic harmonisation, free trade and fair competition, justification for
action on the environment is based, as Grant comments, 'on a wide view of
the Community's interests in the impact of environmental issues on existing
policies in such areas as commerce, agriculture and fisheries'.[22]

So far, attention has been focused on such matters as the control of
pollution and Community policy has had no direct influence on mainstream
planning law in Scotland. However, the Community have had under
consideration for some time a draft Directive on environmental assessment.

[22]   M. Grant, *Urban Planning Law*, p. 66.

If and when the Directive is finally adopted by the Community, it seems likely that some adjustment of the planning legislation will be needed to accommodate a requirement to subject major development proposals to a form of environmental assessment.

B. MALADMINISTRATION

So far in this chapter we have been concerned with the public authorities involved in the administration of planning and with the way in which they are organised for the discharge of their functions. Considerable attention is given in this book to the remedies available under statute and at common law to those affected by the discharge of these functions. There are, however, other, 'non-legal', remedies open to a person who feels himself aggrieved, perhaps not so much by a particular planning proposal or decision, but by the way in which that proposal or decision has been arrived at. The cause of this type of grievance is commonly referred to as 'maladministration'. 'What every form of government needs', comments Wade, 'is some regular and smooth-running mechanism for feeding back the reactions of its disgruntled customers, after impartial assessment, and for correcting whatever may have gone wrong.'[23] One mechanism which has been established for investigating complaints of maladministration by public authorities in the discharge of their functions is the 'ombudsman'.

Ombudsmen operate at different levels. The office of parliamentary ombudsman, or more correctly, the Parliamentary Commissioner for Administration, was established to investigate complaints of maladministration against government departments, including complaints against the Scottish Development Department about the way in which it has discharged its functions under the planning legislation. The office of local ombudsman (the Commissioner for Local Administration) was established to investigate complaints about the way in which local authorities have discharged their functions. Both are concerned principally with the correct functioning of the administrative machine. The remainder of the chapter is given over to a brief description of the way in which the ombudsmen operate.

1. *The Parliamentary Commissioner for Administration*

The office of the Parliamentary Commissioner for Administration was established by the Parliamentary Commissioner Act 1967. The Commissioner is appointed by the Crown and holds office during good behaviour. His function is to investigate complaints by members of the public who claim to have suffered 'injustice in consequence of maladministration' by a government department.[24] A complaint must be made in writing and must be submitted through a member of the House of Commons. The intention is that members should filter out cases which are inappropriate for consideration by the ombudsman; it would seem, however, that members generally prefer to let the ombudsman make the decision about the appropriateness of

---

[23]   H.W.R. Wade, *Administrative Law*, 5th ed., p. 74.
[24]   1967 Act, s.5(1)

D

a complaint. Complaints must generally be lodged within twelve months of the date when the aggrieved person first knew of the matters alleged in the complaint.

A number of matters are specifically excluded from the ombudsman's jurisdiction.[25] Amongst these are contractual and commercial transactions, other than the acquisition of land compulsorily or by agreement and the disposal of surplus land so acquired. Furthermore, the ombudsman may not investigate a case where the person aggrieved has or had a remedy in any court of law, or a right of appeal, reference or review in any statutory or prerogative tribunal[26] unless it would not have been reasonable in the particular circumstances of the case to expect the remedy or right to be invoked.[27]

'Maladministration' is not defined in the 1967 Act but it includes what is generally referred to as the 'Crossman catalogue'[28] of bias, neglect, inattention, delay, incompetence, ineptitude and arbitrariness. And although the ombudsman may not question the merits of a decision taken without maladministration by a government department in the exercise of discretionary powers[29]—for example, a decision on an appeal against a refusal of planning permission—this has not prevented him from questioning discretionary decisions which are thoroughly bad on their merits. As Wade observes 'bad decisions are bad administration and bad administration is maladministration'.[30]

The ombudsman has a discretion whether to investigate a complaint. Any investigation is conducted in private and, subject to limited exceptions, the ombudsman may call for information and papers from any person.

The report of his investigation is submitted to the government department in question, and to the member through whom the case was referred. Although the ombudsman has no sanction to support any recommendation in his report, he has in practice been very successful in securing a remedy for complaints where maladministration has been found to cause injustice. In one case investigated by the Commissioner, for example, neighbours who had made objection to proposed development were not informed by the Minister of Housing and Local Government that an appeal relating to the proposals was to be dealt with by written representations and were given no opportunity to state their case; the ministry refused at first to revoke the planning permission granted for the development but re-opened the matter after the Parliamentary Commissioner had found maladministration in the ministry's handling of the appeal.[31]

Although the office of Parliamentary Commissioner has become well-established, the number of investigations into planning matters in Scotland has been small.

[25] 1967 Act, s.5(3) and Schedule 3.
[26] 1967 Act, s.5(2).
[27] For example, where the law is in doubt.
[28] H. C. Deb., Vol. 734, Col. 51 (18th October, 1966); and see note 38 below.
[29] 1967 Act, s.12(3).
[30] H.W.R. Wade, *Administrative Law*, 5th ed., p. 83.
[31] Case 473/67.

2. The Commissioner for Local Administration

The office of the Commissioner for Local Administration, the local ombudsman, is of more recent creation. It came into existence at the same time as local government reorganisation in 1975 but was not a direct product of the Wheatley Royal Commission's report.

The commission had taken a cautious view of the problem of complaints from the public and had suggested that, in the early stages of reorganisation, the traditional role of the councillor in the redress of grievances should be relied upon. Only when things had settled down should a decision be made about the need for new complaints machinery. But in a rather pained footnote the commission had to admit that they had been overtaken by events. As their Report went to press the Prime Minister chose that moment to announce the government's acceptance of the principle that an ombudsman system should be established for local government.[32] The Scottish local ombudsman was created by Part II of the Local Government (Scotland) Act 1975, very much in the image of the Parliamentary Commissioner.[33]

The Commissioner himself is a Crown appointment and he holds office during good behaviour.[34] He is secure in his office until he either voluntarily resigns, or is removed for incapacity or misbehaviour, or reaches the retiring age of 65. His task is to investigate complaints from members of the public who claim to have sustained injustice in consequence of maladministration in connection with action taken by local authorities in the exercise of their administrative functions. A complaint has to be in writing and must be forwarded to the ombudsman by a member of the council against whom the complaint is made unless the ombudsman is satisfied that a councillor has refused to forward a complaint, when he may take it direct.[35] A complaint must normally be made within 12 months of the date of the complainant's first knowledge of the matters alleged in the complaint. The ombudsman must not investigate a complaint unless satisfied that the authority have been informed of it and given a reasonable opportunity to respond.[36]

There are other restrictions upon the ombudsman's general power to investigate, only some of which bear upon the field of planning. He cannot

---

[32] Cmnd. 4150, pp. 235-266. See also the JUSTICE report proposing local ombudsmen, *The Citizen and his Council* (1969).

[33] For England, the Commission for Local Administration (with three Commissioners) was established by the Local Government Act 1974. See also the Commissioner for Complaints Act (N.I.) 1969.

[34] On these and subsequent aspects of the Commissioner's appointment, powers and procedures see the 1975 Act, Part II and Schedules 4 and 5.

[35] It has been argued that automatic direct access to the ombudsman should be provided. See JUSTICE, *The Local Ombudsman: A Review of the First Five Years* (1980). (This also provides useful discussion of other jurisdictional and procedural aspects of the ombudsman's work.) The Commissioner himself has advocated direct access. See e.g. Annual Reports for years ended March 1983 and March 1984 (H.M.S.O.).

[36] In addition to this statutory pre-requisite to formal investigation, there have been introduced 'revised operating procedures' under which authorities are given notice by the ombudsman of complaints against them. This can lead to a speedy resolution—whether in favour of the complainant or not—without the need for formal investigation.

investigate action taken in respect of personnel matters (including appoint-ments, pay and discipline) nor action which in his opinion affects all or most of the inhabitants of the area of the authority concerned. This last restriction prevents investigation of matters extending beyond the ambit of individual complaint such as the fixing of the rate. On the other hand, complaints need not come from single individuals. They may be made by groups of people or by companies. Community councils have complained to the ombudsman. Local authorities themselves, nationalised industries and quangos are barred.

The investigation conducted by the ombudsman, and by investigating officers on his behalf, is private. He has the power, enforceable by the Court of Session if necessary, to require the attendance of witnesses and production of documents. Following his investigation, the ombudsman reports upon it to the complainant, councillor and authority. Within two weeks of receiving the report, the authority must give public notice (including newspaper advertisement) of its availability for inspection.

If the report is one in which the ombudsman has made no finding of injustice in consequence of maladministration, the authority need take no further action. If such an injustice is reported (and, if it is, it will normally be accompanied by a recommendation as to its removal), then the authority must consider the report and notify the ombudsman of the action they have taken or propose to take. Failing such notification or if the ombudsman is not satisfied with action taken or proposed, he may issue a further report explaining his dissatisfaction. That further report must also be given publicity and it is there that the ombudsman's formal powers stop. Like the Parliamentary Commissioner, he has no power to order a remedy for injustice found. He may recommend a remedy and reinforce that recom-mendation in a further report but that, at present, is the limit. He does not even have the powerful support available to his Parliamentary counterpart in the shape of Parliament itself, the Commons Select Committee and the procedures for ensuring ministerial accountability. This vulnerability of the local ombudsman to being ignored by the authorities he criticises has encouraged some commentators and indeed the Commissioner himself to advocate the legal enforceability of his findings.[37]

It is not a simple matter to assess the actual impact of the local ombudsman upon the planning system during the decade of his operation. In particular, it is difficult to judge how far decisions on particular complaints affect general decision-making processes either within the authority con-cerned or more widely. The statistical returns in the commissioner's annual reports do, however, provide a starting point and show a steady stream of rather more than 50 complaints received about planning matters in each of the years ending in March 1982, 1983 and 1984. This puts planning in second place, a long way behind housing, in the league table of complaints. Thereafter, however, only 24 planning complaints in total were accepted for investigation over the three year period and in only 6 cases (i.e., 2 each year)

---

[37] See Annual Report, 1984, pp. 4-5.

was there a finding of injustice in consequence of maladministration. Numbers of investigations and complaints upheld are, therefore, small and it is not easy to draw general conclusions about the forms of maladministration in planning—alleged and upheld—with which the ombudsman has been concerned. Not very much light has been shed upon the interpretation in practice of the statutorily imprecise concepts of 'injustice' and 'maladministration'.[38] In reviews of reported investigations it has, however, been shown[39] that the ombudsman has acknowledged that complaints of maladministration may include complaints by planning objectors that they have been inadequately informed or consulted about applications; complaints that misleading statements have been made; complaints about delay; and complaints of inconsistency in handling allegedly similar planning applications. Of course, not all complaints framed in these terms have been upheld on their particular facts and commissioners have been loath to interfere with decisions made within the scope of the discretion of planning authorities. Attempts to demonstrate maladministration in the selective use of powers of enforcement have met with a singular lack of success.[40]

[38] For judicial (Lord Denning M.R.) confirmation that 'maladministration' includes the list of observations in the 'Crossman catalogue' of 'bias, neglect, inattention, delay, incompetence, ineptitude, perversity, turpitude, arbitrariness and so on' see *R.* v *Local Commissioner for Administration, ex parte Bradford Metropolitan City Council* [1979] Q.B. 287, at pp. 311-312.

[39] See C.M.G. Himsworth, 'The Maladministration of Information' 1981 S.P.L.P. 30; 'Failure to Take Enforcement Action' 1981 S.P.L.P. 56; 'Misleading Statements' 1982 S.P.L.P. 57; 'Injustice in Consequence of Inconsistency' 1983 S.P.L.P. 56; and 'A Question of Inconsistent Administration—or Aesthetic Judgment?' 1983 S.P.L.P. 89.

[40] See J. Rowan-Robinson, E. Young and I. McLarty, *The Enforcement of Planning Control in Scotland* (S.D.D., 1984), chapter 7.

CHAPTER 4

NATIONAL PLANNING POLICY

Planning legislation subjects proposals for the development of land to a comprehensive system of control. The way in which the control is applied in a given case is a matter, in the first instance, for the discretion of the planning authority and, in the event of appeal, for the Secretary of State. These characteristics of comprehensiveness and discretion make the preparation of policy guidelines desirable so as to secure a measure of consistency in the application of control in day to day practice and to ensure some co-ordination between the different levels—district, regional and national—at which the system operates. It would seem to be equally desirable that those concerned with the development of land, whether as promoters or as 'third parties', should be able to obtain guidance on the policies which underlie the exercise of control.

Part II of the 1972 Act accordingly imposes an obligation upon planning authorities to prepare policy statements dealing with the development and use of land in their areas (see chapter 5). These statements are prepared at the regional (or sub-regional) and local levels in the form of structure and local plans. Whilst the Secretary of State exercises some control over the content of these plans, planning authorities are left with considerable freedom to develop policies appropriate to the circumstances of their areas and to implement these through the operation of the development control process and through other planning powers.

There is no corresponding obligation upon the Secretary of State to prepare national policy statements on land use and in the past he has tended to refrain from doing so except where a clear indication of the 'national interest' was seen to be required. Nevertheless, he has quite frequently issued what might be termed 'operational advice' on aspects of the planning process, often in the form of circulars related to changes in legislation. However, for reasons which are considered below, during the last ten years there has been a significant increase in the amount of land use policy guidance; the flow of operational advice has continued at much the same level.

Our principal concern in this chapter is with sources of national planning policy. However, in practical terms a discussion about sources of policy cannot be entirely divorced from consideration of the way in which policy is formulated, communicated and implemented. In view of the varied and unstructured way in which national policy may emerge some general observations on these matters would seem to be appropriate.

National policy may, for example, emerge incrementally as the sum of a series of decisions on individual proposals for development. National policy, commented the Outer Circle Policy Unit, is 'secreted in the interstices of individual decisions and evolves over time as a consequence of the decisions that are taken and carried out'.[1] It is, for example, difficult to find that there was ever a major assessment of the thermal reactor programme, yet the sum of the decisions on the individual nuclear power stations amounts to a major national programme.

In a similar way, the present government's policy on the emphasis to be given to the allocation of an adequate supply of land for private house building first emerged in Scotland in incremental fashion during the approval processes for the Lothian and Strathclyde structure plans. The policy subsequently appeared in specific form as a national planning guideline and has since been given further emphasis in S.D.D. Circular 21/1983, 'Private House Building Land Supply: Joint Venture Schemes'.

Inevitably, proposals for development which raise national implications will come forward from time to time in what might be described as a policy vacuum. The proposal in 1973 to establish a yard for the construction of oil production platforms at Port Cam, Drumbuie and the proposal in 1981 to extend the downhill skiing facilities on Cairngorm into Lurcher's Gully are examples. Both raised important policy issues and were in consequence called in for decision by the Secretary of State. Considerable time was devoted at the subsequent public inquiries to argument over where the 'national interest' lay. In such cases, the inquiry becomes a part of the policy formulation exercise and the eventual decision (both were refused) is an important indicator of national policy. Both proposals were followed by the production of national planning guidelines (see below), the first setting out a planning framework within which oil- and gas-related developments in coastal areas should be considered, the second giving advice on an acceptable balance between development and conservation policies in the selection of areas for skiing facilities.

In other cases there may be an explicit policy formulation exercise, such as occurred with the designation of national scenic areas as a framework for landscape conservation,[2] and such as is currently in progress over guidelines for development in the countryside.[3]

Those involved in planning practice will wish to know where to look for guidance on national planning policy, however formulated. Policy, particularly on land use issues, may well be communicated to practitioners in a single statement. The national planning guidelines are a good example of this. On the other hand, where land use policy emerges in incremental

[1] The Outer Circle Policy Unit in association with JUSTICE and the Council for Science and Society, *The Big Public Inquiry* (1979).
[2] See S.D.D. Circular 20/1980.
[3] See the draft circular and national planning guideline on 'Development in the Countryside' issued for consultation in March, 1984.

fashion, the best way to obtain information may be to examine past decisions on development plans and planning appeals.[4]

Operational policy on a specific aspect of the planning process is generally communicated through a combination of legislation, primary or delegated, and circular. Recent revisions in policy on the exercise of planning control over hazardous development, for example, resulted in two sets of amending regulations,[5] the making of a direction by the Secretary of State[6] (a form of sub-delegated legislation—see below) and the issuing of S.D.D. Circular 9/1984.

Until recently, the operation of the planning process was not a matter which divided the main political parties.[7] There was a tendency to adopt what might be described as an *ad hoc* approach to operational policy. Changes were made in piecemeal fashion to specific parts of the process as occasion required. However, the present government appears to have fairly definite ideas about what is required of the planning system as a whole and has been carrying through a programme of change to translate these ideas into practice. There was a need, said Mr. Malcolm Rifkind, then Minister for Home Affairs and the Environment at the Scottish Office, in a speech in 1980, to release 'the spirit of enterprise'. The importance of speeding up decision-making processes and relaxing unnecessary controls was stressed. To this end, legislation, both primary and delegated, was introduced to speed up the development plan process and to relax some of the rigour of development control.[8] The determination of nearly all planning appeals was delegated to reporters;[9] enterprise zones, in which planning and fiscal controls are relaxed, were designated in some areas of economic decline;[10] and numerous minor controls were abolished.[11] Consultation papers have been issued proposing the broadening of the Use Classes Order in respect of

[4]   The appeal decision letters and inquiry reports are available for reference at the National Library of Scotland and the Planning Exchange Library. *Scottish Planning Appeal Decisions (SPADS)*, published monthly by the Planning Exchange, provides brief summaries of all Scottish appeal decisions. Selected appeal decisions, mainly concerned with matters of law and procedure, are discussed in *Scottish Planning Law and Practice*.

[5]   The Town and Country Planning (General Development) (Scotland) Amendment Order 1983; and the Town and Country Planning (Use Classes) (Scotland) Amendment Order 1983.

[6]   The Town and Country Planning (Notification of Applications) (Scotland) (Amendment) (No. 2) Direction 1984 (see Annex 1 to S.D.D. Circular 9/1984).

[7]   With the important exception of the compensation/betterment question which is discussed in chapter 1.

[8]   See, for example, the Local Government (Miscellaneous Provisions) (Scotland) Act 1981, s.25 and Schedule 2; the Local Government and Planning (Scotland) Act 1982, ss.36-40, 46, 48 and Schedule 2; the Town and Country Planning (General Development) (Scotland) Order 1981; and the Town and Country Planning (Structure and Local Plans) (Scotland) Regulations 1983.

[9]   The Town and Country Planning (Determination of Appeals by Appointed Persons) (Prescribed Classes) (Scotland) Regulations 1980.

[10]   See, for example, City of Glasgow District and Clydebank District Enterprise Zone Designation Order, 1981.

[11]   See the Local Government (Miscellaneous Provisions) (Scotland) Act 1981, s.25 and Schedule 2.

certain categories of development[12] and the introduction of simplified planning zones within which planning authorities could issue a general planning permission for certain activities.[13] The legislation has been supported by a number of circulars explaining and enlarging upon the provisions and stressing the importance of clear policy guidance and of swift and sound decision taking.[14] The cumulative effect has, therefore, been a decided shift in operational policy under the present administration in the direction of a reduced burden of planning control.

Where policy has been formulated at the national level, the Secretary of State has at his disposal, as is indicated in chapter 3, a number of devices for ensuring the implementation of the policy at the local level. He has indicated that development plans should reflect the national interest in the way a land resource should be used or safeguarded for future use and in development planning priorities;[15] he has wide powers to refuse or modify structure plan policies which do not adequately reflect these considerations;[16] and he may call in local plans for approval.[17] As regards development control, he has directed that certain applications which may have national implications are to be notified to him either upon receipt or in the event of the planning authority proposing to grant permission so that he may consider whether to call them in for a decision.[18] Furthermore, he is the ultimate arbiter on matters of planning policy in the event of an appeal by an applicant from an adverse decision by a planning authority.[19]

Whilst, therefore, planning authorities in practice exercise considerable freedom in the day to day operation of the planning process, there is no doubt that the Secretary of State is well equipped to ensure that day to day practice accords with national policies. Furthermore, there is no doubt that national policy now exerts a greater influence on day to day practice than it did ten years ago.

The remainder of this chapter is given over to a more detailed examination of the four main sources of national planning policy[20]—legis-

[12] See the consultation papers noted at 1983 S.P.L.P. 66 and 1984 S.P.L.P. 66.
[13] See the consultation paper 'Simplified Planning Zones' issued by the S.D.D. in May 1984.
[14] See in particular S.D.D. Circulars 24/1981, 'Development Control'; 21/1983, 'Private House Building Land Supply: Joint Venture Schemes'; and 32/1983, 'Structure and Local Plans'.
[15] See S.D.D. Circular 32/1983, 'Structure and Local Plans'; S.D.D. National Planning Guidelines: 'Priorities for Development Planning', 1981; and *Planning Advice Notes 27* and *30*.
[16] Town and Country Planning (Scotland) Act 1972, s.7.
[17] Town and Country Planning (Scotland) Act 1972, s.12(3) and (4), as substituted (as regards s.12(4)) by the Local Government (Scotland) Act 1973, s.175(2).
[18] The Town and Country Planning (Notification of Applications) (Scotland) Direction 1981 (see Annex B to S.D.D. Circular 24/1981), as amended by the Town and Country Planning (Notification of Applications) (Scotland) (Amendment) (No. 2) Direction 1984.
[19] Town and Country Planning (Scotland) Act 1972, s.33.
[20] There are, of course, numerous other sources of national planning policy such as white papers, statements in Parliament, press releases, ministerial speeches and so on. Technical guidance on specific topics may be obtained from the series of Planning Information Notes issued by the S.D.D.

lation, national planning guidelines, circulars and planning advice notes—
and to a consideration of the weight which they carry in practice.

1. *Legislation*

Policy decisions, particularly on the operation of the planning process, may
well be implemented through legislation. Access to such legislation, primary
or delegated, should present little difficulty to those concerned with the
development of land or, at least, to their legal advisers. Section 273 of the
1972 Act provides that nearly all delegated legislation on planning matters is
to be made by way of statutory instrument; it is therefore subject to the
publication requirements of s.2 of the Statutory Instruments Act 1946.
Although the publication requirements extend only to general statutory
instruments (i.e., those having application throughout Scotland), a list of
local instruments—for example, orders designating enterprise zones—
appears in the official bound volumes of statutory instruments published
annually by H.M.S.O. The S.D.D. will supply on request a list of current
general Acts and statutory instruments relevant to planning (together with
the current circulars and memoranda). The list is updated periodically.

Although most planning legislation is concerned with the rules governing
the operation of the process, it should be noted that special development
orders[21] and orders designating enterprise zones[22] (both are types of
delegated legislation) implement policy decisions to grant planning permission for a particular development or particular classes of development in
a defined area. The most notable example is the special development orders
which have been made in respect of the new towns of Livingston,
Cumbernauld, East Kilbride and Irvine. These orders grant planning
permission to the Development Corporations for any development to be
undertaken by themselves within the designated area of the relevant new
town, provided the proposal accords with a scheme of development, a sort of
local plan, which has been approved by the Secretary of State under s.6(1) of
the New Towns (Scotland) Act 1968. The development orders also grant
permission, subject to the same proviso, for proposals submitted by third
parties to whom the Corporations have leased or sold land.

In June 1981 the Secretary of State for the Environment issued a
consultative document suggesting the possibility of a much wider use of
special development orders. Such orders, it was suggested, might be used to
grant planning permission for specified categories of development—for
example, industrial and residential development in accord with local plans
and the intensification or extension of development in areas already
developed with uses acceptable to the relevant planning authority. The
object of using special development orders in this way would be to provide
developers with the prospect of speed and certainty of decision with a
minimum of red tape. The consultative document was the subject of a
considerable volume of criticism from local authority associations and

---

[21]   Made under s.21 of the Town and Country Planning (Scotland) Act 1972.
[22]   Made under s.179 of and Schedule 32 to the Local Government, Planning and Land Act
       1980.

others involved in planning on the grounds that it would remove control of individual proposals from the local level and preclude public consultation. Nothing further has been done about this suggestion and no similar proposal has been made in Scotland. In the meantime, however, the Department of the Environment and the S.D.D. have issued consultation papers on simplified planning zones[23] which would enable local authorities to give general planning permission for specified categories of development in defined parts of their areas. New primary legislation would be required to confer the necessary powers on planning authorities to introduce such zones.

Access to what is sometimes termed 'sub-delegated legislation' may well be more difficult for those concerned with the development of land. Sub-delegated legislation is a reference to a rule made under the authority of an instrument of delegated legislation. For example, Article 3 of the Town and Country Planning (General Development) (Scotland) Order 1981 grants planning permission for the classes of development listed in Schedule I. Article 4 provides that the Secretary of State or a planning authority may direct that the permission granted by Article 3 shall not apply to the development or classes of development specified. Such a direction is a form of sub-delegated legislation. Other powers to issue directions are scattered throughout the general development order.

For those interested in the effect of sub-delegated legislation the main difficulty relates to publication. Directions issued, for example, by planning authorities under Article 4 of the general development order will have local application and in some cases will be communicated direct to the affected parties. Directions made by the Secretary of State will often have more general application. For example, the Town and Country Planning (Restriction of Permitted Development) (National Scenic Areas) (Scotland) Direction 1980 withdraws for the purposes of National Scenic Areas the planning permission granted by Article 3 of the general development order in respect of the three categories of development listed in the direction. The difficulty is that this direction is not published in any formal way and it is not mentioned in the list of Departmental Circulars and Memoranda, Acts and Statutory Instruments. It is tucked away, together with several other directions, at the end of S.D.D. Circular 20/1980, 'Development Control in National Scenic Areas'. Another recent example is the Town and Country Planning (Notification of Applications) (Scotland) Direction 1981 which lists the categories of applications for planning permission which are likely to have national implications and which must be notified to the Secretary of State. This Direction appears as Annex B to S.D.D. Circular 24/1981. Although the relevant circular in each case makes reference to the appropriate direction, the circulars themselves are not published but are merely available on request from the S.D.D. It is therefore difficult to see how those concerned with development can readily inform themselves of relevant sub-delegated legislation.[24]

[23] See 'Simplified Planning Zones' (S.D.D., May 1984).
[24] The principal directions having general application are listed in Appendix 4 (p. 551 below).

2. *National planning guidelines*

National planning guidelines have three objectives:

(i)   they define land-based resources or potential for development which are of national significance;

(ii) they suggest safeguarding policies to be incorporated in regional reports, structure plans or local plans;

(iii) where appropriate, they specify those development proposals which, because they might impinge unacceptably on a particular resource or potential, should be notified to the Secretary of State so that he might consider whether he should take the decision.[25]

The guidelines, which may be obtained from the S.D.D.,[26] are, therefore, an important source of national planning policy for those concerned with the development of land.

The origin of the series of guidelines lies in a recommendation from the Select Committee on Land Resource Use in Scotland.[27] There was, said the Committee, a need 'to strike a balance between on the one hand, too specific guidelines which produce an over-rigid system in this age of fluctuating population trends, rapidly changing technology, and surprising discovery of natural resources and on the other hand an insufficiency of national policy guidelines which result in excessively overlapping claims being embodied in development plans and an insufficiency of information being available to entrepreneurs anxious to exploit some new opportunity'. The Committee recommended that a national structure plan should be prepared embodying a national industrial strategy with a system of advance zoning. The government in their observations on the report[28] accepted the need for more central guidance but considered that the preparation of a rigid national structure plan would be impracticable. Instead, they stated their intention 'to intensify the efforts to give central guidance, and to build up as quickly as possible a set of guidelines on those aspects of land use which should be examined for Scotland as a whole'.

The catalyst which led to the production of the first national planning guidelines was the environmental problems which arose in the early 1970s as a result of the lack of any clear policy on the location of sites for oil platform construction yards. These problems were highlighted during the public inquiry in November 1973 into the planning application to locate such a yard

---

[25]   See the preface to the National Planning Guidelines (1981).

[26]   Copies of the guidelines appear in R. C. Henderson and D. J. Hogarth (eds.), *Scottish Planning Sourcebook* (Park Place Publishing, 1984).

[27]   Select Committee on Scottish Affairs, *Land Resource Use in Scotland, Vol. 1: Report and Proceedings* (House of Commons Paper 511-i, Session 1971-72, H.M.S.O., 1972).

[28]   *Land Resource Use in Scotland: The Government's Observations on the Report of the Select Committee on Scottish Affairs* (Cmnd. 5428, 1973).

at Port Cam, Drumbuie.[29] The S.D.D. responded by issuing a discussion paper which suggested a planning framework within which oil- and gas-related developments in coastal areas should be considered. This was followed by the production in August 1974 of 'Coastal Planning Guidelines'. The guidelines were concerned with location policy and designated 16 preferred development zones where oil-related development would be encouraged and 26 preferred conservation zones where such development should be discouraged. The Secretary of State indicated that he would take decisions on individual applications within the context of these guidelines and that he expected planning authorities to relate their development plans and development control decisions to them.

Further guidelines were issued in May 1977 as part of central government's policy of disengagement from day to day supervision of the planning process.[30] These related to large industrial sites, petrochemical developments and rural conservation and indicated broad policies to be followed in the preparation of development plans and in the exercise of development control functions. Land use summary sheets accompanied the guidelines and provided background information on the individual subject areas.

Guidelines on aggregates were added to the series in December 1977[31] and on the location of major shopping developments in October 1978.[32] In 1981 revised guidelines for large industrial sites and for petrochemicals were issued, reflecting progress made in the identification of areas suitable for such development.[33] At the same time, the rural conservation guidelines were replaced with new guidelines on agricultural land, land for housing, rural planning priorities, national scenic areas, nature conservation and forestry. Guidelines for skiing development were added in July 1983[34] and in June 1984 draft guidelines on 'Development in the Countryside' were issued by the S.D.D. for consultation. Consideration is also being given to the preparation of guidelines to safeguard sites for high-technology industry from premature or piecemeal development.

[29] For a useful discussion of the policy issues underlying this inquiry see John Uden, 'Public Inquiries and the Planning Decision-Making Process' (University of Glasgow Discussion Papers in Planning, Department of Town and Regional Planning, University of Glasgow, 1976).

[30] S.D.D. Circular 19/1977, 'National Planning Guidelines'.

[31] S.D.D. Circular 51/1977, 'National Planning Guidelines: Aggregates'.

[32] S.D.D. Circular 65/1978, 'National Planning Guidelines on the Location of Major Shopping Developments'.

[33] S.D.D., 'National Planning Guidelines: Priorities for Development Planning' (1981).

[34] Letter and accompanying guidelines issued by S.D.D. in February 1984.

TABLE 3
Current National Planning Guidelines (1.1.85)

North Sea oil and gas: coastal planning guidelines (1974)
Aggregate working (1977)
Location of major shopping developments (1978)
Agricultural land (1981)
Land for housing (1981)
Land for large industry (1981)
Land for petrochemical development (1981)
Rural planning priorities (1981)
National scenic areas (1981)
Nature conservation (1981)
Forestry (1981)
Skiing development (1984)

National planning guidelines are unique to Scotland. They may be distinguished from the *Development Control Policy Notes* issued in England and Wales[35] on two counts. Although the policy notes and the guidelines both represent an attempt to draw together in an explicit and systematic way central government policy on certain aspects of development control, the guidelines go much further in some cases and actually designate zones where particular categories of development should be encouraged or discouraged. Furthermore, the guidelines set out to define the land-based resources or potential for development which are considered to be of national significance.

The guidelines, which have no statutory force, set out to steer a difficult course between 'unhelpful generalisations and unwelcome direction'[36] and do so with some apparent success. 'Guidance from central government', says Diamond, 'has previously been in respect of the procedures to be followed and in the provision of information and only in the most general terms in respect of objectives. Now we have objectives taking on a more defined shape through the indication of some priorities, criteria for evaluation, and the designation of locations.'[37] Diamond sees three obvious benefits accruing from the series of guidelines. First of all, planning authorities will now be able to explain to a much greater extent than was previously possible the way in which their structure and local plans have taken account of national policies and this should result in more realistic plans. Secondly, a higher degree of co-ordination and compatability should emerge between the various sectors within central government. Thirdly, the sharper definition of central government objectives facilitates the separation of issues of national significance in which the Secretary of State must retain an interest from those that are genuinely local matters and which can be left entirely to the planning authorities.

[35] See Ministry of Housing and Local Government Circular 23/69.
[36] S.D.D., 'National Planning Series', General Introduction (1977).
[37] Derek Diamond, 'The Uses of Strategic Planning: The Example of the National Planning Guidelines in Scotland' (1979) 50 *Town Planning Review* 18.

Diamond considers that two further benefits could be achieved. First of all, the list of topics could be extended so that the series forms a comprehensive picture of government policy. At present, as Wannop points out: 'Much is missing. There are no Guidelines for resources which are not natural. There are no Guidelines for power generation purposes. Financial resources for urban renewal and change are not covered—not surprisingly, but inconsistent with any intention to make the Guidelines a comprehensive framework for regional and district planning.'[38] In other words, the series is still some way short of being the 'compendium of all that can usefully be said about the national framework for land use planning'.[39]

Secondly, Diamond suggests that major benefit could derive from the successful harnessing of the participatory potential of the Guidelines. It would seem that this benefit has not been realised. Consultation has generally been limited to civil servants and selected agencies including planning authorities. There are no prescribed procedures for the preparation of guidelines and there has been no attempt to consult the public at large in their formulation. Yet it would appear that this has not been the cause of any widespread dissatisfaction. This may be because, as Wannop observes, in the absence of expenditure and social priorities, the guidelines remain largely apolitical.[40]

3. *Circulars*

Circulars are widely used by the Secretary of State in the planning process. They serve two main purposes. First of all, they draw the attention of planning authorities to new legislation, both primary and delegated, and explain its operation. For example, S.D.D. Circulars 29/1982 and 6/1984 give advice on the planning provisions of the Local Government and Planning (Scotland) Act 1982 and on related regulations; and S.D.D. Circular 33/1983 draws attention to the new regulations on fees for applications and deemed applications. Secondly, they give advice on policy, both operational and land use. S.D.D. Circular 24/1981, for example, sets out the Secretary of State's priorities for development control; S.D.D. Circular 21/1983 is concerned to ensure that the needs of the private housebuilding industry are recognised by local authorities; and S.D.D. Circular 32/1983 describes the general principles which the minister considers should be borne in mind by planning authorities in the preparation of development plans and in alterations to them.

Quite often both purposes will be accomplished in the same circular. S.D.D. Circular 10/1984, for example, introduced the new advertisement control regulations and also indicated the considerations which should guide the control of advertisements in the interests of amenity and public safety.

---

[38] Urlan Wannop, 'Scottish Planning in Practice: Four Distinctive Characteristics' *The Planner*, 1980, p. 64.

[39] Cmnd. 5428 (above).

[40] U. A. Wannop, 'National Planning Guidelines 1981: Priorities for Development Planning' (1982) 53 *Town Planning Review* 226.

Occasionally, circulars offer advice on the interpretation of the law. S.D.D. Circular 22/1984, for example, gives advice on the scope of the power in s.50 of the 1972 Act to enter into planning agreements; and Department of the Environment Circular 1/85 contains guidance on the scope of the power to impose conditions on a grant of planning permission.[41]

Circulars do not generally have the force of law.[42] Support for this view is to be found in the decision of the Lands Tribunal for Scotland in *Inglis* v *British Airports Authority*.[43] The respondent authority urged the tribunal to be guided in their construction of certain provisions in the Land Compensation (Scotland) Act 1973 by Memorandum 85/1973 issued by the S.D.D. The respondents had, it was said, relied upon it in other cases. The tribunal declined to be guided by the Memorandum. It was, said the tribunal, 'purely an administrative circular designed to give guidance to public authorities on the scope of the new enactment. It cannot provide a gloss on the actual words used by Parliament nor can it be used by a judicial tribunal as an aid to construing the wording of a statute or as a guide to the intention of Parliament. To use a departmental memorandum in this way would indeed tend to undermine the rule of law as enacted by Parliament.'

Nonetheless, although circulars do not have the force of law, there is no doubt that they exert a very considerable influence upon the day to day operation of the planning system. There are three reasons for saying this. First of all, as Lord Wilberforce commented in *Coleshill and District Investment Co. Ltd.* v *Minister of Housing and Local Government*,[44] on a circular dealing, *inter alia* with the meaning of 'development', the circular had 'acquired vitality and strength when, through the years, it passed as it certainly did, into planning practice and text books, [and] was acted upon, as it certainly was, in planning decisions.' Secondly, the Secretary of State, through his appellate role in the development control process, is in a strong position to ensure that policy advice given in circulars is implemented.[45] Thirdly, planning authorities are required to have regard to all 'material

---

[41] In a letter published at 1983 S.P.L.P. 90 A. G. Bell, the Chief Reporter at the Scottish Office Inquiry Reporters' Unit, commented that M.H.L.G. Circular 5/1968 (which was replaced by D.o.E. Circular 1/85) had 'been generally regarded in Scotland as authoritative as to the correct planning practice'.

[42] As we have already mentioned, directions made by the Secretary of State under powers conferred in the planning legislation and issued as an annex to a circular will have legislative force.

[43] 1978 S.L.T. (Lands Tr.) 30. See also *Lewisham Borough Council* v *Roberts* [1949] 2 K.B. 608; and *dicta* of Lord Wilberforce in *Coleshill and District Investment Co. Ltd.* v *Minister of Housing and Local Government* [1969] 1 W.L.R. 746, at p. 765; and Lord Scarman in *Newbury District Council* v *Secretary of State for the Environment* [1981] A.C. 578, at p. 621. Contrast *Blackpool Corporation* v *Locker* [1948] 1 K.B. 349; and *Patchett* v *Leatham* (1949) 65 T.L.R. 69. And see, generally, S. M. Nott and P. H. Morgan, 'The Significance of Department of the Environment Circulars in the Planning Process' [1984] J.P.L. 623. As circulars have no legal force, it follows that a circular which conflicts with the law should be disregarded (see, for example, *R.* v *Worthing Borough Council* [1984] J.P.L. 261).

[44] [1969] 1 W.L.R. 746, at p. 765.

[45] For an explicit statement on these lines see S.D.D. Circular 21/1983, 'Private House Building Land Supply: Joint Venture Schemes', para. 8.

considerations' when determining a planning application[46] and it would appear that relevant ministerial policies set out in departmental circulars are 'material considerations' and must be taken into account.[47] The courts have not, of course, gone so far as to say that the advice in a circular must be followed, since that would remove the planning authority's discretion altogether; nevertheless, the requirement to take such policy statements into account must in practice be an important limitation on the exercise of discretion. The overall effect is that policies in circulars are in many cases every bit as influential as formal legislative rules.

No procedures are prescribed for the preparation and issuing of a circular. However, prior consultation commonly takes place with the Convention of Scottish Local Authorities and with a number of other selected agencies, and in recent years the S.D.D. have made a practice of issuing some circulars in draft form for consultation with a wider group of agencies, including planning authorities.

There are more than a hundred current Scottish circulars relating to planning policy matters.[48] Policy, is of course, a protean word and many of these circulars are directed at relatively narrow and technical areas of planning practice. Nevertheless, the general way in which the principal legislation is framed allows circulars to be used to accomplish considerable changes of emphasis in the planning process. For example, in introducing Department of the Environment Circular 22/80, 'Development Control', Tom King, then Minister for Local Government, said: 'I regard this circular as a most important advance in the evolution of the British planning system. Hitherto, there has been too much emphasis on restraint and restriction. From now on, we intend to ensure that positive attitudes prevail.'[49] The significant point is that this 'important advance' was made without recourse to legislation.

4. Planning advice notes

Planning advice notes were introduced to assist regional and islands councils in the preparation of the first round of regional reports (see chapter 5). In Circular 4/1975, 'Town and Country Planning—Regional Reports', the S.D.D. stated that other departments of the Scottish Office and other public agencies whose responsibilities impinged on physical planning would issue guidance on the services and policy areas with which they were concerned.

---

[46] Town and Country Planning (Scotland) Act 1972, s.26(1).

[47] See p. 221 below.

[48] See Appendix 3 (p. 546 below). These circulars are not formally published but are listed by the S.D.D. in the 'List of Department Circulars and Memoranda, Acts and Statutory Instruments' which is updated periodically. Copies of the more important circulars together with a comprehensive list also appear in R. C. Henderson and D. J. Hogarth (eds.), Scottish Planning Sourcebook (Park Place Publishing, 1984). Individual circulars are available on request from the S.D.D. In 'Use of English Circulars, etc., in Scotland' 1984 S.P.L.P. 8 George Jamieson comments that reliance in Scotland upon Department of the Environment circulars, although not very extensive, is not uncommon and appears to be increasing. D.o.E. Circulars are published by H.M.S.O.

[49] D.o.E. Press Notice No. 507, 1st December 1980.

Between July and October 1975 twelve advice notes were prepared by the relevant agencies and issued by the S.D.D. dealing with such matters as 'Agriculture in Scotland', 'The Countryside', 'Planning and Electricity', and 'Demographic Analysis for Planning Purposes'.

Planning Advice Note 13, 'Planning and Geology', issued in December 1975 was not linked in any direct way to the preparation of regional reports and was the first of a series of notes of more general application. It was produced as a result of a marked increase in the number and complexity of issues in which planning authorities were involved which required expert geological advice. The object of the note was to help planning authorities by setting out the information and services available through the government geological service by indicating some of the typical situations in which geological advice should be brought to bear.

Planning advice notes having general application have continued to emerge from the S.D.D. over the intervening years (see table 4 below). Some (PAN 17, 'High Pressure Methane Gas Pipelines', and PAN 25, 'Commercial Pipelines') provide information on statutory procedures, technical requirements and planning considerations concerning the subject in question. Others (PAN 24, 'Design Guidance', PAN 26, 'Disposal of Land and the Use of the Developer's Brief', PAN 29, 'Planning and Small Businesses', PAN 27, 'Structure Planning' and PAN 30, 'Local Planning') go further and give guidance on the way in which planning authorities might discharge particular functions. PAN 24, 'Design Guidance', for example, comments that there is 'a widespread acknowledgement that planning authorities can and should help to safeguard the scale and character of existing areas by influencing the form of new development'; and PAN 29, 'Local Planning and Small Businesses' recommends that: 'Local plans ought to contain policies which are more flexible than the rigid zoning policies in many of the older development plans and give greater consideration to allowing mixed uses.'

In his report on the advisory and monitoring functions of the S.D.D. with respect to planning authorities, J. S. B. Martin recommended that planning advice notes should only be produced when there is a very clear need for advice and no one other than central government can provide it.[50] It seems likely, therefore, that there will be few additions to the series in the years ahead.

Planning Advice Notes are not formally published, but are available on request from the S.D.D.

---

[50]   S.D.D., 1980.

TABLE 4
Current S.D.D. Planning Advice Notes (January 1985)

PAN 1*	Agriculture in Scotland (July 1975)
PAN 2*	Forestry Guidelines (July 1975)
PAN 3*	The Countryside (July 1975)
PAN 4*	Forecasting Employment for Regional Reports and Structure Plans (July 1975)
PAN 5*	Planning for Sport, Outdoor Recreation and Tourism (September 1975)
PAN 6*	National Coal Board Scottish Areas (August 1975)
PAN 7*	Planning and Electricity (August 1975)
PAN 8*	Demographic Analysis for Planning Purposes (July 1975)
PAN 9*	Nature Conservation Guidelines (August 1975)
PAN 10*	British Rail (August 1975)
PAN 12*	The Scottish Fishing Industry (October 1975)
PAN 13*	Planning and Geology (December 1975)
PAN 17	High Pressure Methane Gas Pipelines (June 1977)
PAN 22	Social Surveys (June 1978)
PAN 23	Scottish Economic Monograph 1978 (December 1978)
PAN 24	Design Guidance (April 1980)
PAN 25	Commercial Pipelines (November 1980)
PAN 26	Disposal of Land and the Use of the Developer's Brief (February 1981)
PAN 27	Structure Planning (November 1981)
PAN 29	Planning and Small Businesses (November 1982) and addendum (January 1985)
PAN 30	Local Planning (September 1984)

* Regional Reports Advice

CHAPTER 5
LOCAL PLANNING POLICY

A. INTRODUCTION

In chapter 4 we discussed planning policy at the national level. However, planning policy is made not only at national level but locally as well; local authorities are policy-making bodies and so far as individual citizens or prospective developers are concerned, local authorities' planning policies may well be of greater significance than those of central government. As with central government, local authority policies emerge in a variety of ways and take many forms. In contrast to central government, however, local authorities are required to produce explicit policy statements on certain matters. One of the most important such duties is the obligation upon authorities to produce development plans.

The Planning Advisory Group described the development plan as the 'key feature' of the planning system.[1] Since 1947 planning authorities have been under an obligation to prepare and publish a development plan for their area. Such a plan sets out policies for the use of land in the years ahead. It also sets out proposals for public sector investment—for example, programmes for the provision of major infrastructure works—which are intended to contribute towards the implementation of the plan.[2]

By effectively nationalising the right to develop land, and thus subjecting all future proposals for development to control by the planning authority, the Town and Country Planning (Scotland) Act 1947 made it theoretically possible for planning authorities to plan the future use of land in their areas. 'The objects of Town and Country Planning', said Lewis Silkin, the Minister of Town and Country Planning, when introducing the 1947 legislation, ' . . . are to secure a proper balance between the competing demands for land, so that all the land of the country is used in the best interests of the people.'[3] Development plans were, and still are, intended to play a central role in securing this 'balance'. 'The overall purpose of development planning', says S.D.D. Circular 32/1983, 'is to set out the planning authority's policies and proposals for the use of land in the best interests of the community . . . '

---

[1] *The Future of Development Plans* (H.M.S.O., 1965).
[2] See chapter 17.
[3] H.C. Deb., Vol. 432, Col. 947 (29th January 1947).

However, as Grant points out, 'the plan may influence, but it cannot control events'.[4] There are two reasons for saying this. The first is that, short of undertaking an extensive programme of land acquisition and development, the planning authority cannot compel investment in accordance with the provisions of their plan. The choice whether to invest remains in large measure with private developers. All that the planning authority can do is resist, through the development control process, proposals which are not in conformity with their plans. This suggests that if policies for the use of land in the years ahead are to be capable of realisation, the planning authority must have due regard to the needs of the market when preparing the development plan.[5]

The second reason for suggesting that the development plan cannot control events is that it is not binding upon the planning authority[6] or the Secretary of State. And it cannot be used as a sort of rubber stamp with which to process planning applications.[7] This contrasts with the municipal zoning ordinances which are the basis of much of the land use planning system in the United States. The hallmark of the development control process in the United Kingdom is its discretionary nature. Each application for permission to develop land must be considered individually. 'It is a fundamental rule for the exercise of discretionary power', says Wade, 'that discretion must be brought to bear on every case: each one must be considered on its own merits and decided as the public interest requires at the time.'[8] The development plan will clearly carry weight in the decision but, subject to certain safeguards,[9] the planning authority may depart from the policies in their plan if they consider that circumstances justify such a decision. This might happen, for example, where a development plan is out of date. In that event it has not been uncommon to find planning authorities looking to other, non-statutory, policy statements prepared by them for guidance. These are considered in more detail below.

Although the development plan cannot control events, it will, subject to what is said above, undoubtedly exert a considerable influence upon them. Developers will take the plan into account when planning investment; and planning authorities and the Secretary of State are required to have regard to the appropriate development plan in exercising their development

---

[4] Malcolm Grant, *Urban Planning Law* (Sweet and Maxwell, 1982), p. 77.
[5] See R. Lamb and J. Brand, 'The Practical Evaluation of Planning Policies' 1983 S.P.L.P. 69. See also the addendum to *Planning Advice Note 29*, 'Planning and Small Businesses' (S.D.D., January 1985); Tony Burton, *Business Involvement in Local Plans* (S.D.D., July 1984); and generally the discussion of the promotional role of development plans in chapter 17.
[6] See *Simpson* v *Edinburgh Corporation* 1960 S.C. 313; 1961 S.L.T. 17.
[7] See *Stringer* v *Minister of Housing and Local Government* [1970] 1 W.L.R. 1281; and *Myton Ltd.* v *Minister of Housing and Local Government* (1963) 61 L.G.R. 1690. And see p. 207 below.
[8] H. W. R. Wade, *Administrative Law* (Clarendon Press, Oxford, 5th ed., 1982), pp. 330 and 331.
[9] See p. 208 below.

control functions[10]—for example, in determining a planning application or deciding what to do about a breach of planning control. 'Individual planning decisions', said Dobry 'should not be made in a vacuum. If decisions are to be correct, fair and above all, consistent, they must be made within a clear and consistently applied framework;'[11] the development plan is intended to provide such a framework. There is a similar statutory requirement to have regard to the development plan when considering whether land should be compulsorily purchased for planning purposes[12] and when making various other sorts of planning decisions. It is in this somewhat indirect manner, therefore, that development plans contribute towards the attainment of the 'proper balance' of which Lewis Silkin spoke.

In view of their influential role in the planning process, it is important that development plans should be realistic. The procedures by which the policies in the plans are determined and the format in which they are presented will clearly have a material bearing on this. Important changes have been made in both procedures and format in recent years.

'Old style' development plans and their shortcomings

Under the 1947 Act[13] it was the duty of every planning authority to submit for the approval of the Secretary of State a development plan indicating the manner in which the authority proposed that land in their area should be used (whether by the carrying out thereon of development or otherwise) and the stages by which any such development should be carried out. Each such 'old style' development plan had to include a written statement, summarising the authority's proposals, and a basic map defining the sites of proposed roads, public buildings, open spaces and so on, and allocating or 'zoning' areas of land for particular purposes.

In the early 1960s development plans made under the 1947 legislation were subjected to increasing criticism. Because of the great amount of detail they contained, plans tended to be inflexible, and although planning authorities were under an obligation to review their development plans at five-yearly intervals, and could, if they wished, put forward amendments at any time, it proved extremely difficult to keep plans up to date and forward-looking. The approval of the Secretary of State was required before the original plan or any amendment could come into operation and there thus came before the minister not only major policy issues but also a mass of detail. The need to examine so much detail and the obligation to afford all objectors the opportunity of a hearing (generally at a public inquiry) meant that a considerable period could elapse before ministerial approval was granted. 'Old style' plans were frequently criticised for the narrowness of

[10]   See, for example, 1972 Act, ss.26(1) and 84(1).
[11]   *Review of the Development Control System: Final Report* (H.M.S.O., 1975), para. 2.64.
[12]   1972 Act, s.102(1A) (inserted by the Local Government, Planning and Land Act 1980, s.92(4)).
[13]   The provisions of the 1947 Act relating to the making and amendment of 'old style' development plans were re-enacted in Schedule 3 to the 1972 Act.

their approach—it was said that they were little more than land use allocation maps, that they often paid insufficient attention to economic realities and investment priorities, and that they were not sufficiently concerned with the fundamental question of whether the physical environment was being properly shaped to meet evolving social and economic needs. The procedure for making 'old style' plans was also criticised as affording insufficient opportunity for public involvement at the formative stage of the plan.

As a result of these and other criticisms, provision was made by the Town and Country Planning (Scotland) Act 1969[14] for a completely new system of development planning designed to overcome the problems of the past.

The new system

Under the new system the development strategy for an area is dealt with separately from detailed local planning policies. There are to be two tiers of plans, structure plans and local plans;[15] the development plan for any area will eventually consist of the provisions of any structure plan relating to the area and the provisions of any relevant local plan.

The structure plan consists, in essence, of a written statement and a key diagram (but not a map). The purpose of a structure plan is to set out the broad policy framework for an area; it is not to be concerned with detailed proposals for the use of particular parcels of land in the area. With its freedom from detail it was hoped that the structure plan would allow strategic issues to be settled more quickly than was possible in the past. Structure plans are prepared by regional and general planning authorities and require ministerial approval.

Detailed planning policies and proposals are set out in local plans. A local plan consists of a map and a written statement. Local plans are normally prepared and adopted by general and district planning authorities; only exceptionally will a local plan require to be approved by the Secretary of State. A local plan has to conform generally to the provisions of any approved structure plan relating to the area.

It was hoped that the new development planning system would avoid the delays of the past and that by making it possible for plans to take effect more quickly, the new procedures would help to reduce uncertainty and blight and would make it easier for authorities to keep plans up to date. It was also hoped that the new plans would prove more responsive to public opinion than were 'old style' development plans. The extent to which these hopes are being realised is considered below.

---

[14] See now Part II of the 1972 Act, as amended by the Local Government (Scotland) Act 1973, the Town and Country Planning (Scotland) Act 1977, the Local Government (Miscellaneous Provisions) (Scotland) Act 1981 and the Local Government and Planning (Scotland) Act 1982.

[15] The form of the 'new style' development plan owes much to the recommendations made by the Ministers' Planning Advisory Group in *The Future of Development Plans* (H.M.S.O., 1965).

Part II of the 1972 Act, which deals with the making of structure and local plans, was brought into force for Orkney on 1st April 1975[16] and for the remainder of Scotland on 16th May 1975.[17] Delays in the preparation and approval or adoption of the 'new style' plans mean that nine years later parts of 'old style' development plans are still relevant in much of Scotland. Before dealing with the new system it is therefore still necessary to consider certain aspects of 'old style' plans and to outline the rather complex arrangements for transition to the new system.

B. OLD STYLE DEVELOPMENT PLANS AND TRANSITION TO THE NEW SYSTEM

As is mentioned above, in a number of contexts statute directs that regard must be had to 'the provisions of the development plan'. For the purposes of the relevant legislation there can, as respects any particular piece of land, only be one development plan in operation at any particular time. During the transition to the new system the component parts of the development plan for an area will, however, vary from time to time.

The 'old style' development plan for an area continues in force and is to be treated as being, or as being comprised in, the development plan for that area until it is either revoked by the Secretary of State or is replaced by an appropriate local plan. It seems likely that in some parts of Scotland 'old style' development plans will continue in force for some time to come and it is therefore necessary to give a brief account of the documents which make up an 'old style' plan.

Form and content of 'old style' development plan

An 'old style' development plan includes 'such maps and such descriptive matter as may be necessary to illustrate the proposals in question with such degree of particularity as may be appropriate to different parts of the district'; in particular, such a plan may define the sites of proposed roads, public or other buildings and works, airfields, parks, pleasure grounds, nature reserves and other open spaces, or allocate areas of land for use for agricultural, residential, industrial or other purposes of any class specified in the plan (1972 Act, Schedule 3, para. 1(3)).

A development plan may define as an area of comprehensive development any area which, in the opinion of the planning authority, should be developed or redeveloped as a whole for any one or more of the following purposes:

(*a*) for the purpose of dealing satisfactorily with extensive war damage or conditions of bad lay-out or obsolete development; or

---

[16] See Town and Country Planning (Scotland) Act 1972 (Commencement No. 1) (Orkney Islands Area) Order 1975.
[17] See Town and Country Planning (Scotland) Act 1972 (Commencement No. 2) Order 1975.

(b) for the purpose of providing for the relocation of population or industry or the replacement of open space in the course of the development or redevelopment of any other area; or

(c) for any other purpose specified in the plan (Schedule 3, para. 1(4)).

The Town and Country Planning (Development Plans) (Scotland) Regulations 1966 provided that a development plan was to consist of a written statement and a basic map and such other map or maps as might be appropriate (reg. 6). The written statement had to include, *inter alia*, a summary of the main proposals of the development plan and an indication of the stages by which the proposals were to be carried out (reg. 7). Regulations 8 and 9 of, and Schedule 1 to, the 1966 Regulations made provision as to the form and content of the obligatory basic map. Any land defined as an area of comprehensive development had to be shown on a comprehensive development area map (reg. 10). A development plan could include a programme map showing the stages by which any proposed development should be carried out; however, such a map ceased to be obligatory in 1966 (see reg. 7(2)).

A development plan is to have effect as if there were incorporated in it the provisions of certain ministerial orders and schemes relating to roads and new towns (1972 Act, Schedule 3, para. 5).

The 1947 Act provided that a development plan might designate land as subject to compulsory acquisition. The statutory provisions relating to such designation were repealed by the 1969 Act; after 8th December 1969 planning authorities had no power to propose the designation of land as subject to compulsory acquisition and on that date any existing designation ceased to have effect (except in relation to compulsory purchase orders made before that date).

Amendment of 'old style' development plan

The provisions of the 1947 Act relating to the making and amendment of 'old style' development plans were re-enacted in Schedule 3 to the 1972 Act. Under paragraph 3 of that Schedule planning authorities[18] were able to submit for the approval of the Secretary of State proposals for alterations or amendments to 'old style' development plans; it was, however, provided that the consent of the Secretary of State had to be obtained before any such proposals for amendment of an 'old style' development plan could be submitted to the minister for his consideration (1972 Act, Schedule 5, para. 1). After the coming into operation of Part II of the 1972 Act (dealing with the making of 'new style' plans) the Secretary of State took the view that any fresh development planning proposals should normally be incorporated in a 'new style' plan rather than in an amendment to an 'old style' development plan; after 16th May 1975 the Secretary of State was therefore prepared to sanction the submission of proposals for amendment of an 'old style' plan only if the need for development planning action was urgent and strictly

[18] i.e., general and district planning authorities.

localised. S.D.D. Circular 28/1976 finally announced that the Secretary of State would not be prepared to grant consent in respect of any proposed amendments to an 'old style' plan submitted to him after 15th May 1977.

The Town and Country Planning (Development Plans) (Scotland) Order 1977 repealed Schedules 3 and 4 to the 1972 Act.[19] These Schedules are mainly concerned with the making and amendment of 'old style' development plans. The repeals took effect on 16th May 1977 except as respects those areas in relation to which the Secretary of State had before him on that date proposals made by the planning authority for amendment of an 'old style' development plan; in the areas in which 'old style' proposals were under consideration by the Secretary of State on that date, the repeals were deferred until the Secretary of State had taken a decision on the proposals. Once Schedules 3 and 4 ceased to have effect in any area there could be no further amendment of the 'old style' development plan relating to that area—the 'old style' plan was in effect 'frozen' until replaced by a 'new style' plan.

The up-to-date effect of the Town and Country Planning (Development Plans) (Scotland) Order 1977 in any area may be ascertained from the register kept by the Secretary of State under s.18(7) of the 1972 Act.

Replacement of 'old style' development plan

The mere repeal, as respects any area, of Schedule 3 to the 1972 Act did not mean that the 'old style' development plan for that area thereupon ceased to have effect—the development plan which was in force before the repeal of Schedule 3 is to continue in force and is to be treated for the purposes of the planning legislation and of the Land Compensation (Scotland) Act 1963 as being comprised in, or as being, the development plan for the area (1972 Act, Schedule 5, para. 2).

Nor does the 'old style' plan cease to have effect on the coming into operation of a structure plan made under the new system; in the absence of a local plan for an area, the approved structure plan and the 'old style' development plan will together make up the development plan for that area (see 1972 Act, Schedule 5, para. 3). In any case of conflict the provisions of the structure plan will for most purposes prevail over those of the 'old style' plan.[20]

Only an appropriate local plan made under the new system can take the place of an 'old style' plan. On the adoption or approval of a local plan for any area, so much of any 'old style' plan as relates to the same area is to cease to have effect unless the Secretary of State, after consulting the planning authority, makes an order directing that all or any of the provisions of the

[19] See too 1972 Act, s.18(2) (as substituted by s.5(1) of the Town and Country Planning (Scotland) Act 1977).

[20] See 1972 Act, Schedule 5, para. 3. For the purposes of the Land Compensation (Scotland) Act 1963, however, a landowner is entitled, in effect, to the benefit of those assumptions, whether derived from the structure plan or from the 'old style' plan, which are more favourable to his claim (see Schedule 5, para. 5).

'old style' plan should continue in force (1972 Act, Schedule 5, para. 5A[21]); such an order would presumably be made on the adoption or approval of a local plan which dealt, for example, with only one or two particular types of development and which was therefore only a partial replacement for the 'old style' plan. The Secretary of State also has power to make an order revoking, in whole or in part, the 'old style' plan for any area (see 1972 Act, Schedule 5, paras. 6 and 7).

When, in the manner outlined above, the 'old style' development plan has ceased to have effect in any area, the development plan for that area will consist of the provisions of any approved structure plan relating to the area and the provisions of any local plan applicable to the area (see below).

C. THE NEW SYSTEM

The legislation on the new type of development plan, originally contained in the Town and Country Planning (Scotland) Act 1969, re-enacted in Part II of the 1972 Act and amended in a number of important respects by the Local Government (Scotland) Act 1973, was finally brought into force in 1975 (see p. 76 above). Further minor amendments to the law on development planning were made by the Town and Country Planning (Scotland) Act 1977, the Local Government (Miscellaneous Provisions) (Scotland) Act 1981 and the Local Government and Planning (Scotland) Act 1982. The legislation relating to the new system of development planning makes provision for the preparation of structure plans and local plans.

Once the 'old style' development plan for an area has ceased to have effect, the development plan for that area will consist of:

(*a*) the provisions of any structure plan relating to the area, together with the Secretary of State's notice of approval of the plan;

(*b*) any alterations to the structure plan, together with the Secretary of State's notices of approval thereof;

(*c*) any provisions of a local plan applicable to the area, together with a copy of the planning authority's resolution of adoption or, as the case may be, the Secretary of State's notice of approval of the local plan; and

(*d*) any alterations to that local plan, together with a copy of the planning authority's resolutions of adoption or, as the case may be, the Secretary of State's notices of approval thereof (see 1972 Act, s.17).

Detailed provision as to the form and content of structure and local plans and as to the procedure for their preparation and approval or adoption is made by the Town and Country Planning (Structure and Local Plans) (Scotland) Regulations 1983. The Regulations require every regional, general and district planning authority to maintain an up-to-date register and index map of structure and local plans affecting their area (see reg. 45).

---

[21] Inserted by the Town and Country Planning (Scotland) Act 1977, s.5(5).

The two parts of the 'new style' development plan, the structure plan and the local plan or plans, are now considered in turn.

1. STRUCTURE PLANS

Section 5(1) of the 1972 Act requires regional and general planning authorities to prepare and submit to the Secretary of State for approval a structure plan for their area. The purpose of the plan is to provide 'a strategic policy framework at regional or sub-regional level for the development and control of the physical environment in the interests of the community'.[22] The procedure for the preparation of the plan is set out below.

(a) *Survey*

The policy framework in the structure plan must be justified by the results of a survey (1972 Act s.5(4)) and the first action taken by a planning authority proposing to prepare a structure plan will be to institute a survey of their area.

Each regional and general planning authority must, in so far as they have not already done so, institute a survey of their area examining the matters which may be expected to affect the development of their area or the planning of its development; there is a continuing obligation to keep all such matters under review (1972 Act, s.4(1)). The range of matters to be so examined and kept under review is wide; matters to be covered include:

(*a*) the principal physical and economic characteristics of the area (including the principal purposes for which land is used) and, so far as relevant, those of any neighbouring areas;

(*b*) the size, composition and distribution of the population of the area (whether resident or otherwise);

(*c*) the communications, transport system and traffic of the area and, so far as relevant, of any neighbouring areas;

(*d*) any other considerations which may be expected to affect any of the foregoing matters;

(*e*) such other matters as may be prescribed by regulations; and

(*f*) any changes already projected in any of the foregoing matters and the effect which those changes are likely to have on the development of the area or the planning of such development (1972 Act, s.4(3)).

Planning authorities are required to prepare a report of survey for submission to the Secretary of State along with the structure plan. Notwithstanding the range of matters to be examined, authorities are discouraged from producing large survey reports.[23] The report should only include material which explains the strategic policy framework. Detailed technical information or raw data should not appear in the document.

[22]   S.D.D. Planning Advice Note 27 (PAN 27).
[23]   See PAN 27.

Although the survey provides the basis for preparation of the structure plan, the survey report does not form part of the plan and is not subject to ministerial approval.

(b) *Preparation of structure plan*

Having completed the survey, the planning authority will analyse the information obtained with a view to preparing the structure plan. The Secretary of State has power to direct each regional and general planning authority to prepare and submit to him within a prescribed period a report of survey and a structure plan (1972 Act, s.5(1)). No period has yet been prescribed.

The legislation provides that a structure plan may, instead of consisting of a single document, consist of a series of plans relating to different parts of the authority's area[24]—a form of development planning by instalments—and may, with the approval of the Secretary of State relate to part only of an authority's area (1972 Act, s.5(7); and Local Government (Scotland) Act 1973, s.174(1)). Three authorities—Central, Fife and Grampian Regions— are proceeding on the latter basis and will eventually have two or more structure plans covering their areas. The legislation, as framed, recognised that some regions may be larger than is appropriate for coverage by one plan. It also allowed for the possibility that parts of some regions or islands areas might never be covered by a structure plan; however, it now seems likely that the initial round of structure plans, when complete, will provide total coverage.

The procedure for preparing a structure plan is very much in the hands of the planning authority. However, they must give public notice of their intention to prepare the plan,[25] and during the preparatory stage the authority are required to carry out certain consultations and to take steps to give publicity to the matters which they propose to include in the plan.

Before submitting a structure plan for approval, a regional planning authority must consult[26] every other planning authority likely to be affected by the proposals (1973 Act, s.174(2)). A regional or general planning authority preparing a structure plan must (a) consult the bodies specified in regulation 4 of the Town and Country Planning (Structure and Local Plans) (Scotland) Regulations 1983; (b) afford the consulted bodies an opportunity to express their views; and (c) take such views into consideration (1983 Regulations, reg. 4).

Before authorities have become firmly committed to particular policies and proposals, they must provide an opportunity for members of the public

[24] See Local Government (Scotland) Act 1973, s.174(1).

[25] See Town and Country Planning (Structure and Local Plans) (Scotland) Regulations 1983, reg. 11.

[26] As to what is involved in a duty to 'consult' another body see *Easter Ross Land Use Committee* v *Secretary of State for Scotland* 1970 S.C. 182; 1970 S.L.T. 317 (which arose out of an amendment to an 'old style' development plan). See also Colin T. Reid, 'A Planning Authority's Duty to Consult' 1982 S.P.L.P. 4.

to put forward their views on the structure plan. Before finally determining the content of a structure plan, a regional or general planning authority must ensure:

(a) that adequate publicity is given to the report of the survey and to the. matters which the authority propose to include in the structure plan;

(b) that persons who may be expected to want to make representations on the matters proposed to be included in the plan are made aware of their right to do so; and

(c) that such persons are given an adequate opportunity to make representations (1972 Act, s.6(1)).

The authority must allow a period of at least four weeks for the making of representations and must consider any representations received within the specified period (1972 Act, s.6(1); 1983 Regulations, reg. 3).

This requirement to involve the public in the structure plan process is commonly referred as the 'participation exercise' although this is not a term which is used in the legislation. The term was much in vogue around the time that the legislation for the 'new style' of development plan was introduced. During the debate in 1968 on the second reading of the Town and Country Planning Bill, for example, the Minister of Housing and Local Government, Anthony Greenwood, said: 'Above all, I am determined that there shall be more real public participation in planning. I want people to have a much better chance of being involved in the planning of the area they live in and of influencing it. Planning is for people and about their activities, not just about areas.'[27]

The somewhat vague terms of the legislation would not seem to do justice to this vision of the development planning process. As McAuslan comments 'the statutes providing for [participation] are so open-ended and vague that it is difficult to see that any duty has been laid on local authorities at all.'[28] The explanation is twofold. First of all, in *People and Planning* (1969) the Committee on Public Participation in Planning recommended that participation should not be a formalised or rigid process but should be flexible enough to meet all types of local need. To allow for flexibility the statutory requirements were kept to a minimum and it was left to individual authorities to decide upon the methods of promoting participation best suited to the requirements of particular areas.[29] The Secretary of State is, however, required, before he considers a structure plan, to satisfy himself that the purposes of the statutory provisions on public involvement have been adequately achieved (see p. 87 below).[30]

[27] H.C. Deb., vol. 757, Col. 1362 (31st January 1968).
[28] P. McAuslan, *The Ideologies of Planning Law* (Pergamon Press, 1980), p. 11.
[29] For an analysis of practice in Scotland see A. W. Burton and R. Johnson, *Public Participation in Planning: A Review of Experience in Scotland* (Planning Exchange Occasional Paper, 1976).
[30] On the question of 'adequacy' see *Publicity and Consultation in Structure and Local Plans* (S.D.D., 1979).

Secondly, notwithstanding the use of the word 'participation' in official advice and guidance, it was clearly intended that responsibility for the content of the plan should remain with the planning authority. 'The main purpose of consultation (whether with official bodies or members of the public) is to ensure that those with an interest in the area have the opportunity to contribute information and opinion before decisions are taken.'[31] The aim of the exercise is, as Grant says, 'to extend the opportunity for the exercise of influence by citizens, not to achieve any transfer of power'.[32] It is presumably for this reason that s.6 of the 1972 Act talks about 'publicity' and 'representations' and not about 'participation'.

The very general terms in which the legislation is framed has permitted some back-tracking in the official guidance on the scope of the publicity and consultation exercise. The word 'participation' has dropped out of official advice and guidance. PAN 27, entitled 'Structure Planning', which outlines a procedure for publicity and consultation, states that the procedure 'can be regarded as standard for all plans and alterations and authorities should consider whether there will be any gain in going beyond it'. The main phase of publicity for the general public, says the Advice Note, 'should be strictly tailored to the nature of the material, the character of the area and the expectations of the public'. The reason for this change of heart would seem to be a desire to speed up the plan making process,[33] and perhaps also a feeling that public consultation has most to contribute to local plans.

(c) *The form and content of a structure plan*

Having consulted the specified bodies and having afforded the public an opportunity to make representations, the authority can proceed to complete their preparation of the structure plan.

Concerned as it is with broad policy, not with the detailed use of particular parcels of land, a structure plan is quite different in form from the 'old style' development plan.[34] A structure plan consists of a written statement supplemented by diagrams; it does not contain a map and does not attempt to show the effect that its proposals may have on individual properties.

Section 5(3) of the 1972 Act provides that the written statement will:

(*a*) formulate the authority's policy and general proposals in respect of the development and other use of land in their area (including measures for the

---

[31] S.D.D. *Planning Advice Note 19* (see now PAN 27).

[32] *Urban Planning Law*, p. 101. For a detailed discussion of the theory and practice of participation see N. Boaden, M. Goldsmith, W. Hampton and P. Stringer, 'Planning and Participation in Practice: A Study of Public Participation in Structure Planning' in *Progress in Planning*, D. Diamond and J. B. McLoughlin, eds., 1981.

[33] See PAN 27 and S.D.D. Circular 32/1983.

[34] It will sometimes be difficult to make a clear distinction between broad policy and its detailed application; see, for example, *Edwin H. Bradley & Sons Ltd.* v *Secretary of State for the Environment* (1982) 47 P. & C.R. 374.

improvement of the physical environment and the management of traffic).[35]

The intention seems to be that this should form the central part of the written statement. PAN 27 makes a distinction between policies and proposals. 'Policies' are defined as statements of attitudes or intentions towards some situation, existing or postulated, requiring action. 'Proposals' are defined as permitted and programmed development by the local authority and other public bodies. Parliament has been concerned to see that planning authorities are realistic in their approach to the formulation of their policies and proposals; authorities must have regard to current policies for the economic planning and development of the region as a whole and to the resources likely to be available. Furthermore, the policy and proposals must be justified by the results of the survey (1972 Act, s.5(4)).

Section 5(3) of the 1972 Act further provides that the written statement will:

(b) state the relationship of those proposals to general proposals for the development and other use of land in neighbouring areas which may be expected to affect that area; and

(c) contain such other matters as may be prescribed in regulations.

The power to prescribe 'other matters' places the scope of the structure plan very largely in the hands of the Secretary of State. In the Town and Country Planning (Structure and Local Plans) (Scotland) Regulations 1983[36] the minister has prescribed certain additional matters which must be contained in the written statement. These are:

(a) the existing social, economic and physical structure of the district to which the plan relates and the needs and opportunities for change;

(b) the resources likely to be available for the carrying out of the policies and general proposals formulated in the plan; and

(c) the broad criteria to be applied as respects the control of development in the area, or any part of the area to which the plan relates, including guidance on the application of these criteria, where appropriate, in local plans.

The structure plan may also contain such other matters as the planning authority consider relevant.

It would seem, therefore, that the structure plan must concern itself with a wide range of matters. In practice, however, the requirements are not as wide as they may appear. There are three reasons for saying this.

First of all, it would seem that the policies and proposals contained in the

---

[35] In *Westminster City Council* v *Great Portland Estates plc* [1984] 3 W.L.R. 1035 the House of Lords held that the broadly similar provision dealing with the content of local plans in the Town and Country Planning Act 1971 was to be construed as imposing on the planning authority an obligation to include in their plan *all* proposals which they may have for the development and use of land (see page 97).

[36] See reg. 7.

plan must serve a planning purpose.[37] In *Westminster City Council v Great Portland Estates plc*,[38] for example, the House of Lords held that a local plan policy directed at safeguarding industrial uses having important linkages with central London activities served a genuine planning purpose. Although the policy incidentally protected certain existing users, its object was to safeguard certain industrial activities considered important to the diverse character, vitality and functioning of Westminster. The policy was, said Lord Scarman, 'a powerful piece of positive thinking within a planning context'.

Secondly, PAN 27 advises planning authorities that structure plans should be concerned solely with the treatment of strategic issues. In other words, the plan should be problem-orientated. The authority should single out for consideration in the plan those land use issues which are significant at national or regional level in terms of the action required. The Advice Note states that it will be for authorities themselves to determine their strategic issues. However, having said that, the Advice Note reminds authorities that national planning guidelines are government statements on land use planning issues of national significance and where they express the national interest either as to the way in which a land resource should be used or safeguarded in future, or as to development planning priorities, that interest should be incorporated into structure plan policies.

The sorts of issues tackled in the initial structure plans have included settlement patterns, the scale and location of industry and employment, and mobility and the transport system. PAN 27 suggests that countryside conservation and recreation and tourism might be appropriate topics where there is a strategic planning interest. Other guidance from the Scottish Development Department draws attention to further possible strategic land use issues. For example, *Planning Advice Note 17* emphasises the importance of ensuring that adequate provision is made for high pressure methane gas pipeline routes in appropriate areas; and S.D.D. Circular 21/1983 states that structure plan allocations of land for private housing should be kept under regular review.

Thirdly, it seems that the structure plan, like the 'old style' development plan, is principally concerned with land use. Section 5(3)(a) of the 1972 Act requires the written statement to formulate the planning authority's policy and general proposals in respect of the *development and other use of land* in the area. Whilst most activities are linked in some way to land use, PAN 27 suggests that it is only if there is 'an imbalance or conflict amongst land uses and activities' requiring strategic planning action that an issue will arise which requires attention in the structure plan. Thus, while reference can be made to the economic, social and other policies of the authority to justify the content of the structure plan, the plan itself should be concerned with tackling the land use and development implications of these policies. The Advice Note distinguishes strategic land use policies and proposals, with

---

[37] For a discussion of the scope of planning purposes see chapter 9.
[38] [1984] 3 W.L.R. 1035.

E

which the plan is primarily concerned, from supporting policies and proposals. The latter are not concerned with strategic physical land use development but are included in the plan because they contribute to the implementation of the land use aspects. It is the strategic land use policies and proposals in the plan to which the Secretary of State's approval will relate.[39]

The written statement is to include a reasoned justification of the policy and general proposals formulated therein (1983 Regulations, reg. 6(2)). The policy and general proposals formulated in the written statement are to be set out in such a way as to be clearly distinguishable from the other contents thereof (reg. 6(1)).

A structure plan is to contain or be accompanied by such diagrams, illustrations and descriptive matter as the authority think appropriate for the purpose of explaining or illustrating the proposals; any such material forms part of the plan (1972 Act, s.5(6)). The 1983 Regulations provide that the structure plan must contain or be accompanied by a diagram, called a key diagram, showing, so far as the authority think practicable, the policy and general proposals formulated in the written statement (reg. 9(1)). No diagram contained in or accompanying a structure plan may be shown on a map base (reg. 9(3)).

In the case of any contradiction between the written statement and any other document forming part of a structure plan, the written statement is to prevail (reg. 10).

PAN 27 asserts that structure plans cannot and should not relate to a fixed end date, but should evolve flexibly. Monitoring of a plan should indicate the need for alteration of different parts of the plan at different times. Each policy or proposal will have its own timescale by which it will contribute to the resolution of a strategic issue. The Advice Note suggests that the policy or proposal can be reviewed when the time expires and new or altered policies or proposals can be brought forward as required.

A structure plan must indicate any area selected as an 'action area' (below).

(d) *Action areas*

A structure plan must 'indicate' any part of the area covered by the plan which the regional or general planning authority have selected for comprehensive treatment, to begin within five years of the approval of the structure plan by the Secretary of State, by means of development, redevelopment or improvement or by a combination of those methods;[40] such an area is termed an 'action area'[41] (1972 Act, s.5(5); 1983 Regulations, reg. 8). The structure plan is to indicate the nature of the proposed treatment. A local plan (an 'action area plan') must be prepared for any action area designated in the structure plan (see p. 96 below); there will

---

[39] See S.D.D. Circular 32/1983.
[40] The structure plan will not, of course, define the boundaries of such an area.
[41] Not to be confused with a housing action area under the housing legislation.

therefore have to be full consultation between a regional planning authority who propose to designate an action area and the appropriate district planning authority (who will be obliged to prepare an action area plan for the area). No 'action areas' have been indicated in the initial round of structure plans.[42]

Areas designated under the old system as comprehensive development areas may be re-designated as action areas or may be allowed to continue under the old system.[43]

(e) *Submission to Secretary of State*

When, under s.5(1) of the 1972 Act, a regional or general planning authority submit the survey report and the structure plan to the Secretary of State, they must also submit to the minister a brief account of the steps they have taken to satisfy the requirements of s.6(1) of the 1972 Act as to public consultation (above) and of the consultations they have had with other bodies (1972 Act, s.6(3); 1983 Regulations, reg. 12).

No later than the date of submission of these documents to the minister the authority must make copies of the submitted documents available for public inspection (see 1972 Act, s.6(2); 1983 Regulations, reg. 42); copies must also be made available for sale (reg. 44). Each copy of the plan is to be accompanied by a statement of the period within which objections may be made to the Secretary of State; that period is six weeks from the date when notice of the submission is first published (1972 Act, s.6(2); 1983 Regulations, reg. 16). The authority must give notice by advertisement that the structure plan has been submitted and is available for inspection (see 1983 Regulations, regs. 2(1) and 13 and Schedule); that notice is to indicate the manner in which and the period within which objections may be made to the Secretary of State (see 1983 Regulations, reg. 16 and Schedule).

(f) *Consideration by Secretary of State: (1) adequacy of public consultation*

PAN 27 suggests that the account of the steps taken by the planning authority to consult the public, which must accompany the structure plan when it is submitted for approval, should be simple. It should demonstrate how representations were considered and what decision resulted. As indicated above, a copy of the statement is to be made available for public inspection.

Before considering any structure plan submitted for his approval, the Secretary of State must satisfy himself that the purposes of paragraphs (a) to (c) of s.6(1) of the 1972 Act (requirements as to public consultation—see p. 81 above) have been adequately achieved by the steps the authority have taken. It would seem that this provision was inserted in the legislation to avoid the possibility of application for judicial review of the planning

---

[42] See A. G. Coon, 'Where Are the Action Area and Subject Plans?' 1983 S.P.L.P. 58.
[43] Some of the considerations bearing upon the choices open to authorities as regards existing comprehensive development areas are set out in S.D.D. Circular 28/1976.

authority's action at a late stage in the preparation of the plan.[44] In satisfying himself as to adequacy of the participation exercise, the minister will clearly be influenced to a very large extent by the document setting out the planning authority's account of the steps they have taken. In S.D.D. Circular 28/1976 it was stated that the minister would require to be satisfied that:

'genuine attempts have been made to inform the public (for example, by newspaper advertising, local radio, exhibition, local "planning work-shop", or otherwise); that organisations and individuals have had a reasonable opportunity to examine the proposals, and make comments and representations, and that the planning authority have given genuine consideration to such representations and have either given effect to them or have explained why they are not prepared to do so.'

S.D.D. Circular 28/1976 has since been replaced by Circular 32/1983 which gives no guidance on the question of adequacy. Instead, as mentioned above, PAN 27 now sets out what is stated to be a standard procedure for publicity and consultation.[45]

If the Secretary of State is not satisfied with the steps the authority have taken, he will return the plan, directing the authority to take such further action as he specifies and thereafter to re-submit the plan with such modifications as they consider appropriate[46] (1972 Act, s.6(4)). No such direction has been issued to date.

(g) Consideration by Secretary of State: (2) objections and examination in public

When the period for submitting objections has expired the Secretary of State will proceed to consider the structure plan. In considering the plan the minister may take into account any matters he considers relevant, whether or not they were taken into account in the submitted plan (1972 Act, s.7(2)).

Unless the Secretary of State decides, as he is entitled to do, that he will reject the structure plan without even going as far as considering objections, then, before determining whether or not to approve the plan, the minister must:[47]

---

[44] *Official Report*, Standing Committee G, Session 1967–1968, Vol. IX, Col. 119 (22nd February 1968).

[45] In *Publicity and Consultation in Structure and Local Plans*, a report of a research project published by the S.D.D. in 1979, it was stated that: 'there can be no blueprint for adequacy; to demonstrate that adequate publicity and consultation have taken place a planning authority will need to show that the characteristics of an area have been taken into account in the selection of techniques and that the response has been fully considered prior to the finalisation of the plan.'

[46] As to procedure to be followed in such a case see 1972 Act, s.6(5)–(7); and 1983 Regulations, regs. 14 and 15.

[47] 1972 Act, s.7(3) (substituted by the Local Government (Scotland) Act 1973, s.175(1) and amended by the Local Government and Planning (Scotland) Act 1982, s.36).

(*a*) consider any objections to the plan,[48] and

(*b*) if, but only if, it appears to him that an examination in public should be held of any matter affecting his consideration of the plan, cause a person or persons, appointed by him for the purpose, to hold such an examination,[49] normally within six months of the submission of the plan.

In this way the Secretary of State will be able to concentrate the public proceedings on those strategic issues (whether or not they happen to be the subject of objection) which he considers merit examination. Though the minister has a duty to consider all objections to the structure plan, he is not obliged to afford an objector (or any other person or body) an opportunity of a hearing; only those persons and bodies invited to do so by the Secretary of State (or by the person or persons appointed to hold the examination) will be able to take part in the examination in public (1972 Act, s.7(5)),[50] if such an examination is to be held. In the selection of participants (who need not have made objections or representations) the criterion will be the effectiveness of the contribution which, from their knowledge or the views they have expressed, they can be expected to make to the discussion of the matters to be examined.

The Secretary of State does not, it seems, intend meantime to make regulations with respect to the procedure to be followed at the public examination of a structure plan but instead has issued a Code of Practice.[51] This is for guidance only and has no statutory force.

The Code provides that the Secretary of State will announce the names of the chairman and any other members of the panel appointed to conduct the examination. In practice the chairman has been drawn from the Scottish Office Inquiry Reporters' Unit. The Secretary of State will also publish a list of the matters to be examined and of those persons or bodies invited to take part. The regional or general planning authority responsible for the structure plan will always be invited. Matters which need to be examined are likely to arise, it seems, from doubts about the validity of forecasts or other justification for the plan; from clashes between the plan and national or regional policies, or the policies of neighbouring planning authorities or district planning authorities within the region; from any conflicts between the various general proposals in the plan; or from issues involving

---

[48] The Secretary of State can, however, disregard objections relating to certain types of development authorised by or under ss.5, 7, 9 or 12 of the Roads (Scotland) Act 1984 and the New Towns legislation (see 1972 Act, s.14, as amended by s.156 of, and Schedule 9 to, the Roads (Scotland) Act 1984).

[49] Substituted by the Local Government (Scotland) Act 1973, s.175(1) and subsequently amended by the Local Government and Planning (Scotland) Act 1982, s.36. The Secretary of State must give at least four weeks notice of his intention to hold such an examination (1983 Regulations, reg. 17). In two cases so far the minister has reached a decision on a structure plan without first convening an examination in public.

[50] See Code of Practice for the Examination in Public of Structure Plans, published on 17th October 1977.

[51] See note 50 above.

substantial controversy which has not been resolved. Publication of the list provides an opportunity for comment on the selection of the issues and the participants prior to the examination. A final list will then be published and participants will be invited to provide, in advance of the examination, a statement specifically directed to the matter or matters for examination with which they are concerned.

The Code describes the examination in public as essentially a probing discussion. It is inquisitorial rather than adversarial in character. Its conduct is in the hands of the chairman. The aim is to create an appropriate atmosphere for intensive discussion and to get away from the formalities of the traditional public inquiry. The chairman and any other members of the panel will take an active part in the examination; an important feature of their role is to ensure that relevant points of view are explored.

Where a matter to be discussed involves the interest of a government department, that department will be invited to send a representative to the examination. He will be there primarily to explain his minister's views about the policies and proposals in the plan and to give appropriate information. The Code states that he will not enter into discussion on the merits of government policy. Representatives of the Scottish Development Department may also participate in the examination by describing and explaining alternative policies and proposals which are not being advocated by the other participants.

On the conclusion of the examination the chairman will prepare and submit his report to the Secretary of State. This will not contain a detailed account of the arguments advanced by participants but should provide a balanced assessment of the issues discussed and will normally include recommendations.

If, after the examination, new information becomes available which is of such importance that it leads the minister to a decision he would not otherwise have taken, the Code states that this information will normally be published and an opportunity provided for written comment. In exceptional cases the Secretary of State may re-open the examination.

The examination in public constitutes a statutory inquiry for the purposes of s.1(1)(c) of the Tribunals and Inquiries Act 1971 but not for any other purpose of that Act (1972 Act, s.7(6)[52]). This means that the procedures are subject to the supervision of the Council on Tribunals.

Concern has, not surprisingly, been expressed about the extent of the Secretary of State's powers in relation to the examination in public. He not only decides whether an examination is to take place, he also selects the chairman and any other members of the panel to conduct the examination, he decides upon the issues to be considered and he selects the persons or bodies to take part in the examination. As the Council on Tribunals feared,[53] the examination has the appearance of an entirely administrative process

[52] Substituted by the Local Government (Scotland) Act 1973, s.175(1).
[53] See *Annual Report for 1971–72*, paras. 27–32.

under the control of the Secretary of State.[54] If this all seems rather arbitrary, the reason given is that the procedure is primarily designed to inform the minister on key issues and not to provide a forum for the hearing of objections.[55] 'The purpose of the examination in public', states the Code of Practice, 'is to provide the Secretary of State with the information and advice he needs, in addition to the material submitted with a structure plan and to the objections and representations made on it, to enable him to reach a decision on the plan.' The interests of the objector are intended to be safeguarded by the requirement imposed on the Secretary of State to consider any objections to the plan before reaching a decision (1972 Act, s.7(3)[56]).

It may be noted that when the legislative framework for the 'new style' development plan was first introduced in 1968 in the Town and Country Planning Bill, assurances were given in Parliament that the traditional right to be heard in support of an objection to the plan would be retained. Provision was accordingly made in the 1969 Act for the holding of public inquiries into objections to finalised structure plans. However, the government's experience in the late 1960s and early 1970s with the Greater London Development Plan (G.L.D.P.) made it think again about the procedure for testing the merits of structure plans. Although there were similarities, the G.L.D.P. was not, in fact, a structure plan—it was an 'old style' development plan. Consequently, it contained a considerable amount of detail. This factor, coupled with the emphasis then being given to participation in the development plan process, resulted in some 28,000 objections, all of which were entitled to be supported at a public inquiry. The resulting inquiry sat for two and a half years. As a direct result of this, the government decided to substitute for the public inquiry and the right to be heard in support of objections to a structure plan the examination in public. 'It is essential', says the Code of Practice, 'to reach decisions on structure plans much more quickly than was customary on "old style" development plans.'

It seems that in practice the examination in public has occupied less time than the traditional public inquiry. Nonetheless, experience suggests that the procedure is not free from problems. First of all, in the absence of cross-examination, the effectiveness of the investigation depends on the extent to which the chairman is prepared to probe issues. The exercise has on occasions been described as superficial. 'It has proved a common complaint', says Grant, 'that using discussion rather than questioning as the basic procedure has led to superficiality of treatment of the issues, that participants have been too readily able to avoid being drawn on the

---

[54] In *Edwin H. Bradley & Sons Ltd.* v *Secretary of State for the Environment* (1982) 47 P. & C.R. 374 Glidewell J. said: 'this procedure is not in the nature of a judicial or quasi-judicial hearing between parties . . . '

[55] See *Official Report*, Standing Committee D, Session 1971–72, Vol. III, Col. 55 (25th April 1972).

[56] Substituted by the Local Government (Scotland) Act 1973, s.175(1).

legitimate arguments raised by other participants, and have been able to hide behind technical jargon and unexamined assumptions.'[57] Secondly, the onus on the chairman to ensure that a probing discussion takes place can result in apparent conflict with the requirement that he should be seen to be impartial.[58] Thirdly, the process has largely failed to involve the public. Few individuals have been selected to take part in the discussion and the public benches have often been empty;[59] whether this is the fault of the examination in public or of the abstract nature of the structure plan is difficult to say. Fourthly, the plan is presented as a coherent whole. The singling out of issues for investigation makes it difficult to break down this coherence so as to allow an effective probing of the individual issues.[60] Finally, and largely as a consequence of the fourth point, it has been argued that the investigation might be more effective if it were to take place earlier in the process, i.e., before the planning authority have determined what policies and proposals to include in the plan. This would allow consideration of alternative strategies.[61]

(h) *Final stages*

After considering a structure plan submitted (or re-submitted) to him, the Secretary of State may approve the plan in whole or in part, and with or without modifications or reservations, or may reject it (1972 Act, s.7(1)).[62] The Secretary of State must give reasons for his decision (1972 Act, s.7(8)[63]), and although such reasons may be short[64] they must nonetheless satisfy the test laid down by Megaw J. in *Re Poyser and Mills Arbitration*:[65] 'The reasons that are set out must be reasons which will not only be intelligible, but which deal with the substantial points that have been raised.'

Where the Secretary of State proposes to modify the structure plan in any material respect, he must notify the regional or general planning authority, advertise the proposed modification and serve notice of the proposed modification on such persons as he thinks fit; the Secretary of State must then consider any objections to the proposed modifications[66] (see 1983 Regulations, reg. 18).

---

[57]   *Urban Planning Law*, p. 108. For a Scottish example see J. Rowan-Robinson, *Orkney Uranium and the Planning Process* (Scottish Planning Law and Practice Occasional Paper No. 1, 1979).

[58]   L. Bridges and C. Vielba, *Structure Plan Examinations in Public: A Descriptive Analysis* (Institute of Judicial Administration, University of Birmingham, 1976).

[59]   R. Boyle, 'E.I.P.s: Scottish Practice Reviewed' *The Planner*, May/June 1980, p. 73.

[60]   L. Bridges and C. Vielba, above.

[61]   L. Bridges and C. Vielba, above.

[62]   See A. Coon, 'Structure Plans: Approved in Parts' 1982 S.P.L.P. 26.

[63]   Substituted by the Local Government (Scotland) Act 1973, s.175(1).

[64]   *Edwin H. Bradley & Sons Ltd.* v *Secretary of State for the Environment* (1982) 47 P. & C.R. 374; and *Westminster City Council* v *Great Portland Estates plc* [1984] 3 W.L.R. 1035.

[65]   [1964] 2 Q.B. 247.

[66]   There is no right to object to 'reservations' contained in the notice of approval of a structure plan.

The Secretary of State's decision on the plan will be notified to the planning authority in writing and the minister will give public notice by advertisement and will serve individual notice on such persons as he thinks fit (1983 Regulations, reg. 19). Copies of an operative structure plan together with the reasoned decision letter (which will form part of the plan) and the report of the examination in public must be available for public inspection and copies of the plan must be placed on sale as soon as possible (see 1983 Regulations, regs. 43 and 44; and the Code of Practice).

(i) Operation and validity of structure plan

A structure plan takes effect on the date appointed for the purpose in the Secretary of State's notice of approval (1972 Act, s.16(4)). The validity of a structure plan may be challenged in the Court of Session within the period specified in s.232 of the 1972 Act (see chapter 21) but is not otherwise to be questioned in any legal proceedings whatsoever (see 1972 Act, s.231). No such challenge has yet been made in Scotland.[67]

(j) Alteration of structure plan

If the structure plan is to serve its purpose it must be kept up to date. In S.D.D. Circular 32/1983 the Secretary of State stressed that 'it is essential that the provisions of completed development plans should be monitored and reviewed'.[68] By monitoring the relationship of the plan to actual changes in the environment, development pressures and political priorities, the authority should obtain information to enable them to judge whether an alteration to the plan is required.

A regional or general planning authority may at any time submit to the Secretary of State proposals for alterations to a structure plan and must submit such proposals if directed to do so by the Secretary of State (1972 Act, s.8(1)).[69] Such proposals may include proposals for the repeal and replacement of a structure plan;[70] in particular, proposals may be made for the repeal of a number of structure plans each covering a part of an authority's area and their replacement by a single structure plan for the whole of the area.[71]

The Secretary of State envisages that development planning activity in the coming years will increasingly be concentrated on keeping plans up to date. With this in mind, modifications were introduced in the Local Government

---

[67] But see the English decision *Edwin H. Bradley & Sons Ltd.* v *Secretary of State for the Environment* (1982) 47 P. & C.R. 374.

[68] Although the circular stresses the importance of review there has been some indication that the S.D.D. consider the continuous review (as opposed to periodic review) of structure plans to be unnecessary.

[69] The authority may, whenever they think fit, institute a fresh survey of their area (1972 Act, s.4(2)).

[70] 1972 Act, s.8(1), as amended by the Local Government and Planning (Scotland) Act 1982, s.37(a)(i).

[71] 1972 Act, s.8(1), as amended by the Local Government and Planning (Scotland) Act 1982, s.37(a)(ii).

and Planning (Scotland) Act 1982 to the procedures for altering a structure plan. The publicity requirements in s.6(1) of the 1972 Act which previously applied to proposals for altering a plan have now been replaced by an obligation to 'give such publicity (if any) to, and undertake such consultations (if any) about, the said proposals as they think fit' (1972 Act s.8(3)[72]). The intention is to expedite the procedure for altering a structure plan by omitting the full publicity and consultation requirements for the preparation of the plan. Planning authorities are urged by the Secretary of State to take 'full advantage' of the revised procedures.[73] The planning authority, when submitting alterations to the Secretary of State, must notify him of the steps taken under s.8(3) and if the Secretary of State is not satisfied he may require further action to be taken (1972 Act, s.8(5)[74]).

(k) *Register*

From the time when copies of a structure plan are made available for inspection under s.6(2) of the 1972 Act, particulars of any action taken in connection with the plan must be entered in the register of structure and local plans which regional, general and district planning authorities are required to maintain under reg. 45 of the 1983 Regulations.

2. LOCAL PLANS[75]

The second tier of the new style development plan comprises the local plan or plans. The structure plan for any area will set out the overall strategy; the local plan interprets that strategy in local site-specific policies and proposals and also includes matters of purely local significance. The two levels of the plan are interdependent. When preparing a local plan, the planning authority must ensure that, where a structure plan has been prepared, their proposals conform generally to the structure plan as it stands at the time, whether or not it has been approved by the Secretary of State (1972 Act, s.9(9)[76]).

In S.D.D. Circular 32/1983 the Secretary of State describes the role which local plans should fulfil. They provide the essential basis for sound development control decisions and for providing clear guidance to potential developers, particularly those engaged in industrial development and housebuilding. A local plan, states the circular, should provide a detailed prospectus for development and set out a firm framework within which decisions on planning applications can be made. It should also inform the public about proposals for development, redevelopment or improvement in

---

[72]   Added by the Local Government and Planning (Scotland) Act 1982, s.37(c).
[73]   S.D.D. Circular 32/1983.
[74]   Added by the Local Government and Planning (Scotland) Act 1982, s.37(c).
[75]   See generally P. Healey, *Local Plans in British Land Use Planning* (Pergamon, 1983); also the Planning Exchange, *An Evaluation of Local Plan Production and Performance* (S.D.D., 1984).
[76]   As amended by the Town and Country Planning (Scotland) Act 1977, s.2(1)(b).

the area. A local plan should, therefore, provide clear statements of the planning authority's development control policies for all parts of the plan area and equally should show the parts of the area where policies of no change will apply.

(a) *Responsibility for preparation and adoption of local plans*

The preparation of local plans is normally the responsibility of general and district planning authorities. Section 177(1) of the Local Government (Scotland) Act 1973 provides that a regional planning authority can, however, assume a district planning authority's functions as to the preparation and making of a local plan if in their opinion:

(*a*) a local plan is urgently required to implement the provisions of an approved structure plan and the district planning authority concerned have failed to adopt an appropriate local plan; or
(*b*) the district of more than one district planning authority is likely to be affected by the local plan in question; or
(*c*) the local plan does not conform to an approved structure plan; or
(*d*) the implementation of the local plan will render unlikely the implementation of any other local plan relating to their district.

Where a regional planning authority propose to assume local plan functions in this way the district planning authority concerned may appeal to the Secretary of State (1973 Act, s.177(3)).

Only in exceptional circumstances will a local plan require the approval of the Secretary of State before it comes into operation (see p. 105 below); normally a local plan will be adopted by the planning authority which prepared it.

(b) *Obligation to prepare local plans for whole of authority's district*

As originally enacted, the 1972 Act obliged planning authorities to prepare a local plan for any area indicated in the structure plan as an action area and conferred upon the Secretary of State powers to direct an authority to prepare a local plan,[77] but otherwise left it to planning authorities themselves to decide which parts of their area needed to be the subject of local plans and when the preparation of any such plan should be begun. Amendments made by the Local Government (Scotland) Act 1973 marked a departure from the original concept that local plans should in general only be prepared as and when the planning authority considered such plans to be necessary; the 1973 Act provides that every general and district authority 'shall, as soon as practicable, prepare local plans for all parts of their district' (1973 Act, s.176(1)). S.D.D. Circular 32/1983 states that the Secretary of State attaches great importance to the need for local plans to be prepared as soon as possible for those areas where development pressures are at present being experienced, or are expected. In areas of low priority it would seem that 'as

---

[77] As to the Secretary of State's powers to give such directions see 1972 Act, s.9(7) and (8).

soon as practicable' could mean several years. The Secretary of State does not propose at present to set a target date for local plan coverage for all or any part of Scotland.

(c) *Types of local plan*

Although the legislation on local plans is, as a result of s.176(1) of the 1973 Act (above), rather less flexible than it originally was, planning authorities still enjoy a good deal of freedom in relation to the preparation of such plans; local plans may serve a variety of purposes and authorities are free to include in a local plan any matter which can properly be the subject of planning policies and proposals.

It is intended that the local plans required by s.176(1) of the 1973 Act (above) should be comprehensive plans. These will deal with all aspects of land use and development. One of their main functions will be to provide guidance for development control. S.D.D. *Planning Advice Note 30* (PAN 30) entitled 'Local Planning' states that priority should be given to comprehensive local plans for those areas where pressure for change is greatest. Unless a district-wide comprehensive plan is being prepared, PAN 30 suggests that the territory should be divided into contiguous areas.

The Town and Country Planning (Structure and Local Plans) (Scotland) Regulations 1983 refer to two specialised types of local plan, action area plans and subject plans (see reg. 23). An action area plan must be prepared for any area—e.g. a town centre which is to be redeveloped—indicated in the structure plan as an action area (1972 Act, s.9(6); see p. 86 above). A subject plan will set out in detail the authority's policy for some particular type of development or use of land; a subject plan might, for example, deal with conservation policies, or with tourism and recreation in a particular area, or with an authority's policy for the working of minerals in their district. A subject plan is to be called by the name of the subject with which it deals (1983 Regulations, reg. 23(6)). PAN 30 suggests that local plans for areas subject to significant pressure for change should usually be prepared before resources are allocated to subject plans. Few subject plans have been prepared to date.[78]

Several different local plans, prepared for different purposes, may be in force at the same time in the same part of the authority's area (see 1972 Act, s.9(4)).

(d) *Form and content of local plan*

The content of a local plan will depend to a considerable extent on the purposes of that particular plan. Every local plan must, however, satisfy certain basic requirements.

Section 9(3) of the 1972 Act provides that a local plan is to consist of a map and a written statement and is to formulate in such detail as the authority

---

[78]   See A. G. Coon, 'Where Are the Action Area and Subject Plans?' 1983 S.P.L.P. 58. See also 'Development Plan Bulletin No. 29' (S.D.D., January 1985).

think appropriate their proposals[79] for the development and other use of land in that part of their district and for any description of development or other use of land (including in either case such measures as the authority think fit for the improvement of the physical environment and the management of traffic).

In *Westminster City Council* v *Great Portland Estates plc*[80] the corresponding provision in the Town and Country Planning Act 1971 was interpreted by the House of Lords as imposing a duty on the planning authority to include in their local plan *all* proposals which they may have for the development and use of land. In that case the City of Westminster Local Plan stated that the authority's offices policy would be to guide office development to locations within a 'central activities zone'; outside that zone office development would not normally be appropriate. The plan went on to say that the exceptional circumstances in which office development might be permitted outside the zone would be dealt with in non-statutory guidance to be prepared following adoption of the local plan. The respondents, who were substantial landowners in the City of Westminster, challenged the validity of the offices policy in the plan on the ground, *inter alia*, that by relying upon non-statutory guidelines, the authority had failed to comply with the statutory requirement that the local plan should contain their proposals for the development and use of land.

Lord Scarman, giving judgment for their Lordships, accepted that development plans are not inflexible blueprints and that a planning authority, in exercising their planning functions, could have regard to other material considerations and that such considerations might, for example, include exceptional hardship to individuals or other special circumstances justifying a departure from proposals in the plan. Generally, there was no obligation to refer to such considerations in the plan. However, where, as in this case, such exceptions or special circumstances amounted to policies (in this case they were labelled by the authority in the plan as non-statutory policies), the authority were failing in their statutory duty by excluding them from the plan. The effect of excluding from the plan their proposals in respect of office development outside the central activities zone was to deprive persons such as the respondents from raising objections and securing a public inquiry into such objections. The paragraphs in the local plan dealing with the offices policy were accordingly quashed.

Section 9(3) of the 1972 Act provides that the level of detail in which proposals are to be formulated in the plan is a matter for the planning authority. However, it may not be easy for an authority to distinguish between proposals which, following *Great Portland Estates*, must be included in the plan and matters of detail relating to proposals which may

---

[79] It is not thought that there is any significance in the omission of the word 'policies' from s.9(3). However, present practice is to distinguish policies from proposals (see, for example, 1983 Regulations, reg. 29); this distinction is explained in PAN 30. In *Westminster City Council* v *Great Portland Estates plc* [1984] 3 W.L.R. 1035 Lord Scarman appeared to interpret 'proposals' as meaning 'proposals of policy'.

[80] [1984] 3 W.L.R. 1035.

appropriately be left for consideration at the planning application stage. In *Sand and Gravel Association Ltd.* v *Buckinghamshire County Council*,[81] for example, a planning authority defined 'preferred areas' for future mineral working in a minerals subject plan. In defining these areas the authority, it was alleged, applied subjective tests and did not permit representations from interested parties. The result was that a person interested in land outside the preferred areas could not establish why his land had been excluded, nor could he ascertain whether the tests had been correctly applied. Furthermore, the opportunity to raise these issues at the local plan inquiry was, it was said, refused by the inspector who limited his consideration to the preferred areas. McNeill J. upheld an application to quash the 'preferred areas' policy in the plan; in his view the subjective tests were more appropriate in the circumstances for consideration at the planning application stage. The result of the authority's action in this case was effectively to exclude any opportunity for challenge of the application of the subjective tests. The authority had, therefore, acted unreasonably in the *Wednesbury*[82] sense in the exercise of their powers. Although a local plan does not bind the planning authority when determining a planning application, a developer's chances, observed McNeill J., of obtaining planning permission for a proposal which was not in accordance with the provisions of the development plan were limited in the extreme. McNeill J's decision was, however, overturned by the Court of Appeal.[83] The Court of Appeal held that by concentrating on the misleading terminology of 'subjective' and 'objective' McNeill J. had slipped into the error of substituting his view for that of the inspector and the planning authority. Purchas L.J. said: 'Where planning criteria are concerned, the distinction between subjectivity and objectivity is in almost all cases a false distinction.' 'Overwhelming' evidence was required before the authority's policy could be rejected as unreasonable in the sense of the *Wednesbury* principle; here there was no such overwhelming evidence.

The local plan written statement is to include, in addition to the matters required by the 1972 Act, the matters set out in reg. 25 of the Town and Country Planning (Structure and Local Plans) (Scotland) Regulations 1983. These are:

(*a*) the character, pattern and function of the existing development and other use of land within the district or part of the district to which the plan relates, and the needs and opportunities for change;

(*b*) the implications of current policies and general proposals contained in the relevant structure plan for the district or any part of the district to which the local plan relates;

(*c*) the resources likely to be available for the carrying out of the policies and proposals formulated in the plan; and

[81]   [1984] J.P.L. 798.
[82]   *Associated Provincial Picture Houses Ltd.* v *Wednesbury Corporation* [1948] 1 K.B. 223.
[83]   Unreported, 14th November 1984.

(d) the criteria to be applied as respects the control of development within the district or any part of the district to which the plan relates.

Apart from these specific requirements, the Secretary of State has also drawn attention in Circulars and Advice Notes to a number of other matters which planning authorities should consider when preparing a local plan. For example, PAN 30 states that: 'National Planning Guidelines are Government statements on land use planning issues of national significance. Where they express the national interest in the way a land resource should be used or safeguarded for future use, or in development planning priorities, that interest should be recognised in structure plans and must then be incorporated into detailed local plan policies.' *Planning Advice Note 24*, 'Design Guidance', comments that local plans are proving to be the appropriate place for those design policies which the planning authority regard as sufficiently important to justify refusal of planning permission or the imposition of conditions on a permission. S.D.D. *Planning Advice Note 29*, 'Planning and Small Businesses', says that local plans have a valuable role to play in enabling developers to know in advance what is likely to receive planning permission, which areas the planning authority would prefer them to avoid, and the authority's attitude to expansion on existing sites; local plans can identify sites and premises for small industrial developments and set out related development control policies. And a consultation paper, 'Listing and Listed Building Control', issued by the S.D.D. in December 1984, suggests that all planning authorities should consider the practice of including in local plans their proposals for new or extended conservation areas and for works to be covered by directions under article 4 of the General Development Order.

Local plans may also contain such other matters as the planning authority consider relevant.[84] Such plans may, therefore, concern themselves with a wide range of matters. Nonetheless, as with structure plans,[85] it would seem that policies and proposals in local plans must serve a planning purpose.[86]

The written statement must contain a reasoned justification for the proposals (1983 Regulations, reg. 24). In *Westminster City Council* v *Secretary of State for the Environment*[87] Mr David Widdicombe Q.C., sitting as a Deputy Judge, used the 'reasoned justification of the proposals' to construe the policies in a local plan.

PAN 30 states that it is unrealistic for a local plan to have a fixed plan period; each policy or proposal will have its own timescale by which it is expected to contribute to the achievement of the plan's objectives.

In contrast to the statutory requirements relating to the structure plan, the map comprised in a local plan—termed the 'proposals map'—is to be based

---

[84] Town and Country Planning (Structure and Local Plans) (Scotland) Regulations 1983, reg. 25.

[85] See page 85.

[86] *Westminster City Council* v *Great Portland Estates plc* [1984] 3 W.L.R. 1035. For a discussion of the scope of planning purposes see chapter 9.

[87] [1984] J.P.L. 27.

on the Ordnance Survey Map (1983 Regulations, reg. 26). Its purpose is to identify those policies and proposals which affect any given piece of land. No particular scale is prescribed for the proposals map, although guidance is given on this in PAN 30.

A local plan may contain or be accompanied by such other diagrams, illustrations and descriptive matter as the authority think appropriate for the purpose of explaining or illustrating their proposals (1972 Act, s.9(5)).

The reconciliation of contradictions in and between local plans is dealt with in reg. 27 of the 1983 Regulations.

(e) *Preparation of local plans*

A general or district planning authority proposing to prepare a local plan must, in so far as they have not already done so, institute a survey of the area to which the plan relates; the survey will have to take into account the matters which the authority think relevant to the formulation of their proposals and these matters will have to be kept under review during and after preparation of the local plan (1972 Act, s.9(4A)[88]).

As mentioned above, all general and district planning authorities are obliged by s.176(1) of the Local Government (Scotland) Act 1973 to prepare local plans for all parts of their area as soon as possible. This has meant that during the early years of the operation of the new system, preparation of local plans has often been proceeding at the same time as the structure plan.

The duty to prepare local plans as soon as practicable is, however, qualified in relation to any area for which a structure plan has not yet been approved. In the case of a *general* planning authority, s.176(6) of the 1973 Act simply provides that the authority may prepare a local plan in advance of an approved structure plan unless they have received a direction to the contrary from the Secretary of State. Where a *district* planning authority propose to prepare a local plan for an area before a structure plan for the area has come into operation, the position is more complex. When the legislative framework for structure and local plans was first introduced in 1969, it was not known that the reorganisation of local government in 1973 would result in the two plans being prepared in most instances by different authorities. Accordingly, the Local Government (Scotland) Act 1973 had to make some provision to eliminate potential conflict where a local plan was being prepared in advance of the approval of a structure plan. It is therefore provided by s.176(3) and (4) of the 1973 Act that a district planning authority must not prepare a local plan in advance of an approved structure plan unless they have first sought and obtained the consent of their regional planning authority. Consent may be withheld or withdrawn by the regional planning authority if a structure plan is in course of preparation or if any decision is likely to be taken shortly by any authority and that plan or decision is likely to have a substantial effect on the contents of the local plan. Consent is not, however, to be unreasonably withheld or withdrawn by the

---

[88]   Inserted by the Town and Country Planning (Scotland) Act 1977, s.2(1).

regional planning authority (1973 Act, s.176(3)). Any question as to whether consent has been unreasonably withheld or withdrawn may be referred by the district planning authority to the Secretary of State;[89] the minister's decision on the matter is final (1973 Act, s.176(5)).

The procedure for preparing a local plan is, to a large extent, in the hands of the planning authority. However, public notice must be given of their intention to prepare a plan; furthermore, before determining the content of the plan, the authority must undertake a participation exercise. The provisions governing this are almost identical to those which apply to the preparation of a structure plan. The authority must ensure that adequate publicity is given to any relevant matters arising out of the survey and to the matters they propose to include in the plan. The authority must also ensure that persons who may be expected to want to make representations on the matters proposed to be included in the plan are made aware of their right to do so; a period of at least four weeks must be allowed for the making of representations to the authority and the authority must consider any representations received within the specified period (1972 Act, s.10(1);[90] 1983 Regulations, reg. 3). The comments made above (see p. 82) in connection with participation in the preparation of a structure plan apply equally to the preparation of a local plan.[91] PAN 30 sets out a procedure which it says can be regarded as standard for all plans and replacement plans, and states that 'authorities should consider whether there will be any gain in going beyond it'.

The main difference in the provisions dealing with participation in the preparation of structure and local plans is that the Secretary of State has no power to judge the adequacy of a local plan participation exercise.[92] While the minister must be notified of the steps taken by the authority, he has no power to require further steps to be taken.

An authority preparing a local plan must consult the bodies specified in regulation 4(2) of the 1983 Regulations, must give the consulted bodies an opportunity to express their views, and must take such views into consideration.

In the preparation of a local plan regard must be had to any relevant regional report (below) and to the Secretary of State's observations on that report (1973 Act, s.173(7)). An authority preparing a local plan must secure that the local plan proposals conform generally to any relevant structure

[89] See, by way of illustration of the sort of difficulties that may arise, A. Grant, 'Gordon District Local Plan' 1980 S.P.L.P. 20.

[90] As amended by the Town and Country Planning (Scotland) Act 1977, s.2(2).

[91] See too R. Boyle and J. Brand, 'Participation in Planning: the Spirit and the Practice' 1981 S.P.L.P. 36. But see the Addendum to *Planning Advice Note 29*, 'Planning and Small Businesses', issued by the S.D.D. in January 1985 which encourages planning authorities to involve representatives of the business community in the preparation of local plans. The Addendum reflects the main findings and conclusions of a report *Business Involvement in Local Plans* by Tony Burton (S.D.D., July 1984).

[92] Provision for this existed in s.10(4) of the 1972 Act but was subsequently repealed by s.41 of and Schedule 4 to the Local Government (Miscellaneous Provisions) (Scotland) Act 1981.

plan as that plan stands for the time being (whether or not it has been approved by the Secretary of State) (1972 Act, s.9(9)[93]).

(f) *Action following preparation of local plan*

A general or district planning authority who have prepared a local plan must send a copy of the plan to any local authority whose area is wholly or partly within the district or part of the district to which the plan relates and to any other local authority whose interests appear likely to be affected by the policies and proposals in the plan (1983 Regulations, reg. 29). This means, for example, that a district planning authority should send a certified copy of the plan to the relevant regional planning authority and that a general planning authority should send a certified copy to the relevant district council.

The planning authority must publish notice indicating where the local plan can be seen (see 1972 Act, s.10(2); 1983 Regulations, regs. 30 and 42). The notice must specify the manner in which and the period (6 weeks after the date of first publication of the notice) within which objections to the plan can be made (see 1972 Act, s.10(2); 1983 Regulations, regs. 30, 31 and 42 and Schedule). To be valid, an objection must be in writing, must state the matters to which it relates and must be received by the planning authority within the specified period[94] (see 1983 Regulations, reg. 31 and Schedule).

Not later than the date on which they first give notice of the preparation of a local plan, the planning authority must send two copies of the plan to the Secretary of State; the authority are also to submit (1) a brief account of the steps they have taken to comply with the requirements of s.10(1) of the 1972 Act as to public consultation (above); and (2) a brief account of the consultations they have had with the bodies specified in reg. 4(2) of the 1983 Regulations (see 1972 Act, s.10(2), (3); 1983 Regulations, reg. 30). However, the Secretary of State no longer has the power to require the planning authority to take further action on consultation.[95]

(g) *Consideration of objections*

Unless the Secretary of State has exercised his 'call in' powers (below), the consideration of objections to a local plan is a matter for the planning authority (1972 Act, s.12(1)). For the purpose of considering objections the authority may, and shall if an objector so requires, cause a public local inquiry or other hearing to be held[96] (1972 Act, s.11(1), as amended by the Local Government and Planning (Scotland) Act 1982, s.38(b); see too 1983

---

[93]   The Town and Country Planning (Scotland) Act 1977 made a small amendment to this subsection to take account of the fact that some parts of a region might never be covered by a structure plan (see 1977 Act, s.2(1)(b)).

[94]   A model form for the making of an objection to a local plan is provided in Appendix 1 to S.D.D. Circular 32/1983.

[95]   See s.41 of and Schedule 4 to the Local Government (Miscellaneous Provisions) (Scotland) Act 1981.

[96]   The Tribunals and Inquiries Act 1971 applies to a local inquiry or other hearing into objections to a local plan (see 1972 Act, s.11(1)(b)).

Regulations, regs. 32 and 34). Any such inquiry or hearing is to be held by a person appointed by the planning authority from a list of persons specified by the Secretary of State (reg. 33). Rules governing the procedures at inquiries and hearings held in connection with local plans have not been made; the Secretary of State has instead issued a Code of Practice.[97]

The Code provides that, subject to the fundamental principles of openness, fairness and impartiality, the main emphasis of the procedure at a local plan inquiry should be on informality. The objective is not any kind of judicial arbitration between opposing parties but a joint attempt, in discussion, to arrive at decisions on future land use which will reflect the overall public interest.[98] The order of proceedings will be for the person conducting the inquiry, the reporter, to determine. Generally he will try to group together objections which have substantial common ground. He will ask each objector to make an opening statement and to call any witnesses; these witnesses may be questioned by the planning authority. The planning authority will then make a statement in reply and may call witnesses; these in turn may be questioned by the objectors. The objectors will be given an opportunity to make a final statement before the inquiry proceeds to consideration of the next objection or group of objections.

Where an objector wishes to suggest one or more alternative sites or areas for the application of particular policies and proposals, these should be notified to the reporter and the planning authority in advance of the inquiry.[99] There will, however, be limits upon the degree to which alternatives can be explored at the inquiry. The inquiry, says the Code, must adhere to discussion of the published plan and objections to it. If the planning authority decide, after the inquiry, to pursue any alternatives put forward, these will need to be advertised as proposed modifications to the plan and an opportunity allowed for objection.

Government departments may be represented at the inquiry but any departmental witness may be questioned on matters of fact or expert opinion only and not on the merits of government policy. The reporter will always make an inspection of the area covered by the local plan.

After the inquiry, the reporter will prepare a report for submission to the planning authority. This will summarise the arguments advanced, either in writing or by the parties at the inquiry, in respect of each objection or group of objections and it will set out his findings of fact and recommendations.

If, after the inquiry, the authority receive any new evidence or take into consideration any new issue of fact which was not raised at the inquiry, and as a result are disposed to disagree with a recommendation of the reporter,

[97] The Code of Practice for Local Plan Inquiries and Hearings was published on 17th October 1977.
[98] Problems encountered in such inquiries in England are considered in M. J. Bruton, G. Crispin and P. M. Fidler, 'Local Plans: Public Local Inquiries' [1980] J.P.L. 374.
[99] The nature of the duty of an inspector (reporter) to entertain evidence on alternative sites was considered by the Court of Appeal in *Sand and Gravel Association Ltd.* v *Buckinghamshire County Council* (unreported, 14th November 1984, overturning the decision of McNeill J. reported at [1984] J.P.L. 798).

they must not adopt the plan without first notifying the parties and allowing a further opportunity for representations.

Where a public local inquiry or other hearing has been held, the planning authority who prepared the plan must, as part of their consideration of objections, consider the report of the person who held the inquiry or hearing and must decide, in the light of that report and each recommendation contained therein, whether or not to take any action as respects the plan; the authority must prepare a statement of their decision, giving reasons therefor[1] (1983 Regulations, reg. 35(1)). That statement is to be published along with the report of the person who held the inquiry or hearing (reg. 35(2)).

Where no local inquiry or other hearing is held for the purpose of considering objections to the local plan, the planning authority must prepare a statement of their decision on each objection together with reasons.

If the authority propose to modify the plan they must give notice of their intention and afford a further opportunity for objection. The planning authority must consider any further objections, and if objection is made to a matter which has not already been considered at a local inquiry then, if the objector so requires, the authority must afford him an opportunity of being heard at a public inquiry or hearing. As regards other objections, the authority have a discretion whether to hold a further inquiry (1983 Regulations, reg. 37). Modifications concerned only with drafting or technical matters of a minor nature and which do not materially affect any policy or proposal in the plan are not required to follow this procedure (1983 Regulations, reg. 37(3)).

Research has shown that there is some dissatisfaction with a process which allows the planning authority to sit in judgment on their own plan.[2] And in *R. v Hammersmith and Fulham London Borough Council, ex parte People Before Profit Ltd.*[3] Comyn J. was critical of the statutory procedures. He said that as the law stood objectors to a local plan may have 'very little real say at all' and that the planning authority were 'in effect judge and jury in their own cause'. He was 'slightly perturbed' to think that the finding of a public inquiry could, as in this case, be so favourable to objectors and yet the authority could dismiss the objections 'virtually out of hand', but it was clear that the authority had the law on their side 'to an extent that may make individuals incredulous'. However, a survey of the outcome of a number of local plan inquiries in Scotland suggests that, notwithstanding that planning authorities are 'judges in their own cause', objectors have been reasonably successful in securing modifications to policies and proposals in local plans.[4]

---

[1]   These reasons may be briefly stated (*Westminster City Council* v *Great Portland Estates plc* [1984] 3 W.L.R. 1035), but must be proper, adequate and intelligible (*Re Poyser and Mills' Arbitration* [1964] 2 Q.B. 247; and *Great Portland Estates*).

[2]   See M. J. Bruton, G. Crispin, P. M. Fidler and E. A. Hill, 'Local Plans P.L.I.s in Practice' *The Planner*, January/February 1982, p. 16.

[3]   (1981) 45 P. & C.R. 364.

[4]   T. Burton, 'Local Plan Inquiries' 1982 S.P.L.P. 8.

(h) *Adoption of local plan*

In some areas it may still be some years before a structure plan is approved. As originally enacted, s.12(2) of the 1972 Act provided, however, that a local plan was not to be adopted unless it conformed generally to the structure plan as approved by the Secretary of State; it would, therefore, have been impossible to adopt a local plan for any area not covered by an approved structure plan. The Town and Country Planning (Scotland) Act 1977 removed this obstacle to the early adoption of local plans; it is now provided that conformity with a structure plan is to be a pre-requisite of adoption of a local plan only where an approved structure plan is in existence (see 1977 Act, s.2(3)).

Before adopting a local plan the planning authority must advertise their intention to adopt the plan and must serve notice on objectors (see 1983 Regulations, reg. 38(1)). They must also send to the Secretary of State a certificate that the required notices have been published and served, together with a certified copy of the local plan in the form in which they propose to adopt it. A district planning authority must send a similar copy of the plan to the regional planning authority (reg. 32(2)). The planning authority may not adopt the plan until at least 28 days have elapsed from the sending of the certificate to the Secretary of State; the minister has power to direct the authority not to adopt the plan until he notifies them that he has decided not to call it in under s.12(3) of the 1972 Act (below) (see reg. 38(3)).

If the Secretary of State does not intervene, the planning authority may, after the expiry of the 28 day period, adopt the plan, either as originally prepared or as modified to take account of objections or of any matters arising out of objections (1972 Act, s.12(1)). When the authority resolve to adopt or abandon a local plan they must give notice as required by reg. 39 of the 1983 Regulations. Copies of any plan adopted by an authority must be sent to the Secretary of State and, where appropriate, to the regional planning authority (reg. 39).

(i) *Intervention by Secretary of State*

A local plan will normally be adopted by the planning authority who prepared it. The Secretary of State may, however, direct that a local plan is not to have effect unless it is approved by him (1972 Act, s.12(3)); the minister can intervene in this way at any time before the plan has been formally adopted by the planning authority. S.D.D. Circular 32/1983 states that the Secretary of State will 'seek to be involved in the preparation of local plans only where issues of national importance are involved or where there is clear evidence that statutory requirements have not been fulfilled'. The procedure to be followed in a case where a local plan has been called in by the Secretary of State is to be found in s.12(4)[5] of the 1972 Act and reg. 40 of the 1983 Regulations.

---

[5] Substituted by the Local Government (Scotland) Act 1973, s.175(2).

(j) *Operation and validity of local plan*

A local plan will come into operation on the date appointed for the purpose in the relevant resolution of adoption or notice of approval (1972 Act, s.16(4)). The validity of a local plan may be challenged by way of application to the Court of Session within the period specified in s.232 of the 1972 Act (see chapter 21) but is not otherwise to be questioned in any legal proceedings whatsoever[6] (1972 Act, s.231).

No such challenge has yet been made in Scotland but in England local plans have been successfully impugned on at least two occasions. In *Westminster City Council* v *Great Portland Estates plc*[7] part of a local plan was quashed by the House of Lords on the ground that the planning authority had failed to comply with the statutory duty to include all proposals for the development and use of land in their local plan. In *Fourth Investments Ltd.* v *Bury Metropolitan Borough Council*[8] McCullough J. granted an application to quash part of a local plan allocating land to the local green belt on the ground that the inspector who conducted an inquiry into objections to the plan had failed to make any assessment of the likely requirement for housing land in the area as a whole over the whole of the plan period and that as a result he could not reasonably have reached a conclusion as to whether the applicants' land should be included in the green belt. In *Sand and Gravel Association Ltd.* v *Buckinghamshire County Council* (see p. 98 above) parts of a local plan were quashed by McNeill J. on the ground that the planning authority had acted unreasonably in drawing up the plan; as mentioned above, that decision was, however, overturned by the Court of Appeal.

(k) *Action following adoption or approval of local plan*

Any operative local plan must be made available for public inspection and copies of the plan must be put on sale as soon as possible (see 1983 Regulations, regs. 42–44).

(l) *Alteration or repeal of local plan*

Each local plan must be kept under review by the planning authority (1972 Act, s.13(1)[9]). The planning authority may at any time make proposals for the alteration, repeal or replacement of a local plan; in the case of a local plan which was approved by the Secretary of State, the consent of the minister must be obtained before proposals to alter, repeal or replace the plan can be made (1972 Act, s.13(1)). The procedures for the alteration,

---

[6]   Once the time limit is up, it may not only be too late to challenge the validity of the plan as such but also too late to challenge the validity of the policies therein in their application to the determination of a planning application—see *Westminster City Council* v *Secretary of State for the Environment* [1984] J.P.L. 27.

[7]   [1984] 3 W.L.R. 1035.

[8]   [1985] J.P.L. 185.

[9]   Substituted by Local Government and Planning (Scotland) Act 1982, s.40(a). On the question of monitoring see A. Prior, 'Local Plans Monitoring' 1984 S.P.L.P. 87.

repeal or replacement of a local plan are similar to those which obtain in relation to the making and adoption of the original plan (see 1972 Act, s.13(3); 1983 Regulations, reg. 41).

S.D.D. Circular 32/1983 stresses the importance which the Secretary of State attaches to the monitoring and review of local plans. With this in mind, an optional expedited procedure for the alteration of local plans was introduced in the Local Government and Planning (Scotland) Act 1982.[10] The procedure is similar to that introduced for the alteration of structure plans (see p. 93 above). If a planning authority do not consider it appropriate, they may omit the publicity and consultation steps normally required in connection with the preparation of a local plan (see 1972 Act, s.10(1)). In that event, the authority must include with copies of the proposed alterations, when they are made available for public inspection, a statement of their reasons for not taking such steps. A copy of the statement must also be sent to the Secretary of State (1972 Act, s.13(4)[11]). Planning authorities are urged by the Secretary of State to take 'full advantage of the revised procedures'.[12]

(m) Register

From the time when copies of a local plan are made available for inspection under s.10(2) of the 1972 Act, particulars of any action taken in connection with the plan must be entered in the register of structure and local plans which regional, general and district planning authorities are required to maintain under reg. 45 of the 1983 Regulations.

3. CONCLUSION

When the framework for the 'new style' development plan was introduced in 1969, the intention was to introduce something more than a new procedure. Development planning was to change in a number of important respects. First of all, it was to become a continuous process. Planning authorities were to move away from the preparation of plans as blueprints for the future. The new plans were to be speedily produced and then monitored and up-dated as required. In this way it was hoped that they would be able to reflect changes in circumstances. Secondly, by involving the public in the plan-making and review process, the hope was that the 'new style' plan would be more responsive to their interests. Thirdly, the preoccupation with land use was to give way to a wider view of the concerns of planning which embraced socio-economic issues. To what extent have these intentions been fulfilled?[13]

Because of the delay in bringing the new development plans into operation it is too early to say whether the new process will be successful in moving away from 'blueprint' planning. However, it appears that the

[10] See s.40(c).
[11] Added by the Local Government and Planning (Scotland) Act 1982, s.40(c).
[12] S.D.D. Circular 32/1983.
[13] Some of these issues are considered in *Structure Plans and Local Plans—Planning in Crisis* (J.P.E.L. Occasional Paper, Sweet and Maxwell, 1983).

Secretary of State has had reservations about the ability of the original procedures to cope with the need for speedily prepared plans which can be kept up to date.[14] As a result, a number of changes have been made in recent years to these procedures, by way of both legislation and official guidance. Participation exercises are being curtailed, particularly as regards alterations to plans, and the right to be heard in support of an objection to a structure plan has disappeared altogether. Unhappily, these changes have been made at the expense of opportunities for public involvement in the process. It is difficult to believe that the 'new style' development planning process has resulted in 'more real public participation in planning'[15] as was originally hoped. However, it is questionable whether these changes have had or will have much effect on the level of public involvement in structure planning. Involvement has been limited.[16] The somewhat abstract form in which issues are discussed does little to stimulate public interest and it may be that consultation through representative groups is the best that can be hoped for. Public participation may, as was suggested in the *Review of the Management of Planning*,[17] have most to contribute to local plans.

The delay in bringing the new plans into operation was caused, initially, by the Secretary of State's postponement of the date for bringing the new legislative framework into operation. It was decided that this should await the reorganisation of local government in May 1975.[18] The postponement proved to be beneficial in some respects. It enabled the Scottish Development Department to observe the difficulties encountered by English planning authorities in the preparation of the first generation of structure plans.[19] It became apparent that there were ambiguities about the intended scope of the new style structure plan.[20] Was it to provide a comprehensive strategy for dealing with social, economic and environmental issues; or was it to be a land use policy statement which merely took account of social and economic policies in so far as they related to land use? In practice, it seems there were serious problems in attempting to use a document prepared under the town and country planning legislation to deal with issues outside

[14] For a statement of development plan progress see the 'Development Plan Bulletins' issued from time to time by the S.D.D.

[15] See the hopes expressed by Mr Anthony Greenwood, H.C. Deb., Vol. 757, Col. 1362 (31st January 1968).

[16] See A. W. Burton and R. Johnson, *Public Participation in Planning: A Review of Experience in Scotland* (Planning Exchange Occasional Paper, 1976). See too N. Boaden, M. Goldsmith, W. Hampton and P. Stringer, 'Planning and Participation in Practice: A Study of Public Participation in Structure Planning' in *Progress in Planning*, D. Diamond and J. B. McLoughlin, eds., 1981.

[17] S.D.D., April 1977.

[18] See S.D.D. Circular 52/1971.

[19] For a discussion of these difficulties see J. B. McLoughlin and J. Thornley, *Some Problems in Structure Planning: a Literature Review* (C.E.S., 1972); and M. Drake, J. B. McLoughlin, R. Thompson and J. Thornley, *Aspects of Structure Planning in Britain* (C.E.S., 1976).

[20] See J. Jowell and D. Noble, 'Planning as Social Engineering: Notes on the First English Structure Plans' (1980) 3 *Urban Law and Policy* 293; and J. Jowell and D. Noble, 'Structure Plans as Instruments of Social and Economic Policy' [1981] J.P.L. 466.

the scope of that legislation and in some cases beyond the jurisdiction of the plan-making authority. In consequence, the Scottish Development Department was able to forestall similar uncertainty in Scotland by declaring that structure plans should concern themselves with key land use issues (to be determined by the authority) and that economic, social and other policies should only be included in so far as they contributed to the land use aspects of the plan.[21] The structure plan, as Robinson aptly observes, 'is not a vehicle for co-ordinating wider policy, but merely for reflecting the implications of it'.[22] The preoccupation with land use therefore remains. However, the Secretary of State's ability to limit the scope of the first structure plans owes much to the preparation of the rather more wide- ranging regional reports that preceded them (see below).

D. REGIONAL REPORTS

A regional or general planning authority may at any time prepare and submit to the Secretary of State a 'regional report' consisting of planning policy proposals (Local Government (Scotland) Act 1973, s.173). The regional report is peculiar to Scotland. It has been described as 'an outstanding "eureka!" happening in recent planning history'[23] although its genesis may lie in the much-discussed need for a corporate approach to policy planning in local government.

The precise object or purpose of the report is not stated in the 1973 Act. However, during the committee stage of the Local Government (Scotland) Bill, Mr George Younger, then Under-Secretary of State at the Scottish Office, said that regional reports might provide 'a basis of discussion between the Secretary of State and regional or island area authorities on general development policy'; alternatively, such a report might 'provide a basis of guidance for the preparation or review of structure plans'; and, 'in the absence of structure plans, or during a period when structure plans have fallen out of date, but have not been reviewed', a regional report might serve as 'a guide to district planning authorities and, indeed, to developers on up-to-date policy trends'. It would seem, therefore, that the report is intended to be a flexible tool for the planning authority.

This flexibility is enhanced by the limited formal procedural requirements governing the preparation of regional reports. Before submitting a regional report to the Secretary of State, a regional planning authority must consult

[21] See, for example, S.D.D. Circular 30/1977.
[22] P. Robinson, 'Regional Reports: A Step in the Right Direction?' *The Planner*, May 1977, p. 73.
[23] S. T. McDonald, 'The Regional Report in Scotland: A Study of Change in the Planning Process' (1977) 48 *Town Planning Review* 215. For further discussion of regional reports see P. Robinson, 'Regional Reports: A Step in the Right Direction?' *The Planner*, May 1977, p. 73; B. Howat, *Policy Planning in the First Regional Reports in Scotland* (Planning Exchange Occasional Paper No. 2, 1976); and M. Wilkinson and B. Howat, *Regional Reports and Structure Plans in Scotland* (Planning Exchange Occasional Paper No. 3, 1977).

every district planning authority within their region and every other planning authority likely to be affected by the report. A regional report is not subject to the approval of the Secretary of State but the minister is required to make observations on each report submitted to him. There is no provision for public involvement in the preparation of a regional report but the regional or general planning authority must publish the report together with the Secretary of State's observations thereon. A regional report does not form part of the statutory development plan, but in the exercise of their planning functions all planning authorities must have regard to any regional report and to any ministerial observations thereon which affect or are likely to affect them (1973 Act, s.173(7)).

Whatever the origins of the regional report, by the time it appeared in legislative form it had become subject to the same sort of ambiguities that underlay the first generation of English structure plans.[24] Section 173(3) of the 1973 Act provides that the report is to be based on the structure plan survey and 'shall consist of planning policy proposals for the district of the authority as a whole or any part of it, as respects the matters mentioned in section 5(3) of [the 1972 Act], having regard to the requirements of section 5(4) of [the 1972 Act]'. The intention of the subsection is not clear. Section 5(3) of the 1972 Act sets out the matters which are to be contained in the structure plan written statement; s.5(4) lists other matters to which the planning authority must have regard in preparing the structure plan. The subsection therefore links the regional report to the sort of issues with which a structure plan might deal. What is not clear is the extent to which the regional report may concern itself with broader issues. The point could be important, as regard must be had to the regional report in the determination of planning applications.

Some indication of the Secretary of State's view is to be found in S.D.D. Circular 4/1975. The minister has power·to direct planning authorities to submit regional reports (1973 Act, s.173(2)). Having decided to postpone the commencement of the new development planning system until after the reorganisation of local government, the Secretary of State gave advance notice in Circular 4/1975 that he proposed to make such a direction requiring all regional and general planning authorities to submit regional reports to him by 15th May 1976. The report, said the circular, should essentially be a short statement of the main policies and priorities carrying implications for land use which had been adopted by the Regional Council. The reports would not be effective unless their physical planning content was based firmly on Regional Councils' views on policies outside the purely physical planning field. Regional Councils would accordingly wish to consider how best to ensure that the regional report fully reflected the corporate approach which their policy and resources committees would be developing towards those economic and social (as well as environmental) problems which have implications for land use. The report would, therefore, concern itself with

---

[24] For a discussion of this see J. B. McLoughlin, *The Evolution of Strategic Planning in Scotland and the Origins of the Regional Report* (S.S.R.C. Working Paper, 1978).

the broader economic, social and environmental issues but only in so far as
they had 'implications for land use'.

The Town and Country Planning (Regional Reports) (Scotland) Direction 1975 directed that each such report should:

(a) cover the whole district of the authority;

(b) identify areas where the authority considered that significant planning
action was needed in the near future; and

(c) indicate what form of planning action was considered necessary in each
of those areas and to what extent this was likely to require a variation of
existing investment patterns.

The result of the direction, as McDonald observes, was that 'within some
15 months of reorganisation Scotland had achieved almost complete
coverage by policy documents offering indications of priorities over broad
policy areas backed up by statements of priorities for physical planning
action.'[25] The reports set out the broad policy framework within which
structure and local plans would be prepared and enabled the Secretary of
State to advise authorities that structure plans should concern themselves
with land use issues and should be problem-orientated.

The value of the first round of regional reports was generally acknowledged. However, in S.D.D. Circular 28/1976 the Secretary of State said that
he did not at that stage intend to require submission of regional reports every
year and it has since been left to individual regional and general planning
authorities to decide whether to produce further reports. Consideration has,
in the meantime, been given to the question of what kind of guidance the
Scottish Office might provide on the form and content of a second round of
reports. S.D.D. Circular 4/1975 emphasised that the form of the first round
should not necessarily be taken as a pattern for future reports. A research
report published by the Scottish Office in 1978 concluded that:

'the statutory provision for the Secretary of State to call for periodic
presentation of Regional Reports offers valuable opportunities for
Regional (and Islands) Councils to draw out a limited range of key issues
which they regard as of strategic concern to them, and systematically to
pursue their implications both for the policy-making processes of the
Regional Councils themselves and for their relationships with central
government, District Councils and other public agencies.'[26]

In his report on the advisory and monitoring functions of the Scottish
Development Department with respect to local planning authorities[27] Mr J.
S. B. Martin recommended that the Secretary of State should consider

[25] S. T. McDonald, 'The Regional Report in Scotland: A Study of Change in the Planning
Process' (1977) 48 *Town Planning Review*, 215.
[26] S.D.D., *Future Regional Reports: A Study of Form and Content*, a report prepared by the
Institute for Operational Research, 1978.
[27] S.D.D.. 1980.

calling for regional reports on a regular basis, arguing that if this were done 'less effort would be required on structure plans and monitoring reports' and 'physical planning and other policies could be better integrated'. However, a letter from the Scottish Development Department to Chief Executives of regional and islands councils in May 1982 stated that very considerable changes had occurred since the submission of the first round of regional reports; problems associated with local government re-organisation had been largely overcome, a range of policy-planning instruments—financial plans, housing plans, and transport policies and programmes—had been developed, and substantial progress had been made on the replacement of 'old style' development plans by structure and local plans. Given the ready availability in these policy-planning documents of information about a wide range of local authority policies and proposals, the Secretary of State saw no need, for his interest, said the letter, to call for a further round of regional reports in the forseeable future.[28] The minister was also reluctant, said the letter, to impose time-consuming tasks upon authorities at a time when manpower constraints had become very much more severe than previously. However, the letter concluded by recognising that some authorities might wish to prepare regional reports for their own purposes (for example, in the context of corporate planning).

E. NON-STATUTORY POLICY STATEMENTS

In their report[29] in 1965 the Planning Advisory Group observed that the result of out of date development plans was an increasing reliance by planning authorities on non-statutory policy statements to deal with emerging planning problems. These statements were not subject to the normal machinery for development plan amendments of publicity, objection and inquiry and could, therefore, be speedily prepared and implemented.

The validity of decisions made in reliance upon this sort of non-statutory policy statement has been accepted by the courts in the past.[30] In *Clyde and Co.* v *Secretary of State for the Environment*[31] Sir David Cairns observed in the Court of Appeal that he could see 'no reason why either the local planning authority or the Secretary of State should have to look for considerations of policy only to the development plan'. *Myton* v *Minister of Housing and Local Government*[32] arose as a result of a recommendation by the Minister of Housing and Local Government in M.H.L.G. Circular 42/55

---

[28]   In *Investment in the Environment* (Aberdeen University Press, 1983) Eric Gillett suggests that there are difficulties in inviting a second round of regional reports because the implication of the legislation is that they were to be preliminary to structure plans.

[29]   *The Future of Development Plans*.

[30]   But see now the decision of the House of Lords in *Westminster City Council* v *Great Portland Estates plc* [1984] 3 W.L.R. 1035 (below).

[31]   [1977] 1 W.L.R. 926.

[32]   (1965) 16 P. & C.R. 240.

that planning authorities should consider the establishment of green belts. The circular suggested the preparation and submission to the minister of a sketch plan setting out the proposed boundaries of the green belt, the intention being that the sketch plan would in due course be converted into a formal amendment to the development plan. The circular recommended that, after submission of the sketch plan, there should be a general presumption against development in the area. Following the preparation and submission of such a sketch plan, a planning authority refused planning permission for residential development of land within a proposed green belt on the basis of the general presumption. A subsequent appeal to the minister was dismissed. The applicant appealed to the High Court and argued, *inter alia*, that the ground for the dismissal of the appeal was, in effect, a decision by the minister to include the land in the green belt without the safeguards of objection and inquiry; as a result he would be seriously prejudiced by the blighting of his land. Widgery J. concluded, however, that the applicant's appeal had been dismissed because the land was, for the time being, included in a sketch plan indicating a proposed green belt, and that, in the circumstances, and pending the full inquiry which would follow before the sketch plan became an amendment to the development plan, it was undesirable that the land should be developed. The applicant would suffer no substantial prejudice as a full opportunity for objection and inquiry would be given before any green belt was formally designated and his land permanently blighted.

With the advent of the 'new style' development plans and given, in particular, the wide range of matters with which local plans can deal, the Scottish Development Department is discouraging authorities from preparing non-statutory policy statements. For example, PAN 30 specifically states that 'any non-statutory policy statements should now be embodied in statutory local plans'. Presumably it is felt that decisions will have greater credibility if they are based on policies which have been subjected to the discipline of publicity, objection and inquiry. Exceptionally, the preparation by authorities of supplementary development guidance is considered a constructive measure calculated to safeguard and enhance design standards and encourage a wider awareness of planning objectives.[33] S.D.D. *Planning Advice Note 24* defines supplementary development guidance under three headings:

(*i*)   site planning briefs: setting out the authority's development aims for a particular location;
(*ii*) developer's briefs: specifying the terms and conditions of the disposal of land as a basis for competitive bids; and
(*iii*) design guides: containing a general set of advisory principles and standards sought by the authority.

Some support for the distinction made by the Scottish Development Department between non-statutory policy statements and supplementary

[33]   S.D.D. *Planning Advice Note 24*, 'Design Guidance' (1980).

development guidance would seem to be derived from the recent decision of the House of Lords in *Westminster City Council* v *Great Portland Estates plc.*[34] In that case the City of Westminster District Plan sought to discourage office development outside a 'central activities zone'. The plan stated that the exceptional circumstances in which office development might be permitted outside the zone were best dealt with by non-statutory guidance to be prepared following adoption of the plan. This part of the plan was successfully challenged on the ground that the planning authority had failed to comply with the statutory requirement that a local plan 'shall formulate in such detail as the authority think appropriate the authority's proposals for the development and use of land in that part of their area'. If a planning authority have policy proposals for the development and use of land, they are failing in their statutory duty, declared Lord Scarman, if they choose to exclude them from the plan.

The decision in *Great Portland Estates* imposes some limit on the use that can be made of non-statutory policy statements. However, it is not a limit that can easily be defined. While the planning authority have a discretion as to the level of detail to be contained in a plan, it may not be easy to say in any particular case whether circumstances are such that proposals are matters of policy to be contained in the plan or matters of detail which may properly be left to be dealt with in extra-statutory guidelines. Neither is it clear what effect reliance upon a non-statutory policy statement (as opposed to supplementary development guidance) will have upon the *vires* of a planning decision.

However, until 'new style' development plans are brought into full operation, planning authorities are likely to attach considerable weight to the policies in their draft structure and local plans (examples of non-statutory policy statements). In *R.* v *City of London Corporation, ex p. Allan*[35] Woolf J. held that policies in a draft local plan were material considerations which a planning authority should take into account in an appropriate case when determining a planning application.[36]

Even when the 'new style' plans come into full operation, it seems doubtful whether planning authorities will readily relinquish the use of non-statutory policy statements. There is evidence to suggest that, despite discouragement from the Secretaries of State, planning authorities in England and Wales and in Scotland are continuing to make widespread use of a variety of such statements.[37] It would seem that the great majority of

---

[34] [1984] 3 W.L.R. 1035. Contrast *Covent Garden Community Association Ltd.* v *Greater London Council* [1981] J.P.L. 183 (failure to propose alteration of local plan not unreasonable).

[35] (1980) 79 L.G.R. 223.

[36] See too p. 210 below.

[37] See, for example, M. J. Bruton and D. J. Nicholson, 'Non-Statutory Local Plans and Supplementary Planning Guidance' [1983] J.P.L. 432; M. J. Bruton and D. J. Nicholson, 'The Use of Non-Statutory Local Planning Instruments in Development Control and Section 36 Appeals' [1984] J.P.L. 552 and 663; Planning Exchange, *An Evaluation of Local Plan Production and Performance* (S.D.D., 1984), para. 137; and District Planning Officers Society, *The Local Plan System: The Need for Radical Change* (1982).

such statements do not threaten the integrity of development plan policies; they operate as a supplement to these policies. Their advantage lies in their flexibility of form, content and procedure. Their disadvantage lies in the uncertainty about the weight that will be given to them on appeal.[38] It is fair to say, nonetheless, that in practice such policy statements exert a considerable influence on day to day development control decisions.

---

[38] While the Secretary of State may take account of informal policies, he may equally take account of informal steps by a planning authority not to follow such policies—see *Philglow Ltd. v Secretary of State for the Environment* [1984] J.P.L. 111.

CHAPTER 6

DEVELOPMENT

Introduction

The system of regulatory planning in Scotland revolves around the definition of 'development' in s.19 of the Town and Country Planning (Scotland) Act 1972. If particular proposals do not constitute 'development', as defined in the 1972 Act, planning permission will not be required for the carrying out of those proposals. If, on the other hand, the proposals fall within the statutory definition, planning permission will almost invariably be necessary.[1] It is not always easy to say whether proposed action comes within the statutory definition of development. As was said by Lord Wilberforce in *Coleshill and District Investment Co. Ltd.* v *Minister of Housing and Local Government*,[2] '"Development" is a key word in the planners' vocabulary but it is one whose meaning has evolved and is still evolving. It is impossible to ascribe to it any certain dictionary meaning, and difficult to analyse it accurately from the statutory definition.'

Subject to the provision which s.19 of the 1972 Act makes in relation to specified operations and changes of use (see p. 152 below), 'development' means 'the carrying out of building, engineering, mining or other operations in, on, over or under land,[3] or the making of any material change in the use of any buildings or other land' (s.19(1)). Although particular activities on land may well involve both 'operations' and a 'material change in the use' of the land, the general scheme of the legislation is, as the Court of Appeal held in *Parkes* v *Secretary of State for the Environment*,[4] to distinguish between the two concepts. In that case Lord Denning M.R. stated that 'operations' comprise activities which result in some physical alteration of land, an alteration which has some degree of permanence in relation to the land itself, whereas 'use' refers to activities which are done in, alongside or on the land, but which do not interfere with the actual physical characteristics of the land. The Court of Appeal held in *Parkes* that the sorting, storing and

---

[1] For exceptions, see chapter 7 below.

[2] [1969] 1 W.L.R. 746.

[3] 'Land' is defined in s.275 of the 1972 Act as including any building (as defined by s.275); it also includes land covered with water. In *Argyll and Bute District Council* v *Secretary of State for Scotland* 1976 S.C. 248; 1977 S.L.T. 33 the Second Division of the Court of Session held that the term 'land' as used in the 1972 Act does not comprehend the seabed below low water mark.

[4] [1978] 1 W.L.R. 1308; see too *Cheshire County Council* v *Woodward* [1962] 2 Q.B. 126, per Lord Parker C.J.

processing of scrap metal was a use of land and not an operation.

Section 275 of the 1972 Act specifically provides that 'use' does not include the use of land for the carrying out of any building or other operations thereon; the fact that one has permission to use land for a certain purpose does not mean that one is entitled to carry out building or other operations for that purpose.[5] It is perhaps curious that although s.275 states that 'use' is not to include building or other operations, there is no mention of engineering or mining operations. In *Parkes* (above) the Court of Appeal left open the question whether these sorts of operations could in some circumstances also constitute a 'use' of land.[6] The distinction between 'operations' and 'use' is important for a number of purposes, especially in connection with the enforcement of planning control (see chapter 13).

The open texture of the statutory definition has meant that a good deal of case law has grown up around the word 'development'. In particular, since the statute provides no specific guidance as to when a change of use is to be regarded as 'material', the courts have been compelled, in order to achieve some degree of certainty and consistency in the application of the legislation, to supplement the statute in a number of important ways. Concepts such as the planning unit, abandonment of use and extinguishment of use provide a legal framework within which the question whether particular proposals amount to development can be considered.

By and large, however, the courts have confined themselves to laying down broad guidelines; it has in the main been left to planning authorities themselves to determine, as a matter of fact rather than as a matter of law, whether particular proposals amount to development. It should, therefore, be emphasised that many decisions on 'development' turn to a very considerable extent on their own particular facts and do not necessarily lend themselves to generalisations. In *Coleshill* (above) Lord Morris of Borth-y-Gest suggested that the 'true path of enquiry' in any particular case (and one which commended itself to the Lands Tribunal for Scotland in *Alexandra Transport Co. Ltd.* v *Secretary of State for Scotland*[7]) first involves ascertaining exactly what it is that it is desired to do, or exactly what it is that has been done, and then ascertaining whether or not that comes within the statutory definition of development. In *Coleshill* the House of Lords refused to consider in the abstract the question whether the demolition of a building involves development and in *Alexandra Transport* the Lands Tribunal refused to decide in the abstract whether the infilling of an excavation constitutes development; whether or not works which might be described as 'demolition' or 'infilling' constitute development depends on the facts of the particular case and it is only when the projected or completed operation or

5   See *Sunbury-on-Thames U.D.C.* v *Mann* (1958) 9 P. & C.R. 309. See too *Western Fish Products Ltd.* v *Penwith District Council* [1981] 2 All E.R. 204.
6   See too *Murfitt* v *Secretary of State for the Environment* (1980) 40 P. & C.R. 254 (in which it seems to have been accepted that the placing of hardcore on a site was such an integral part of the use of the site for vehicle parking that it should not be treated separately). See also the decisions on tipping of material on land mentioned at p. 162 below.
7   (1972) 25 P. & C.R. 97.

F

change of use is fully and clearly described that the statutory definition can be applied.

A. OPERATIONS

In terms of the 'operations' limb of the statutory definition, the carrying out of 'building, engineering, mining or other operations in, on, over or under land' amounts to development.

Some works may be too trifling to be regarded as 'operations' and may be disregarded for planning purposes.[8]

(a) *Building operations*

'Building operations' include 'rebuilding operations, structural alterations of or additions to buildings, and other operations normally undertaken by a person carrying on business as a builder',[9] while 'building' includes 'any structure or erection, and any part of a building, as so defined, but does not include plant or machinery comprised in a building' (s.275).

It can be difficult to determine whether a particular object (to use a neutral term) is a 'building' and whether, therefore, its erection or installation or alteration amounts to development. In *Barvis Ltd.* v *Secretary of State for the Environment*[10] the appellants owned a tower crane which they used on contract sites. Having no immediate use for it on a contract site, they erected and used the crane at their depot. The crane stood eighty-nine feet high and ran on rails fixed in concrete. Its dismantling and re-erection was a specialist operation which took several days and cost about £2,000. It was the appellants' declared intention to use the crane on contract sites when business needs dictated but they could give no positive indication as to when it was likely to be moved from the depot. The English minister concluded that the erection of the crane constituted an 'operation' within the statutory definition of development. In dismissing an appeal against the minister's decision, the Divisional Court expressed the view that in determining whether an object or installation was a 'structure or erection', assistance was to be derived from a passage in *Cardiff Rating Authority* v *Guest Keen Baldwin's Iron & Steel Co. Ltd.*[11] in which it was suggested that the following factors might be relevant: Is the object in question of substantial size? Is it something that either has been or normally would be built or constructed on site as opposed to being brought on to the site ready made? Has it some degreee of permanence[12] in that it would normally remain *in situ* and only be

---

[8] See, for example, *SPADS* No. A3237 (P/PPA/SL/78, 30th January 1980); [1977] J.P.L. 122; and [1978] J.P.L. 395. See too the remarks of Lord Pearson in *Coleshill* (above). Contrast *SPADS* No. A3268 (P/ENA/CB/23 and 24, 3rd March 1980); *United Refineries* v *Essex County Council* [1978] J.P.L. 110; and appeal decision noted in [1979] J.P.L. 125.

[9] See *United Refineries Ltd.* v *Essex County Council* [1978] J.P.L. 110 (stripping of topsoil a building operation).

[10] (1971) 22 P. & C.R. 710.

[11] [1949] 1 K.B. 385.

[12] See, for example, [1978] J.P.L. 487.

removed by a process amounting to pulling down or taking to pieces? Is it physically attached to the land? The court emphasised, however, that size is not necessarily conclusive, nor is the fact that 'by some feat of engineering or navigation it is brought to the hereditament in one piece', and the fact that an object has a limited degree of mobility or that it is not physically attached to the land does not necessarily prevent it being a 'structure or erection'.

The English minister has held that a free-standing carport to which small wheels had been attached so as to make it mobile was a building;[13] that the erection of a timber building, bolted together and resting on concrete padstones, was a building operation;[14] and that the installation of vending machines secured to the ground by bolts amounted to an operation for the purposes of the planning legislation.[15] In *Buckinghamshire County Council* v *Callingham*[16] the Court of Appeal held that a model village and toy railway came within the definition of 'building'. On the other hand, the Divisional Court held in *James* v *Brecon County Council*[17] that the minister had not erred in deciding that the installation on land of a battery of six fairground swing-boats capable of being removed as a whole by six men or of being dismantled in an hour, did not constitute development, whether or not the swing-boats were fixed to the land. In *Cheshire County Council* v *Woodward*[18] the court held that the minister was entitled to find that the placing on land of a wheeled coal hopper and conveyor some sixteen to twenty feet in height did not constitute development, even though, having regard to the nature of the particular site, it would have been difficult to move either piece of equipment. The parking of a caravan on land has generally been treated as a 'use' of land rather than an operation.[19]

Though the expression 'building operations' clearly embraces a wide range of activities, its scope is limited to some extent by s.19(2)(a) of the 1972 Act, which provides that 'the carrying out of works for the maintenance, improvement or other alteration of any building, being works which affect only the interior of the building or which do not materially affect the external appearance of the building' is not to constitute development.[20] Works for the alteration of a building by providing additional space therein below ground are not, however, within this exception[21] (see s.19(2)(a)); such

---

[13] [1967] J.P.L. 552; see too [1963] J.P.L. 198; and [1965] J.P.L. 687.

[14] [1968] J.P.L. 352; see too [1975] J.P.L. 368; [1977] J.P.L. 47; and [1978] J.P.L. 571.

[15] *Bulletin of Selected Appeal Decisions*, 2nd Series, II/40.

[16] [1952] 2 Q.B. 515.

[17] (1963) 15 P. & C.R. 20.

[18] [1962] 2 Q.B. 126. See, however, the comments made upon this case in *Barvis* (above).

[19] See *Guildford R.D.C.* v *Penny* [1959] 2 Q.B. 112; *Britt* v *Buckinghamshire C.C.* (1963) 14 P. & C.R. 332; *Bulletin of Selected Appeal Decisions*, IX/8; and IX/18; and [1982] J.P.L. 267; see, however, *Wealden District Council* v *Secretary of State for the Environment* [1983] J.P.L. 234; *SPADS* Nos. A3373 (P/ENA/D/37, 1st July 1980); A3930 (P/ENA/SR/3, 21st October 1981); and A3964 (P/PPA/D/90, 23rd November 1981); [1964] J.P.L. 495; and J. Alder, *Development Control*, p. 46.

[20] As to the enlargement, improvement or other alteration of dwellinghouses, see too p. 175 below.

[21] Unless the works were begun before 8th December 1969.

works as the carrying out of excavations in order to create a basement or to lower the floor level of a building[22] are therefore likely to constitute development.

The line between works of maintenance, improvement or other alteration of a building (which do not constitute development) and rebuilding works (which will involve development even though the external appearance of the building is not to be altered) can be difficult to draw. Where, for example, it was discovered in the course of repairing a building that structural defects were more serious than had initially been realised, with the result that additional work had to be undertaken until there remained of the original building nothing but the front facade and the main side walls, the minister, though he accepted that the original intention was to carry out maintenance work only, and that the external appearance of the building had not been materially altered, took the view that the original building had ceased to exist and that the operations which had been carried out were works in connection with the erection of a new building and therefore involved development.[23]

Whether particular works materially affect the external appearance of a building is a question of fact. Such operations as altering an existing window or cutting a window in an otherwise blank wall have been treated as having a material effect on a building's appearance.[24] In *Hillhead Housing Association* v *Stewart*[25] the Sheriff (D.J.B. Robertson) held that structural work to the gable wall of a tenement block, the repair and cleaning of external stonework, retiling of the roof with a different type of tile, the fitting of external doors to closes and the provision in back court areas of new walls, paved and grassed areas, paths and facilities for clothes-drying, bin-storage and seating involved development since each of these operations resulted in a significant change in the external appearance of the building.[26] On the other hand, repairs to the tenement's chimneys could not be said to have a material effect on the external appearance of the building.

In *Kensington and Chelsea Royal London Borough Council* v *C.G. Hotels*[27] it was held that the placing of floodlights on a building had not materially affected the appearance of the building; and even if the floodlighting materially affected the appearance of the building at night, that result was brought about by the running of electricity through the apparatus (which could not amount to development). When considering whether

22   See *SPADS* No. A3254 (P/PPA/CC/43; P/DEV/1/CC/1, 15th February 1980).
23   [1968] J.P.L. 414. See too *Street* v *Essex County Council* (1965) 193 E.G. 537; *Hewlett* v *Secretary of State for the Environment* [1981] J.P.L. 187; *Bulletin of Selected Appeal Decisions*, 2nd Series, III/65; [1966] J.P.L. 601; [1967] J.P.L. 351; [1970] J.P.L. 165; [1971] J.P.L. 230; [1972] J.P.L. 345; [1974] J.P.L. 162 and 555; [1977] J.P.L. 608; and [1980] J.P.L. 422. See too p. 176 below.
24   See, for example, *SPADS* No. A3315 (P/ENA/LB/18, 22nd April 1980); [1969] J.P.L. 151; [1979] J.P.L. 326; and [1984] J.P.L. 258. Contrast appeal decision noted in *Selected Enforcement and Allied Appeals*, p. 34.
25   Sheriff Court, Glasgow, 5th November 1984 (unreported).
26   Contrast *SPADS* No. A5039 (P/ENA/SP/16, 2nd April 1984).
27   (1980) 41 P. & C.R. 40.

particular works will materially affect the external appearance of a building, it would seem that it is with the appearance of the building at the time of the decision that comparison must be made and not with its appearance at some earlier time.[28]

As mentioned above, the definition of 'building' includes any part of a building. The appellants in *Coleshill and District Investment Co. Ltd.* v *Minister of Housing and Local Government*[29] had acquired disused explosives stores and magazines; these buildings were surrounded by blast walls against which had been heaped protective banks of rubble and soil. Without obtaining planning permission the appellants removed the embankments, with the result that the unsightly blast walls were exposed. They proposed also to remove the blast walls. The minister concluded that the blast walls and embankments were an integral part of each building and that the removal of the blast walls would, as an alteration which would materially affect the external appearance of the buildings, constitute building operations. The House of Lords held that there was no error of law in treating the walls and embankments, though physically discontiguous from the buildings they surrounded, as integral parts of the buildings.[30] Lord Pearson declared that 'the character of the whole structure in each case as a purpose-built magazine is an important reason for treating it as a single unit (*unum quid* in the convenient Scottish phrase)'.

In *Glasgow District Council* v *Secretary of State for Scotland*[31] the Lord Justice-Clerk (Lord Wheatley) and Lord Dunpark were prepared to hold that the partial demolition of a building was a building operation as involving a material alteration in the building's external appearance.

(b) *Engineering operations*

The expression 'engineering operations' is not defined in the 1972 Act but in *Fayrewood Fish Farms Ltd* v *Secretary of State for the Environment*[32] Mr David Widdicombe Q.C., sitting as a deputy High Court judge, said that the term should be given its ordinary meaning of operations of a kind usually undertaken by, or calling for the skills of, an engineer.[33] Engineering operations can therefore embrace activities ranging from bridge-building to the installation of a fuel storage tank.[34] In *Coleshill* (above) Lord Pearson accepted that while some works may be too small to be 'dignified with the title of an engineering operation', the removal, by excavator and lorry, of large soil and rubble embankments was of sufficient magnitude to constitute an engineering operation.

---

[28] See [1979] J.P.L. 117. See too *SPADS* No. A3254 (P/PPA/CC/43; P/DEV/1/CC/1, 15th February 1980).

[29] [1969] 1 W.L.R. 746.

[30] As to the meaning of 'part of a building' see too *Cooper* v *Bailey* (1956) 6 P. & C.R. 261.

[31] 1980 S.C. 150; 1982 S.L.T. 28. See p. 124 below.

[32] [1984] J.P.L. 267.

[33] See too *Hamilton District Council* v *Alexander Moffat and Son (Demolition) Ltd.* (p. 125 below).

[34] See [1972] J.P.L. 216.

Among the activities which have been treated as involving engineering operations are the drilling of exploratory bore holes,[35] turf-stripping,[36] the carrying out of substantial infilling or other works in a private garden,[37] the laying of tarmac,[38] and the formation of a hardstanding for vehicles.[39] Although the deposit of refuse on land is declared to involve a material change in the use of that land (see p. 162 below), the deposit of material on land will in some circumstances involve engineering or other operations.[40]

The 1972 Act specifically provides that engineering operations include 'the formation or laying out of means of access to roads'; 'means of access' is defined as including 'any means of access, whether private or public, for vehicles or for foot passengers, and includes a road' (s.275(1), as amended by the Roads (Scotland) Act 1984).[41] Works for the maintenance or improvement of a road, carried out by a local roads authority on land within the boundaries of the road, do not constitute development (s.19(2)(b)), nor do works (including the breaking open of any road or other land) carried out by a local authority or statutory undertakers for the purpose of inspection, repair or renewal of sewers, pipes, cables or other apparatus (s.19(2)(c)).

(c) Mining operations[42]

The 1972 Act does not define mining operations but states that the word 'minerals' includes 'all minerals and substances in or under land of a kind ordinarily worked for removal by underground or surface working' (s.275). Such substances as sand, gravel and peat would thus seem to be included in the definition. 'Mining operations' will include the extraction of minerals by surface working or quarrying.

As a result of an amendment to the 1972 Act made by the Town and Country Planning (Minerals) Act 1981, mining operations include:

(a) the removal of material of any description:
    (i)   from a mineral-working deposit;
    (ii) from a deposit of pulverised fuel ash or other furnace ash or clinker; or

---

[35] See [1975] J.P.L. 609.
[36] See [1981] J.P.L. 829.
[37] See *SPADS* Nos. A3752 (P/PPA/LA/132, 29th May 1981); and A3262 (P/ENA/CC/7, 25th February 1980).
[38] See [1982] J.P.L. 800.
[39] See *SPADS* No. A4856 (P/ENA/LA/62, 4th October 1983).
[40] See *Northavon District Council* v *Secretary of State for the Environment* (1980) 40 P. & C.R. 332; *SPADS* No. A4622 (P/DEV/1/LC/1, 9th May 1983); and appeal decisions noted in [1982] J.P.L. 263; [1983] J.P.L. 561; and *Selected Enforcement and Allied Appeals*, p. 50. Contrast, however, appeal decisions noted in [1978] J.P.L. 494; [1979] J.P.L. 495; [1980] J.P.L. 348; [1981] J.P.L. 135; and [1983] J.P.L. 618. See too C.M. Brand and D.W. Williams, 'Tipping on Land' [1984] J.P.L. 158.
[41] As to what amounts to the formation or laying out of a means of access, see *SPADS* No. A3039 (P/ENA/SA/11, 28th June 1979); [1970] J.P.L. 543; [1972] J.P.L. 109; [1977] J.P.L. 121; and [1981] J.P.L. 380.
[42] Mineral operations are subject to a special regime of control—see p. 469 below.

(iii) from a deposit of iron, steel or other metallic slags; and
(b) the extraction of minerals from a disused railway embankment.[43]

In *Thomas David (Porthcawl) Ltd.* v *Penybont R.D.C.*[44] the Court of Appeal held that in mining operations each cut by the bulldozer constitutes a separate act of development (see p. 311 below).

(d) *'Other operations'*

It is not altogether clear what operations are covered by this phrase. It has been suggested that the expression should be construed *eiusdem generis* with building, engineering and mining operations. In *Ross* v *Aberdeen County Council*[45] the Sheriff said, however, that in his view these operations did not constitute a *genus*. In *Coleshill and District Investment Co. Ltd.* v *Minister of Housing and Local Government*[46] it was argued that building, engineering and mining were all positive or constructional operations and that 'other operations' could not therefore include demolition, an operation of a destructive character; Lord Guest said that he was 'unable to detect a positive or constructional *genus*' since mining operations are not constructional.[47] Lord Morris of Borth-y-Gest considered, however, that 'the word "other" must denote operations which could be spoken of in the context of or in association with or as being in the nature of or as having relation to building operations or engineering operations or mining operations'.

It may be that 'other operations' include excavation and levelling works (so far as not included in mining or engineering operations). In some circumstances the deposit of materials (other than refuse) may come within this category.[48]

(e) *Demolition*

In *Control of Demolition*[49] Mr. George Dobry Q.C. declared: 'Most lawyers would agree that no clear guidance can be derived from the . . . authorities as to when demolition does or does not amount to development . . .' The Dobry Report recommended that the position should be clarified by legislation and that the definition of 'development' should be amended to include total or partial demolition of a building. No action was taken on this recommendation.

Shortly after the 1947 Act came into operation, the view was expressed by the Secretary of State for Scotland that demolition did not of itself constitute

---

[43] 1972 Act, s.19(3A) (added by s.19 of the Town and Country Planning (Minerals) Act 1981). This provision had not been brought into force at the time of writing.
[44] [1972] 1 W.L.R. 1526.
[45] 1955 S.L.T. (Sh.Ct.) 65.
[46] [1969] 1 W.L.R. 746.
[47] See, however, the comments of Lord Robertson in *Glasgow District Council* v *Secretary of State for Scotland* 1980 S.C. 150; 1982 S.L.T. 28 (see p. 124 below).
[48] See, for example, [1982] J.P.L. 741; and see p. 162 below.
[49] H.M.S.O., 1974.

development and did not therefore require planning permission.[50] Similarly, in *Howell* v *Sunbury-on-Thames U.D.C.*[51] Marshall J. stated: 'To describe the clearing of a site of all buildings and no more as "developing a site" is to do violence to the accepted meaning of the word "development".'

In the *Coleshill* case,[52] however, Lord Morris said that although it may well be that 'some operations which could conveniently be called demolition' would not come within the statutory definition of development, the question whether 'demolition' constitutes development, 'neat and arresting as the question so expressed may seem to be', is not sufficiently precise. 'It is', he said, 'unnecessary and may be misleading to give the work or operation some single labelling word and then try to apply the definition to that word.' In *Coleshill* the House of Lords held unanimously that the minister had not erred in law in deciding that the removal of rubble embankments surrounding ammunition stores constituted an engineering operation and that the proposed removal of blast walls surrounding the stores would amount to a structural alteration of the buildings and would therefore involve a building operation.

The question whether the demolition of the top three storeys of a five-storey building involved development was raised in *Glasgow District Council* v *Secretary of State for Scotland.*[53] The Lord Justice-Clerk (Lord Wheatley) and Lord Dunpark were prepared to accept that the works which had been carried out, involving as they did a material alteration in the external appearance of the building, came within the statutory definition of development. Their Lordships were not prepared to accept the argument that the existence of specific statutory provisions prohibiting the demolition of listed buildings[54] indicated that the demolition of an unlisted building was not to be treated as development. Both the Lord Justice-Clerk and Lord Dunpark left open the question whether the total demolition of a building involves development, Lord Dunpark saying that it was arguable that the total removal of a building could not reasonably be described as a structural alteration.

Lord Robertson rejected the planning authority's argument as expressed in its widest form—that all and any demolition of a building, or part of a building, *ipso facto* involves development. He said: 'Had Parliament intended demolition to be included in "development" as defined in s.19, it would have been simple to say so. The emphasis is on developments producing results of a constructive, positive, identifiable character.'[55] Lord Robertson thought it significant that Parliament had considered it necessary to deal specifically with the demolition of listed buildings.

In the rather special circumstances of the *Glasgow District* case the court found that planning permission was not required (see p. 229 below).

[50] See D.H.S. Circular 16/1949.
[51] (1963) 15 P. & C.R. 26.
[52] See p. 121 above.
[53] 1980 S.C. 150; 1982 S.L.T. 28.
[54] See chapter 19 below.
[55] See *Coleshill* (above), per Lord Wilberforce.

In *Hamilton District Council* v *Alexander Moffat & Son (Demolition) Ltd.*[56] the Sheriff (I.A. Macmillan) held, after considering the *Coleshill* and *Glasgow District* cases, that the demolition of a railway viaduct was an engineering operation. The Sheriff's decision appears to have been strongly influenced by the skilled and specialised nature of the proposed works.

The demolition of a building may well form part of a building operation or lead to the making of a material change in the use of the land upon which the building stood.[57] In *Iddenden* v *Secretary of State for the Environment*[58] the Court of Appeal took the view, however, that where nissen huts had been demolished and a new building erected on the site, all without planning permission, the demolition and the building operations were in planning law separate operations, although, as Lord Denning said: 'No doubt the pulling down of the old and the erection of the new was all one combined operation by the workmen.' The Court held that although the erection of the new building was a breach of planning control, the pulling down of the old buildings did not constitute development and therefore did not amount to a breach of planning control.

B. MATERIAL CHANGE OF USE

Introduction

It is not every change in the use of a building or land that constitutes development; only when a change of use is 'material' does development occur. The 1972 Act makes specific provision in relation to certain changes of use (see p. 152–163 below), but contains no general guidance as to the circumstances in which a change of use is to be regarded as material. Whether or not a particular change of use is such as to constitute development is very largely a matter of fact and degree (see, in particular, p. 133 below); a number of general principles have, however, developed over the years and these provide something in the nature of a framework within which that question is to be considered.

For planning purposes a distinction must, at the outset, be drawn between the primary or predominant use or uses of land and any uses which are merely ancillary to the primary use or uses. In considering whether or not a proposed change of use would be 'material' it is with the primary use of the land that any proposed change of use must be compared.

The operation of this principle is to be seen in the decision of the Second Division of the Court of Session in *Alexandra Transport Company Ltd.* v *Secretary of State for Scotland.*[59] In that case land had been used as a quarry

[56] Sheriff Court, Hamilton, 16th February 1984 (unreported, but see 1984 S.P.L.P. 76). See too appeal decision noted in [1983] J.P.L. 616.
[57] See *London County Council* v *Marks and Spencer Ltd.* [1953] A.C. 535.
[58] [1972] 1 W.L.R. 1433.
[59] 1974 S.L.T. 81; see too *G. Percy Trentham Ltd.* v *Gloucestershire C.C.* [1966] 1 W.L.R. 506; *Shephard* v *Buckinghamshire County Council* (1967) 18 P. & C.R. 419; *Williams* v *Minister of Housing and Local Government* (1967) 18 P. & C.R. 514; *Brazil (Concrete) Ltd.* v *Amersham R.D.C.* (1967) 18 P. & C.R. 396; and *L.R. Jillings* v *Secretary of State for the Environment* [1984] J.P.L. 32.

under a planning consent which contained a condition that all waste material was to be backfilled into the quarry workings. The land having been sold, the question arose whether use of the quarry as a tip for refuse brought in from outside amounted to a material change of use. The appellants argued that planning permission had been granted, albeit subject to conditions, for the deposit of waste materials on the land, that the only change in the situation was in the type of waste materials which were being deposited, and that that change did not amount to a material change of use. The court held, however, that a material change of use had occurred. Lord Milligan pointed out that the deposit of quarry refuse had to be treated as an ancillary use of the land; the primary use had been use for quarrying purposes. The primary use of the land, not the ancillary use, determined the character of the use and thus when the land ceased to be used as a quarry and became a 'dump' a material change of use took place.

The fact that, for change of use purposes the law focuses upon the primary use of land and has little concern with ancillary uses, has a number of important consequences. These are considered below.

(a) The planning unit

(i) *General.* In terms of the 1972 Act, development occurs when there is a material change in the use of 'any buildings or other land', but the statute provides no guidance as to the 'buildings or other land' which it may be appropriate to consider in any particular case. When considering whether or not a material change of use has taken place or whether particular proposals will amount to a material change of use, the first logical step therefore is to identify the 'planning unit', i.e. the area of land to be looked at in considering the materiality or otherwise of the particular change of use.

The main importance of identifying the planning unit correctly is that the answer to the question 'Has a material change of use occurred?' may depend upon the area selected for consideration.[60] In *Williams* v *Minister of Housing and Local Government*,[61] for example, the owner of a nursery garden who had for several years sold the produce of the garden from a timber building situated on the land began also to sell produce not grown on the land. The planning authority took enforcement action, alleging development by use of the building as a retail shop. Taking the nursery garden together with the building as the appropriate planning unit, the minister upheld the enforcement notice; the primary use of that unit was use for agricultural purposes (including, but only as ancillary to that primary use, sale of the agricultural produce of the unit), but once 'imported' produce was brought on to the land

---

[60] In *Thomas David (Porthcawl) Ltd.* v *Penybont R.D.C.* [1972] 1 W.L.R. 1526 the concept of the planning unit was employed by the Court of Appeal in connection with *operational* development (see p. 311 below). See too *Welsh Aggregates Ltd.* v *Secretary of State for the Environment* [1983] J.P.L. 50. The term 'planning unit' has acquired an additional, and rather different, meaning in connection with the extinguishment of existing use rights—see p. 144 below.

[61] (1967) 18 P. & C.R. 514.

for purposes of sale a change in the character of use occurred—there was then, in effect, use as a general greengrocer's shop. The Divisional Court heid that the minister had not erred in treating the whole premises as the proper planning unit. The importance of selecting the right planning unit was emphasised by Widgery J., who pointed out that if the unit for consideration had been the building in isolation, it might well have been contended that since it had been used all along for sale by retail, no material change of use had occurred.

(ii) *Identification of the planning unit.* Prior to the decision in *Burdle* v *Secretary of State for the Environment*[62] the phrase 'planning unit' was quite frequently employed but the criteria for identifying the unit were not at all clear.[63] In *Jennings Motors Ltd.* v *Secretary of State for the Environment*[64] the Court of Appeal approved what was described as the 'extremely helpful general test' contained in the judgment of Bridge J. in *Burdle*. The threefold guide set out by Bridge J. in that case can be reconciled with most of the earlier decisions on the subject[65] and has been frequently applied and cited by the courts and ministers.[66]

In *Burdle* Bridge J., while not, he said, 'presuming to propound exhaustive tests apt to cover every situation', considered that it might be helpful to sketch out certain broad criteria appropriate to the determination of the planning unit.[67]

First, he said, whenever it is possible to recognise a single main purpose of the occupier's use of his land (whether or not there are secondary activities which are ancillary to that main purpose) the planning unit is the whole unit of occupation. That proposition emerged clearly, said Bridge J., from the decision of the Court of Appeal in *G. Percy Trentham Ltd.* v *Gloucestershire County Council.*[68]

As a working rule, therefore, one starts off with the presumption that the unit of occupation is the appropriate planning unit. That presumption will only be displaced if some smaller unit can be discerned (below). In general, the 'unit of occupation' is the area occupied[69] as a single holding by an

---

[62] [1972] 1 W.L.R. 1207.
[63] For detailed discussion of the earlier decisions see W. Parkes, 'Determination of the Planning Unit' [1972] J.P.L. 605; S.N.L. Palk, 'The Planning Unit' (1973) 37 Conv. 154; and Neil Hawke, 'Recognising the Planning Unit' [1974] J.P.L. 399. On later developments see E. Young, 'The Planning Unit: Judicial Creativity in a Statutory Context' (1983) 28 J.L.S.S. 339 and 371.
[64] [1982] Q.B. 541.
[65] See, for example, *Bendles Motors Ltd.* v *Bristol Corporation* [1963] 1 W.L.R. 247; *G. Percy Trentham Ltd.* v *Gloucestershire County Council* [1966] 1 W.L.R. 506; *Brazil (Concrete) Ltd.* v *Amersham Rural District Council* (1967) 18 P. & C.R. 396; *Williams* v *Minister of Housing and Local Government* (1967) 18 P. & C.R. 514; and *Brooks* v *Gloucestershire County Council* (1968) 19 P. & C.R. 90.
[66] In *Duffy* v *Secretary of State for the Environment* [1981] J.P.L. 811 Glidewell J. described Bridge J.'s judgment as the 'classic exposition' of the law on the subject.
[67] The other members of the Divisional Court agreed with Bridge J.'s judgment.
[68] [1966] 1 W.L.R. 506 (considered below).
[69] The question of ownership of the land appears not to be relevant to identification of the unit.

individual occupier or by joint occupiers.[70] Before land can be treated as comprising a single unit of occupation, that land must, it seems, be capable of being regarded as a single holding or entity.[71] Although a single planning unit can clearly extend over a group of buildings[72] or several parcels of land, a significant degree of physical separation may be a major factor leading to the conclusion that particular buildings or pieces of land do not form a single planning unit, even though those buildings or pieces of land are occupied by a single occupier for related purposes. In *Duffy* v *Secretary of State for the Environment*[73] Glidewell J. accepted the inquiry inspector's view that buildings lying on opposite sides of a major road and 150 yards from each other did not form part of the same planning unit, even though the buildings were apparently used together for hotel purposes.

Secondly, where the occupier carries on a variety of activities on the unit of occupation and it is not possible to say that one activity is ancillary to another (as in the case of a 'composite use' where the component activities are not confined within separate and physically distinct areas of land), the entire unit of occupation will again be the planning unit.

Thirdly, however, where within a single unit of occupation two or more physically separate and distinct areas are occupied for substantially different and unrelated purposes, each area used for a different main purpose (together with its incidental and ancillary activities) ought to be considered as a separate planning unit. On Bridge J.'s criteria, therefore, it is only if some unit smaller than the unit of 'occupation' can be recognised as the site of activities which amount in substance to a separate use both physically and functionally that the unit of occupation is displaced by the unit of 'activity' as the appropriate planning unit.

Bridge J. added:

'To decide which of these three categories apply to the circumstances of any particular case at any given time may be difficult . . . There may indeed be an almost imperceptible change from one category to another. Thus, for example, activities . . . once properly regarded as incidental to another use or as part of a composite use may be so intensified in scale and physically concentrated in a recognisably separate area that they produce a new planning unit the use of which is materially changed.'

It would seem that so long as the right criteria are applied, the choice of the planning unit is for the planning authority or the Secretary of State to make as a matter of fact and degree in the circumstances of the particular

---

[70] See *Johnston* v *Secretary of State for the Environment* (1974) 28 P. & C.R. 424, per Lord Widgery C.J. See, however, *Kwik Save Discount Group* v *Secretary of State for Wales* (1978) 37 P. & C.R. 170 (below).

[71] On incorporation of one piece of land with another see *TLG Building Materials* v *Secretary of State for the Environment* (1980) 41 P. & C.R. 243.

[72] See, for example, *Vickers-Armstrong* v *Central Land Board* (1957) 9 P. & C.R. 33.

[73] [1981] J.P.L. 811. See too appeal decision noted in [1973] J.P.L. 386.

case;[74] provided that the criteria are not applied unreasonably by the planning authority or the minister, the courts will not intervene.

(iii) *Application of principles.* The presumption in favour of the unit of occupation as the appropriate planning unit appears to be a strong one, and Bridge J.'s 'working rule' has been employed in many of the cases where a question as to the correct planning unit has arisen.[75] Sometimes this will be of advantage to the 'developer',[76] sometimes not.[77] The presumption in favour of the unit of occupation is particularly strong in the case of dwellinghouses. In *Wood* v *Secretary of State for the Environment*[78] (in which it was held that the minister had been wrong to treat as a separate planning unit a conservatory attached to a farmhouse and used for retail sales) the view was expressed by Lord Widgery C.J. that 'it can rarely if ever be right to dissect a single dwellinghouse and to regard one room in isolation as being an appropriate planning unit . . .'

The broad significance of correct identification of the planning unit has been mentioned above but some examples of the operation of Bridge J.'s three criteria and some of the consequences of the application of those criteria should perhaps be mentioned here. It may be noted, however, that these consequences might well be complicated by the terms of a specific planning permission relating to the land in question.

1. *Single main use.* In terms of the first of Bridge J.'s guidelines, where several activities are carried on upon the unit of occupation but it is possible to recognise one of those activities as the primary use of the land and the others as ancillary thereto, it is, of course, the primary use which determines the use of the unit as a whole for planning purposes and the materiality of any change of use must be considered in the context of that primary use.[79]

The facts of *Johnston* v *Secretary of State for the Environment*[80] provide a good illustration of the operation of this principle. In that case premises consisting of forty-four garages were originally used for the garaging of taxis belonging to the landowner. Over the years the garages came to be let singly

---

[74] See, for example, *Johnston* v *Secretary of State for the Environment* (1974) 28 P. & C.R. 424; and *London Borough of Camden* v *Secretary of State for the Environment* [1979] J.P.L. 311. However, in one or two earlier cases the courts appear to have treated identification of the unit as a matter of law—see, for example, *G. Percy Trentham Ltd.* v *Gloucestershire C.C.* [1966] 1 W.L.R. 506.

[75] See, for example, *Burdle* (above); *Wood* v *Secretary of State for the Environment* [1973] 1 W.L.R. 707; *Johnston* v *Secretary of State for the Environment* (1974) 28 P. & C.R. 424; *Wakelin* v *Secretary of State for the Environment* (1978) 77 L.G.R. 101; and *Hilliard* v *Secretary of State for the Environment* (1978) 37 P. & C.R. 129; and appeal decisions noted in [1976] J.P.L. 117 and 120; [1977] J.P.L. 188, 195 and 611; [1978] J.P.L. 54 and 784; [1980] J.P.L. 693; [1981] J.P.L. 382; and [1982] J.P.L. 115 and 534.

[76] See, for example, *Burdle* and *Wood* (above).

[77] See, for example, *Williams* (above).

[78] Above: see too *Brooks* v *Gloucestershire County Council* (1968) 19 P. & C.R. 90.

[79] See, for example, appeal decisions noted in [1979] J.P.L. 54; and [1981] J.P.L. 382.

[80] (1974) 28 P. & C.R. 424.

or in groups to different persons. Some of the garages came to be used for vehicle repairs as opposed to garaging *simpliciter*. The appellants contended that the planning authority and the minister should have treated the entire group of forty-four garages as the planning unit. In that case one would have had to consider the materiality of the change in the use of a few of the garages in the context of the whole group; thus regarded, it is conceivable that the change of use might not have been considered a material one. The Divisional Court held that the Secretary of State's conclusion that each garage or small group of garages separately occupied was a separate planning unit could not be criticised. In these circumstances the minister had been entitled to find in relation to the appropriate planning unit that a material change of use had occurred.

Looked at in the context of the primary use of the planning unit, various sorts of change in the activities carried on upon the unit will not involve a material change of use. Uses ancillary to the main use can, for example, be given up or changed, new ancillary uses may be introduced and ancillary uses may be absorbed by the main use (see p. 147 below).

2. *Mixed use.* Bridge J.'s second category would seem to embrace all those cases where several distinct activities are carried on upon the unit of occupation but the different activities are not confined within physically separate areas.[81] This he describes as a composite use but it might be better described as a mixed use.

If a case falls into this category it may well not be a material change of use to change the location of the various uses within the unit, so long as the 'mix' of uses does not change materially.[82]

3. *Dual use.* As regards the third of Bridge J.'s criteria, it may well be difficult to know when 'physically separate and distinct areas' within a single unit of occupation are occupied for 'substantially different and unrelated purposes' and when, therefore, such areas should be treated as separate planning units, the 'unit of activity'—i.e. the area upon which a particular activity is carried on—being in this situation preferred to the unit of occupation. Again this is largely a question of fact.[83]

An example of a case which was treated as falling into this category is *David W. Barling Ltd.* v *Secretary of State for the Environment*.[84] In this case an area of land had been used for the storage of building materials in connection with the building on another part of the site of two houses for the

---

[81] See, for example, appeal decisions noted in [1973] J.P.L. 261; and [1977] J.P.L. 195.

[82] See the comments of Lord Widgery C.J. in *de Mulder* v *Secretary of State for the Environment* [1974] Q.B. 792 and in *Hilliard* v *Secretary of State for the Environment* (1977) 34 P. & C.R. 193. See too *Bromsgrove* v *Secretary of State for the Environment* [1977] J.P.L. 797. And see p. 147 below.

[83] See *London Borough of Camden* v *Secretary of State for the Environment* (1978) 252 E.G. 275, per Lord Widgery C.J.

[84] [1980] J.P.L. 594. See too *Vyner* v *Secretary of State for the Environment* [1977] J.P.L. 795; *Warnock* v *Secretary of State for the Environment* [1980] J.P.L. 590; and appeal decisions noted in [1970] J.P.L. 43; and [1973] J.P.L. 386.

occupiers of the whole site. After completion of the houses the storage use continued in connection with the running of a general building business and at that time the area used for storage was fenced off from the houses. The Divisional Court accepted the Secretary of State's conclusion that when it was fenced off the storage area became a separate planning unit with an independent use for commercial purposes.

In *Barling* physical division of the land by fencing would seem to have been relevant. Absence of such division will not, however, tell decisively in favour of a single planning unit. Where part of an old, and apparently largely disused, orchard possessed existing use rights as a caravan site, the Divisional Court held that although the orchard was not physically divided in any way, the caravan site was severable from the remainder of the orchard, and the introduction of caravans on the rest of the orchard constituted a change from agricultural use.[85] On the other hand, in *East Barnet U.D.C.* v *British Transport Commission*[86] the Divisional Court took the view that an area of land which had not been used for many years should, 'as a matter of common sense', be treated as an unused part of a larger planning unit rather than as a separate unit in its own right, with the result that there was no material change of use when the unused parcel came to be used for the same purpose as the rest of the unit.

(iv) *Sub-division and merger of planning units.* It seems clear from Bridge J.'s judgment in *Burdle* that certain sorts of change in occupation or activity will result in the creation of a new planning unit.[87] This may happen (1) if two or more planning units are merged;[88] (2) if a planning unit is sub-divided into areas in separate occupation;[89] or (3) if a unit is divided into distinct geographical areas devoted to unrelated uses.[90] In the last case a material change of use will inevitably occur. However, the creation of a new planning unit by methods (1) and (2) will not necessarily result in a material change of use, though it may be the first step towards the making of such a change.

Where, for example, a part of shop premises has been used for office purposes ancillary to the main (shop) use of the planning unit, and the planning unit is then sub-divided with the result that the office part of the premises comes into separate and independent occupation, a material change of use will occur; there has been a change from shop to office use. Until recently, however, there was no suggestion that the sub-division of a

---

[85] *Williams-Denton* v *Watford R.D.C.* (1963) 15 P. & C.R. 11; see too *Brookes* v *Flintshire C.C.* (1956) 6 P. & C.R. 140; and *R.* v *Axbridge R.D.C.* [1964] 1 W.L.R. 422.

[86] [1962] 2 Q.B. 484. Contrast appeal decision noted in [1979] J.P.L. 247.

[87] The possibility that a 'new planning unit' may be created by the erection of a building etc. is considered separately below.

[88] See, for example, *TLG Building Materials* v *Secretary of State for the Environment* (1980) 41 P. & C.R. 243.

[89] See, for example, *G. Percy Trentham Ltd.* (discussed below). See too *SPADS* No. A3640 (P/PPA/CA/16, 10th March 1981).

[90] See, for example, *David W. Barling Ltd.* (above). As was the case in *Barling* this may happen where an ancillary use loses its ancillary status.

planning unit or the amalgamation of two units *automatically* resulted in a material change of use. Where, for example, premises formerly used as one shop come to be used as two shops in separate occupation, comparison of the use of either of the new units with the use of the former unit would suggest that no material change of use has occurred.[91]

However, in *Wakelin* v *Secretary of State for the Environment*[92] the Court of Appeal accepted that the selling off for separate occupation of a large house and lodge forming part of a single planning unit would involve a material change of use. Lord Denning M.R. declared: 'if you divide a large house and grounds into two units . . . that is a material change of use'. In *Winton* v *Secretary of State for the Environment*[93] Woolf J. said that *Wakelin* undoubtedly broke new ground; he did not, however, accept that Lord Denning was expressing a general view that the sub-division of a planning unit in itself amounted to a material change of use. Distinguishing *Wakelin*, Woolf J. held that if the division of a single planning unit into two separate units has no planning consequences, then it does not amount to development.[94]

In *Johnston* v *Secretary of State for the Environment*[95] Lord Widgery C.J. pointed out that there was at that time no reported case in which the appropriate planning unit had been held to comprise areas of land in different occupation. However, in *Kwik Save Discount Group* v *Secretary of State for Wales*[96] the Divisional Court held that areas in different occupation *could* form a single planning unit. In this case the occupiers of a garage complex obtained planning permission to change the use of a workshop to a retail showroom. The appellants acquired the workshop and proceeded to use it as a retail supermarket, claiming that with the severance of the workshop from the remainder of the site so far as activities and control were concerned, a new planning unit had come into existence, a planning unit which could be used for any form of retail sales.

The Divisional Court did not think one could create a new planning unit out of a complex of buildings such as these, which were supplementary to one another, simply by selecting one of the buildings and conveying it to an owner or occupier different from the owner or occupier of the rest of the site. The planning unit remained the same throughout, notwithstanding the severance. Lord Widgery stated that planning units were 'not primarily matters of title but of activity'. The planning authority were therefore entitled to restrain the supermarket use as being a material change from the garage use. The Divisional Court's decision in *Kwik Save* was upheld by the Court of Appeal, but on different grounds.[97] The Court of Appeal did not

[91]   See, for example, *SPADS* No. A3735 (P/PPA/TB/10, 20th May 1981).
[92]   (1978) 77 L.G.R. 101.
[93]   (1982) 46 P. & C.R. 205. See too appeal decision noted in [1984] J.P.L. 892.
[94]   A consultation paper issued by the Scottish Development Department on 31st July 1984 suggested that it should be made clear by future legislative amendment that the division of a planning unit other than a dwellinghouse does not of itself involve a material change of use.
[95]   (1974) 28 P. & C.R. 424.
[96]   (1978) 37 P. & C.R. 170.
[97]   (1980) 42 P. & C.R. 166.

find the question of the planning unit important or helpful in deciding the case.

Contrary to what Lord Widgery said in *Kwik Save* it is *occupation* rather than *activity* which has generally been treated as important in determining the planning unit; it is only if the unit of occupation cannot be justified in a particular case that the question of activity arises. The Divisional Court's decision seems to run counter to the Court of Appeal's reasoning in *G. Percy Trentham Ltd.* v *Gloucestershire County Council*[98] in which the severance of part of a farm was treated as creating a new planning unit. The decision in *Trentham* also shows that the result in *Kwik Save* would have been the same if the areas of separate occupation had been treated as separate planning units.

In *Trentham* the appellants, building and civil engineering contractors, purchased a farmhouse, yard and farm buildings which, prior to the purchase, had formed part of a 75 acre farm. Without obtaining planning permission the appellants proceeded to use some of the farm buildings, which had been used to house agricultural vehicles and machinery and to store corn and hay, for the storage of building materials, plant and equipment. It was argued for the appellants that the use of the buildings both before and after the sale was use as a warehouse or repository and that there had therefore been no material change of use. The Court of Appeal held that the former use was not use as a 'repository' but that in any event, taking as the proper planning unit the whole area purchased, the previous use of the land was for agricultural purposes and that there had been a change from an agricultural use as farm buildings to a store for other purposes. The storage use prior to the appellants' purchase of the land was merely ancillary to the dominant agricultural use and even though the particular use of the particular buildings remained use for storage, the dominant use had changed materially.

It might be suggested that the Divisional Court's approach in *Kwik Save* introduces an unnecessary complication into the law on the planning unit.

(b) *'Material' change*

The use in s.19(1) of the word 'material' to qualify 'change in the use of any buildings or other land' makes clear that no slight or trivial change of use, having regard to the use of the whole planning unit, will amount to development. Some changes of use may be too insubstantial or too brief to be regarded as having any planning significance.[99]

It may sometimes be fairly obvious that a particular change of use is, or would be, material—for example a change from use as a dwelling-house to

---

[98] [1966] 1 W.L.R. 506.

[99] See, for example, *Kwik Save Discount Group* v *Secretary of State for the Environment* (1980) 42 P. & C.R. 166 (offering of five cars for sale for a period of about one month in a building with a floor space of about 20,000 square feet). See too *Paul* v *Ayrshire County Council* 1964 S.C. 116; 1964 S.L.T. 207, per Lord Justice-Clerk Grant; [1963] J.P.L. 692; [1969] J.P.L. 99; [1971] J.P.L. 583; [1972] J.P.L. 341; and [1974] J.P.L. 300 and 733.

use as a shop—but in some cases it can be very difficult to determine whether a particular change of use is a material one.[1] Is there, for example, a material change of use if a house formerly occupied all the year round by a single family comes to be used for holiday letting to a succession of families?[2]

The courts will not generally interfere with the decision of a planning authority or the Secretary of State on the issue of the materiality of a particular change unless the decision is one that no reasonable authority or minister, properly advised as to the law, could have reached. Thus, while a court may, for example, concern itself with the question whether a particular type of change of use is capable of amounting to development[3] or whether irrelevant factors have been taken into account by the Secretary of State in reaching his decision,[4] it has frequently been said that whether a particular change is material is very largely a matter of fact and degree[5] and the court will not intervene where the law has been properly applied, even if on the facts the court itself might have been inclined to reach a different conclusion.[6] In *Bendles Motors Ltd.* v *Bristol Corporation*,[7] for example, the minister concluded that the placing of a vending machine on the forecourt of a garage involved a material change in the use of the premises. The minister having correctly considered the materiality of the change in relation to the use of the planning unit as a whole, the Divisional Court could not say that his decision was wrong, though they themselves might have been inclined to treat the introduction of the machine as *de minimis*.

So much is the matter one of fact and degree that it is very difficult to formulate any helpful general principles as to when a change of use is material. An early circular[8] declared that: 'A change in kind [of use] will always be material—e.g. from house to shop or from shop to factory. A change in the *degree* of an existing use may be "material" but only if it is very marked. For example, the fact that lodgers are taken privately in a family dwellinghouse would not in the Secretary of State's view constitute a

---

[1]   When considering whether a proposed change of use will be material, the proposed use must be compared with the last operative use of the land; regard cannot properly be had to a use for which planning permission has been granted but which has not been commenced—see ministerial decision noted in [1975] J.P.L. 616.
[2]   See, for example, *Blackpool Borough Council* v *Secretary of State for the Environment* (1980) 40 P. & C.R. 104.
[3]   See, for example, *Birmingham Corporation* v *Minister of Housing and Local Government* [1964] 1 Q.B. 178; and *Lewis* v *Secretary of State for the Environment* (1971) 23 P. & C.R. 125.
[4]   See, for example, *Lewis* (above); *Snook* v *Secretary of State for the Environment* (1975) 33 P. & C.R. 1; and *Winmill* v *Secretary of State for the Environment* [1982] J.P.L. 445.
[5]   See, for example, *Marshall* v *Nottingham City Corporation* [1960] 1 W.L.R. 707; *East Barnet U.D.C.* v *British Transport Commission* [1962] 2 Q.B. 484; *Bendles Motors Ltd.* v *Bristol Corporation* [1963] 1 W.L.R. 247; *Gray* v *Oxfordshire County Council* (1963) 15 P. & C.R. 1; *Howell* v *Sunbury-on-Thames U.D.C.* (1963) 15 P. & C.R. 26; and *Braddon* v *Secretary of State for the Environment* [1977] J.P.L. 450.
[6]   See, however, *Emma Hotels Ltd.* v *Secretary of State for the Environment* (1980) 41 P. & C.R. 255.
[7]   [1963] 1 W.L.R. 247.
[8]   D.H.S. Circular 16/1949.

material change of use in itself so long as the use of the house remains substantially that of a private residence.[9] On the other hand, the change from a private residence with lodgers to a declared guest house, boarding-house or private hotel would be "material".'

The concept of a change in 'kind' of use as contrasted with a change in the degree of an existing use may sometimes prove to be a useful initial approach and it has frequently been said that the question to be asked in considering whether or not a proposed change of use is a material one is whether the character of the existing use of land will be substantially altered by the proposed change. The easier it is to typify the present use of land as being of a different 'kind' or 'character' to the proposed use, the more likely it is that a change from the former to the latter is material. A change, for example, from shop to office use will clearly be a material one.

However, for the purpose of gauging the materiality of a change of use, the identification of a change in the 'kind' or 'character' of use can pose very considerable difficulties, especially where the uses under consideration have some features in common. Uses of land can be typified with varying degrees of particularity—for example, a general word like 'hostel' embraces a number of different types of accommodation[10]—and the problem with making an abstract comparison of 'kinds' of use is to know the level of generality at which the uses in question should be categorised. As Lord Parker C.J. put it in *East Barnet U.D.C.* v *British Transport Commission*,[11] the difficulty is to know whether, for the purpose of comparing one use with another, it is right to consider what he called the 'general purpose' to which land is put or whether one should 'descend to the particular' and consider whether the particular purpose is different. He said:

'To take an example, is the purpose for which a shop is occupied the purpose of a retail shop quite generally, or is it the narrower purpose of being used as a retail shop for the sale of a particular commodity? If the former is correct, then a change in the nature of the article sold would not be development; if the latter, it would.'

The *East Barnet* case demonstrates that where the kind of use, the general purpose, to which land is put remains the same, but there is, in Lord Parker's words,[12] 'a change from one particular purpose to another particular purpose'—where, for example, land continues to be used for storage purposes but the commodity stored is changed—it may be right to conclude

---

[9] See, however, appeal decision noted in [1983] J.P.L. 824 (use of two bedrooms of four-bedroomed house for overnight accommodation for paying guests held to involve a material change of use).

[10] See *Commercial and Residential Property Development Co.* v *Secretary of State for the Environment* (1981) 80 L.G.R. 443, per Glidewell J.

[11] [1962] 2 Q.B. 484.

[12] *Devonshire C.C.* v *Horton* (1962) 14 P. & C.R. 444.

that the change of use is not a material one. In the *East Barnet* case[13] land had previously been used by the British Transport Commission as a coal storage depot, all of the coal being transported to and from the depot by rail. The land came to be used by a motor manufacturing company as a transit depot for the storage and handling of motor vehicles, virtually all of which were transported by rail. The Divisional Court held that the magistrates had been entitled to find that no material change of use had taken place.[14] In *Lewis* v *Secretary of State for the Environment*[15] the Divisional Court held that the minister had erred in law in treating as material a change in the use of premises from use for maintenance and repair of vehicles belonging to a particular company to use for maintenance and repair of vehicles belonging to the public at large; the use throughout having, in the court's view, remained the same, the change could not be material.[16]

On the other hand, even though the 'general purpose' remains the same, a change of use within that general purpose *can* be material. Various sorts of use can, for example, be described at a general level as 'residential' but it is clear that a change within that broad category of use may be material. In *Birmingham Corporation* v *Minister of Housing and Local Government*[17] houses formerly in single-family occupation came to be used as houses let in lodgings to a number of different occupants. The minister decided that since the houses had remained in residential use throughout, the change in the type of occupancy could not as a matter of law be material. The Divisional Court held that the minister had erred in law. Merely because the uses in question could be described as residential did not debar the minister from considering whether, as a matter of fact and degree, a material change of use had occurred.

---

[13] Above. See too *Marshall* v *Nottingham City Corporation* [1960] 1 W.L.R. 707 (change from manufacture and sale of wooden buildings to sale of caravans not material); *Devonshire C.C.* v *Allens Caravans (Estates) Ltd.* (1962) 14 P. & C.R. 440; and *Devonshire C.C.* v *Horton* (1962) 14 P. & C.R. 444 (change from use of land for camping in tents to use as a caravan site not material); and *Blackpool Borough Council* v *Secretary of State for the Environment* (1980) 40 P. & C.R. 104 (holiday letting of dwelling to succession of families not material). See too *SPADS* No. A2306 (P/ENA/GA/1 and 2, 22nd March 1977) (change from storage of steel and ironmongery to storage of furniture not material); and [1980] J.P.L. 342; and [1981] J.P.L. 612 (use of dwelling for holiday lettings not a material change).

[14] One might, however, contrast the appeal decision noted in [1976] J.P.L. 248 (change from storage of coal to storage of cars held a material change of use). See too [1978] J.P.L. 343.

[15] (1971) 23 P. & C.R. 125; see too *Snook* v *Secretary of State for the Environment* (1975) 33 P. & C.R. 1; and *Philip Farrington Properties Ltd.* v *Secretary of State for the Environment* [1982] J.P.L. 638.

[16] However, as Lord Widgery pointed out in *Jones* v *Secretary of State for the Environment* (1974) 28 P. & C.R. 362, there are circumstances in which a material change of use can occur even though the type of activity on the land has been constant throughout; there may, for example, be a material change where an existing use is intensified (see p. 139 below) or where a use which was previously ancillary to another use has become the primary use of the land (see p. 148 below).

[17] [1964] 1 Q.B. 178. See too *Borg* v *Khan* (1965) 17 P. & C.R. 144; and *SPADS* No. A2194 (P/ENA/GLW/54 and 58-62, 18th October 1976).

A change in the use of premises from use as a single-family private residence to use for multiple paying occupation[18] can amount to a material change of use;[19] and the courts have held the minister entitled to find that a material change of use occurred where there was a change from student hostel to residential hotel;[20] where there was a change from bed-sitting accommodation to hotel;[21] where there was a change from single-family occupation of a house to use as accommodation for hotel staff;[22] where there was a change from guest house to residential accommodation;[23] and where there was a change from one type of social club to another.[24] It would seem that in appropriate circumstances a change from use as a private dwelling-house to use for short holiday lettings could amount to a material change of use,[25] as could a change from a short-stay hostel to a long-stay hostel.[26]

Other examples of changes within the same broad category of use being treated as material might be cited. The courts have, for example, held the minister entitled to find that a change from use for lock-up garages to use for the storage and maintenance of a coach fleet was material;[27] that a change from selling eggs at the farm door to selling eggs by means of a roadside vending machine was a material change;[28] and that a change from plant nursery to garden centre was material.[29]

Decisions such as those mentioned above appear to indicate that abstract comparisons of the character of uses of land may not be very helpful in considering whether a particular change of use is material. It is often more useful to ask whether, as between two uses exhibiting some similarities, the change from one to the other will have consequences which are material or relevant in own planning terms.[30] There is a good deal of judicial support for

---

[18] On the meaning of 'multiple occupation' see *Duffy* v *Pilling* (1977) 33 P. & C.R. 85; *Lipson* v *Secretary of State for the Environment* (1976) 33 P. & C.R. 95; *Winmill* v *Secretary of State for the Environment* [1982] J.P.L. 445; *Breachberry Ltd.* v *Secretary of State for the Environment* [1985] J.P.L. 180; and appeal decision noted in [1979] J.P.L. 123.

[19] See, for example, ministerial decisions noted in [1965] J.P.L. 47 and 144; [1976] J.P.L. 55; [1977] J.P.L. 535; [1984] J.P.L. 822; and *SPADS* No. A2251 (P/ENA/LA/4, 12th January 1977). Contrast [1978] J.P.L. 270 and 578.

[20] *Mornford Investments* v *Minister of Housing and Local Government* [1970] 2 All E.R. 253.

[21] *Mayflower Cambridge Ltd.* v *Secretary of State for the Environment* (1975) 30 P. & C.R. 28.

[22] *Clarke* v *Minister of Housing and Local Government* (1966) 18 P. & C.R. 82.

[23] *Breachberry Ltd.* v *Secretary of State for the Environment* [1985] J.P.L. 180.

[24] *Burkmar* v *Secretary of State for the Environment* (1984) 271 E.G. 377.

[25] See the comments of Jupp J. in *Blackpool Borough Council* v *Secretary of State for the Environment* (1980) 40 P. & C.R. 104 (although in that case the court upheld the minister's decision that no material change of use had occurred).

[26] See *Commercial and Residential Property Development Co.* v *Secretary of State for the Environment* (1981) 80 L.G.R. 443, per Glidewell J. See too *SPADS* No. A2548 (P/ENA/LA/8, 12th January 1978) (change of use from guest house to hostel treated as material).

[27] *Gray* v *Oxfordshire County Council* (1963) 15 P. & C.R. 1.

[28] *Hidderley* v *Warwickshire County Council* (1963) 14 P. & C.R. 134.

[29] *T.A. Miller* v *Minister of Housing and Local Government* (1968) 19 P. & C.R. 263.

[30] One is not, of course, considering in this context the *desirability* of the particular change of use.

such an approach.[31] In *Devonshire County Council* v *Allens Caravans (Estates) Ltd.*,[32] for example, Lord Parker C.J. said: 'The materiality to be considered is a materiality from a planning point of view and, in particular, the question of amenities.' Though difficult questions may arise as to whether or not a particular matter is relevant to planning, it is clear that the effect which a particular change will have on a locality will often be important.[33] Matters such as increased noise,[34] changes in the volume of traffic or other activity or on-site sales generated by a new use,[35] increased demands on public services,[36] and provision of services and residents' length of stay in residential accommodation[37] may all be relevant.

In determining an appeal against an enforcement notice served in respect of the selling of a certain amount of heated food from a shop which sold a range of household convenience goods the reporter took account of the fact that only some of the food for sale in the shop was heated, that the sale of heated food only took place for a two hour period in the middle of the day, that the means employed for heating food did not have adverse environmental effects and that the premises continued to have the appearance and character of an ordinary retail shop rather than a hot food shop. The reporter's conclusion that there had not been such a change as to amount to a material change of use[38] was upheld by the Inner House of the Court of Session.[39]

Considerations which are not relevant to planning must, of course, be disregarded. It has been held that the identity of the person carrying on an

---

[31] See dicta in *Marshall* v *Nottingham City Corporation* [1960] 1 W.L.R. 707; *East Barnet U.D.C.* v *British Transport Commission* [1962] 2 Q.B. 484; *Devonshire County Council* v *Allens Caravans (Estates) Ltd.* (1962) 14 P. & C.R. 440; *Wilson* v *West Sussex C.C.* [1963] 2 Q.B. 764; *Williams* v *Minister of Housing and Local Government* (1967) 18 P. & C.R. 514; *Commercial and Residential Property Development Co.* v *Secretary of State for the Environment* (1981) 80 L.G.R. 443; and *Burkmar* v *Secretary of State for the Environment* (1984) 271 E.G. 377. See too appeal decisions noted in [1980] J.P.L. 282; and [1981] J.P.L. 612.

[32] Above.

[33] See, for example, appeal decisions noted in [1971] J.P.L. 72; [1980] J.P.L. 282 and 476; [1981] J.P.L. 612; and [1982] J.P.L. 199.

[34] See *Ross* v *Aberdeen County Council* 1955 S.L.T. (Sh.Ct.) 65; and appeal decisions noted in [1971] J.P.L. 172; [1972] J.P.L. 219; and [1979] J.P.L. 633. See too *Gray* v *Oxfordshire County Council* (1963) 15 P. & C.R. 1.

[35] See, for example, *Costas Chrysanthou* v *Secretary of State for the Environment* [1976] J.P.L. 371, per Lord Widgery C.J.; *Snook* v *Secretary of State for the Environment* (1975) 33 P. & C.R. 1, per Bridge J.; and *SPADS* Nos. A2286 (P/PPA/SD/2, 3rd March 1977); and A3256 (P/ENA/HA/7, 18th February 1980).

[36] See *Guildford R.D.C.* v *Penny* [1959] 2 Q.B. 112, per Lord Evershed M.R.

[37] See *Commercial and Residential Property Development Co.* v *Secretary of State for the Environment* (1981) 80 L.G.R. 443; *Winmill* v *Secretary of State for the Environment* [1982] J.P.L. 445; and *Breachberry Ltd.* v *Secretary of State for the Environment* [1985] J.P.L. 180.

[38] See *SPADS No.* A4367 (P/ENA/SL/161, 11th November 1982).

[39] *City of Glasgow District Council* v *Secretary of State for Scotland* 1985 S.L.T. 19.

activity,[40] a change in the ownership or source of supply[41] or means of subsequent disposal[42] of articles dealt with on the premises in question, and the degree of control exercised over parts of the premises by the individual occupiers of residential premises[43] are not relevant for this purpose.

(c) Intensification of use

Intensification of an existing use of land can have significant town planning consequences and may, if marked, amount to a material change in the use of the land.

In this connection the word 'intensification', according to Widgery J., 'is normally used to describe the situation which arises where an area of land is used throughout the relevant time for the same purpose but the intensity of the activity varies; a field may have been used for car-breaking at all material times, but for only three cars at one time and for thirty-three on another occasion.'[44] In *Royal Borough of Kensington and Chelsea v Secretary of State for the Environment*[45] Donaldson L.J. said that the word 'intensification' had to be used with very considerable circumspection; in this context 'intensification' meant a change to something different. The question is whether the intensification is so great as to affect what Lord Evershed M.R. called 'a definable character of the land and its use'.[46] We would therefore suggest that an intensification of use can only amount to a material change of use if it is in some way significant from a planning viewpoint.[47]

In *Guildford R.D.C. v Penny*[48] the Court of Appeal indicated (though it was not necessary to decide the point) that in appropriate circumstances increase or intensification of use was capable of constituting development and in *James v Secretary of State for Wales*[49] it was held that an increase from

[40] See *Lewis v Secretary of State for the Environment* (1971) 23 P. & C.R. 125; *East Barnet U.D.C. v British Transport Commission* [1962] 2 Q.B. 484; *Snook v Secretary of State for the Environment* (1975) 33 P. & C.R. 1; *Shephard v Buckinghamshire C.C.* (1966) 18 P. & C.R. 419; *Rael Brook v Minister of Housing and Local Government* [1967] 2 Q.B. 65; and appeal decisions noted in [1967] J.P.L. 173; [1971] J.P.L. 653; and [1981] J.P.L. 375.
[41] See *Lewis v Secretary of State for the Environment* (1971) 23 P. & C.R. 125; see too *Marshall v Nottingham City Corporation* [1960] 1 W.L.R. 707; and appeal decision noted in [1973] J.P.L. 654. However, as Lord Widgery pointed out in *Costas Chrysanthou v Secretary of State for the Environment* [1976] J.P.L. 371, cases such as *Williams v Minister of Housing and Local Government* (1967) 18 P. & C.R. 514 show that there can be a material change of use if a change in the ownership or source of supply of the articles dealt with is such as to greatly increase the volume of traffic, business or activity on the land. See too *Jones v Secretary of State for the Environment* (1974) 28 P. & C.R. 362.
[42] See *Snook v Secretary of State for the Environment* (1975) 33 P. & C.R. 1.
[43] See *Winmill v Secretary of State for the Environment* [1982] J.P.L. 445.
[44] *Brooks v Gloucestershire County Council* (1967) 19 P. & C.R. 90.
[45] [1981] J.P.L. 50.
[46] *Guildford R.D.C.v Penny* [1959] 2 Q.B. 112.
[47] See, for example, appeal decision noted in [1982] J.P.L. 534.
[48] Above: see too *dicta* in *East Barnet U.D.C. v British Transport Commission* [1962] 2 Q.B. 484; *Marshall v Nottingham City Corporation* [1960] 1 W.L.R. 707; and *de Mulder v Secretary of State for the Environment* [1974] Q.B. 792.
[49] [1966] 1 W.L.R. 135 (reversed in the House of Lords on other grounds: [1968] A.C. 409).

one to four in the number of caravans on a site could be a material change of use. In another case[50] Lord Denning M.R. said: 'I doubt very much whether the occupier could increase from twenty-four to seventy-eight [caravans] without permission. An increase in intensity of that order may well amount to a material change of use.'

In *Peake* v *Secretary of State for Wales*[51] the appellant had, as a part-time but profitable hobby, used his private garage for the repair and maintenance of vehicles; after being declared redundant in his employment in 1968 he carried on the business of vehicle maintenance at the garage on a full-time basis. The Divisional Court held that although the change from part-time to full-time activity could not of itself amount to a material change of use, the Secretary of State had been entitled to find that a material change of use had occurred by intensification in 1968.[52] In *Brooks and Burton* v *Secretary of State for the Environment*[53] the Court of Appeal held that there was ample evidence to support the Secretary of State's conclusion that there had been a material change of use by intensification where the manufacture of concrete blocks had increased from under 300,000 blocks per annum to about 1,200,000 blocks per annum. (It was, however, held that the change of use did not involve development since both uses fell within the same use class in the Use Classes Order.[54])

It may be difficult to judge in any particular case whether as a matter of fact and degree there has been such a change in the degree of an existing use as to constitute a material change of use. Where, for example, the number of lorries parked on a site was increased from one or two to about forty, the English minister decided that a material change of use had taken place.[55] On the other hand, in a Scottish appeal in 1981 the reporter took the view that where the number of paying guests living in a guest house had increased from about eight or ten to eighteen there had not been such an intensification as to amount to a material change in the use of the premises.[56]

(d) *When does a change of use occur?*

In *Caledonian Terminal Investments Ltd.* v *Edinburgh Corporation*[57] a majority of the Second Division of the Court of Session took the view that where planning permission has been granted for a change in the use of land,

---

[50] *Esdell Caravan Parks Ltd.* v *Hemel Hempstead R.D.C.* [1966] 1 Q.B. 895.

[51] (1971) 22 P. & C.R. 889; see too *Dyble* v *Minister of Housing and Local Government* (1966) 197 E.G. 457; and *Hipsey* v *Secretary of State for the Environment* [1984] J.P.L. 806.

[52] See also ministerial decision noted in [1974] J.P.L. 490.

[53] [1977] 1 W.L.R. 1294.

[54] See p. 160 below.

[55] [1960] J.P.L. 807. Other examples of intensification of a use being found to amount to a material change of use are to be found in *SPADS* Nos. A2314 (P/PPA/ST/1, 7th April 1977); and A3679 (P/PPA/GB/38, 16th April 1981); [1970] J.P.L. 717; [1974] J.P.L. 100 and 733; and [1977] J.P.L. 123.

[56] *SPADS* No. A3795 (P/ENA/LA/17, 29th June 1981). See too [1964] J.P.L. 363; [1970] J.P.L. 653; [1972] J.P.L. 270; [1973] J.P.L. 264; [1974] J.P.L. 101; [1978] J.P.L. 270 and 395; [1980] J.P.L. 771; and [1982] J.P.L. 534.

[57] 1970 S.C. 271; 1970 S.L.T. 362 (see p. 381 below).

the change of use does not take place until the land is actually put to the new use.[58] To similar effect, the English minister has expressed the view that where a new building is erected, either with or without planning permission, it has no use for the purposes of the planning legislation until it is actually used.[59] However, in *Impey* v *Secretary of State for the Environment*[60] Donaldson L.J. expressed the view that a change of use can take place before premises have actually been put to a new use, saying that in a case where premises had been converted for residential use and put on the market as available for letting, it was plain that there had on these facts been a change of use. We would submit that although the physical state of a building may be closely linked to a change in the use of that building there is much to commend the approach adopted in *Caledonian Terminal Investments*; an intention to make a change in the use of premises is very different from an actual change of use.

A material change of use may take place gradually over a period—for example, where an existing use is intensified; in such a case difficult questions of fact can arise as to precisely when the material change (and therefore development) occurred.

(e) *Discontinuance and abandonment of use*

The mere suspension of a use does not of itself amount to a material change in the use of land. In *Paul* v *Ayrshire County Council*[61] the Second Division of the Court of Session held that the exclusion of the public from a strip of ground did not constitute a material change in the use of the land, being merely a discontinuance of a use. The Lord Justice-Clerk (Lord Grant) declared: 'A discontinuance of use . . . is not a change of use; it is merely the first step towards a change, and there is no change until the second step (use for some different purpose) is taken.' He added:

'I can find nothing in the 1947 Act to indicate . . . that I need planning permission to cease using my residence as a dwellinghouse and leave it empty and abandoned. The question of permission arises only if I begin to use it as, for example, a shop or an office . . . The simple reason is that discontinuance of the previous use is not a material change of use and accordingly needs no planning permission.'

Similarly, as Ashworth J. said in *Hartley* v *Minister of Housing and Local Government*:[62] 'If land is put to more than one use, usually referred to as a

---

[58]   Section 275(5) of the 1972 Act, which deals with the 'initiation' of development, is not relevant in this context—see *Burn* v *Secretary of State for the Environment* (1971) 219 E.G. 586; *Impey* v *Secretary of State for the Environment* (1980) 47 P. & C.R. 157; and *Backer* v *Secretary of State for the Environment* (1982) 47 P. & C.R. 149.

[59]   See [1975] J.P.L. 616.

[60]   (1980) 47 P. & C.R. 157. See too *Backer* v *Secretary of State for the Environment* (1982) 47 P. & C.R. 149.

[61]   1964 S.C. 116; 1964 S.L.T. 207.

[62]   [1969] 2 Q.B. 46.

composite use, the cessation of one of the uses does not of itself constitute development.'[63] (If, however, as in *Wipperman* v *Barking London Borough Council*,[64] one of the component uses is allowed to absorb the site to the exclusion of another use, there can be a material change of use.)

Where the use of land has been suspended and is thereafter resumed without there having been any intervening different use, then *prima facie* the resumption does not constitute development.[65] However, in *Hartley* v *Minister of Housing and Local Government*[66] Lord Denning M.R. said: 'When a man ceases to use a site for a particular purpose, and lets it remain unused for a considerable time, then the proper inference may be that he has abandoned the former use.' Once a use has been abandoned, the landowner cannot, said Lord Denning, 'start to use the site again, unless he gets planning permission; and this is so even though the new use is the same as the previous one'.[67] In *Hartley's* case the Court of Appeal held, affirming the decision of the Divisional Court, that there were sufficient grounds to support the minister's finding that the previous use of a site for car sales, suspended between 1961 and 1965, had been abandoned and that the resumption of that use amounted, as a change from 'non-use' to a positive use, to a material change of use.[68]

It may be difficult to determine whether a use has merely been temporarily suspended or whether it has been abandoned. In *Hartley's* case Widgery L.J. treated the occupier's intention not to resume a use as an important indicator of abandonment, whereas Lord Denning appeared to favour the more objective test of whether a reasonable man would conclude from all the circumstances that a use had been abandoned.

However, in considering whether or not a use has been abandoned, the intention with which the use was ended would appear to be an important factor.[69] An intention to abandon a use might be inferred from the taking of some action inconsistent with retention of the right to resume that use—the removal, for example, of petrol pumps and the taking of action to render petrol storage tanks useless may indicate a clear intention to abandon the

[63]   See *Philglow* v *Secretary of State for the Environment* (1984) 270 E.G. 1192.
[64]   (1965) 17 P. & C.R. 225 (see p. 151 below).
[65]   See *Hartley* v *Minister of Housing and Local Government* [1969] 2 Q.B. 46, per Ashworth J.
[66]   [1970] 1 Q.B. 413.
[67]   In *Pioneer Aggregates (U.K.) Ltd.* v *Secretary of State for the Environment* [1984] 3 W.L.R. 32 (see p. 270 below) the House of Lords held that a planning permission could not be abandoned, but cast no doubt on the concept of abandonment of existing use rights.
[68]   See too *Miller-Mead* v *Minister of Housing and Local Government* [1963] 2 Q.B. 196; *T.A. Miller* v *Minister of Housing and Local Government* (1968) 19 P. & C.R. 263; *Draco* v *Oxfordshire C.C.* (1972) 224 E.G. 1037; *Ratcliffe* v *Secretary of State for the Environment* (1975) 235 E.G. 901; and *Nicholls* v *Secretary of State for the Environment* [1981] J.P.L. 890.
[69]   See, for example, *Gredley (Investment Developments) Co. Ltd.* v *London Borough of Newham* (1973) 26 P. & C.R. 400; and *Wheatfield Inns (Belfast) Ltd.* v *Croft Inns Ltd.* [1978] N.I. 83; see too appeal decisions noted in [1973] J.P.L. 48; [1980] J.P.L. 759; [1982] J.P.L. 119, 194 and 801; and [1983] J.P.L. 129 and 375.

use of the land in question as a petrol filling station.[70] If, after suspension of a particular use, land has been put to some different use, that fact may be relevant as indicating an intention to abandon the original use.[71] Where, however, a change has been made from one use to another without any intervening period of non-use, there is no place for the concept of abandonment.[72] The making of a planning application for a different use of the land may provide some indication of the landowner's intentions[73] but is clearly not conclusive evidence of an intention to abandon a use.[74]

The length of the period of discontinuance of a use will usually be relevant but even a long period may not be conclusive evidence of an intention to abandon the use.[75] The physical condition of the land or any building may also be a relevant factor. In one Scottish appeal, for example, the ruinous state of a cottage was one of the factors which led the Secretary of State to conclude that the residential use of the premises had been abandoned.[76]

In *Grover's Executors* v *Rickmansworth U.D.C.*[77] the Lands Tribunal held that the fact that the use of land had been brought to an end and the land offered for sale with vacant possession did not show an intention to abandon the use; such action was consistent with a desire to obtain a more favourable price for the land. Nor did the service of a purchase notice provide a conclusive indication of intention to abandon the use.

(f) *Seasonal or periodic uses*

Where land is put to a seasonal or periodic use—where, for example, land is used as a fairground in the summer months or where it is used as a racecourse for only a few days each year—and is not used for any other purpose for the remainder of the year, the cessation and resumption each year do not amount to a material change of use.[78]

---

[70] [1972] J.P.L. 577 (upheld in *Draco* (above)). See too [1971] J.P.L. 457; and [1977] J.P.L. 326.

[71] See *Grillo* v *Minister of Housing and Local Government* (1968) 208 E.G. 1201; *Maddern* v *Secretary of State for the Environment* [1980] J.P.L. 676; *Balco Transport Services* v *Secretary of State for the Environment* (1981) 45 P. & C.R. 216; [1969] J.P.L. 707; and [1984] J.P.L. 451.

[72] See *Young* v *Secretary of State for the Environment* (1983) 47 P. & C.R. 165 (C.A.) (This point was not considered in the House of Lords: [1983] 2 A.C. 662). See too *Balco Transport Services Ltd.* v *Secretary of State for the Environment* (1981) 45 P. & C.R. 216; and appeal decision noted in [1982] J.P.L. 798.

[73] See appeal decision noted in [1981] J.P.L. 914.

[74] See, for example, *SPADS* No. A4013 (P/PPA/FB/82; P/DEV/1/FB/2, 19th January 1982) (in which the reporter concluded that although the owners of a building had at one stage conceived of abandoning a particular use, the intention to abandon the use had itself been abandoned). See too [1971] J.P.L. 244.

[75] See, for example, *Fyson* v *Buckinghamshire County Council* [1958] 1 W.L.R. 634; and appeal decisions noted in [1982] J.P.L. 794; [1983] J.P.L. 129; and [1984] J.P.L. 207.

[76] *SPADS* No. A3254 (P/PPA/CC/43; P/DEV/1/CC/1, 15th February 1980). See too appeal decisions noted in [1978] J.P.L. 651; and [1979] J.P.L. 551.

[77] (1959) 10 P. & C.R. 417.

[78] See *Hawes* v *Thornton Cleveleys U.D.C.* (1965) 17 P. & C.R. 22.

In *Webber* v *Minister of Housing and Local Government*[79] the Court of Appeal held (disapproving *dicta* in earlier cases) that where land had been used over a period of years for agriculture in the winter and for camping in the summer, the seasonal change from camping to agriculture or vice versa did not involve a material change of use for the purposes of the planning legislation; the 'normal use' of the land from year to year was for two purposes and so long as that normal use continued from year to year there was no material change of use.

(g) *Extinguishment of use*

In *Petticoat Lane Rentals Ltd.* v *Secretary of State for the Environment*[80] Widgery L.J. said that the 'question of how far existing planning rights can be lost by the occupier obtaining and implementing an inconsistent planning permission has not as yet been fully developed in the authorities'. That is probably still the case but the opinions of the House of Lords in *Newbury District Council* v *Secretary of State for the Environment*[81] and the decision of the Court of Appeal in *Jennings Motors Ltd.* v *Secretary of State for the Environment*[82] shed a good deal of light on how this question should be approached. Although it is clear, as Lord Scarman said in one case,[83] that 'existing use rights are hardy beasts with a great capacity for survival', in the *Newbury* case the House of Lords agreed that if the carrying out of development on land resulted in the creation of a 'new planning unit' or the beginning of a 'new chapter of planning history', the consequence was that existing use rights attaching to the land in question were extinguished.[84] The main question to be considered, therefore, is what are the circumstances in which a 'new planning unit' is created or a 'new chapter in the planning history' of a site begun.

The early decisions. The earliest decision on this matter is *Prossor* v *Minister of Housing and Local Government*.[85] In that case planning permission had been obtained for the rebuilding of a petrol filling station subject to a condition that no retail sales other than of motor accessories should take place on the site. The appellant displayed on the site second-hand cars for sale, claiming that there was attached to the land an existing use right for the display and sale of cars. Though it was held that he had not been able to establish this claim, the Divisional Court also held that the appellant was bound by the condition attached to the planning permission. Lord Parker C.J. stated:

---

[79] [1968] 1 W.L.R. 29. See too [1981] J.P.L. 449.
[80] [1971] 1 W.L.R. 1112; and see E. Young, 'The Planning Unit' (1983) 28 J.L.S.S. 339 and 371.
[81] [1981] A.C. 578.
[82] [1982] Q.B. 541.
[83] *Pioneer Aggregates (U.K.) Ltd.* v *Secretary of State for the Environment* [1984] 3 W.L.R. 32.
[84] Existing use rights can also be lost by the implementation of a planning permission imposing conditions on the future use of the land (see p. 241 below).
[85] (1968) 67 L.G.R. 109.

'by adopting the permission granted . . . the appellant's predecessor . . . gave up any possible existing use rights in that regard which he may have had. The planning history of this site, as it were, seems to me to begin afresh . . . with the grant of this permission, a permission which was taken up and used.'

One phase of the planning history had been brought to an end and another had started.

In *Leighton and Newman Car Sales Ltd.* v *Secretary of State for the Environment*[86] the Court of Appeal held, on facts very similar to those in *Prossor*, that premises which had been rebuilt under a planning permission constituted a completely new and different planning unit to which the previous use of the original premises was irrelevant.

In *Petticoat Lane Rentals* v *Secretary of State for the Environment*[87] planning permission was granted for the erection of a building on a cleared site which had previously been used as an open-air market. The open ground floor of the building was to be used for car parking and loading. The planning permission expressly provided that this ground floor area might be used for market trading on Sundays but said nothing about such trading on weekdays. After the permission had been implemented the ground floor area was used for market trading on weekdays as well as on Sundays. The Divisional Court held that where a clear area of ground is developed by the erection of a building over the whole of the land, the previous planning unit ceases to exist; the land as such is merged in the new building and a new planning unit with no planning history results. Any existing rights attaching to the previous planning unit are automatically extinguished and any use not authorised by the planning permission can be restrained. As the planning permission in this case did not authorise use for market trading on weekdays, that use was a breach of planning control. A majority of the court reserved for future consideration what the position would be if the whole of the land was not redeveloped by being covered by a building; that matter is considered below.

As is evident from the cases mentioned above, judges have sometimes spoken, in the context of the extinguishment of existing use rights, of the creation of a 'new planning unit', sometimes of a 'new chapter in planning history' being started. Any difference between the terms is, it seems, largely a matter of semantics.[88] The important point is that both phrases are used to

---

[86] (1976) 32 P. & C.R. 1. See too *J. Toomey Motors Ltd.* v *Basildon District Council* [1982] J.P.L. 775.

[87] [1971] 1 W.L.R. 1112.

[88] See the judgments of the majority of the Court of Appeal in *Jennings Motors* (above); see too the opinions of Lord Scarman and Lord Lane in *Newbury* (above). In extinguishment cases the term 'planning unit' is being employed in a primarily temporal sense, rather than in the primarily 'territorial' sense considered above (see pp. 126–133). The use of the same term in these rather different senses might be thought unfortunate but in *Jennings Motors* the majority of the Court of Appeal considered that the expression 'new planning unit' was hallowed by usage and should be retained to include the concept of a break in the planning history of a site. Lord Denning thought otherwise.

describe the situation where, as in the *Prossor, Leighton and Newman* and *Petticoat Lane Rental* cases, a change in the physical nature of premises or in their planning status is so radical as to give rise to the inference that any prior use is being given up and a new planning history begun. In effect, the slate is wiped clean. In *Jennings Motors Ltd.* v *Secretary of State for the Environment*[89] the Court of Appeal held that it was in every case a question of fact and degree whether an alteration in the physical nature of a site or in its planning status was so radical as to lead to the extinguishment of existing use rights.

When are rights extinguished? In *Aston* v *Secretary of State for the Environment*[90] the Divisional Court had to consider the position where a new building did not cover the whole of the site in question. Lord Widgery expressed the view that whenever a new building was erected, that part of the land covered by the new building was merged with it and a new planning unit was thereby created. 'One starts', he said, 'with a new planning unit that has no permitted planning uses except those derived from the planning permission, if any, and from section 33(2) of the Act of 1971,[91] which allows such a building . . . to be used for the purpose for which it was designed.' If, as was the case in *Aston*, the building was erected without planning permission, it had, the Divisional Court agreed, no permitted use at all.

However, in *Jennings Motors* the Court of Appeal held that the mere erection of a new building does not automatically create a new planning unit. It is merely one of the factors to be taken into account in considering whether, in Oliver L.J.'s words, 'there has taken place in relation to the particular land under consideration a change of so radical a nature as to constitute a "break in the planning history" or a "new planning unit"'. The principle enunciated by Lord Widgery in *Aston* was therefore too widely expressed. However, the majority of the Court of Appeal considered there was no ground for thinking *Aston* to have been wrongly decided on its facts. In *Aston* the new building replaced an earlier building, destroyed eight years previously, that had covered less than half the available area. The new building covered 90 per cent of the available area. There had therefore been a very substantial change in the physical nature of the site.

In *Jennings Motors* the Secretary of State, in deciding an enforcement appeal, had taken the view that the unauthorised erection of a building occupying about 6 per cent of the area of a particular site automatically resulted in the creation of a new planning unit, and therefore of a building which had no permitted use.[92] The Court of Appeal held that the Secretary of State had misdirected himself in law; it was a question of fact and degree

---

[89] [1982] Q.B. 541.
[90] (1973) 43 P. & C.R. 331.
[91] Section 33(2) of the Town and Country Planning Act 1971 is similar in its terms to s.30(2) of the 1972 Act—see p. 257 below.
[92] The planning authority could, of course, have taken enforcement action in respect of the unauthorised building operation but chose instead to serve an enforcement notice alleging that a material change in the use of the site had taken place.

whether the change in question was so radical as to lead to the extinguishment of existing use rights.[93] Where the erection of a new building does not
effect such a radical change as to result in the loss of existing use rights, those
use rights will continue to attach to the site inside the new building.

Physical operations are more likely to lead to the application of the
doctrine of extinguishment of use than a mere change in the use of land,[94] but
the view was expressed by the House of Lords in the *Newbury* case and by
the majority of the Court of Appeal in *Jennings Motors* that a change in the
planning status of a site, such as its sub-division into smaller units or its
incorporation into a larger planning unit, may lead to the inference that a
new chapter in planning history has been started. It might be suggested that
the same principle will apply to the demolition of a building.[95]

(h) *Multiple uses*

Primary and ancillary uses. Where several activities are carried on within a
single 'planning unit' it may be possible to recognise a single primary
purpose to which the land is put and to which the other uses of the land are
ancillary or incidental. In such a case it is the primary purpose which
determines the use of the unit as a whole.[96] This principle was well illustrated
by Lord Denning M.R. in *Brazil (Concrete) Ltd.* v *Amersham R.D.C.*[97] His
Lordship said:

> 'Take for instance, Harrods Store. The unit is the whole building. The
> greater part is used for selling goods: but some parts are used for ancillary
> purposes, such as for offices and for packing articles for dispatch. The
> character of the whole is determined by its primary use as a shop. It is
> within Class I of the Use Classes Order. The ancillary use of part as an
> office does not bring it within Class II: and the ancillary use of part for
> packing does not make it a light industrial building within Class III.'

Rights to change within unit. Where part of a single planning unit has been
put to a use different from, but ancillary to, the primary use of the unit, it
would seem that no development will be involved in using that part for the
main use or for another use ancillary to the main use.[98] Where, for example,
it was proposed to use as offices a caretaker's flat in an office block, the
proposed change was held not to involve development.[99] And where the

---

[93] See too *Joyce Shopfitters Ltd.* v *Secretary of State for the Environment* [1976] J.P.L. 236;
      Hilliard v *Secretary of State for the Environment* (1978) 37 P. and C.R. 129; and Oliver
      L.J.'s comment on those cases in *Jennings Motors.*
[94] See, however, *J. Toomey Motors Ltd.* v *Basildon District Council* [1982] J.P.L. 775.
[95] See *Joyce Shopfitters Ltd.* v *Basildon District Council* [1976] J.P.L. 236.
[96] See p. 125 above.
[97] (1967) 18 P. & C.R. 396.
[98] See, for example, *Vickers-Armstrong* v *Central Land Board* (1957) 9 P. & C.R. 33; and
      Bulletin of Selected Appeal Decisions, XI/21.
[99] [1975] J.P.L. 685. See too appeal decisions noted in [1977] J.P.L. 464; [1978] J.P.L. 578;
      [1979] J.P.L. 784; and [1982] J.P.L. 534.

primary use of a site was boat-building and repair, the English minister quashed an enforcement notice which alleged that a change in the use of part of the site from car parking to boat sales constituted a breach of planning control; both these uses were ancillary to the primary use and in giving his decision the minister stated: 'It is not considered that the change of use of the appeal land from one purpose ancillary to the business use of the premises to another ancillary use of the premises can be said to involve a material change of use which would constitute development requiring a grant of planning permission.'[1]

In like manner, the introduction upon land of a new use which is merely ancillary to the primary use of the planning unit will not amount to a material change of use. In *Borough of Restormel* v *Secretary of State for the Environment*,[2] for example, a caravan was stationed in the grounds of a hotel. The caravan was to provide sleeping accommodation for two waitresses in the summer season but was not capable of being used as a self-contained living unit. Forbes J. upheld the inspector's conclusion that the use was ancillary to that of the hotel and did not therefore involve development.

So long as it remains ancillary to the main use, the scale of an ancillary use may be varied without there being any material change in the use of the planning unit but if an ancillary use develops to such an extent as to become the main use of the unit or to become a separate use in its own right, it may be that the right conclusion on the facts is that a material change of use has occurred. In *Jones* v *Secretary of State for the Environment*,[3] for example, it was held that the minister was entitled to find that a material change of use had occurred when the use of premises for the purpose of a road haulage business with ancillary manufacture of trailers was changed to the manufac-ture of trailers for outside sale. The activity formerly carried on as ancillary to the primary use had itself become 'level to the standard of a primary use'.

The right to use land for some ancillary purpose will, of course, be lost when the primary use ceases.

When is a use ancillary? The question whether a particular use is ancillary to another use or is itself a separate and distinct use will not always admit of an easy answer; factors such as the character and intensity of the uses in question, the proportion of the planning unit devoted to each activity and the degree to which one of the uses is dependent on another would appear to

[1]   [1972] J.P.L. 37. See too [1979] J.P.L. 54.
[2]   [1982] J.P.L. 785.
[3]   (1974) 28 P. & C.R. 362. See too *Frith* v *Minister of Housing and Local Government* (1969) 210 E.G. 213; *Snook* v *Secretary of State for the Environment* (1975) 33 P. & C.R. 1; *Costas Chrysanthou* v *Secretary of State for the Environment* [1976] J.P.L. 371; *Pollock* v *Secretary of State for the Environment* (1979) 40 P. & C.R. 94; *L.R. Jillings* v *Secretary of State for the Environment* [1984] J.P.L. 32; and appeal decisions noted in [1973] J.P.L. 666; [1974] J.P.L. 614; [1975] J.P.L. 687; [1976] J.P.L. 196; [1977] J.P.L. 190; [1983] J.P.L. 400; and *SPADS* Nos. A3922 (P/PPA/ST/32; P/ENA/ST/21, 14th October 1981); A3930 (P/ENA/SK/3, 12th October 1981); and A4886 (P/ENA/FB/47, 1st November 1983).

be relevant.[4] A flat situated over a shop might, for example, be regarded as being used for a purpose ancillary to the shop if the occupier of the flat carried out duties connected with the shop, so that his living on the premises facilitated the operation of the shop; a different conclusion would probably be appropriate in a case where it would make little difference to the operation of the shop if the occupant of the flat lived elsewhere.[5] Where two thirds of the output of a bakery was sold from a shop in the same building, the English minister held the bakery use to be ancillary to the shop use,[6] but where, on the other hand, a bakery in a yard behind a shop supplied not only that shop but also several other shops, the minister concluded that the bakery was a light industrial use in its own right.[7]

In *Emma Hotels Ltd.* v *Secretary of State for the Environment*[8] the Secretary of State had taken the view that the use of part of a private hotel as a non-residents' bar was not an incident of the hotel use but a separate use in its own right. The minister had regard to the scale of use of the bar by non-residents, the manner in which the bar was operated and advertised, its distinctive character and appearance and the fact that it could be readily isolated physically from the remainder of the premises. The Divisional Court held, however, that the matters relied on by the Secretary of State were insufficient to justify his conclusion that the non-residents' bar was not an incident of the hotel use.

The question whether one use is ancillary to another can arise in a great variety of contexts. Although the decision in each case will depend very much on the facts and circumstances of that particular case, a few examples may be of interest.

The English minister has held, for example, that tyre fitting and wheel balancing were ancillary to the use of premises for the retail sale of tyres;[9] that the use of the basement of a hotel as a night club was ancillary to the hotel use;[10] that the residential use of a flat above a bank was ancillary to the bank use;[11] that servicing of vehicles and the carrying out of minor repairs was incidental to the sale of vehicles;[12] that the stationing of several caravans on a site was incidental to the main use of the land as a holiday camp;[13] and

---

[4]   See, for example, appeal decisions noted in *Scottish Bulletin of Selected Appeal Decisions*, I/8; [1976] J.P.L. 328; [1980] J.P.L. 58; [1984] J.P.L. 826; and *SPADS* Nos. A3881 (P/PPA/FC/36; P/ENA/FC/10, 4th September 1981); and A3021 (P/PPA/SL/56, 19th June 1979).

[5]   See *Vyner* v *Secretary of State for the Environment* [1977] J.P.L. 795.

[6]   *Bulletin of Selected Appeal Decisions*, XIII/24.

[7]   *Bulletin of Selected Appeal Decisions*, XIII/25. See too *Costas Chrysanthou* v *Secretary of State for the Environment* [1976] J.P.L. 371. But contrast *SPADS* No. A3768 (P/ENA/LA/36, 11th June 1981).

[8]   (1980) 41 P. & C.R. 255; and see [1979] J.P.L. 390. See, however, the comment on *Emma Hotels* in *Lydcare Ltd.* v *Secretary of State for the Environment* (1983) 47 P. & C.R. 336. Contrast *SPADS* No. A3127 (P/PPA/SQ/59, 10th September 1979).

[9]   *Selected Enforcement and Allied Appeals*, p. 33.

[10]   [1978] J.P.L. 869.

[11]   [1978] J.P.L. 333.

[12]   [1974] J.P.L. 41.

[13]   [1980] J.P.L. 126.

that the use of a shop forecourt for parking was incidental to the shop use.[14]

On the other hand, it has been held that the storage and sale of furniture in a church building, though for the benefit of the church and other charities, was not ancillary to the church use;[15] that the use of a school for social functions was not incidental to the overall use of the planning unit for educational purposes;[16] that the showing of films in booths was not ancillary to the use of premises as a shop;[17] that the sale of petrol was not ancillary to the use of premises for car sales and repairs;[18] that the sale of food and household goods was not ancillary to use as a petrol filling station;[19] that use of part of a farm for the keeping of cattle in transit was not ancillary to the agricultural use of the land;[20] that the installation of amusement machines in a fish and chip shop[21] or in a retail shop[22] was not ancillary to the shop use; that the keeping and ritual slaughter of poultry in shop premises was not ancillary to the shop use;[23] and that the sale of alcoholic drinks to significant numbers of customers who were not also having meals on the premises was not ancillary to the use of premises as a restaurant.[24]

The retail sale from an agricultural holding of the produce of that holding is normally accepted as being a use ancillary to the use of the land for agriculture,[25] but 'the adaptation for sale of that produce on the holding is not regarded as ancillary to the use of the land for agriculture, and neither is the sale of the produce from the holding after processing elsewhere'.[26]

Dwellings. It would seem that the use, beyond the merely trivial, of even a small part of a private residence for the carrying on of commercial or industrial activities is normally to be regarded as involving a material change

---

[14] See, for example, [1956] J.P.L. 74; [1959] J.P.L. 812; and [1972] J.P.L. 474. See too *SPADS* No. A2868 (P/ENA/SC/8, 15th December 1978) (storage of pallets and crates in the forecourt of a dairy held ancillary to the dairy use of the premises); and [1984] J.P.L. 889.

[15] [1978] J.P.L. 126.

[16] [1978] J.P.L. 51.

[17] [1980] J.P.L. 58; and see *S.J.D. Properties Ltd.* v *Secretary of State for the Environment* [1981] J.P.L. 673; and *Lydcare Ltd.* v *Secretary of State for the Environment* (1983) 47 P. & C.R. 336, upheld by the Court of Appeal: [1984] J.P.L. 809.

[18] See *Ben Jay Auto Sales* v *Minister of Housing and Local Government* (1964) 16 P. & C.R. 50.

[19] [1975] J.P.L. 687.

[20] See *Warnock* v *Secretary of State for the Environment* [1980] J.P.L. 590.

[21] See *SPADS* No. A4715 (P/ENA/CB/45, 7th July 1983).

[22] See *SPADS* No. A4621 (P/ENA/CB/37, 9th May 1983). Contrast *SPADS* No. A4390 (P/ENA/GE/5, 29th November 1982).

[23] See *Hussain* v *Secretary of State for the Environment* (1971) 23 P. & C.R. 330; and *Ahmed* v *Birmingham Corporation* (1972) 224 E.G. 689.

[24] See *SPADS* Nos. A4933 (P/DEV/1/SL/2, 13th December 1983); and A4966 (P/PPA/SD/23, 24th January 1984).

[25] See, for example, *Haigh* v *Secretary of State for the Environment* [1983] J.P.L. 40; and appeal decision noted in [1974] J.P.L. 165. A retail sales use will only be ancillary to an agricultural use of land if most of the produce sold is grown on the land—see, for example, ministerial decision noted in [1973] J.P.L. 386.

[26] [1974] J.P.L. 165; and [1977] J.P.L. 740. See too *London Borough of Bromley* v *George Haeltschi & Son Ltd.* [1978] J.P.L. 45.

DEVELOPMENT

151

in the use of the premises;[27] the use for commercial or industrial purposes involves a completely different kind of use, a use which cannot normally be regarded as ancillary or incidental to the main use of the premises as a dwelling-house.[28] Use of the living room of a private house on three evenings per week for the receipt of taxi bookings by telephone and for the radio control of fifteen taxis (none of which normally called at the house) was, for example, held by the English minister to involve a material change in the use of the premises.[29] Section 19(2)(d) of the 1972 Act specifically provides that use of the curtilage of a dwelling-house for any purpose incidental to the enjoyment of the dwelling-house as such does not involve development (see p. 152 below).

Multiple use—other aspects. Where several activities are being carried on upon the planning unit, one of those activities may be so insignificant that it can, for planning purposes, be disregarded. Where, for example, the dining room of a flat was used for business purposes but no clients visited the premises, all the business was conducted by telephone, and no one but the occupier of the flat worked on the premises, the reporter concluded that no material change in the use of the flat had taken place.[30]

Where two or more separate uses are carried on within a single planning unit, the mere cessation of one of the component activities does not in itself amount to a material change of use but if one of the component activities is allowed to absorb the entire site to the exclusion of the other uses, there may be a material change of use.[31] In *Hartley* v *Minister of Housing and Local Government*[32] Ashworth J. said:

---

[27] See, for example, ministerial decisions noted in [1968] J.P.L. 485; [1971] J.P.L. 287; [1972] J.P.L. 339; and [1974] J.P.L. 554. Contrast decisions noted in [1963] J.P.L. 677; and [1971] J.P.L. 529.

[28] In an early circular (D.H.S. Circular 16/1949) the Secretary of State said that he would not regard it as a material change of use for a professional man such as a doctor or dentist to use one or two rooms in his private dwelling for consultation purposes, so long as that use remained ancillary to the main residential use. One might now doubt whether such use can automatically be regarded as ancillary to the residential use of premises: see appeal decision noted in [1984] J.P.L. 599.

[29] [1971] J.P.L. 533; see too *Cook* v *Secretary of State for Wales* (1971) 220 E.G. 1433; *SPADS* Nos. A4900 (P/ENA/D/53, 14th November 1983); and A4977 (P/PPA/SP/65, 14th February 1984). Contrast *SPADS* No. A4712 (P/ENA/FB/43, 6th July 1983).

[30] *SPADS* No. A3767 (P/ENA/SL/139, 11th June 1981). Contrast decision noted in [1982] J.P.L. 330. See too [1974] J.P.L. 490 (part-time work from home); and [1972] J.P.L. 273 (occasional retail sales from warehouse).

[31] See *Wipperman* v *Barking London Borough Council* (1965) 17 P. & C.R. 225; *Brooks* v *Gloucestershire County Council* (1968) 19 P. & C.R. 90; *Emma Hotels* v *Secretary of State for the Environment* [1979] J.P.L. 390, per Bridge L.J.; and *Cook* v *Secretary of State for the Environment* [1982] J.P.L. 644; and appeal decisions noted in [1974] J.P.L. 677; [1978] J.P.L. 871; and [1981] J.P.L. 449. In *Bromsgrove District Council* v *Secretary of State for the Environment* [1977] J.P.L. 797 Forbes J. seems to have regarded the *Wipperman* decision as depending on intensification of use. However, the principle in *Wipperman* seems rather different.

[32] [1969] 2 Q.B. 46.

'If one of two or more composite uses is discontinued and thereafter resumed, the question whether such resumption constitutes development is a question of fact to be determined in the light of all the relevant circumstances. Much will depend on the nature of the uses, what portion of the site was devoted to the discontinued use, what use (if any) was made of that portion during the period of discontinuance, how long the discontinuance lasted and so on.'

What might appear to be separate uses of land may have to be treated for planning purposes as a single use. This possibility is illustrated by the decision in *Re St. Winifred's, Kenley*.[33] In that case premises used partly as offices and partly as laboratories were held to have a single use as an industrial research establishment, which use involved elements of laboratory work and of office work but was distinct from use as either laboratories or offices alone; 'what one has here', said Pennycuick J., 'is a single use involving widely disparate activities'.

C. USES SPECIFICALLY DECLARED NOT TO INVOLVE DEVELOPMENT

Section 19(2) of the 1972 Act has the effect of excluding from the definition of development certain changes of use. Since 'use' does not include the use of land for the carrying out of any building or other operations thereon (s.275), such operations are not excepted from the statutory definition by the provisions of s.19(2).

1. *Use of curtilage of dwellinghouse*
The use of any buildings or other land within the curtilage of a dwellinghouse for any purpose incidental to the enjoyment of the dwellinghouse as such does not involve development (s.19(2)(d)).[34]

The word 'curtilage' is not defined in the 1972 Act but in *Sinclair-Lockhart's Trustees* v *Central Land Board*[35] Lord Mackintosh declared that:

'ground which is used for the comfortable enjoyment of a house or other building may be regarded in law as being within the curtilage of that house or building and thereby as an integral part of the same, although it has not been marked off or enclosed in any way. It is enough that it serves the

---

[33] (1969) 20 P. & C.R. 583. See too appeal decisions noted in [1980] J.P.L. 693; and [1982] J.P.L. 115.

[34] Since it is now clear that the use of land for a purpose which is merely ancillary to the main use of that land does not involve development (see above), it may be that this specific provision is unnecessary.

[35] 1951 S.C. 258; 1951 S.L.T. 121. See too *Re St. John's Church, Bishop's Hatfield* [1967] P. 113; *Methuen-Campbell* v *Walters* [1979] Q.B. 525; *Attorney-General* v *Calderdale Borough Council* [1983] J.P.L. 310; *SPADS* No. A3353 (P/PPA/SH/21; HJM/A/SH/3, 12th June 1980); and appeal decision noted in [1983] J.P.L. 68.

purposes of the house or building in some necessary or reasonably useful way.'

That statement was approved by the Second Division of the Court of Session in *Paul* v *Ayrshire County Council.*[36]

In *Paul* the owner of a house acquired a strip of ground which lay adjacent to his property and which had previously been used by the public as a means of access to a golf course. The landowner proceeded to enclose the land and to incorporate it into his garden. It was held that the use of the strip of land as garden ground was, in terms of the legislation, a use of land within the curtilage of a dwellinghouse for a purpose incidental to the use of the dwellinghouse as such and thus did not constitute development. The reasoning behind the court's decision in *Paul* that the strip of ground was within the curtilage of the dwellinghouse at the time of the change of use is somewhat difficult to understand; it may be that the timetable of events in this case—the purchase of the unfinished house and the incorporation of the strip of ground into the garden could apparently be regarded as a 'single operation' on the part of the landowner—was a significant factor in the decision. In general, one would expect that where land previously used for agriculture or for some other purpose which is not incidental to the use of a dwellinghouse has been brought into the curtilage of a dwelling and used as garden ground or for some other purpose incidental to the enjoyment of the dwellinghouse, it will be held that development of the land has taken place.[37]

The word 'dwellinghouse' is not defined in the 1972 Act. In *Gravesham Borough Council* v *Secretary of State for the Environment*[38] McCullough J. held that the question whether or not a particular building is a dwellinghouse is one of fact but that a distinctive characteristic of a dwellinghouse is its ability to afford the facilities required for day-to-day private domestic existence. The English minister has expressed the view that for the purposes of the present statutory provision a 'dwellinghouse' means 'a single private dwellinghouse used for occupation by one family only[39] and does not include a house or bungalow used exclusively for letting to holidaymakers throughout the year'.[40] That statement was made in the letter giving the minister's decision on an appeal which concerned, *inter alia*, the use of land within the

---

[36] 1964 S.C. 116; 1964 S.L.T. 207.

[37] See *Sampson's Executors* v *Nottingham County Council* [1949] 2 K.B. 439, per Lord Goddard; *SPADS* No. A3921 (P/PPA/SS/53; P/ENA/SS/27-30, 12th October 1981); and [1979] J.P.L. 189.

[38] (1982) 47 P. & C.R. 142. See too *Scurlock* v *Secretary of State for Wales* (1977) 33 P. & C.R. 202; *SPADS* No. A3254 (P/PPA/CC/43, 15th February 1980); and appeal decision noted in [1976] J.P.L. 326. Where operations are carried out to convert a building to a dwelling, the change of use to dwellinghouse can, it seems, take place before the building is actually used for the new purpose—see p. 141 above.

[39] See, however, *SPADS* No. A3801 (P/PPA/D/69; P/ENA/D/39 and 40, 3rd July 1981) in which the reporter was satisfied that although the appeal property was occupied by three households, in the absence of any sub-division of the property it was still appropriate to treat it as a 'dwellinghouse' for the purposes of s.19(2)(d).

[40] [1974] J.P.L. 241.

curtilage of a dwellinghouse for the stationing of a caravan used to accommodate paying guests who could not be found sleeping accommodation in the house itself. The minister concluded that the use of the caravan 'as an integral part of the commercial use' of the dwellinghouse could not be regarded as 'incidental to the personal enjoyment or domestic needs of a private occupier' and therefore did not come within the subsection; the use of the caravan in this way constituted development.

Whether or not a particular use is for a purpose 'incidental to the enjoyment of the dwellinghouse as such' is generally a question of fact and degree. Use of land within the curtilage of a dwellinghouse for parking a private car or for storing a private caravan will come within s.19(2)(d),[41] whereas the parking of commercial vehicles may well fall outside it.[42] Where a building or caravan situated within the curtilage of a house is used or is capable of use as a separate residential unit it will not normally be possible to treat that use as being for a purpose incidental to the enjoyment of the dwellinghouse as such;[43] where, however, such a building or caravan is merely used to provide additional sleeping or living accommodation for persons who also make some substantial use of the dwellinghouse, the position may well be different.[44] The use of land or buildings within the curtilage of a dwellinghouse for the purposes of a hobby or spare-time activity will normally come within the exception but may cease to do so if the hobby or activity grows into a purely commercial use or comes to be carried on on a very substantial scale.[45]

2. Use for agriculture or forestry

The use of any land[46] for the purposes of agriculture or forestry (including afforestation) and the use for any of those purposes of any building occupied together with land so used is not to be taken to involve development (s.19(2)(e)). Whatever the previous use of land, a change to use for the

---

[41]   See, for example, *SPADS* No. A3237 (P/PPA/SL/78, 30th January 1980).

[42]   See, for example, *SPADS* Nos. A2815 (P/ENA/LA/15, 12th October 1978) (parking of ice-cream van); A3030 (P/ENA/LA/20, 26th June 1979) (parking of taxi); and A4856 (P/ENA/LA/62, 4th October 1983) (parking of mobile shop). See too [1971] J.P.L. 646; [1974] J.P.L. 610 and 672; [1976] J.P.L. 529; [1977] J.P.L. 397; [1978] J.P.L. 789; and [1980] J.P.L. 209.

[43]   See, for example, *SPADS* Nos. A2833 (P/ENA/HA/4, 17th October 1978); A3444 (P/ENA/HC/9, 23rd September 1980); A3445 (P/PPA/HC/47; P/ENA/HC/11, 23rd September 1980); A3616 (P/PPA/D/78, 18th February 1981); [1965] J.P.L. 319; and [1971] J.P.L. 187.

[44]   See, for example, *SPADS* No. A3373 (P/ENA/D/37, 1st July 1980); [1970] J.P.L. 233; and [1976] J.P.L. 586.

[45]   See, for example, *SPADS* No. A2965 (P/ENA/FA/7, 19th April 1979); [1971] J.P.L. 642; [1972] J.P.L. 339; [1976] J.P.L. 588; [1977] J.P.L. 116 and 192; [1978] J.P.L. 200; [1980] J.P.L. 472; and [1984] J.P.L. 288 and 291.

[46]   'Land' includes buildings (see 1972 Act, s.275) and accordingly the use of a building for an agricultural purpose is not development and does not require planning permission even if the agricultural use is in no way dependent upon the land on which the building stands—*North Warwickshire Borough Council* v *Secretary of State for the Environment* [1984] J.P.L. 434.

purposes of agriculture or forestry[47] does not, therefore, constitute development.

In *Hidderley* v *Warwickshire County Council*[48] it was held that the installation of an egg-vending machine was not a use of the land 'for the purposes of agriculture' so as to bring it within the statutory exception, Lord Parker C.J. saying that the expression 'for the purposes of agriculture' clearly refers to 'the productive processes' of agriculture.

The word 'agriculture' is given a wide definition by s.275 of the 1972 Act. That definition encompasses 'the breeding and keeping of livestock (including any creature kept for the production of food, wool, skins or fur, or for the purpose of its use in the farming of land)'. In *Belmont Farm Ltd.* v *Minister of Housing and Local Government*[49] the Divisional Court held that, taking account of the words in brackets, the phrase 'breeding and keeping of livestock' had to be restrictively construed and did not cover the breeding and training of horses for show-jumping. However, the statutory definition of 'agriculture' also includes 'the use of land as grazing land' and in *Sykes* v *Secretary of State for the Environment*[50] it was held that these words should be given their natural meaning and that the use of land for the grazing of horses came within the definition of agriculture.

It has been held that the use of land for allotments falls within the definition of 'agriculture'[51] but that the use of land for the keeping of animals in transit does not.[52] The statutory definition of 'agriculture' is wide enough to include fox-farming,[53] mink-farming[54] and fish-farming[55] but not the keeping and boarding of dogs.[56] In *Northavon District Council* v *Secretary of State for the Environment*[57] it was held that the depositing of materials on agricultural land for the purpose of improving the land did not involve a material change in the use of the land.

3. *Use Classes Order*

Section 19(2)(f) of the 1972 Act provides that in the case of buildings or other land 'used for a purpose of any class specified in an order made by the Secretary of State under this section, the use thereof for any other purpose of the same class' is not to involve development. Under s.19 there has been

---

[47] As to consultations between the Forestry Commission and planning authorities on forestry policy see, however, S.D.D. Circular 7/1984.
[48] (1963) 14 P. & C.R. 134.
[49] (1962) 13 P. & C.R. 417. See too *Minister of Agriculture, Fisheries and Food* v *Appleton* [1970] 1 Q.B. 221.
[50] (1980) 42 P. & C.R. 19. Contrast appeal decision noted in [1984] J.P.L. 527.
[51] *Crowborough Parish Council* v *Secretary of State for the Environment* (1980) 43 P. & C.R. 229.
[52] *Warnock* v *Secretary of State for the Environment* [1980] J.P.L. 590.
[53] See *SPADS* No. A3410 (P/ENA/HD/7, 26th August 1980).
[54] See decision of Secretary of State for Scotland, reference P/PPR/R/1, 16th August 1978.
[55] See [1980] J.P.L. 480.
[56] See [1970] J.P.L. 156; and [1980] J.P.L. 420.
[57] (1980) 40 P. & C.R. 332.

made the Town and Country Planning (Use Classes) (Scotland) Order 1973 ('the U.C.O.'), the Schedule to which sets out seventeen use classes. Each use class consists of a collection of broadly similar uses; Article 3(1) of the U.C.O. provides that a change from a use within one of these classes to another use within the same class does not constitute development.[58] The Town and Country Planning (Use Classes) (Scotland) Amendment Order 1983 has the effect of excluding from all of the specified classes any use of a building or land which involves the presence on the site of a notifiable quantity of a hazardous substance.[59]

A consultation paper issued by the Scottish Development Department on 28th July 1983[60] stated that the purpose of the U.C.O. is to avoid the need for planning applications wherever possible. This simplifying function of the U.C.O. does, however, mean that changes in matters such as the intensity of use of premises, traffic density and labour intensity (which can sometimes be of concern to planning authorities[61]) are outside the scope of planning control.

Although many different uses are specified in the Use Classes Order, the Order does not in any way purport to cover all possible uses of land and there are in fact many uses which do not come within any of the use classes.[62] It is, as was said in a Scottish appeal decision in 1976, 'a misconception to assume that for purposes of the planning legislation any use to which premises might be put must somehow be fitted into one of the Classes defined in the [Use Classes] Order'.[63]

In *Tessier* v *Secretary of State for the Environment*[64] Lord Widgery C.J. said that it was desirable not to stretch the Use Classes Order 'to embrace activities which do not clearly fall within it'; in his Lordship's view it was 'no bad thing that unusual activities should be treated as *sui generis* for this purpose'. However in *Forkhurst* v *Secretary of State for the Environment*[65]

---

[58] This provision is not applicable to a division of a unit into sub-units—see *Winton* v *Secretary of State for the Environment* (1982) 46 P. & C.R. 205. The provisions of the U.C.O. will not operate if the previous use was so insubstantial that it can be disregarded for planning purposes—see *Kwik Save Discount Group* v *Secretary of State for the Environment* (1980) 42 P. & C.R. 166; and *SPADS* No. A5064 (P/PPA/CB/83, 19th April 1984).

[59] 'Hazardous substance' and 'notifiable quantity' are defined in Article 2(2) of the U.C.O. (as amended by the 1983 Order).

[60] The consultation paper contains proposals for certain (relatively minor) amendments to the U.C.O.

[61] See, for example, J.B. McLoughlin, *Control and Urban Planning* (Faber & Faber, 1973).

[62] See, for example, *Brazil (Concrete) Ltd.* v *Amersham R.D.C.* (1967) 18 P. & C.R. 396 (builder's yard—see too [1974] J.P.L. 239; [1975] J.P.L. 614; [1978] J.P.L. 343; and *SPADS* No. A4744 (P/ENA/FB/44, 28th July 1983); but contrast *Scottish Bulletin of Selected Appeal Decisions*, III/84). See too *Re St. Winifred's, Kenley* (1969) 20 P. & C.R. 583 (industrial research establishment); *Mornford Investments* v *Minister of Housing and Local Government* [1970] 2 All E.R. 253 (students' hostel); *Farm Facilities Ltd.* v *Secretary of State for the Environment* [1981] J.P.L. 42 (motor hire business); and *SPADS* Nos. A3896 (P/PPA/SL/87; P/ENA/SL/127, 16th September 1981) (composite use as shop and bakery); and A4701 (P/ENA/GA/43, 30th June 1983) (operation of vehicle hire fleet).

[63] *SPADS* No. A2005 (P/ENA/EDB/28, 19th January 1976).

[64] (1975) 35 P. & C.R. 161.

[65] (1982) 46 P. & C.R. 89.

Hodgson J. stated that although *Tessier* was undoubtedly authority for the proposition that there can be uses which do not fall within any use class, he did not agree with Lord Widgery's view that the U.C.O. should be interpreted narrowly. In Hodgson J.'s view there was no warrant in the legislation for either restricting or stretching the U.C.O., and it could not be said to be either a good thing or a bad thing to treat unusual uses as *sui generis*.

The Use Classes Order may not be easy to apply in practice; it can, for example, be difficult to decide if on the facts of the case a particular use is an industrial use[66] and, if it is, into which use class it falls.

Class I of the U.C.O. relates to use as a shop for any purpose except as (i) a shop for the sale of hot food;[67] (ii) a tripe shop; (iii) a shop for the sale of pet animals; (iv) a cats-meat shop; and (v) a shop for the sale of motor vehicles.[68] 'Shop' is defined in the U.C.O. as 'a building used for the carrying on of any retail trade or retail business wherein the primary purpose is the selling of goods by retail'[69] but also includes a building used for the purposes of a hairdresser, undertaker, travel agency, ticket agency or post office or for the reception of goods to be washed, cleaned or repaired;[70] it does not include a building used as a fun fair, amusement arcade, pin-table saloon, garage, launderette, petrol filling station, office, betting office, hotel, restaurant,[71] snack bar or cafe, or premises licensed for the sale of excisable liquor for consumption on the premises (Article 2(2)).[72] By virtue of the provisions of s.19(2)(f) and the U.C.O., the use as two shops of premises previously used as a single shop will not involve development.[73]

Class II relates to use as an office for any purpose. 'Office' includes a bank and premises occupied by an estate agency, building society or employment agency or (for office purposes only) for the purpose of car hire or driving instruction; it does not, however, include a post office or betting office (Article 2(2)).[74]

---

[66] See, for example, *Tessier* (above) (use of premises as a sculptor's workshop not an industrial use for the purposes of the U.C.O. even though industrial machinery used in the making of sculptures).

[67] In *City of Glasgow District Council* v *Secretary of State for Scotland* 1985 S.L.T. 19 Lord Grieve said that it was clear that all shops which sell hot food are not necessarily 'shops for the sale of hot food' for this purpose (see p. 138 above).

[68] Development consisting of a change of use from a hot food shop, pet shop or betting office to use as any type of shop other than hot food shop, pet shop or betting shop is permitted by the General Development Order (see p. 178 below).

[69] On the application of this phrase see *Lydcare Ltd.* v *Secretary of State for the Environment* (1983) 47 P. & C.R. 336; upheld by the Court of Appeal: [1984] J.P.L. 809.

[70] Use of a dry-cleaning unit will take premises outside the definition of 'shop'—see [1981] J.P.L. 439.

[71] A change from use as a restaurant to use for any purpose within Class I of the U.C.O. is permitted by the G.D.O.—see p. 178 below.

[72] On the meaning of 'shop' see too *Horwitz* v *Rowson* [1960] 1 W.L.R. 803; and *Tandridge District Council* v *Secretary of State for the Environment* [1983] J.P.L. 667.

[73] See *Bulletin of Selected Appeal Decisions*, IX/10; and [1979] J.P.L. 705.

[74] On the meaning of 'office' see too *Shephard* v *Buckinghamshire C.C.* (1966) 18 P. & C.R. 419; *Re St. Winifred's, Kenley* (1969) 20 P. & C.R. 583; and appeal decision noted in [1980] J.P.L. 346.

Classes III to IX deal with industrial uses.[75] Class III relates to use as a light industrial building for any purpose, and Class IV to use as a general industrial building for any purpose, while Classes V to IX, Special Industrial Groups A to E, group together certain industrial uses[76] which may be particularly objectionable because of smell, noise, fumes, etc. 'Industrial building' is defined in Article 2(2) of the Order as a building used for the carrying on, in the course of trade or business other than agriculture, of any process for or incidental to specified purposes including the making, altering, repairing, adapting for sale or breaking up of any article or the getting, dressing or treatment of minerals. In *Rael Brook Ltd.* v *Minister of Housing and Local Government*[77] the Divisional Court held that neither the making of profit nor any commercial activity is essential before a process may be said to be carried on 'in the course of trade or business' for the purpose of the definition of 'industrial building', and that a cooking centre for school meals run by a local authority came within that definition.

A 'light industrial building' means an industrial building (not being a special industrial building) in which the processes carried on or the machinery installed are such as could be carried on or installed in any residential area without detriment to the amenity of that area[78] by reason of noise, vibration, smell, fumes, smoke, soot, ash, dust or grit; a 'special industrial building' is an industrial building used for one or more of the purposes specified in Classes V-IX; and a 'general industrial building' means an industrial building other than a light or special industrial building (Article 2(2)). In *Scrivener* v *Minister of Housing and Local Government*[79] Widgery J. (delivering the judgment of the Divisional Court) said:

[75]   For decisions concerning particular industrial uses see *Brain* v *London County Council* (1957) 9 P. & C.R. 113 (L.T.) (garage use treated as within Class III); *George Cohen 600 Group Ltd.* v *Minister of Housing and Local Government* [1961] 1 W.L.R. 944; (whether recovery of scrap metal in Class IV); *Scrivener* v *Minister of Housing and Local Government* (1966) 18 P. & C.R. 357 (whether cellulose spraying took industrial use into Class VIII); *Walter Chadburn & Son* v *Leeds Corporation* (1969) 20 P. & C.R. 241 (whether use in Class IV or Special Industrial Group D); *Forkhurst* v *Secretary of State for the Environment* (1982) 46 P. & C.R. 89 (Class IV). See too *SPADS* Nos. A2312 (P/ENA/SL/50-52, 31st March 1977) (scrap yard and haulage contractor's yard in Class IV); A3573 (P/PPA/ST/28, 12th January 1981) (car repairs and coal yard within Class IV); A3882 (P/ENA/LD/8, 4th September 1981) (scrap yard and servicing of motor vehicles in Class IV); A3884 (P/ENA/D/42, 7th September 1981) (whether spray painting took vehicle repair use into Class VIII); A4063 (P/ENA/SL/6, 11th March 1982) (use as a civil engineering contractors' yard within Class IV); and A4880 (P/ENA/TC/37, 25th October 1983) (Class VI).
[76]   In contrast to Classes III and IV, not limited to activities within a building. See, however, Article 2(3) of the U.C.O. (below).
[77]   [1967] 2 Q.B. 65. But see too *Tessier* v *Secretary of State for the Environment* (1975) 31 P. & C.R. 161 (use of premises by sculptor not an industrial use); and ministerial decision noted in *Selected Enforcement and Allied Appeals*, p. 29.
[78]   Whether or not detriment is caused to the amenity of the particular area in which the building is situated is irrelevant—see *W. T. Lamb Properties Ltd.* v *Secretary of State for the Environment* [1983] J.P.L. 303; and appeal decision noted in [1975] J.P.L. 552.
[79]   (1966) 18 P. & C.R. 357. See too *Essex County Council* v *Secretary of State for the Environment* (1973) 229 E.G. 1733; and *Brooks and Burton* v *Secretary of State for the Environment* [1977] 1 W.L.R. 1294.

'To decide into which of these three main categories an industrial building falls involves a process of elimination. It must first be considered whether the building is a special industrial building; if not, whether it is a light industrial building; and if the answer is in the negative in each case the building falls into the residual category of a general industrial building . . . [I]n our opinion the division of industrial buildings into "light", "general" and "special" is done with a view to classifying them according to the extent to which they may cause nuisance or inconvenience in the neighbourhood and thus according to the degree of care required in their siting.[80] In this connection it is not the ultimate purpose of the use which matters but the processes employed on the premises, and the definition of a light industrial building clearly underlines this. We do not think that the intention of this Order can be achieved unless the nature of the "process" is given the same significance when distinguishing general and special industrial buildings as it is when distinguishing general and light industrial buildings . . . [W]e are satisfied that when construing the word "purposes" in Class VIII one must not confine it to the single or overall purposes of the occupier's use of the building but must treat it as referring also to the processes employed.'

Article 3(2) of the Order provides that where a group of contiguous or adjacent buildings used as parts of a single undertaking includes buildings used for purposes falling within two or more of Classes III to IX, those particular two or more classes may, in relation to that group of buildings, be treated as a single class for the purposes of the Order, provided that the area occupied in that group of buildings by either general or special industrial buildings is not substantially increased thereby. This provision therefore permits the interchange of industrial uses between the various buildings and in an appropriate case will permit an increase in the area occupied by light industrial buildings at the expense of general or special industrial use.[81]

Each of the other use classes, Classes X to XVII, groups together a number of similar uses. Class X, for example, relates to use as a boarding or guest house or a hotel providing sleeping accommodation (except where licensed for the sale of excisable liquor other than to non-residents or persons consuming meals on the premises),[82] while Class XIII relates to use as a home or institution providing for the boarding, care and maintenance of children, old people or persons under disability, a convalescent home, a nursing home, a sanatorium or a hospital.[83]

It would seem to be settled law that in determining whether a change of use is permitted under the Use Classes Order, the 'planning unit' (above)

[80] For an example of the application of this principle see [1975] J.P.L. 484.
[81] See too the provisions of the General Development Order (p. 178 below).
[82] In *Mornford Investments* v *Minister of Housing and Local Government* [1970] 2 All E.R. 253 it was held that a students' hostel was not within this class. See too the comments of Glidewell J. in *Commercial and Residential Property Development Co.* v *Secretary of State for the Environment* (1981) 80 L.G.R. 443.
[83] On the interpretation of this class, see *Rann* v *Secretary of State for the Environment* (1980) 40 P. & C.R. 113.

must be looked at as a whole and that a use which is incidental to the main use of the land cannot be treated as an independent use for the purposes of the Order.[84]

The Order provides that a use which is ordinarily incidental to and included in any use specified in the Schedule to the Order is not excluded from that use as an incident thereto merely by reason of its specification in the Schedule as a separate use (Article 3(3)). In *Scrivener* v *Minister of Housing and Local Government*[85] the Divisional Court held that the use of the word 'ordinarily' in this provision makes clear that any ancillary use imported by this Article must be incidental to the class of use in general and not merely to a particular example of that class; for example, when applying Article 3(3) of the Order to Class I—'use as a shop for any purpose'—the ancillary use must be ordinarily incidental to the activities carried on in shops generally and not merely to the requirements of a particular trade in a particular shop.[86] Intensification of use,[87] within the same use class, does not amount to development.[88]

Article 2(3) of the Use Classes Order provides that references in the Order to a building 'may, except where otherwise provided, include references to land occupied therewith and used for the same purposes'. In *Brooks and Burton* v *Secretary of State for the Environment*[89] it was held that the identical provision appearing in the English order was to be given its plain meaning; the Court of Appeal held that the test to be applied in determining whether, for the purpose of Article 2(3), land which was occupied with an industrial building had itself been used as an 'industrial building', was not whether the process carried on upon the land was ancillary to or dependent on the use of the building, but whether the land had been used for the same purpose as the building and could therefore be regarded as one unit with it.

Article 3(4) of the Use Classes Order states that nothing in the Order is to be taken as limiting the power of a planning authority under ss.26 and 27 of the 1972 Act to impose conditions on a grant of planning permission. In *City of London Corporation* v *Secretary of State for the Environment*[90] it was held that in granting planning permission for a use within one of the use classes the planning authority are entitled to impose a condition which has the effect

---

[84] See *Brazil (Concrete) Ltd.* v *Amersham R.D.C.* (1967) 18 P. & C.R. 396; *G. Percy Trentham Ltd.* v *Gloucestershire County Council* [1966] 1 W.L.R. 506; *Shephard* v *Buckinghamshire County Council* (1966) 18 P. & C.R. 419; *L.R. Jillings* v *Secretary of State for the Environment* [1984] J.P.L. 32; and see p. 147 above.

[85] (1966) 18 P. & C.R. 357.

[86] See *Hussain* v *Secretary of State for the Environment* (1971) 23 P. & C.R. 330 (slaughtering of poultry on the premises not ordinarily incidental to shop use); and *Lydcare Ltd.* v *Secretary of State for the Environment* (1983) 47 P. & C.R. 336; upheld by the Court of Appeal: [1984] J.P.L. 809 (showing of films in shop).

[87] On intensification of use see p. 139 above.

[88] See *Brooks and Burton* v *Secretary of State for the Environment* [1977] 1 W.L.R. 1294.

[89] Above. See too *North Sea Land Equipment* v *Secretary of State for the Environment* [1982] J.P.L. 384.

[90] (1971) 23 P. & C.R. 169; see too Sir Douglas Frank's comments in *Carpet Decor (Guildford) Ltd.* v *Secretary of State for the Environment* [1981] J.P.L. 806.

of prohibiting a change to other uses within that use class, even though such a change does not, in terms of the Order, involve development.[91]

While the Use Classes Order provides that a change within the same use class does not constitute development, it is not necessarily the case (though it often will be so) that development is involved in a change from a use within one of the use classes to a use within a different use class or to a use not falling within any of the use classes;[92] whether or not any such change of use involves development depends upon whether the change is a material one.

D. USES SPECIFICALLY DECLARED TO INVOLVE DEVELOPMENT

Three specific changes of use are declared by the 1972 Act to involve a material change in the use of the land.

1. Use of dwellinghouse as two or more separate dwellings

The 1972 Act declares 'for the avoidance of doubt' that the use as two or more separate dwellinghouses of any building previously used as a single dwellinghouse[93] involves a material change in the use of the building and of any part thereof which is so used (s.19(3)(a)).[94]

For the purposes of this provision multiple occupation of a dwellinghouse is not enough (though multiple occupation may so alter the character of the use of a house previously occupied as a single-family dwelling as to amount to a material change of use).[95] In *Ealing Borough Council* v *Ryan*[96] it was submitted on behalf of the planning authority that if people were found to be living separately in a building then there were bound to be separate dwellings. The Divisional Court rejected that proposition, Ashworth J. saying that 'a house may well be occupied by two or more persons, who are to all intents and purposes living separately, without that house being thereby used as separate dwellings. In other words persons may live separately under one roof without occupying separate dwellings.' Whether or not there is use as two or more separate dwellinghouses will often be a question of fact and degree; in the *Ealing* case Ashworth J. suggested that such factors as the existence or absence of any form of physical reconstruction and the extent to which the allegedly separate dwellings are self-contained and independent of other parts of the same property might be relevant. It seems doubtful whether principles enunciated in cases under the

[91] In *Caledonian Terminal Investments Ltd.* v *Edinburgh Corporation* 1970 S.C. 271; 1970 S.L.T. 362 it seems to have been accepted that such a condition might validly be imposed.
[92] See Sir Douglas Frank's comments in *Rann* v *Secretary of State for the Environment* (1980) 40 P. & C.R. 113.
[93] As to what constitutes a 'dwellinghouse' see p. 153 above.
[94] See too *Wakelin* v *Secretary of State for the Environment* (1978) 77 L.G.R. 101 (p. 132 above).
[95] See p. 136 above.
[96] [1965] 2 Q.B. 486.

Rent Acts are of any assistance where the question of separate dwellings arises under the planning legislation.[97]

Section 19(3)(a) is only concerned with dwellinghouses and with change to use as two or more separate dwellinghouses; the English minister determined in one case that a change of use from two flats to use as a single dwellinghouse did not constitute development.[98] In *Peaktop Properties (Hampstead) Ltd.* v *Camden London Borough Council*[99] the Court of Appeal held that s.22(3)(a) of the Town and Country Planning Act 1971 (corresponding to s.19(3)(a) of the 1972 Act) had no application where it was proposed to add an extra storey to a block of flats; the proposals did not involve creating two dwellings out of one.

2. *Deposit of refuse on site already used for that purpose*

Section 19(3)(b) of the 1972 Act provides that 'the deposit of refuse or waste materials[1] on land involves a material change in the use thereof, notwithstanding that the land is comprised in a site already used for that purpose, if either the superficial area of the deposit is thereby extended, or the height of the deposit is thereby extended and exceeds the level of the land adjoining the site'.[2]

Thus, despite the fact that land is comprised in a site already used for the deposit of refuse or waste materials, further deposits on that land will in the specified circumstances involve a material change in the use of the land.[3] It would seem that if refuse is deposited on land such as a former quarry which has already been used for tipping, then so long as the refuse does not extend above the level of the adjoining land or cover more than the area of the quarry, no material change of use will be involved.[4]

[97] See *Ealing Borough Council* (above); and *Birmingham Corporation* v *Minister of Housing and Local Government* [1964] 1 Q.B. 178.

[98] *Bulletin of Selected Appeal Decisions*, IX/15; see too [1982] J.P.L. 119.

[99] (1983) 82 L.G.R. 101.

[1] Whether material is refuse or waste is a matter of fact. The English minister has treated subsoil as coming within the statutory provision—see [1981] J.P.L. 911.

[2] In *Bilboe* v *Secretary of State for the Environment* (1980) 39 P. & C.R. 495 the Court of Appeal held that tipping for the purpose of disposing of waste material is to be regarded as a use of land and not an operation. (See too *Roberts* v *Vale Royal District Council* (1977) 39 P. & C.R. 514; and *R.* v *Derbyshire County Council, ex p. North East Derbyshire District Council* (1979) 77 L.G.R. 389). However, the tipping of material for some purpose other than the mere disposal of the material—e.g. in order to make land fit for building or agriculture—may, independently of change of use, amount to development as involving engineering or other operations—see p. 121 above. Where materials are deposited for the purpose of improving agricultural land there will be no material change in the use of the land (see *Northavon District Council* v *Secretary of State for the Environment* (1980) 40 P. & C.R. 332); such tipping may in some circumstances amount to building or engineering operations requisite for the use of the land for agriculture and may therefore be permitted development under the G.D.O. (see p. 179 below).

[3] See *Alexandra Transport Company Ltd.* v *Secretary of State for Scotland* 1974 S.L.T. 81 in which the Court of Session considered the corresponding provision of the 1947 Act (from which, however, certain apparently otiose words were omitted on consolidation in the 1972 Act). It is probably the case that a material change of use occurs on each occasion when waste material is deposited on the site in such a way as to extend the superficial area or height of the deposit—see *Bilboe* (above); and appeal decision noted in [1981] J.P.L. 907.

[4] See *Ratcliffe* v *Secretary of State for the Environment* (1975) 235 E.G. 901.

The meaning of the phrase 'already used', as employed in this sub-section, was considered in *Macdonald v Glasgow Corporation.*[5] In that case the proprietor of an area of land which had been used since 1955 for the deposit of waste materials appealed against an enforcement notice, contending, *inter alia,* that planning permission was not required because at the date of his purchasing the land in 1958 the land was 'already used' for the purpose of depositing waste materials within the meaning of the statute. The Sheriff-Principal held that planning permission was required for the continued use of the land for the deposit of waste materials since the words 'already used' referred to use prior to the coming into operation of the 1947 Act. It was also contended for the appellant that the whole area of the site could be raised by the deposit of waste materials to the level of the highest points of any adjoining land; though it was not necessary to decide this point, the Sheriff-Principal 'inclined to the view that the proper levels to be applied . . . are the varying contours of the immediately adjoining lands'.

3. *Display of advertisements*

Use for the display of advertisements of any external part of a building not normally used for that purpose is to be treated as involving a material change in the use of that part of the building (s.19(4)). Where, however, the display of advertisements in accordance with regulations made under the Planning Act[6] involves development, planning permission for that development is deemed to be granted by virtue of s.62 of the 1972 Act and no application for planning permission under Part III of the Act is necessary.

E. APPLICATION TO DETERMINE WHETHER PLANNING PERMISSION REQUIRED

From what has been said above it will be seen that it may well be difficult to decide whether proposed operations or a proposed change of use will constitute development. Under the 1972 Act the planning authority may be asked to determine whether particular proposals amount to development. If any person who proposes to carry out any operations on land, or to make any change in the use of land, wishes to have it determined whether the carrying out of those operations, or the making of that change, would constitute or involve development of the land, he may, either as part of an application for planning permission or independently of any such application, apply to the planning authority to determine that question (s.51(1)). If the authority consider that the proposals will involve development they must then determine whether an application for planning permission in respect thereof is required under Part III of the 1972 Act, having regard to the provisions of

---

[5]   1960 S.L.T. (Sh.Ct.) 21.

[6]   The Town and Country Planning (Control of Advertisements) (Scotland) Regulations 1984 are dealt with in chapter 19 below.

the development order[7] and of any enterprise zone scheme[8] (1972 Act, s.51(1)[9]).

The procedure to be followed in making application for such a determination is similar to that laid down in connection with an application for planning permission (see chapter 9) and is set out in Article 9(2) of the General Development Order. It is there provided that an application is to be in writing, is to contain a description of the operations or change of use proposed, together with certain other prescribed particulars, and is to be accompanied by a plan sufficient to identify the land to which the application relates. The Town and Country Planning Act 1984 provides (s.1) that for the purpose of enabling Crown land to be disposed of with the benefit of a determination under s.51, application for such a determination may be made by the government department or other Crown body responsible for the land or by someone authorised by the appropriate authority[10] (see p. 169 below). The planning authority are to keep a register of applications for determinations under s.51 (see 1972 Act, s.31(2) and 51(2), and G.D.O., Art. 17(3)).

It seems clear that a determination under s.51 cannot be made retrospectively and that an application cannot competently be made in respect of operations or a change of use already carried out.[11] The Secretary of State has no power under s.51 to decide upon the validity of a planning permission,[12] nor is he able under this provision to interpret a specific grant of planning permission.[13]

Although there are no Scottish court decisions directly in point, it would seem that where a planning authority or one of its officers has expressed the view that particular proposals will not involve development, such an expression of view will in certain limited circumstances be binding upon the authority even though the statutory formalities relating to application for and making of a determination have not been observed. The leading English cases on the application of the doctrine of estoppel (personal bar) in a town planning context are considered in greater detail above,[14] but it would seem to be the case that an effective determination can be made even though a formal application for such a determination has not been submitted.

---

[7]   Planning permission is automatically granted for certain types of development by the G.D.O. (see p. 171 below).

[8]   An order designating an enterprise zone will operate as a grant of planning permission for specified types of development (see p. 272 below).

[9]   As amended by the Local Government, Planning and Land Act 1980, Sched. 32, para. 19(3).

[10] Certain provisions of the 1972 Act are modified for this purpose by the Town and Country Planning (Crown Land Applications) (Scotland) Regulations 1984.

[11] See, for example, *SPADS* Nos. A3397 (P/DEV/1/SP/1, 13th August 1980); and A3611 (P/DEV/1/SC/2, 13th February 1981).

[12] *Edgwarebury Park Investments* v *Minister of Housing and Local Government* [1963] 2 Q.B. 408.

[13] See appeal decision noted in [1982] J.P.L. 115.

[14] See p. 34 above.

In *Wells* v *Minister of Housing and Local Government*[15] the Court of Appeal held (Russell L.J. dissenting[16]) that where, following the making of an application for planning permission, the planning authority's surveyor wrote to the applicants stating that the works in question were permitted development and that the authority did not propose to consider the application, that letter amounted to a valid determination under the planning legislation—there had either been a waiver by the planning authority of any formal application for a determination or the application for planning permission contained an implied invitation to the authority to make such a determination if they thought fit. The Court of Appeal also held, however, that only a positive statement by the planning authority can constitute a valid determination and that the deletion, on a printed bye-law consent notification, of a sentence warning against acting on the faith of the bye-law approval without obtaining planning permission could not be regarded as a determination under the planning legislation that planning permission was not required.

In *Western Fish Products Ltd.* v *Penwith District Council*[17] the Court of Appeal expressed the view (*obiter*) that the legislation contemplates a considerable degree of formality in applications and determinations as to whether planning permission is required and that while an application for planning permission impliedly contains an invitation to determine that permission is not required,[18] and accordingly in such a case a formal written application for a determination is not necessary, that exception should not be extended beyond cases in which there has been an application for planning permission.[19]

In *Glasgow District Council* v *Secretary of State for Scotland*[20] planning permission for certain proposals had been refused by the planning authority. On appeal, the Secretary of State concluded that the works in question did not involve development. It was argued for the planning authority that in the absence of an application for a s.51 determination, the Secretary of State had no power to make such a decision. For the Secretary of State it was argued, citing *Wells* (above), that an application for planning permission contains an implied invitation to make a determination that planning permission is not required. Though it was not necessary for the Second Division to decide this point, both Lord Dunpark and Lord Robertson set out their reasons for rejecting the planning authority's argument. Their

[15] [1967] 1 W.L.R. 1000; applied in *English-Speaking Union* v *City of Westminster London Borough Council* (1973) 26 P. & C.R. 575. See too *Property Investment Holdings Ltd.* v *Secretary of State for the Environment* [1984] J.P.L. 587.
[16] In *Western Fish Products Ltd.* v *Penwith District Council* [1981] 2 All E.R. 204 the Court of Appeal stated that they found Russell L.J.'s judgment 'very powerful'.
[17] [1981] 2 All E.R. 204.
[18] See *Property Investment Holdings Ltd.* v *Secretary of State for the Environment* [1984] J.P.L. 587.
[19] It might be suggested that this represents a very narrow view of the *ratio* in *Wells*. In *English-Speaking Union* (above) the doctrine in *Wells* was applied to a mere exchange of letters.
[20] 1980 S.C. 150; 1982 S.L.T. 28.

Lordships found it unnecessary to rely on *Wells*. Lord Dunpark did not think that s.51 could be applied to the facts of this case; there was no application under s.51 and he did not think the Secretary of State's decision fell to be construed in the sense of a s.51 determination—it was a decision in an appeal against refusal of planning permission. Lord Robertson said that s.51 was conceived for the benefit of developers and applicants for planning permission. It did not limit the powers of the planning authority or the Secretary of State. He was unable to see any reason why the wide discretion conferred on the Secretary of State by s.33(3) of the 1972 Act (dealing with the minister's powers on appeal against the decision of a planning authority—see p. 267 below) should be limited by refusing him power to decide that an application for planning permission was unnecessary.

There is a right of appeal to the Secretary of State against a determination made by a planning authority; appeal can also be made on the failure of a planning authority to give notice of their determination within the prescribed period (see s.51(2)). The Secretary of State can 'call in' for decision by himself an application for a determination (s.51(2)). In any case where the minister determines that development is involved, that decision is not to be taken as final for the purposes of any appeal under the provisions of the 1972 Act relating to the enforcement of planning control (s.51(3)).

Either the applicant or the planning authority, if dissatisfied with a decision of the Secretary of State under s.51, may appeal to the Court of Session or require the minister to state a case for the opinion of the Court (s.234).[21]

The 1972 Act is silent as to the precise effect of a determination under s.51. It would seem that a determination that development is not involved is as good as a grant of planning permission and is, in the words of Lord Denning, 'irrevocable by the planning authority, just as is a planning permission'.[22] In *English-Speaking Union of the Commonwealth* v *City of Westminster London Borough Council*[23] a determination had been made by the planning authority to the effect that in terms of the Use Classes Order a proposed change of use would not involve development; it was held that this determination was not invalidated by a change made in the relevant provision of the Use Classes Order before the development was carried out. 'The determination', said Pennycuick V.-C., 'established the right of the plaintiff once and for all and, as held in the *Wells* case, was as good as planning permission.'[24]

---

[21] There would seem to be nothing to prevent a developer seeking a declarator that particular proposals do not require planning permission: see *Pyx Granite Co.* v *Minister of Housing and Local Government* [1960] A.C. 260.

[22] *Wells* v *Minister of Housing and Local Government* (above).

[23] (1973) 26 P. & C.R. 575.

[24] For persuasive criticism of this decision see [1974] J.P.L. 141 (W.A. Leach).

CHAPTER 7

DEVELOPMENT NOT REQUIRING SUBMISSION OF A PLANNING APPLICATION

Certain exceptional categories of development, set out in s.20 of the 1972 Act, are declared not to require planning permission. Nor does development by the Crown require such permission. Otherwise, planning permission is required for the carrying out of any development[1] of land (1972 Act, s.20(1)). However, an express grant of planning permission by the planning authority may not be necessary in order to allow development to proceed; in certain circumstances planning permission for development is deemed to be granted and in other circumstances permission is granted by development order. These cases are considered in this chapter.

A. DEVELOPMENT NOT REQUIRING PLANNING PERMISSION

Section 20 of 1972 Act

Section 20 of the 1972 Act makes a number of exceptions to the general rule that planning permission is required for the development of land.[2] The more important of these exceptional cases are as follows[3]:

(a) Where on the appointed day (1st July 1948) land was normally used for one purpose and was also used on occasions,[4] whether at regular intervals or not, for another purpose, then provided that the land was used for that other purpose on at least one similar occasion between the appointed day and the beginning of 1969, planning permission is not required in respect of the use of the land for that other purpose on similar occasions (s.20(3)(b)).

(b) Where planning permission to develop land has been granted for a limited period, planning permission is not required for the resumption, at the end of that period, of the use of the land for the purpose for which it was normally used before the permission was granted, provided that the 'normal use' was not begun in contravention of Part II of the 1947 Act or Part III of the 1972 Act (s.20(5), (6), (10)[5]).

---

[1] 'Development' is defined in s.19 of the 1972 Act—see chapter 6.
[2] See Michael Purdue, 'The Right to Revert to Earlier Uses of Land' [1984] J.P.L. 6.
[3] A consultation paper issued by the Scottish Development Department on 31st July 1984 proposes amendment of s.20 to provide a right of reversion to a previous use after a personal permission ceases to be exercised.
[4] On the meaning of the expression 'on occasions' as used in this context see *Smyth* v *Minister of Housing and Local Government* (1966) 18 P. & C.R. 351.
[5] On the interpretation of the corresponding provisions in the English legislation see *Smith* v *Secretary of State for the Environment* (1982) 47 P. & C.R. 194.

(c) Where planning permission has been granted subject to limitations by a development order, planning permission is not required to resume the normal use of the land, provided that such 'normal use' was not begun in contravention of Part II of the 1947 Act or Part III of the 1972 Act (s.20(8), (10)).

(d) Where an enforcement notice has been served in respect of any development of land, planning permission is not required for the use of that land for the purpose for which, in accordance with the provisions of Part III of the 1972 Act, it could lawfully have been used if that development had not been carried out (s.20(9)). A 'lawful use' for this purpose is one begun with the benefit of a valid planning permission or, alternatively, one begun before 1st July 1948 and not since abandoned or replaced by another use (other than another use begun with the benefit of a planning permission for a limited period or begun in breach of planning control and in respect of which enforcement action has been taken).[6] A use begun in contravention of Part III of the 1972 Act does not constitute a 'lawful' use for the purposes of this sub-section, even though that use has acquired immunity from enforcement action; if therefore a use which was instituted in breach of planning control but which has acquired immunity from enforcement action is discontinued in favour of a fresh use involving development, and enforcement action is taken in respect of that new use, the occupier will have no right to revert to the former use.[7] An occupier of land can revert to a previous lawful use only if that use immediately preceded the use enforced against; if the immediately preceding use is unlawful he cannot go back to earlier uses until he reaches the last lawful use.[8]

Development by Crown

Crown land is in large measure exempt from the provisions of the planning legislation. 'The reason it is exempt', said Lord Denning M.R. in *Ministry of Agriculture, Fisheries and Food* v *Jenkins*,[9] 'is, not by virtue of any provision in the Act itself, but by reason of the general principle that the Crown is not bound by an Act unless it is expressly or impliedly included.' However, certain exceptions to the general principle are made by ss.253 to 255 of the 1972 Act and by the Town and Country Planning Act 1984.[10]

---

[6] See *LTSS Print and Supply Services Ltd.* v *Hackney London Borough Council* [1976] Q.B. 663.

[7] *Young* v *Secretary of State for the Environment* [1983] 2 A.C. 662; *LTSS Print and Supply Services Ltd.* (above); and see *SPADS* Nos. A2548 (P/ENA/LA/8, 12th January 1978); and A2709 (P/ENA/SL/76, 12th July 1978). See too Nigel P. Gravells, 'Reversion to Previous Land Use Following Enforcement Proceedings' [1984] Conv. 339.

[8] *Young* v *Secretary of State for the Environment* (above) (overruling on this point *Balco Transport Services Ltd.* v *Secretary of State for the Environment* (1981) 45 P. & C.R. 216). See too *Denham Developments Ltd.* v *Secretary of State for the Environment* (1983) 47 P. & C.R. 598.

[9] [1963] 2 Q.B. 317.

[10] For an account of the provisions of the 1984 Act see 1984 S.P.L.P. 44 (H. McN. Henderson).

'Crown land' is defined in s.253(7) of the 1972 Act as land in which there is a Crown interest, that is, an interest belonging to Her Majesty in right of the Crown, or belonging to a government department, or held in trust for Her Majesty for the purposes of a government department. The 1972 Act provides that certain planning powers may be exercised in relation to such land. It is provided, for example, that a development plan may include proposals relating to the use of Crown land; that a building which is for the time being Crown land may be 'listed' as a building of special architectural or historic interest; and that certain provisions of the 1972 Act, in particular the provisions of Part III of the Act, relating to general planning control, are to apply to Crown land to the extent of any interest therein which is for the time being held otherwise than by or on behalf of the Crown[11] (s.253).

Not only does the Crown not need to obtain planning permission for development, until the coming into operation of the 1984 Act government departments and other Crown bodies were unable to apply for planning permission or other consents under Parts III and IV of the 1972 Act. This could give rise to problems in connection with the disposal of Crown land and the 1984 Act provides for the making of applications for planning permission (see p. 191 below), listed building consent, consent to demolish an unlisted building in a conservation area, or a determination under s.51 of the 1972 Act in anticipation of disposal of such land. The 1984 Act also permits the making of tree preservation orders in anticipation of disposal of Crown land and makes provision for the enforcement of planning control in respect of development carried out on Crown land by trespassers (see p. 309 below).

Parts III and IV of the 1972 Act are not applied to Crown land in which no interest is held otherwise than by or on behalf of the Crown, with the result that the Crown does not require planning permission (or other consents) under those Parts of the Act. However, S.D.D. Circular 21/1984 specifies certain non-statutory procedures to be followed in the consideration of the planning aspects of proposals for development by government departments and other bodies entitled to Crown exemption from the provisions of the planning legislation.

Where a government department or other Crown body propose to carry out development of a type which would, if carried out by a private developer, require a specific grant of planning permission, the department or body will consult the appropriate planning authority.[12] Even where consultation on that basis would not be necessary departments will notify the planning authority of development proposals which are likely to be of special concern to the authority or to the public—for example, where there could be a very substantial effect on the character of a conservation area.

---

[11] Section 4(1) of the 1984 Act resolves possible doubts as to the categories of persons possessing an interest in Crown land by providing that a person who is entitled to occupy Crown land by virtue of a written contract is to be treated as having an interest in the land.

[12] The circular states, however, that the consultation procedure cannot fully apply to proposals involving national security.

The developing department will send to the planning authority a Notice of Proposed Development; the authority are to treat this Notice in the same way as they would an application for planning permission and will, *inter alia*, undertake the usual consultations. Although development proposals by government departments are not subject to statutory publicity requirements, it is intended that they should be given just as much publicity as if the Notice of Proposed Development were an application for planning permission (see p. 194 below). After taking account of the views of any bodies they have consulted and of any comments received in response to the publicity given, the planning authority should, within two months, send the developing department their views on the proposed development, stating whether they find it acceptable and, if so, on what conditions (if any), or whether they find it unacceptable. The terms of the Town and Country Planning (Notification of Applications) (Scotland) Direction 1981[13] (see p. 201 below) and of the Town and Country Planning (Development Contrary to Development Plans) (Scotland) Direction 1981[14] (see p. 209 below) should be observed in dealing with government departments' proposals.

Where the planning authority object to the Notice of Proposed Development or to any detailed proposal submitted after a Notice of Proposed Development in outline, or where there is any unresolved disagreement, the developing department will, if they wish to proceed, notify the Scottish Development Department. In all cases where there have been objections the planning authority, the developing department and other interested parties will be given an opportunity to express their views. The circular states that it is expected that the written representations method will be suitable for most cases. However, in some cases it may be desirable to hold a non-statutory public inquiry.

General and district planning authorities are recommended to keep a non-statutory addendum to the planning register in respect of Notices of Proposed Development.

Since the Crown is not subject to planning control, any use of land instituted by the Crown, even if intended to be only temporary, can be continued indefinitely by a third party such as a purchaser of the land or the owner of land of which the Crown is a lessee. Section 5 of the Town and Country Planning Act 1984 provides machinery by which the planning authority may achieve a greater degree of control in such circumstances. The planning authority may enter into an agreement with the appropriate government department when a material change of use is made or is intended to be made by the Crown. The effect of such an agreement is that if the land ceases to be used by the Crown for the purpose specified in the agreement, the use instituted by the Crown is to be treated as having been authorised by a planning permission granted subject to a condition requiring its discontinuance on the date the Crown ceases to use the land. The result is that planning permission will normally be needed for continuance of the use

---

[13]   As amended.
[14]   As amended.

by someone other than the Crown. The provisions of s.20(5) of the 1972 Act (above) will, however, apply and will authorise the resumption of the use to which the land was normally put prior to the commencement of the use which is the subject of the agreement.

B. PLANNING PERMISSION DEEMED TO BE GRANTED

In certain circumstances planning permission for development is deemed to be granted. Among the more important such cases are the following:

(a) Where an advertisement is displayed in accordance with the Town and Country Planning (Control of Advertisements) (Scotland) Regulations 1984,[15] planning permission is deemed to be granted for development involved in such display (1972 Act, s.62).

(b) Where the sanction of a government department is required by virtue of any enactment in respect of development to be carried out by a local authority or statutory undertakers,[16] that department may, on granting such sanction, direct that planning permission for the development shall be deemed to be granted[17] (1972 Act, s.37[18]).

(c) Where a planning authority require planning permission for development in their own area, and that development is not 'permitted development' in terms of the General Development Order (below) or development for which permission is deemed to have been granted under s.37 of the 1972 Act (above), they must follow the procedure set out in the Town and Country Planning (Development by Planning Authorities) (Scotland) Regulations 1981.[19] The regulations, which are outlined at p. 273 below, provide that in specified circumstances the Secretary of State is deemed to have granted planning permission for the development in question.

(d) The Secretary of State may, when granting an authorisation for pipe line construction under the Pipe-lines Act 1962, direct that planning permission shall be deemed to be granted for that development.

C. PERMISSION GRANTED BY DEVELOPMENT ORDER

Where it is proposed to carry out development requiring planning permission, application to the planning authority for such permission is not always necessary; the proposed development may be authorised by a development order made by the Secretary of State. A development order may grant

---

[15]   See chapter 19.
[16]   Planning permission for certain types of development carried out by local authorities and statutory undertakers is granted by the General Development Order (below).
[17]   The Secretary of State for Energy is, for example, authorised to grant 'deemed' planning permission for power stations under the Electric Lighting Act 1909 and the Electricity Act 1957.
[18]   As amended by the Local Government and Planning (Scotland) Act 1982, Schedule 4.
[19]   As amended by the Town and Country Planning (Development by Planning Authorities) (Scotland) Amendment Regulations 1984.

planning permission for development specified in the order or for development of any class so specified (1972 Act, s.21(2)(a)). Such an order may be made either as a general order, applicable (subject to such exceptions as may be specified therein) to all land, or as a special order, applicable only to such land as is specified therein (s.21(3)). Planning permission granted by a development order may be granted unconditionally or subject to such conditions or limitations as may be specified in the order (s.21(4)).

The General Development Order: 'permitted development'

The general development order presently in force is the Town and Country Planning (General Development) (Scotland) Order 1981[20] ('the G.D.O.'). Except where its application is limited by a special development order,[21] the G.D.O. is applicable to all land in Scotland (G.D.O., Art. 1(1)).

Under Article 3(1) of the G.D.O.[22] planning permission is granted by the order for development falling within any of the 22 classes specified in the First Schedule to the G.D.O. and such development may be undertaken without the permission of any planning authority or of the Secretary of State.[23]

It is provided, however, that nothing in Article 3 of, or the First Schedule to, the G.D.O. is to operate so as to permit any development contrary to a condition imposed in any planning permission granted or deemed to be granted otherwise than by the order (G.D.O., Art. 3(2)). In granting permission for a dwelling-house, for example, the planning authority might impose a condition to the effect that, notwithstanding any provision of the G.D.O., no garage is to be erected within the curtilage of the house except with the authority's consent; that condition will override the general permission granted by the G.D.O. for the erection of such a garage and the authority can thus retain control over such matters as the external

---

[20] As amended by the Town and Country Planning (General Development) (Scotland) Amendment Order 1983 and the Town and Country Planning (General Development) (Scotland) Amendment Order 1984.

[21] See p. 184 below.

[22] As substituted by the Town and Country Planning (General Development) (Scotland) Amendment Order 1983.

[23] A number of changes in permitted development rights as they affect agriculture, telecommunications and cable systems, the Civil Aviation Authority and warehouses and repositories were proposed in a consultation paper issued by the Scottish Development Department on 23rd January 1984. A press release issued by the Scottish Information Office on 25th October 1984 announced the amendments which the government proposes to make to the G.D.O. as it affects telecommunications developments. First, the installation of specified types of minor telecommunication apparatus by operators to whom the powers in the Telecommunications Code (contained in Schedule 2 to the Telecommunications Act 1984) have been applied is to enjoy permitted development status under the G.D.O. Secondly, permitted development rights are, subject to certain limitations, to be generally available (i.e. not only to operators to whom the Telecommunications Code applies) for the erection of up to two microwave dish aerials on non-domestic property.

appearance and siting of any such garage.[24]

It is also provided that the G.D.O. is not to permit any development which involves, or is likely to involve, the laying or construction of a notifiable pipeline or the presence of a notifiable quantity of a hazardous substance or, where a hazardous substance is already on the land in a notifiable quantity, development which would, or is likely to, lead to a more than three-fold increase in the amount present[25] (G.D.O., Art. 3(1)(b) and 3(2A)[26]).

Permission granted by the G.D.O. in respect of development of any class specified in the First Schedule is subject to any condition or limitation imposed in the First Schedule in relation to that class. If any such condition or limitation is not complied with, enforcement action may be taken by the planning authority. Where a limitation in the G.D.O. is exceeded—as, for example, by the extension of a house by an amount exceeding that permitted by the G.D.O.—the whole development, and not just the excess, is unauthorised.[27]

In *Wood* v *Secretary of State for the Environment*[28] it was held that where an addition is made to a building under the G.D.O. permission, that addition takes upon itself the characteristics of the original building in all respects and that accordingly the permitted uses of a conservatory were the same as the permitted uses of the house to which the conservatory had been added as 'permitted development' under the G.D.O.

Many of the classes of 'permitted development' are governed by one or both of the two 'standard conditions' set out in Part II of the First Schedule to the G.D.O.:

1. that the permission is not to authorise any development which involves

---

[24] Although Lord Parker C.J. said in *East Barnet U.D.C.* v *British Transport Commission* [1962] 2 Q.B. 484 that he was unable to accede to the argument that a specific condition imposed on a grant of permission by a planning authority overrode an unlimited permission granted by the G.D.O., these remarks would seem to be *obiter* and may be doubted, particularly as they appear to be contrary to the reasoning in *City of London Corporation* v *Secretary of State for the Environment* (1971) 23 P. & C.R. 169 (see p. 160 above) and *Kingston-Upon-Thames Royal London Borough Council* v *Secretary of State for the Environment* [1973] 1 W.L.R. 1549 (see p. 242 below). See too the comments of the Lord President (Lord Emslie) in *British Airports Authority* v *Secretary of State for Scotland* 1979 S.C. 200; 1979 S.L.T. 197, of Sir Douglas Frank in *Carpet Decor (Guildford) Ltd.* v *Secretary of State for the Environment* [1981] J.P.L. 806, and of Forbes J. in *Dawson* v *Secretary of State for the Environment* [1983] J.P.L. 544.

[25] As to the meanings of 'notifiable pipeline', 'hazardous development' and 'notifiable quantity' see Art. 2(1) of the G.D.O. (as amended by the Town and Country Planning (General Development) (Scotland) Amendment Order 1983).

[26] Added by the Town and Country Planning (General Development) (Scotland) Amendment Order 1983.

[27] See, for example, *Garland* v *Minister of Housing and Local Government* (1968) 20 P. & C.R. 93; *Rochdale Metropolitan Borough Council* v *Simmonds* (1980) 40 P. & C.R. 432; and *Ewen Developments Ltd.* v *Secretary of State for the Environment* [1980] J.P.L. 404.

[28] [1973] 1 W.L.R. 707.

the formation, laying out or material widening of a means of access to a trunk or classified road;[29] and

2. that no development is to be carried out which creates an obstruction to the view of persons using any road used by vehicular traffic at or near any bend, corner, junction or intersection so as to be likely to cause danger to such persons.

Certain of the classes of 'permitted development' relate to relatively minor sorts of development while others relate to development by public authorities and statutory undertakers, apparently on the assumption that such developments require less scrutiny than the proposals of private developers.[30] The classes of 'permitted development' are mainly expressed in terms of the type of development rather than of its impact on the environment and have been criticised on the ground that they disregard some of the potential planning problems attendant on the changes thus permitted.[31] There are mentioned below those classes of permitted development which appear to be of most general interest.

Class I—Development within the curtilage[32] of a dwelling-house

Class I permits three types of 'householder' development. Permitted development rights under Class I cannot be claimed in respect of a flat.[33] It appears that Class I can only apply in relation to premises which are used solely as a dwelling-house and that it cannot apply to premises with a dual use—for example, for residential and business purposes.[34]

In *Sainty v Minister of Housing and Local Government*[35] the Divisional Court approved the minister's decision that Class I 'must refer to a dwelling-house which is in existence when the operations mentioned in the Class are being carried out'. If, therefore, there is no building capable of use, if need be after repair, for ordinary residential purposes,[36] or if the use of a building as a dwelling-house has been abandoned,[37] Class I will not apply. Whether a particular building is a dwelling-house is largely a question of fact;[38] however, the factors which may be of assistance in answering that

---

[29] 'Road', 'trunk road' and 'classified road' are defined in Article 2(1) of the G.D.O.; and see the Roads (Scotland) Act 1984. See too *SPADS* Nos. A3039 (P/ENA/SA/11, 28th June 1979); and A3246 (P/PPA/FB/42, 11th February 1980); also *Young v Neilson* (1893) 20 R. (J.) 62.

[30] See J. B. McLoughlin, *Control and Urban Planning* (Faber & Faber, 1973), chapter 2.

[31] See, for example, *Control and Urban Planning* (above).

[32] The meaning of 'curtilage' is considered at p. 152 above.

[33] For the purposes of the G.D.O. 'dwelling-house' does not include a building containing one or more flats, or a flat contained within such a building (G.D.O., Art. 2(1)).

[34] See *Scurlock v Secretary of State for Wales* (1976) 238 E.G. 47; and appeal decision noted in [1981] J.P.L. 441.

[35] (1964) 15 P. & C.R. 432.

[36] See, for example, appeal decisions noted in *SPADS* No. A3254 (P/PPA/CC/43, 15th February 1980); [1977] J.P.L. 258; [1982] J.P.L. 806; and [1984] J.P.L. 282.

[37] See, for example, [1979] J.P.L. 117.

[38] As to the meaning of 'dwelling-house' see p. 153 above.

question were considered in *Gravesham Borough Council* v *Secretary of State for the Environment*.[39]

(1) *Enlargement, improvement or alteration of dwelling-house.*

Paragraph (1) of Class I permits the enlargement, improvement or other alteration of a dwelling-house so long as:

(*a*) the cubic content of the original[40] dwelling-house (as ascertained by external measurement[41]) is not exceeded by more than

    (i) in the case of a terrace house,[42] 50 cubic metres or one tenth, whichever is the greater; or

    (ii) in any other case, 50 cubic metres or one fifth, whichever is the greater,

subject (in either case) to a maximum of 115 cubic metres;

(*b*) the height of the building as so enlarged, altered or improved does not exceed the height of the highest part of the roof of the original dwelling-house;

(*c*) no part of the building as so enlarged, altered or improved projects beyond the forwardmost part of any wall of the original dwelling-house which fronts on a road;

(*d*) in the case of an enlargement, improvement or other alteration comprising a projection from the roof of the dwelling-house, the projection does not exceed specified limits as to roof area and height above the roof line of the dwelling-house;[43]

(*e*) where any part of the dwelling-house will as a result of the development lie within a distance of five metres from an existing garage[44] or coach-house, that building shall (for the purposes of the calculation of cubic content) be treated as forming part of the dwelling-house as enlarged, altered or improved;

(*f*) no part of the building (as so enlarged, improved or altered) which lies within a distance of two metres from any boundary of the curtilage of the dwelling-house has, as a result of the development, a height exceeding four metres;

(*g*) the area of ground covered by buildings within the curtilage (other than the original dwelling-house) does not exceed half the total area of the curtilage excluding the ground area of the original dwelling-house.

The erection of a garage or coach-house within the curtilage of the dwelling-house is to be treated as the enlargement of the dwelling-house for

---

[39] (1982) 47 P. & C.R. 142.

[40] i.e., the dwelling-house as existing on 1st July 1948, or in the case of a dwelling-house built on or after that date, as so built (G.D.O., Art. 2(1)).

[41] On the method of calculation see appeal decision noted in [1983] J.P.L. 67.

[42] 'Terrace house' is defined in Art. 2(1) of the G.D.O.

[43] As a result of this limitation, the provision of dormer windows will almost always require express permission.

[44] 'Garage' includes, it seems, a car-port—see [1971] J.P.L. 290.

all purposes of this permission (including the calculation of cubic content) if any part of that building lies within a distance of five metres from any part of the dwelling-house. The erection of a stable or loose-box anywhere within the curtilage of the dwelling-house is to be treated as the enlargement of the dwelling-house for all purposes of this permission (including the calculation of cubic content). Permission under Class I(1) is subject to standard conditions 1 and 2 (above).

Since works which do not materially affect the external appearance of a building do not constitute development,[45] permission under Class I(1) will only be relevant where there is to be an alteration in a building's external appearance.

It can sometimes be difficult to determine whether particular works fall within Class I(1).[46] It does not cover the complete rebuilding of a dwelling-house; in *Sainty v Minister of Housing and Local Government*[47] the minister's conclusion that 'After a dwelling-house is demolished that building is no longer capable of being enlarged, improved or altered and is therefore unable to benefit from the general permission contained in the Order' was upheld by the Divisional Court.[48] However, it will not always be easy to draw the line between 'improvement' or 'alteration' (which comes within Class I(1)) and 'rebuilding' (which does not).[49] And, as was pointed out by Lord Parker C.J. in *Sainty* (above), 'it may well be that it is possible to arrive at what in effect is a new erection by stages, each stage of which can be said to be an improvement.'

Difficulties can arise in the application of the phrase 'beyond the forwardmost part of any wall . . . which fronts on a road'.[50] In *Bradford Metropolitan District Council v Secretary of State for the Environment*[51] artificial stone cladding had been applied to the front wall of a dwelling-house. It was held that the Secretary of State had not erred in treating projecting window sills as part of the wall and in reaching the conclusion that since the stone cladding did not project beyond the sills, it was permitted development.[52] In *North West Leicestershire District Council v Secretary of State for the Environment*[53] an extension to an 'L-shaped' house with two

---

[45] 1972 Act, s.19 (2)(a) (see p. 119 above).
[46] See, for example, appeal decisions noted in [1969] J.P.L. 92; [1970] J.P.L. 165; [1974] J.P.L. 373; and [1978] J.P.L. 640.
[47] (1964) 15 P. & C.R. 432.
[48] See too *C. W. Larkin v Basildon District Council* [1980] J.P.L. 407; *SPADS* No. A2104 (P/PPA/PK/270, 2nd July 1970); and appeal decisions noted in [1974] J.P.L. 162 and 555; [1975] J.P.L. 418; [1976] J.P.L. 249; and [1978] J.P.L. 49. Contrast [1979] J.P.L. 332 (appeal decision).
[49] See F. J. B. Bourne, 'Dwelling-houses—Rebuild or Permitted Development' [1981] J.P.L. 567 and appeal decisions cited in that article.
[50] See, for example, *SPADS* Nos. A3246 (P/PPA/FB/42, 11th February 1980); A3801 (P/PPA/D/69, 3rd July 1981); and A4097 (P/PPA/FB/101, 6th April 1982); and appeal decisions noted in [1973] J.P.L. 107; [1982] J.P.L. 53; and [1983] J.P.L. 405 and 750.
[51] (1977) 35 P. & C.R. 387. See too appeal decision noted in [1982] J.P.L. 531.
[52] Contrast *SPADS* No. A4637 (P/PPA/FB/117, 17th May 1983).
[53] (1982) 46 P. & C.R. 154.

walls fronting a road had been carried out behind the further forward of the two walls but in front of the recessed wall. It was held that the inspector who determined an appeal against an enforcement notice served in respect of the extension had not erred in concluding that since the extension was behind the line produced by a projection of the forwardmost wall, it fell within Class I(1).

It seems clear that any earlier enlargement carried out under permission granted by the G.D.O. counts against the limits specified in Class I(1). However, it seems that an enlargement carried out under an express planning permission does not do so.[54]

(2) *Buildings, etc. for incidental purposes.* Under paragraph (2) of Class I there is permitted the erection, construction or placing and the maintenance, improvement or other alteration, within the curtilage of a dwelling-house, of any building or enclosure[55] (other than a dwelling, stable or loose-box)[56] required for a purpose incidental to the enjoyment of the dwelling-house as such, including the keeping of poultry,[57] bees, pet animals,[58] birds or other livestock for the domestic needs or personal enjoyment of the occupants of the dwelling-house, so long as:

(*a*) no part of such building or enclosure projects beyond the forwardmost part of any wall of the original dwelling-house which fronts on a road;

(*b*) in the case of a garage or coach-house, no part of the building is within a distance of five metres from any part of the dwelling-house;

(*c*) the height does not exceed, in the case of a building with a ridged roof, four metres or, in any other case, three metres;

(*d*) the area of ground covered by buildings within the curtilage (other than the original dwelling-house) does not thereby exceed half the total area of the curtilage excluding the ground area of the original dwelling-house.

(3) *Oil storage tanks.* The erection or placing within the curtilage of a dwelling-house of a tank for the storage of oil for domestic heating is permitted, subject to compliance with certain conditions, by paragraph (3) of Class I.

Class II—Minor operations

Paragraph (1) of Class II permits the erection or construction of gates,

---

[54] *Dawson v Secretary of State for the Environment* [1983] J.P.L. 544.
[55] A boundary wall or fence cannot, apparently, be regarded as an 'enclosure' for this purpose—see [1973] J.P.L. 320. 'Means of enclosure' come within Class II (1) (below).
[56] The Secretary of State for the Environment has expressed the view that this provision does not cover the erection of any accommodation which could be regarded as adding to or extending the normal living accommodation of the dwelling-house—see [1983] J.P.L. 683. Contrast the appeal decision noted at [1980] J.P.L. 198.
[57] See *Scottish Bulletin of Selected Appeal Decisions*, III/92 (deep-litter poultry shed for the keeping of up to twenty-five hens for domestic needs held to be permitted development).
[58] See, for example, appeal decision noted in [1982] J.P.L. 60.

fences, walls or other means of enclosure not exceeding 1 metre in height where abutting[59] on a road used by vehicular traffic or 2 metres in height in any other case;[60] maintenance, improvement or other alteration of such means of enclosure is also permitted. In *Prengate Properties Ltd.* v *Secretary of State for the Environment*[61] it was held that the construction of a wall was not authorised under Class II(1) unless it had some function of enclosure. Standard conditions 1 and 2 govern this permission.

Paragraph (2) grants permission for the painting or colouring of the exterior of any building or works otherwise than for purposes of advertisement, announcement or direction.

Class III—Changes of use

Permission is granted for development consisting of a change of use to:

(*a*) use as a general industrial building (as defined by the Use Classes Order[62]) from use as a special industrial building (as so defined);

(*b*) use as a light industrial building (as defined by the U.C.O.) from use as a special industrial building or a general industrial building (as so defined);

(*c*) use as a light industrial building (as defined by the U.C.O.) from use as a repository or warehouse[63] (used solely for wholesale to traders and not for trade with the public) or vice versa, provided that the total floor area does not exceed 235 square metres;

(*d*) use as any type of shop[64] other than those listed below from use as:

(i)   a shop for the sale of hot food;
(ii) a shop for the sale of pet animals or birds;
(iii) a betting office;[65]

(*e*) use for any purpose within Class I of the Schedule to the Use Classes Order (i.e. shop use) from use as a restaurant.

Class IV—Temporary buildings and uses

Paragraph (1) of Class IV grants permission for the erection or construction

---

[59]   A wall or fence does not need to be immediately adjacent to a road for it to be said to be 'abutting on' the road—see *Simmonds* v *Secretary of State for the Environment* [1981] J.P.L. 509. See too *Lewisham Borough Council* v *South Eastern Ry.* (1910) 8 L.G.R. 403 (applied in *SPADS* No. A3039 (P/ENA/SA/11, 28th June 1979)); and appeal decisions noted in [1969] J.P.L. 526; [1976] J.P.L. 190; [1981] J.P.L. 70; [1982] J.P.L. 129; and [1984] J.P.L. 295.

[60]   As to the point from which the height is to be measured see *SPADS* No. A2374 (P/ENA/HF/6, 13th June 1977); and [1979] J.P.L. 492.

[61]   (1973) 25 P. & C.R. 311. See too *Ewen Developments Ltd.* v *Secretary of State for the Environment* [1980] J.P.L. 404; and appeal decisions noted in [1979] J.P.L. 492; and [1982] J.P.L. 197.

[62]   See p. 158 above.

[63]   As to the meaning of 'repository or warehouse' see *Newbury District Council* v *Secretary of State for the Environment* [1981] A.C. 578. See too *Hooper* v *Slater* [1978] J.P.L. 252.

[64]   'Shop' is defined in Article 2(1) of the G.D.O.

[65]   Compare the provisions of Class I of the Use Classes Order—see p. 157 above.

of temporary buildings, works, plant or machinery in connection with certain operations carried out in pursuance of planning permission.[66]

Paragraph (2) permits the use of land (other than a building or the curtilage of a building) for any purpose except as a caravan site[67] or an open air market on not more than 28 days in total in any calendar year, and the erection or placing of moveable structures on the land for the purposes of that use. The benefit of this permission is not available to a person intending to use a site on a permanent basis—e.g. as a permanent motor racing circuit once a week. A permanent use of land and a temporary casual use for up to 28 days in any year are quite different things; the main test would seem to be the subjective one of the developer's intention.[68] In a case where substantial works of a permanent nature were necessary before land could be used for car racing and it was intended that the racing should be a permanent feature with a planned programme of up to twenty-eight meetings a year, the English minister concluded that such a use could not be said to be of a temporary nature and held that the general permission granted by the G.D.O. was not available.[69]

Class V—Agricultural buildings, works and uses

Paragraph (1) of Class V permits, subject to certain limitations, the carrying out on agricultural land,[70] having an area of more than 0.4 hectare and comprised in an agricultural unit,[71] of building or engineering operations requisite for the use of that land for the purposes of agriculture,[72] other than the placing on land of structures not designed for those purposes or the provision and alteration of dwellings.

Permitted development rights under Class V(1) can only be claimed where there is a subsisting agricultural use of land (and not merely prospective agricultural use) at the time the operations in question are carried out.[73] Further, to satisfy the definition of 'agricultural land', the land must be in use for a trade or business.[74]

The phrase 'operations requisite for the use of that land for agriculture' has given rise to difficulties. In *MacPherson* v *Secretary of State for Scotland*[75] the Inner House of the Court of Session accepted that the word 'requisite' as used in Class V(1) should be interpreted as equivalent to 'reasonably

[66] The meaning of this provision was considered in *Sunbury-on-Thames U.D.C.* v *Mann* (1958) 9 P. & C.R. 309 and in *Brown* v *Hayes and Harlington U.D.C.* (1963) 62 L.G.R. 66.

[67] Temporary use of land as a caravan site is dealt with in Class XXI (below).

[68] See *Miller-Mead* v *Minister of Housing and Local Government* [1963] 2 Q.B. 196; and *Tidswell* v *Secretary of State for the Environment* (1976) 34 P. & C.R. 152.

[69] *Selected Enforcement and Allied Appeals*, p. 27.

[70] As defined in the Agriculture (Scotland) Act 1948 (G.D.O., Art. 2(1)).

[71] As defined in the Agriculture (Scotland) Act 1948.

[72] See the definition of 'agriculture' in s.275 of the 1972 Act; see also p. 155 above.

[73] *Jones* v *Stockport Metropolitan Borough* (1983) 269 E.G. 408; and see, for example, appeal decisions reported in [1981] J.P.L. 129; [1983] J.P.L. 178; and [1984] J.P.L. 535.

[74] See, for example, appeal decisions reported in [1978] J.P.L. 864; and [1983] J.P.L. 687.

[75] 1985 S.L.T. 134.

necessary'.[76] The developer's opinion as to whether particular works are 'requisite' for agriculture may carry little or no weight; the test is an objective one. In *MacPherson* it had been contended on appeal to the Secretary of State that a proposal to tip approximately 1.5 million cubic metres of demolition material on a twenty acre site, and thus to fill a glen to an average depth of twenty metres, was requisite for agricultural purposes in that it would ultimately provide a higher quality of grazing land. Lord Cameron (with whom Lords Grieve and Wylie agreed) held that in determining the appeal the reporter had applied his mind to the right question—whether these engineering operations[77] were reasonably necessary for the use of the land for agriculture—and that in concluding that the operations did not fall within the ambit of Class V(1) the reporter had properly taken account of the scale of the operation, the time over which it would extend, and the absence of any explanation of the need for such a depth of infilling.[78]

As regards the erection of buildings 'requisite' for agriculture, the views expressed by the Secretary of State for the Environment on the interpretation of the corresponding provision of the English G.D.O. could, said Purchas L.J. in *Jones* v *Stockport Metropolitan Borough*,[79] 'only be described as vacillating'.[80] In *Jones* the Court of Appeal expressed the view that there was 'no basis for implying a limitation that the use of the building must be ancillary to the use of the parts of the land on which the building is not put, or that the use of the building must be in some way dependent on the use of the parts of the land on which the building is not put'; in the court's view all one need do is ask whether the building in question is reasonably necessary for the use of the land for agriculture.[81]

Buildings are only permitted under Class V(1) if they are designed for agricultural purposes. In *Belmont Farm Ltd.* v *Minister of Housing and*

[76] See too *Jones* v *Stockport Metropolitan Borough* (1983) 269 E.G. 408; and *R.* v *Secretary of State for the Environment, ex parte Powis* [1981] 1 W.L.R. 584.
[77] In a number of appeals the English minister has held that the tipping of materials on land did not amount to an engineering operation and was therefore outwith the scope of this Class—see, for example, [1978] J.P.L. 494; [1980] J.P.L. 348; [1981] J.P.L. 135; and [1983] J.P.L. 618. Contrast, however, *Fayrewood Fish Farms Ltd.* v *Secretary of State for the Environment* [1984] J.P.L. 267; and appeal decisions noted in [1979] J.P.L. 118; [1982] J.P.L. 263; and [1983] J.P.L. 561.
[78] See too *SPADS* No. A4622 (P/DEV/1/LC/1, 9th May 1983); and [1983] J.P.L. 561. Contrast *Northavon District Council* v *Secretary of State for the Environment* (1980) 40 P. & C.R. 332; and appeal decisions noted in [1976] J.P.L. 655; [1978] J.P.L. 118; and [1984] J.P.L. 196.
[79] (1983) 269 E.G. 408.
[80] See, for example, the appeal decisions reported in [1977] J.P.L. 47; [1981] J.P.L. 604; and [1982] J.P.L. 126 and 584; and see J. H. Dolman, 'Agricultural Permitted Development—Intensive Livestock Units' [1981] J.P.L. 795; F. J. B. Bourne, 'Class VI Again' [1982] J.P.L. 423; and F. J. B. Bourne, 'Class VI—Yet Again' [1983] J.P.L. 156.
[81] This seems to accord with the interpretation adopted by the Secretary of State for Scotland—see *SPADS* No. A3410 (P/ENA/HD/7, 26th August 1980); and ministerial decision reference P/PPR/R/1, 16th August 1980.

Local Government[82] it was held that a building 'designed' for the purposes of agriculture meant one so designed 'in the sense of its physical appearance and layout'; on that test an aircraft hangar was not a building designed for agricultural purposes.

Permission is granted under paragraph (2) of Class V for the erection etc. of roadside stands for milk churns, and under paragraph (3) for the winning and working of minerals required for agricultural purposes.

In *Jones* (above) Purchas L.J. said of the corresponding Class in the English G.D.O. that 'the statutory provisions have fallen far behind developments in the farming world', and suggested that the time had come for re-drafting the provisions. In a consultation paper on proposed amendments to the G.D.O. issued on 23rd January 1984 the Scottish Development Department stated that it was proposed to reword Class V in such a way as to provide a clear test in respect of agricultural buildings and engineering operations permitted under the Class. The consultation paper also stated that it was proposed to give planning authorities increased power to control piggeries and poultry buildings near residential areas, and to exclude fish farming from Class V(I). An earlier consultation paper, issued in July 1983, proposed that 'permitted development' status should no longer be accorded to (a) operations involving the deposit of waste material not generated on the agricultural unit itself and (b) operations involving the winning and working of minerals which are then moved off the agricultural unit.

Class VI—Forestry buildings and works

This Class permits the carrying out of certain building and other operations on land used for the purposes of forestry.

Class VII—Development for industrial purposes

Under Class VII permission is granted for the carrying out of specified types of development by industrial undertakers[83] on land used for industrial purposes. Development thus permitted includes (subject to certain limitations and conditions) extension or alteration of buildings,[84] provision of private ways[85] and railways, installation or erection of certain plant and

---

[82] (1962) 13 P. & C.R. 417. See too *Harding* v *Secretary of State for the Environment* [1984] J.P.L. 503; and appeal decisions noted in [1978] J.P.L. 867; [1981] J.P.L. 129; and [1982] J.P.L. 55.

[83] 'Industrial undertakers' means undertakers by whom an industrial process is carried on (G.D.O., Art. 2(1)); the term does not therefore include a person who merely owns land which is used for industrial purposes—see *Selected Enforcement and Allied Appeals*, p. 36. See too *Welsh Aggregates Ltd.* v *Secretary of State for the Environment* [1983] J.P.L. 50.

[84] So long as the height of the 'original building' is not exceeded, the cubic content is not exceeded by more than one fifth or the aggregate floor space by more than 1,000 square metres, and the operations do not materially affect the external appearance of the premises. As to the meaning of 'original building' see p. 175 above: and appeal decisions noted in [1982] J.P.L. 457: and [1984] J.P.L. 199.

[85] See *Welsh Aggregates* (above).

H

machinery, and deposit of waste materials. It is only if the existing use of the land is lawful (and not merely immune from enforcement action) that permission is granted by the G.D.O.[86]

Class XVI—Development by mineral undertakers

Class XVI applies *inter alia*, to the carrying out by mineral undertakers[87] of certain types of development, including the erection, alteration or extension of buildings, plant or machinery required in connection with the winning and working of minerals,[88] and the deposit (subject to certain limitations) of waste materials. It may be noted, however, that the planning authority have limited powers of control in connection with the erection, alteration or extension of a building[89] by mineral undertakers. Development by the National Coal Board is dealt with in Class XVII.

Class XVIII—Peat

Permission is granted, subject to standard condition 1, for the winning and working of peat by any person for the domestic requirements of that person.

Class XX—Development by planning authorities

Under this Class permission is granted for the carrying out (within their own area) by a regional, general or district planning authority of:

(*a*) works for the erection, enlargement, improvement or other alteration of dwelling-houses in accordance with a local plan or 'old style' development plan;

(*b*) any other development under the Housing (Scotland) Acts 1966 to 1980 in accordance with a local plan or 'old style' development plan;

(*c*) any development the estimated cost of which does not exceed £50,000, other than: (i) development to which paragraphs (a) or (b) above apply; (ii) 'bad neighbour' development (see p. 197 below); or (iii) development which constitutes a material change in the use of any buildings or other land.

Class XXI—Use as caravan site

In certain cases in which a site licence under the Caravan Sites and Control of Development Act 1960 is not required (relating in the main to temporary and minor uses), planning permission is granted for the use of land as a caravan site.

---

[86] See *Brooks and Burton* v *Secretary of State for the Environment* [1977] 1 W.L.R. 1294.

[87] As defined in Article 2(1) of the G.D.O. The meaning of the phrase 'mineral undertakers' (and of other terms used in this Class) was discussed in *English Clays Lovering Pochin & Co. Ltd.* v *Plymouth Corporation* [1973] 1 W.L.R. 1346; [1974] 1 W.L.R. 742.

[88] 'Building' does not, for the purposes of the G.D.O., include plant or machinery (G.D.O., Art. 2(1)).

[89] See *South Glamorgan County Council* v *Hobbs (Quarries) Ltd.* [1980] J.P.L. 35.

Class XXII—Development on licensed caravan sites

Under this Class permission is granted in respect of development required by the conditions of a site licence issued under the Caravan Sites and Control of Development Act 1960.

Directions restricting permitted development

Either the Secretary of State or a planning authority may, by direction under Article 4 of the G.D.O., direct that permission granted by Article 3 of the G.D.O. is not to apply (a) to all or any development of all or any of the classes specified in the First Schedule to the G.D.O., or (b) to any particular development within any of those classes. The making and effects of such a direction are considered in chapter 16 below.

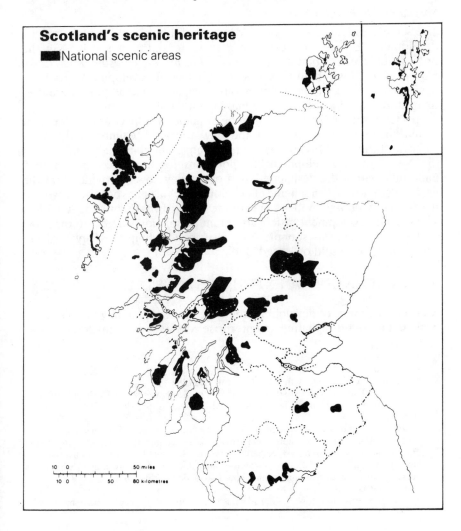

Scotland's scenic heritage

National scenic areas

In exercise of these powers the Secretary of State has made the Town and Country Planning (Restriction of Permitted Development) (National Scenic Areas) (Scotland) Direction 1980.[90] The Direction provides, because of the effect that such developments can have on scenery, that in the National Scenic Areas[91] (see the map reproduced above) the following classes of development are not to enjoy 'permitted development' status (and will therefore require express planning permission): (i) all buildings and structures over 12 metres high (including agricultural and forestry developments); (ii) vehicle tracks above 300 metres altitude except upland forestry tracks which are part of an afforestation proposal agreed by the planning authority; and (iii) all local roads authority roadworks outside present road boundaries costing more than £100,000.

Special development orders

The Secretary of State is empowered by s.21 of the 1972 Act to make special development orders, applicable only to such land as is specified in the order.[92] In *Essex County Council* v *Minister of Housing and Local Government*[93] it was held that in making a special development order the minister acts in a purely administrative capacity and is not, therefore, obliged to hear objections before making the order.

Special development orders have been made in respect of development within the designated areas of the new towns of Cumbernauld, East Kilbride, Irvine and Livingston.[94] The orders grant planning permission to the New Town Development Corporations for any development they undertake within the designated area of the new town, provided that the proposal accords with a scheme of development which has been approved by the Secretary of State under s.6(1) of the New Towns (Scotland) Act 1968. The special development orders also grant permission, subject to the same proviso, for proposals submitted by persons to whom the Development Corporation have sold or leased land.

D.   DESIGNATION OF ENTERPRISE ZONES

Certain categories of development may be granted planning permission by way of an order designating an enterprise zone (see p. 272 below).

---

[90]   The Direction was issued with S.D.D. Circular 20/1980.
[91]   The National Scenic Areas are defined in Part II of 'Scotland's Scenic Heritage', published by the Countryside Commission for Scotland on 26th April 1978—see S.D.D. Circular 20/1980.
[92]   In June 1981 the Secretary of State for the Environment issued a consultation paper suggesting that greater use might be made of special development orders. Such orders could grant planning permission for specified types of development in specified areas. No action has followed the consultation paper and no indication has been given as to whether the Secretary of State for Scotland is minded to take action of this kind.
[93]   (1967) 18 P. & C.R. 531.
[94]   The other Scottish new town, Glenrothes, is not covered by a special development order.

CHAPTER 8

CONTROL OF DEVELOPMENT
1: PLANNING APPLICATIONS

Introduction

Unless granted in one of the ways mentioned above, planning permission must be obtained from the planning authority (or the Secretary of State) before any particular development of land can be carried out (1972 Act, s.20(1)). It is this case by case consideration of development proposals that gives the British planning system its flexibility.

Development control—the day to day control exercised by planning authorities over the development of land—is that part of the planning system with which the individual citizen, whether as landowner, developer or affected neighbour, is most likely to come in contact. Development control is also, as McAuslan says,[1] 'the major area for legal expertise in the planning process'. 'The law', continues McAuslan, 'may be said to be concerned with three things here: (i) it sets out a procedure to be followed for the seeking of, and the giving of decisions on, planning permissions; (ii) it sets out the limits within which planning controls operate and is therefore inevitably involved in making decisions on whether these limits have been overstepped; and (iii) it provides mechanisms and remedies for legal challenges to the process if people feel aggrieved with it.'

However, as McAuslan cautions, just because the role of the law is important here, one should guard against assuming that it is all-important. Matters such as the detailed operation of development control in practice, the variety in local authority practice, and questions about the objectives and impact of development control are important but are beyond the scope of this work.[2] However, although this and the following three chapters are mainly concerned with statutory procedures and the controls exercised by the courts over the decision-making activities of planning authorities, it is worthy of mention that in recent years there has been a growth of general interest in and criticism of the role of development control. As one commentator put it:[3] 'Indeed, from being the Cinderella of the [town

---

[1] Patrick McAuslan, *Land, Law and Planning* (Weidenfeld and Nicolson, 1975), p. 350.

[2] For consideration of such matters see, for example, J. B. McLoughlin, *Control and Urban Planning* (Faber, 1973); J. Underwood, *Development Control: A Review of Research and Current Issues* (Pergamon Press, 1981); and M. L. Harrison, 'Development Control: the Influence of Political, Legal and Ideological Factors' (1972) 43 T.P. Rev. 254.

[3] H. W. E. Davies, 'The Relevance of Development Control' (1980) 51 T.P. Rev. 7.

planning] profession, development control has become a fully paid up ugly sister in the eyes of many of its critics.'

Criticism has been levelled both at the nature of the decisions taken and at the way in which these decisions are taken. Not all of the criticisms can be reconciled. Development control processes are, as the S.D.D. discussion paper, *Review of the Management of Planning*,[4] said: 'criticised as being too lengthy, as holding up vital investment, and as damaging the local, regional and national economy, but also as taking too little account of different points of view'. However, as the same paper points out, 'if there is to be more consultation and consideration, there cannot be significantly greater speed in decision taking'. In the last few years the various criticisms and suggestions have resulted in a number of changes in procedures. In particular, 'neighbour notification' of planning applications has given members of the public an increased opportunity for making their voices heard on planning proposals.

At the same time, attempts have been made to speed up decision making. The statutory procedures, many of them designed to ensure that competing considerations are properly taken into account and that the policies and objectives of different bodies are co-ordinated, and which are virtually the same whatever the scale of the proposed development, can be time-consuming. Steps have been taken by legislative and administrative means to try to reduce the time needed to arrive at decisions. S.D.D. Circular 24/1981, which stresses the importance of giving quick and sympathetic treatment to development proposals that will generate jobs and wealth, suggests that savings in time could result from revised local authority procedures such as the delegation of decision-making to officers and small sub-committees, the regular monitoring of the progress of applications and the prompt issuing of decisions. Inadequate documentation by applicants and consultations with outside bodies are acknowledged to be factors contributing to delay. To help eliminate delays caused by the latter, a code of practice was issued with the circular and authorities were encouraged to limit consultation on proposed developments to those bodies clearly affected by the proposals.

Application for planning permission

Although a person proposing to carry out development may well have had preliminary discussions with the planning authority about his proposals (and S.D.D. Circular 26/1984 recommends that planning authorities should encourage their staff to advise intending applicants about adjustments to proposals and plans which would improve an application's chances of success), it is the formal application for planning permission that sets the statutory machinery of development control in motion.

An application may be made for planning permission *simpliciter* (i.e. full permission) or for outline permission; the former will include details of the

[4]   S.D.D., April 1977.

proposed development[5] whereas, in a case where it is desired to obtain a decision in principle on a proposal to carry out building or other operations, an application for outline permission, which need only be accompanied by a site plan, may be made (below). In either case the principle of the development is placed in issue.[6]

An application for planning permission is to be made to the district or general planning authority in whose area the development is to take place (G.D.O., Art. 8(1)). Application is to be made on a form issued by and obtainable from the planning authority and is to include the particulars required by that form; the application is to be accompanied by a plan sufficient to identify the land to which it relates and by such other plans and drawings as are necessary to describe the proposed development, together with such additional number of copies (not exceeding three) of the form and plans as may be required by the planning authority (G.D.O., Art. 8(1)).

The planning authority may direct the applicant to supply further information and may require the production of evidence to verify any information required.

Where development for which planning permission was granted has not yet commenced and the time limit within which development must be begun or within which an application for approval of reserved matters must be submitted (see p. 261 below) has not yet expired, a fresh application for planning permission for that development may be made without submission of the detail required in the initial application (see G.D.O., Art. 8(3)). All that is required is that the application be made in writing and provide sufficient information to enable the authority to identify the previous grant of permission.

Application for planning permission may be made in respect of buildings or works constructed or carried out, or a use of land instituted, before the date of the application, whether the buildings or works were constructed or carried out, or the use instituted, without planning permission or in accordance with planning permission granted for a limited period (1972 Act, s.29(1) and (2)). Application may also be made to retain buildings or works or continue the use of land without complying with a condition subject to which a previous permission was granted (1972 Act, s.29(1)(b)[7]).

In *Britannia (Cheltenham) Ltd.* v *Secretary of State for the Environment*[8] Sir Douglas Frank thought it competent for the applicants and the planning authority to agree to a variation of an application at any time up to

[5] However, even though full details have been submitted, the planning authority may, of their own initiative, impose a condition requiring that the authority's subsequent approval be obtained in regard to specified matters (see p. 192 below).
[6] See *Alexander Russell Ltd.* v *Secretary of State of Scotland* 1984 S.L.T. 81.
[7] Inserted by the Local Government and Planning (Scotland) Act 1982, Sched. 2, para. 7. A consultation paper issued by the Scottish Development Department on 31st July 1984 proposed that the planning legislation be amended to provide for the making at any time of an application for the removal or variation of a condition attached to a grant of planning permission.
[8] [1978] J.P.L. 554. See too *Centre Hotels (Cranston) Ltd.* v *Secretary of State for the Environment* [1982] J.P.L. 108.

determination of the application. However, in *Bernard Wheatcroft Ltd.* v *Secretary of State for the Environment*[9] (see p. 255 below) Forbes J. stressed the importance of not depriving those who should have been consulted on an application of the opportunity to comment, and in view of the statutory provisions on publicity for and consultations on applications it is suggested that it would not be proper, after these steps have been taken, for an application to be amended so as to make it substantially different from that submitted; in such circumstances a completely fresh application would seem to be appropriate.

Application for outline planning permission

By making application for outline planning permission it may be possible for an intending developer to ascertain, without spending time and money upon the preparation of detailed plans, whether the planning authority are prepared to give approval in principle to the carrying out of operations on a particular site.

'Outline planning permission' means a planning permission for the carrying out of building or other *operations*[10] which is granted subject to a condition (in addition to any other conditions which may be imposed) requiring subsequent approval to be obtained from the planning authority with respect to one or more 'reserved matters' (below) of which details have not been given in the application (G.D.O., Art. 2(1)).

An application for outline permission is to be made on a form issued by the planning authority, must describe the development to which it relates and must be accompanied by a site plan; the application may contain such further information as the applicant desires to submit (G.D.O., Art. 8(2)).

Matters in respect of which details have been included in an application for outline permission cannot, it seems, be treated as 'reserved matters'; if, therefore, an applicant wishes to give some purely illustrative indication of how the development might ultimately be carried out, the fact that these details do not form part of the application should be made clear. Where the planning authority are not prepared to approve of some matter of which details have been submitted, they may impose a condition requiring their subsequent approval of that matter, not as a 'reserved matter' under the G.D.O., but as an ordinary planning condition.[11] The subsequent approval would not be for approval of 'reserved matters' but for any 'consent, agreement or approval . . . required by a condition imposed on a grant of planning permission' (see p. 192 below).

If the planning authority are of the opinion that they ought not to consider a particular application for outline permission separately from the consideration of any one or more 'reserved matters' they may inform the

---

[9]   (1980) 43 P. & C.R. 233.

[10]   And not for a change of use alone—see, for example, *Glacier Metal Co. Ltd.* v *London Borough of Hillingdon* (1975) 239 E.G. 573.

[11]   See, for example, *Sutton London Borough Council* v *Secretary of State for the Environment* (1975) 29 P. & C.R. 350.

applicant that they are unable to entertain the application unless further details on such matters as they may specify are submitted (G.D.O., Art. 8(2)). The applicant is entitled to appeal to the Secretary of State against such a decision.

Every outline planning permission is subject to a condition that application for approval of reserved matters must be made within a specified time limit (see p. 262 below).

Application for approval of reserved matters

An application for approval of reserved matters is not an application for planning permission; it is, in Lord Wheatley's words, 'just a step in the process of applying for planning permission and is part and parcel of the application for planning permission'.[12] An application for approval of reserved matters need not therefore be accompanied by a certificate under s.24 of the 1972 Act[13] (see. p. 193 below).

'Reserved matters' are any matters in respect of which details have not been given in an outline application and which concern the siting, design, or external appearance of any building to which the outline permission relates, or the means of access to such a building, or the landscaping[14] of the site in respect of which the application was made (G.D.O., Art. 2(1)).

The courts have not, in general, adopted a strict approach towards applications for approval of reserved matters.[15]

In *Inverclyde District Council* v *Inverkip Building Co. Ltd.*[16] outline planning permission was granted for housing development subject to a condition that further approval was to be obtained with respect to the density of the proposed development; the means of drainage and disposal of sewage; the landscaping[17] and treatment of boundary walls and fences; and the reservation of a specified area for such educational, social, commercial and recreational development as the planning authority might approve. The planning authority sought reduction of the outline permission on the ground that it was *ultra vires* to reserve these matters for subsequent approval as they did not fall within the definition of 'reserved matters'. The Second Division of the Court of Session held that whether a particular condition fell to be treated as a condition relating to a reserved matter depended on the circumstances of the individual case, and that on a broad common-sense approach and having regard to the nature of the development, the matters specified in the condition at issue in this case, apart from the reservation of

---

[12] *Inverclyde District Council* v *Secretary of State for Scotland* 1980 S.C. 363; 1981 S.L.T. 26.

[13] *R.* v *Bradford-on-Avon U.D.C., ex parte Boulton* [1964] 1 W.L.R. 1136.

[14] 'Landscaping' is defined in Art. 2(1) of the G.D.O.

[15] See, for example, *Cardiff Corporation* v *Secretary of State for Wales* (1971) 22 P. & C.R. 718 (an application which bore to be for full planning permission in respect of a development for which outline permission had previously been granted could be treated as a valid application for approval of reserved matters).

[16] 1983 S.L.T. 563; and see comment in 1982 S.P.L.P. 76 and 1983 S.P.L.P. 47.

[17] 'Landscaping' was not included in the definition of reserved matters in the G.D.O. of 1950 (as amended) which was in operation at the time the permission was granted.

the specified area, were 'reserved matters' within the meaning of the G.D.O.;[18] in particular, 'density' concerned siting, design and external appearance and could affect means of access; drainage and disposal of sewage concerned siting and to some extent design; and landscaping and treatment of boundary walls and fences concerned siting and design.

On the other hand in *Grampian Regional Council* v *Secretary of State for Scotland*[19] it was doubted whether an anticipated traffic problem at a road junction about one and a half kilometres from the application site was a matter which could be reserved as concerning 'means of access' in terms of the G.D.O.

An application for approval of reserved matters must be within the ambit of the outline planning permission,[20] must not depart from it in a material way (though an application for something outwith the scope of the outline permission need not invalidate the application—see below), and must be in accordance with the conditions annexed to the outline permission.[21] However, in *Inverclyde District Council* v *Secretary of State for Scotland*,[22] in which the original application for approval of details fell outwith the scope of the outline permission, the Second Division of the Court of Session saw no reason why the application could not be amended to bring it into line with the outline permission.

Application for approval of reserved matters is to be in writing, is to give particulars sufficient to identify the outline planning permission in relation to which it is made, and is to include such particulars and be accompanied by such plans and drawings as the authority consider necessary to enable them to deal with the application (G.D.O., Art. 9(1)). In *Inverclyde District Council* v *Secretary of State for Scotland*[23] the House of Lords held that the requirements as to the particulars to be submitted with the application were directory only, so that a failure to comply did not invalidate an application. Lord Keith stated that there was no reason why further particulars should not be allowed to be proferred at a later stage.

There would seem to be no reason why application for approval of reserved matters should not be made by stages[24] or relate to part only of the site covered by the outline permission.[25] The planning authority might, however, refuse approval of a 'piecemeal' application on the ground that

---

[18] The Lord Ordinary (Lord McDonald) took a rather different view—see *Inverclyde District Council* v *Inverkip Building Co. Ltd.* 1981 S.C. 401; 1982 S.L.T. 401.

[19] 1983 S.L.T. 526.

[20] It can relate to more than one outline permission—see *Lobb* v *Secretary of State for the Environment* [1984] J.P.L. 336.

[21] See *Inverclyde District Council* v *Secretary of State for Scotland* 1980 S.C. 363; 1981 S.L.T. 26 (Second Division); and 1982 S.L.T. 200 (H.L.); *Heron Corporation Ltd.* v *Manchester City Council* [1978] 1 W.L.R. 937; and see p. 258 below.

[22] Above.

[23] 1982 S.L.T. 200; and see comment in 1982 S.P.L.P. 47.

[24] See *R.* v *Secretary of State for the Environment, ex p. Percy Bilton Industrial Properties Ltd.* (1975) 31 P. & C.R. 154.

[25] See *Inverclyde District Council* v *Secretary of State for Scotland* 1980 S.C. 363; 1981 S.L.T. 26 (Court of Session); 1982 S.L.T. 200 (H.L.).

they considered that the various reserved matters should not be dealt with separately. There is no reason in law why, where there has been a grant of approval of reserved matters, those reserved matters should not be revised or varied by a further submission of reserved matters under the same outline permission.[26] In *Inverclyde District Council* v *Secretary of State for Scotland* (above) the House of Lords held that although an application for approval of all reserved matters has to be made within the statutory time limit (see p. 262 below), there was no good reason why amendment of an application for approval of reserved matters should not be permitted at any stage, even outside the time limit, provided it was still within the ambit of the outline permission.[27]

An application for planning permission and an application for approval of reserved matters may be contained in the same document. In *Inverclyde District Council* v *Secretary of State for Scotland* (above) application was made in 1976 for 'any permission' required under the Planning Acts for the erection of houses on an area for which outline permission had been granted in 1974. The 1974 permission showed an area reserved for 'educational, social, commercial and recreational development'. The 1976 application showed the proposed housing development extending over this reserved area. The House of Lords held that in so far as the application related to the reserved area, it was to be regarded as a fresh application for planning permission for that area.

In *Etheridge* v *Secretary of State for the Environment*[28] Woolf J. held that a full planning permission for houses on part of a site for which outline permission had previously been granted for housing served also as approval of details reserved in the original outline permission.

Application for planning permission in anticipation of disposal of Crown land

Until the coming into operation of the Town and Country Planning Act 1984 government departments and other Crown bodies were unable to apply for planning permission when they wished to dispose of Crown land (see p. 169 above). Prior to the 1984 Act two procedural devices were employed to overcome this difficulty. First, there was a procedure under which an informal opinion as to acceptable uses of Crown land could be sought from the planning authority or, in cases of disagreement, from the Secretary of State. However, in *R.* v *Worthing Borough Council*[29] it was held that the giving of such an opinion by the Secretary of State was an unlawful fetter on the discretion of the planning authority. Secondly, a third party might be

---

[26] See *Heron Corporation Ltd.* v *Manchester City Council* [1978] 1 W.L.R. 937.

[27] For an example of a case in which it was considered that proposed amendments to an application would have the effect of altering the whole character of the application, see *SPADS* No. A4709 (P/PPA/GA/52, 5th July 1983).

[28] (1983) 48 P. & C.R. 35; see too *Cardiff Corporation* v *Secretary of State for Wales* (1971) 22 P. & C.R. 718.

[29] [1984] J.P.L. 261.

asked to submit a planning application in respect of the land; however, in 1983 the government was advised that the planning legislation precluded the making of such an application.

Under the 1984 Act an application for planning permission may be made by the appropriate authority (the government department owning or managing the land or the Crown Estate Commissioners) or by any person authorised by that authority (s.1(1),(2)). Where such an application is made, the statutory provisions relating to the making and determination of a planning application are to apply as if the land were not Crown land (s.1(2)), subject to the modifications made by the Town and Country Planning (Crown Land Applications) (Scotland) Regulations 1984. The 1984 Act provides that a grant of planning permission is to apply only to development carried out after the land has ceased to be Crown land or to development carried out by virtue of a private interest in the land (s.1(3)). Section 1(8) validates any permission which may have been granted in respect of Crown land in which there was no other interest.

Application for consent, agreement or approval

The planning legislation recognises[30] that a planning authority may attach to a grant of planning permission a condition, distinct from a condition requiring the subsequent approval of 'reserved matters', requiring the subsequent consent, agreement or approval of the planning authority to be obtained for a specified aspect of a proposed development.[31] The planning authority might, for example, require that before a permitted use is commenced, provision for the abatement of noise should be made in accordance with a scheme approved by the authority. An application for such consent, agreement or approval is not a planning application and does not attract a fee.

Application for variation of planning permission

After planning permission has been granted for a development the developer may wish to make some minor alteration to the approved proposal. Section 31A of the 1972 Act[32] provides that the planning authority may, at the request of the grantee or his agent, vary a planning permission in

---

[30]   See 1972 Act, s.28(dd) (inserted by the Local Government and Planning (Scotland) Act 1982, Sched. 2, para. 6) and ss.33 and 34 (as amended by the 1982 Act, Sched. 2, paras. 11 and 12).

[31]   See *Sutton London Borough Council* v *Secretary of State for the Environment* (1975) 29 P. & C.R. 350; *Roberts* v *Vale Royal D.C.* (1977) 39 P. & C.R. 514; and *Bilboe* v *Secretary of State for the Environment* [1979] J.P.L. 100 (Divisional Court); and (1980) 39 P. & C.R. 495 (C.A.).

[32]   Inserted by s.46 of the 1982 Act.

a case where they are satisfied that the variation is not material.[33] An application for a non-material variation of this kind is not subject to the statutory requirements on publicity, nor does it attract a fee.

Notification of application for planning permission to owners and agricultural tenants

An applicant for planning permission need not have any legal interest in the land to which the application relates,[34] nor does he require the consent of the owner, but if the applicant is not the owner of the land, he will have to give notice of the making of the planning application to the owner. Notice of the making of an application must in every case be given to any agricultural tenant of the land.

Section 24(1) of the 1972 Act[35] provides that a planning authority shall not entertain an application for planning permission unless it is accompanied by one of the four certificates specified in that sub-section. Unless the applicant can certify that at the beginning of the period of twenty-one days ending with the date of the application, no person other than the applicant himself was the owner[36] of any of the land to which the application relates, he must certify that he has given notice of the application to all persons who, at the beginning of the period of 21 days ending with the date of the application, were owners of any of the land to which the application relates; if, after taking reasonable steps, the applicant has been unable to ascertain the names and addresses of some or all of the owners, he must so certify and must also certify that notice of the application has been published in a local newspaper (s.24(1),(2)).

Owners of mineral rights in land are to be notified of an application for the winning and working of minerals in the same way as owners of the land (see p. 477 below). In the case of applications for underground mining the requirements as to notification are modified to take account of the difficulty that may be encountered in ascertaining the names and addresses of all owners (see p. 477 below).

Any certificate issued for the purposes of s.24 must contain either a statement to the effect that none of the land to which the application relates constitutes or forms part of an agricultural holding[37] or a statement that the

---

[33] This appears to give statutory effect to Lord Denning's statement in *Lever Finance Ltd.* v *Westminster (City) London Borough Council* [1971] 1 Q.B. 222 that a planning permission covers the work in the approved plans together with any immaterial variation thereof. See too *Kerrier District Council* v *Secretary of State for the Environment* (1980) 41 P. & C.R. 284.

[34] See *Hanily* v *Minister of Housing and Local Government* [1952] 2 Q.B. 444, per Parker J.

[35] As amended by the Local Government, Planning and Land Act 1980.

[36] For the purposes of s.24 'owner' includes a lessee under a lease with not less than seven years to run (s.24(7), as amended by the Local Government, Planning and Land Act 1980, s.92(2),(3); and the Local Government and Planning (Scotland) Act 1982, Sched. 2, para. 3(c)).

[37] As defined in the Agricultural Holdings (Scotland) Act 1949 (see 1972 Act, s.24(7)). The grant of planning permission may result in loss of the security of tenure which an agricultural tenant enjoys under the Agricultural Holdings (Scotland) Acts.

applicant has given the requisite notice to any agricultural tenant (s.24(4) and s.26(3)).

Any notice or certificate issued for the purposes of s.24 is to be in the form set out in Schedule 3 to the G.D.O. (G.D.O., Art. 6). Any person who knowingly or recklessly issues a false certificate is guilty of an offence (s.24(5)).

An owner or agricultural tenant has a period of at least 21 days within which he may make representations on the application to the planning authority. The authority may not decide the application before the expiry of that period (s.24(4)).

As mentioned above, the planning authority are not to entertain an application for planning permission unless it is accompanied by a certificate under s.24. It would seem that failure to furnish any certificate or failure to furnish a certificate in the correct form will deprive the planning authority of jurisdiction to deal with the application.[38] A factual error in a certificate may be no more than a mere irregularity that does not go to the jurisdiction of the planning authority to entertain the application for planning permission; however, an error may be so gross as to render the certificate a complete nullity, and a defect which is more that a mere irregularity may entitle the court to strike down a subsequent grant of planning permission.[39] D.H.S. Circular 66/1959 stated that while it is not the duty of the planning authority to check the accuracy of a certificate, 'this does not preclude them from questioning the statements in a certificate if they see good reason to do so.'

Publicity for applications[40]

The planning legislation of 1947 proceeded on the basis that an application for planning permission concerned only the applicant and the planning authority. Although the legislation required an application for planning permission to be recorded in the register of planning applications (see p. 261 below), and in that way every application was, in a sense, a matter of public knowledge, there was no obligation on the applicant or the planning authority to give any public notice of the application or to notify neighbours or other 'third parties'.

The absence of any machinery for involving the public in development control was defended on grounds of principle as well as of administrative convenience. Planning, it was said, was concerned to ensure that development was controlled in the public interest; it was not the function of planning

---

[38]   See appeal decisions noted in [1966] J.P.L. 492; and [1973] J.P.L. 612.

[39]   See *Main* v *Swansea City Council* (1984) 49 P. & C.R. 26, applying *Co-operative Retail Services Ltd.* v *Taff-Ely Borough Council* (1979) 39 P. & C.R. 223 and *London and Clydeside Estates Ltd.* v *Aberdeen District Council* 1980 S.C. (H.L.) 1; 1980 S.L.T. 81; and considering *R.* v *Bradford-on-Avon Urban District Council, ex parte Boulton* [1964] 1 W.L.R. 1136.

[40]   See C. M. Brand and Brian Thompson, 'Third Parties and Development Control—A Better Deal for Scottish Neighbours?' [1982] J.P.L. 743; and C. M. Brand, 'Neighbour Notification' 1982 S.P.L.P. 72.

to seek to protect the private interests of members of the public against the activities of others. On the other hand, it can be argued, as the Scottish Law Commission did in a Memorandum issued in 1967,[41] that 'the state of public opinion, whether of fairly immediate neighbours or of a substantial part of the community as a whole, is part of the information which an elected representative ought to have before him when he is making up his mind' on a planning application. The Commission expressed the view that the general lack of opportunity for the expression of public opinion on planning applications could have the effect 'of shaking the general faith in what should be a democratic process' and recommended that all applications should be publicised.

Over the years governments made concessions in the face of continuing pressure from various quarters for increased publicity for planning applications[42] and the point has now been reached where all planning applications are publicised in some way.[43] The publicising of applications means that persons who wish to do so have an opportunity to make representations to the planning authority. In general, the period allowed is 14 days (see G.D.O., Art. 10(3)[44]) but a period of 21 days applies in respect of publicity arranged for the purposes of s.25 of the 1972 Act (below).

Planning authorities proposing to carry out development must comply with the statutory requirements on publicity as if they were making application for planning permission (see p. 273 below). Although development proposals of government departments are not subject to statutory publicity, it is intended that they should be publicised in the same way as if the Notice of Proposed Development given by a department were an application for planning permission (S.D.D. Circular 21/1984, see p. 170 above).

(i) *Neighbour notification.*[45] Under Article 7[46] of the G.D.O. it is, in general, the duty of an applicant for planning permission or for approval of reserved matters[47] to serve on any person who holds a 'notifiable interest' in

---

[41] Memorandum No. 4, *Applications for Planning Permission.*

[42] For an account of the development of publicity arrangements for planning applications see Eric Young, 'Publicity for Planning Applications' 1974 S.L.T. (News) 19.

[43] Planning authorities have also been encouraged to be on the alert to advertise any application which might be of wide interest—see S.D.D. Circulars 49/1971 and 59/1974.

[44] As substituted by the Town and Country Planning (General Development) (Scotland) Amendment Order 1984.

[45] The questions whether the notification procedure is mandatory or directory and whether the procedure confers *locus standi* on a neighbour so that he might be able to challenge a planning decision are considered by C. M. Brand and Brian Thompson in 'Third Parties and Development Control—A Better Deal for Scottish Neighbours?' [1982] J.P.L. 743.

[46] Made under s.23 of the 1972 Act, as substituted by s.41 of the 1982 Act. A new Article 7 was inserted by the Town and Country Planning (General Development) (Scotland) Amendment Order 1984.

[47] The requirements do not extend to applications for any consent, agreement or approval required by a condition attached to a grant of planning permission but the planning authority may at their discretion publicise such an application if they think it ought to be drawn to public attention.

'neighbouring land' a copy of the application, together with a notice[48] stating:

(a) that the plans or drawings relating to the application may be inspected in the register kept by the planning authority;

(b) the address at which the plans may be so inspected if different from the address of the planning authority shown on the application; and

(c) the period within which the plans may be inspected (G.D.O., Art. 7(1)).

'Neighbouring land' is defined in Article 2(1) of the G.D.O.; the basis of definition is land which is conterminous with or within 4 metres of the boundary of the land for which development is proposed (with the qualification that any part of the land must be within 90 metres of any part of the development in question) but there are somewhat complex provisos dealing with buildings divided into separate units and extending the definition where a road is adjacent to or near the land on which development is proposed.

The parties holding a 'notifiable interest' in neighbouring land are (a) in the case of lands and heritages entered in the valuation roll, the persons appearing therefrom to be owners, lessees and occupiers; and (b) in any other case, the owners, lessees and occupiers of the land.

The planning authority are not to entertain an application unless it is accompanied by a certificate[49] stating:

(a) that notices have been served in terms of Article 7(1) of the G.D.O.; or

(b) that no notification in terms of Article 7(1) is required; or

(c) that the applicant has taken such steps as are reasonably open to him (specifying them) to ascertain the names and addresses of all the parties holding a notifiable interest in neighbouring land, and either:

(i) that the names and addresses of the parties holding a notifiable interest in neighbouring land have not been ascertained and no notice has been served in terms of Article 7(1); or

(ii) that notices have been served in terms of Article 7(1) on one or more of the parties holding a notifiable interest in neighbouring land but that the names and addresses of the other parties holding a notifiable interest have not been ascertained;

(d) where appropriate, the names and addresses of all those parties having a notifiable interest in neighbouring land who have been notified in terms of Article 7(1) (G.D.O., Art. 7(3)).

---

[48] The notice is to be in the form set out in Part IV of Schedule 3 to the G.D.O. or in a form substantially to the like effect—G.D.O., Art. 7(1).

[49] The certificate is to be in the form set out in Part V of Schedule 3 to the G.D.O., or in a form substantially to the like effect.

The planning authority may dispense with the requirements for neighbour notification in relation to neighbouring land separated by a road from the land on which the development is proposed (G.D.O., Art. 7(4)). S.D.D. Circular 6/1984 states that the dispensation power, intended to relieve applicants of the normal statutory requirements where these would be unduly onerous, should be exercised sparingly and normally only where the proposed development is taking place in a tenement or similar building and the neighbouring land is predominantly or exclusively of a tenemental or similar nature.

Where the applicant has been unable to notify all those with a notifiable interest or the authority have granted a dispensation under Article 7(4) of the G.D.O., the planning authority must advertise the application in a local newspaper (below).

(ii) *Press advertisement.* Article 7(5) of the G.D.O. provides that in certain circumstances applications must be advertised by the planning authority in a newspaper circulating in the locality in which the land is situated.[50] These are:

(a) where the applicant has submitted a certificate under Article 7(3)(c) of the G.D.O. (above) to the effect that he has failed to notify all those with a notifiable interest in neighbouring land;

(b) where, in terms of Article 7(4) of the G.D.O. (above), the planning authority have dispensed with the requirement to notify those with a notifiable interest in neighbouring land across the road; and

(c) where the application relates to development of one or more of the classes of development specified in Schedule 2 to the G.D.O.[51] These are developments which may have a significant and possibly adverse effect on amenity and are often referred to as 'bad neighbour' developments. The following classes of development are specified for this purpose:

1. the construction of buildings for use as a public convenience;
2. the construction of buildings or other operations, or use of land, for the disposal of refuse or waste materials, or for the storage or recovery of re-usable metal;
3. the construction of buildings or other operations (other than the laying of sewers, the construction of pumphouses in a line of sewers, the construction of septic tanks and cesspools serving single dwelling-houses, or single buildings in which not more than 10 people will normally reside, work or congregate and works ancillary thereto) or use of land for the retention, treatment or disposal of sewage, trade-waste, or effluent;

---

[50] In Northern Ireland it has been held that a failure to comply with a statutory provision requiring advertisement of a planning application rendered the planning permission *ultra vires*—see *Morelli* v *Department of the Environment* [1976] N.I. 159. See too appeal decision reported in [1983] J.P.L. 138.

[51] As substituted by the Town and Country Planning (General Development) (Scotland) Amendment Order 1984.

4. the construction of buildings or other operations or use of land as a scrap yard or coal yard, or for the winning or working of minerals;

5. the construction of buildings or use of land for the purposes of a slaughterhouse or knacker's yard; or for the killing or plucking of poultry;

6. the construction of buildings and use of buildings for any of the following purposes, namely, as a theatre, cinema, music hall, dance hall, fun fair, bingo hall, casino, skating rink, swimming bath, gymnasium (not forming part of a school, college or university), building for indoor games, Turkish or other vapour or foam bath, licensed premises,[52] or hot food shop;

7. the construction of buildings and the use of buildings or land as a zoo, or wildlife park, or for the business of boarding or breeding cats or dogs;

8. the construction of buildings and use of buildings or land as a crematorium, or use of land as a cemetery;

9. the construction of buildings and use of buildings or land for motor car or motor cycle racing;

10. construction of a building to a height exceeding 20 metres;

11. the construction of buildings, operations, and use of buildings or land which will alter the character of an area of established amenity;

12. the construction of buildings, operations, and use of buildings or land which will introduce significant change into a homogeneous area;

13. the construction of buildings, operations, and use of buildings or land which will affect residential property by reason of fumes, noise, vibration, smoke, artificial lighting, or the discharge of any solid or liquid substance;

14. the construction of buildings, operations, or use of buildings or land which will bring crowds into a generally quiet area;

15. the construction of buildings, operations, or use of buildings or land which will cause activity and noise between the hours of 8 p.m. and 8 a.m.

To avoid duplication, the above requirements as to press advertisement are not to apply where a notice has been published in accordance with s.24(2) of the 1972 Act (relating to notification of owners and agricultural tenants—see p. 193 above) or is required to be published by the planning authority in accordance with s.25(2)(a) of the 1972 Act (relating to publicity for applications affecting conservation areas—below) (G.D.O., Art. 7(6)).

Where the planning authority are required to publish a notice in a newspaper in accordance with Article 7(5) of the G.D.O. (above), the applicant is to pay the cost to be incurred by the authority at the time of submitting his application (G.D.O., Art. 7(7)). The press advertisement should be in the form set out in Part VI of Schedule 3 to the G.D.O. This provides for a number of applications to be advertised jointly in a 'block' advertisement. S.D.D. Circular 6/1984 recommends that authorities should arrange for such advertisements to be placed at regular intervals in the same newspaper so that members of the public become familiar with the pattern of their appearance.

Under s.25 of the 1972 Act[53] it is the responsibility of the planning

---

[52]   The term 'licensed premises' is defined in Article 2(1) of the G.D.O.

[53]   As amended by the Town and Country Amenities Act 1974.

authority to publicise any application for planning permission in respect of development which would, in the opinion of the authority, (a) affect the character or appearance of a conservation area or (b) affect the setting of a listed building. In such a case the planning authority must publish notice of the application in a local newspaper and, for not less than 7 days, display a notice on or near the land. A period of at least 21 days is allowed for representations on such an application (s.25(3)).

The Town and Country Planning (Development Contrary to Development Plans) (Scotland) Direction 1981 (as amended) provides that before granting permission for development which does not accord with the provisions of the development plan, the application must have been advertised in a local newspaper and a period of 21 days allowed for representations (see p. 209 below).

Where a planning authority require planning permission for development which they propose to carry out, they must give notice of their intention to develop in a local newspaper, indicating where plans of the development may be inspected and allowing a period of 21 days for representations to be made to the authority (see p. 273 below).

Fees for applications and deemed applications

Under s.87 of the Local Government, Planning and Land Act 1980 the Secretary of State is empowered to make regulations prescribing fees for planning applications. The government's aim in introducing fees was simply to offset some of the costs of administering development control. Prior to the introduction of fees it was said that it was the government's intention that the scheme should be simple; however, the regulations currently in force, the Town and Country Planning (Fees for Applications and Deemed Applications) (Scotland) Regulations 1983, are fairly complex.[54]

Fees are payable in respect of applications for planning permission; applications for approval of reserved matters; applications for consent to display advertisements; and deemed applications arising from enforcement appeals and established use certificate appeals. Fees are not payable in respect of other types of application. The level of fees is related broadly to the scale of the development in question. The scale of fees is contained in Part II of the Schedule to the fees regulations;[55] that scale is summarised in Appendix 2 (p. 544 below).

The regulations exempt certain categories of application from the requirement to pay a fee. The exempted classes include applications for certain alterations to a dwellinghouse which is the residence of a disabled person; applications for alterations to provide access for disabled persons to buildings to which the public have access; applications which are required to be made only because of the withdrawal of 'deemed' permission under the G.D.O. by means of an Article 4 direction (see p. 386) or by way of a

[54] Helpful guidance is to be found in S.D.D. Circular 33/1983.
[55] Experience since the introduction of fees in 1981 suggests, however, that the fees may well be subject to increase at regular intervals.

condition attached to a planning permission; and applications for the erection of agricultural buildings (other than dwellinghouses) (see regs. 4 and 5).

Where an application is withdrawn or permission is refused by the planning authority or by the Secretary of State, the applicant may submit, without payment of a fee, one further application for development of the same character or description on the same site (reg. 7); in such a case the revised application must be made within 12 months of the withdrawal or the refusal of permission. A similar exemption is made in respect of applications to vary planning permission (reg. 6).

Reduced fees are payable in respect of duplicate applications made within 28 days of each other;[56] applications for development crossing local authority boundaries; applications containing alternative schemes for the development of the same land; applications made by community councils; applications by non-profit-making clubs or sporting or recreational organisations relating to playing fields for their own use; applications to continue an existing use or retain an existing building without complying with a condition requiring cessation of the use or removal of the building; and certain 'reserved matters' applications.

The statutory period for determination of an application does not begin to run until the appropriate fee has been paid (G.D.O., Art. 10(6)).[57] The fees regulations do not prescribe a procedure for the resolution of disputes about the amount of the fee payable in any particular case; where, however, the applicant seeks to appeal against the non-determination of an application within the prescribed period, the Secretary of State will have to take a view on the correct fee as this will affect his jurisdiction to determine the appeal.

Examination and acknowledgement of application by planning authority

On receipt of an application for planning permission or for approval of reserved matters and the fee (if any) required to be paid, the planning authority are to send the applicant an acknowledgement (G.D.O., Art. 10(2) and Sched. 4). Article 10(6)[58] of the G.D.O. makes clear that an application is not to be taken to have been received until any certificate required by the 1972 Act has been received, any fee payable in respect of the application has been paid, and, in a case where the applicant was required to pay the cost of advertisement of the application (see p. 197 above), that sum has been paid.

---

[56] Applicants sometimes submit duplicate applications in order that they can appeal on one in the event of failure on the part of the planning authority to determine the application within the prescribed period, while still negotiating with the planning authority on the other application.

[57] In a consultation paper issued on 31st July 1984 the Scottish Development Department proposed that the planning legislation be amended to make the validity of an application for planning permission dependent upon the correct fee having been paid.

[58] As amended by the Town and Country Planning (General Development) (Scotland) Amendment Order 1984.

Where, after sending an acknowledgement of an application to the applicant, the planning authority form the opinion that the application may be invalid by reason of failure to comply with the requirements of Article 8 or Article 9 of the G.D.O. or with any other statutory requirement, they must as soon as possible inform the applicant of that fact (G.D.O., Art. 10(4)).

Notification of applications to Secretary of State

In order to ensure that national policy objectives are not frustrated, the Secretary of State has power to 'call in' from a planning authority for decision by himself (see below) development proposals which are of national interest. However, some form of notification system is required so that the Secretary of State is made aware of the making of an application for such development. Provision for such notification is made by the Town and Country Planning (Notification of Applications) (Scotland) Direction 1981.[59]

The Notification Direction of 1981 divides development proposals into two groups.[60] Those in Part A of the Schedule to the Direction are to be notified to the Secretary of State on receipt of the application, while those in Part B are to be notified only if the planning authority propose to grant planning permission. In both cases a district planning authority are to notify their regional planning authority.

The categories of development in Part A comprise all major oil-related proposals and industrial development requiring more than 100 hectares of land. Category B proposals include proposals affecting important nature conservation sites; developments which might sterilise aggregate resources; certain proposals to develop agricultural land; proposals which have major hazard implications; certain proposals for development affecting trunk and special roads; and development contrary to a structure or local plan approved by the Secretary of State.[61]

The Town and Country Planning (Notification of Applications) (Scotland) Direction 1980[62] requires planning authorities to notify the Secretary of State[63] where they propose to grant planning permission for specified types of development within the National Scenic Areas[64] but only if the Countryside Commission for Scotland have advised against the grant of permission or have recommended conditions which the planning authority

---

[59] As amended by the Town and Country Planning (Notification of Applications) (Scotland) (Amendment) Direction 1984 and the Town and Country Planning (Notification of Applications) (Scotland) (Amendment) (No. 2) Direction 1984 (see S.D.D. Circulars 24/1981, 6/1984 and 9/1984).

[60] Several of the matters in which there is a national interest are the subject of national planning guidelines (see p. 64 above) which set out in more detail the reasons for the notification requirement.

[61] See p. 209 below.

[62] Issued with S.D.D. Circular 20/1980.

[63] And in the case of a district planning authority, the regional planning authority.

[64] See p. 184 above.

do not propose to impose on a grant of permission.

The main purpose of the Notification Directions is to give the Secretary of State an opportunity to consider whether to call in the application (below). If the Secretary of State has not exercised his call in powers within the period specified in the direction then the planning authority may proceed to determine the application.

Reference of application to the Secretary of State

Under s.32 of the 1972 Act[65] the Secretary of State has power to direct that an application for planning permission or for approval of reserved matters or for any consent, agreement or approval required by a condition attached to a grant of planning permission should be referred to him instead of being dealt with by the planning authority. Where an application is thus 'called in' by the Secretary of State, the planning authority must inform the applicant of that fact and of any reasons given by the Secretary of State for issuing the direction (G.D.O., Art. 15).

If either the planning authority or the applicant so desire, the Secretary of State must afford to each of them an opportunity of appearing before and being heard by a person appointed by the minister for the purpose; such a hearing will normally take the form of a public local inquiry. A decision made by the Secretary of State on an application for planning permission referred to him under s.32 can be challenged in the Court of Session on the grounds specified in s.233 of the 1972 Act (see chapter 21).

The legislation makes no provision for the making by any person or body of a formal request that the Secretary of State call in an application. In *R. v Secretary of State for the Environment, ex parte Newprop*[66] a decision of the Secretary of State not to call in an application because he considered it to be of purely local concern was unsuccessfully challenged. Forbes J. said that the Secretary of State's discretion was 'wholly at large' and that his decision could only be challenged if 'wildly perverse'; the Secretary of State had not fettered his discretion unlawfully by adopting a policy that applications for planning permission would only be called in if planning issues of more than local importance were involved.[67]

Reference of application to regional planning authority

While development control is primarily the responsibility of district and general planning authorities, there are available to regional planning authorities reserve powers enabling them, in specified circumstances, to act in place of a district planning authority and thus ensure that the region's strategic planning policies are protected.

---

[65] As amended by the Local Government and Planning (Scotland) Act 1982, Schedule 2 para. 10 and Schedule 4; and the Town and Country Planning (Minerals) Act 1981, Schedule 2, para. 2.

[66] [1983] J.P.L. 386.

[67] So far as Scotland is concerned, S.D.D. Circular 24/1981 states that intervention by the Secretary of State should be confined to 'exceptional circumstances'.

Under s.179 of the Local Government (Scotland) Act 1973[68] a regional planning authority have power in certain circumstances (below) to direct that an application for planning permission or for any approval required by a development order or for any consent, agreement or approval required by a condition attached to a grant of planning permission should be referred to them for decision instead of being dealt with (as would normally be the case) by a district planning authority within the region.[69] In order to facilitate a regional planning authority's consideration of whether such action on their part is necessary, district planning authorities are required to furnish weekly lists of planning applications to the appropriate regional planning authority.[70]

The regional planning authority can call in an application where:

(a) the proposed development does not conform to a structure plan approved by the Secretary of State; or
(b) the proposed development raises a major planning issue of general significance to the district of the regional planning authority (s.179(2)).

The Secretary of State considers that regional call in powers should only be exercised in exceptional circumstances and that once structure plans resolving the major planning issues for any district are in operation, major planning issues not anticipated in the plan should arise only very rarely (see S.D.D. Circular 6/1984).

The regional authority's call in power can only be exercised where the application has not been called in by the Secretary of State; in any event, an application referred to the region can be called in by the Secretary of State (1972 Act, s.32(7)[71]). Where an application is called in by the regional planning authority the district planning authority must inform the applicant of that fact (G.D.O., Art. 15).

The district planning authority are entitled to appeal to the Secretary of State against a call in direction issued by the region (1973 Act, s.179(4)). The principles by which the Secretary of State considers regional and district planning authorities should be guided in deciding respectively whether to issue a direction calling in an application and whether to lodge an appeal against such a direction are set out in Annex C to S.D.D. Circular 6/1984. The Secretary of State will be guided by the same principles in determining an appeal against call in by a district planning authority. The Secretary of State has not exercised his power to impose time limits upon such appeal

[68] As substituted by the Local Government and Planning (Scotland) Act 1982, Schedule 3, para. 24 (taking account of recommendations made by the Committee of Inquiry on Local Government in Scotland (Cmnd. 8115, 1981)).
[69] For discussion of the use of these powers (prior to their amendment by the 1982 Act) see Eric Young, 'Call in of Planning Applications by Regional Planning Authorities' [1979] J.P.L. 358.
[70] See the Town and Country Planning (Planning Applications—Weekly Lists) (Scotland) Direction 1984 (issued with S.D.D. Circular 6/1984).
[71] Inserted by the Local Government and Planning (Scotland) Act 1982, Schedule 2, para. 10.

procedures. However, he expects regional planning authorities to come to a prompt decision on whether to exercise their powers and expects any appeal against call in to be lodged expeditiously. In the event of an appeal, the Secretary of State will call for the regional planning authority and the district planning authority to submit their statements to him within 21 days and will reach his decision within 14 days of receiving the statements. Appeals will normally be decided on the basis of written submissions.

A regional planning authority will deal with an application called in by them in the same fashion as a district or general planning authority would. If the regional authority have not notified the applicant of their decision within three months, the applicant is entitled to appeal to the Secretary of State as if the application had been refused.

The call in by a regional planning authority of two planning applications was challenged by applicants for planning permission in *Bellway Ltd.* v *Strathclyde Regional Council.*[72] Lord Brand thought it clear from the legislation that the applicants had no title or interest to challenge the validity of the call in. His Lordship pointed out that the applicants had a right to appeal to the Secretary of State against the regional planning authority's decision on the planning applications; in determining such an appeal the Secretary of State has power to deal with an application as if it had been made to him in the first place and is therefore able to rectify any antecedent defect. Lord Brand also expressed the view that the Secretary of State's decision to uphold the call in by the regional authority could not be questioned since the 1973 Act provides[73] that the minister's decision is 'final'.

Consultations on applications

Article 13 of the G.D.O. provides that a planning authority must, before granting planning permission (either conditionally or unconditionally) for specified types of development, consult[74] with specified bodies or persons; these include the Secretary of State, adjoining planning authorities, the National Coal Board, the Nature Conservancy Council, the river purification authority and the Health and Safety Executive.[75] The Secretary of State has power to direct planning authorities in any particular case or class of cases to carry out consultations with any body or person named in the direction[76] (G.D.O., Art. 13(2)).

Consulted bodies must be given at least 14 days notice and the planning

[72]   1979 S.C. 92; 1980 S.L.T. 66; and see comment in 1981 S.P.L.P. 43.
[73]   Section 179(4).
[74]   See Colin T. Reid, 'A Planning Authority's Duty to Consult' 1982 S.P.L.P. 4.
[75]   On consultation with the Health and Safety Executive see too S.D.D. Circular 9/1984.
[76]   See, for example, the Town and Country Planning (Aerodromes) (Scotland) Direction 1982, relating to consultation on development within an area shown on an aerodrome safeguarding map; and the Town and Country Planning (Notification of Applications) (Scotland) Direction 1980, requiring consultation with the Countryside Commission in relation to specified types of development within the National Scenic Areas (see p. 201 above).

authority are not to determine the application before the expiry of that time. A Code of Practice on Consultation was issued with S.D.D. Circular 24/1981. It is open to bodies which have to be consulted under the G.D.O. to waive their consultation rights in relation to particular categories of development or for particular geographical areas where they think consultation on individual applications unnecessary.

The Secretary of State has on several occasions asked planning authorities to consult certain bodies in connection with particular types of application.[77] In addition, planning authorities may, of their own initiative or following a request, consult other bodies such as community councils.

Determining an application: matters to be taken into account

In determining an application for planning permission the planning authority must have regard to a number of matters specifically prescribed by the legislation. The principal such matters are:

(1) The provisions of the development plan so far as material to the application (1972 Act, s.26(1));

(2) Any other material considerations (1972 Act, s.26(1));

(3) The regional report and the observations of the Secretary of State thereon (1973 Act, s.173(7));

(4) Any representations made to the planning authority within the prescribed period (see p. 193 above) by an owner of land or an agricultural tenant who has received notification in terms of s.24 of the 1972 Act (1972 Act, s.26(3));

(5) Any representations made to the planning authority within the prescribed period in response to 'neighbour notification' or press advertisement of an application under s.23 of the 1972 Act and Article 7 of the G.D.O. (see p. 194 above) (1972 Act, s.26(2)[78]);

(6) Any representations made to the planning authority within the prescribed period (see p. 198 above) in respect of development to which s.25 of the 1972 Act applies (development affecting a conservation area or the setting of a listed building) (1972 Act, s.26(4));

(7) Any representations made to the planning authority within the prescribed period (see p. 204 above) in response to consultations carried out under Article 13 of the G.D.O. (G.D.O., Art. 13(3)); and

(8) Any representations received by the planning authority within the prescribed period (see p. 209 below) in respect of an application to which the Town and Country Planning (Development Contrary to Development Plans) (Scotland) Direction 1981 (as amended) applies.

---

[77] See, for example, S.D.D. Circulars 51/1974 (on development affecting fishery interests); 77/1975 (on development of agricultural land); 38/1978 (on consultation with the Royal Fine Art Commission); 53/1978 (on proposals relating to theatres); and 39/1980 (on development in the vicinity of methane pipelines).
[78] As amended by the 1982 Act, Schedule 2, para. 5.

Of the matters listed above, the provisions of the development plan and any other material considerations raise particular problems which are discussed in the following chapter. As regards any representations received under heads (4) to (8) above, there is no obligation on the planning authority to grant a hearing to any person or to have organised consultations (other than as specified by statute).[79] Nor are the authority obliged to inform the applicant of any representations made or to give him an opportunity to comment thereon.[80] An authority may, however, be prepared to accede to a request for a hearing from an applicant or other interested person or may take the initiative in arranging such a hearing.

Determining an application: the planning authority's discretion

Subject to the constraints imposed by the legislation and by the courts, in considering an application a planning authority have a wide discretion as to whether or not to grant planning permission and as to the conditions (if any) to be imposed on a grant of planning permission. The limitations on authorities' powers to attach conditions to a grant of planning permission are considered in chapter 10 while aspects of the more general control exercised by the courts over planning authorities' decision-making powers are considered in chapter 11.

---

[79] See *R*. v *Sheffield City Council, ex parte Mansfield* (1978) 37 P. & C.R. 1.

[80] Even if the applicant is made aware or becomes aware of representations there is no statutory obligation on the authority to disclose the contents of such representations or of the names of the people making them and it has been suggested that it is proper for the authority not to do so without consent—see [1981] J.P.L. 622 and [1984] J.P.L. 696; and see letter in 1983 S.P.L.P. 26.

CHAPTER 9

CONTROL OF DEVELOPMENT
2: THE DEVELOPMENT PLAN AND OTHER MATERIAL CONSIDERATIONS

As we mentioned above, of particular importance among the matters to which a planning authority must have regard in determining a planning application[1] are 'the provisions of the development plan, so far as material to the application', and 'any other material considerations' (1972 Act, s.26(1)). These matters are considered in this chapter.

Development plans and development control

An important function of a development plan[2] is to provide guidelines for development control. However, in the words of Lord Widgery C.J.,[3] 'every recipient of a discretion who has to exercise that discretion is required to consider all the circumstances of the case.' While, therefore, planning authorities are obliged to have a general policy in planning matters, that policy must not be of such a nature as to prevent an authority considering each planning application on its own merits. In *Stringer* v *Minister of Housing and Local Government*[4] it was held, for example, that an agreement between a planning authority and a university to the effect that no development would be permitted in the vicinity of Jodrell Bank telescope was *ultra vires* the planning authority in that the agreement obliged the authority to disregard considerations—the provisions of the development plan and other material considerations—to which they were bound by statute to have regard.

The corollary of this is that the planning authority are not obliged to follow the provisions of the development plan when determining a planning application. In *Simpson* v *Edinburgh Corporation*[5] Edinburgh university obtained planning permission for the construction of modern university buildings in George Square, Edinburgh, which required the demolition of two sides of the square and the destruction of its characteristic Georgian

---

[1] And in the making of various other sorts of decisions.

[2] Whatever combination of structure, local and 'old style' plans the particular development plan consists of for the time being.

[3] *R.* v *Secretary of State for the Environment, ex p. Reinisch* (1971) 22 P. & C.R. 1022.

[4] [1970] 1 W.L.R. 1281. See too *H. Lavender & Son Ltd.* v *Minister of Housing and Local Government* [1970] 1 W.L.R. 1231; and *Link Homes Ltd.* v *Secretary of State for the Environment* [1976] J.P.L. 430.

[5] 1960 S.C. 313; 1961 S.L.T. 17. Followed in *Enfield London Borough Council* v *Secretary of State for the Environment* (1974) 233 E.G. 53. See too *R.* v *Hammersmith and Fulham Borough Council, ex p. People Before Profit Ltd.* (1981) 45 P. & C.R. 364.

appearance. The grant of permission was challenged by the owner of a dwelling in George Square as being contrary to the provisions of the development plan and therefore *ultra vires*. The Lord Ordinary, Lord Guest, said:

'It was argued for the pursuer that this section [now s.26 of the 1972 Act] required the planning authority to adhere strictly to the development plan. I do not so read this section. "To have regard to" does not, in my view, mean "slavishly to adhere to". It requires the planning authority to consider the development plan, but it does not oblige them to follow it.'

Lord Guest added that if the requirement to have regard to the plan was to be regarded as requiring strict adherence to the plan then the addition of the words requiring the authority to have regard to 'any other material considerations' could mean that the authority might be faced with the impossible task of reconciling the two. Lord Guest said: 'In my opinion, the meaning of [s.26(1)] is plain. The planning authority are to consider all the material considerations, of which the development plan is one.'

However, a decision on a planning application will be open to challenge in the courts if it can be shown that the planning authority (or the Secretary of State on appeal) failed to have regard to the development plan.[6] Further, a planning authority (or the Secretary of State) will be treated as having failed in their duty to have regard to the development plan if they misinterpret the provisions of the plan.[7]

The courts' influence is, however, necessarily marginal in nature. If development plans are to retain credibility they should exert an important influence on development control decisions. The plans have been the subject of a public participation exercise and an objection procedure and should not lightly be set aside. Three safeguards exist with this in mind.

First of all, the Notification of Applications Direction 1981 (see p. 201 above) provides that the Secretary of State must be informed if a planning authority propose to grant planning permission for development which conflicts with an approved structure plan or with a local plan which has been

---

[6]   See *Holmes* v *Secretary of State for the Environment* [1983] J.P.L. 476; and *London Borough of Richmond upon Thames* v *Secretary of State for the Environment* [1984] J.P.L. 24. In *R.* v *Sevenoaks District Council, ex p. W. J. Terry* [1984] J.P.L. 420 Glidewell J. found that a planning authority had failed to take account of a policy contained in a structure plan but exercised his discretion not to quash the authority's decision on the ground that they would have reached the same decision even if the relevant policy had been considered.

[7]   See *Niarchos (London) Ltd.* v *Secretary of State for the Environment* (1977) 35 P. & C.R. 259; *Pyrford Properties Ltd.* v *Secretary of State for the Environment* (1977) 36 P. & C.R. 28; *Moldene Ltd.* v *Secretary of State for the Environment* [1979] J.P.L. 176; *Bell and Colvill Ltd.* v *Secretary of State for the Environment* [1980] J.P.L. 823; *J.A. Pye (Oxford) Estates Ltd.* v *Secretary of State for the Environment* (1981) 261 E.G. 368; *Troman's* v *Secretary of State for the Environment* [1983] J.P.L. 474; *Westminster Renslade Ltd.* v *Secretary of State for the Environment* (1983) 48 P. & C.R. 255; *Federated Estates Ltd.* v *Secretary of State for the Environment* [1983] J.P.L. 812; and *Westminster City Council* v *Secretary of State for the Environment* [1984] J.P.L. 27.

'called in' and approved by the Secretary of State. This gives the Secretary of State an opportunity to consider whether the application should be transferred to him for a decision under s.32 of the 1972 Act or whether he should issue a direction restricting the grant of planning permission under Article 11 of the G.D.O.; planning authorities are not otherwise required to notify the Secretary of State of an application for planning permission solely because the proposed development does not accord with the provisions of the development plan. In addition, where a regional planning authority propose to grant permission for a development contrary to a structure plan approved by the Secretary of State, they must send prescribed information to the appropriate district planning authority.[8]

Secondly, in those parts of Scotland where a two-tier planning system is in operation, the regional planning authority may direct a district planning authority to refer to them (the region) for a decision any application for development which does not conform to an approved structure plan, provided the application is not already the subject of a direction from the Secretary of State under s.32 of the 1972 Act.[9] S.D.D. Circular 6/1984 suggests that the criterion for regional call-in should normally be that a proposed development significantly conflicts with a structure plan policy.[10]

Thirdly, the Town and Country Planning (Development Contrary to Development Plans) (Scotland) Direction 1981[11] provides that a planning authority may grant planning permission for development which does not accord with the provisions of the development plan so long as the application has not been called in by the Secretary of State or by a regional planning authority, and is not the subject of a direction by the Secretary of State under Article 11 of the G.D.O. However, before granting such a permission the planning authority must comply with the following procedure:

1. The application must have been advertised by a notice given by the planning authority in a local newspaper circulating in the district, and the planning authority must have considered any representations made within 21 days of first publication of the notice;

2. In the case of a district planning authority, they must have sent to the regional planning authority a copy of the application and a statement of their reasons for proposing to grant planning permission, and have considered any representations received from the regional planning authority within 21

[8] See Town and Country Planning (Notification of Applications) (Scotland) (Amendment) Direction 1984 (Annex B to S.D.D. Circular 6/1984).
[9] See Local Government (Scotland) Act 1973, s.179 (as substituted by para. 24 of Schedule 3 to the Local Government and Planning (Scotland) Act 1982).
[10] Annex C, para. 3.
[11] Annex C to S.D.D. Circular 24/1981, as amended by the Town and Country Planning (Development Contrary to Development Plans) (Scotland) (Amendment) Direction 1984 (Annex C to S.D.D. Circular 6/1984). The Directions were made under (inter alia) s.28(1)(b) of the 1972 Act and Article 12 of the G.D.O.; these provisions are, it seems, purely procedural in character and do not affect jurisdiction—see Simpson (above); and Co-operative Retail Services Ltd. v Taff-Ely Borough Council (1979) 39 P. & C.R. 223.

days of that authority's receipt of the information. Where the application conflicts with an approved structure plan, the regional planning authority may not be content with making representations to the district and may prefer, as mentioned above, to call it in for decision by themselves.

3. In the case of a regional planning authority proposing to grant planning permission for development contrary to an approved or adopted local plan, the regional planning authority must have sent to the appropriate district planning authority a statement of their reasons for proposing to grant permission, and have considered any observations received from the district authority within 21 days of that authority's receipt of the statement.

The Development Contrary to Development Plans Direction does not apply to development to be carried out by general or district planning authorities themselves.

S.D.D. Circular 24/1981 states that in the case of adopted local plans and 'old style' development plans, the Secretary of State expects planning authorities to take full account of objections to proposals for non-conforming development and to offer objectors an opportunity, if they have so requested, of appearing before them to state and explain their objections. Where an objector is to appear before the planning authority then the circular recommends that the applicant should also be offered an opportunity to appear and defend his application.

Draft development plans and non-statutory policy statements[12]

A matter which has given rise to some practical difficulty in recent years has been the weight to be given when determining a planning application to draft development plans, particularly draft local plans. The difficulty arises in this way. The planning authority puts forward certain proposals for the use of land in its draft plan. Local people object to these proposals and a public inquiry is arranged. In the meantime, a planning application is submitted to the planning authority for the development of the land. If the application is in accord with the proposals in the draft plan the planning authority may be minded to grant permission. Such a step would effectively pre-empt the decision on the objections to the local plan, and the objectors would, understandably, feel aggrieved. On the other hand, the planning authority may decide to postpone a decision on the application until the local plan proposals have been settled. As this may be some time away the applicant may well feel aggrieved. This difficulty serves to highlight the relationship between development plans and development control.

---

[12] It seems clear that draft development plans are not 'development plans' for the purposes of s.26(1) of the 1972 Act but 'other material considerations'—*Clyde & Co.* v *Secretary of State for the Environment* [1977] 1 W.L.R. 926. Non-statutory policy statements would appear to fall into the same category—*Myton Ltd.* v *Minister of Housing and Local Government* (1965) 16 P. & C.R. 240.

In *Link Homes Ltd.* v *Secretary of State for the Environment*[13] Willis J. commented that the fact that a development plan was in course of preparation was not a reason which could be used as a rubber stamp objection to refuse all planning applications until the plan had been approved or adopted. On the other hand, in *R.* v *City of London Corporation, ex parte Allan*[14] Woolf J. held that a draft plan must be taken into account if it is material to an application, although, as with approved plans, the contents will not bind the authority. What this seems to amount to is that an application for planning permission may properly be refused on the ground that the development will be likely to prejudice the outcome of a draft development plan[15] but that there is no obligation to refuse the application in such circumstances.[16] All that is required is that the effect of the proposed development on the policies and proposals in the draft plan should be properly considered before the application is determined.[17]

Similar difficulties arise over the weight which may be given to non-statutory policy statements, whether adopted or in course of preparation. These are policy statements on specific topics which are prepared and adopted by planning authorities and used to guide development control decisions. No formal procedures govern their preparation and the extent to which the public can influence such policies is entirely in the hands of the planning authority. It would seem that such policy statements may properly be taken into account in determining a planning application,[18] and that failure to take account of such a statement may render a decision *ultra vires*.[19] As with development plans, a statement of this kind must not bind the authority but should be weighed against any other material considerations.

---

[13] [1976] J.P.L. 430. See also *Myton Ltd.* v *Minister of Housing and Local Government* (1965) 16 P. & C.R. 240; and *Thornville Properties* v *Secretary of State for the Environment* [1981] J.P.L. 116.

[14] (1980) 79 L.G.R. 223 (cited with approval by the Court of Appeal in *Davies* v *London Borough of Hammersmith and Fulham* [1981] J.P.L. 682).

[15] See, for example, *Governors of Rugby School* v *Secretary of State for the Environment* (1975) 234 E.G. 371. In *Thornville* (above) Sir Douglas Frank held that reasons must be given why the application, if granted, would prejudice the plan.

[16] *Davies* v *London Borough of Hammersmith and Fulham* [1981] J.P.L. 682; *R.* v *City of London Corporation, ex p. Allan* (1980) 79 L.G.R. 223. See also ministerial decisions noted in [1979] J.P.L. 494; [1981] J.P.L. 65 and 541; and [1982] J.P.L. 322.

[17] See, for example, *R.* v *Hammersmith and Fulham Borough Council, ex p. People Before Profit Ltd.* (1981) 45 P. & C.R. 364.

[18] *Myton Ltd.* v *Minister of Housing and Local Government* (1965) 16 P. & C.R. 240. In *Philglow Ltd.* v *Secretary of State for the Environment* [1984] J.P.L. 111 (reversed on other grounds: (1984) 270 E.G. 1192) the Secretary of State for the Environment was held entitled to take account of a local planning authority's change of attitude on a policy document prepared by the authority.

[19] See *J.A. Pye (Oxford) Estates Ltd.* v *Secretary of State for the Environment* (1981) 261 E.G. 368. As to the difficulties which may arise over non-statutory policies see, however, *Westminster City Council* v *Great Portland Estates plc* [1984] 3 W.L.R. 1035 (p. 114 above).

'Any other material considerations'[20]

In determining an application, a planning authority must have regard not only to the development plan and to the other matters listed at p.205 above but also to 'any other material considerations' (1972 Act, s.26(1)). A decision which fails to take account of material considerations or which is based on matters which are not material may be quashed by the courts[21] on the ground that it is *ultra vires* the authority.[22] It is therefore, important to define the scope of the matters embraced by this term. As one writer has put it: 'The question of material considerations is a crucial one for development control, and indeed for the whole town and country planning system, since it is through this concept that the limits to public intervention in the planning sphere are defined.'[23]

These 'other material considerations' are not specifically defined in the 1972 Act and it is difficult to discern their scope by implication from the legislation. The courts, for their part, have tended to confine themselves to deciding upon the validity of the particular consideration in issue in any given case and to eschew the giving of general guidance about their range. As a great deal turns on the particular circumstances of each case, it is not possible to reconcile all the decisions in this area and it is difficult to extract from them any yardstick which may readily be used as a measure of the validity of any given consideration.

Although it is well established that these 'other material considerations' must be of a 'planning' nature,[24] this merely serves to rephrase the question

[20]   See Eric Young, 'Planning Considerations' 1975 S.L.T. (News) 245; Michael Purdue, 'The Scope of Planning Authorities' Discretion: or What's Material?' [1977] J.P.L. 490; Martin Loughlin, 'The Scope and Importance of "Material Considerations" ' (1980) 3 *Urban Law and Policy* 171; and Paul Q. Watchman, 'Planning Considerations' 1983 S.P.L.P. 36 and 72.

[21]   The onus of proving that an irrelevant consideration was taken into account or a relevant one ignored rests with the person seeking to challenge the decision—see, for example, *Fawcett Properties Ltd.* v *Buckingham County Council* [1959] Ch. 543, per Pearce L.J.; and *Bell and Colvill Ltd.* v *Secretary of State for the Environment* [1980] J.P.L. 823.

[22]   *Associated Provincial Picture Houses Ltd.* v *Wednesbury Corporation* [1948] 1 K.B. 223. The presence of an irrelevant factor or a failure to take account of a relevant factor may not be fatal if the court considers that the defect did not affect the decision, or operated in favour of the complainant—see, for example, *Hanks* v *Secretary of State for the Environment* [1963] 1 Q.B. 999; *Bradwell Industrial Aggregates* v *Secretary of State for the Environment* [1981] J.P.L. 276; and *Chichester District Council* v *Secretary of State for the Environment* [1981] J.P.L. 591. It seems that any relevant matter arising up to the date of the decision (e.g. between the holding of a public inquiry and the decision) must be taken into account—see, for example, *J.A. Pye (Oxford) Estates Ltd.* v *West Oxfordshire District Council* (1982) 47 P. & C.R. 125; and *Price Brothers (Rode Heath) Ltd.* v *Secretary of State for the Environment* (1978) 38 P. & C.R. 579. A person exercising a statutory discretion may be under a duty to call his own attention to relevant matters—see, for example, *Prest* v *Secretary of State for Wales* (1982) 81 L.G.R. 193; and *Francis Joseph Tierney* v *Secretary of State for the Environment* [1983] J.P.L. 799.

[23]   J. Underwood, *Development Control: A Review of Research and Current Issues* (Pergamon Press, 1981), p. 199.

[24]   *East Barnet U.D.C.* v *British Transport Commission* [1962] 2 Q.B. 484; *Stringer* v *Minister of Housing and Local Government* [1970] 1 W.L.R. 1281; *Newbury District Council* v *Secretary of State for the Environment* [1981] A.C. 578, per Lords Scarman and Fraser; and *Westminster City Council* v *Great Portland Estates plc* [1984] 3 W.L.R. 1035.

in terms of 'what is planning'? Here, too, there is a lack of definition. There is no explicit statement in the 1972 Act of the objectives of planning or of the planning system. This may be because planning is not an end in itself. It is not the function of the system to build houses or roads or hospitals but rather to provide a framework within which such investments can be made. The nearest that the Act comes to a statement of an objective is the very generally expressed requirement that development plans should set out policies and proposals for the development and the use of land in the planning authority's area.[25] This suggests that the scope of development plans is delimited by physical land use factors. Although the Structure and Local Plans Regulations prescribe a range of matters that must be contained in such plans, including a statement of the regard that has been paid to social and economic policies, it appears that policies and proposals in the plans are concerned with the implications which these matters may have for the physical environment.[26]

As the control of development is intended to operate within the framework of the policies and proposals in the development plan, it would seem to follow that the development control process is similarly circumscribed by physical land use factors. Although 'other material considerations' are matters outwith the development plan, it appears that they too must follow this general pattern and be concerned with the use of land. In *Stringer* v *Minister of Housing and Local Government*[27] Cooke J. defined these other considerations as 'any consideration which relates to the use and development of land'.

However, as a yardstick for measuring the validity of a consideration this definition clearly has its problems. The list of matters which could be said to be concerned with the use and development of land is open-ended, as the courts are beginning to recognise.[28] Some further qualification of the yardstick is desirable. This further qualification is a test of remoteness. The consideration must be shown to be 'material' to the particular application. In *Stringer* Cooke J. went on to say: 'Whether a particular consideration falling within that broad class is material in any given case will depend on the circumstances.'

Thus although the list of considerations could be said to be open-ended, a planning authority in determining an application must take into account only those planning considerations which are relevant in the particular circumstances of the case. In some cases the courts have been prepared to determine whether a particular factor, relevant to planning in general, is in

---

[25] 1972 Act, ss.5(3) and 9(3).
[26] See in particular *Planning Advice Notes 27* and *28*, issued by the Scottish Development Department in November 1981; also S.D.D. Circular 28/1976 and the Procedure Notes which replaced it on 29th December 1976.
[27] [1970] 1 W.L.R. 1281.
[28] See, for example, *Clyde & Co.* v *Secretary of State for the Environment* [1977] 1 W.L.R. 926, per Sir David Cairns. In general, however, the courts treat it as a matter of statutory interpretation, and therefore as a matter for judicial determination, whether a particular consideration is capable in law of being relevant to town and country planning.

fact relevant in the circumstances of a particular case;[29] in other cases it has, however, been said that it is for the planning authority (or the minister) to decide whether, in the circumstances of an individual case, a particular issue is material.[30] The weight to be attached to a particular consideration is generally for the planning authority or the Secretary of State to determine;[31] however, if the authority or the minister attach undue or insufficient weight to a particular consideration the court may be prepared to intervene and quash the decision as perverse or unreasonable.[32]

It would seem, therefore, that the 'other material considerations' in s.26(1) must satisfy two tests. First of all, they must be 'planning' considerations, that is they must have consequences for the use and development of land. Secondly, they must be material in the circumstances of the case, that is they must be prompted by the application. It would appear, however, that material considerations are not confined to the consequences of the proposed development looked at in isolation (although if the development is approved then any conditions imposed on the planning permission must be fairly and reasonably related to the development—see chapter 10). The decisions of the courts make clear that planning authorities are not, for example, confined to the question 'whether the character of the building or the proposed building is objectionable in itself'[33] and it has been held to be quite proper for a planning authority to refuse an application, which might be unobjectionable in itself, on the grounds that it was desirable to preserve an existing permitted use of the land[34] or that if permission were granted it would be difficult to resist further applications for the development of other sites.[35]

Clearly, such tests provide only general guidance for those engaged in the development control process. Difficult questions will inevitably arise at the margins and much will depend on the particular circumstances of each case. In town and country planning the doctrine of relevant and irrelevant considerations has given rise to what H. W. R. Wade describes[36] as 'incessant litigation' and some illustration of the scope of the matters which have been accepted or rejected in particular cases as 'other material considerations' may therefore be helpful.

---

[29] See, for example, *Brown v Secretary of State for the Environment* (1978) 40 P. & C.R. 285.

[30] See, for example, *Sovmots Investments Ltd. v Secretary of State for the Environment* [1977] Q.B. 411, per Forbes J.; and *Wordie Property Company Ltd. v Secretary of State for Scotland* 1984 S.L.T. 345 (and comment in 1983 S.P.L.P. 75).

[31] See *Sovmots* (above), per Forbes J.; and *Clyde & Co. v Secretary of State for the Environment* [1977] 1 W.L.R. 926.

[32] See, for example, *South Oxfordshire District Council v Secretary of State for the Environment* [1981] 1 W.L.R. 1092. See too *Niarchos (London) Ltd. v Secretary of State for the Environment* (1977) 35 P. & C.R. 259.

[33] *Clyde & Co. v Secretary of State for the Environment* [1977] 1 W.L.R. 926, per Sir David Cairns.

[34] *Clyde & Co.* (above).

[35] *Collis Radio Ltd. v Secretary of State for the Environment* (1975) 29 P. & C.R. 390.

[36] *Administrative Law* (Clarendon Press, Oxford, 5th ed., 1982), p. 370.

'*Amenity*'. In *Stringer* (above) Cooke J. found it impossible to accept that planning considerations are limited to matters relating to amenity.[37] 'Amenity' considerations are, however, often important in the determination of planning applications. Though the concept of 'amenity' is impossible to define with precision—one official report described it as 'that element in the appearance and lay-out of town and country which makes for a comfortable and pleasant life [and] the quality which a well-designed building estate or neighbourhood will have'[38]—it is clear that the scope of amenity considerations is very wide. As the same report put it: 'Anything ugly, dirty, noisy, crowded, destructive, intrusive or uncomfortable may "injure the interests of amenity" and, therefore, be of concern to the planning authority.' In *Copeland Borough Council* v *Secretary of State for the Environment*,[39] for example, Lord Widgery C.J. said that 'the purpose of all town and country planning is to preserve amenities and the sensible and attractive layout of properties.'

Compatibility with other uses. In *Collis Radio Ltd.* v *Secretary of State for the Environment*[40] Lord Widgery C.J. declared:

'Planning . . . deals with localities and not individual parcels of land and individual sites. In all planning cases it must be of the greatest importance when considering a single planning application to ask oneself what the consequences in the locality will be . . . In so far as an application for planning permission on site A is judged according to the consequence on sites B, C and D, in my judgment no error of law is disclosed but only what is perhaps the most elementary principle of planning practice is being observed.'

Thus in *Stringer* (above), after quoting Widgery J.'s dictum that 'an essential feature of planning must be the separation of different uses or activities which are incompatible the one with the other',[41] Cooke J. held that the likelihood that a proposed development would interfere with the work of the Jodrell Bank telescope was a material planning consideration. Similarly, in *R.M.C. Management Services Ltd.* v *Secretary of State for the Environment* [42] it was held that in dealing with an application for a

---

[37] See too the comments of Sir David Cairns in *Clyde & Co.* v *Secretary of State for the Environment* [1977] 1 W.L.R. 926.

[38] Ministry of Town and Country Planning, *Town and Country Planning Progress Report 1943–1951* (Cmd. 8204, 1951).

[39] (1976) 31 P. & C.R. 403.

[40] (1975) 29 P. & C.R. 390.

[41] See *Fitzpatrick Developments Ltd.* v *Minister of Housing and Local Government* (1965) 194 E.G. 911.

[42] (1972) 222 E.G. 1593. See too, for example, appeal decisions noted in *Scottish Bulletin of Selected Appeal Decisions*, II/54 and III/81; *SPADS* Nos. A2308 (P/PPA/TA/3, 23rd March 1977); A2922 (P/PPA/SU/4, 27th February 1979); A3009 (P/PPA/SL/49, 6th June 1979); A3380 (P/PPA/GE/19, 11th July 1980); [1973] J.P.L. 120; [1974] J.P.L. 425; and [1983] J.P.L. 398.

ready-mixed concrete plant, the planning authority could properly take into account the effect which dust created by the concrete plant would have on neighbouring factories manufacturing precision products and requiring clean air.

The desirability of preserving a balance of uses (e.g. in a shopping area) will be a material consideration, and it will, it seems be proper to take account of the desirability of safeguarding the future development potential of neighbouring land,[43] and of the danger that development would prejudice public proposals for the land in question.[44] The number of unimplemented permissions in the area for development similar to that which is the subject of the application under consideration is a material consideration.[45]

Private interests. In *Stringer*[46] Cooke J. could not accept that the planning authority 'must have regard only to public interests as opposed to private interests', and declared that in his view 'the protection of the interests of individual occupiers is one aspect, and an important one, of the public interest as a whole'. He considered that in this context no assistance was to be derived from the decisions in *Buxton* v *Minister of Housing and Local Government*,[47] *Simpson* v *Edinburgh Corporation*[48] and *Gregory* v *Camden London Borough Council*;[49] these cases were, he said, 'concerned with the right of an individual to maintain proceedings in the courts. An individual may well have no such rights and yet be a person whose interests may very properly be considered at an anterior stage when the question whether or not to grant planning permission is being dealt with.'

It is, for example, a material consideration that a proposed development would result in loss of privacy, sunlight, daylight or amenity enjoyed by a neighbouring householder.[50] However, the fact that neighbours have not objected to a proposed development is not necessarily a strong factor in favour of the development.[51]

Retaining the existing use. The desirability of retaining the existing permitted use of premises is a matter which can validly be taken into account in determining a planning application, provided that the planning authority's reason for seeking the continuation of the existing use is a proper planning

---

[43]   See appeal decision reported in [1977] J.P.L. 685.
[44]   See, for example, *SPADS* No. A3425 (P/PPA/FB/49, 8th September 1980).
[45]   See, for example, *SPADS* No. A3252 (P/NP/7/1/HF/1C9, 15th February 1980).
[46]   [1971] 1 W.L.R. 1281.
[47]   [1961] 1 Q.B. 278.
[48]   [1960] S.C. 313; 1961 S.L.T. 17.
[49]   [1966] 1 W.L.R. 899.
[50]   See, for example, *Barratt Developments (Eastern) Ltd.* v *Secretary of State for the Environment* [1982] J.P.L. 648; and *SPADS* Nos. A2240 (P/PPA/LA/31, 21st December 1976); A2299 (P/PPA/FB/8, 10th March 1977); A2414 (P/PPA/CC/10, 18th August 1977); A2551 (P/PPA/CA/6, 12th January 1978); A2863 (P/PPA/TC/52, 11th December 1978); A2884 (P/PPA/SU/44, 17th January 1979); and A3477 (P/PPA/CC/57, 23rd October 1980).
[51]   See, for example, *SPADS* No. A2441 (P/PPA/SB/3, 22nd September 1977).

one.[52] In *Clyde & Co.* v *Secretary of State for the Environment*,[53] for example, the Court of Appeal held that permission for a change from residential to office use could properly be refused on the ground that the existing residential use of the building in question was one which, given the shortage of housing accommodation in the area, ought to continue.[54]

Alternative permitted uses, if any, may also be taken into account,[55] and it is likely to be material to consider what could happen if an application is refused.

In *Westminster City Council* v *British Waterways Board*[56] Dunn L.J. held that preservation of the existing use of land is not to be confused with the preservation of use by a particular existing occupier, which is not generally a material planning consideration; planning is concerned, he said, 'with development of land, and not with the protection of existing occupiers'.

Precedent. As each application for planning permission must be considered on its own merits, it might be thought that fear of creating an undesirable precedent was not a proper planning consideration. In *Collis Radio Ltd.* v *Secretary of State for the Environment*,[57] however, the Divisional Court held that a planning authority can properly take into account the possibility that to grant planning permission for a particular development, unobjectionable in itself, might set a precedent and make it difficult for the authority to refuse planning permission for similar development on other sites and thus lead to undesirable proliferation of such development.

Further, as was pointed out by the reporter in a Scottish planning appeal, consistency in decision-making has an important role to play in ensuring the continued public acceptability of development control.[58]

---

52 See *Clyde & Co.* v *Secretary of State for the Environment* [1977] 1 W.L.R. 926; *Granada Theatres Ltd.* v *Secretary of State for the Environment* (1980) 43 P. & C.R. 253; *L.O. Finn & Co.* v *Secretary of State for the Environment* [1984] J.P.L. 734; and *SPADS* No. A3104 (P/PPA/SA/45, 22nd August 1979). In *Clyde & Co.* Sir David Cairns said that it was enough that there was 'at least a fair chance' that the refusal of permission for the proposed use would result in the existing use being continued. However, in *Westminster City Council* v *British Waterways Board* [1984] 3 W.L.R. 1047 Lord Bridge expressed the view that a rather higher standard was appropriate; in his view it was necessary to show 'a balance of probability' that a refusal would result in the preferred use being continued.

53 [1977] 1 W.L.R. 926.

54 Since the discontinuance of a use is not in itself development, the planning authority have no way of ensuring that premises are actually used for the permitted purpose; the owner might simply prefer to leave the premises empty.

55 *South Oxfordshire D.C.* v *Secretary of State for the Environment* [1981] 1 W.L.R. 1092 (see p. 222 below).

56 (1983) 82 L.G.R. 44 (C.A.); upheld in the House of Lords: [1984] 3 W.L.R. 1047. Contrast *Westminster City Council* v *Great Portland Estates plc* [1984] 3 W.L.R. 1035.

57 (1975) 29 P. & C.R. 390; followed in *Tempo Discount Warehouses Ltd.* v *London Borough of Enfield* [1979] J.P.L. 97; and *Anglia Building Society* v *Secretary of State for the Environment* [1984] J.P.L. 175. See too *SPADS* Nos. A2032 (P/PPA/RN/345, 25th February 1976); A4093 (P/PPA/SC/75, 5th April 1982); and A4132 (P/PPA/SC/80, 7th May 1982). Contrast *Walter Hermanns & Sons Ltd.* v *Secretary of State for the Environment* (1974) 234 E.G. 47.

58 See *SPADS* No. A5133 (P/PPA/HF/60, 5th June 1984).

Safety. The possible consequences of a development on the safety of the public and of users of the premises, whether from its potentially hazardous nature or from its likely effect on traffic flow, has been regarded as a planning matter.[59] Indeed, planning authorities are required by the G.D.O. to have regard to representations made to them in appropriate cases by the Health and Safety Executive and by the highway authority.[60]

In *Stringer*[61] Cooke J. said: 'if permission is sought to erect an explosives factory adjacent to a school, the Minister must surely be entitled and bound to consider the question of safety.' However, so far as the safety of the design of a particular building is concerned, Lord Dunpark said in *Ravenseft Properties Ltd.* v *British Gas Corporation*[62] that it was certainly 'not self-evident that this was a planning matter'.

Economic and financial considerations.[63] Difficult questions arise as to how far the economic or financial implications of a proposed development are relevant planning considerations.

In *J. Murphy & Sons Ltd.* v *Secretary of State for the Environment*[64] the minister, in considering whether to grant planning permission for local authority development, had refused to take into account the fact that the site would, because of its nature and situation, be a particularly expensive one to develop. Ackner J. held 'as a matter of law' that the minister's view was correct; there was nothing in the planning legislation which required a planning authority to look beyond the proposed development's effect on land use and to enquire into costs.[65] 'The planning authority', said Ackner J., 'exercises no paternalistic or avuncular jurisdiction over would-be developers to safeguard them from their financial follies.' To somewhat similar effect, Sir Douglas Frank stated in *Walters* v *Secretary of State for the Environment*[66] that if the inquiry inspector's decision letter in that case were

---

[59]   See, for example, S.D.D. Circular 9/1984 on planning controls over hazardous development; S.D.D. *Planning Advice Note 25*, 'Commercial Pipelines'; *Development Control Policy Note No. 1* (M.H.L.G., 1969); and appeal decisions noted in [1975] J.P.L. 751; *Scottish Bulletin of Selected Appeal Decisions*, III/91; and *SPADS* Nos. A3405 (P/PPA/CB/ 37, 21st August 1980); A3569 (P/PPA/GB/35, 12th January 1981); A5063 (P/PPA/SU/139, 19th April 1984); A5066 (P/PPA/TB/73, 24th April 1984); and A5076 (P/SLR/11/FA/1, 27th April 1984).

[60]   Art. 13.

[61]   [1971] 1 W.L.R. 1281.

[62]   Court of Session, 31st January 1979 (unreported, but see 1981 S.P.L.P. 76). See too the appeal decisions concerning site stability noted at p. 227 below.

[63]   For analyses of the courts' decisions on this matter see M. Purdue, 'The Economics of Development—Its Status as a Planning Consideration' [1979] J.P.L. 146; J. Alder, 'Planning Permission and the Eccentric Millionaire' (1979) 129 New L.J. 704; M. Loughlin, 'Planning Control and the Property Market' (1980) 3 *Urban Law and Policy* 1; and A. F. Footner, 'The Financial Consequences to an Applicant—Are They Material in Determining a Planning Application?' [1983] J.P.L. 724.

[64]   [1973] 1 W.L.R. 560.

[65]   However, in *Hambledon and Chiddingfold Parish Councils* v *Secretary of State for the Environment* [1976] J.P.L. 502 Ackner J. said he might have stated the general principle too widely in *Murphy*.

[66]   (1979) 77 L.G.R. 529.

to be construed 'as conveying that permission would be refused if it were shown that the development could only be carried out at a loss because of design constraints and the market demand, then I would hold he was wrong'.

However, in *Sovmots Investments Ltd. v Secretary of State for the Environment*[67] Forbes J. said (obiter) that if Ackner J. was intending to say in *Murphy* that cost could never be a relevant planning consideration, he was unable to agree. In Forbes J.'s view planning authorities were entitled to bear in mind the likelihood of a development being carried into effect.

In *Sosmo Trust Ltd. v Secretary of State for the Environment*[68] Woolf J. said that although the various authorities on the relevance of the cost or economic viability of a proposed development appeared at first sight to be in conflict, it was possible to reconcile these authorities once it was appreciated that 'what could be significant was not the financial or lack of financial viability of a particular project but the consequences of that financial viability or lack of financial viability'. In that case planning permission for office development had been refused. On appeal to the Secretary of State' the applicants argued that if their scheme was not approved, the site would remain derelict. However, in the letter giving the decision on the appeal it was said that in general the financial aspects of a proposed development were not relevant to planning. Founding strongly on what was said by Forbes J. in *Sovmots* (above), Woolf J. held that the present case was one where no reasonable Secretary of State could have concluded that the economic factor was not relevant. It must, said Woolf J., 'be a planning consideration that a consequence of not granting planning permission was that an existing building was going to be left unoccupied and derelict'.

Woolf J.'s view that the cost or viability of a proposed development will be relevant where it is likely to have some significance in planning terms would seem to be borne out by the decisions in a significant number of cases.[69] In *Brighton Borough Council v Secretary of State for the Environment*,[70] for example, planning permission had been refused for residential development on an unused part of playing fields attached to a school. The school building was 'listed' as a building of special architectural or historic interest and occupied a prominent position in a conservation area. The inspector who

[67] [1977] Q.B. 411.

[68] [1983] J.P.L. 806.

[69] See *Kent Messenger Ltd. v Secretary of State for the Environment* [1976] J.P.L. 372; *Clyde & Co. v Secretary of State for the Environment* [1977] 1 W.L.R. 926; *Niarchos (London) Ltd. v Secretary of State for the Environment* (1977) 35 P. & C.R. 259; *Richmond-upon-Thames L.B.C. v Secretary of State for the Environment* [1979] J.P.L. 175; *James Miller & Partners (Guildford) Ltd. v Secretary of State for the Environment* [1980] J.P.L. 264; *Brighton Borough Council v Secretary of State for the Environment* (1980) 39 P. & C.R. 46; *Calflane Ltd. v Secretary of State for the Environment* [1981] J.P.L. 879; *R. v East Yorkshire Borough of Beverley Council, ex p. Wilson* [1983] C.L.Y. 3721; and *Wordie Property Company Ltd. v Secretary of State for Scotland* 1984 S.L.T. 345. See too *Prest v Secretary of State for Wales* (1982) 81 L.G.R. 193; and *Green v Secretaries of State for the Environment and Transport* (1984) 271 E.G. 550 (decisions on compulsory purchase orders). See too *SPADS* No. A3547 (P/PPA/TB/28, 17th December 1980).

[70] (1980) 39 P. & C.R. 46.

determined the appeal against the refusal of permission took account of the fact that the building's future would only be assured if capital could be realised from the proposed development. Sir Douglas Frank held that the building's restoration was an important planning matter and that the inspector was therefore entitled to take into account the possibility that a planning benefit would result from the grant of permission.

In *Sosmo Trust* (above) it was also argued that the economic viability of the proposed development itself was not a relevant consideration. It was not necessary for Woolf J. to decide this point but he said that while some support for that argument was to be found in *Walters* (above), he had reservations about the general applicability of what had been said in that case. In Woolf J.'s view the accumulation of planning permissions which were incapable of implementation could be undesirable. Further, what was said in *Walters* was to some extent contrary to Forbes J.'s view in *Sovmots* that it would be right for a planning authority to treat more favourably a wise commercial development than one which could only be implemented by an eccentric millionaire.

There is little doubt that the general economic impact of a development is a proper planning consideration. It is common practice for a developer to support his application by reference to the economic benefits, whether national, regional or local, which will flow from it (sometimes expressed in terms of economic 'need'), and a planning authority will clearly have these in mind when reaching a decision.[71] Equally, planning authorities will wish to take account of any undesired economic effects which may result from the proposal and it would seem to be quite proper to do so. In giving his decision on a hypermarket application in 1972, for example, the English minister expressed the view that 'while it is not the function of land use planning to prevent competition between retailers or between different methods of retailing, the effects of competition on existing shopping centres and on the future prospects of the redevelopment of those centres are, in fact, material considerations . . .'[72]

The adequacy of existing public services to serve the needs of a proposed development and the cost of providing necessary new infrastructure are planning considerations;[73] on applications requiring the provision of

---

[71] In one Scottish appeal, for example, the desirability of facilitating the economic contribution of small businesses was regarded as relevant—see *SPADS* No. A4402 (P/PPA/LB/46, 6th December 1982). See too S.E.P.D. Circular 2/1978.

[72] [1972] J.P.L. 403. See too *J. Sainsbury Ltd.* v *Secretary of State for the Environment* [1978] J.P.L. 378; S.D.D. Circular 65/1978 'National Planning Guidelines on the Location of Major Shopping Developments'; and ministerial appeal decisions noted in [1980] J.P.L. 546 and 549; and *Scottish Bulletin of Selected Appeal Decisions*, I/27. In one Scottish appeal the reporter, while accepting that the protection of existing shopping centres was not an extraneous objective, expressed the view that it was not a proper use of planning powers to seek to restrict 'the precise range of goods which a retail firm may legitimately offer for sale'—see *SPADS* No. A5136 (P/PPA/TB/59, 18th June 1984).

[73] See, for example, *Esdell Caravan Parks Ltd.* v *Hemel Hempstead R.D.C.* [1966] 1 Q.B. 895; and *SPADS* Nos. A2008 (P/PPA/AB/247, 27th January 1976); and A3471 (P/PPA/HF/34, 17th October 1980).

substantial new infrastructure such as schools, roads, water and sewerage S.D.D. Circular 64/1976 declared that 'a major function of planning legislation is to ensure that the community's overall interest in the sensible and economic use of land is fully borne in mind in considering the merits of proposed developments' and that refusal of planning permission would be justified where unnecessary or excessive commitment of public resources would be involved.

However, it seems that the conferring of a direct financial benefit on the planning authority (or the avoidance of direct financial disadvantage to them) cannot be a material consideration in dealing with a planning application.[74] The fact that an applicant for planning permission has offered to provide some form of 'planning gain'[75] which will overcome some planning objection to the proposal may justify the grant of planning permission where it would otherwise have had to be refused, but failure to provide any 'planning gain' or to offer to carry out something which it is the planning authority's duty to do is not in itself a legitimate reason for refusal of permission.[76]

Circulars, etc.[77] In *J.A. Pye (Oxford) Estates Ltd.* v *Wychavon District Council*[78] Glidewell J. held that ministerial policies set out in departmental circulars[79] were material considerations which had to be taken into account in determining an appeal; he also held that interpretation of a circular is a matter of law on which the court may review a decision.[80] In *Hatfield Construction Ltd.* v *Secretary of State for the Environment*[81] Mr. David Widdicombe Q.C., sitting as a deputy High Court judge, held that departmental circulars and development control policy notes were part of the background of every planning appeal and must be presumed to have been taken into account in the determination of an appeal unless there was evidence to the contrary.

---

[74] See appeal decision noted in [1975] J.P.L. 424. In *Davy* v *Spelthorne Borough Council* [1984] A.C. 262 Lord Fraser doubted if it would be proper for a planning authority to allow themselves to be influenced by the threat of an action for damages.

[75] See p. 278 below.

[76] See *Westminster Renslade Ltd.* v *Secretary of State for the Environment* (1983) 48 P. & C.R. 255; and *London Borough of Richmond upon Thames* v *Secretary of State for the Environment* [1984] J.P.L. 24.

[77] See Brian Thompson, 'Development Control's "Circular" Triangle' 1984 S.P.L.P. 36; and S. M. Nott and P. H. Morgan, 'The Significance of Department of the Environment Circulars in the Planning Process' [1984] J.P.L. 623. On the use and relevance in Scotland of English departmental guidance see G. Jamieson, 'Use of English Circulars, etc. in Scotland' 1984 S.P.L.P. 8.

[78] [1982] J.P.L. 575.

[79] In *Peak Park Joint Planning Board* v *Secretary of State for the Environment and Cyril Kay* [1979] J.P.L. 618 Sir Douglas Frank considered that advice in a departmental circular relating to the renewal of planning permission was merely some form of administrative policy and was not a relevant planning consideration.

[80] On this point see too *Tameside Metropolitan Borough Council* v *Secretary of State for the Environment* [1984] J.P.L. 180.

[81] [1983] J.P.L. 605. See too *New Forest District Council* v *Secretary of State for the Environment* [1984] J.P.L. 178.

However, in *J.A. Pye (Oxford) Estates Ltd.* v *West Oxfordshire District Council*[82] Mr. David Widdicombe Q.C., sitting as a deputy High Court judge, expressed the view that a *draft* circular was not a material consideration—it might be amended or might never be issued. In that case the circular in question came into operation between the submission of the inquiry inspector's report and the issue of the decision letter; the decision was therefore quashed because of the minister's failure to take it into account. In both *London Borough of Richmond upon Thames* v *Secretary of State for the Environment*[83] and *Westminster City Council* v *Secretary of State for the Environment*[84] the report of the Property Advisory Group on 'Planning Gain' was held to be a material consideration; despite its purely advisory status it represented the views of a government-appointed committee. In the latter case Mr. David Widdicombe Q.C. stood by what he had said on the status of draft circulars in *J.A. Pye (Oxford) Ltd.* (above) but in the former case Glidewell J. said that he did not agree that a draft circular could never be a material consideration.

Existing rights and planning history. Existing use rights attaching to the land in question and its planning history may be relevant considerations. Thus in *Wells* v *Minister of Housing and Local Government*[85] the fact that planning permission had already been granted (though not implemented) for a particular development was held to be a matter which ought to have been taken into account in considering whether planning permission should be granted for a similar,[86] though larger, development. In *South Oxfordshire District Council* v *Secretary of State for the Environment*[87] Woolf J. held that a time-expired planning permission was a relevant consideration; the minister was, however, wrong to regard such a permission as a 'vitally material consideration'.

The purpose for which land is presently used and the fact that a particular use is immune from enforcement action may be relevant considerations in considering whether planning permission should be granted for the erection

[82] (1982) 47 P. & C.R. 125.
[83] [1984] J.P.L. 24.
[84] [1984] J.P.L. 27.
[85] [1967] 1 W.L.R. 1000; see too *Millard* v *Secretary of State for the Environment* (1979) 254 E.G. 733; *Spackman* v *Secretary of State for the Environment* [1977] 1 All E.R. 257; and appeal decision reported in [1984] J.P.L. 132.
[86] The existence of a permission for development of a different kind is not likely to be relevant—see *North Surrey Water Company* v *Secretary of State for the Environment* [1977] J.P.L. 100.
[87] [1981] 1 W.L.R. 1092. However, in *Peak Park Joint Planning Board* v *Secretary of State for the Environment and Cyril Kay* [1979] J.P.L. 618 Sir Douglas Frank expressed the view that an expired planning permission was no longer of any account. In *Regina (Thallon)* v *Department of the Environment* [1982] N.I. 26, an invalid planning permission was held not to be a material consideration—see Brian Thompson, 'Relevance in the Determination of Planning Applications' [1983] J.P.L. 97.

of buildings to be used for that purpose.[88] It may also be relevant to consider the uses to which land could be put without the risk of enforcement action being taken, so long as there is a likelihood of such a use being taken up.[89] However, whether the planning history of a site is a material consideration will depend greatly on the circumstances of the individual case.[90] Where a building had been destroyed by fire the Secretary of State for the Environment considered that some weight had to be given to the fact that but for the fire, the premises would still have been in use.[91]

Social considerations. There is some uncertainty about how far what might be described as social considerations may be taken into account in determining planning applications. In *R.* v *Hillingdon London Borough Council, ex parte Royco Homes Ltd.*[92] the Queens Bench Division quashed a planning permission for the development of land for residential purposes which was subject to conditions restricting the first occupiers of the proposed houses to persons on the council's housing waiting list and according them security of tenure for ten years. The court took the view that the conditions effectively required the applicants to take on a significant part of the local authority's housing duties and, as such, were unreasonable. Again, in *David Lowe & Sons Ltd.* v *Musselburgh Town Council*[93] the First Division of the Court of Session quashed a planning permission for residential development which was subject to a condition allocating four out of every five of the houses to meet local authority housing needs. Although the court's decision turned upon ambiguity in the phrasing of the condition, both the Lord President (Lord Emslie) and Lord Cameron would have been prepared to hold that a planning permission could not competently be qualified by such a condition; in their view the condition went far beyond matters relating to the development of land.

On the other hand, the Structure and Local Plans Regulations (see p. 84 above) specifically require planning authorities to have regard to social policies and considerations in the preparation of development plans and it would seem strange that they should be ignored for the purposes of development control. In *Clyde & Co.* v *Secretary of State for the Environ-*

---

[88] *Western Fish Products Ltd.* v *Penwith District Council* [1981] 2 All E.R. 204; *Newbury District Council* v *Secretary of State for the Environment* [1983] J.P.L. 381; and *Philglow Ltd.* v *Secretary of State for the Environment* [1984] J.P.L. 111 (reversed on other grounds: (1984) 270 E.G. 1192).

[89] *Snowden* v *City of Bradford Metropolitan Council* [1980] J.P.L. 749; and *Lewstar Ltd.* v *Secretary of State for the Environment* [1984] J.P.L. 116.

[90] See *London Borough of Tower Hamlets* v *Secretary of State for the Environment* [1983] J.P.L. 315; and *Peacock Homes Ltd.* v *Secretary of State for the Environment* [1983] J.P.L. 541 (planning history relevant); and *Chris Fashionware (West End) Ltd.* v *Secretary of State for the Environment* [1980] J.P.L. 678; and *George A. Whistlecraft* v *Secretary of State for the Environment* [1983] J.P.L. 809 (planning history not relevant).

[91] [1977] J.P.L. 608.

[92] [1974] Q.B. 720.

[93] 1973 S.C. 130; 1974 S.L.T. 5.

ment[94] Sir David Cairns accepted that 'the need for housing is clearly a planning consideration'; and in *Bradwell Industrial Aggregates* v *Secretary of State for the Environment*[95] Sir Douglas Frank listed among the questions which the minister should have asked himself the question 'how important, taking into account economic and social factors, was the continuance of this undertaking?'

Need. Whilst it seems that the need for a particular development or type of development in economic or social terms may be a valid consideration,[96] the Secretary of State for Scotland has expressed the view that, generally speaking, lack of need for a particular development is not a planning reason which would support its refusal.[97] However, it appears that lack of need may be material in areas subject to restrictive policies. Department of Health for Scotland Circular 40/1960, for example, recommends that in areas of open countryside new houses should not normally be permitted unless, on the merits of the case, a special need can be shown.

Alternative sites. The question whether a better alternative site is available for a proposed development can be a material consideration.[98] For example, a proposal to site a development in a green belt may be supported by the applicant on the ground that the need for the development in that area outweighs its disadvantages. In such a case, the question of whether there is a suitable alternative site outside the green belt is likely to be material. In *R.* v *Berkshire County Council, ex parte Mangnall*[99] Nolan J. held that although it was the duty of the planning authority to consider and evaluate a suggested alternative site, the planning legislation did not require the comparative evaluation of the two sites to be carried out on an equal basis in order to choose the 'better' site; it was sufficient for the planning authority to have proper regard to the suggested other site as a possible alternative. In *Ynystawe, Ynyforgan and Glais Gipsy Site Action Group* v *Secretary of State for Wales*[1] Glidewell J. stated that an inspector at a public inquiry was not

94 [1977] 1 W.L.R. 926.
95 [1981] J.P.L. 276. See also *Commercial and Residential Property Development Company Ltd.* v *Secretary of State for the Environment* (1981) 80 L.G.R. 443; and appeal decisions noted in [1979] J.P.L. 418; and [1980] J.P.L. 843 and 853.
96 See *Stringer* v *Minister of Housing and Local Government* [1970] 1 W.L.R. 1281, per Cooke J.; and *Clyde & Co.* v *Secretary of State for the Environment* [1977] 1 W.L.R. 926, per Sir David Cairns.
97 *SPADS* No. A2061 (P/PPA/GLW/955, 9th April 1976); see too *Scottish Bulletin of Selected Appeal Decisions*, 1/27.
98 See *Rhodes* v *Minister of Housing and Local Government* [1963] 1 W.L.R. 208; *Banks Horticultural Products* v *Secretary of State for the Environment* (1979) 252 E.G. 811; *Brown* v *Secretary of State for the Environment* (1978) 40 P. & C.R. 285; *Ynystawe, Ynyforgan and Glais Gipsy Site Action Group* v *Secretary of State for Wales* [1981] J.P.L. 874; and *Prest* v *Secretary of State for Wales* (1982) 81 L.G.R. 193.
99 *The Times*, 31st October 1984.
1   [1981] J.P.L. 874.

bound to look around for alternatives, but if evidence about suitable alternatives was offered to him in such a case, he was bound to consider and evaluate it.

Personal circumstances and attributes. Where an adverse decision on a planning application would cause an applicant great hardship then it seems that, other considerations being equal, this factor may tip the balance in favour of a grant of permission.[2] For example the English minister has said that where a dwelling has been destroyed by fire or other disaster or is to be demolished because of, say, road proposals, an application for a replacement dwelling has 'a very strong claim to sympathetic consideration'.[3]

Otherwise, it seems that the personal circumstances or attributes of the applicant will not generally be of much relevance in the consideration of a planning application.[4] Nor will the identity[5] or attributes of the person who is to occupy premises normally be a material consideration. In *Birmingham Corporation* v *Minister of Housing and Local Government* [6] Lord Parker C.J. accepted that a planning authority were not concerned with the characteristics of the particular people living in a house, whether unruly or well behaved.

The comfort and convenience of occupants. It would appear to be proper for a planning authority to concern themselves with matters relating to the comfort and convenience of those who will ultimately occupy the development for which application has been made.[7] It may thus be proper to refuse planning permission for dwellinghouses because the proposed houses lack privacy[8] or because the site has an unsatisfactory noise climate.[9]

However, so far as the internal space standards of proposed houses are concerned, it has been held in a number of appeal decisions made by the English minister or his inspectors that these are matters for the developer and his customers and not for the planning authority.[10] Once a building has

2 See *New Forest District Council* v *Secretary of State for the Environment* [1984] J.P.L. 178; *Tameside Metropolitan Borough Council* v *Secretary of State for the Environment* [1984] J.P.L. 180; and *Westminster City Council* v *Great Portland Estates plc* [1984] 3 W.L.R. 1035. And see, for example, *Scottish Bulletin of Selected Appeal Decisions*, III/80; *SPADS* No. A2076 (P/PPA/AR/254, 19th May 1976); and [1969] J.P.L. 159.
3 [1973] J.P.L. 123.
4 See, however, *Scottish Bulletin of Selected Appeal Decisions*, III/93.
5 See *Westminster City Council* v *British Waterways Board* [1984] 3 W.L.R. 1047.
6 [1964] 1 Q.B. 178. See too *R.* v *Hillingdon London Borough Council, ex p. Royco Homes Ltd.* and *David Lowe & Sons Ltd.* v *Musselburgh Town Council* (see p. 223 above). Contrast, however, *Fawcett Properties Ltd.* v *Buckingham County Council* [1961] A.C. 636 (see p. 234 below).
7 See, for example, *Scottish Bulletin of Selected Appeal Decisions*, III/91.
8 See, for example, *Scottish Bulletin of Selected Appeal Decisions*, II/29; and *SPADS* No. A3469 (P/PPA/LC/41, 17th October 1980).
9 See, for example, *SPADS* No. A2016 (P/PPA/RC/89, 5th March 1976); and [1973] J.P.L. 436.
10 See, for example, [1978] J.P.L. 579; [1979] J.P.L. 191; [1980] J.P.L. 704; and [1983] J.P.L. 407, 694 and 836. See, however, *R.* v *Hillingdon London Borough Council, ex parte Royco Homes Ltd.* [1974] Q.B. 720.

been erected, internal alterations can be made without the need for planning permission and it can therefore be argued that the internal arrangements of a building for which planning permission is sought cannot generally be a proper planning consideration. That question was, however, left open by Lord Widgery C.J. in *R.* v *Hillingdon London Borough Council, ex parte Royco Homes Ltd.*[11] It is not clear how far planning control can properly be used to regulate the quality of work carried out under planning permission.[12]

Miscellaneous. Moral considerations cannot properly be taken into account by the planning authority[13] but in *Marie Finlay* v *Secretary of State for the Environment*[14] it was held to be a material consideration that the showing of sexually explicit films in premises might be detrimental to the character and amenities of the area.

In *Bearsden Town Council* v *Glasgow Corporation*[15] it was held that undertakings given by the applicants, though not legally enforceable, were material considerations which could properly be taken into account in considering a planning application. In *McLaren* v *Secretary of State for the Environment*[16] it was held that the minister was entitled to take account of the fact that the planning authority and the applicants proposed to enter into an agreement relating to certain aspects of a proposed development if permission were granted.

Fairness to the applicant may be a relevant, though probably not important, consideration. In *Ynys Mon—Isle of Anglesey Borough Council* v *Secretary of State for Wales*[17] it was held that provided other planning considerations did not compel a different view, the Secretary of State was entitled to treat it as a factor supporting the grant of planning permission that, having regard to the planning history of the surrounding area, it would be inequitable to refuse permission.

Among the matters which cannot, it seems, properly be taken into account by the planning authority are the existence of title restrictions which

---

[11] [1974] Q.B. 720. Internal arrangements were treated as relevant in a Scottish appeal in which permission would have been granted for accommodation for an agricultural worker but not for holiday accommodation—see *SPADS* No. A3152 (P/ENA/GD/11, 12th October 1979).
[12] See *Sutton London Borough Council* v *Secretary of State for the Environment* (1975) 29 P. & C.R. 350; see also appeal decisions noted at [1980] J.P.L. 704; and [1981] J.P.L. 108.
[13] See, for example, appeal decision reported in [1968] J.P.L. 108; and the decisions noted in 1983 S.P.L.P. 54.
[14] [1983] J.P.L. 802. See too appeal decision reported in [1980] J.P.L. 58.
[15] 1971 S.C. 274; 1971 S.L.T. (Notes) 66. See too *Augier* v *Secretary of State for the Environment* (1978) 38 P. & C.R. 219 (in which it was, however, said that the applicants would be barred from going back on their undertakings).
[16] [1981] J.P.L. 423.
[17] [1984] J.P.L. 646.

might prevent the carrying out of the proposed development.[18]

Provision of access for the disabled is, it seems, a proper planning consideration.[19]

Planning and other controls. Given the nature of planning, there will be occasions when 'planning' considerations may overlap with 'highway' or 'housing' or 'educational' considerations and so on. An attempt to further delimit the scope of 'other material considerations' has sometimes been made by those who argue that planning powers should not be used to regulate matters which can be dealt with under other, more specific, statutes. This is a view which has been expressed by the Secretary of State for Scotland and Scottish Office reporters on a number of occasions.[20] In giving his decision, for example, on an appeal against a refusal of planning permission for the working of sand and gravel in the bed of a loch, the Secretary of State stated that the question whether the proposed operations would have an adverse effect on water supplies was a matter for the river purification authority and not one which should be dealt with under the planning legislation.[21]

It has also been said in Scottish appeal decisions that the need for a public house[22] and the desirability of, or need for, bingo facilities[23] or amusement arcades[24] are matters for the appropriate licensing authorities, that questions of safety in public places[25] and matters of hygiene[26] are more appropriately dealt with under other legislation and that the adequacy of a water supply for fire-fighting purposes is a matter for the building authority.[27] In one appeal decision the view was expressed that the site's stability was a matter to be dealt with under the building legislation[28] but in other cases site stability has

[18] See note attached to decision of Lands Tribunal for Scotland in *Gorrie & Banks Ltd.* v *Musselburgh Town Council* 1974 S.L.T. (Lands Tr.) 5, in which the planning history of a particular site is recounted. See too appeal decision reported in [1983] J.P.L. 764 (right of way). It may, however, be relevant to take into account the fact that a neighbour's legal rights might have the effect that the applicant could not implement some aspect of the proposed development without which it should not be allowed to proceed—see *SPADS* No. A2911 (P/PPA/SL/58, 15th February 1979).
[19] See, for example, appeal decision reported in [1983] J.P.L. 136.
[20] See, for example, *Scottish Bulletin of Selected Appeal Decisions*, III/66 (fire risk from petrol pumps more properly dealt with under Petroleum Acts); and I/26 (more appropriate for authority to use powers under the roads legislation to secure the lowering of a wall).
[21] *Scottish Bulletin of Selected Appeal Decisions*, III/87. As to the dangers of such a restrictive approach, see *Harwich Harbour Conservancy Board* v *Secretary of State for the Environment* [1975] 1 Lloyds Rep. 334.
[22] *SPADS* Nos. A2750 (P/PPA/LA/67, 23rd August 1978); and A2752 (P/PPA/TB/11, 25th August 1978).
[23] *SPADS* No. A2100 (P/PPA/ML/179, 29th June 1976).
[24] *SPADS* No. A3678 (P/PPA/LD/31, 16th April 1981).
[25] *SPADS* Nos. A2314 (P/PPA/ST/1, 7th April 1977); and A3678 (above).
[26] *SPADS* Nos. A2314 (above); and A2747 (P/PPA/HD/11, 21st August 1978).
[27] *SPADS* No. A2300 (P/PPA/SP/2, 15th March 1977).
[28] *SPADS* No. A2719 (P/PPA/CB/22, 24th July 1978).

been treated as a material planning consideration.[29] It has also been said that it is not appropriate to use ordinary development control powers to restrict the display of advertisements since advertisements are subject to their own specific controls.[30] In one Scottish appeal it was held that it would not be right for the planning authority to concern themselves with the possibility that a proposed development would interfere with radio and television reception in the area;[31] south of the border differing views have been expressed.[32]

The fact that an action might lie at common law to restrain noise or smell or some other adverse effect that might result from a proposed development does not prevent the planning authority taking account of that factor but it may be relevant to consider whether some potential damage to amenity could be reduced by private law remedies.[33]

There is a principle of statutory interpretation that general powers in an Act should not derogate from powers granted specifically in other legislation—*generalia specialibus non derogant*. However, powers will often not be truly concurrent, as different statutes have different purposes and contexts, and so far as planning and other statutes are concerned the courts have shown little inclination to construe different statutory codes as if Parliament had allocated mutually exclusive areas of jurisdiction to each code. In any event, the presumption would seem to be specifically rebutted by s.274 of the 1972 Act which provides that powers conferred by the planning legislation may be exercised in relation to any land notwithstanding any provision for regulating development of land made by an enactment in force at the passing of the 1947 Act.[34] In *Esdell Caravan Parks Ltd.* v *Hemel Hempstead R.D.C.*[35] the Court of Appeal held that the various considerations relating to the use of land as a caravan site could not be divided into two watertight groups, one a group of 'planning' considerations which might relevantly be taken into account by the planning authority considering the grant of permission for the site and the other a group of 'site' considerations

---

[29] *SPADS* Nos. A3369 (P/PPA/ML/141, 30th June 1980); A3959 (P/PPA/SS/61, 16th November 1981); and A4128 (P/PPA/SS/68, 4th May 1982). See too [1981] J.P.L. 298.

[30] *SPADS* Nos. A4129 (P/PPA/HF/45, 4th May 1982); and A4254A (P/PPA/CC/83, 6th August 1982). In England a planning condition prohibiting the display of advertisements has been treated as *ultra vires*—see [1982] J.P.L. 733.

[31] *SPADS* No. A4844 (P/PPA/FB/128, 26th September 1983). Contrast, however, *SPADS* No. A5257 (P/ENA/FB/48, 31st August 1984).

[32] See [1981] J.P.L. 842; [1983] J.P.L. 760; and [1984] J.P.L. 297 (treated as material); [1982] J.P.L. 132; [1983] J.P.L. 75; and [1984] J.P.L. 298 (held not material).

[33] See *Fitzpatrick Developments Ltd.* v *Minister of Housing and Local Government* (1965) 194 E.G. 911, per Widgery J.

[34] The reference to an enactment in force at the passing of the 1947 Act appears to include a later re-enactment of the same provision—see *Westminster Bank Ltd.* v *Minister of Housing and Local Government* [1971] A.C. 508, per Lord Reid.

[35] [1966] 1 Q.B. 895. See too *Hanks* v *Minister of Housing and Local Government* [1963] 1 Q.B. 999 (a rigid distinction could not be drawn between 'planning' and 'housing' considerations). 'Housing need' was upheld as a material consideration in *Clyde & Co.* v *Secretary of State for the Environment* [1977] 1 W.L.R. 926.

which could properly be taken into account only by the authority considering the grant of a caravan site licence; many considerations fell into both categories and could therefore be taken into account by both authorities.[36]

In *Westminster Bank Ltd.* v *Minister of Housing and Local Government*[37] it was held that in refusing an application for planning permission on the ground that the land would be required for future road widening the planning authority had not acted outwith their powers, even though the result of using planning powers rather than highway powers to achieve this objective was to deprive the landowners of a right to immediate payment of compensation. The House of Lords held that as Parliament had imposed no limit on the use of either method of preventing development which would interfere with road proposals, the use of one method rather than the other was not an abuse of power.[38]

In *Ladbroke (Rentals) Ltd.* v *Secretary of State for the Environment*[39] it was argued that, having regard to the specific powers of the licensing authority under the gaming legislation to impose restrictions on permitted opening hours in order to prevent disturbance to occupiers of property in the vicinity, it was not open to the Secretary of State to impose such restrictions in the exercise of his powers under the planning legislation. Sir Douglas Frank said that while it would no doubt be right 'as a matter of sensible administration' that such matters should be left to the licensing authority, the court was not entitled to imply that simply because the licensing authority possessed these express powers, the wide powers given to planning authorities were thereby diminished. It may therefore be appropriate for a planning authority to ask (as did Parker J. in his capacity as inspector at the Windscale inquiry) whether some other system of control can be relied upon to achieve the desired result; if it can, he said, 'it is the task of that system to afford the necessary protection and not that of the planning authority.'[40]

That duality of control may give rise to legal difficulties is, however, demonstrated by the decision of the Court of Session in *City of Glasgow District Council* v *Secretary of State for Scotland*.[41] The court held that where

[36] Some matters will, of course, be more appropriately dealt with under one or other of the codes—see *Esdell*. And in *SPADS* No. A3857 (P/ENA/CB/31, 24th August 1981) the reporter considered that matters of public health, safety and hygiene would more appropriately be dealt with by the site licensing authority.
[37] [1971] A.C. 508. See also *Hoveringham Gravels Ltd.* v *Secretary of State for the Environment* [1975] Q.B. 754 (the fact that a site was known to the planning authority to be a site of great archaeological importance was 'a perfectly legitimate reason for refusing planning permission'); *Allnatt (London) Properties Ltd.* v *Middlesex County Council* (1964) 15 P. & C.R. 288; and *Maurice* v *London County Council* [1964] 2 Q.B. 362.
[38] However, in *British Airports Authority* v *Secretary of State for Scotland* 1979 S.C. 200; 1979 S.L.T. 197 Lord Cameron appears to have drawn support for his view that a condition was *ultra vires* for unreasonableness from the fact that the matter in question could more appropriately be dealt with under other legislation.
[39] [1981] J.P.L. 427.
[40] Report of the Windscale Inquiry, p. 41, quoted in *Planning for Industry* (J.P.E.L. Occasional Paper, 1980), p. 62.
[41] 1980 S.C. 150; 1982 S.L.T. 28 (see p. 124 above).

development is carried out under the compulsion of a building authority in the interests of public safety, the work is not subject to planning control. The problem facing the court was whether the building or planning code took priority in the exceptional situation in which the landowner found himself—on the one hand he was faced with a requirement to demolish his building but on the other hand was refused planning permission for the work. Faced with two such conflicting orders, the landowner was entitled to know where he stood. The court concluded that in such circumstances common sense demanded that public safety should prevail.

CHAPTER 10

CONTROL OF DEVELOPMENT
3: CONDITIONS

General

In terms of s.26(1) of the 1972 Act planning authorities are empowered to grant planning permission 'subject to such conditions as they think fit'. Section 27(1), which is expressed to be without prejudice to the generality of s.26(1), goes on to list certain specific types of condition which may be imposed. These may regulate the development or use of any land under the control of the applicant (whether or not it is land in respect of which the application is made) or require the carrying out of works on any such land, 'so far as appears to the planning authority to be expedient for the purposes of or in connection with the development authorised by the permission' (s.27(1)(a)).

It is not clear whether s.27(1)(a) should be construed as amplifying or restricting the scope of the general power conferred on planning authorities by s.26(1). The relationship between the two provisions has been aptly described as 'somewhat obscure'.[1] In *British Airports Authority* v *Secretary of State for Scotland*[2] the First Division of the Court of Session appear to have taken the view that all conditions must satisfy the 'expediency' test contained in s.27(1)(a). Lord Cameron stated, for example, that: 'The power to impose conditions is governed by s.27(1)(a) of the Act of 1972 and the "expediency" there referred to is "for the purposes of or *in connection with*" . . . the development authorised by that permission.' However, in *Hall & Co. Ltd.* v *Shoreham-by-Sea Urban District Council*[3] the Court of Appeal rejected the argument that the 'expediency' test should be treated as restricting a planning authority's general powers to impose conditions. Willmer L.J. pointed out that the subsection in which the 'expediency' test appears—the subsection conferring the special powers on conditions, equivalent to s.27(1)(a) of the Scottish Act—declares those special powers to be without prejudice to the more general powers on conditions. He therefore refused to treat the provision relating to the special powers 'as imposing a limitation on the wide words' of the general provision.

The Court of Session's approach in *British Airports Authority* appears to necessitate a somewhat strained construction of the legislation. It seems much more natural to read s.27(1)(a) as amplifying rather than restricting

---

[1]   See [1979] J.P.L. 315.
[2]   1979 S.C. 200; 1979 S.L.T. 197.
[3]   [1964] 1 W.L.R. 240.

the scope of the power conferred by s.26(1). Section 27(1)(a) would appear to be intended to permit the planning authority to impose particular types of condition which might not otherwise be competent. In particular, s.27(1)(a) seems to extend the planning authority's powers (which under s.26(1) appear to relate only to land comprised in the application) by enabling them to impose conditions affecting other land under the applicant's control. The relationship between s.26(1) and s.27(1)(a) is important in view of the decision in *British Airports Authority* that it cannot be 'expedient' to impose a condition which is unnecessary and that such a condition may be quashed (see p. 247 below).

Section 27(1)(b) provides for what may be described as a 'limited period permission'. This is a permission granted subject to a condition requiring the removal of any buildings or works authorised by the permission, or the discontinuance of any use of land so authorised, at the end of a specified period, and the carrying out of any works required for the reinstatement of land at the end of that period. A grant of planning permission for development consisting of the winning and working of minerals might be described as a special type of limited period permission. Section 41A of the 1972 Act[4] provides that every such permission shall be subject to a condition as to the duration of the development (see p. 471 below).

In addition to the general provisions of ss.26 and 27, there are a number of provisions in the 1972 Act dealing with particular types of condition. Section 27A[5] provides that where planning permission for mineral workings is granted subject to a condition requiring the restoration of the site on completion of the development, then the planning authority may also impose what is termed an 'aftercare' condition requiring certain steps to be taken to bring the land up to a specified standard (see p. 475 below). Sections 38 and 39 and Schedule 22 provide that, subject to certain exceptions, every planning permission shall be subject to a condition that the development must commence within a stipulated period, failing which the permission will lapse (see p. 261 below). Section 57 imposes a duty on the planning authority to ensure, whenever it is appropriate, that in granting planning permission for any development adequate provision is made, by the imposition of conditions, for the preservation or planting of trees.

Although the general power to impose conditions in s.26(1) is, in the words of Lord Jenkins, 'expressed in language apt to confer an absolute discretion on a local planning authority to impose any condition of any kind they may think fit',[6] the power has not been interpreted as unlimited by the courts and there are several possible grounds on which a condition may be challenged (either in the courts or on appeal to the Secretary of State) as

---

4   Added by the Town and Country Planning (Minerals) Act 1981, s.24.
5   Added by the Town and Country Planning (Minerals) Act 1981, s.22.
6   *Fawcett Properties Ltd.* v *Buckingham County Council* [1961] A.C. 636.

being invalid in law.[7]

In *Pyx Granite Co. Ltd.* v *Minister of Housing and Local Government*,[8] Lord Denning declared, in the course of a judgment approved by the House of Lords in *Fawcett Properties Ltd.* v *Buckingham County Council*:[9]

'Although the planning authorities are given very wide powers to impose "such conditions as they think fit", nevertheless the law says that those conditions, to be valid must fairly and reasonably relate to the permitted development. The planning authority are not at liberty to use their powers for an ulterior object, however desirable that object may seem to them to be in the public interest.'

'It follows', said Viscount Dilhorne in *Newbury District Council* v *Secretary of State for the Environment*,[10] 'that the conditions imposed must be for a planning purpose and not for any ulterior one[11], and that they must fairly and reasonably relate to the development permitted. Also they must not be so unreasonable that no reasonable planning authority could have imposed them.' In addition to the three tests laid down by Viscount Dilhorne, conditions may also be void for uncertainty[12] and it seems that they may now be open to challenge on the ground that they are unnecessary.[13] These tests are considered in turn.

The condition must be imposed for a planning purpose and not for an ulterior one

This is another way of saying that in deciding to impose conditions a planning authority may be influenced only by planning considerations. The difficulty of defining the proper scope of planning considerations was discussed in the preceding chapter and that discussion is relevant here. To say that these considerations or purposes are to be derived from the development plan so far as material to the application, from the regional report together with the observations of the Secretary of State thereon, from

---

[7] See Mungo Deans, 'Planning Conditions and the Courts' 1984 S.P.L.P. 10. Department of the Environment Circular 1/85 provides guidance on the use of conditions in planning permissions. In a letter published at 1983 S.P.L.P. 90 A.G. Bell, the Chief Reporter at the Scottish Office Inquiry Reporters' Unit, commented that M.H.L.G. Circular 5/68 (the predecessor of Circular 1/85) had 'been generally regarded in Scotland as authoritative as to the correct planning practice'. See also S.D.D. Circular 22/1984.

[8] [1958] 1 Q.B. 554.

[9] [1961] A.C. 636; and in *Mixnam's Properties Ltd.* v *Chertsey U.D.C.* [1965] A.C. 735; and *Newbury District Council* v *Secretary of State for the Environment* [1981] A.C. 578.

[10] [1981] A.C. 578.

[11] In the same case Lord Fraser said that a condition 'may have other purposes as well as its planning purpose. But if it is imposed solely for some other purpose or purposes, such as furtherance of the housing policy of the local authority, it will not be valid as a planning condition.'

[12] *Fawcett Properties Ltd.* v *Buckingham County Council* [1961] A.C. 636; *David Lowe & Sons Ltd.* v *Musselburgh Town Council* 1973 S.C. 130; 1974 S.L.T. 5.

[13] *British Airports Authority* v *Secretary of State for Scotland* 1979 S.C. 200; 1979 S.L.T. 197.

the response to publicity and consultations and from any other material considerations does little to narrow the field.

Argument about the proper scope of planning has occurred in the context of conditions imposing a limitation on the class of people who may occupy development. Planning control is concerned primarily with the use of land rather than with the user.[14]

However, provided the purpose of a condition is one which relates to the use of the land, it would seem that this purpose may be secured through a condition which has the consequence of limiting the categories of user.[15] In *Fawcett Properties Ltd.* v *Buckingham County Council*[16] planning permission for a pair of cottages had been granted subject to a condition providing that occupation of the cottages was to be limited to persons employed in agriculture or forestry. The House of Lords held that although the wording of the condition might be open to criticism and might produce anomalies, the condition was reasonably related to planning purposes—in particular, the furtherance of the planning authority's green belt policy—and did not place an unreasonable restriction on the use of the cottages.

It was specifically held in *Fawcett* that it is within the power of the planning authority to impose a condition relating to the class of persons who may occupy a building[17] and it is somewhat difficult to reconcile certain statements made in *David Lowe & Sons Ltd.* v *Musselburgh Town Council*[18] with the decision in *Fawcett*. In *David Lowe* planning permission had been granted to a local authority for residential development of certain sites subject to a condition in the following terms: 'The sites are approved for the burgh's estimated future local authority and private housing needs over the next 20 years which cannot be accommodated within the existing burgh boundaries, in the proportion of one private house to four local authority houses.' The First Division of the Court of Session held that the condition was so ambiguous as to be unenforceable but, had it been necessary to do so, both the Lord President (Lord Emslie) and Lord Cameron would have been prepared to hold that a planning permission could not competently be qualified by such a condition. Lord Cameron said: 'this condition goes much further than one which is related to the development of the land with which planning legislation is concerned. It plainly purports to limit the uses which owners or occupiers of buildings to be erected are to make of them . . . ' The Lord President quoted the statutory definition of 'development' and stated that the planning legislation 'is concerned with the control of development

---

[14] See *Westminster City Council* v *Great Portland Estates plc* [1984] 3 W.L.R. 1035; and *Westminster City Council* v *British Waterways Board* [1984] 3 W.L.R. 1047.

[15] *Westminster City Council* v *Great Portland Estates plc* [1984] 3 W.L.R. 1035; and *Fawcett Properties Ltd.* v *Buckingham County Council* [1961] A.C. 636. But see *David Lowe & Sons Ltd.* v *Musselburgh Town Council* 1973 S.C. 130; 1974 S.L.T. 5.

[16] [1961] A.C. 636.

[17] In *Fawcett* Lord Keith said, however: 'There might be personal attributes or circumstances required of the occupants which had no conceivable relevance to planning policy and, if so, such requirements would be bad. But that cannot, in my opinion, be said here.'

[18] 1973 S.C. 130; 1974 S.L.T. 5. See Eric Young, 'Planning Condition Apportioning Land Between Private and Local Authority Housing' [1975] J.P.L. 139.

thus defined, and for the purposes of planning permission is not concerned with ownership or occupation of land or buildings'. *Fawcett* was apparently cited in argument but was not mentioned by either the Lord President or Lord Cameron.

In practice, planning authorities have shown a continuing interest in the use of occupancy conditions, most commonly to restrict new houses in the countryside to agricultural workers.[19] The English minister has accepted that occupancy conditions may have a role to play in the control of office and industrial development, although he has emphasised the importance of wording the condition so that a developer can ascertain with a degree of certainty whether a particular prospective occupier is included in the specified class.[20]

An example of conditions held to have been imposed for an ulterior purpose is provided by *R. v Hillingdon London Borough Council, ex parte Royco Homes Ltd.*[21] The conditions in question provided that the first occupiers of the residential development in question should be persons on the council's housing waiting list and that for a period of ten years from the date of first occupation the occupiers of the dwellings should have security of tenure under the Rent Acts. In the Divisional Court Lord Widgery C.J., who delivered the main judgment, considered that the conditions were 'the equivalent of requiring the applicants to take on at their own expense a significant part of the duty of the council as housing authority'; 'however well intentioned and however sensible such a desire on the part of the council may have been', there was, in Lord Widgery's view, no doubt that these conditions were *ultra vires*.

The condition must fairly and reasonably relate to the development permitted

Not only must a condition be imposed for a planning purpose, there must also be a direct relationship between the development proposed and the condition. This is a rather more stringent test than is applied to grounds of refusal. The latter must be supported by a sound planning reason but the link between the particular development proposed and the ground of refusal can be relatively slight.[22]

Inevitably, difficult questions can arise in determining whether there is a sufficiently direct relationship between a particular development and a

[19] See *Alderson* v *Secretary of State for the Environment* [1984] J.P.L. 429 (p. 246 below).
[20] See, generally the decisions of the English minister noted at [1975] J.P.L. 556; [1979] J.P.L. 412 and 414; [1980] J.P.L. 212 and 845; [1981] J.P.L. 918; [1982] J.P.L. 543; and [1984] J.P.L. 368.
[21] [1974] Q.B. 720. See 'The *Hillingdon ("Royco")* Case' [1974] J.P.L. 507. See too *Hall & Co. Ltd. v Shoreham-by-Sea U.D.C.* [1964] 1 W.L.R. 240 (below); and the comments of Forbes J. in *Westminster Renslade Ltd. v Secretary of State for the Environment* (1983) 48 P. & C.R. 255.
[22] See, for example, *Collis Radio Ltd. v Secretary of State for the Environment* (1975) 29 P. & C.R. 390; *Clyde & Co. v Secretary of State for the Environment* [1977] 1 W.L.R. 926; and *Ynystawe, etc. Gipsy Site Action Group v Secretary of State for Wales* [1981] J.P.L. 874. See too appeal decision reported in [1983] J.P.L. 833.

condition attached to permission for that development. In *British Airports Authority* v *Secretary of State for Scotland*[23] it was argued that before a condition could be said to be fairly and reasonably related to the permitted development there had to be a causal relationship between the development and the mischief which the condition was designed to suppress. Lord Cameron did not consider this method of approach to be of real assistance, saying:

> 'It does not in my opinion really matter whether the development can be said to be directly causative of the state of affairs to which the condition is intended to apply, or whether that state of affairs is merely consequential upon the use to which the development is or will be or may be applied. It is enough that there should be a recognised and real relationship between the development and the condition and that it can be affirmed that it is one that is fair and reasonable.'

The courts will only intervene on the ground of gross unreasonableness or if the planning authority or the Secretary of State misdirect themselves in law.[24]

The application of this test in practice may be illustrated by reference to three cases: *Pyx Granite Co. Ltd.* v *Minister of Housing and Local Government*,[25] *British Airports Authority* v *Secretary of State for Scotland*[26] and *Newbury District Council* v *Secretary of State for the Environment*.[27]

In *Pyx Granite* the Court of Appeal had to consider whether conditions, affecting plant situated on land which was not the subject of the planning application, were reasonably related to the quarrying operations with which the planning permission was concerned. As mentioned above, the planning authority are entitled to impose conditions on land under the applicant's control, whether or not it is land in respect of which the application was made, but only 'so far as appears to the planning authority to be expedient for the purposes of or in connection with the development authorised by the permission'. The Court of Appeal held the conditions valid; they were imposed for a proper planning purpose and they required the carrying out of works on land which was so near to the site of the permitted quarrying operations as to make the works 'expedient for the purposes of or in

[23]   1979 S.C. 200; 1979 S.L.T. 197.
[24]   *Newbury District Council* v *Secretary of State for the Environment* [1981] A.C. 578.
[25]   [1958] 1 Q.B. 554 (reversed on other grounds by the House of Lords: [1960] A.C. 260).
[26]   1979 S.C. 200; 1979 S.L.T. 197.
[27]   [1981] A.C. 578. See too *Kingston-Upon-Thames Royal London Borough Council* v *Secretary of State for the Environment* [1973] 1 W.L.R. 1549; *A.I. & P. (Stratford) Ltd.* v *London Borough of Tower Hamlets* (1976) 237 E.G. 416; and *Kember* v *Secretary of State for the Environment* [1982] J.P.L. 383. Also *Selected Enforcement and Allied Appeals*, pp. 44 and 45; and ministerial decisions noted in *SPADS* Nos. A2270 (P/PPA/KD/78, 11th February 1977); A3551 (P/PPA/SR/22, 19th December 1980); A3790 (P/PPA/GD/59, 26th June 1981); A4254A (P/PPA/CC/83, 6th August 1982); 1981 S.P.L.P. 88; 1982 S.P.L.P. 54; 1983 S.P.L.P. 87; [1977] J.P.L. 742; [1983] J.P.L. 259, 762, 764 and 833; and [1984] J.P.L. 199.

connection with' that development. Lord Denning considered that it might have been otherwise had there been an attempt 'to impose like conditions about plant and machinery a mile or so away . . . But here the plant and machinery is on the spot and the conditions are so closely "in connection with" the permitted development as to be valid.'

In *British Airports Authority* v *Secretary of State for Scotland* the First Division of the Court of Session had to consider the validity of conditions, varied by the Secretary of State on appeal, attached to three permissions for development at Aberdeen Airport. The first application was by the British Airports Authority for permission to construct a new terminal building and improved aircraft handling facilities. The permission was subject to conditions restricting operational hours so as to prevent night flying and limiting the direction of take off and landing so as to avoid over-flying built up areas. The Court held that the conditions were designed to serve a proper planning purpose, namely the protection of the area surrounding the airport by limiting the time and place of aircraft noise. They also held that the Secretary of State was entitled to find on the evidence that the development was required to cater for the intensification of the use of the airport as such. There was a close relationship between the permitted development and future noise levels and the conditions designed to control the mischief of aircraft noise were fairly and reasonably related to that development.

The second application was by Bristow Helicopters Ltd. for permission to extend their terminal building. The permission was subject to a condition restricting operational hours to prevent night flying. Here, too, the court held that the Secretary of State was entitled to find on the evidence that the development was required to enable the company to handle the expected growth in helicopter traffic and that there was, accordingly, a clear relationship between the appellants' future use of the airport for helicopter traffic and the permitted development of their terminal.

The third application was by British Airways Helicopters Ltd. for permission to erect a one storey building as an office for their flight operations headquarters for the United Kingdom and as accommodation for ground training for flying personnel. This permission was also subject to a condition restricting operational hours so as to avoid night flying. In this case the court found that there was no connection whatever between the permitted development and the helicopter operations of the appellants at the airport. The condition could not therefore be said to be fairly and reasonably related to the development in question and was quashed.

In *Newbury District Council* v *Secretary of State for the Environment* planning permission had been granted in 1962 for the use of two existing hangars on a disused airfield as warehouses. The permission was subject to a condition requiring the removal of the buildings at the end of 1972. The buildings were not removed and in due course an enforcement notice was served. On appeal, the Secretary of State decided that the condition was not sufficiently related to the change of use for which the planning permission had been granted and that the 1962 permission was therefore void. The planning authority appealed and the matter eventually came before the

238 SCOTTISH PLANNING LAW AND PROCEDURE

House of Lords. The court held that the condition had been imposed for a planning purpose, the hangar being an undesirable intrusion into the landscape. However, they found that on the evidence the Secretary of State was entitled to conclude that the condition requiring the removal of the hangars was not fairly and reasonably related to the permission for a temporary change in their use and was therefore *ultra vires*.[28]

Conditions must not be unreasonable

A condition may be imposed for a planning purpose and be fairly and reasonably related to the permitted development, yet be so unreasonable as to be *ultra vires* the planning authority. As was pointed out by Lord Reid in *Westminster Bank Ltd.* v *Minister of Housing and Local Government*,[29] the word 'unreasonable' as used in this context has a somewhat artificial meaning; a condition attached to a grant of planning permission will be held by the courts to be void for 'unreasonableness' only if it is one 'which no reasonable authority acting within the four corners of their jurisdiction could have decided to impose'.[30] There may well be room for disagreement as to whether a particular condition is unreasonable or not.[31]

Situations in which conditions have been challenged as unreasonable may be divided for illustrative purposes into three broad categories:[32] (1) factors beyond the control of the applicant, (2) restrictions on existing use rights, and (3) financial and other obligations. These categories are considered in turn.

(1) *Factors beyond the control of the applicant*

In *British Airports Authority* v *Secretary of State for Scotland*[33] Lord Cameron said:

---

[28] The House of Lords did not rule out the possibility, though it might only arise in exceptional cases, that a condition requiring the removal of a building might fairly and reasonably relate to a grant of permission for a change in the use of the building.

[29] [1971] A.C. 508. See too *Kent County Council* v *Kingsway Investments (Kent) Ltd.* [1971] A.C. 72.

[30] *Associated Provincial Picture Houses Ltd.* v *Wednesbury Corporation* [1948] 1 K.B. 223, per Lord Greene M.R. See also *Wordie Property Co. Ltd.* v *Secretary of State for Scotland* 1984 S.L.T. 345, per Lord Emslie.

[31] Contrast, for example, Lord Reid's view of the conditions at issue in *Mixnam's Properties Ltd.* v *Chertsey U.D.C.* [1965] A.C. 735 with that of Lord Upjohn in the same case, or the judgment of Salmon L.J. with that of Diplock L.J. in *Westminster Bank Ltd.* v *Beverley Borough Council* [1969] 1 Q.B. 499. See too the divergent views expressed in *Kent County Council* v *Kingsway Investments (Kent) Ltd.* [1969] 2 Q.B. 332 (C.A.); and [1971] A.C. 72 (H.L.)

[32] It may also be that a condition which has the effect of making a planning permission radically different from what was applied for would be treated as unreasonable—see the remarks of Forbes J. in *Bernard Wheatcroft Ltd.* v *Secretary of State for the Environment* (1980) 43 P. & C.R. 233 (p. 255 below).

[33] 1979 S.C. 200; 1979 S.L.T. 197. Contrast *Kent County Council* (above). See too ministerial decision noted in 1982 S.P.L.P. 85.

'A condition imposed under the planning legislation can be enforced by enforcement orders in terms of s.84 of the 1972 Act. Failure to comply with such an order involves exposure to substantial penal sanctions. In my opinion it follows from this that the necessary assumption on which this structure of conditions and powers of enforcement rests, is that nothing shall be imposed upon a developer with which it is plain he does not possess the capacity to comply.'

In that case a condition imposed on the applicants, the British Airports Authority, an obligation to control the direction of take off and landing of aircraft at Aberdeen Airport. That was a matter which only the Civil Aviation Authority could control and there were no steps which the applicants could take to secure the result required by the condition. The requirement was therefore 'no "condition" at all' and was *ultra vires*.[34]

However in *Grampian Regional Council* v *City of Aberdeen District Council*[35] the House of Lords held that a condition which prescribed that development was not to begin until a particular result had been achieved was, in the circumstances of the case, valid, notwithstanding that it did not lie within the applicants' sole power to bring about the result required by the condition. In that case the reporter who had held a public inquiry into a deemed refusal of planning permission said in his decision letter that he would have favoured granting permission had it not been that increased traffic from the proposed development would in his view result in unacceptable traffic danger at a road junction some distance from the appeal site. He considered that a condition requiring closure of part of the road between the appeal site and the junction would be incompetent since the applicants could not themselves ensure closure of the road. (A closure order would be open to objection and would require confirmation by the Secretary of State.)

Before the Court of Session[36] the applicants accepted that on the authority of *British Airports Authority* (above) a condition requiring them to secure the road's closure would have been invalid for unreasonableness. They argued, however, that the reporter had misdirected himself in failing to

---

[34] The decision suggests that the fact that the applicants would not be able to comply with the condition and the fact that it would be unenforceable were both factors demonstrating the condition's unreasonableness. In *Peak Park Joint Planning Board* v *Secretary of State for the Environment* (1979) 39 P. & C.R. 361 Sir Douglas Frank said that an unenforceable condition (which may well also be impossible to comply with) had to be distinguished from one which might be difficult to enforce; he did not think it anything to the point that a condition otherwise desirable should not be imposed merely because it might be difficult to enforce. See too *Bizony* v *Secretary of State for the Environment* (1975) 239 E.G. 281. In *R. Bell & Co. (Estates) Ltd.* v *Department of the Environment for Northern Ireland* [1982] N.I. 322 (and see 1983 S.P.L.P. 79) it was held that a condition which, though capable of implementation at the time of its imposition, had subsequently become impossible, had to be disregarded. And see *Commercial & Residential Property Development Co. Ltd.* v *Secretary of State for the Environment* (1981) 80 L.G.R. 443.

[35] 1984 S.L.T. 197.

[36] *Grampian Regional Council* v *Secretary of State for Scotland* 1983 S.L.T. 526.

consider whether to impose a condition to the effect that development was not to commence until the road in question had been closed. That argument found favour with the First Division.

On appeal to the House of Lords, the planning authority attacked the First Division's decision on the ground that the imposition on a planning permission of any negative condition relating to the occurrence of an uncertain event was unreasonable. They argued that there was no practical distinction between a positive condition requiring the road to be closed (which had been conceded to be *ultra vires*) and the negative condition sanctioned by the Court of Session; in either case the practical effect was to require the applicants to bring about something that was not within their power to secure. It was further argued for the planning authority that it was undesirable that there should be prolonged uncertainty as to whether the development would be able to proceed.

The House of Lords held that there was no substance in the planning authority's contentions. In the first place, there was in this context a crucial difference between the positive and negative type of condition; the latter was enforceable while the former was not. Secondly, the reasonableness of any condition had to be considered in the light of the circumstances of the individual case and in this case the applicants' proposals had been found by the reporter to be generally desirable in the public interest; the only aspect he considered disadvantageous was the traffic problem and that could be solved in a way which had reasonable prospects of coming about. Not only, therefore, would it not have been unreasonable to grant planning permission subject to the suspensive condition, it would have been highly appropriate to do so. Further, in the House of Lords' view, s.198 of the 1972 Act (which makes provision for the stopping up of highways in order to enable development to be carried out) told strongly in favour of the reasonableness of a negative condition relating to road closure; it could be inferred that such a condition was contemplated by the legislature. As to the argument on uncertainty, it was, the House of Lords considered, sufficient to notice that ss.38 and 39 of the 1972 Act make provision as to the duration of planning permission (see p. 261 below) and thus recognise that development which has been granted planning permission may not be carried out within any particular time scale or at all; uncertainty might be said to be a natural feature of the planning process.

Although s.27(1)(a) of the 1972 Act makes clear that a condition may be validly imposed in respect of land other than the land which is the subject of the application for planning permission,[37] in terms of that provision such other land must be under the 'control' of the applicant.[38] In *Birnie* v *Banff*

---

[37] A condition relating to land which, though not under the applicant's control, is included by the applicant in the application for planning permission is valid—see *Atkinson* v *Secretary of State for the Environment* [1983] J.P.L. 599. In that case Woolf J. recommended that in such a case the condition should be framed in such a way as to ensure that the developer is in a position to comply with the condition before the development is begun.

[38] The relevant time is, it seems, the date of the decision rather than the date of the application—see *Atkinson* (above).

County Council,[39] for example, feuars of a piece of ground were granted planning permission for the erection of a house, the permission being subject to a condition that an access lane be formed on unfeued ground immediately to the rear of the feu. The condition was not complied with and the planning authority served an enforcement notice requiring the feuars to form the lane. The Sheriff held that the condition sought to be enforced was *ultra vires* in that it required the carrying out of works on land which was not under the applicant's control.

To avoid such problems the planning authority may have to refuse planning permission until the necessary land is brought within the applicant's control. However, in *George Wimpey & Co. Ltd.* v *New Forest District Council*[40] Sir Douglas Frank stated that 'control' did not necessarily involve 'having an estate or interest in the land but only such right as was required to implement the condition'. It was 'a question of fact and degree for the Secretary of State whether the control was of a degree and kind sufficient to satisfy him that the condition would be complied with'. It was, however, held in this case that the Secretary of State ought to have considered the possibility of overcoming a difficulty over access to a site by imposing a negative condition to the effect that development should not commence until satisfactory arrangements had been made.

(2) *Restrictions on existing use rights*

The effect of the 1947 planning legislation was to subject all new development to control by planning authorities but to leave landowners with the right to carry on the existing use of the land. In general, the only way in which the planning authority can of their own initiative require the discontinuance of an existing lawful use of land, or impose conditions on the continuance of such a use, or require the removal of existing buildings or works, is by making an order under s.49 of the 1972 Act; compensation is payable in respect of any loss suffered as a result of the making of such an order.[41]

It would seem, however, that in granting planning permission for the development of land the planning authority may be able, without payment of compensation, to impose a condition which has the effect of restricting 'existing use' rights, provided the condition is imposed for a planning purpose and is fairly and reasonably related to the permitted development.

---

[39] 1954 S.L.T. (Sh.Ct.) 90. See too *Peak Park Joint Planning Board* v *Secretary of State for the Environment* (1979) 39 P. & C.R. 361; *Ladbroke (Rentals) Ltd.* v *Secretary of State for the Environment* (1981) 258 E.G. 973; *SPADS* Nos. A2004 (P/PPA/RC/75, 14th January 1976); A2384 (P/ENA/FB/5, 30th June 1977); A2809 (P/PPA/TB/12, 6th October 1978); A3367 (P/PPA/SS/41, 30th June 1980); A3503 (P/PPA/TC/86, 11th November 1980); and A4494 (P/PPA/FB/110, 15th February 1983); and English ministerial decisions noted in [1967] J.P.L. 615 and 617; [1968] J.P.L. 306; and [1980] J.P.L. 423. Contrast, however, the decision noted in [1983] J.P.L.

[40] [1979] J.P.L. 314. See too *Hayns* v *Secretary of State for the Environment* (1977) 37 P. & C.R. 317; *Augier* v *Secretary of State for the Environment* (1978) 38 P. & C.R. 219; and appeal decision noted in [1980] J.P.L. 425.

[41] See chapter 16.

Where, for example, an authority grant planning permission for the extension of an existing factory, they may be entitled to impose a condition requiring the formation of a new access to the site and the closing of an existing access.[42] This would seem to be borne out by the wording of s.27(1) which authorises the imposition of a condition for regulating not only the development but also the *use* of any land under the control of the applicant. It was thus possible for Talbot J. to hold in *City of London Corporation* v *Secretary of State for the Environment*[43] that a condition which had the effect of prohibiting change from one use to another use within the same class in the Use Classes Order—a change which would not amount to development—was valid. It is, of course, the case that if the applicant does not wish to comply with a condition restricting 'existing use' rights he need not implement the permission.

The power of a planning authority to attach to a grant of planning permission conditions abrogating 'existing use' rights was considered by the Divisional Court in *Kingston-upon-Thames Royal London Borough Council* v *Secretary of State for the Environment.*[44] In that case the planning authority granted planning permission for the reconstruction of a railway station subject to a condition that an area of land, shown on the plan which accompanied the application as allocated for car parking purposes, should be available for those purposes at all times and should be used for no other purpose. Compliance with the condition would have necessitated the removal from this area of land of the main electric traction cable. Reconstruction of the station was carried out but the condition was not complied with. Following an appeal against an enforcement notice issued by the planning authority, the Secretary of State held the condition *ultra vires* in that its effect would be to restrict, without payment of compensation, existing activities which would be legal under planning law if the permitted development had not taken place.

Though the minister's conclusion appeared to be supported by the decision of the House of Lords in *Hartnell* v *Minister of Housing and Local Government*,[45] by the decision of Glyn-Jones J. in *Allnatt London Properties* v *Middlesex County Council*[46] and by a dictum of Lord Denning in *Pyx Granite Co. Ltd.* v *Minister of Housing and Local Government*,[47] the Divisional Court held in the *Kingston* case that the proposition relied on by

[42] See, for example, [1969] J.P.L. 287.

[43] (1971) 23 P. & C.R. 169. See also *SPADS* No. A4254A (P/PPA/CC/83, 6th August 1982). In *Carpet Decor (Guildford) Ltd.* v *Secretary of State for the Environment* [1981] J.P.L. 806 Sir Douglas Frank appeared to accept that a planning authority could exclude the operation of the General Development Order by condition on a planning permission.

[44] [1973] 1 W.L.R. 1549. See too *Prossor* v *Minister of Housing and Local Government* (1968) 67 L.G.R. 109; *Leighton and Newman Car Sales Ltd.* v *Secretary of State for the Environment* (1975) 30 P. & C.R. 23, per Lord Widgery C.J.; *Peak Park Joint Planning Board* v *Secretary of State for the Environment* (1979) 39 P. & C.R. 361; and *Penwith District Council* v *Secretary of State for the Environment* (1977) 34 P. & C.R. 269.

[45] [1965] A.C. 1134.

[46] (1964) 15 P. & C.R. 288.

[47] [1958] 1 Q.B. 554.

the minister was untenable and that the condition, being reasonably related to the permitted development and not unreasonable, was valid. Lord Widgery C.J. considered that *Hartnell's* case 'was a very special one . . . decided purely on its own facts' and that it 'had nothing to do with the present case except that the phrase about removing existing use rights without compensation may have found its roots in those very different factual circumstances'. His Lordship did not cast doubt upon the correctness of the decision in *Allnatt's* case but considered that the reason given for the decision in that case was wrongly expressed.

A similar view was expressed by the Lord President (Lord Emslie) in *British Airports Authority v Secretary of State for Scotland*.[48] After examining a number of authorities he stated that he was:

'clearly of the opinion that they do not establish the particular proposition for which they were cited, namely that the powers of s.27(1) may never be used to restrict, without compensation, existing rights of use of land under the control of an applicant for planning permission. There is, in my opinion, no such general principle to be discovered from a construction of the 1972 Act.'

(3) *Financial and other obligations*

Difficult questions can arise over conditions which require a payment in money or in kind by the developer. Department of the Environment Circular 1/85 states that:[49]

'No payment of money or other consideration can be required when granting a permission or any other kind of consent required by a statute, except where there is specific statutory authority. Conditions requiring for instance, the cession of land for road improvements or for open space, or requiring the developer to contribute money towards the provision of public car parking facilities, should accordingly not be attached to planning permissions.'

The English minister has on several occasions expressed the opinion that the making of a payment to the planning authority—for example, as a contribution to infrastructural costs[50] or to the cost of provision of parking spaces by the planning authority—cannot properly be made a condition of a planning permission. In a recent appeal decision an inspector concluded: 'Government advice and Ministerial decision, however, combine to make clear that in lieu of providing parking spaces, either on-site or on other nearby land available to him, the option of offering a commuted sum towards the cost of providing additional public car parking is one which at

---

[48] 1979 S.C. 200; 1979 S.L.T. 197.
[49] Para. 63.
[50] See, for example [1974] J.P.L. 106; and [1980] J.P.L. 841. Woolf J. appeared to agree in *McLaren v Secretary of State for the Environment* [1981] J.P.L. 423.

first instance is exercisable solely at the discretion of the developer.'[51] The minister has also said that it is improper to impose a condition requiring a developer to make over land to the planning authority[52] or to find security for the fulfilment of a condition contained in a planning permission[53] or requiring a developer to enter into an agreement with the planning authority.[54]

The principle that no payment of money or other consideration can be required when granting planning permission appears to be derived from the well-settled rule of law that any charge upon a subject may only be imposed by clear and unambiguous language in a statute.[55]

An example of clear and unambiguous language in a statute is provided by the Offshore Petroleum Development (Scotland) Act 1975, s.9 of which relates to the reinstatement of land which is to be developed for certain purposes connected with the exploitation of offshore petroleum. That section provides that where planning permission for such oil-related development is granted subject to a reinstatement condition, the planning authority may, subject to the approval of the Secretary of State, require the developer, before the start of development, to find security for fulfilment of the reinstatement condition. Any requirement imposed under s.9 of the 1975 Act is to have effect as a further condition of the planning permission and is to be enforceable accordingly.

The nearest the 1972 Act comes to a clear and unambiguous provision is to be found in s.27(1)(a). This provides that, without prejudice to the general power in s.26(1), conditions may be imposed on a grant of planning permission requiring the carrying out of works on the land which is the subject of the application and on any other land under the control of the applicant.

Such conditions must fulfil the tests discussed earlier in this chapter. Thus they must be imposed for a planning purpose and be fairly and reasonably related to the permitted development. A condition requiring the provision of, or a contribution towards the cost of providing, infrastructure unrelated to the development would therefore be *ultra vires* the planning authority.[56] On the other hand, it is commonplace to find conditions on planning permissions requiring the provision of car parking, the carrying out of landscaping, the planting of trees and so on—conditions which impose a financial burden on the developer but which serve a planning purpose, are fairly and reasonably related to the development and are reasonable in the circumstances.

However, in *Hall & Co. Ltd.* v *Shoreham-by-Sea U.D.C.*[57] the Court of

---

51 [1982] J.P.L. 463. See also the ministerial decisions noted at [1967] J.P.L. 493; [1975] J.P.L. 620; and [1982] J.P.L. 665. See also the Appendix to S.D.D. Circular 22/1984.

52 *Bulletin of Selected Appeal Decisions*, II/17 and XI/1.

53 *Bulletin of Selected Appeal Decisions*, III/16.

54 See [1980] J.P.L. 841.

55 See J.M. Evans, *de Smith's Judicial Review of Administrative Action* (4th ed., Stevens, 1980), p. 100.

56 *R.* v *Bowman* [1898] 1 Q.B. 663.

57 [1964] 1 W.L.R. 240.

Appeal categorised as unreasonable a condition which required the developers of an industrial site to construct, at their own expense, a service road along the frontage of the site and to give a right of passage over the road to and from adjoining sites. The object sought to be obtained by the planning authority—a restriction on the number of access points to a congested main road—was a proper planning purpose and the condition was held to be fairly and reasonably related to the permitted development. However, the court took the view that the condition effectively took away the plaintiffs' rights of property without compensation by requiring them to construct at their own expense what would virtually amount to a public highway and was thus unreasonable and *ultra vires*. A similar conclusion was reached by Woolf J. in *M.J. Shanley Ltd. (in liquidation) v Secretary of State for the Environment*[58] about a proposed condition which would have required the provision for public recreation of 40 acres of land.

Just how far a planning authority can go in using conditions to redistribute the cost of infrastructure provision from the public to the private sector is uncertain. For example, a condition requiring the provision of a children's play area in a residential development may be said to serve a planning purpose and if the need for the provision of such infrastructure arises solely from the development in question then the condition is fairly and reasonably related to the proposal. The question is whether such conditions are unreasonable in terms of the decision in *Hall*.

The decisions in *Britannia (Cheltenham) Ltd. v Secretary of State for the Environment* and *Robert Hitchins Builders Ltd. v Secretary of State for the Environment*[59] suggest that such conditions may be valid in respect of matters which are incidental or ancillary to the permitted development, provided they are to be located on land within the control of the developer. In these cases, which were heard together, Sir Douglas Frank held that permission for large scale residential development could properly be made the subject of conditions requiring the provision and layout of adequate play areas and open spaces although he accepted that a requirement to dedicate them to the public would be unreasonable.

It seems unlikely that conditions can be used to require the provision of infrastructure, or a contribution towards the cost of its provision, on land beyond the control of the developer, even if the need for it derives solely from the development. The planning authority in such circumstances can, of course, refuse the application on the ground that the present systems of sewage disposal, water supply, roads, etc. are inadequate or that the development is premature, although this may, in some cases, seem an unduly negative response. Alternatively, and in order to overcome such a blockage of his application, a developer may voluntarily agree to provide, or to contribute towards the cost of, the necessary infrastructure. In view of the

---

[58] [1982] J.P.L. 380. See also the decision by the English minister reported in [1979] J.P.L. 485.

[59] [1978] J.P.L. 554 (subsequently quashed on other grounds by the Court of Appeal: [1979] J.P.L. 534).

uncertainty in this area it is not uncommon to find such matters dealt with by way of planning agreements (see chapter 12).

Uncertainty

In addition to the three tests laid down by Viscount Dilhorne in *Newbury District Council* v *Secretary of State for the Environment*,[60] a condition attached to a grant of planning permission may be held void for uncertainty. In *Fawcett Properties Ltd.* v *Buckingham County Council*[61] the House of Lords held by a majority of 4 to 1 that although the wording of a particular condition was imperfect and might give rise to problems of construction, the condition was not void for uncertainty. Lord Denning declared: 'a planning condition is only void for uncertainty if it can be given no meaning or no sensible or ascertainable meaning and not merely because it is ambiguous or leads to absurd results. It is the daily task of the courts to resolve ambiguities of language and to choose between them; and to construe words so as to avoid ambiguities or to put up with them.'

Applying that dictum, the Second Division of the Court of Session held in *Caledonian Terminal Investments Ltd.* v *Edinburgh Corporation*[62] that although a condition which provided that office premises were to be used only by a professional person providing a professional or scientific service falling within certain categories of the Standard Industrial Classification might give rise to doubts and ambiguities in the future, the condition could be given a sensible and ascertainable meaning and was therefore not void for uncertainty.

In *David Lowe & Sons Ltd.* v *Musselburgh Town Council*,[63] however, the First Division adopted a test which appears capable of being more easily satisfied by a person challenging the validity of a condition. In that case the court held that mere ambiguity was enough to render a condition ineffective.

It would seem that the standard of certainty required may vary according to whether the permission is granted on an application for full planning permission or merely for outline permission.[64]

---

[60] [1981] A.C. 578.

[61] [1961] A.C. 636. See too *Hall & Co. Ltd.* v *Shoreham-by-Sea U.D.C.* [1964] 1 W.L.R. 240; and *M.J. Shanley Ltd. (in liquidation)* v *Secretary of State for the Environment* [1982] J.P.L. 380.

[62] 1970 S.C. 271; 1970 S.L.T. 362. See also *Harris* v *Secretary of State for Scotland*, Court of Session, 14th February 1980 (unreported, but see 1980 S.P.L.P. 18); *Inverclyde District Council* v *Inverkip Building Co. Ltd.* 1981 S.C. 401; 1982 S.L.T. 401; *Alderson* v *Secretary of State for the Environment* [1984] J.P.L. 429 (word 'locally', as used in a condition restricting occupation of a dwelling to a person employed locally in agriculture held by the Court of Appeal to have a perfectly intelligible meaning). See, however, appeal decision noted in [1984] J.P.L. 837 (condition restricting sale of produce from farm shop to 'locally-grown' fruit and vegetables too imprecise and not capable of enforcement).

[63] 1973 S.C. 130; 1974 S.L.T. 5.

[64] See *Inverclyde District Council* v *Inverkip Building Co. Ltd.* 1981 S.C. 401; 1982 S.L.T. 401; and *Britannia (Cheltenham) Ltd.* v *Secretary of State for the Environment* [1978] J.P.L. 554.

Necessity[65]

Department of the Environment circular 1/85 suggests that in deciding whether to impose a condition consideration should be given by the planning authority to the need which the condition will fulfil.[66] In *British Airports Authority* v *Secretary of State for Scotland*[67] the First Division of the Court of Session broke new ground in holding that certain conditions which they found to be unnecessary were 'inexpedient' and therefore *ultra vires* in terms of s.27(1)(a) of the 1972 Act. The permission granted to the British Airports Authority for development at the airport was subject to a condition which stated that the developers 'shall take such steps as are necessary to secure that all aircraft using the airport, shall, whenever it is safe and practicable to do so, take off towards the north and land from the north'. One of the grounds on which this condition was challenged by the applicants was that it was unnecessary; by the time the Secretary of State came to make his decision the Civil Aviation Authority had taken the steps necessary to ensure that aircraft landed and took off in the desired direction. This submission was upheld by the court. The Lord President (Lord Emslie) declared that 'it can never be "expedient . . . in connection" with a permitted development within the meaning of s.27(1) of the 1972 Act, to impose a condition which is unnecessary'. Lord Cameron, agreeing with the Lord President, drew attention to the existence of other statutory powers, specifically intended for the regulation of the matters with which the condition was concerned; these showed, he said, 'that in a very real sense the imposition of the condition is unnecessary for the purpose for which it was apparently designed'.

In the same case a condition attached to the planning permission granted to one of the companies engaged in helicopter operations at the airport was challenged on similar grounds. The condition prohibited night flying from the company's helicopter terminal. It was pointed out by the company that there had been no evidence before the Secretary of State that there was any likelihood of helicopters operating from this land. They argued that the Secretary of State's planning objective in imposing the condition—the control of aircraft noise—was covered by a condition attached to the planning permission granted to the British Airports Authority, since it was from their runways that all flying took place. The court accepted that the condition was 'both pointless and unnecessary'. It could not be said to be 'expedient' and was therefore *ultra vires*.

Whilst it is clearly desirable that conditions should serve some worthwhile purpose, the full implications of this particular aspect of the judgments are difficult to foresee. The issue of necessity was not dealt with at any length and it is uncertain what measure of need the courts will apply and what effect it may have, for example, on the use of overlapping and concurrent powers (see p. 227 above).

[65] See Eric Young, 'Is an Unnecessary Condition *Ultra Vires*?' [1983] J.P.L. 357.
[66] Paras. 12-14.
[67] 1979 S.C. 200; 1979 S.L.T. 197.

Severance of invalid conditions

If a condition is held to be void there may have to be considered the question whether the planning permission to which the condition was attached remains in force, shorn of the invalid condition, or whether the whole permission falls with the invalid condition. In the first place it must be considered whether it is a decision of a planning authority that is being questioned or whether it is a decision of the minister on appeal or on a 'called in' application.

In the latter case, the decision can only be challenged by an aggrieved person by way of an application to the Court of Session in terms of s.233(1)(b) of the 1972 Act. Section 233(4)(b) provides, *inter alia*, that if the Court is satisfied that the action of the minister is not within the powers of the Act it may quash the action (see chapter 21). In *British Airports Authority* v *Secretary of State for Scotland*[68] the First Division of the Court of Session held that the word 'action' in s.233(4)(b) referred to the 'decision' of the minister and the 'decision' in that case was the composite confirmation of the grant of planning permission subject to certain conditions. Section 233(4)(b) did not empower the Court to excise the *ultra vires* conditions from the decision. If the conditions were *ultra vires*, the whole composite decision failed and would be quashed. It would seem therefore, that if the decision in question is that of the minister then the possibility of the severance of invalid conditions does not arise.

Where the decision in question is that of a planning authority (and not therefore subject to the statutory provisions on challenge) then the law is not clear. It has been said on the one hand, that it is never possible to mutilate a planning permission by removing a condition and that if any one of the conditions attached to a grant of permission is held to be bad, the whole planning permission falls with it.[69] At the other extreme the view has been expressed that an *ultra vires* condition is always severable, since if it is void it can have no effect on the force of the planning permission itself.[70]

The most widely held view appears to be that severance of an invalid condition is possible in some circumstances.[71] In *Hall & Co. Ltd.* v *Shoreham-by-Sea U.D.C.*[72] the Court of Appeal, having held certain conditions void for unreasonableness, held that the conditions were not severable—they were fundamental to the planning permission in the sense

[68] 1979 S.C. 200; 1979 S.L.T. 197.
[69] See *Pyx Granite Co. Ltd.* v *Minister of Housing and Local Government* [1958] 1 Q.B. 554, per Hodson L.J.; and *Kent County Council* v *Kingsway Investments (Kent) Ltd.* [1971] A.C. 72, per Lord Guest.
[70] See *Kent County Council* v *Kingsway Investments (Kent) Ltd.* [1969] 2 Q.B. 332, per Winn L.J.
[71] See *Fawcett Properties Ltd.* v *Buckingham County Council* [1958] 1 W.L.R. 1161, per Roxburgh J.; *Hall & Co. Ltd.* v *Shoreham-by-Sea U.D.C.* [1964] 1 W.L.R. 240; *Allnatt London Properties Ltd.* v *Middlesex County Council* (1964) 15 P. & C.R. 288; *Kent County Council* v *Kingsway Investments (Kent) Ltd.* [1969] 2 Q.B. 332 (C.A.) and [1971] A.C. 72 (H.L.); and *R.* v *Hillingdon London Borough Council, ex parte Royco Homes Ltd.* [1974] Q.B. 720.
[72] [1964] 1 W.L.R. 240; followed in *Royco Homes* (above).

that the planning authority would not have granted planning permission without the conditions and thus the whole planning permission fell with the conditions.

In *Kent County Council v Kingsway Investments (Kent) Ltd.*[73] the House of Lords held by a 3 to 2 majority that a condition requiring approval of detailed plans within three years of the grant of outline planning permission was not void for unreasonableness. Though it was not necessary to the decision, the majority (Lords Morris of Borth-y-Gest, Donovan and Guest) expressed the view that if the condition had been invalid it could not have been severed from the outline permission. The minority (Lords Reid and Upjohn) differed from the majority in both respects. All of their Lordships except Lord Guest considered that severance of an invalid condition was possible in certain circumstances but the judgments exhibit considerable differences of view as to what those circumstances are.

In *British Airports Authority*[74] the Lord President (Lord Emslie) summarised the position in this way:

'A number of English cases were cited to us—all actions for a declaration in respect of planning permissions granted by a local planning authority subject to conditions—from which it may be taken that if a condition held to be *ultra vires* is important and not trivial there can be no question of quashing only that condition. The whole of the planning permission must be quashed on the view that it might not have been granted at all if it had been appreciated that the condition objected to could not properly be attached to it.'

Had it been proper to apply this test in this case, Lord Emslie would have been inclined to say that the inept conditions could not safely be regarded as unimportant and the planning permission as a whole would have had to be quashed.

A similar view was expressed by the Lord Justice-Clerk (Lord Wheatley) in *Inverclyde District Council v Inverkip Building Co. Ltd.*[75] His Lordship said that he saw 'no reason why a condition which is undoubtedly *ultra vires* but which is trivial and not material, which does not alter the character of the deed, and which could be excised without doing any material damage to the nature and purpose of the deed should not be severable', but that, agreeing with the Lord Ordinary (Lord McDonald),[76] he would have held, had it been necessary to decide the point, that the conditions at issue in the case before him were material and not trivial and that the permission to which they were attached would have had to be reduced.

From the point of view of the applicant there would thus seem to be a considerable risk in challenging the validity of a condition.

[73] [1971] A.C. 72.
[74] 1979 S.C. 200; 1979 S.L.T. 197. See too *Newbury District Council v Secretary of State for the Environment* [1981] A.C. 578.
[75] 1983 S.L.T. 563. Lord Robertson expressed his agreement on this point.
[76] 1981 S.C. 401; 1982 S.L.T. 401.

The question of severance was not raised in *Birnie* v *Banff County Council*[77] but it may be mentioned that in that case the planning authority apparently argued that having acted upon a planning permission to which a condition was attached, the applicants had to be taken to have accepted the condition and were not entitled to dispute its validity. The sheriff said of this argument that 'the doctrine of approbate and reprobate is not among the canons of statutory construction. If the condition was invalid, and this is the assumption underlying the argument, it has no effect and it cannot be given effect by an appeal to the doctrine of personal bar . . .' A similar conclusion was reached by Lord McDonald in *Inverclyde District Council* v *Inverkip Building Co. Ltd.*[78] who, while stressing that his opinion on this point was *obiter*, expressed himself to be 'strongly attracted to the proposition that once a document has been shown to be *funditus* null whether because of *vires* or any other reason, no amount of personal bar can make it valid'.

---

[77] 1954 S.L.T. (Sh.Ct.) 90.
[78] 1981 S.C. 401; 1982 S.L.T. 401. See also *Newbury District Council* v *Secretary of State for the Environment* [1981] A.C. 578, per Lord Fraser.

CHAPTER 11
CONTROL OF DEVELOPMENT
4: PLANNING AUTHORITY'S DECISION AND OTHER MATTERS

Having considered an application for planning permission, the planning authority may:

(*a*) grant planning permission unconditionally, or
(*b*) grant planning permission subject to such conditions as they think fit, or
(*c*) refuse planning permission (1972 Act, s.26(1)).

So long as they confine themselves to proper planning considerations and observe the appropriate procedural requirements (see chapters 8 and 9), planning authorities have a wide discretion to grant or refuse planning permission.

Planning authorities also enjoy a wide discretion to attach conditions to a grant of planning permission; some control over that discretion is, however, exercised by the courts (see chapter 10). The courts also exercise a certain amount of control over the more general powers of planning authorities to determine planning applications.

The scope of the planning authority's discretion: limitations

While the planning authority must take account of the various matters mentioned in chapters 8 and 9,[1] they are in no way bound by these matters and must consider each planning application on its own merits. They must not (in the absence of statutory authorisation) act under the dictation of another person or body[2] or so tie their hands in advance as to disable

---

[1] In *R. v London Borough of Haringey, ex parte Barrs* [1983] J.P.L. 54 (below) one of Comyn J.'s reasons for holding a grant of planning permission *ultra vires* for unreasonableness was that the authority did not appear to have paid any real attention to objections. Contrast, however, *R. v Hammersmith and Fulham Borough Council, ex parte People Before Profit Ltd.* (1981) 45 P. & C.R. 364.
[2] See, for example, *Lavender v Minister of Housing and Local Government* [1970] 1 W.L.R. 1231, in which the minister's decision was held *ultra vires* in that he had in effect surrendered his discretion to another minister. See too *R. v Worthing Borough Council* [1984] J.P.L. 261, in which an expression of opinion by the Secretary of State for the Environment as to the future use of a piece of Crown land was held to be an unlawful constraint on the free exercise of the planning authority's discretion.

themselves from properly exercising their discretion.[3] In *Steeples* v *Derbyshire County Council*[4] Webster J. considered that a planning authority's prior obligation to use their best endeavours to obtain planning permission for a particular development would have indicated to a reasonable man that the planning authority had imposed upon themselves a fetter on their freedom to discharge their statutory duty and would have suggested to the reasonable man that there was a real likelihood that the authority would be biased in their consideration of an application for planning permission for the development in question; the grant of planning permission was held to be in breach of the rules of natural justice and *ultra vires*.

In *R.* v *Amber Valley District Council, ex parte Jackson*[5] a meeting of the local Labour party decided, prior to consideration of a planning application for a particular development, to support the development in question. The Labour group were in control on the council. Objectors to the proposed development sought an order of prohibition to prevent the authority considering the application, arguing that any reasonable person knowing the relevant facts would regard the outcome of the planning application as a foregone conclusion and that in the circumstances the planning authority could not fairly determine the application. Woolf J. held that although there was an obligation on the planning authority to act fairly and without bias on an application for planning permission, here there was no evidence of bias. Woolf J. said that all that the evidence indicated was that the planning authority were 'politically predisposed' in favour of the development; it was, in his view, 'almost inevitable now that party politics played so large a part in Local Government, that the majority group on a Council would decide on the Party line', but it would be wrong to infer that the planning committee would not take into account all relevant factors.[6] It may be, however, that a decision taken on the basis of a pre-determined group policy which members felt themselves obliged to follow would be of questionable validity; in such circumstances it might be inferred that members had closed their minds to matters they were bound to take into account.[7]

On the basis of the '*Wednesbury* principles' the courts also exercise a degree of control over discretionary decision-making through the concepts of relevancy, reasonableness and purpose (see chapter 2). All three

[3]   See chapters 9 and 12.
[4]   [1985] 1 W.L.R. 256. Contrast *R.* v *St. Edmondsbury Borough Council, ex parte Investors in Industry Commercial Properties Ltd., The Times*, 12th April 1985.
[5]   [1985] 1 W.L.R. 298.
[6]   See too *Cardiff Corporation* v *Secretary of State for Wales* (1971) 22 P. & C.R. 718 in which Thesiger J. said that 'local planning authorities consist of democratically elected members and the members are, in my view, in practice constantly considering what their voters want and may, in dealing with any question, deal with it in accordance with what they think will be satisfactory to those whose votes they have solicited in the past and intend to solicit in the future.'
[7]   See *Innes* v *Royal Burgh of Kirkcaldy* 1963 S.L.T. 325; and the Report by Mr. Manuel Kissen Q.C. on the local inquiry in the matter of a review of rents of council houses in Dundee (H.M.S.O., 1963).

concepts are considered in chapter 10 in connection with the imposition of conditions on planning permissions, while the concept of relevancy in the determination of applications is considered in chapter 9. However, brief mention may be made here of examples of cases in which the courts have treated decisions on planning applications as *ultra vires* for unreasonableness or as involving a use of discretionary powers for an ulterior purpose or improper motive.[8]

In *Niarchos (London) Ltd.* v *Secretary of State for the Environment*[9] a planning authority had refused to grant a further temporary permission for the use of premises as offices, the development plan containing a policy to the effect that temporary office permissions should not be renewed in respect of any premises 'reasonably capable' of adaptation for residential use. On appeal, the minister refused planning permission, stating that he did not think that the financial considerations which allegedly made conversion of the offices to houses unprofitable were of such importance as to merit an exception to the development plan policy. Sir Douglas Frank, sitting as a deputy judge of the High Court, held that the minister had misinterpreted the policy. What he should have asked himself was whether the premises could reasonably be adapted for housing. The deputy judge considered that the minister should have taken the financial implications into account and that had he done so the inevitable conclusion would have been that the premises could not reasonably be adapted for residential use. (The inspector who held the inquiry into the appeal had concluded that the only alternative to continuation of the office use was that the premises would be left empty.) The minister's decision was therefore, unreasonable and had to be quashed.

Though much quoted and analysed, the '*Wednesbury*' test for unreasonableness is, however, notoriously difficult to apply in practice. In *R.* v *Haringey London Borough Council, ex parte Barrs*[10], for example, a local planning authority, having purchased a site with an existing planning permission for four houses, subsequently granted themselves planning permission for seven houses. Comyn J. held, applying the *Wednesbury* principles, that the permission was *ultra vires* for unreasonableness in that the facts suggested that the authority had granted themselves a permission they would not have granted to a private individual. On appeal, however, the members of the Court of Appeal found themselves unable to conclude on the evidence that the planning authority had acted unreasonably.

---

[8]   As Lord Greene pointed out in *Associated Provincial Picture Houses Ltd.* v *Wednesbury Corporation* [1948] 1 K.B. 223, the various grounds on which a discretionary decision may be attacked run into one another and some of the decisions dealt with in chapter 9 in the context of 'material considerations' could equally be treated under the heading of 'improper purpose'.

[9]   (1977) 35 P. & C.R. 259. Contrast *Granada Theatres Ltd.* v *Secretary of State for the Environment* (1980) 43 P. & C.R. 253; and *Wessex Regional Health Authority* v *Salisbury District Council* [1984] J.P.L. 344. In *Bell & Colvill Ltd.* v *Secretary of State for the Environment* [1980] J.P.L. 823 Forbes J. said that he 'profoundly disagreed' with the decision in *Niarchos*.

[10] *The Times*, 1st July, 1983, reversing [1983] J.P.L. 54. See too *Sand and Gravel Association* v *Buckinghamshire County Council* (unreported, 14th November 1984 (C.A.)).

Decisions were quashed as perverse or unreasonable in *South Oxfordshire District Council* v *Secretary of State for the Environment*[11] and *Niarchos (London) Ltd.* v *Secretary of State for the Environment (No. 2).*[12]

So far as concerns the use of development control powers for an ulterior object or for improper purposes, it has been held that a planning authority are not entitled to refuse planning permission to the owners of land simply in order to protect the authority's own possession of the property,[13] that it is improper to use planning powers to impose on a developer some burden which should properly be shouldered by the planning authority themselves in some other capacity,[14] and that a planning authority are not entitled to refuse planning permission for a private hospital in order to protect National Health Service staffing resources.[15] In *Paul* v *Ayrshire County Council*[16] the Lord Justice-Clerk (Lord Grant) and Lord Strachan said that it would clearly be a misuse of planning powers for a planning authority to attempt by means of a refusal of planning permission to create a right of way.

The exercise of a planning authority's discretion may be restricted in two further ways. Firstly, the Secretary of State has power to give directions restricting the grant of planning permission by any planning authority, either indefinitely or during such period as may be specified in the direction, in respect of any development or class of development (G.D.O., Art. 11). Secondly, the planning authority may have bound themselves by an agreement under s.50 of the 1972 Act to deal with a planning application in a certain way (see chapter 12).

The decision on an application for planning permission

The question whether a planning authority may grant a planning permission which departs from the terms of the application made to them—whether, for example, the authority may grant planning permission for the erection of 30 houses on a site for which application was made to build 40 houses—does not admit of a straightforward answer. In *Glacier Metal Co. Ltd.* v *London Borough of Hillingdon*[17] Judge Stabb declared that a planning authority 'may grant planning permission if they approve the whole of the application, but must refuse if they disapprove of part, because they have no power to grant planning permission as to part only'.[18] However, though it seems clear

---

[11]   [1981] 1 W.L.R. 1092.

[12]   [1981] J.P.L. 118.

[13]   *Westminster City Council* v *British Waterways Board* [1984] 3 W.L.R. 1047. Contrast *Westminster City Council* v *Great Portland Estates plc* [1984] 3 W.L.R. 1035.

[14]   See *Westminster Renslade Ltd.* v *Secretary of State for the Environment* (1983) 48 P. & C.R. 255; *Hall & Co. Ltd.* v *Shoreham-by-Sea U.D.C.* [1964] 1 W.L.R. 240 (see p. 244 above); and *R.* v *Hillingdon London Borough Council, ex parte Royco Homes Ltd.* [1974] Q.B. 720 (see p. 235 above).

[15]   See *SPADS* No. A4594 (P/PPA/LB/48, 20th April 1983); see too appeal decision reported in [1983] J.P.L. 142.

[16]   1964 S.C. 116; 1964 S.L.T. 207.

[17]   (1975) 239 E.G. 573.

[18]   Judge Stabb suggested, however, that the powers of the minister on appeal might be rather wider.

that an authority are not entitled to grant planning permission for a development substantially different from that for which application was made, Judge Stabb's statement appears to be too sweeping.

In *Kent County Council* v *Secretary of State for the Environment*[19] Sir Douglas Frank accepted that where an application was made up of a number of separate and divisible elements, it was lawful for these elements to be separately dealt with; it was held in this case that the decision of the minister to grant permission for part of the development applied for and to refuse permission for the remainder was valid. A rather different approach was adopted in *Bernard Wheatcroft Ltd.* v *Secretary of State for the Environment*.[20] In this case the minister had concluded that where application had been made for planning permission for the erection of 420 houses on 35 acres of land, the proposed development was not severable and that it would therefore be improper for him to grant planning permission for an alternative scheme, put forward by the applicants, for 250 houses on 25 acres. Forbes J. held that there was no principle of law that unless the proposed development was severable there could not be imposed on a planning permission a condition which would have the effect of reducing the permitted development below that for which planning permission had been sought. Accordingly, the Secretary of State had misdirected himself in law. The true test was whether the effect of the conditional planning permission would be to allow development which was in substance not that for which planning permission had been sought. Forbes J. expressed the view that the main, but not the only, criterion for judging whether the substance of an application would be altered is whether the development 'is so changed that to grant it would be to deprive those who should have been consulted on the changed development of the opportunity of consultation'. Where, as in the case before him, the proposed development had been the subject of consultation and had produced root-and-branch opposition to any development at all, it was difficult to accept that it should be necessary to repeat the consultation process on a smaller development.[21] Forbes J. said that he had come to his general conclusion 'with a certain feeling of satisfaction', as it seemed to him 'to permit a welcome degree of flexibility in the conduct of planning applications and appeals while at the same time maintaining adequate safeguards for the interests of those in whose favour the provisions for consultation were enacted'.

On the other hand, in *Britannia (Cheltenham) Ltd.* v *Secretary of State for the Environment*[22] (which was not referred to in *Wheatcroft*) Sir Douglas Frank said that it must be beyond doubt that the development described in a planning application includes any development ancillary or incidental to the proposed development. He concluded in that case that conditions requiring

[19] (1976) 33 P. & C.R. 70.
[20] (1980) 43 P. & C.R. 233; followed in *Wessex Regional Health Authority* v *Salisbury District Council* [1984] J.P.L. 344.
[21] See, however, *Wessex Regional Health Authority* (above).
[22] [1978] J.P.L. 554 (reversed on different grounds by the Court of Appeal: [1979] J.P.L. 534).

that provision be made in the plans for public open space and a social and shopping centre were incidental to an application for a large housing development; and that in dealing with an application for outline planning permission it was permissible to attach conditions excluding an area from development in order to preserve it for some type of development other than that for which application had been made.[23]

Planning authorities sometimes seek to limit the scope of a planning permission, not by way of condition but by way of a restriction contained in the permission itself—for example, by granting planning permission for the use of a building for agricultural purposes. In *Wilson v West Sussex County Council*,[24] for example, planning permission was granted for an 'agricultural cottage'. The Court of Appeal held that since the permission specifically incorporated the terms of the application for permission it was necessary to refer to the application in construing the permission (see p. 272 below), and that the word 'agricultural' had a functional significance and was to be construed as limiting the proposed dwelling to one intended to be occupied by an agricultural worker. In *Waverley District Council v Secretary of State for the Environment*[25] permission for the use of buildings as a 'depot for cattle lorries' had been granted following an application for permission to use land and buildings for agricultural purposes. Hodgson J. held that it could not be said that the use of the buildings for general haulage purposes unconnected with agriculture came within the terms of the permission.

It appears that in the *Waverley* case the restriction was capable of enforcement.[26] However, restrictions contained in a planning permission will not always be enforceable. In *East Suffolk County Council v Secretary of State for the Environment*,[27] for example, the Divisional Court held that the minister had not erred in law in ruling that where planning permission had been granted for the erection of a house 'for the purpose of dwelling accommodation for an agricultural worker', a change from occupation by an agricultural worker to occupation by someone who was not so employed was not a material change of use and that the restriction in the permission could not therefore be enforced. It seems that in such circumstances a planning authority should impose a specific condition rather than rely on a restriction in the permission itself.

Although planning permission is normally to enure for the benefit of the land and of all persons for the time being interested therein (see 1972 Act, s.30(1)), in appropriate circumstances the planning authority may grant a 'personal' planning permission, expressed to be for the benefit of a particular individual only. Permission may be granted for a limited period (s.27(1), (2)—see p. 232 above).

[23] See too *Inverclyde District Council v Inverkip Building Co. Ltd.* 1983 S.L.T. 563.
[24] [1963] 2 Q.B. 764. See too *East Suffolk County Council v Secretary of State for the Environment* (1972) 70 L.G.R. 595; *Williamson v Stevens* (1977) 34 P. & C.R. 117; and *Kwik Save Discount Group Ltd. v Secretary of State for Wales* (1980) 42 P.& C.R. 166.
[25] [1982] J.P.L. 105.
[26] Contrast, however, *Carpet Decor (Guildford) Ltd. v Secretary of State for the Environment* [1981] J.P.L. 806.
[27] (1972) 70 L.G.R. 595.

The planning authority may grant planning permission for the retention on land of buildings or works constructed or carried out before the date of the application or for the continuance of a use of land instituted before the date of the application, whether the development in question was carried out without permission or under a permission granted for a limited period; any such permission may be expressed to have retrospective effect (s.29). Permission can also be granted for the retention of such buildings or works or the continuation of such a use without complying with some condition subject to which a previous planning permission was granted (s.29(1)(b)[28]).

Planning permission granted for the erection of a building may specify the purposes for which the building may be used; if no purpose is specified, the permission is to be construed as including permission to use the building for the purpose for which it is designed (s.30(2)).[29] Thus, a building designed for use as a factory could, unless a particular class of industry is specified in the permission, be used for any factory purpose consistent with its design.

When granting planning permission relating to a building or premises in respect of which a duty exists to include, where it is reasonable and practicable to do so, provision for the needs of the disabled,[30] the planning authority are to ensure that the applicant is aware of the duty (1972 Act, s.26(4A)[31]).

S.D.D. Circular 26/1984 recommends that in appropriate cases planning authorities should point out to applicants who have been refused planning permission adjustments to their proposals which might allow them to proceed.

Outline planning permission and approval of reserved matters

Having granted an application for outline planning permission (see p. 188 above), the planning authority have in effect committed themselves in principle to the type of development specified in the permission. 'Once granted', said Lord Robertson in *Inverclyde District Council* v *Secretary of State for Scotland*,[32] 'it is a valuable commodity which is annexed to, and runs with, the land from purchaser to purchaser.' The subsequent approval of the planning authority is, however, required with regard to 'reserved matters', i.e., matters of detail which are reserved by way of condition in the outline permission for later consideration (see p. 189 above).

In *Inverclyde District Council* v *Inverkip Building Co. Ltd.*[33] the Second Division of the Court of Session held that although a particular matter included in a condition attached to a planning permission under the umbrella of 'reserved matters' did not in fact relate to a matter which was

---

[28] Added by the 1982 Act, Schedule 2, para. 7.
[29] The effect of this provision was considered in *Wilson* v *West Sussex C.C.* [1963] 2 Q.B. 764; see too *Peake* v *Secretary of State for Wales* (1971) 22 P. & C.R. 889; and *Wood* v *Secretary of State for the Environment* [1973] 1 W.L.R. 707.
[30] See the Chronically Sick and Disabled Persons Act 1970.
[31] Added by the Local Government (Miscellaneous Provisions) (Scotland) Act 1981, s.36.
[32] 1980 S.C. 363; 1981 S.L.T. 26.
[33] 1983 S.L.T. 563.

capable of being a reserved matter in terms of the G.D.O., its inclusion as a 'reserved matter' did not make the grant of outline permission invalid. In this case the Lord Justice-Clerk (Lord Wheatley) expressed the opinion that the distinction between conditions relating to reserved matters and 'ordinary' conditions imposed under ss.26 and 27 of the 1972 Act[34] is that in respect of reserved matters the planning authority *must* impose conditions reserving these matters for their subsequent approval whereas any other conditions attached to a grant of planning permission are at the discretion of the planning authority.

Having granted outline planning permission and thus given their approval in principle to the type of development proposed, it is not open to the planning authority, in dealing with a subsequent application for approval of reserved matters, to refuse approval except on grounds which arise from and relate to matters which were reserved in the outline permission.[35] The planning authority cannot at the stage of consideration of reserved matters consider such questions as whether the development is desirable in principle or is premature. An application for approval of reserved matters must, however, be within the ambit of the outline permission and must accord with the conditions annexed to that permission,[36] and where what purports to be an application for approval of details does not accord with the terms of the outline permission, the planning authority are entitled to treat the later application as a completely new application and to refuse it on grounds of principle.[37] Where, for example, outline planning permission had been granted for a warehouse for wholesale and retail distribution, the planning authority were held entitled to refuse an application for approval of details which was not in accordance with the outline permission in that it showed that the applicants' real intention was to erect a supermarket.[38] Where, however, an application for approval of reserved matters includes matters which are not within the ambit of the outline permission, it may sometimes be possible for the planning authority to grant only that part of the application falling within the scope of the outline permission.[39]

Application for approval of reserved matters must be made within a specified time limit (see p. 262 below). However, in *Cardiff Corporation* v

---

[34] As to which see chapter 10.

[35] See *Cardiff Corporation* v *Secretary of State for Wales* (1971) 22 P. & C.R. 718; *Chelmsford Corporation* v *Secretary of State for the Environment* (1971) 22 P. & C.R. 880; *Lewis Thirkwell Ltd.* v *Secretary of State for the Environment* [1978] J.P.L. 844; and appeal decisions noted in [1969] J.P.L. 156; and [1976] J.P.L. 555 and 726.

[36] See *Inverclyde District Council* v *Secretary of State for Scotland* 1980 S.C. 363; 1981 S.L.T. 26 (Second Division); and 1982 S.L.T. 200 (H.L.); *Heron Corporation Ltd.* v *Manchester City Council* [1978] 1 W.L.R. 937; and see p. 190 above.

[37] See *Shemara Ltd.* v *Luton Corporation* (1967) 18 P. & C.R. 520; *Calcaria Construction Co. (York) Ltd.* v *Secretary of State for the Environment* (1974) 27 P. & C.R. 435; *Chalgray Ltd.* v *Secretary of State for the Environment* (1976) 33 P. & C.R. 10; *SPADS* Nos. A2713 (P/PPA/SU/21, 19th July 1978); A2313 (P/PPA/CB/6, 5th April 1977); A2918 (P/PPA/AL/167, 21st February 1979); and A3330 (P/PPA/SE/6, 12th May 1980); and appeal decision noted in [1974] J.P.L. 45.

[38] *Calcaria Construction* (above).

[39] See *Inverclyde District Council* v *Secretary of State for Scotland* 1982 S.L.T. 200.

Secretary of State for Wales[40] Thesiger J. said that 'a local planning authority cannot eliminate an outline planning permission merely by failing to consider and approve the detailed plans which have been submitted in time for an appeal to be entered to the Minister against either a refusal or a mere failure to approve.'

On an application for approval of reserved matters it is not clear whether the planning authority have power to impose further conditions relating to that matter[41] or whether their powers at this stage are restricted to outright approval or rejection of the detailed proposals. This point was raised in *Chelmsford Corporation* v *Secretary of State for the Environment*[42] and was said by Browne J. to raise 'very difficult and fundamental problems', but in the circumstances of that case it was not necessary to deal with the question.

Notice of decision

Notice of the planning authority's decision on an application for planning permission or for approval of reserved matters is to be in writing (G.D.O., Art. 10(7)). Though the matter is perhaps not yet entirely free from doubt,[43] English case law appears to have established that it is the notice of the authority's decision rather than the resolution of the authority which constitutes the grant or refusal of permission.[44]

It is important for some purposes—for example, in determining the time within which an appeal is to be lodged or in determining whether development has been begun within the statutory time limit—to establish the exact date when a decision on a planning application was made. Section 30A of the 1972 Act[45] provides that the date of the granting or of the refusal of an application for planning permission or for an approval required by a development order or for any consent, agreement or approval required by a condition imposed on a grant of planning permission shall be the date on which the notice of the planning authority's decision bears to have been signed on behalf of the authority.

The period within which the planning authority are to give notice to an applicant of their decision or of the reference of the application to the

---

[40] (1971) 22 P. & C.R. 718.

[41] However, such a decision seems to be envisaged by Article 10(7) of the G.D.O.

[42] (1971) 22 P. & C.R. 880.

[43] See, for example, J.F. Garner, 'When is a Planning Permission?' [1972] J.P.L. 194; and M. Albery, 'What and When is a Planning Decision?' (1974) 70 L.Q.R. 351.

[44] See *R.* v *Yeovil Borough Council, ex parte Trustees of Elim Pentecostal Church* (1971) 33 P. & C.R. 39; and *Co-operative Retail Services* v *Taff-Ely Borough Council* (1978) 38 P. & C.R. 156. See too *Slough Estates Ltd.* v *Slough Borough Council (No. 2)* [1969] 2 Ch. 305 (C.A.); and [1971] A.C. 958 (H.L.). It may, however, be possible to show that what purports to be a planning permission is in fact no permission at all because it was issued by mistake (see *Norfolk County Council* v *Secretary of State for the Environment* [1973] 1 W.L.R. 1400) or because it was issued without authority (see *Attorney-General, ex rel. Co-operative Retail Services Ltd.* v *Taff-Ely Borough Council* (1979) 39 P. & C.R. 223 (C.A.) and (1981) 42 P. & C.R. 1 (H.L.); in such circumstances the decision will be invalid but may sometimes be given effect by the doctrine of personal bar (see p. 34 above).

[45] Added by the 1982 Act, Schedule 2, para. 8.

Secretary of State or to the regional planning authority is two months,[46] commencing on the date of receipt of the application[47] or (except where the applicant has already given notice of appeal to the Secretary of State) such extended period as may be agreed in writing between the applicant and the planning authority (G.D.O., Art. 10(5)). If the planning authority do not give notice of their decision within the proper period, the applicant is entitled to appeal to the Secretary of State as if permission had been refused (1972 Act, s.34). S.D.D. Circular 26/1984 advises planning authorities that if it becomes clear in the course of negotiations with an applicant that such negotiations could profitably continue beyond the statutory two months' limit, the authority should endeavour to reach agreement on a specific extension of the time allowed. On the other hand, says the circular, should it appear that further discussion is unlikely to be fruitful, the authority should proceed to take a decision on the application as soon as possible so that uncertainty is removed.

In *Bovis Homes (Scotland) Ltd.* v *Inverclyde District Council*[48] the planning authority failed to give notice of their decision on an application for approval of reserved matters within two months of receipt of the application. The applicants raised an action seeking (1) declarator that the planning authority were bound to consider the application and give notice of their decision thereon; and (2) decree ordaining the authority to give such notice within two months of decree. The planning authority argued that the applicants could have appealed to the Secretary of State within the six month period following the 'deemed refusal' of planning permission and that since they had not done so their action was incompetent because a common law remedy was not available to the pursuers where they had failed to avail themselves of the statutory machinery for appeal. The planning authority also argued that even if there was a duty upon them to give a decision within the two month period following receipt of the application, the duty 'flew off' at the end of that period. Founding strongly upon the decision in *London and Clydeside Estates Ltd.* v *Aberdeen District Council*[49] (in which the House of Lords had to consider similar provisions in the Land Compensation (Scotland) Act 1963), Lord Wylie held that the obligation to deal with an application was a continuing one, notwithstanding the expiry of the two month period specified in the G.D.O.;[50] decree *de plano* was therefore granted.

---

[46] In the case of an application called in by a regional planning authority the period is three months (see p. 204 above).

[47] As to the date on which an application is to be taken as having been received, see Article 10(6) of the G.D.O. (p. 200 above).

[48] 1982 S.L.T. 473; and see comment in 1982 S.P.L.P. 46. See too *James* v *Minister of Housing and Local Government* [1966] 1 W.L.R. 135 (C.A.) (overruled on other grounds in the House of Lords: [1968] A.C. 409); and *London Ballast Co. Ltd.* v *Buckinghamshire County Council* (1966) 18 P. & C.R. 446.

[49] 1980 S.C. (H.L.) 1; 1980 S.L.T. 81.

[50] The G.D.O. of 1975, which applied in *Bovis Homes*, referred to agreed extension of the two month period 'at any time'. The G.D.O. of 1981 omits these words but it seems unlikely that this change would have led to a different decision in *Bovis Homes*.

Where, on an application for planning permission or for approval of reserved matters, the planning authority decide to grant permission or approval subject to conditions or to refuse permission or approval, the notice is to state the reasons for the decision (G.D.O., Art. 10(7)). Failure to give any reason for the imposition of a condition does not, however, invalidate the condition.[51] Where no reasons are given the court is, it seems, entitled to look at all the surrounding circumstances in order to ascertain what the authority's reasons were.[52] It is the duty of the planning authority to give all their reasons and not just some of them.[53]

Notice of a refusal or conditional grant of planning permission or of a refusal or conditional grant of approval of reserved matters is to be accompanied by a notification informing the applicant of his right to appeal to the Secretary of State and of his rights in certain circumstances to serve a purchase notice or make a claim for compensation[54] (G.D.O., Art. 10(7) and Schedule 4, Part II).

Register

Under s.31 of the 1972 Act[55] it is the duty of every general and district planning authority to keep a register containing prescribed information with respect to planning applications. The register is to be available for inspection by the public at all reasonable hours (s.31). The register is to be kept in two parts[56] (G.D.O., Art. 17). Part I is to contain a copy of every application for planning permission and of every application for approval of reserved matters submitted to the authority and not finally disposed of, together with copies of plans and drawings submitted in relation thereto. In this way full information about any application which has not been finally disposed of is available to the public. Part II of the register provides a record in summary form of every application made to the authority. Every entry in the register is to be made within seven days of the receipt of an application or of the giving or making of the relevant direction, decision or approval, as the case may be. Planning authorities are empowered to keep copies of the relevant part of the register at local offices. The register is to include an index in the form of a map for enabling a person to trace any entry in the register.

Time limits upon planning permission

Before the coming into operation of the Town and Country Planning

[51] *Brayhead (Ascot) Ltd.* v *Berkshire County Council* [1964] 2 Q.B. 303. See too *SPADS* No. A2509 (P/PPA/LA/42, 23rd November 1977).
[52] See *R.K.T. Investments Ltd.* v *Hackney London Borough Council* (1978) 37 P. & C.R. 442.
[53] *Hamilton* v *West Sussex C.C.* [1958] 2 Q.B. 286.
[54] The effects of failure to comply with similar statutory provisions relating to the issue of a certificate of appropriate alternative development were considered by the House of Lords in *London and Clydeside Estates Ltd.* v *Aberdeen District Council* 1980 S.C. (H.L.) 1; 1980 S.L.T. 81.
[55] As amended by the 1982 Act, Schedule 2, para. 9.
[56] In *Steeples* v *Derbyshire County Council* [1985] 1 W.L.R. 256 it was held that the keeping of a file of all applications could not be said to amount to the keeping of a register.

(Scotland) Act 1969 a planning permission which was not acted upon remained effective for an indefinite period; unless there was imposed upon the grant of permission a condition setting a time limit for the commencement or completion of development or for the submission for approval of 'reserved matters' following an outline planning permission,[57] a developer could be as dilatory as he pleased over beginning or completing a development or over submission of detailed plans. Provision was, however, made by the 1969 Act for the imposition of time limits upon planning permissions; that Act also enabled a planning authority to take certain action where there is unreasonable delay in completing development.

The 1972 Act, re-enacting the provisions of the 1969 Act, provides that, subject to certain exceptions, every planning permission[58] shall be granted or, as the case may be, shall be deemed to be granted, subject to a condition that the development must be begun not later than the expiration of:

(a) five years beginning with the date on which the permission is granted or deemed to be granted; or

(b) such other period (whether longer or shorter) as the authority concerned with the terms of the planning permission[59] may direct, having regard to the provisions of the development plan and to any other material considerations (s.38(1)).

If a time limit is not imposed by express condition attached to a grant of planning permission, that permission is deemed to have been granted subject to a condition that development must be begun within five years (s.38(2)).

There is excluded from the operation of s.38:[60]

(a) any planning permission granted by a development order;

(b) any planning permission granted for a limited period;

(c) any planning permission granted under s.29 of the 1972 Act on an application relating to buildings or works completed, or a use of land instituted, before the date of the application;

(d) any outline planning permission (such permission is dealt with separately under s.39 (below)); or

(e) any planning permission granted or deemed to have been granted before 8th December 1969 (below).

Section 39 provides that every outline planning permission (as defined in s.39(1)) shall be granted subject to conditions to the following effect:

---

[57] A condition requiring approval of reserved matters within a specified period was held valid in *Kent County Council* v *Kingsway Investments (Kent) Ltd.* [1971] A.C. 72.
[58] As regards planning permission for mining operations see p. 471 below.
[59] That authority is defined in s.40(4).
[60] See 1972 Act, s.38(3) and Sched. 22, para. 14.

(a) that application for approval of any reserved matter must be made within three years[61] of the grant of outline permission;[62] and

(b) that the development must be begun before the expiry of five years from the date of the outline permission or before the expiry of two years from the date of final approval of any reserved matter, whichever is the later (s.39(2)).

If these time limits are not imposed by express condition, they are deemed to have been imposed on a grant of outline planning permission (s.39(3)). The authority concerned with the terms of an outline permission may substitute for the periods of five, three and two years referred to in the statute such other periods as, having regard to the provisions of the development plan and to any other material considerations, they consider appropriate (s.39(4), (6)).

The time limit for submission of an application for approval of details is extended in certain cases. Where an application for approval of details has been refused or an appeal against such a refusal dismissed, one further application for approval of reserved matters may be made within six months of the date of such refusal or dismissal, even though three years from the date of the grant of outline permission have expired (1972 Act, s.39(2)(a)[63]). In this way a developer has a final opportunity to revise his proposals so as to make them acceptable to the planning authority or the Secretary of State.

Sections 38 and 39 do not apply to any planning permission or outline planning permission granted before 8th December 1969, but, unless development under such a permission had been started before the beginning of 1969, any such permission was deemed to have been granted subject to the time limits specified in paragraphs 15 and 16 of Schedule 22 to the 1972 Act.[64] There is no statutory time limit in a case where development under a permission was begun before the beginning of 1969; this means that in such a case no completion notice (see p. 265 below) can be issued and the developer can take as long as he pleases over completing the development.

In *R.* v *Secretary of State for the Environment, ex parte Percy Bilton*

---

[61] In *R.* v *Bromley London Borough Council, ex parte Sievers* (1980) 41 P. & C.R. 294 outline planning permission had been granted on 24th June 1974. An application for approval of details was completed on Saturday 22nd June 1977 but the planning authority's offices were shut on that and the following day, with the result that the application was not handed in until 24th June. Shaw L.J. held that the Saturday and Sunday did not count in computing the time and that the lateness of the application, if any, was *de minimis* and had to be disregarded.

[62] This would seem to mean that the applicant 'is entitled to submit plan after plan, details after details, within the three years in the hope of getting them approved; but, if none of those is approved, the condition prevents any more being submitted after the three years' (*Kingsway Investments (Kent) Ltd.* v *Kent County Council* [1969] 2 Q.B. 322, per Lord Denning M.R.) See too *Cardiff Corporation* v *Secretary of State for Wales* (1971) 22 P. & C.R. 718; and appeal decision noted in [1975] J.P.L. 364.

[63] As amended by the 1982 Act, Schedule 2, para. 13.

[64] See *Alexander Russell Ltd.* v *Secretary of State for Scotland* 1984 S.L.T. 81.

Industrial Properties Ltd.[65] outline planning permission had been granted in respect of a 22 acre site in 1952 and parts of the site had been developed in accordance with subsequent detailed approvals. Applications made in 1973 for approval of details in respect of undeveloped portions of the site were held invalid by the English minister as having been made outwith the statutory time limits. The Divisional Court held, however, that for the purposes of the statutory provisions on the duration of planning permission, the 22 acre site was not to be treated as consisting of separate parcels of land and that development had to be taken to have begun on the whole site; the land was not therefore subject to the statutory time limits.

For the purposes of ss.38 and 39 development is to be taken to be begun on the earliest date on which any 'specified operation' comprised in the development is carried out (s.40(1)). The 'specified operations', detailed in s.40(2), include any work of construction in the course of the erection of a building, the digging of a trench for the foundations of a building, the laying of any underground main or pipe to the foundations, any operation in the course of laying out or constructing a road or part of a road, and any change in the use of land, where that change constitutes 'material development' as defined in s.40(3).

As Eveleigh L.J. said in *Malvern Hills District Council* v *Secretary of State for the Environment*:[66] 'Very little need be done to satisfy the section.[67] That which is done, however, must genuinely be done for the purpose of carrying out the development.' Marking out an estate road with pegs has been held to amount to a 'specified operation',[68] as has the digging of trenches which were immediately back-filled.[69] To qualify as a 'specified operation' the work must, however, involve implementation of the development authorised by the permission.[70]

There is a right of appeal against conditions imposed by virtue of ss.38 and 39(s.40(6)) but the imposition of such conditions is mandatory and an appeal in respect of the imposition of a time limit can in effect be made only against the specified period and not against the principle of such a condition.

---

[65] (1975) 31 P. & C.R. 154. See too *Salisbury District Council* v *Secretary of State for the Environment* [1982] J.P.L. 702; and *Etheridge* v *Secretary of State for the Environment* (1983) 48 P. & C.R. 35.

[66] (1982) 46 P. & C.R. 58.

[67] For an example of works which were held not to satisfy the section see *SPADS* No. A4104 (P/ENA/GA/29, 16th April 1982).

[68] *Malvern Hills* (above). See too *Spackman* v *Secretary of State for the Environment* [1977] 1 All E.R. 257; and *United Refineries Ltd.* v *Essex County Council* [1978] J.P.L. 110.

[69] *High Peak Borough Council* v *Secretary of State for the Environment* [1981] J.P.L. 366.

[70] See *South Oxfordshire District Council* v *Secretary of State for the Environment* [1981] 1 W.L.R. 1092; and appeal decisions noted in *SPADS* No. A3206 (P/PPA/GC/38, 13th December 1979); and [1980] J.P.L. 764. For development to be 'begun' it will normally have to be authorised by the permission in question (see *Etheridge* v *Secretary of State for the Environment* (1983) 48 P. & C.R. 35), but development in breach of a condition may suffice (see *Clwyd County Council* v *Secretary of State for Wales* [1982] J.P.L. 696 (upheld on other grounds by the Court of Appeal *sub. nom. Welsh Aggregates Ltd.* v *Secretary of State for the Environment* [1983] J.P.L. 50)).

If a condition imposed under s.38 or s.39 is not complied with, the planning permission lapses at the end of the specified period (s.40(7)).

Where development has not been started, application for renewal of a permission which is subject to a time limit under s.38 or s.39 can be made at any time before the expiry of the time limit simply by making written application to the planning authority, giving sufficient information to enable the authority to identify the previous grant of permission; there is no need to supply plans and drawings with such an application (G.D.O., Art. 8(3)). If such an application is refused there is a right of appeal to the Secretary of State.

The conditions referred to in ss.38 and 39 cannot found a compensation claim, nor can such conditions give rise to a purchase notice (see 1972 Act, ss.136, 158, 226 and 169).

Completion notice

Once development has been begun under a planning permission, that permission is given an indefinite life, subject, however, to the right of the planning authority to serve a completion notice under s.41 of the 1972 Act. A completion notice can be served where:

(*a*) a planning permission is, by virtue of ss.38 or 39 or paragraphs 15 or 16 of Schedule 22, subject to a condition that development must be begun before the expiration of a particular period; and

(*b*) the development has been begun within that period but the period has elapsed without the development having been completed; and

(*c*) the planning authority are of opinion that the development will not be completed within a reasonable period (s.41(1), (2)).

A completion notice is to state that the planning permission will cease to have effect at the expiration of a period specified in the notice, being a period of not less than twelve months after the notice takes effect (s.41(2)). The notice is to be served on the owner and on the occupier of the land and on any other person who, in the opinion of the planning authority, will be affected by the notice (s.41(3)(a)). It is to take effect only if and when it is confirmed by the Secretary of State (s.41(3)(b)). If, within such period (being a period of not less than 28 days from service of the notice) as may be specified in a completion notice, any person on whom the notice is served so requires, the Secretary of State must afford to that person and to the planning authority an opportunity of being heard by a person appointed for the purpose by the Secretary of State (s.41(4)). In confirming a notice the Secretary of State may substitute some *longer* period for that specified in the notice as the period at the expiry of which the planning permission is to cease to have effect (s.41(3)(b)).

If a completion notice takes effect, the planning permission referred to in the notice, in so far as it relates to development not carried out, becomes invalid at the expiration of the specified period (s.41(5)). The planning authority may withdraw a completion notice at any time before the expiry of the period specified in the notice (s.41(6)).

Duration of mineral permissions

Any planning permission for the winning and working of minerals has a defined life (see p. 471 below).

Appeal to Secretary of State

Where application is made to a planning authority for planning permission or for any approval required under a development order, or for any consent, agreement or approval required by a condition imposed on a grant of planning permission, and that permission, consent, agreement or approval is refused by the authority or is granted by them subject to conditions, the applicant,[71] if he is aggrieved[72] by the decision, is entitled to appeal to the Secretary of State (1972 Act, s.33[73]).

Where the planning authority fail to give notice of their decision within the prescribed period (see p. 259 above), appeal may be made to the Secretary of State as if the application had been refused and notification received by the applicant at the end of the prescribed period (s.34[74]).

The procedure for making an appeal to the Secretary of State is set out in Article 16 of the G.D.O. Notice of appeal, stating the grounds on which the appeal is made, is to be given to the Secretary of State, on a form obtained from him, within six months of the decision or of the expiry of the time allowed for the giving of notice of the planning authority's decision or within such longer period as the Secretary of State may at any time allow. With the notice of appeal the appellant is to furnish the Secretary of State with a copy of the application made to the planning authority and all relevant plans and documents submitted with it, a copy of the notice of the decision and all other relevant correspondence with any planning authority. Notice of the appeal must be given to owners and agricultural tenants of the land and to neighbours (1972 Act, s.33(5)[75]).

---

[71] An appeal under s.33 is only valid if made by the applicant himself—see, for example, *SPADS* Nos. A2004 (P/PPA/RC/75, 14th January 1976); and A2035 (P/PPA/GLW/949, 25th February 1976).

[72] In a case in which the appellant's interest in an appeal site was not one which would enable him to implement any planning permission and the planning authority, as owners of the site, confirmed that they would not be prepared to dispose of the land to the appellant, the Secretary of State took the view that the appellant could not be regarded as being 'aggrieved' by the planning authority's decision and dismissed the appeal as 'inappropriate'—see *SPADS* No. A3298 (P/PPA/SL/84, 3rd April 1980). See too *SPADS* No. A3314 (P/PPA/ST/29, 21st April 1980); and appeal ref. P/PPA/LD/35, 10th July 1981 (see 1982 S.P.L.P. 34). Contrast, however, *SPADS* Nos. A2314 (P/PPA/ST/1, 7th April 1977); and A2449 (P/PPA/LR/636, 29th September 1977).

[73] As amended by the 1982 Act, Schedule 2, para. 11.

[74] Amended by the 1982 Act, Schedule 2, para. 12. As to the scope of s.34 see the decision of the Second Division in *Inverclyde District Council* v *Secretary of State for Scotland* 1980 S.C. 363; 1981 S.L.T. 26; and see comment in 1982 S.P.L.P. 47. This matter was not pursued in the House of Lords: 1982 S.L.T. 200.

[75] As amended by the 1982 Act, Schedule 2, para. 11.

The Secretary of State is to inform the planning authority of the appeal and is to transmit to them a copy of the notice of appeal and copies of such other documents as he deems necessary for the purpose of the appeal (G.D.O., Art. 16(3)). Within two months from the date when the Secretary of State notifies them of the appeal, the planning authority are to submit to the minister a statement of their observations on the appeal, together with, in any appropriate case, a copy of any certificates provided by the applicant (G.D.O., Art. 16(4)).

Where the appeal is against the decision of a district planning authority, the Secretary of State must serve a copy of the notice of appeal on the regional planning authority (G.D.O., Art. 16(5)). If the regional planning authority wish to take part in the appeal proceedings they must, within one month of receiving the copy of the notice of appeal, so notify the Secretary of State and must, within one month thereafter, send to the Secretary of State and to the appellant a statement of their observations on the appeal (G.D.O., Art. 16(6)). Similar provision is made for notification of the district authority and their taking part in an appeal against a decision made by the regional planning authority (see G.D.O., Art. 16(8)).

If the planning authority or the regional planning authority fail to comply with the time limits mentioned above or if there is a failure on the part of the appellant or one of the authorities to submit any observations or documents required by the Secretary of State within any time specified by him, the minister may simply proceed to determine the appeal (G.D.O., Art. 16(7)).

Most planning appeals are now determined by persons appointed for the purpose by the Secretary of State—see chapter 20. Appeal procedures are discussed in that chapter.

The Secretary of State or appointed person may allow or dismiss an appeal against the decision of a planning authority, or may reverse or vary[76] any part of the authority's decision, whether the appeal relates to that part of the decision or not, and may deal with the application as if it had been made to him in the first instance;[77] since the whole matter is before him, the Secretary of State or appointed person may, for example, have to consider whether, instead of refusing planning permission, there is any form of condition which might achieve a satisfactory result.[78] Where the Secretary of State or appointed person proposes to reverse or vary any part of the planning authority's decision to which the appeal does not relate, he must give notice of his intention to the applicant and to the planning authority and must afford to each of them an opportunity of making representations on the matter (s.33(3)). An appellant should therefore bear in mind that in

[76] See p. 254 above. As to amendment of the application at this stage see *Inverclyde District Council* v *Secretary of State for Scotland* 1980 S.C. 363; 1981 S.L.T. 26 (Second Division); and 1982 S.L.T. 200 (H.L.).
[77] This means that the Secretary of State has power to deal with the application even though the decision of the planning authority from which the appeal arose is in fact a nullity—see *Stringer* v *Minister of Housing and Local Government* [1970] 1 W.L.R. 1281.
[78] See, for example, *Grampian Regional Council* v *Secretary of State for Scotland* 1983 S.L.T. 526; and *George Wimpey & Co. Ltd.* v *New Forest District Council* [1979] J.P.L. 314.

determining an appeal against a conditional grant of planning permission the Secretary of State or appointed person is entitled to impose more onerous conditions or even to refuse planning permission altogether.[79]

The decision on a planning appeal will often turn on the application of principles of good planning to the facts of the particular case but elements of law and of ministerial policy may also be relevant. Though one cannot, of course, speak of 'precedent' in connection with planning appeals, it may sometimes be useful to consider previous appeal decisions as indicating ministerial policy on particular matters. *Scottish Planning Appeal Decisions* (*SPADS*), published by the Planning Exchange, Glasgow, provides summaries of all Scottish appeal decisions. Many decisions of interest are also to be found in the three *Scottish Bulletins of Selected Appeal Decisions*, in the two series of *Bulletins* containing decisions of the English minister and in the *Journal of Planning and Environment Law*. Notes and comments on interesting Scottish appeal decisions appear in *Scottish Planning Law and Practice*. Guidance as to the Secretary of State's policy on particular matters is to be found in departmental circulars and the National Planning Guidelines (see chapter 4).

The decision on any appeal under s.33 is declared to be final (s.33(6)). Any person aggrieved by the decision is, however, entitled to make application to the Court of Session under s.233 of the 1972 Act (see chapter 21 below).

Reference to Planning Inquiry Commission

The 1972 Act empowers the Secretary of State to refer development proposals of a far-reaching or novel character to a Planning Inquiry Commission constituted by the minister under s.44 of the Act (see p. 517 below).

Effect of planning permission

The 1972 Act provides that any grant of planning permission to develop land shall (except in so far as the permission otherwise provides and without prejudice to the statutory provisions as to duration, revocation or modification of permission) enure for the benefit of the land and of all persons for the time being interested therein (s.30(1)).

Any number of planning applications may be made in respect of the same land, even though the proposals in the applications are mutually inconsistent, and the planning authority are obliged to deal with each application on its own merits, regarding each application as a proposal for separate and independent development.[80] There can therefore be a number of unimplemented planning permissions outstanding in respect of the same area of land and the owner of land may be able to choose which of several mutually inconsistent planning permissions he will exercise. Where, however, one of

[79] See, for example, *SPADS* No. A3161 (P/PPA/D/51, 24th October 1979); [1974] J.P.L. 482 and 739; and [1975] J.P.L. 556.
[80] See *Pilkington* v *Secretary of State for the Environment* [1973] 1 W.L.R. 1527.

two or more permissions is acted upon, it will not thereafter be possible for the landowner to implement any other inconsistent permission.[81] In *Pilkington v Secretary of State for the Environment*[82] permission had been granted in 1953 for the erection of a bungalow at the northern end of a strip of land, the bungalow to be ancillary to a smallholding which was to occupy the remainder of the land. In 1954 permission was given for the erection of a house in the centre of the strip of land, the remainder of the strip again being shown as associated with the permitted development. The 1954 permission was implemented. It was then proposed (and would have been physically possible) to erect the bungalow referred to in the 1953 permission. The Divisional Court held that the 1953 permission could not now be implemented—it permitted a house on the site as ancillary to the smallholding which was to occupy the rest of the site and it was not now possible, consistently with the (implemented) 1954 permission, to erect a house on those terms.

It would seem, however, that a planning permission can sometimes be regarded as divisible, and in *F. Lucas & Sons Ltd. v Dorking and Horley R.D.C.*[83] Winn J. held that a developer who had been granted two planning permissions in respect of the same area of land, the earlier permission allowing the erection of twenty-eight houses on the site, the later permitting six houses in accordance with a quite different layout plan for the same site, was entitled to develop part of the land in accordance with the later permission and the remainder of the site in accordance with the earlier permission. Winn J. considered that the planning permission for twenty-eight houses was not to be regarded as permitting only the complete development but was properly to be regarded as allowing the erection of any one or more of the houses comprised in the scheme.[84]

The mere fact that planning permission has been applied for and granted does not in itself detract from existing use rights in any way; it is only if the permission is acted upon that any such question can arise[85] and there is, of

---

[81] A consultation paper issued by the Scottish Development Department on 31st July 1984 stated that it had been suggested that some high-technology enterprises may experience difficulty as a result of a certain lack of flexibility in planning law. In particular, if planning permission is granted for alternative uses (e.g. industrial and office) and is then implemented in respect of one of those uses, there is no right to change to the alternative use without obtaining a further planning permission. It is therefore proposed to provide that in these circumstances a change of use will not require planning permission. It would, however, be open to the planning authority to impose a condition preventing such a change of use.

[82] [1973] 1 W.L.R. 1527; approved by the Court of Appeal in *Hoveringham Gravels Ltd. v Chiltern District Council* (1977) 76 L.G.R. 533; and by the House of Lords in *Pioneer Aggregates (U.K.) Ltd. v Secretary of State for the Environment* [1984] 3 W.L.R. 32. See too *Ellis v Worcestershire C.C.* (1961) 12 P. & C.R. 178; and *Lobb v Secretary of State for the Environment* [1984] J.P.L. 336. Contrast *Salisbury District Council v Secretary of State for the Environment* [1982] J.P.L. 702.

[83] (1964) 17 P. & C.R. 111; compare ministerial decision noted in [1974] J.P.L. 45.

[84] See too *Sheppard v Secretary of State for the Environment* (1975) 233 E.G. 1167.

[85] See p. 144 above on the circumstances in which implementation of a planning permission may lead to the creation of a new planning unit or to a new chapter in the planning history of the site.

course, no compulsion upon a landowner to implement a permission. A grant of planning permission does not preclude the landowner subsequently contending that no such permission was necessary.[86]

It is, of course the case that it is only if a planning permission is implemented that any condition attached to the permission can come into effect.[87] However, even though a particular development departs from the terms of a planning permission, carrying out the development may be treated as an implementation of the permission with the result that a condition attached to the permission can be enforced.[88]

In *Pioneer Aggregates (U.K.) Ltd.* v *Secretary of State for the Environment*[89] Lord Scarman said that planning control was a creature of statute and that it was a field of law in which the courts should not introduce principles or rules derived from private law unless expressly authorised to do so by Parliament or unless it was necessary in order to give effect to the purpose of the legislation. His Lordship pointed out that planning permission was not a private right but a right which is declared by statute to enure for the benefit of the land (see 1972 Act, s.30(1)—above); the House of Lords therefore held that there is no principle in planning law that a valid planning permission capable of being implemented can be held to have been abandoned or lost by the act of a person entitled to the benefit of the permission.[90] The Court of Appeal were therefore held to have erred in law in holding in *Slough Estates Ltd.* v *Slough Borough Council (No. 2)*[91] that by taking action inconsistent with the retention of any rights under a planning permission a landowner might be held to have waived or abandoned his rights under the permission.

Conditions cannot be implied from the wording of a planning permission.[92] In the somewhat special circumstances of the case it was held in *R.* v *Derbyshire County Council, ex parte North East Derbyshire District*

---

[86] *Newbury District Council* v *Secretary of State for the Environment* [1981] A.C. 578. See too *Mounsdon* v *Weymouth & Melcombe Regis Borough Council* [1960] 1 Q.B. 645; *East Barnet U.D.C.* v *British Transport Commission* [1962] 2 Q.B. 484; and *Sheppard* v *Secretary of State for the Environment* (1975) 233 E.G. 1167.

[87] See *Sheppard* (above).

[88] See, for example, *Kerrier District Council* v *Secretary of State for the Environment* (1980) 41 P. & C.R. 284; and *J. Toomey Motors Ltd.* v *Basildon District Council* [1982] J.P.L. 775 (see p. 299 below).

[89] [1984] 3 W.L.R. 32.

[90] However, although existing use rights are, as Lord Scarman said in *Pioneer Aggregates* 'hardy beasts with a great capacity for survival', they can be lost by abandonment—see p. 141 above.

[91] [1969] 2 Ch. 305.

[92] See *Trustees of Walton-on-Thames Charities* v *Walton and Weybridge U.D.C.* (1970) 68 L.G.R. 488. See too *East Suffolk C.C.* v *Secretary of State for the Environment* (1972) 70 L.G.R. 595; *Sutton London Borough Council* v *Secretary of State for the Environment* (1975) 29 P. & C.R. 350; and *Carpet Decor (Guildford) Ltd.* v *Secretary of State for the Environment* [1981] J.P.L. 806. Contrast, however, *Kwik Save Discount Group Ltd.* v *Secretary of State for Wales* (1980) 42 P. & C.R. 166, in which, on the interpretation of the permission in question, a restriction could be implied on the goods to be sold in a showroom; and see p. 256 above.

Council[93] that a condition attached to a grant of planning permission might be treated in effect as granting permission for that which the condition required.

Even though a planning permission contains an error it will, it seems, be effective 'if it so accurately describes the development to be carried out that anyone taking the permission and its accompanying plans and applications to the land will be able to see, without doubt, precisely what it is which has been authorised.'[94]

The mere grant of planning permission for development may not, of course, be enough to enable a developer to proceed with the projected development; he may, for example, require consents under other legislation. The fact that planning permission has been granted for a particular development is no defence to a nuisance action in respect of the activities authorised by the permission. A grant of planning permission does not override any land obligation to which the land in question may be subject but the fact that such permission has been granted or refused may be taken into account by the Lands Tribunal for Scotland in considering an application under the Conveyancing and Feudal Reform (Scotland) Act 1970 for variation or discharge of a land obligation. In *Main* v *Lord Doune*,[95] for example, the tribunal declared:

'Although planning permissions are granted in the light of a conception of the public interest (the safeguarding of private rights being merely incidental thereto) nevertheless they may provide some guide as to whether a use being impeded is reasonable or whether a land obligation has become unreasonable or inappropriate.'

Construction of planning permission

In *Miller-Mead* v *Minister of Housing and Local Government*[96] Lord Denning M.R. said: 'A grant of [planning] permission runs with the land and may come into the hands of people who have never seen the application . . .' In general, such people may take a planning permission at face value in that it is generally competent, in construing a planning permission, to consider only material to be found within the four corners of the document granting planning permission,[97] including any reasons stated therein.[98] It is

---

[93] (1979) 77 L.G.R. 389. See too *Irlam Brick Company* v *Warrington Borough Council* [1982] J.P.L. 709; and *Welsh Aggregates Ltd.* v *Secretary of State for the Environment* [1983] J.P.L. 50. Contrast *Alexandra Transport Company Ltd.* v *Secretary of State for Scotland* 1974 S.L.T. 81.

[94] See *R.* v *Secretary of State for the Environment, ex parte Reinisch* (1971) 22 P. & C.R. 1022, per Lord Widgery C.J.

[95] 1972 S.L.T. (Lands Tr.) 14.

[96] [1963] 2 Q.B. 196.

[97] *Slough Estates Ltd.* v *Slough Borough Council (No. 2)* [1971] A.C. 958; *Miller-Mead* (above); and appeal decisions noted in [1980] J.P.L. 61 and 352.

[98] *Crisp from the Fens Ltd.* v *Rutland C.C.* (1950) 1 P. & C.R. 48; *Fawcett Properties Ltd.* v *Buckingham County Council* [1961] A.C. 636; *Centre Hotels (Cranston) Ltd.* v *Secretary of State for the Environment* [1982] J.P.L. 108; and *Irlam Brick Company* v *Warrington Borough Council* [1982] J.P.L. 709.

not normally permissible to look at the application for permission as an aid to interpretation.[99] Where, however, the planning permission expressly incorporates the application or a plan which accompanied the application or correspondence relating to the application, it will be proper and necessary to have regard to the incorporated documents.[1]

It is not normally competent to consider the resolution of the planning authority in order to construe or explain the terms of a permission.[2] Where, however, the issue is whether planning permission was in fact granted or whether the decision was within the power of the planning authority, the court is entitled to go behind the document in question in order to ascertain the true facts.[3]

A planning permission is not to be construed *contra proferentes.*[4]

Enterprise zones and planning permission

The Local Government, Planning and Land Act 1980[5] makes provision for the designation of enterprise zones, the purpose of such designation being to encourage industrial and commercial activity in such areas through the removal or streamlining of certain statutory or administrative controls and the removal of certain fiscal burdens. The procedure under which an area may be designated an enterprise zone (by order made by the Secretary of State) and the effects of such designation are set out in Schedule 32 to the 1980 Act.[6]

One of the important effects of an order designating an enterprise zone is that planning permission is thereby granted for any particular development specified in the enterprise zone scheme[7] or for development of any class so specified; such permission may be subject to conditions or limitations and certain matters may be reserved for approval by the enterprise zone authority. If the Secretary of State approves, the enterprise zone authority may direct that any permission granted by the scheme is not to apply in relation to a specified development or class of development or to a specified class of development in a specified area within the zone.

---

[99] See *Slough Estates* and *Miller-Mead* (above).

[1] *Wilson v West Sussex C.C.* [1963] 2 Q.B. 764; *Slough Estates* (above); *Chalgray v Secretary of State for the Environment* (1976) 33 P. & C.R. 10; *Manning v Secretary of State for the Environment* [1976] J.P.L. 634; *Kwik Save Discount Group Ltd.* v *Secretary of State for Wales* (1980) 42 P. & C.R. 166; and *Edmunds v Secretary of State for Wales* [1981] J.P.L. 52 (competent to have regard to letter 'inextricably attached' to the planning application).

[2] *Slough Estates Ltd.* v *Slough Borough Council (No. 2)* [1969] 2 Ch. 305, per Lord Denning M.R.

[3] *Attorney-General, ex rel. Co-operative Retail Services Ltd.* v *Taff-Ely Borough Council* (1979) 39 P. & C.R. 233 (C.A.) and (1981) 42 P. & C.R. 1 (H.L.); and *Norfolk County Council v Secretary of State for the Environment* [1973] 1 W.L.R. 1400.

[4] *Crisp from the Fens Ltd.* v *Rutland C.C.* (1950) 1 P. & C.R. 48, per Singleton J.

[5] See s.179 and Schedule 32.

[6] See too 1980 S.P.L.P 15; and 1981 S.P.L.P. 38.

[7] An enterprise zone scheme is to be prepared, on the invitation of the Secretary of State, by a district or general planning authority.

Development by local authorities

Where a local authority propose to carry out development they must, unless planning permission for that development is granted by development order (see p. 171 above) or is deemed to be granted as a result of a direction attached to a sanction granted by a government department (see p. 171 above), obtain planning permission in one of the following ways.

Regional councils which are not planning authorities and district councils which are not planning authorities must obtain planning permission from the planning authority in the normal way.

Where a local authority require planning permission for development which they propose to carry out[8] in the area for which they are themselves the planning authority, the procedures contained in the Town and Country Planning (Development by Planning Authorities) (Scotland) Regulations 1981[9] apply. The planning authority are to comply with the statutory requirements as to the notification of owners and agricultural tenants (see p. 193 above) and as to neighbour notification (see p. 195 above). Consultations must be carried out under Article 13(1) of the G.D.O. (see p. 204 above). The authority are then to give notice of their intention to develop in a local newspaper, indicating where plans of the development may be inspected and allowing a period of 21 days for representations to be made to the authority.[10]

If no representations are made to the planning authority within the prescribed periods, planning permission is deemed to be granted by the Secretary of State. Otherwise, the planning authority must give notice of intention to develop to the Secretary of State. Unless the Secretary of State directs the authority to submit a formal application for planning permission, permission is deemed to be granted on the expiry of 28 days from receipt of the notice. Where the Secretary of State directs the authority to make a formal application, that application is deemed to have been referred to the Secretary of State under s.32 of the 1972 Act (see p. 202 above) and will be determined accordingly. Any planning permission deemed to be granted to a planning authority under the regulations applies only to a development by the planning authority concerned and does not run with the land.

---

[8] This does not perhaps include the situation where a development is to be a joint venture with private developers on a profit-sharing basis—see *Sunbell Properties Ltd.* v *Dorset County Council* (1979) 253 E.G. 1123.

[9] As amended by the Town and Country Planning (Development by Planning Authorities) (Scotland) Amendment Regulations 1984.

[10] In *R.* v *Lambeth London Borough Council, ex parte Sharp, The Times,* 28th December 1984 Croom-Johnson L.J. held that certain provisions of the Town and Country Planning General Regulations 1976, which prescribe the procedure to be followed by local authorities seeking to carry out development in England and Wales (but which differ somewhat from the Scottish regulations) were mandatory; failure to observe the requirements of the regulations that the notice published by the authority should specify the period for making objections and should state that objections are to be in writing invalidated a deemed grant of planning permission.

Development by statutory undertakers

Except where planning permission is deemed to be granted or is granted by the G.D.O. (see p. 171 and p. 172 above), statutory undertakers[11] must make application for planning permission in the normal way before carrying out development. Where, however, an application is made by statutory undertakers in respect of their 'operational land'[12] or certain other land, and that application is 'called in' by the Secretary of State or an appeal is made to the Secretary of State from the planning authority's decision on such an application, the application or appeal is to be dealt with by the Secretary of State acting jointly with the 'appropriate Minister', i.e. the minister responsible for the undertaking in question[13] (s.214). Special provision is made in a number of respects by the 1972 Act in relation to the operational land of statutory undertakers (see Part XI of the Act and ss.235 and 236).

Stopping up and diversion of roads, etc

In order that development of land may be carried out in terms of a planning permission, it may be necessary to stop up or divert a road; there are contained in Part X of the 1972 Act[14] provisions which enable such action to be taken.

Where he is satisfied that it is necessary to do so in order to enable development to be carried out in accordance with planning permission or to be carried out in accordance with an enterprise zone scheme or to be carried out by a government department, the Secretary of State may by order authorise the stopping up or diversion of any road[15] (s.198(1)). Such an order may deal with the provision or improvement of any other road and may contain such other incidental and consequential provisions as appear to the Secretary of State to be necessary or expedient (s.198(2), (3)); in particular, the order may require a specified authority or person to pay, or to make contributions in respect of, the cost of the carrying out of any work provided for by the order or of any increased expenditure attributable to the order. In this way the person carrying out the development which necessitates the stopping up may have to contribute towards the cost of the closure.

Section 204 lays down the procedure to be followed in connection with the making by the Secretary of State of such an order. If any objection to the making of the order is received by the Secretary of State a local inquiry will be held unless the Secretary of State is satisfied that 'in the special

---

[11] As defined in s.275 of the 1972 Act. See too *British Airports Authority* v *Secretary of State for Scotland* 1979 S.C. 200; 1979 S.L.T. 197.

[12] On the meaning of 'operational land' see ss.211 and 212. See too *SPADS* No. A3722 (P/PPA/SL/59, 15th May 1981).

[13] As defined in s.64 of the 1972 Act.

[14] Certain of the provisions of Part X of the 1972 Act were amended by the Roads (Scotland) Act 1984—see, in particular, Schedule 9, paras. 70(8)–(18) and (22), and Schedule 11 to the 1984 Act.

[15] Although this provision cannot be used where the permitted development has been completed, it can be employed if development has been started but not completed—see *Ashby* v *Secretary of State for the Environment* [1980] 1 W.L.R. 673.

circumstances of the case' the holding of such an inquiry is unnecessary (s.204(3)). If objection is made by an authority or person required to make a financial contribution under the order, the order is to be subject to special parliamentary procedure (s.204(5)). It was formerly the case that the procedure for making an order stopping up or diverting a road could not be begun until planning permission for the development to which the order related had been granted. It is now provided, however, that in specified circumstances—where, for example, an application for planning permission has been 'called in' or where an appeal has been made to the Secretary of State—the procedure for making the order may be carried on concurrently with the proceedings relating to planning permission (s.205). In this way the stopping up order may be made earlier than would otherwise be possible; the order cannot, however, be finally made until planning permission has been granted (s.205(5)).

Planning authorities may themselves[16] make orders stopping up or diverting roads (other than trunk roads), footpaths or bridleways if this is necessary in order to enable development to be carried out in accordance with planning permission or in accordance with an enterprise zone scheme or to be carried out by a government department (1972 Act, ss.198A[17] and 199). Such orders are advertised and, if no objections are received, are confirmed by planning authorities themselves. If objections are received, the order is to be submitted to the Secretary of State for confirmation (s.206 and Schedule 18). A draft order may be published in anticipation of planning permission being granted (s.205A[18]). Planning authorities have a broad discretionary power to recover some or all of the costs they incur when making orders stopping up or diverting roads or paths at the request of third parties (1972 Act, s.210A[19]).

Section 203[20] of the 1972 Act provides for the extinguishment of public rights of way over land held by a local authority for planning purposes.

---

[16] After consultation with the roads authority.
[17] Added by the Local Government (Miscellaneous Provisions) (Scotland) Act 1981, Schedule 2, para. 25.
[18] Added by the 1981 Act, Schedule 3, para. 16.
[19] Added by s.45 of the 1982 Act.
[20] As amended by the 1981 Act, Schedule 2, para. 28.

CHAPTER 12
PLANNING AGREEMENTS

Introduction

Section 50 of the 1972 Act provides that a planning authority may enter into an agreement with any person interested in land in their area for the purpose of restricting or regulating the development or use of the land. Recent research has shown widespread use of the equivalent provision in the English legislation[1] and an increasing use of such agreements in Scotland.[2]

The purpose of this sort of agreement, said Walton J. in *Western Fish Products Ltd.* v *Penwith District Council*,[3] is to 'enable the local planning authority to control matters which it might otherwise have no power to control by the imposition of conditions on any planning permission'. Such agreements are also used, it would seem, to duplicate normal development control powers; they offer an alternative enforcement mechanism and their content is not susceptible to variation or discharge by way of an appeal to the Secretary of State.[4]

Section 50 enables planning authorities to achieve these purposes by empowering them to enter into a special form of contract. The contract is special in two ways. First of all, if recorded in the Register of Sasines or in the Land Register, as appropriate, it will be enforceable at the instance of the planning authority against singular successors in title (s.50(2)). Local authorities have a general power to enter into contracts in pursuance of their functions. That power is given statutory recognition in s.69 of the Local Government (Scotland) Act 1973, which empowers local authorities to do anything which is calculated to facilitate or is conducive or incidental to the

---

[1]   See, in particular, J. Jowell 'Bargaining in Development Control' [1977] J.P.L. 414; and J. N. Hawke, 'Planning Agreements in Practice' [1981] J.P.L. 5 and 86.
[2]   J. Rowan-Robinson and E. Young, *Planning by Agreement in Scotland: The Law and Practice* (Scottish Planning Law and Practice Occasional Paper No. 4, 1982).
[3]   Unreported, 19th November 1977.
[4]   See *S.P.L.P Occasional Paper No. 4* (above). In *Avon County Council* v *Millard, The Times*, 11th February 1985, the Court of Appeal held a planning authority entitled to seek an injunction to restrain a company with whom they had entered into an agreement under s.52 of the Town and Country Planning Act 1971 (which is similar in its terms to s.50 of the Scottish Act) from acting in contravention of the agreement. The company's contention that the action was premature because the planning authority had not exhausted the enforcement machinery contained in the planning legislation (which provides for the service of an enforcement notice in respect of a breach of planning control—see chapter 13 below) was held not to be well-founded.

discharge of any of their functions. A planning authority may, therefore, enter into an agreement with a landowner for the purpose of restricting or regulating the development or use of land without recourse to s.50 of the 1972 Act. However, whilst such an agreement may be adequate where an immediate 'one off' obligation is involved, it may be of limited value if the development which underlies the agreement is to be carried out by some third party or if the agreement imposes a postponed or continuing obligation. Such an agreement will be enforceable between the original contracting parties but will not bind successors in title. Section 50 of the 1972 Act overcomes this difficulty by providing that an agreement made under that section, if recorded in the Register of Sasines or in the Land Register, as appropriate, may be enforced by the planning authority against persons deriving title to the land from the person with whom the agreement was entered into (1972 Act, s.50(2)).

Secondly, an agreement under s.50 is special in the sense that it enables the planning authority to impose some fetter on the exercise of their discretionary powers. It is often said that public bodies which have been entrusted with the exercise of statutory powers and duties 'cannot enter into any contract or take action incompatible with the due exercise of their powers or the discharge of their duties'.[5] A public authority cannot, as it were, disable itself by contract from exercising its powers or from performing its statutory duties. However, as Wade says: 'There will often be situations where a public authority must be at liberty to bind itself for the very purpose of exercising its powers effectively.'[6] The problem is that the courts have not provided any very clear guidelines as to how and where the line is to be drawn between, on the one hand, a contract which is an improper restriction on an authority's discretion and, on the other hand, a contract which is a legitimate exercise of that discretion. This is not the place for a detailed discussion of this very difficult area of law,[7] but it is of some importance to consider how far planning authorities can, by means of agreements, validly restrict the future exercise of their powers. Can they, for example, bind themselves to grant planning permission or to refrain from taking enforcement action? These are questions we examine in more detail below; at this stage it is sufficient to say that s.50(3) appears to go some way towards allowing for this.

There is nothing very new about the power to enter into agreements for planning purposes; what is new is the extent to which the power is now being used. Provision for planning agreements was first made, in a somewhat more

---

[5] *Birkdale District Electricity Supply Company* v *Southport Corporation* [1926] A.C. 355, per Lord Birkenhead.

[6] H. W. R. Wade, *Administrative Law* (Clarendon Press, Oxford, 5th ed., 1982), p. 339.

[7] For such discussion see J. M. Evans, *de Smith's Judicial Review of Administrative Action*, (Stevens, 4th ed., 1980), pp. 317–320; H. W. R. Wade, *Administrative Law* (above), pp. 335–341; P. Rogerson, 'On the Fettering of Public Powers' [1971] P.L. 288; and E. Young and J. Rowan-Robinson, 'Section 50 Agreements and the Fettering of Powers' [1982] J.P.L. 673.

limited form, in the Town and Country Planning (Scotland) Act 1932.[8] The object of that provision would seem to have been to enable planning authorities to keep land free of development without becoming liable to pay compensation. The power was subsequently extended almost to its present form by the Town and Country Planning (Scotland) Act 1947, although the exercise of the power was subjected to ministerial approval. There seems little doubt that the requirement to obtain this approval had an inhibiting effect on the use of agreements.[9] The requirement was abolished by the Town and Country Planning (Scotland) Act 1969. Since then, and particularly since local government reorganisation in 1975, there has been a very substantial increase in the use of such agreements.[10]

The increasing use of agreements has, not surprisingly, caused some concern, particularly amongst developers. The main focus of concern has been the use of agreements to secure what is commonly referred to as 'planning gain'.[11] The term has no precise definition but generally refers to some sort of benefit to the community which was not part of the original proposal by a developer, and was therefore negotiated, and is not of itself of any commercial advantage to the developer. There is, broadly, some attempt to extract a community benefit from the profits of a particular development. The use of agreements for this purpose would seem to have been more common in England than in Scotland.

As a result of this concern, the Property Advisory Group was asked by the Secretary of State for the Environment in 1980 to prepare a report on the subject of 'planning gain'. Their report, published in 1981,[12] was very critical of the practice of bargaining for planning gain. Subject to certain exceptions, the Property Advisory Group categorised the practice as unacceptable, their main objection being that if planning decisions were generally to be linked to the willingness of developers to offer collateral benefits by way of

8   In *Ransom & Luck* v *Surbiton Borough Council* [1949] Ch. 180 it was held that the sole purpose of the corresponding provision of the English legislation was to allow local authorities to accept undertakings from landowners and to enable authorities to enforce such undertakings; it did not permit a local authority to contract not to use its statutory powers or to use those powers in a particular way.
9   In a thesis entitled 'Section 50 Agreements', submitted for the Diploma in Town Planning, University of Strathclyde, in 1979, I. Bruce states that between 1946 and the coming into operation of the Town and Country Planning (Scotland) Act 1969, only six agreements were made in Scotland.
10   See *S.P.L.P. Occasional Paper No. 4* (above).
11   See, for example, J. Jowell, 'Bargaining in Development Control' [1977] J.P.L. 414; J. Jowell, 'The Limits of Law in Urban Planning' [1977] C.L.P. 63; M. Grant, 'Developers' Contributions and Planning Gain: Ethics and Legalities' [1978] J.P.L. 8; S. Byrne, 'Conditions and Agreements: The Local Authority's Viewpoint', in J.P.E.L. Occasional Paper, *Development Control—Thirty Years On* (Sweet and Maxwell, 1979); Sir D. Heap and A. J. Ward, 'Planning Bargaining: The Pros and Cons' [1980] J.P.L. 631; J. Ratcliffe, 'Planning Gain—An Overview' (1981) 258 E.G. 407; and I. Simpson, *Planning Gain: the Implications for Planning in the U.K.* (University of Strathclyde, 1984).
12   *Planning Gain* (H.M.S.O., 1981). And see *Richmond upon Thames L.B.C.* v *Secretary of State for the Environment* [1984] J.P.L. 24; and *Westminster City Council* v *Secretary of State for the Environment* [1984] J.P.L. 27.

agreements, the whole planning system would fall into disrepute. The report went on to advocate the provision of guidance by the Secretary of State. Such guidance was subsequently issued by the Secretary of State for the Environment in D.o.E. Circular 22/83 and by the Secretary of State for Scotland in S.D.D. Circular 22/1984. In general terms, S.D.D. Circular 22/1984 recommends that obligations imposed by agreement should be reasonable in the circumstances, should be fairly and reasonably related in scale and kind to the development proposed and should represent a reasonable charge on the developer.

Whilst considerable attention has been focused on attempts by some planning authorities to secure planning gain, rather less attention has been given to the consequences of the use of agreements on the development control process as a whole. Development control is a process of regulation; the planning authority 'adjudicates' in public on proposals for development. Planning by agreement might fairly be described as the antithesis of this; the process of public adjudication gives way to negotiation carried on in private. Although the development control process can accommodate with advantage the occasional use of agreements to overcome objections to development which might otherwise prove insurmountable, it would seem that the widespread use of agreements could only be accommodated at a cost to the adjudicatory nature of the process. As Grant says of the position in England: 'The consequence of increased reliance by authorities on planning agreements as an instrument in development control was that the traditional regulatory model of control in many cases was superseded by a consensual, negotiated model.'[13] Nonetheless, it is clear from the overall scheme of the legislation that the role of the planning authority was never intended to be solely one of regulation; the authority is endowed with wide promotional powers (see chapter 17). The difficulty lies in the reconciliation of these powers when they are used in combination.

Section 50 is one of the more complex provisions of the 1972 Act. The remainder of this chapter is given over to an examination of some of these complexities.

The parties

Section 50(1) provides that a planning authority (a term which for this purpose refers to a regional, general or district planning authority[14]) 'may enter into an agreement with any person interested in land in their area (in so far as the interest of that person enables him to bind the land) . . . ' Subsection (2) states that such an agreement shall, if recorded in the Register of Sasines (or in the Land Register, as appropriate), 'be enforceable at the instance of the planning authority against persons deriving title to the land from the person with whom the agreement was entered into'.

The phrase 'any person interested in land' is one that gives rise to some

---

[13] Malcolm Grant, *Urban Planning Law*, (Sweet and Maxwell, 1982), p. 364.
[14] Local Government (Scotland) Act 1973, s.172 and Schedule 22; and Local Government and Planning (Scotland) Act 1982, s.48 and Schedule 2.

difficulty. In *Pennine Raceway Ltd.* v *Kirklees Metropolitan Borough Council*[15] Eveleigh L.J. observed that the corresponding English provision was not confined to interests in land in the strict conveyancing sense. However, the words 'in so far as the interest of that person enables him to bind the land', which appear in brackets in subsection (1) of s.50 of the 1972 Act and for which there is no equivalent in the English legislation, suggest that in Scotland at least the phrase may have to be construed in a strict conveyancing sense and that a recordable interest will be required. The agreement must be recorded if it is to be capable of enforcement against persons deriving title to the land from the person with whom the agreement was entered into. There is, of course, no obligation to record a s.50 agreement.

It would seem, though, as we have already indicated, that a planning authority could, under other powers,[16] make a valid contract with a person who does not possess a sufficient interest in terms of s.50. Such an agreement—with, for example, a person who is interested in the development of land but who has not yet acquired title to it[17]—will bind the individual but would not be binding upon the land.

A person with a sufficient interest can, of course, only bind his own interest. A landlord cannot, for example, burden a tenant's interest (unless there is some provision to that effect in the lease). It appears, therefore, that the planning authority will have to make sure that any person with whom they propose to enter into an agreement under s.50 has the necessary capacity to do so. They will have to investigate the title and they will have to consider whether, in order to ensure that the agreement is effective, other parties with different interests in the land need to be joined.[18]

If an obligation affecting land is to be effective in the short term as well as in the longer term, then it may be that all persons who currently have some interest in the land should be joined as parties to the agreement, including those with interests which are incapable of binding the land. If the latter were omitted, they might be able to ignore the agreement for as long as their interest subsists. It may be necessary for the planning authority to employ other powers to achieve the desired effect.

Subsection (2) of s.50 provides that:

' . . . no such agreement shall at any time be enforceable against a third party who shall have in bona fide onerously acquired right (whether completed by infeftment or not) to the land prior to the agreement being recorded as aforesaid or against any person deriving title from such third party.'

---

[15]   [1983] Q.B. 382.
[16]   For example, Local Government (Scotland) Act 1973, s.69.
[17]   See, for example, *Jones* v *Secretary of State for Wales* (1974) 28 P. & C.R. 280. See too *Augier* v *Secretary of State for the Environment* (1978) 38 P. & C.R. 219 (reported sub. nom. *Hildenborough Village Preservation Association* v *Secretary of State for the Environment* [1978] J.P.L. 708).
[18]   For further discussion on this point see D. Cockburn, 'Section 50 Agreements: Some Conveyancing Aspects', 1984 S.P.L.P. 38.

The meaning of the words 'bona fide' as used in this provision could be very important in a case where a landowner who had entered into a s.50 agreement proposed to dispose of the land before the agreement had been recorded. Would a purchaser acquiring the land for value be free from the obligation contained in the agreement? Subsection (2) of s.50 has not been subjected to judicial scrutiny but we would tentatively suggest that the answer to that question will simply depend on whether or not the purchaser had knowledge of the existence of the agreement. We think some support for this view can be derived from *Stodart v Dalzell*[19] and *Rodger (Builders) Ltd. v Fawdry*.[20]

'Restricting or regulating'

Subsection (1) of s.50 provides that a planning authority may enter into an agreement with any person interested in land:

> 'for the purpose of restricting or regulating the development or use of the land . . . and any such agreement may contain such incidental and consequential provisions (including provisions of a financial character) as appear to the planning authority to be necessary or expedient for the purposes of the agreement.'

The phrase 'for the purpose of restricting or regulating' the development or use of land appears to impose some limit upon the scope of agreements but it is a limit which it is difficult to define with any precision. While the words 'restricting or regulating' clearly permit the inclusion in a s.50 agreement of negative obligations—for example, provisions placing restrictions upon the use of premises—the extent to which the agreement can impose obligations of a positive nature—obligations requiring, for example, the provision of infrastructure or the allocation of land for some public purpose—is far from clear.

There has been a good deal of discussion in academic and professional texts and journals of the question of the *enforceability* of positive obligations contained in agreements made under the identical provision in the English Act,[21] but much of this discussion is not directly relevant to Scotland. In England, positive covenants imposed on a sale of land can bind the person who originally undertakes the obligation but can never, either at common law or in equity, bind his successors in title. Negative or restrictive covenants will bind successors in title in equity provided the covenants conform to certain strict requirements.[22] The wording of the provision in the English Act

---

[19] (1876) 4 R. 236 (distinguished in *Wallace v Simmers* 1960 S.C. 255).
[20] 1950 S.C. 483.
[21] See in particular J. F. Garner, 'Agreements Under Section 25' [1949] J.P.L. 628; Malcolm Grant, 'Planning by Agreement' [1975] J.P.L. 501; Michael Aves, 'Enforcing Section 52 Agreements' [1976] J.P.L. 216; John Alder, *Development Control* (Sweet and Maxwell, 1979), pp. 129–132; L. R. Tucker, 'Planning Agreements—The Twilight Zone of Ultra Vires' [1978] J.P.L. 806; and M. Loughlin, 'Planning Gain: Law, Policy and Practice' (1981) 1 Oxford Jo. of Legal Studies 61.
[22] These requirements were spelt out in *Tulk v Moxhay* (1884) 2 Ph. 774.

appears to be designed to put the planning authority notionally in a position whereby they could conform to these strict requirements and thus enforce negative or restrictive covenants through the medium of an agreement which will bind successors in title. The wording does not appear to enlarge upon the common law position so as to allow positive covenants in an agreement to bind successors in title, although that has subsequently been achieved through other legislation.[23]

So far as the law of Scotland is concerned there is no such general restriction as exists south of the border in relation to the enforcement of positive obligations relating to land. The question of the type of obligation which may validly be included in a s.50 agreement is, therefore, entirely a matter of the interpretation of the words of the statute and, in particular, of the phrase 'for the purpose of restricting or regulating'.

This is not a matter which has, so far, had to be considered by the courts[24] and all we can do is speculate as to how the provisions might be interpreted. Whether at the end of the day a judge adopts a literal or a purposive approach to the construction of the legislation, he will of necessity look fairly closely at the actual words used in the section.

It seems clear that an agreement can only be said to 'restrict' the development or use of land if it is of a negative character, in the sense that it imposes some prohibition or limitation upon what is to be done on the land or permits the doing of something subject to conditions or within certain limits.

'Regulating' presents rather more difficulty. The ordinary meaning seems to overlap with that of 'restrict'.[25] In so far as they are distinguishable, 'restrict' would seem to be concerned primarily with limiting what can be done, whereas 'regulate' is concerned with ensuring that something is done in a particular way.

However, we think it unlikely that a court would insist that every provision in an agreement must be of a restrictive or regulatory nature. It seems to us that the question that has to be asked in every case is whether the agreement, taken as a whole, could properly be said to have been made for the purpose of restricting or regulating the development or use of land. Such an approach opens the door to the inclusion in a s.50 agreement of obligations which are positive in character. 'Provided', says Grant, 'that the main clear purpose of an agreement is to restrict or regulate use or development, that purpose may be achieved through positive or negative consequential or incidental terms.'[26]

Whether, read as a whole, a particular agreement can be said to be restrictive or regulatory of the development or use of land is a question

---

[23] See s.126 of the Housing Act 1974, now superseded by s.33 of the Local Government (Miscellaneous Provisions) Act 1982; see M. Grant, *Urban Planning Law*, pp. 373 and 374.

[24] But see *Attorney-General* v *Barnes Corporation and Ranelagh Club* [1939] Ch. 110.

[25] The *Shorter Oxford English Dictionary* (1978), for example, defines 'regulate' as 'to control, govern or direct by rule or regulation; to subject to guidance or restrictions; to adjust, in respect of time, quantity, etc.'

[26] Paper presented to a conference on 6th June 1979, quoted in (1979) 251 E.G. 1262.

which will depend very largely on the terms of the agreement and generalisations on the question would appear to be unsafe. Nevertheless, we find it difficult to see how an agreement which, for example, required a developer to make what amounted to a gift of works unconnected with a development could be said to be restrictive or regulatory in nature. On the other hand, a provision in an agreement requiring a financial guarantee for the reinstatement of land would seem to come within the scope of s.50, the reinstatement of the land being the main purpose of the agreement.

Difficult questions arise in connection with agreements which impose an obligation on a developer to provide or to contribute towards the cost of providing sewers, roads, open spaces and so on generated by a proposed development. However, we think such a requirement might fairly be said to be regulatory of the development in the sense of ensuring that it meets a certain standard and that such an obligation could be described as 'incidental or consequential' on the attainment of that purpose.

Development or use of land

The object of an agreement under s.50 will be to restrict or regulate 'the development or use of land'. Research carried out in both England and Scotland[27] shows that the great majority of planning agreements are related in some way to the development control functions of planning authorities. Agreements have been used for a great variety of purposes. They have been used, for example, to duplicate or supplement conditions on planning permissions or as a substitute for such conditions, to regulate matters which could not be subject to ordinary planning control, to achieve modification or cessation of development which was originally unauthorised, to extinguish existing use rights and to transfer infrastructure costs to a developer.

It is clear that in very many cases agreements are linked in fairly direct fashion to an application for planning permission, though the subject matter of the agreement may well be something that was not included in the application for permission originally made. Planning agreements can, however, be used for wider purposes. Section 50 encompasses any development or use of land. It is, therefore, perfectly possible for an agreement to restrict or regulate matters which do not amount to 'development' within the meaning of s.19 of the 1972 Act. If, for example, a planning authority wished to ensure that a wilderness area or a mixed woodland was not lost as a result of agricultural or forestry operations (which are generally outside the scope of planning control), an agreement could provide a means of restricting or regulating such operations. However, in the absence of an application for planning permission, the authority would probably need to offer some service or financial inducement to persuade a landowner to accept such control.[28]

---

[27] J. Jowell, 'Bargaining in Development Control' [1977] J.P.L. 414; J. N. Hawke, 'Planning Agreements in Practice' [1981] J.P.L. 5 and 86; and *S.P.L.P. Occasional Paper No. 4* (above).

[28] There are, in any event, alternative and more specific powers available for securing agreement in this sort of situation; see Countryside (Scotland) Act 1967, ss.13(1) and 49A. See also the Local Government and Planning (Scotland) Act 1982, s.15.

Agreements and the planning authority's discretion

From the point of view of the planning authority, one of the attractions of planning agreements is that they enable the authority to broaden the scope of their development control powers. In particular, an agreement under s.50 can enable a planning authority to get round some of the limitations and uncertainties connected with planning conditions (see chapter 10). Planning authorities clearly have a wide discretion to enter into agreements under s.50 and a further wide discretion as to the content of any such agreement, but there are, inevitably, certain legal constraints.

In the first place, since the power to make agreements under s.50 is conferred by the planning legislation, it seems reasonable to suppose that the courts would require a planning authority to demonstrate that a s.50 agreement had been entered into for a 'planning' purpose. It is clear that the scope of the planning legislation is wide. In *Stringer* v *Minister of Housing and Local Government*[29] Cooke J. commented: 'In principle, it seems to me that any consideration which relates to the use and development of land is capable of being a planning consideration.' On this view, the requirement that an agreement must have a 'planning' purpose would not seem to impose much of a constraint. However, somewhat narrower views of the legislation's scope have sometimes been expressed.[30]

Secondly, and more significantly, if an agreement relates in some way, as the great majority do, to the exercise by a planning authority of their development control powers—for example, the granting of planning permission or the taking of enforcement action—then the agreement is likely to have to be confined to dealing with matters which can be said to be 'material planning considerations'. The reason for this is that sections 26 and 84 of the 1972 Act stipulate the matters which may be taken into account by a planning authority in determining a planning application or in deciding whether or not to take enforcement action. The principal such matters are the development plan and 'any other material considerations'. In deciding whether or not to grant permission or serve an enforcement notice the authority may well be influenced by the outcome of any negotiations over a planning agreement. Such agreements must, therefore, either be the consequence of a policy or proposal in the development plan or a 'material consideration'. If they are not, then the validity of the development control decision (although not, it would seem, the agreement) may be open to question on the ground that it has been influenced by an immaterial consideration.

Agreements which are the consequence of a policy or proposal in the development plan are exceptional at present, but a number of examples

---

[29] [1970] 1 W.L.R. 1281; see also *Westminster City Council* v *Great Portland Estates plc* [1984] 3 W.L.R. 1035, per Lord Scarman, and generally the discussion in chapter 9.

[30] See, for example, *David Lowe and Sons Ltd.* v *Musselburgh Town Council* 1973 S.C. 130; 1974 S.L.T. 5.

have been noted in England.[31] The position may change in the future as a result of the encouragement given to planning authorities in S.D.D. Circular 22/1984 to give guidance in their development plans about the circumstances in which agreements may be sought. Where a development plan contains a policy statement of this kind, then a failure to have regard to the policy when determining an application or an appeal in an appropriate case will lay the decision open to challenge.[32]

The expression 'material considerations' would appear to be narrower in scope than 'planning considerations'. In *Stringer* (above) Cooke J. said: 'Whether a particular consideration falling within that broad class [i.e. of planning considerations] is material in any given case will depend on the circumstances.' In other words, it would seem that material considerations are those considerations relating to the use and development of land which arise out of or are relevant to the matter in hand. A planning permission which was dependent on an agreement which, for example, sought to impose on a developer the cost of providing public services unrelated to his development would arguably be concerning itself with something that was not a material consideration.

Equally, the planning authority will have to ensure that the advantages they envisage arising from an agreement do not cause them to ignore other relevant considerations. Failure in this respect will also lay their decision on the planning application open to challenge.[33]

It would seem that if the parties to a planning appeal indicate their willingness to enter into an agreement, that is a matter which the Secretary of State will have to take into account in reaching his decision.[34]

Agreements and the fettering of powers

We mentioned earlier that a public authority cannot disable itself by contract from exercising its powers and from performing its statutory duties.[35] For example, in *Stringer* (above) an undertaking given by a planning authority to Manchester University to the effect that they would discourage development which might prejudice the operation of the Jodrell Bank telescope was held by Cooke J. to be inconsistent with the proper

---

[31] See, for example, M. Grant, 'Developers' Contributions and Planning Gain: Ethics and Legalities' [1978] J.P.L. 8; M. Loughlin, 'Planning Gain: Law, Policy and Practice' (1981) 1 Oxford Jo. of Legal Studies 61; and *Planning Gain* (Report of the Property Advisory Group, H.M.S.O., 1981).

[32] *Richmond upon Thames L.B.C.* v *Secretary of State for the Environment* [1984] J.P.L. 24.

[33] See, for example, *J. J. Steeples* v *Derbyshire County Council* [1985] 1 W.L.R. 526. Contrast *R.* v *Sevenoaks District Council, ex parte W. J. Terry* [1984] J.P.L. 420.

[34] See *McLaren* v *Secretary of State for the Environment* [1981] J.P.L. 423. Compare, however, *Tarmac Properties* v *Secretary of State for Wales* (1977) 33 P. & C.R. 103 in which it was held that the Secretary of State had not acted unreasonably in not taking into account an agreement which had been drafted but never executed by the parties.

[35] For discussion of the application of this doctrine see E. Young and J. Rowan-Robinson, 'Section 52 Agreements and the Fettering of Powers' [1982] J.P.L. 673 and the texts and articles cited in that article. See too *R.* v *Sevenoaks District Council, ex parte W. J. Terry* [1984] J.P.L. 420.

performance of the authority's statutory duties. The effect of the agreement was to bind the authority to disregard considerations relevant to a planning application, considerations which, under the planning legislation, the authority were obliged to take into account.

The presumption underlying the decision in *Stringer* is that Parliament cannot have intended that authorities should be able, by agreement, to disable themselves from carrying out their statutory responsibilities. If, however, Parliament manifests an intention that authorities should be able to bind themselves in particular ways, there is, of course, no place for the operation of such a presumption. As regards planning agreements, it can be argued that such a manifestation of Parliamentary intention appears in subsection (3) of s.50. That subsection is somewhat obscurely worded but it would seem that it is intended to preserve the exercise of any planning powers in accordance with the provisions of the development plan or in accordance with any direction given by the Secretary of State as regards matters to be included in such a plan, notwithstanding anything to the contrary contained in an agreement.[36] Put another way, subsection (3) would seem to mean that an authority may by agreement pre-determine the way in which it will exercise a particular power—for example, the determination of a planning application or a decision on enforcement action—but such an agreement will not bind the authority if it requires an exercise of power contrary to the provisions of the development plan or of a direction by the Secretary of State.

The corresponding subsection in the English Act of 1971 came under judicial scrutiny in *Windsor and Maidenhead Royal Borough Council* v *Brandrose Investments*.[37] In that case, a planning authority, in accordance with an agreement made under s.52 of the Town and Country Planning Act 1971, granted planning permission for the redevelopment of a site. The development necessarily involved the demolition of buildings on the site. Before demolition of these buildings took place, the planning authority decided to extend an existing conservation area in such a way that it included the development site. One effect of the designation of an area as a conservation area is that the consent of the planning authority is required for the demolition of any buildings in the area. When the developers began to demolish buildings on the development site, the planning authority sought an injunction to restrain them from doing so. The main issue before the court was whether the authority could lawfully enter into an agreement which would operate so as to exclude the exercise of the authority's statutory powers to prevent the demolition of buildings on the site.

Fox J., at first instance, held that an agreement under s.52 could validly fetter such powers. There was, he said, 'nothing in principle to prevent the exercise of a statutory power being limited by the previous exercise of

---

[36] For an account of the origins of the equivalent provision in the English legislation see Malcolm Grant, *Urban Planning Law*, p. 368.

[37] [1981] 1 W.L.R. 1083; [1983] 1 W.L.R. 509 (C.A.); and see the comment on the Court of Appeal decision at 1983 S.P.L.P. 52; also Malcolm Grant, 'The Planning After Effects of the Brandrose Litigation', *Local Government Chronicle*, 15th July 1983, p. 768.

another statutory power'. This was the effect of the s.52 agreement and the planning authority were, accordingly, not entitled to use their statutory powers to prevent such demolition.

The Court of Appeal held, however, that local planning authorities were not empowered to inhibit themselves by agreement from including land in a conservation area or from requiring consent for the demolition of buildings in such an area. In the court's judgment subsection (3) could not be construed 'as restricting the exercise by a local planning authority of any of their statutory powers which they have a public duty to exercise'.

It seems clear that the Court of Appeal considered that an authority cannot restrict the exercise of positive *duties* imposed upon them by statute. It is not clear, however, whether it was also the court's view that authorities are prohibited from fettering the future exercise of mere *powers*.[38] It is of course the case that duties cannot always be readily distinguished from mere powers—in the context of the present case, for example, there is inherent in the 'duty' as to the designation of conservation areas a large area of discretion on the part of the planning authority—but if the Court of Appeal's judgment is read as implying that planning authorities cannot fetter their powers, subsection (3) would appear to be completely redundant. The court did not, however, address itself to the important and difficult question of what the subsection means, confining itself to saying that 'whatever s.52(3) means' (and on that matter the court shared, it was said the 'bemusement' of counsel), the subsection did not empower authorities to restrict their powers relating to demolition of buildings in a conservation area.

Variation and termination of s.50 agreements[39]

Section 50(1) states that agreements may be entered into 'either permanently or during such period as may be prescribed by the agreement'.

The agreement itself may provide for its termination either after a prescribed period or after the carrying out of specified works. It may sometimes be implicit that the agreement is to end after certain works have been carried out.

An agreement may become less relevant with the passage of time. For example, planning policies may change, there may be a change of circumstances, or the planning permission to which the agreement is related may be revoked. It may be desirable to make provision in the agreement for revocation or modification of the agreement in such circumstances. The parties can of course agree to a revocation or modification at any time.

In England and Wales, an application can be made to the Lands Tribunal under s.54 of the Law of Property Act 1925 for the variation or discharge of a covenant contained in an agreement made under s.52 of the Town and Country Planning Act 1971.[40] We are doubtful, however, about the

---

[38] For further discussion of this point see the article cited in n.35.
[39] See 'Section 50 Agreements. Report by Society of Directors of Administration', 1984 S.P.L.P. 40.
[40] See *Gee* v *National Trust* [1966] 2 W.L.R. 170; *Re Beecham Group Ltd's Application* (1980) 256 E.G. 829; and *Re Bovis Homes Southern Ltd's Application* [1981] J.P.L. 368.

competence of an application to the Lands Tribunal for Scotland for the variation or discharge of obligations imposed by an agreement under s.50 of the 1972 Act. Such an application would need to be made under s.1 of the Conveyancing and Feudal Reform (Scotland) Act 1970 which is concerned with the variation and discharge of land obligations. We do not consider that an obligation imposed by a s.50 agreement falls within the definition of a 'land obligation' in s.1(2) of the 1970 Act.

CHAPTER 13

THE ENFORCEMENT OF PLANNING CONTROL

Introduction

There is not much point in having a sophisticated system for controlling development unless there are effective provisions for enforcing control. Part V of the 1972 Act provides the machinery for enforcement.

The present chapter is primarily concerned with those provisions of Part V which deal with the enforcement of control over development which has been carried out without planning permission or in contravention of a condition or limitation attached to a grant of planning permission.[1] The remaining provisions of Part V, which relate to the enforcement of control in relation to listed buildings, trees, advertisements and orders under s.49 of the 1972 Act, are summarised in the chapters dealing with those matters.

In 1975 Dobry commented that: 'Over the years, enforcement, because of legal technicalities involved, has probably been the weakest link in the planning control system.'[2] Dobry's comment was directed at the position in England but since 1969, apart from a tendency to lag about a year behind with legislative changes, the law relating to enforcement has been broadly the same in Scotland.[3] The provisions of Part V of the 1972 Act have twice been amended (by the Town and Country Planning (Scotland) Act 1977 ('the 1977 Act') and the Local Government and Planning (Scotland) Act 1982 ('the 1982 Act')) in an effort to overcome some of the weaknesses highlighted by Dobry and others.[4] These changes, together with the less strict approach to the construction of enforcement notices adopted by the English courts,[5] may have gone a little way towards reducing the technical complexity of this area of planning law but it is doubtful if they have done much to reduce the cumbersome and time-consuming nature of the enforcement process.

---

[1] This chapter is almost entirely concerned with law and procedure. The results of a study of enforcement practice in Scotland are contained in J. Rowan-Robinson, E. Young and I. McLarty, *The Enforcement of Planning Control in Scotland* (S.D.D., 1984). See too T. Ramsay and E. Young (eds.), *Enforcement of Planning Control: Law and Practice* (University of Strathclyde, 1980).

[2] G. Dobry Q.C., *Review of the Development Control System: Final Report* (H.M.S.O., 1975).

[3] The Scottish legislation does, however, differ on numerous matters of detail from that applying in England and Wales.

[4] See, for example, 1981 S.P.L.P. 89.

[5] See, for example, *Miller-Mead v Minister of Housing and Local Government* [1963] 2 Q.B. 196, per Lord Denning M.R.; and *Eldon Garages Ltd.* v *Kingston-Upon-Hull County Borough Council* [1974] 1 W.L.R. 276, per Templeman J.

A. TAKING ENFORCEMENT ACTION

Power to serve an enforcement notice

A breach of planning control may take one of three forms:

(i) an unauthorised operation;
(ii) an unauthorised material change of use;
(iii) a breach of a condition or limitation subject to which planning permission has been granted.

Although a breach of planning control is unlawful,[6] it is not, of itself, a criminal offence.[7] Instead, s.84 of the 1972 Act provides that, where it appears[8] to a planning authority that a breach of planning control has occurred since 1964, then they may serve what is termed an 'enforcement notice' requiring the breach to be remedied. Contravention of the terms of an effective enforcement notice may result in sanctions, including in some cases prosecution.

The bodies primarily responsible for the enforcement of planning control are the district and general planning authorities.[9] However, regional planning authorities may, after consultation with the appropriate district planning authority, serve an enforcement notice in respect of a breach of control which in their opinion materially prejudices an approved structure plan.[10] If, after consultation with the appropriate planning authority, the Secretary of State considers it expedient to do so, he may himself serve an enforcement notice (s.260(5)).

There is no obligation on a planning authority to serve an enforcement notice in respect of a breach of control; subject to what is said below, they have a discretion, and a refusal to take enforcement action will normally be unchallengeable.[11] The authority may, for example, decide that they have no

---

[6] Section 20(1) of the 1972 Act requires planning permission to be obtained for the development of land.

[7] Contrast the situation where there has been an infringement of listed building control (s.53 of the 1972 Act).

[8] It is enough that a *prima facie* case exists—see *Miller-Mead* v *Minister of Housing and Local Government* [1963] 2 Q.B. 196; see also *Jeary* v *Chailey R.D.C.* (1973) 26 P. & C.R. 280. The planning authority are under no obligation to satisfy themselves prior to serving an enforcement notice that the development in question is not permitted by the G.D.O.; they are entitled to serve an enforcement notice on the basis that no planning permission has been granted, leaving it to the developer to establish, if he can, that the development is outwith control—see *Tidswell* v *Secretary of State for the Environment* (1976) 34 P. & C.R. 152.

[9] Where service of an enforcement notice was authorised by the chairman of an authority's planning committee, the Secretary of State for the Environment took the view that the notice was a nullity in that a planning authority cannot delegate their powers to a single member—see [1982] J.P.L. 48 and [1983] J.P.L. 323.

[10] 1972 Act, s.84A (added by s.43 of the 1982 Act).

[11] See *Perry* v *Stanborough (Developments) Ltd.* (1977) 244 E.G. 551. However, in *Davy* v *Spelthorne Borough Council* [1984] A.C. 262 Lord Fraser doubted if it would be proper for a planning authority to allow their decision on whether to take enforcement action to be influenced by the threat of a possible action for damages. And see *R.* v *Stroud District*

objection to the unauthorised development and that enforcement action should not be taken.[12] Where, however, an authority consider that they would be likely to grant planning permission for an apparently unauthorised development, S.D.D. Circular 33/1983 recommends that the authority should notify the developer of the apparent breach (which might create difficulties in connection with disposal of the land), invite him to submit a planning application, and, if he declines to do so, warn him that the development will remain at risk of enforcement action.

The planning authority may be content with an unauthorised development only if certain changes are made or if it is subjected to certain conditions; this may result in negotiations between the developer and the planning authority leading to a retrospective grant of planning permission. However, the planning authority may, 'if they consider it expedient to do so having regard to the provisions of the development plan and to any other material considerations',[13] serve an enforcement notice. The reference to 'the provisions of the development plan and to any other material considerations' emphasises that a decision to serve such a notice must be prompted solely by planning considerations and not by a desire to penalise a developer for contravening the law. If, in deciding to serve an enforcement notice, the planning authority take account of irrelevant factors or fail to take account of relevant factors then the notice will be *ultra vires* and a nullity (see p. 339 below).

Although the power to take enforcement action is discretionary, the exercise of discretion is restricted in three ways. First, the planning authority may bind themselves by an agreement under s.50 of the 1972 Act not to exercise their enforcement powers or to exercise them in a certain way.[14] Secondly, if action which constitutes a breach of planning control has been taken on the strength of informal or erroneous assurances given on behalf of the planning authority, the authority may in certain limited circumstances be barred from serving an enforcement notice in respect of that breach (see p. 34 above). Thirdly, any breach of planning control which took place

---

Council, ex. p. Goodenough (1980) 43 P. & C.R. 59 (see p. 444 below). In *Costello* v *Dacorum District Council* (1983) 81 L.G.R. 1 the Court of Appeal held it was not an abuse of their powers for a planning authority to acquire land in order, *inter alia*, to put an end to a use for which the Secretary of State had on appeal granted temporary planning permission.

[12] It is not uncommon for members of the public to seek to persuade an authority to take enforcement action. Failure to act, or a delay in taking action, may result in a complaint of maladministration to the Commissioner for Local Administration in Scotland—see C. M. G. Himsworth, 'Failure to Take Enforcement Action' 1981 S.P.L.P. 56.

[13] The phrase 'having regard to the provisions of the development plan and to any other material considerations' is discussed in chapter 9 above. Where, at the time of service, an enforcement notice was not authorised by the local planning authority, the Secretary of State for the Environment took the view that the notice, though subsequently ratified by the authority, was a nullity in that the authority could not at the date of service have considered it expedient to take action—see [1977] J.P.L. 604. Cf. planning appeal reported in [1980] J.P.L. 618.

[14] See chapter 12 above. See, however, *Windsor and Maidenhead Royal Borough Council* v *Brandrose Investments Ltd.* [1983] 1 W.L.R. 509.

before the end of 1964 is immune from enforcement action and certain types of breach become immune from enforcement action four years after the occurrence of the breach (see p. 310 below).

There is nothing to prevent a planning authority taking enforcement action while an appeal against a refusal of planning permission is pending.[15]

Entry and information

If a planning authority believe that a breach of planning control has occurred, they will, before embarking upon formal enforcement action, wish to ensure that they are in possession of as much information as possible as to the activities carried on upon the land in question and as to the persons having an interest in the land. Section 265 of the 1972 Act allows a person duly authorised in writing by the planning authority to enter upon land for the purpose of surveying it in connection with the service of an enforcement notice. Admission to occupied land cannot, however, be demanded as of right unless twenty-four hours notice has been given (s.266). In addition, s.270 of the 1972 Act[16] empowers an authority to serve a notice on the occupier of land, or on a person in receipt of rent from the land, requiring him to state the nature of his interest in the land, the name and address of any other person known to him as having an interest in the land,[17] and details of the purposes for which the land is currently being used. Failure to respond to the notice or knowingly to make a mis-statement in response to the notice is a criminal offence. However, a planning authority may still have difficulty in ascertaining the planning history of a site; unlike the corresponding English provision,[18] s.270 of the 1972 Act does not allow for inquiry as to the time when uses or activities being carried on upon the site began.

Service of an enforcement notice

An enforcement notice is to be served on the owner, lessee and occupier of the land to which it relates, and on any other person having an interest in that land if, in the authority's opinion, that interest is materially affected by the notice[19] (s.84(5)). Service is to be effected by service of a copy of the notice

---

[15]   See *Davis* v *Miller* [1956] 1 W.L.R. 1013.

[16]   As amended by s.5(4) of the 1977 Act.

[17]   The decision in *McDaid* v *Clydebank District Council* 1984 S.L.T. 162 (below) demonstrates how important this information can be to the planning authority.

[18]   See s.284(1A) of the Town and Country Planning Act 1971 (added by s.3 of the Town and Country Planning (Amendment) Act 1977).

[19]   'Interest' probably means a legal interest of some sort in the land—see *Stevens* v *Bromley London Borough Council* [1972] Ch. 400, per Salmon L.J.; and appeal decision reported in [1976] J.P.L. 113. See too [1983] J.P.L. 826. In a case where there had been a failure to serve an enforcement notice on heritable creditors, the reporter was not satisfied that the creditors' interest was materially affected by the notice—see *SPADS* No. A2194 (P/ENA/GLW/54,58–62, 18th December 1976).

on each such person.[20] This makes it clear that there is only one notice in respect of a breach of control but that copies of it must be served on each person with an interest in the land.[21] Where there are several such persons, the notice need not be served on each of them on the same day but it cannot take effect until a period of not less than twenty-eight days has elapsed from the date on which the last person is served (see p. 306 below).[22]

The statutory requirements may well mean that an enforcement notice has to be served on a person who is not responsible for the breach. As was said by the reporter in one appeal: 'The Act does not make provision for apportioning blame or the cost of complying with the requirements of an enforcement notice.'[23]

Difficult questions can arise as regards the definition of 'occupier' for the purposes of s.84(5). In *Stevens* v *London Borough of Bromley*[24] a majority of the Court of Appeal took the view that it is in each case a question of fact and degree whether a licensee, such as a person permitted to station a caravan on land, is an 'occupier' for the purpose of the statutory requirement as to service of an enforcedment notice;[25] in that case the court held (distinguishing *Munnich* v *Godstone R.D.C.*[26]) that where the owner of a caravan had, under a licence from the owner of the land, stationed the caravan on a site, had used it as a permanent home for some seven months, and appeared 'to have exercised a degree of control on the site indistinguishable from that of a tenant', he was in all the circumstances an occupier of the land in the sense of the statute and was therefore entitled to be served with an enforcement notice relating to the land.

In *Scarborough Borough Council* v *Adams*[27] Watkins L.J. concluded that in view of the length of time and the exclusive nature of their occupation, mere squatters were, in the circumstances of the case, 'occupiers' for the purposes of the planning legislation. In that case it was held that so far as service of an enforcement notice was concerned it was irrelevant and had no effect on the validity of the notice that the recipients were described as

---

[20] See 1972 Act, s.84(5A) (added by 1982 Act, s.48 and Schedule 2, para. 19(b)). S.D.D. Circular 6/1984 states that the Secretary of State considers that, in order to meet the requirements of s.84(5A), the planning authority should prepare a properly authorised document for retention in their records; copies of that document should be served on the specified parties. Section 269 of the 1972 Act sets out the ways in which service may be effected; see too *Hammersmith London Borough Council* v *Winner Investments* (1968) 20 P. & C.R. 971; *Moody* v *Godstone R.D.C.* [1966] 1 W.L.R. 1085; *Hewitt* v *Leicester Corporation* [1969] 1 W.L.R. 855; and appeal decision reported at [1979] J.P.L. 693.

[21] This would seem to overcome the difficulty that occurred in *Skinner and King* v *Secretary of State for the Environment* [1978] J.P.L. 842.

[22] 1972 Act, s.84(9) (substituted by 1982 Act, s.48 and Schedule 2, para. 19(d)). This overcomes the difficulty encountered in *Bambury* v *London Borough of Hounslow* [1966] 2 Q.B. 204. The notice will take effect on the same date for all persons served.

[23] *SPADS* No. A3815 (P/ENA/SC/18, 15th July 1981).

[24] [1972] Ch. 400. See too ministerial decision noted in [1976] J.P.L. 113.

[25] It may be noted, however, that the English statute does not specifically mention service on a lessee.

[26] [1966] 1 W.L.R. 427.

[27] (1983) 47 P. & C.R. 133. See too *SPADS* No. A2384 (P/ENA/FB/5, 30th June 1977).

'occupiers' even if they were only trespassers. In considering what the word 'occupier' means for the purposes of the planning legislation it is doubtful whether much assistance is to be derived from decisions on the meaning of the word in other branches of the law.[28]

The fact that the legislation requires service on certain classes of people does not preclude the planning authority serving notice on someone who does not belong to those classes.[29]

Section 85(1)(e) of the 1972 Act provides that any person on whom an enforcement notice is served or any other person with an interest in the land may appeal to the Secretary of State on the ground that the notice was not served as required by s.84(5) (see p. 324 below). In terms of s.85(10) of the 1972 Act, the validity of an enforcement notice 'shall not, except by way of appeal [to the Secretary of State], be questioned in any proceedings whatsoever' on grounds which include that specified in s.85(1)(e), relating to a failure in service.

The effect of these provisions was considered in *McDaid* v *Clydebank District Council*.[30] In that case the planning authority served three enforcement notices on the occupier of land but omitted to serve the owners. The occupier failed to appeal against the notices and the owners did not become aware of the notices until after the time for appeal to the Secretary of State had expired. The owners petitioned the Court of Session for suspension of the notices and for interdict prohibiting the authority taking action on the notices. The Lord Ordinary (Lord Allanbridge) refused the petition on the ground that s.85(10) excluded the court's jurisdiction.

However, on appeal, the First Division held that the court's powers were not excluded by s.85(10) and that as the enforcement notices had not been properly served, they were nullities. This was not, said Lord Cameron, 'a mere error in the manner or requirements of service; so far as the petitioners are concerned there was no service on them at all'. Since the notice was lacking 'an essential element',[31] it was 'not such a notice as the statute required and thus a nullity'. The petitioners had lost their right of appeal as a result of a breach of precise obligations laid on the planning authority and the authority ought not to be entitled, the court thought, to take advantage of their failure to comply with the legislation. While it is easy to appreciate the potential injustice to the owners which led the court to this decision, justice may have been bought at the price of certainty; it is possible that an enforcement notice might be challenged on such grounds years after the event.

Section 85(4)(b) of the 1972 Act provides that in a case where it would otherwise be a ground for determining an appeal against an enforcement

---

[28]   See *Caravans and Automobiles Ltd.* v *Southall Borough Council* [1963] 1 W.L.R. 690, per Lord Parker C.J.

[29]   See *Scarborough Borough Council* (above).

[30]   1984 S.L.T. 162.

[31]   It may be noted that in *Scarborough Borough Council* v *Adams* (above) Watkins L.J. said that the legislation makes it 'imperative' that the planning authority serve notice on certain classes of people.

notice in favour of an appellant that a person required by s.84(5) to be served with the notice was not served, the Secretary of State (or appointed person) may disregard that fact if neither the appellant nor that person has been substantially prejudiced by the failure to serve him. This is a power which has been frequently exercised. For example, in an appeal against an enforcement notice which had been served on the landowner's husband but not on the owner herself, the reporter considered that he would be justified in disregarding the failure in that he was satisfied that neither husband nor wife had been substantially prejudiced by the failure.[32]

However, in view of the decision in *McDaid* (above), the scope of the power conferred by s.85(4)(b) may be much narrower than was previously thought. In that case Lord Cameron said that the statutory provisions allowing the Secretary of State to disregard a failure in service 'are merely expository of the powers of the Secretary of State in dealing with an appeal competently before him, but are quite irrelevant to the case of a person entitled to receive service but on whom no notice has been served'.

The planning authority may withdraw an enforcement notice at any time before it takes effect; for example, it may have come to their notice that the breach of control is immune from enforcement action or that the notice has been wrongly served. Notice of the withdrawal must be given to every person who was served with the enforcement notice (s.84(10)). Any such withdrawal does not prevent the authority serving a fresh enforcement notice in respect of the breach of control. A second enforcement notice can, it seems, be served before the first has become effective.[33]

Where an enforcement notice is a nullity or is quashed for material error there would seem to be nothing to prevent a planning authority from serving a fresh enforcement notice in respect of the breach of control unless in the meantime the breach has become immune from enforcement action under one of the 'limitation periods'.

The content of an enforcement notice

There is no prescribed form of notice but a model form is attached to S.D.D. Circular 6/1984. In terms of the 1972 Act (as amended) an enforcement notice must specify certain matters. These are:

1. the matters alleged to constitute a breach of planning control (s.84(7));
2. the steps required to be taken to restore the land to its condition before the breach took place; the notice may also specify, as an alternative, the

---

[32] *SPADS* No. A3735 (P/ENA/TB/10, 20th May 1981). For examples of appeals in which the exercise of this power was considered see *SPADS* Nos. A2183 (P/ENA/D/1 and 2, 8th October 1976); A2186 (P/ENA/LA/1, 12th October 1976); A3193 (P/ENA/LB/14, 16th November 1979); A3208 (P/ENA/HF/19 and 20, 14th December 1979); [1973] J.P.L. 381; [1974] J.P.L. 41 and 248; [1975] J.P.L. 230; [1976] J.P.L. 710; [1979] J.P.L. 403, 693 and 701; [1981] J.P.L. 382; and [1983] J.P.L. 271; and *Selected Enforcement and Allied Appeals*, pp. 18–22. See too *Skinner and King v Secretary of State for the Environment* [1978] J.P.L. 842.

[33] See *Edwick v Sunbury-on-Thames U.D.C. (No. 2)* (1965) 17 P. & C.R. 1.

steps required to bring the land to a condition acceptable to the planning authority (s.84(7)[34]);

3. the date on which the notice is to take effect (s.84(9)[35]);

4. the period or periods within which any steps specified are to be carried out (s.84(7A)(a)[36]);

5. the precise boundaries of the land to which the notice relates;[37]

6. the reasons why the authority consider it expedient to serve an enforcement notice;[37] and

7. an explanation of the rights of persons to appeal against the enforcement notice.[37]

Each of these matters is considered below.

Since 1947 there has been much litigation about the way in which the prescribed matters should be dealt with in enforcement notices and in several decisions under the Town and Country Planning Act 1947 the English courts adopted a very strict approach.[38] However, the substantial amendments to the English legislation on enforcement notices which were effected in 1960 (similar changes in the Scottish legislation being made in 1969) were such that Lord Denning was able to say in *Miller-Mead* v *Minister of Housing and Local Government*[39] that the legislature had 'disposed of the proposition that there must be a strict and rigid adherence to formalities'. It is only, he said, if an 'informality, defect or error is a material one', that is, only if it is 'such as to produce injustice', that an enforcement notice should be quashed; a defect which 'does not go to the substance of the matter' can be corrected by the Secretary of State (see p. 328 below). In the same case Upjohn L.J. said that an inaccuracy or misrecital will not of itself make an enforcement notice bad, provided that the notice tells the recipient fairly 'what he has done wrong and what he must do to remedy it'.

The test propounded by Upjohn L.J. in *Miller-Mead* was approved by the Court of Appeal in *Munnich* v *Godstone R.D.C.*,[40] and has been applied in a number of English cases.[41]

In *Ormston* v *Horsham R.D.C.*,[42] for example, the Court of Appeal held that a notice which required the restoration of land to its condition before

---

[34] The alternative was added by the 1982 Act, s.48 and Schedule 2, para. 19(c).
[35] As substituted by the 1982 Act, s.48 and Schedule 2, para. 19(d).
[36] As substituted by the 1982 Act, s.48 and Schedule 2, para. 19(c).
[37] See 1972 Act, s.84(7A) and (12) (added by 1982 Act, s.48 and Schedule 2, paras. 19(c) and (e)); and the Town and Country Planning (Enforcement of Control) (Scotland) Regulations 1984.
[38] See, for example, *Francis* v *Yiewsley and West Drayton U.D.C.* [1958] 1 Q.B. 478; and *Cater* v *Essex County Council* [1960] 1 Q.B. 424.
[39] [1963] 2 Q.B. 196.
[40] [1966] 1 W.L.R. 427.
[41] See, in particular, *London Borough of Hounslow* v *Secretary of State for the Environment* [1981] J.P.L. 510, per Ackner L.J. See also *Watford Borough Council* v *Secretary of State for the Environment* [1982] J.P.L. 518; *Curtis* v *David O'Morgan* [1982] J.P.L. 581; and *Ormston* v *Horsham R.D.C.* (1965) 17 P. & C.R. 105.
[42] (1965) 17 P. & C.R. 105.

unauthorised development took place but did not specify the land's condition prior to the development was sufficiently certain. The owner knew what the site was like before he began the development and could therefore restore it accordingly. In *Bath City Council* v *Secretary of State for the Environment*[43] it was held (in the context of a listed building enforcement notice) that there would be nothing uncertain in a requirement to restore the roof of a building to its condition prior to the carrying out of unauthorised works. Woolf J. said that it would not be open to the landowner in such a case to say that he could not remember the precise state of the roof at the appropriate time; in such circumstances it may, he said, be an indirect consequence of unauthorised development that the person who carried out the works has to carry out more work to comply with an enforcement notice than is strictly required by the notice, but that would not be a ground for challenging the validity of the notice—the person who carried out the unauthorised works should be in the best position to know what steps are required to rectify the breach and if he does not know, he cannot complain if it means he has to do more work than would otherwise be necessary.

However, it seems that a somewhat stricter test may still apply in Scotland. In *McNaughton* v *Peter McIntyre (Clyde) Ltd.*[44] the High Court of Justiciary stated that 'a notice should be precise so that a person on whom a notice is served knows exactly what he should do.' The court held that a notice which required the removal of 'stone, rubble, timber and metal objects and other material on land namely the foreshore *ex adverso* the boatyard occupied by you . . .' was bad for lack of specification. The land in question had been used since 1938 as part of the boatyard and quantities of stone and rubble had from time to time been deposited for the maintenance of slipways and the provision of an area of hardstanding and for their protection against erosion by the sea. Against that physical background it was quite impossible to know what had to be removed. Furthermore, the court refused to accept that the notice could be saved by the state of knowledge of the recipients, saying that 'this suggestion fails to meet the criticism that the complaint and the enforcement notice themselves should state clearly and in precise terms what is to be done and what should have been done in terms of the enforcement notice. Section 86 [of the 1972 Act] is a penal section which prescribes penalties for non-compliance with enforcement notices. Persons and companies, like the respondents who are exposed to penal consequences are entitled to know, precisely and unambiguously, from the notice and the complaint what they are required to do and why they are required to do it if they are to avoid penal consequences.'

The judgment in *McNaughton* makes no mention of the test propounded in *Miller-Mead*. It is difficult to know, therefore, whether it should be viewed as requiring a greater measure of formality in the way in which the prescribed matters are to be dealt with in enforcement notices in Scotland or

---

[43] (1983) 47 P. & C.R. 663. See too *Eldon Garages Ltd.* v *Kingston-Upon-Hull County Borough Council* [1974] 1 W.L.R. 276, per Templeman J.

[44] High Court of Justiciary, 21st March 1978 (unreported, but see 1981 S.P.L.P. 15).

298 SCOTTISH PLANNING LAW AND PROCEDURE

whether it should be treated as an example of a notice so lacking in specification that it failed to tell the recipient fairly what he had done wrong and what he had to do to remedy the breach. The facts of the case would seem to support the latter view. An enforcement notice which is so uncertain that the recipient cannot tell what steps he has to take to comply with it is a nullity and in these circumstances the recipient's state of knowledge is immaterial. The distinctions between notices which are nullities, those which must be quashed and those which may be corrected or varied are discussed more fully later in this chapter.

Whatever view is taken of the decision in *McNaughton*, there is no doubt that an enforcement notice must, at the very least, tell the recipient fairly what he has done wrong and what he must do to remedy the breach.[45] The application of this test is now considered in more detail in the context of the several matters which the notice must specify.

1. *Matters alleged to constitute a breach of control*

An enforcement notice must specify the matters alleged to constitute a breach of planning control (s.84(7)(a)).

It is probably still the case that the notice must make clear which of two types of breach of planning control is alleged; the notice must allege either that development has been carried out without a grant of planning permission or that there has been a breach of a condition subject to which planning permission was granted. If the notice alleges one of these two types of development when it should have alleged the other it will be quashed. In *Kerrier District Council* v *Secretary of State for the Environment*[46] Lord Lane C.J. said:

'It is clearly established by many decisions that, if a planning authority wishes to serve an enforcement notice, it must decide whether the breach alleged is development without planning permission or failure to comply with some condition or limitation. If, on the facts of any particular case, the planning authority puts the case in the wrong pigeon-hole, the enforcement notice will be set aside.'

In allocating the breach of control to the appropriate 'pigeon-hole' it is not necessary to incorporate the actual words used in the legislation. On the

---

[45] *Miller-Mead* v *Minister of Housing and Local Government* [1963] 2 Q.B. 196, per Upjohn L.J.
[46] (1980) 41 P. & C.R. 284. See also *East Riding County Council* v *Park Estates (Bridlington) Ltd.* [1957] A.C. 223; *Francis* v *Yiewsley and West Drayton U.D.C.* [1958] 1 Q.B. 478; *Miller-Mead* v *Minister of Housing and Local Government* [1963] 2 Q.B. 196; and *Eldon Garages Ltd.* v *Kingston-Upon-Hull County Borough Council* [1974] 1 W.L.R. 276. Cf. *Garland* v *Minister of Housing and Local Government* (1968) 20 P. & C.R. 93, per Lord Denning M.R.; *Pilkington* v *Secretary of State for the Environment* [1973] 1 W.L.R. 1527, per Lord Widgery C.J.; *Rochdale Metropolitan Borough Council* v *Simmonds* (1980) 40 P. & C.R. 432 (in which the Divisional Court rejected this argument but was apparently not referred to the earlier decisions); and *SPADS* No. A3268 (P/ENA/CB/23 and 24, 3rd March 1980).

other hand, it is unlikely to be sufficient merely to state the facts alleged to constitute the breach of control. In *Eldon Garages Ltd.* v *Kingston-Upon-Hull County Borough Council*[47] Templeman J. said:

'Facts can only constitute a breach if either, firstly, they amount to development without the grant of planning permission, or, secondly, they amount to a breach of condition. In my judgment, construing the Act simply as it stands, the notice must make clear whether the authority is alleging that the recipient is guilty of development without planning permission or guilty of a breach of a condition subject to which planning permission was granted.'

The decision of the Divisional Court in *Rochdale Metropolitan Borough Council* v *Simmonds*[48] suggests that there may be sufficient compliance with the requirement if the nature of the breach of control can be discovered by implication from the notice as a whole.

Selecting the correct 'pigeon-hole' will not always be easy. In *Kerrier District Council* (above), for example, planning permission was granted for the erection of a bungalow subject to a condition restricting the occupation of the dwelling to persons employed in agriculture. The bungalow when built was occupied by people who were not 'agricultural workers' within the meaning of the condition. The planning authority served an enforcement notice on the occupiers alleging a breach of the condition. On appeal, the Secretary of State found that the bungalow as built differed materially from that which had been approved. It included a basement not shown on the plans attached to the grant of planning permission. The minister therefore concluded that the bungalow had been built without planning permission and that, as the planning permission which had been granted had not been implemented, there could be no question of a breach of condition; the enforcement notice would have to be quashed as it alleged the wrong type of breach. The Divisional Court took a different view. They considered that without the grant of planning permission the bungalow would never have been built. 'Having relied on the permission to build a house, it would seem strange that the occupiers should not be bound by the condition, particularly if it was by reason of their own default that the plans were not complied with. If the house had complied with the plans, the occupiers would have been bound by the condition. They can hardly be in a better position because the house did not comply with the plans.'

The decision in *Kerrier District Council* suggests that development carried out on the strength of a grant of planning permission will bring any conditions into operation and allow for their enforcement notwithstanding that the development departs in a material way from the grant of permission. Donaldson L.J. reached a similar conclusion in *J. Toomey Motors Ltd.* v

[47] [1974] 1 W.L.R. 276.
[48] (1980) 40 P. & C.R. 432.

Secretary of State for the Environment.[49] He did not think 'that it was possible to repudiate a permission, where one was doing that which one had been given planning permission to do, and there was no other basis upon which one could do it'.

There will, of course, be cases where the development being carried on departs to such an extent from any grant of planning permission that it will, as a matter of fact and degree, have to be treated as development without planning permission rather than as a breach of condition.

In *Hilliard* v *Secretary of State for the Environment*,[50] the Divisional Court accepted that it may be possible on occasions to allocate a breach of control to either 'pigeon-hole', i.e. development without planning permission or the breach of a condition or limitation. In that case planning permission had been granted for the erection of a building on a farm subject to a condition that the building should only be used for the storage of agricultural produce and farm implements in conjunction with the use of the farm for agricultural purposes. Subsequently, it was used for the storage and wholesale distribution of fruit and vegetables not produced on the farm. The planning authority served an enforcement notice alleging an unauthorised material change of use. The appellant argued that the authority were wrong in law to assert a material change of use and that they ought to have alleged a breach of condition. This argument was rejected by the Divisional Court. Lord Widgery said: 'I think it was a strange administrative action to take the course which the council took but to say that it was wrong in law is something which I cannot accept. I think that if the council could make out their case either on breach of condition or intensification of activity it was up to them as a matter of law to choose which they wanted.' However, in *London Borough of Camden* v *Backer and Aird*[51] Donaldson L.J. expressed some doubt about whether the same activity could amount to both unauthorised development and a breach of a condition. In that case planning permission was granted for the erection of a second storey on a building for use as a loft. The permission was subject to a condition restricting the use of the loft to storage in connection with the residential use of the remainder of the premises. The loft was subsequently occupied as a separate residential unit and the planning authority served an enforcement notice alleging breach of the condition. The notice was quashed for reasons which are not material to the present discussion. However, Donaldson L.J. went on to say that it seemed to him to be arguable 'that the condition applied and limited and restricted the loft user, and that it was only if you were using the premises as a loft otherwise than in accordance with the condition that then it can be said to be a breach of the condition'. If you were not using it as a loft at all, he would have thought it arguable that you were simply acting without planning permission.

---

[49] [1981] J.P.L. 418; affirmed by the Court of Appeal: (1982) 264 E.G. 141. See also *Clwyd County Council* v *Secretary of State for Wales* [1982] J.P.L. 696.
[50] (1979) 37 P. & C.R. 129; see too the comments of Shaw L.J. giving the judgment of the Court of Appeal: (*loc. cit.*).
[51] [1982] J.P.L. 516 (C.A.).

In *Britt* v *Buckinghamshire County Council*[52] it was held that the planning authority could overcome any difficulty about selecting the correct 'pigeon-hole' by serving two enforcement notices making alternative allegations, provided that the authority made clear that the notices were served in the alternative.

On appeal against an enforcement notice, the Secretary of State is empowered to correct certain defects (see p. 328 below) but if the notice seriously misdescribes the breach, that will be a fatal defect. The decision in *Copeland Borough Council* v *Secretary of State for the Environment*[53] illustrates the degree of precision that may be required. In that case planning permission had been granted for the erection of a house, the plans indicating that the roof was to be constructed of tiles of a particular colour. The wrong colour of tiles was used and the planning authority served an enforcement notice describing the breach as consisting of construction of the roof with the wrong colour of tiles. The court held that in reality the breach consisted of the erection of a building which did not comply with the approved plans; the enforcement notice contained what Lord Widgery described as a 'gross error' and was 'so groggy' that it could not be saved.

Section 84(2) of the 1972 Act provides that there is a breach of planning control 'if any . . . limitations subject to which planning permission was granted have not been complied with'.[54] The word 'limitations' is not defined in the Act and in *Peacock Homes Ltd.* v *Secretary of State for the Environment*[55] Dillon L.J. said that the word does not carry any technical meaning and would seem to be surplus in that any limitation on a planning permission would have to be imposed by way of a condition;[56] he said, however, that insofar as it has any weight, the word 'limitations' would seem apt to cover a limitation in time subject to which planning permission is granted.

As was pointed out in *Rochdale Metropolitan Borough Council* v *Simmonds*,[57] where there is a failure to comply with a condition or limitation the planning authority's powers extend no further than to require steps to be taken for the purpose of securing compliance with the condition or limitation, whereas if there is development without planning permission, the planning authority are entitled to require restoration of the land to its condition before the development took place. The English courts have

---

[52] (1963) 14 P. & C.R. 332. See too *Harding* v *Secretary of State for the Environment* [1984] J.P.L. 503.

[53] .(1976) 31 P. & C.R. 403. And see the cases mentioned at pp. 330–331 below.

[54] Section 84(11) of the 1972 Act provides that the validity of an enforcement notice is not to depend on whether the non-compliance to which the notice relates is described as non-compliance with a condition or with a limitation. The description in the notice is to be construed as the notice requires.

[55] (1984) 48 P. & C.R. 20.

[56] However, in *Wilson* v *West Sussex County Council* [1963] 2 Q.B. 764 the Court of Appeal held that in a planning permission for an agricultural cottage, the word 'agricultural' had a functional significance and was to be construed as limiting the proposed building to one intended to be occupied by an agricultural worker or by a person engaged in agriculture.

[57] (1980) 40 P. & C.R. 432.

taken the view that the limit on cubic capacity prescribed in relation to certain types of development permitted by the General Development Order is not a 'limitation' on the permission; where the limit prescribed by the G.D.O. has been exceeded, the whole of any such development is unauthorised and an enforcement notice should treat the breach as the carrying out of development without planning permission.[58]

So long as it specifies the alleged breach with sufficient clarity, an enforcement notice need not specify the former use of the land.[59] There is no reason why an enforcement notice should not specify two separate breaches of planning control.[60] It seems that it is not necessary for an enforcement notice to state that the alleged breach consists of 'operations' or 'a material change of use'.[61] An enforcement notice is not a nullity merely because it overstates the case and alleges more than can be proved; any such error can be corrected on appeal.[62]

2. Steps required to be taken to remedy the breach of planning control

An enforcement notice must specify the steps required by the authority to be taken to remedy the breach of planning control. In effect, this means that the notice must set out the steps required to restore the land to its condition before the breach took place;[63] the notice may also specify, as an alternative to requiring the restoration of the land to its previous condition, steps to be taken to put the land into a condition acceptable to the planning authority (s.84(7)[64]).

The alternative disposes of lingering doubts as to whether a planning authority may 'under-enforce'.[65] If, for example, the breach of planning control consists of the erection of a building without planning permission, the notice must require the removal of the building but it may now, as an alternative, require specified steps to be taken to put the building into a

---

58   See *Garland* v *Minister of Housing and Local Government* (1968) 20 P. & C.R. 93; *Copeland Borough Council* v *Secretary of State for the Environment* (1976) 31 P. & C.R. 403; and *Rochdale Metropolitan Borough Council* v *Simmonds* (1980) 40 P. & C.R. 432.

59   See *Ross* v *Aberdeen County Council* 1955 S.L.T. (Sh.Ct.) 65; *Clarke* v *Minister of Housing and Local Government* (1966) 18 P. & C.R. 82; and *City of Westminster* v *Secretary of State for the Environment* [1983] J.P.L. 602. An error as to the previous use can be corrected on appeal—see appeal decision noted in [1982] J.P.L. 121.

60   See appeal decision noted in [1979] J.P.L. 547.

61   See *Scott* v *Secretary of State for the Environment* [1983] J.P.L. 108. However, if an enforcement notice alleges one of these types of development when it ought to have alleged the other, it may be bad—see appeal decisions noted in [1979] J.P.L. 489; and [1982] J.P.L. 267. See too *Wealden District Council* v *Secretary of State for the Environment* [1983] J.P.L. 234.

62   *Brooks and Burton* v *Secretary of State for the Environment* [1977] 1 W.L.R. 1294.

63   The Secretary of State for the Environment takes the view that it is not enough simply to require the taking of steps to remedy the alleged breach: specific steps must be required—see [1979] J.P.L. 633.

64   Substituted by the 1982 Act, s.48 and Schedule 2, para. 19(c).

65   See, for example, *Iddenden* v *Secretary of State for the Environment* [1972] 1 W.L.R. 1433. Cf. *Copeland Borough Council* v *Secretary of State for the Environment* (1976) 31 P. & C.R. 403.

condition which will make it acceptable to the planning authority. The recipient of the notice may then choose whether to remove the building completely or alter it as required.

To achieve the restoration or alteration of the land, the steps specified in the notice may include the demolition or alteration of any building or works, the discontinuance of any use of land, or the carrying out on land of any building or other operations (s.84(8)). However, as the Lord Justice-Clerk (Lord Grant) pointed out in *Paul* v *Ayrshire County Council*,[66] while the planning authority may 'enforce the discontinuance of a new use and the restoration of land to its previous *state*, there is no power to compel the restoration and continuance of the previous *use*'.

Although there are some doubts about the measure of formality required in specifying the steps to be taken (see p. 296 above), there is no doubt that an enforcement notice which is very imprecise or ambiguous as to the steps to be taken will be treated as a nullity. In *Metallic Protectives Ltd.* v *Secretary of State for the Environment*,[67] for example, an enforcement notice alleged a breach of a condition which provided in effect that no nuisance was to be caused to the residential properties in the area by reason of the emission from a factory of noise, vibration, smoke, smell, fumes, soot, ash, dust or grit. The notice required the appellants to install satisfactory sound-proofing for a compressor and to take all possible action to minimise the effects of using acrylic paint. The Divisional Court considered that these requirements were far too imprecise; the notice was so defective as to be a nullity and incapable of amendment. Similarly, in *London Borough of Hounslow* v *Secretary of State for the Environment*,[68] the Divisional Court concluded that two enforcement notices which required the recipients 'to comply or seek compliance' with a condition attached to a planning permission did not tell the recipients with sufficient clarity what steps they had to take and were so ambiguous as to be nullities.

The steps which may be required to be taken are limited to those required to remedy the breach of control described in the notice. In *Cleaver* v *Secretary of State for the Environment*,[69] an enforcement notice described the breach of control as 'the carrying out of unauthorised development, namely the reception, storage and breaking up of any vehicle, metal, wood, plastic, asbestos or product of metal, wood, plastic or asbestos or any other such items'. The notice went on to require the recipient, amongst other things, to 'discontinue the operation of a trade or business comprising the sale or exchange of any such item or material'. The notice was successfully challenged in the Divisional Court on the ground that the steps required to be taken exceeded what was necessary to remedy the breach. In particular, while the notice required the recipient to discontinue business activities, the

---

[66] 1964 S.C. 116; 1964 S.L.T. 207.

[67] [1976] J.P.L. 166.

[68] [1981] J.P.L. 510. See also *Sykes* v *Secretary of State for the Environment* (1980) 42 P. & C.R. 19.

[69] [1981] J.P.L. 38. See too *Bath City Council* v *Secretary of State for the Environment* (1983) 47 P. & C.R. 663 (listed building enforcement notice).

breach alleged in the notice made no reference to such activities. Whilst the steps proscribed the sale of items of the sort described in the breach, the notice did not relate the retail activity to the storage and breaking business.

The steps required to be taken in a notice may also be treated as excessive if they purport to restrict established rights. This is sometimes referred to as the '*Mansi* rule' after the decision in *Mansi* v *Elstree R.D.C.*[70] In that case an enforcement notice alleged a material change in the use of a glasshouse from use for agriculture to use for the sale of goods and required the latter use to be discontinued. The appellant argued that the notice purported to restrict his activities further than it legitimately might by forbidding all sales, including subsidiary sales of home-grown produce and other goods which had previously been carried on quite lawfully in association with the use of the glasshouse for agricultural purposes. This argument was accepted by the court, Widgery J. saying: 'True that use was a subsidiary one, but nevertheless it should be protected and, in my judgment, this appeal should be allowed to the extent that the decision in question should be sent back to the Minister with a direction that he ought to amend the notice so as to safeguard the appellants' established right . . . ' This decision was followed in *Newport* v *Secretary of State for the Environment*[71] in which Waller L.J. commented that 'it is important, where criminal prosecution is a possibility, that the limits of what can and what cannot be done should be set out.'

Just what rights are to be safeguarded in the notice may be difficult to determine, particularly where a material change through intensification has occurred. In *de Mulder* v *Secretary of State for the Environment*,[72] enforcement notices were served in respect of an intensification of use and required the recipients to reduce the activities on the site to their level in 1970, being the point in time when it was alleged that the intensification had become material. Lord Widgery C.J. said:

'In those so-called intensification cases the material change of use occurs at a point when the landowner has already exercised every right which the planning Acts give him, in other words it is not until the material change of use occurs that enforcement action can be taken, and when the enforcement action is taken any latitude of the kind to which I referred in *Mansi*'s case has already been absorbed and enjoyed. It seems to me, therefore, in the present case if the Secretary of State is allowed to do as he has purported to do, namely, to cut the appellant down to the level of general dealing appropriate in April 1970, he will on the way, as it were, have made the necessary adjustment required in *Mansi*'s case.'

[70] (1964) 16 P. & C.R. 153. See M. Purdue, 'The Complexities of Enforcing the Development Control System and the *Mansi* Rule' [1981] J.P.L. 154.

[71] (1980) 40 P. & C.R. 261. See also *Trevors Warehouses Ltd.* v *Secretary of State for the Environment* (1972) 23 P. & C.R. 215; *Day and Mid-Warwickshire Motors Ltd.* v *Secretary of State for the Environment* (1979) 78 L.G.R. 27; *Isaac Lee* v *London Borough of Bromley* [1982] J.P.L. 778; *Richard Haigh* v *Secretary of State for the Environment* [1983] J.P.L. 40; *Choudry* v *Secretary of State for the Environment* [1983] J.P.L. 231; and *Denham Developments Ltd.* v *Secretary of State for the Environment* (1983) 47 P. & C.R. 598.

[72] [1974] Q.B. 792.

Although the '*Mansi* rule' needs to be borne in mind when specifying the steps to be taken to remedy a breach of planning control, an enforcement notice must be read as a whole and there are circumstances in which it will be unnecessary for the notice to spell out established rights. It is not, it seems, 'necessary for the Secretary of State or the local authority to have to go so far as to put in an enforcement notice that which must be obvious to everybody'.[73] In particular, it is not necessary for the notice to make specific provision for safeguarding a use which is obviously ancillary to the permitted use of the premises. In *Monomart (Warehouses) Ltd.* v *Secretary of State for the Environment*,[74] for example, planning permission had been granted, *inter alia*, for a 'builders' merchants' warehouse'. The appellants used the premises as a 'do-it-yourself supermarket', retailing builders' supplies. The planning authority served an enforcement notice requiring the discontinuance of the retail sales. The Secretary of State on appeal added the words 'except as may be incidental to the use of the premises as a builders' merchants' warehouse'. The Divisional Court considered that the addition was not strictly necessary. Construing the notice as a whole, it was clear that the breach with which the notice was concerned was retail sales in excess of retail sales permissible as ancillary or incidental to the main use. It was quite impossible to make sense of the notice unless it was assumed that the reference to the retail sale of goods was a reference to the retail sale of goods in excess of the rights which might be incidental to the warehouse use.

Similarly, in *Jones* v *Secretary of State for the Environment*,[75] Lord Widgery stated that he could see 'no reason in law or commonsense' why an enforcement notice should make provision for safeguarding an ancillary use which had ceased by the time enforcement had become necessary. This is presumably because the steps required to be taken can only relate to the alleged breach of control and if an activity is not being carried on at the time when the breach occurs, then there can be no question of the activity being discontinued.

Clearly, there will be occasions when it may be difficult to determine whether the '*Mansi* rule' applies. In *Cord* v *Secretary of State for the Environment*[76] Donaldson L.J. suggested that:

'It might be a useful test, where this question arose, to write out the terms of the enforcement notice and then to write below it the things which the person concerned was entitled to do without further planning permission. They should then consider whether the second paragraph derogated from the first paragraph. If one was plainly a derogation from the other there was a strong case for writing it into the enforcement notice for the avoidance of doubt. But if the chronicle of matters which the landowner was entitled to do did not constitute a derogation from the requirements

---

[73] *Cord* v *Secretary of State for the Environment* [1981] J.P.L. 40, per Kilner-Brown J.
[74] (1979) 34 P. & C.R. 305. See also *Cord* (above); and *North Sea Land Equipment* v *Secretary of State for the Environment* [1982] J.P.L. 384.
[75] (1974) 28 P. & C.R. 362.
[76] [1981] J.P.L. 40.

of the enforcement notice it was a waste of time and might even, in some circumstances, be a source of confusion to specify what was obvious.'

The '*Mansi* rule' does not apply to cases involving operational development (as opposed to cases involving change of use). A planning authority may, for example, quite properly require the demolition of the whole of an unauthorised extension to a house; there is no obligation upon the authority to safeguard in the enforcement notice that part of the extension which would have been permitted under the general development order.[77] This is because the building of the extension is treated as one operation and not as a series of separate operations.[78]

3. *The date on which the notice is to take effect*

An enforcement notice must specify the date on which it is to take effect.[79] This must be a period of not less than 28 days from the date of service of the notice. However, where there are several parties to be served, copies of the notice may have to be served on different days. There is, nonetheless, only one notice and it can, therefore, have only one effective date. In the situation where parties are served on different days, s.84(9) provides that the period at the end of which the notice will take effect is to be a period of not less than 28 days from the date of the latest service.[80]

If there is an appeal to the Secretary of State against an enforcement notice, the notice is of no effect pending the final determination or withdrawal of the appeal (s.85(3)). It seems, however, that it is unnecessary to state in the notice that the specified date is subject to the provisions of s.85(3) although in the interests of clarity this may be desirable.[81]

4. *The period for compliance with the notice*

In addition to specifying the date on which it is to take effect, an enforcement notice must also specify the period for compliance with the notice. In other words, it must state the period, commencing with the date when the notice takes effect, within which the steps specified in the notice are required to be taken (s.84(7A)(a)). Different periods may be prescribed for different steps. It is a ground of appeal against an enforcement notice

---

[77] But see now s.84(7) of the 1972 Act (as substituted by s.48 of, and para. 19(c) of Schedule 2 to, the Local Government and Planning (Scotland) Act 1982) which permits a planning authority to 'under-enforce'.

[78] *Prengate Properties Ltd.* v *Secretary of State for the Environment* (1973) 25 P. & C.R. 311; *Ewen Developments Ltd.* v *Secretary of State for the Environment* [1980] J.P.L. 404; and *Rochdale Metropolitan Borough Council* v *Simmonds* (1980) 40 P. & C.R. 432.

[79] A notice which fails to do so is a nullity—see, for example, *SPADS* No. A2671 (P/ENA/GD/2, 16th June 1978).

[80] This provision, substituted by s.48 of, and para. 19(d) of Schedule 2 to, the 1982 Act, disposes of the sort of problem that arose in *Bambury* v *London Borough of Hounslow* [1966] 2 Q.B. 204.

[81] *King and King* v *Secretary of State for the Environment* [1981] J.P.L. 813.

that the period specified for compliance falls short of what should reasonably be allowed.

A notice which fails to specify this period is a nullity.[82] It seems that there will be sufficient compliance with the statutory provisions if a notice requires the steps to be taken by a certain date rather than within a specified period. All that is required is that the period should be capable of deduction within the four corners of the notice, if necessary by subtracting the date on which the notice is to take effect from the date specified for compliance.[83] However, an enforcement notice must specify separately the date on which it is to take effect and the time within which the steps required by the notice are to be taken; a notice which does not specify both of these is a nullity. Thus in *Burgess* v *Jarvis*[84] an enforcement notice which required the demolition of houses built without planning permission 'within five years after the date of service' of the notice but which did not specify the date when the notice took effect was held to be bad.

5. *Boundaries of the land.*

An enforcement notice must specify the precise boundaries of the land to which it relates, whether by reference to a plan or in words.[85] The Secretary of State considers that this identification is best done by a plan attached to the notice and indicating the boundaries of the land by means of a coloured line.[86]

In determining whether a material change of use has occurred, regard must be had to the correct 'planning unit'.[87] And when an enforcement notice is served alleging a material change of use, it is, as was said by Widgery L.J. in *Hawkey* v *Secretary of State for the Environment*:[88] 'always open to the landowner to contend, if he can, that the planning unit is something larger than that specified in the notice and that, if the true planning unit is looked at, no material change of use has occurred at all' (and that there has, therefore, been no breach of planning control).

Although the enforcement notice has to specify the land on which it is alleged that a breach of planning control has taken place, it is not essential that the enforcement notice should identify the planning unit.[89] Nor is it necessary that the enforcement notice be directed towards the whole planning unit; it is open to the authority to bring enforcement proceedings either in respect of the whole planning unit or in respect of some smaller

[82] See, for example, *SPADS* No. A2738 (P/ENA/SQ/1, 15th August 1978).
[83] *King and King* v *Secretary of State for the Environment* (above).
[84] [1952] 2 Q.B. 41; followed in *Mead* v *Chelmsford R.D.C.* [1953] 1 Q.B. 32; *Swallow and Pearson* v *Middlesex County Council* [1953] 1 W.L.R. 422; and *Godstone R.D.C.* v *Brazil* [1953] 1 W.L.R. 1102.
[85] 1972 Act, s.84(7A) and (12) (added by the 1982 Act, s.48 and Schedule 2, para. 19(e)); and Town and Country Planning (Enforcement of Control) (Scotland) Regulations 1984, reg. 3.
[86] See S.D.D. Circular 6/1984.
[87] The question of the appropriate planning unit is discussed in chapter 6.
[88] (1971) 22 P. & C.R. 610.
[89] See *Hawkey* (above.

portion on which the alleged breach of planning control has occurred.[90] In *de Mulder* v *Secretary of State for the Environment*[91] Lord Widgery C.J. put the matter thus: 'It is in my judgment quite proper . . . for the planning authority to say: although the material change of use is to be observed all over the site, the activities which give rise to that are in one place or in one corner, and we will direct our enforcement action to the place where the offensive activity takes place.'

In *de Mulder* the planning authority had, however, served a number of enforcement notices, each directed to a different part of a farm which was the appropriate planning unit. The separate enforcement notices had the effect of restricting the appellants' use of the land to the intensity of use existing in each of the separate areas on a particular date, whereas if a single enforcement notice relating to the whole planning unit had been served, the appellants would have been able to increase the intensity of use in any one of those separate areas so long as the overall intensity of use of the planning unit did not exceed the level existing on the date in question. The Divisional Court held that a planning authority could not, by arbitrarily dividing up a site into a number of smaller areas and directing a separate enforcement notice to each of those smaller areas, impose more severe restrictions on a landowner than might have been imposed on him by a single enforcement notice applicable to the whole planning unit and that in this case the separate enforcement notices were therefore unduly restrictive.[92]

In *Thomas David (Porthcawl) Ltd.* v *Penybont R.D.C.*[93] the Court of Appeal employed the concept of the appropriate 'planning unit' in order to determine the question whether too wide an area had been specified in an enforcement notice concerned with unauthorised operations.[94] In that case a company had for some time carried on, without the grant of planning permission, mining operations on two small areas of land. The enforcement notice served by the planning authority was not, however, confined to the two areas actually being worked but required the company to discontinue[95] the extraction of sand and gravel from any part of a much larger area which included the two small areas. A licence granted by the owners of the land entitled the company to work an area rather larger than that to which the notice applied. The company argued that the notice was invalid in that it

---

[90] See *Hawkey* (above) and *Morris* v *Secretary of State for the Environment* (1975) 31 P. & C.R. 216. See too ministerial decisions noted in [1976] J.P.L. 120, 590 and 710; [1977] J.P.L. 264; and [1978] J.P.L. 338.

[91] [1974] Q.B. 792.

[92] See also *Burdle* v *Secretary of State for the Environment* [1972] 1 W.L.R. 1207, per Bridge J.; *T.L.G. Building Materials Ltd.* v *Secretary of State for the Environment* (1980) 41 P. & C.R. 243; and *Dunton Park Caravan Site Ltd.* v *Secretary of State for the Environment* [1981] J.P.L. 511.

[93] [1972] 1 W.L.R. 1526.

[94] Prior to this case the concept of the planning unit had been employed only in cases involving change of use.

[95] Generally, an enforcement notice cannot require the discontinuance of 'operations' but the discontinuance of mining operations is treated for this purpose as a use of land (see Town and Country Planning (Minerals) (Scotland) Regulations 1971, reg. 4(b)).

should have been confined to the two areas actually worked. The Court of Appeal held that the notice was valid; as the planning unit was not confined to the two small areas worked but 'extended to the whole area which might be regarded as suitable for excavation by the developers if they could get planning permission for it', the notice was not too wide. In the Divisional Court[96] Lord Widgery C.J. declared:

'I do not think that it can possibly have been the intention of Parliament that, when an enforcement notice is served in regard to mining operations such as the present, the effect of the enforcement notice should be meticulously restricted to the very square yardage which is being the subject of an actual cut by the shovel or bulldozer as the case may be. I think it is permissible and indeed right in mining operation cases to ask whether the land on which the actual cut is taken is not in truth and in fact part of a wider area which is being started in development by the particular immediate activity referred to. If as a matter of fact and common sense it is clear that the first cut is a cut relative to a larger area, then it is right for the tribunal of fact to determine if it thinks fit that the larger area is a planning unit for present purposes.'

6. Reasons for notice

In any enforcement notice they serve, the planning authority must specify the reasons why they consider it expedient to serve the notice.[97] The Secretary of State regards this as an important initial means of enabling the recipient of a notice to understand from the outset the reasons why the planning authority have taken this course of action.

7. Explanatory note

An enforcement notice is to include a note explaining the rights of appeal against the notice.[98] The terms of this notice are prescribed by regulation 4 of the Town and Country Planning (Enforcement of Control) (Scotland) Regulations 1984.

Crown land

Provided that the Crown grants consent to the service of an enforcement notice, enforcement action is competent against a person who holds an interest in Crown land (see 1972 Act, s.253). Any person entitled to occupy Crown land by virtue of a contract in writing is deemed to have an interest in the land for this purpose.[99]

Where unauthorised development was carried out on Crown land by a person without an interest in the land (in Parliament the example mentioned

---

[96] [1972] 1 W.L.R. 354.
[97] 1972 Act, s.84(7A) and (12) (added by the 1982 Act, s.48 and Schedule 2, para. 19(e)); and Town and Country Planning (Enforcement of Control) (Scotland) Regulations 1984, reg.3.
[98] 1972 Act, s.84(12) (added by the 1982 Act, s.48 and Schedule 2, para. 19(e)).
[99] See Town and Country Planning Act 1984, s.4.

M

was that of mobile snack bars operating on laybys on trunk roads) it was
formerly impossible to take enforcement action. The Town and Country
Planning Act 1984 seeks to close this loophole by providing in s.3 that a
planning authority may, with the consent of the appropriate government
department, serve a 'special enforcement notice'. This is somewhat
narrower in scope than an ordinary enforcement notice and the grounds of
appeal are more restricted. The Secretary of State is empowered to make
regulations applying to Crown land such provisions of the 1972 Act as he
considers expedient.[1]

Register of enforcement notices, etc.

Section 87A of the 1972 Act[2] imposes a duty on all district and general
planning authorities to maintain a register of enforcement notices, stop
notices and waste land notices. The information to be kept in this register is
prescribed by regulation 7 of the Town and Country Planning (Enforcement
of Control) (Scotland) Regulations 1984.

B. IMMUNITY FROM ENFORCEMENT ACTION

The question whether the operations or uses being carried on upon land are
subject to the risk of enforcement action will clearly be an important factor
in any transaction affecting that land. In order to introduce some certainty
into this area, it has been considered desirable to impose what might be
described as 'limitation periods' on the power to take enforcement action.
Somewhat paradoxically, therefore, it can sometimes be advantageous for a
developer to seek to prove that a breach of planning control has persisted for
some time.

Limitation periods

For this purpose breaches of planning control may be divided into the
following five categories:

1. An enforcement notice may only be served within four years of the
carrying out of an unauthorised building, engineering, mining or other
operation (s.84(3)(a)).

Building and engineering operations may be made up of many component
parts. The building of a house, for example, might be said to comprise the
laying of foundations, the construction of walls and the placing of the roof.
However, it seems that, subject to any special provision in the planning
permission itself, building or engineering operations are to be treated as a

---

[1]   See the Town and Country Planning (Special Enforcement Notices) (Scotland) Regulations
   1984.
[2]   Inserted by s.44 of the 1982 Act.

single operation and not as a multitude of operations.[3] Thus the building of a house will be treated as one operation. The difficulty is that the various parts of the operation may be carried out over a period of time and this has given rise to some uncertainty as to the date from which the four year period is to be calculated. The reference in s.84(3)(a) to 'the carrying out' of the operation suggests that if activities are to be treated as one operation then time runs from the date of substantial completion and it now seems clear that this is the correct approach.[4] In *Ewen Developments Ltd.* v *Secretary of State for the Environment,*[5] for example, the local planning authority served an enforcement notice requiring the removal of a number of embankments which had been constructed over a period of years. The developer argued that he could only be required to reduce the height of the embankments to the height at which they were four years before the enforcement proceedings began. The Divisional Court rejected this argument, holding that the construction of the embankments should be viewed as one operation and that individual elements of the construction could not be singled out as time-barred.

It seems that the question whether particular building works should be viewed as a single operation or as two or more separate operations will normally depend on the appearance of the building in question.[6]

Although time appears to run from the date of substantial completion of building and engineering operations, there is nothing to prevent a planning authority serving an enforcement notice as soon as unauthorised operations are started.

Different considerations would seem to apply as regards the 'limitation period' for mining operations. In *Thomas David (Porthcawl) Ltd.* v *Penybont Rural District Council,*[7] the Court of Appeal had to consider the effect of an enforcement notice which required a company to discontinue mining operations carried out without the·grant of planning permission on two areas of land. The company claimed that as the extraction of sand and gravel from the two areas had begun more than four years before service of the enforcement notice, the operations were immune from enforcement action and the company was entitled to continue mining operations in the future within the two areas. The Court of Appeal held that in mining operations each shovelful extracted or each cut by the bulldozer is a separate act of development in itself and is not merely part of one continuing

---

3   See *Ewen Developments Ltd.* v *Secretary of State for the Environment* [1980] J.P.L. 404; *Copeland Borough Council* v *Secretary of State for the Environment* (1976) 31 P. & C.R. 403. See too *Garland* v *Minister of Housing and Local Government* (1968) 20 P. & C.R. 93; and ministerial decisions noted in *Selected Enforcement and Allied Appeals,* pp. 48–52. Compare, however, *F. Lucas & Sons Ltd.* v *Dorking and Horley R.D.C.* (1964) 17 P. & C.R. 111; and the judgment of Stephenson L.J. in *Thomas David (Porthcawl) Ltd.* v *Penybont R.D.C.* [1972] 1 W.L.R. 1526.
4   See *Howes* v *Secretary of State for the Environment* [1984] J.P.L. 439; and *Ewen Developments Ltd.* v *Secretary of State for the Environment* [1980] J.P.L. 404.
5   Above.
6   See *Worthy Fuel Injection Ltd.* v *Secretary of State for the Environment* [1983] J.P.L. 173.
7   [1972] 1 W.L.R. 1526.

development; in this case, therefore, the court held that although those mining operations which had taken place more than four years before service of the enforcement notice were not subject to enforcement action, the enforcement notice had been validly served in respect of extractions made within the four years preceding the notice.

It would seem that there will be occasions when building, engineering, mining or other operations which are themselves immune from enforcement action under the four year limitation period may nonetheless be caught by an enforcement notice alleging an unauthorised material change of use. In *Murfitt* v *Secretary of State for the Environment* [8] an enforcement notice required the discontinuance of the use of a site for the parking of heavy goods vehicles and the restoration of the site in accordance with a scheme to be agreed with the local planning authority or in default of agreement to be determined by the Secretary of State. The developer argued that the requirement to restore the site could not include a requirement to remove hardcore which had been laid on the site more than four years before the date of service of the notice; that was an 'operation' which was protected by the limitation period. The Divisional Court disagreed. After pointing out that s.87(6) of the Town and Country Planning Act 1971 (corresponding to s.84(7) of the 1972 Act) specifically requires that an enforcement notice should set out the steps to be taken to restore the land to its condition before the unauthorised development took place, Stephen Brown J. said:

'That is, of course, a mandatory duty that is placed on a local authority, and it would make a nonsense of planning control, in my judgment, if it were to be considered in the instant case that an enforcement notice requiring discontinuance of the use of the site in question for the parking of heavy goods vehicles should not also require the restoration of the land, as a physical matter, to its previous condition, that requirement, of necessity, being the removal of the hardcore.'

The decision in *Murfitt* was followed in *Perkins* v *Secretary of State for the Environment*. [9]

There was some suggestion by counsel for the Secretary of State in *Murfitt* that a 'change of use' enforcement notice could catch only those operations which were integral to the change of use but the judgments of Stephen Brown J. and Waller L.J. are couched in terms which appear to be wide enough to catch any sort of operations, integral or otherwise. [10] Section 84(7) of the 1972 Act [11] now provides that an enforcement notice may, as an alternative to requiring the restoration of the land to its condition before the unauthorised development took place, set out the steps to be

[8]   (1980) 40 P. & C.R. 254.
[9]   [1981] J.P.L. 755.
[10]   See too the judgment of Glidewell J. in *Perkins*, above.
[11]   As amended by the 1982 Act, Schedule 2, para. 19(c).

taken to bring the land to a condition acceptable to the planning authority. The result may be that the sort of situation which arose in *Murfitt* and *Perkins* will be a more common occurrence.

Quite apart from the situation which arose in *Murfitt* and *Perkins*, there will be occasions where the carrying out of operations may be accompanied by a material change in the use of the land on which the operations have taken place. In a case where four years have elapsed since operations were carried out and no enforcement notice can, therefore, be served in respect of those operations, it would seem that it may still be possible in some circumstances to serve an enforcement notice in respect of a change of use which accompanied the carrying out of the operations and to which the four year limitation does not apply.[12]

2. An enforcement notice may only be served within four years of a failure to comply with a condition or limitation which relates to the carrying out of building, engineering, mining or other operations and subject to which planning permission was granted (s.84(3)(b)).

In *Peacock Homes Ltd.* v *Secretary of State for the Environment*[13] the Court of Appeal held that this limitation period applies to every condition attached to a planning permission involving operational development and not merely to a condition which itself requires or involves the carrying out of operations. The Court of Appeal held in this case that a condition, attached to a planning permission for the erection of a building, which provided that the use was to be discontinued and the building demolished at the end of a specified period could fairly be said to relate to the erection of the building.

In the case of mining operations, the four-year period runs from the date when non-compliance with the condition has come to the planning authority's knowledge.[14]

3. An enforcement notice may only be served within four years of the making without planning permission of a change of use of any building to use as a single dwelling-house (s.84(3)(c)).

Such a change of use can, it seems, take place before the building is actually used as a dwelling-house.[15] The phrase 'use as a single dwelling-house' is narrower in its meaning than 'residential use'.[16]

4. An enforcement notice may only be served within four years of a failure to comply with a condition which prohibits, or has the effect of preventing, a

---

[12] See *Burn* v *Secretary of State for the Environment* (1971) 219 E.G. 586; and appeal decision reported in [1974] J.P.L. 733. One could thus have a building which the planning authority cannot require to be demolished but which cannot lawfully be used.

[13] (1984) 48 P. & C.R. 20.

[14] See Town and Country Planning (Minerals) (Scotland) Regulations 1971, reg. 5.

[15] See *Impey* v *Secretary of State for the Environment* (1980) 47 P. & C.R. 157; and *Backer* v *Secretary of State for the Environment* (1982) 47 P. & C.R. 149.

[16] see *Backer* (above.)

change of use of a building to use as a single dwelling-house (s.84(3)(d)[17]).

5. All other breaches of control, i.e. all unauthorised material changes of use other than to a single dwelling-house, and all breaches of conditions or limitations other than those falling within categories 2 and 4 above, are immune from enforcement action if the breach occurred before 1965 (s.85(1)(d)).[18]

The courts have not given any very clear guidance on the application of the time limits to a breach of a condition attached to a planning permission (categories 2, 4 and 5 above). If, for example, a condition prohibiting a certain use was first broken prior to the end of 1964 and the breach has continued since that date, is it now too late to serve an enforcement notice or can the planning authority still serve a notice on the basis that there has been a breach of planning control after the end of 1964? In *Bilboe* v *Secretary of State for the Environment*[19] an application to use an old stone quarry as a tip was granted in 1950 subject to a condition requiring the approval of the planning authority to be obtained for the materials to be deposited. Between 1950 and 1963 rubble was tipped on the site without the approval of the planning authority having been obtained. No further tipping took place until after 1975 when, although the planning authority's approval was obtained for the deposit of certain materials, other materials which had not been approved were tipped on the site. An enforcement notice was served alleging a breach of the condition attached to the permission of 1950. The Court of Appeal held that non-compliance with the condition had taken place once and for all in or about 1950, so that the breach of control was now immune from enforcement action. No consideration appears to have been given to whether this might have been a 'continuing' as opposed to a 'once and for all' breach.

In a case where sales of certain categories of articles took place intermittently in breach of a condition prohibiting the sales of such articles, the Minister of Housing and Local Government took the view that as there was no connection or continuity between one sale in breach of the condition and another such sale on another date, each sale constituted a complete and separate breach in itself and the time for serving an enforcement notice therefore began afresh from the date of each breach.[20] Where, on the other hand, the failure to comply with a condition has been continuous, the English minister has, in a number of cases where the 'four year rule' applied, quashed enforcement notices served more than four years after the initial breach, holding that the time for service began to run from the first date of

[17]   Added by the 1982 Act, Schedule 2, para. 19(a). This provision fills the gap noted by the Divisional Court in *Backer* v *Secretary of State for the Environment* (1980) 42 P. & C.R. 98 (upheld by the Court of Appeal sub. nom. *London Borough of Camden* v *Backer and Aird* [1982] J.P.L..516).

[18]   A consultation paper issued by the Scottish Development Department on 31st July 1984 proposed the removal of this limitation period (see p. 317 below).

[19]   (1980) 39 P. & C.R. 495.

[20]   See [1961] J.P.L. 691.

non-compliance with the condition.[21] Even though a particular breach of a condition has in this way become immune from enforcement action, that does not necessarily mean, however, that the condition is entirely un-enforceable—such a condition could still be enforced, according to the English minister, 'if any further breaches of a demonstrably different nature occurred'.[22]

If, in a case where the 'four year rule' applies (categories 1 to 4 above), any dispute arises as to the date on which such a breach of planning control occurred, the onus of proof rests on the person claiming the benefit of the rule (s.84(4)).

The operation of the time limits on service of an enforcement notice can clearly give rise to difficult problems. In the case of an unauthorised change of use there may well be practical difficulties in determining when the material change of use occurred, especially if the change took place gradually over a period.[23] In order to alleviate such difficulties, a person having an interest in the land in question may, except in cases to which the four year time limit applies (categories 1 to 4 above), ask the planning authority to issue an 'established use certificate'.[24]

If granted, this establishes conclusively for the purposes of an appeal against an enforcement notice that the use in question has secured immunity from enforcement action.

Certification of established use

In the case of all unauthorised material changes of use (except those relating to a change to use as a single dwelling-house) the only restriction on service of an enforcement notice is that the breach of planning control must have occurred after the end of 1964 (see p. 314 above). This might make it difficult for a person with an interest in land to establish (notably for the benefit of intending purchasers) that the use to which the land is being put is safe from enforcement. In order to overcome this difficulty, which is likely to increase with the passage of time, the 1972 Act provides that where a person having an interest in land[25] claims that a particular use of that land has become 'established', he may apply to the planning authority for a certificate to that

---

[21] See, for example, [1963] J.P.L. 813; [1966] J.P.L. 348; [1968] J.P.L. 294 and 351; and [1971] J.P.L. 57.
[22] [1968] J.P.L. 294.
[23] See *Britt* v *Buckinghamshire County Council* (1963) 14 P. & C.R. 332, per Widgery J.
[24] See 1972 Act, s.90 (below).
[25] The Secretary of State for Scotland seemingly takes the view that the phrase 'person with an interest in the land' includes a person who is bound by contract, or who has an option, to purchase the land or to take a lease of it.

effect (s.90(2)). Such a certificate is termed an established use certificate.[26]

An established use certificate is, as regards the matters stated therein, conclusive[27] for the purposes of an appeal against an enforcement notice served in respect of any land to which the certificate relates, provided that application for the certificate was made before the notice was served (s.90(7)). An established use certificate is not equivalent to a grant of planning permission (see p. 320 below); it merely provides a protection against enforcement action.

For the purposes of Part V of the 1972 Act, a use of land is established if:

(a) it was begun before the beginning of 1965 without planning permission in that behalf and has continued since the end of 1964; or

(b) it was begun before the beginning of 1965 under a planning permission in that behalf granted subject to conditions or limitations,[28] which either have never been complied with or have not been complied with since the end of 1964; or

(c) it was begun after the end of 1964 as a result of a change of use not requiring planning permission and there has been, since the end of 1964, no change of use requiring planning permission (s.90(1)).

Paragraph (c) would seem to be intended to cover the case where the use which is claimed to have become established was begun after the end of 1964 but the previous use was in the same use class, with the result that the change of use was not such as to require planning permission. As was stated in S.D.D. Memorandum 37/1970: 'There may be several links in the chain, all of them involving no more than a change within the same use class, provided that the chain goes back to 1964 or earlier.'

Before it can be claimed that a use has become established in terms of paragraph (a) or paragraph (b) above, it must be shown that there has been a *continuous* breach of planning control from a date before 1st January 1965; a use cannot, therefore, become established under s.90 of the 1972 Act if there has been a grant of planning permission which, for any part of the time since

---

[26] A consultation paper issued by the Scottish Development Department on 31st July 1984 stated that with the passage of time applications and appeals relating to established use certificates are becoming increasingly difficult to decide; in particular, it is increasingly difficult to obtain firm factual evidence on which to base a decision. The consultation paper therefore proposed that the statutory provisions relating to the making of applications for established use certificates should be repealed. A lengthy period of grace would be allowed before these changes became operative in order to allow persons who wished to secure immunity from enforcement action to apply for a certificate. An established use certificate would still, as at present, provide conclusive evidence that the use specified therein was immune from enforcement action.

[27] The certificate cannot subsequently be 'explained' by evidence as to the actual use at the time the certificate was granted—see *Broxbourne Borough Council* v *Secretary of State for the Environment* [1980] Q.B.1 (below).

[28] Presumably this means that the permission may be one granted by the G.D.O.

31st December 1964, rendered the use lawful or made the condition inoperative, as the case may be.[29]

Subsection (2) of s.90 provides that application may be made for an established use certificate where it is claimed that a 'particular use' of land has become established. The Secretary of State for the Environment takes the view that by virtue of that subsection a certificate can be sought only in respect of the particular purpose for which the land was used at the appropriate time and that it is not, for example, open to the planning authority or the minister 'to issue a certificate generally for "industrial use" or for "use for industrial purposes":[30] these are not descriptions of particular uses of land but general references to a type of use.'[31] A class of use specified in the Schedule to the Use Classes Order cannot be regarded as a 'particular use'; the certificate must specify the precise use to which the land was put, e.g. timber storage ancillary to the use of the adjoining land as a sawmill and wood products factory.[32] An application for an established use certificate must relate to the primary use of the planning unit.[33]

Application for an established use certificate may only be made in respect of a use subsisting at the time of the application (s.90(2)). In one appeal the Secretary of State for Scotland accepted that even though a use had been interrupted for a lengthy period and was not being actively carried on at the time of the application, the use was still 'subsisting' within the meaning of the statute.[34] In order to establish that a use is not subsisting at the date of the application, there has to be, in the opinion of the Secretary of State for the Environment, 'positive evidence either of a change of use or of abandonment of the former use'.[35] The Secretary of State for the Environment takes the view that a use carried on in defiance of an effective enforcement notice cannot be accepted as a subsisting use.[36] An application for an established use certificate may not be made in respect of the use of land as a single dwelling-house (s.90(2)). The English minister has held that this provision did not bar an application in which it was alleged that a condition relating to the class of persons who might occupy a dwelling-house had not been complied with; such a condition, the minister thought, 'did not itself concern the use of the building as a single dwelling-house'.[37]

Detailed provision as to the method of applying for an established use certificate and as to the procedure on appeal against refusal of such a

---

[29] See *Bolivian and General Tin Trust* v *Secretary of State for the Environment* [1972] 1 W.L.R. 1481; see too appeal decisions reported in [1972] J.P.L. 226 and 230; and [1974] J.P.L. 239.

[30] Unless the use in question is so general it cannot be described with greater precision—see appeal decision noted in [1981] J.P.L. 449 ('general storage').

[31] [1971] J.P.L. 463: See also [1972] J.P.L. 171; [1974] J.P.L. 293; and [1981] J.P.L. 449.

[32] See [1971] J.P.L. 463.

[33] See appeal decision reported in [1977] J.P.L. 188.

[34] *SPADS* No. A2082 (P/EUC/EDB/3, 18th May 1976).

[35] [1971] J.P.L. 463. See also [1981] J.P.L. 449; and [1982] J.P.L. 800.

[36] See, for example, [1972] J.P.L. 230; [1974] J.P.L. 490; [1975] J.P.L. 106 and 686; [1976] J.P.L. 247 (referring to *Glamorgan County Council* v *Carter* [1963] 1 W.L.R. 1); and [1981] J.P.L. 691.

[37] [1971] J.P.L. 417.

certificate is made by Schedule 12 to the 1972 Act and Article 18 of, and Schedules 5 and 6 to, the G.D.O. An application for an established use certificate must describe the use in respect of which a certificate is sought and, if there is more than one use of the land on the date when the application is made, there must be provided a full description of all uses of the land at the date of the application, giving, where appropriate, an indication of the part of the land to which each of the uses relates (G.D.O., Art. 18(1)). Unless the applicant is himself the owner of the whole of the land to which the application relates he must give notice of the application to all owners of the land (G.D.O., Art. 18(2)).[38] It is an offence to give false information or to withhold material information in order to procure a particular decision on an application for an established use certificate (s.90(8)). An application for an established use certificate may be accompanied by an application for planning permission to continue the use; S.D.D. Memorandum 37/1970 stated: 'The fact that such an application for planning permission is made is not to be regarded as an admission of doubt about the immunity of a use from enforcement nor should it be allowed to prejudice the full consideration on its merits of the claim for an established use certificate.'

If and in so far as they are satisfied that the applicant's claim is made out, the planning authority must grant an established use certificate (s.90(4)). The onus is therefore on the applicant to establish his claim[39] but the planning authority may, of course, take account of any information in their possession. The decision of the planning authority (or of the Secretary of State on appeal) is limited to the question whether the particular use specified in the application has been established; an established use certificate cannot be granted for a 'lesser use' than the one specified.[40] A certificate may be granted either for the whole of the land specified in the application or for a part of it (s.90(3)); the Secretary of State for the Environment has, however, expressed the view that since a use of land attaches to the planning unit as a whole, an established use certificate must similarly relate to the whole of the planning unit. Thus in one case, where it was agreed that the planning unit comprised two fields amounting to some 12 acres in extent, the minister held that it was wrong for the planning authority to seek to restrict the established use of the two fields for tented camping to a particular portion of the planning unit notwithstanding his inspector's conclusion that the camping use had only become established on a part of the unit.[41] The minister nonetheless considered that matters such as the number

---

[38] 'Owner' is defined in Article 18(2) of the G.D.O. and includes an occupier for the time being of any part of the land.

[39] See appeal decisions noted in [1979] J.P.L. 247 and 780. The standard of proof is 'the balance of probabilities' rather than 'beyond all reasonable doubt'—see [1981] J.P.L. 527.

[40] See *Hipsey* v *Secretary of State for the Environment* [1984] J.P.L. 806.

[41] [1981] J.P.L. 527. See also appeal decision reported in [1977] J.P.L. 188; and the comments of Woolf J. in *Enticott and Fullite Ltd.* v *Secretary of State for the Environment* [1981] J.P.L. 759.

of tents and the length of the season could properly be included in the certificate.

The importance of describing the established use with some precision in the certificate is borne out by the decision of the Divisional Court in *Broxbourne Borough Council* v *Secretary of State for the Environment*.[42] The planning authority granted an established use certificate certifying that 'the use of the above land and building for the storage, sawing, re-sawing and disposal of timber in the round and the storage, maintenance, repair and overhaul of vehicles and plant incidental thereto' was established. The site subsequently changed hands and in due course came to be used, amongst other things, as a bulk storage depot for timber planks. The planning authority took enforcement action requiring the discontinuance of the use of the land for the purpose of the stacking and storage of planks of timber. On appeal the Secretary of State considered that the present use of the site was not so different from that described in the established use certificate as to constitute a material change of use. The court upheld the Secretary of State's decision. The certificate was wholly silent as to the scope and intensity of the use at the time it was issued and the established use was therefore to be treated as without limit as regards these matters; the whole purpose of an established use certificate was to preclude the necessity of reopening investigation of past events. As Robert Goff J. commented, the case demonstrated 'that planning authorities should exercise great care concerning the terms of established use certificates which they issue'.

An application for an established use certificate may specify two or more uses, in which case the certificate may be granted either for all those uses or for some one or more of them (s.90(3)). S.D.D. Memorandum 37/1970 stated that a certificate may not be granted in respect of use not described in the application and the English minister has expressed a similar opinion.[43]

If an application for an established use certificate is refused in whole or in part by the planning authority or if the authority fail to give notice of their decision within two months (or such extended period as may be agreed) the applicant may appeal to the Secretary of State (s.91(2)).[44] Before determining an appeal, the Secretary of State must, if either the applicant or the planning authority so desire, afford to each of them an opportunity of appearing before and being heard by a person appointed by the Secretary of State for the purpose (s.91(4)).[45] Where the planning authority have granted an established use certificate in respect of part of the land covered by an application and an appeal is made in respect of the remaining part of the land, the Secretary of State has no power to revoke the certificate already granted.[46] In determining an appeal the Secretary of State is, however,

---

[42] [1980] Q.B. 1.
[43] See [1971] J.P.L. 467.
[44] For procedure, see 1972 Act, Schedule 12; and G.D.O., Art. 18.
[45] For procedure, see the Town and Country Planning (Inquiries Procedure) (Scotland) Rules 1980 or the Town and Country Planning Appeals (Determination by Appointed Person) (Inquiries Procedure) (Scotland) Rules 1980, as appropriate.
[46] See the comments of Woolf J. in *Cottrell* v *Secretary of State for the Environment* [1982] J.P.L. 442.

entitled to uphold the planning authority's decision on grounds different from those of the authority.[47]

On an appeal under s.91(2) the Secretary of State may grant planning permission in respect of any use of land for which an established use certificate is not granted (s.91(3)); in the case of any use of land for which the Secretary of State has power to grant planning permission under s.91, the appellant is deemed to have made application for such permission (s.91(5)) and a fee must be paid to the minister.[48] The fee is due at the time when written notice of the appeal is given to the Secretary of State but will be refunded in the event of an established use certificate being granted.

An established use certificate is not equivalent to a grant of planning permission—an established use certificate would not, for example, be a substitute for the express grant of planning permission which is necessary before a caravan site licence can be granted—so that in some cases it might be wise for an applicant for an established use certificate to apply also for planning permission in order that the two applications can be dealt with together. It would seem, by virtue of s.90(2), which provides that application for a certificate can only be made in respect of a use subsisting at the time of the application, that the Secretary of State has no jurisdiction to grant planning permission under s.91 for a use not subsisting at that date.[49]

Except as provided in s.233 of the 1972 Act, the validity of any decision of the Secretary of State on an appeal relating to an established use certificate shall not be questioned in any legal proceedings whatsoever (s.231) (see chapter 21).

A form of established use certificate is set out in Part II of Schedule 6 to the General Development Order. The date on which application for the certificate was made is to be the date at which the use is certified as established (1972 Act, Schedule 12, para. 4). The form of established use certificate contains a note emphasising that the certificate is not a grant of planning permission and that it 'does not necessarily entitle the owner or occupier of the land to any consequential statutory rights which may be conferred where planning permission has been granted under Part III of the Town and Country Planning (Scotland) Act 1972'. Thus the fact that a use is referred to in a certificate will not imply that it is a use of land which can lawfully be resumed without planning permission under the provisions of s.20(5), (6) and (8) of the 1972 Act[50] (see p. 167 above). Similarly, even though an established use certificate has been granted, planning permission will still be required for a change from the 'established' use to another use within the same class.

A register of established use certificates must be maintained by the planning authority.[51]

---

[47] *Cottrell* (above).
[48] See Town and Country Planning (Fees for Applications and Deemed Applications) (Scotland) Regulations 1983.
[49] See appeal decisions noted in [1971] J.P.L. 463 and 467; and [1974] J.P.L. 293.
[50] See appeal decision noted in [1976] J.P.L. 117.
[51] 1972 Act, Sched. 12, para. 6; and G.D.O., Art. 18.

C. CHALLENGING ENFORCEMENT NOTICES

Introduction

The legislation on enforcement appears to be designed to ensure that in the majority of cases a person who wishes to challenge an enforcement notice should, in the first place at least, follow the statutory avenue of appeal to the Secretary of State for which provision is made by s.85(1) of the 1972 Act. The eight grounds of appeal set out in that subsection, which include certain matters of fact, planning merits and law, cover the matters on which one is most likely to wish to challenge an enforcement notice. In providing that an enforcement notice is not to be questioned on specified grounds other than by way of appeal to the Secretary of State, the legislation seeks to ensure that in the majority of cases it is only after the appeal process has been exhausted that enforcement action may be challenged in the courts. Certain of the grounds on which it might otherwise have been possible to attack the *vires* of an enforcement notice in court are thus made the exclusive preserve of the Secretary of State and if in such a case the notice is not challenged by way of appeal the opportunity to challenge the notice may be lost for good. Further, in determining an appeal the Secretary of State or appointed person may correct certain types of defects in enforcement notices; the scope for challenging notices in the courts on technical grounds is thus reduced.

Although the grounds on which appeal to the Secretary of State may be made embrace a number of matters on which the *vires* of a notice might, in the absence of the specific statutory provisions, be open to attack in the courts, they do not cover all the grounds on which it may be possible to challenge the validity of an enforcement notice; in some circumstances it is possible to challenge the *vires* of an enforcement notice in court, either directly or as a defence to proceedings for non-compliance with an enforcement notice. In theory, it has been said, 'the statutory appeals system and the challenge of notices by other means ought to be mutually exclusive',[52] and that the matters which may be the subject of an appeal to the minister do not go to the *vires* of a notice. The distinction has, however, been blurred both by the way in which the legislation is drafted and by the courts. The interplay between the statutory provisions and the courts' general powers have resulted in very considerable complexity in this area.[53]

This section deals firstly with appeal to the Secretary of State and then with challenge in the courts.

---

[52] J. Davis, 'Enforcement', in *Development Control—Thirty Years On* (J.P.E.L. Occasional Paper, 1979); see also J. Alder, *Development Control* (Sweet and Maxwell, 1979), pp. 148–150.

[53] See H. M. Purdue, 'The Methods of Challenging Enforcement Notices' [1973] J.P.L. 84; J. E. Alder, 'Challenging Enforcement Notices' [1978] J.P.L. 160; and M. Purdue, 'The Secretary of State's Power to Repair Defective Enforcement Notices' [1981] J.P.L. 483.

Appeal to the Secretary of State

A person on whom an enforcement notice has been served or any other person having an interest in the land[54] may appeal to the Secretary of State on grounds specified in s.85(1) of the 1972 Act (below). While it is not a ground of appeal to the Secretary of State that a notice is *ultra vires*, as was said in one appeal,[55] 'where in the course of an appeal such issues are raised the Secretary of State has no alternative but to consider them, since they go to the question of his jurisdiction.' The minister, and indeed the court in the event of a challenge of the minister's decision on the appeal,[56] may conclude that the notice is a nullity.[57] In any case, since it may not be clear, until a court pronounces on it, that an enforcement notice is *ultra vires*, even if it is decided to challenge a notice in the court, it may be wise to consider also the lodging of an appeal to the Secretary of State, thus safeguarding this avenue of challenge in the event of the court action proving unsuccessful. Where the minister or appointed person concludes that the notice is *ultra vires*, the notice is incapable of correction or variation by the minister because the appeal cannot validate a nullity.[58] Indeed, the appeal itself might arguably be regarded as a nullity. Unlike appeals under s.33 of the 1972 Act (see p. 267 above) the minister, in determining an appeal under s.85 of the Act, may not deal with the matter anew. The notice could merely be disregarded but, so that there should be no doubt on the matter, the minister may decide that it should be formally quashed.[59]

When an appeal is lodged, the enforcement notice is of no effect pending the final determination[60] or withdrawal of the appeal (s.85(3)); in the meantime, unless a stop notice has also been served (see p. 344 below), the breach of control may continue. An appeal can therefore serve as a holding device and a high proportion of enforcement appeals are withdrawn prior to determination.

Grounds of appeal

Appeal to the Secretary of State may be made on any one or more of the eight grounds set out in s.85(1) of the 1972 Act.[61] If made out, certain of the grounds of appeal lead inevitably to the quashing of the enforcement notice. The grounds of appeal are as follows:

[54]   See appeal decision reported in [1983] J.P.L. 826.
[55]   [1982] J.P.L. 48.
[56]   See 1972 Act, ss.231 and 233 (as amended by s.47 of the 1982 Act).
[57]   See, for example, *Metallic Protectives Ltd.* v *Secretary of State for the Environment* [1976] J.P.L. 166; and *London Borough of Hounslow* v *Secretary of State for the Environment* [1981] J.P.L. 510.
[58]   *Ridge* v *Baldwin* [1964] A.C. 40.
[59]   See, for example, *London Borough of Hounslow* v *Secretary of State for the Environment* [1981] J.P.L. 510.
[60]   Where an appeal against an enforcement notice has been dismissed by or on behalf of the Secretary of State, the notice takes effect from the date of the dismissal; the coming into force of the notice is not delayed until the time for appeal to the court has expired—see *Dover District Council* v *McKeen, The Times*, 18th March 1985 (distinguishing *Garland* v *Westminster City Council* (1970) 21 P. & C.R. 555).
[61]   As amended by the 1982 Act.

(*a*) That planning permission ought to be granted for the development to which the enforcement notice relates or, as the case may be, that a condition or limitation alleged in the enforcement notice not to have been complied with ought to be discharged.

Section 85(7) provides that where an appeal is brought against an enforcement notice, the appellant shall be deemed to have made an application for planning permission. It would seem, therefore, that the planning merits of the alleged breach of control will be in issue in the appeal whether or not ground (*a*) is specifically pleaded.

(*b*) That the matters alleged in the enforcement notice do not constitute a breach of planning control.

The appellant may be able to show, for example, that the activity complained of does not constitute 'development' within the meaning of s.19 of the 1972 Act (see chapter 6) or that the development is permitted by the general development order (see chapter 7). In an appeal on ground (*b*) the question whether a breach of planning control has occurred is to be judged as at the date the enforcement notice was served.[62] The fact that planning permission has been sought and granted subject to a condition does not preclude a later appeal on ground (*b*).[63]

(*bb*) That the breach of planning control alleged in the notice has not taken place.

This ground of appeal was introduced by the Local Government and Planning (Scotland) Act 1982[64] and meets the point made by Lord Widgery C.J. in *Hammersmith London Borough Council* v *Secretary of State for the Environment*[65] in which his Lordship said: 'It is a little odd that the Act of 1971 at no point authorises the Secretary of State to accept an appeal against an enforcement notice merely because the allegation in the notice does not fit the factual position on the ground.' The new provision allows an appeal to be lodged on the ground that there has 'in fact', as opposed to 'in law' (ground (*b*)), been no breach of planning control.

(*c*) In the case of a notice which, by virtue of s.84(3) of the 1972 Act, may be served only within the period of four years from the date of the breach of planning control to which the notice relates, that the period has elapsed at the date of service.

(*d*) In the case of a notice not falling within paragraph (*c*) (above), that the breach of planning control alleged by the notice occurred before the beginning of 1965.[66] Grounds (*c*) and (*d*) allow for an appeal on the basis that

---

[62] *Prengate Properties Ltd.* v *Secretary of State for the Environment* (1973) 25 P. & C.R. 311.

[63] See *East Barnet U.D.C.* v *British Transport Commission* [1962] 2 Q.B. 484.

[64] See s.48 and Schedule 2, para. 20.

[65] (1975) 30 P. & C.R. 19. See, however, *Jeary* v *Chailey R.D.C.* (1973) 26 P. & C.R. 280.

[66] A consultation paper issued by the Scottish Development Department on 31st July 1984 proposed that this ground of appeal should be replaced by a ground that a valid established use certificate (see p. 315 above) has been granted in respect of the use of the land to which the enforcement notice relates. If effect is given to this proposal it will mean that a person who failed to obtain an established use certificate while it was still possible to do so (it is also proposed to abolish the right to apply for a certificate—see p. 316 above) will lose the right he presently has to carry on a use which has continued since before the beginning of 1965.

the breach of control is immune from enforcement action under one or other of the 'limitation periods' (see p. 310 above). These grounds are mutually exclusive.

(e) That the enforcement notice was not served as required by s.84(5) of the Act (see p. 294 above).

(f) That the steps required by the notice to be taken exceed what is necessary to remedy any breach of planning control. This would include the plea successfully advanced in *Mansi* v *Elstree R.D.C.*[67] that the notice seeks to restrict a use of the land which may legitimately be carried on (see p. 304 above). To succeed on this ground the appellant must show that the enforcement notice requires more than is necessary to undo the contravention;[68] if it is desired to argue that it would be reasonable to require something less than full restoration, that argument should be made under ground (a).

(g) That the specified period for compliance with the notice falls short of what should reasonably be allowed. It would seem that the reasonableness of the period allowed is to be tested as at the date of service of the notice.[69] In considering whether in terms of ground (g) the specified period falls short of what should reasonably be allowed, the minister is apparently entitled to take into account the previous planning history of the site. In *Mercer* v *Uckfield Rural District Council*[70] an appeal against a refusal of planning permission was dismissed in November 1959. In December 1960 an enforcement notice was served requiring the owner to remove vehicles and other articles from the site within 28 days of the notice taking effect. At the date of service there were some 300 vehicles on the site and the owner appealed to the minister on the ground that the period allowed for compliance with the notice was unreasonably short. Taking the previous planning history of the site into account, the minister found the period reasonable. The Divisional Court held that the owner, knowing that an enforcement notice could have been served at any time after November 1959, kept the vehicles on the site after that date at his peril and that the previous planning history was relevant and was properly taken into account by the minister.

Appeal procedure

An appeal must be made in writing to the Secretary of State (s.85(2)[71]) and must be made before the date specified in the enforcement notice as the date on which it is to take effect (s.85(1)[72]). The Secretary of State has no power to extend the time for appeal. It is not enough that an appeal is posted before

---

[67] (1964) 16 P. & C.R. 153.
[68] See, for example, *SPADS* No. A2978 (P/ENA/LB/9 and 10, 27th April 1979).
[69] *Smith* v *King* (1969) 21 P. & C.R. 560.
[70] (1963) 14 P. & C.R. 32.
[71] As substituted by the 1982 Act, s.48 and Schedule 2, para. 20(b).
[72] As amended by the 1982 Act, s.48 and Schedule 2, para. 20(a)(i).

the specified date; the notice of appeal must be received by the Secretary of State before the relevant date.[73]

There is no prescribed form for a notice of appeal and in *Pirie* v *Bauld*[74] it was held that a letter which referred to s.85 but did not specifically state that it was intended to give notice of appeal was to be treated as a valid appeal. A person giving notice of an appeal must submit to the Secretary of State a statement specifying the grounds on which he is appealing against the enforcement notice and stating briefly the facts[75] on which he proposes to rely in support of each of these grounds; if this statement is not submitted at the time of making the appeal, or any statement received is inadequate and the Secretary of State has to request further information, the minister may require the information to be supplied within 28 days.[76] If that requirement is not complied with, the Secretary of State may dismiss the appeal (s.85(2C)(a)).

Planning authorities have been asked to send the recipient a duplicate copy of an enforcement notice, which can be sent to the Secretary of State with any appeal which may be made.[77]

A fee is generally payable in respect of the 'deemed' planning application associated with the enforcement appeal (above) and should be paid to the Secretary of State when the appeal is lodged.[78] The fee will be refunded if the Secretary of State declines jurisidiction, or if the enforcement notice is withdrawn, or if the appeal is withdrawn before the date of the public inquiry or site inspection, or if the appeal succeeds on any of the grounds (*b*) to (*e*) in s.85(1). A fee is payable in respect of each appeal made by different persons against an enforcement notice.

Within 28 days of the Secretary of State notifying them of the appeal, the planning authority must submit to the Secretary of State and to the appellant a statement of the submissions which they propose to put forward.[79] This statement is to include a summary of the authority's response to each ground of appeal advanced by the appellant and a statement as to whether the authority would be prepared to grant planning permission for the development alleged in the enforcement notice to have been carried out, and, if so,

---

[73] See *Lenlyn Ltd.* v *Secretary of State for the Environment*, *The Times*, 5th December 1984. In *R.* v *Melton and Belvoir Justices, ex p. Tynan* (1977) 33 P. & C.R. 214 notice of appeal was sent one day late but was initially accepted by the Secretary of State; the Divisional Court took the view that the purported acceptance did not render the appeal valid.

[74] 1975 S.L.T. (Sh.Ct.) 6.

[75] It is necessary to state facts even if it is proposed only to raise matters of law on appeal—see *P.A.D. Entertainments Ltd.* v *Secretary of State for the Environment* [1982] J.P.L. 706.

[76] 1972 Act, s.85(2A) (added by the 1982 Act, s.48 and Schedule 2, para. 20) and Town and Country Planning (Enforcement of Control) (Scotland) Regulations 1984, reg. 5. These provisions give statutory recognition to the decision in *Howard* v *Secretary of State for the Environment* [1975] Q.B. 235.

[77] See S.D.D. Circulars 33/1983 and 6/1984.

[78] See the Town and Country Planning (Fees for Applications and Deemed Applications) (Scotland) Regulations 1983, reg. 8; and S.D.D. Circular 33/1983, Appendix A.

[79] 1972 Act, s.85(2B) (added by the 1982 Act, s.48 and Schedule 2, para. 20); and the Town and Country Planning (Enforcement of Control) (Scotland) Regulations 1984, reg. 6.

the details of any conditions they would wish to attach to such a permission.

If the authority's statement is not submitted within the 28 day period, the Secretary of State may allow the appeal without further procedure and quash the enforcement notice.[80] The Secretary of State will, it seems, invoke this power when he considers the planning authority to have delayed their submission unreasonably.[81]

The appeal procedure is similar to that for appeals against refusal or conditional grant of planning permission (see p. 266 above and chapter 20). The Secretary of State must, if either the appellant or the planning authority so desire, afford to each of them an opportunity of appearing before, and being heard by, a person appointed by the minister for the purpose[82] (s.85(2D) and Schedule 7, paragraph 2(2)). Appeals against enforcement notices are among the classes of appeals which have been delegated to appointed persons (see chapter 20); however, the Secretary of State retains power to direct that any particular appeal is to be determined by him.[83] Whether the appeal is to be decided by written submissions or after a public inquiry, notice of the appeal will be given in the local press. S.D.D. Circular 6/1984 states that it is only in exceptional circumstances that the Secretary of State will exercise his powers to direct the planning authority to take further steps to give notice of the appeal.

In *Ross* v *Aberdeen County Council*[84] the Sheriff held, in an appeal against an enforcement notice, that in accordance with the principle that the onus of proof 'rests with the party who would fail if no evidence was adduced on either side', it was for the appellant to make good his grounds of appeal. A similar conclusion was reached by Widgery J. in *Nelsovil* v *Minister of Housing and Local Government.*[85] However, in *L.W.T. Contractors Ltd.* v *Secretary of State for the Environment*[86] Woolf J. stressed that the burden of proof in enforcement appeals was not the criminal burden of 'beyond reasonable doubt' but the ordinary civil burden of 'the balance of probabilities'.

Determination of appeal

On the determination of an appeal against an enforcement notice the

---

[80] 1972 Act, s.85(2C)(b) (added by the 1982 Act, s.48 and Schedule 2, para. 20).

[81] See S.D.D. Circular 6/1984, para. 19.

[82] The procedures for such a hearing, generally dealt with by way of local inquiry, are governed by the Town and Country Planning (Inquiries Procedure) (Scotland) Rules 1980, or the Town and Country Planning Appeals (Determination by Appointed Person) (Inquiries Procedure) (Scotland) Rules 1980, as appropriate.

[83] See the Town and Country Planning (Determination of Appeals by Appointed Persons) (Prescribed Classes) (Scotland) Regulations 1980.

[84] 1955 S.L.T. (Sh.Ct.) 65.

[85] [1962] 1 W.L.R. 404. See also *Britt* v *Buckinghamshire County Council* (1964) 1 Q.B. 77; and *Wild* v *Secretary of State for the Environment* [1976] J.P.L. 432.

[86] [1981] J.P.L. 815; see too *Thrasyvoulou* v *Secretary of State for the Environment* [1984] J.P.L. 732.

Secretary of State (or, in a delegated case, the appointed person[87]) is to give directions for giving effect to his determination including, where appropriate, directions for quashing the enforcement notice or for varying the terms of the notice *in favour of the appellant* (s.85(5)). A notice might, for example, be varied where the minister considered the allegations in the notice not fully justified, or considered the requirements of the notice excessive or the time allowed for compliance too short.

The Secretary of State may grant planning permission for the development to which the enforcement notice relates (s.85(5)(a)) or for such other development on the land to which the notice relates as he considers appropriate (s.85(5)(aa)).[88] It would seem that it is not open to the minister to grant planning permission in respect of land which was not covered by the notice.[89] A grant of planning permission may include permission for the retention or completion of any buildings or works without compliance with a condition attached to a previous planning permission (s.85(6)(a)). The permission may also be subject to such conditions as the Secretary of State thinks fit (s.85(6)(b)). In considering whether to grant planning permission, the minister must, as in a planning appeal, have regard to the provisions of the development plan, so far as material to the subject matter of the enforcement notice, and to any other material considerations (s.85(6)).

The Secretary of State may discharge any condition or limitation on a grant of planning permission for the development to which the enforcement notice relates (s.85(5)(a)); it appears that this power is not confined to a condition or limitation in respect of which a breach of planning control is alleged. Furthermore, he may substitute for it any other condition or limitation (s.85(6)).

The Secretary of State may also determine any purpose for which the land may, in the circumstances obtaining at the time of the determination, be lawfully used,[90] having regard to any past use thereof or to any planning permission relating to the land (s.85(5)(b)). A determination under this provision will make clear the use to which the land may lawfully be put and will avoid the need for exploratory applications for planning permission. A determination under s.85(5)(b) does not, of course, oblige a person with an interest in the land to use the land in accordance with the determination, but

---

[87] In the determination of an enforcement notice appeal the appointed person has the same powers and duties as are conferred upon the Secretary of State by s.85(4)–(6) of the 1972 Act (1972 Act, Schedule 7, para. 2(1)).

[88] Added by the 1982 Act, s.48 and Schedule 2, para. 20. This provision overcomes the difficulties highlighted in *Richmond-upon-Thames Borough Council* v *Secretary of State for the Environment* (1972) 224 E.G. 1555 (in which it was held that it was not open to the Secretary of State to grant planning permission for development different from the unauthorised development which was the subject of the enforcement notice) and in *Hansford* v *Minister of Housing and Local Government* (1969) 213 E.G. 637 (in which it was held that planning permission could not be granted for part only of the offending development).

[89] See appeal decision noted in [1973] J.P.L. 261.

[90] As to the meaning of 'lawful use' see p. 168 above.

he may do so at any time after the determination without further authorisation under the planning legislation. The English minister will apparently not make such a determination unless specifically asked to do so by one of the parties and even when asked has sometimes had to decline to do so because insufficient evidence was presented to the inquiry to enable him to form a view on the question.[91]

Even if appeal to the Secretary of State against an enforcement notice has not been made on ground (a) of s.85(1) (i.e., on the ground that planning permission ought to be granted for the development to which the enforcement notice relates or, as the case may be, that a condition or limitation alleged in the enforcement notice not to have been complied with ought to be discharged), the appellant is deemed to have made an application for planning permission for the development to which the notice relates (s.85(7)).

A decision that a use is immune from enforcement action because it began before the beginning of 1965 is not equivalent to a grant of planning permission (see p. 320 above) and even where an appeal succeeds on ground (d) of s.85(1) (i.e., that the alleged breach occurred before the beginning of 1965) and the enforcement notice is quashed, the Secretary of State will still have to consider the application for planning permission which the appellant is, by virtue of s.85(7), deemed to have made.

Defects in enforcement notices

On an appeal against an enforcement notice, the Secretary of State or appointed person may correct any informality, defect or error in the notice if he is satisfied that the informality, error or defect is not material (s.85(4)(a)). However, some defects will be regarded as so serious as to render the notice *ultra vires*, with the result that no question of correction can arise.

In *Miller-Mead* v *Minister of Housing and Local Government*[92] Upjohn L.J. stated that if on its face the notice does not comply with the requirements of [s.84] then it is a nullity and 'so much waste paper'. He said: 'A notice has to specify certain matters. If it does not so specify, the notice is plainly inoperative as a notice under the Act.' It would seem, therefore, that a failure to specify the breach of control, the steps required to be taken to remedy the breach, the date on which the notice is to take effect and the period for compliance will nullify the notice. Thus in *Burgess* v *Jarvis*[93] the Court of Appeal held that a notice which did not specify the period at the expiration of which it was to take effect was a nullity.

Upjohn L.J. went on to define a further category of defects which will nullify a notice. He said:

---

[91]   See *Selected Enforcement and Allied Appeals*, p. 62.
[92]   [1963] 2 Q.B. 196.
[93]   [1952] 2 Q.B. 41.

'Supposing, then, on its true construction the notice was hopelessly ambiguous and uncertain, so that the owner or occupier could not tell in what respect it was alleged that he had developed the land without permission or in what respect it was alleged that he had failed to comply with a condition or, again, that he could not tell with reasonable certainty what steps he had to take to remedy the alleged breaches. The notice would be bad on its face and a nullity.'

This category may be illustrated by the decision of the Divisional Court in *Metallic Protectives Ltd.* v *Secretary of State for the Environment.*[94] The Court considered that a notice which required the installation of satisfactory sound-proofing of a compressor and for all possible action to be taken to minimise the effects created by the use of acrylic paint was so uncertain in its terms as to be a nullity. As such, it was incapable of amendment.

Certain matters on which it might have been possible to challenge the *vires* of an enforcement notice at common law are included in the statutory grounds of appeal to the Secretary of State under s.85 (above) and the provision of a statutory right of appeal suggests that these matters do not go to the *vires* of an enforcement notice.[95] As a result of his powers of correction the Secretary of State will in some circumstances be able to uphold an enforcement notice which might otherwise have had to be quashed as invalid. The answer to the question whether the Secretary of State is able to correct an error in an enforcement notice will, of course, be important for the recipient of the notice because if the power of correction is not available then the notice will have to be quashed by the minister. For the recipient the end result may, therefore, be much the same as if the notice was a nullity.

Speaking of the similarly-worded provision in the Town and Country Planning Act 1962, Lord Denning said in *Miller-Mead* that the minister

'can correct errors so long as, having regard to the merits of the case, the correction can be made without injustice. No informality, defect or error is a material one unless it is such as to produce injustice. Applied to misrecitals, it means this—if the misrecital goes to the substance of the matter then the notice may be quashed, but, if the misrecital does not go to the substance of the matter and can be amended without injustice, it should be amended rather than that the notice should be quashed or declared a nullity.'

Generalisations about when the correction of an informality, defect or error will be regarded as material must be treated with caution. Much will

---

[94] [1976] J.P.L. 166. See also *McNaughton* v *Peter McIntyre (Clyde) Ltd.*, High Court of Justiciary, 21st March 1978 (unreported, but see 1981 S.P.L.P. 15).
[95] See, however, *McDaid* v *Clydebank District Council* 1984 S.L.T. 162 (below).

depend on the circumstances of each case.[96] However, it would seem that if the planning authority allege the wrong breach of control—for example, if they allege development without planning permission when the notice should refer to a breach of a condition—then the error will be regarded as material and incapable of correction.[97] In *Kerrier District Council* v *Secretary of State for the Environment*[98] Lord Lane C.J. said: 'If, on the facts of any particular case, the planning authority puts the case in the wrong pigeon-hole, the enforcement notice will be set aside.' Furthermore, it seems that if the planning authority put the case in the right 'pigeon-hole' but seriously misdescribe the breach, that error, too, will be incapable of correction.[99]

In *Royal Borough of Kensington and Chelsea* v *Secretary of State for the Environment and Mia Carla Ltd.*[1] Donaldson L.J. said that the power to correct a notice was 'distinctly limited'. It would not extend to correction of a misdescription in the alleged unauthorised material change of use. The notice in that case referred to 'a material change in the use of the garden of the said land to a use for the purposes of a restaurant'. The planning authority argued that it could be amended so as to refer instead to a material change of use by way of intensification of the restaurant use. 'Plainly', said Donaldson L.J., 'such an amendment would not be the correction of any informality or defect; it would be producing a totally different enforcement notice.'

The decision in *Mia Carla* appears to go further than that in *Birmingham Corporation* v *Minister of Housing and Local Government*.[2] There Lord Widgery C.J. said that the minister was perfectly right to refuse to amend a notice which alleged as the breach of control 'house-let-in-lodgings' rather than 'use as separate dwellings'. Lord Widgery did not specifically rule out such an amendment but stated that 'it would be wrong in these circum-stances for the minister to amend an enforcement notice to cover a development which had never been put forward or argued' at the inquiry into the appeal. In other words, such an amendment or correction would cause injustice.

Misdescriptions of the breach of control which are not of a serious nature would seem to be capable of correction. Thus, in *Hammersmith London*

---

[96] See M. Purdue, 'The Secretary of State's Power to Repair Defective Enforcement Notices' [1981] J.P.L. 483. Examples of appeal decisions raising the question whether correction could be made are to be found in *SPADS* Nos. A2959 (P/ENA/HF/8, 17th April 1979); A4234 (P/ENA/SL/152, 21st July 1982); A4471 (P/ENA/D/45–47, 31st January 1983); A4701 (P/ENA/GA/43, 30th June 1983); A4921 (P/ENA/W/27, 5th December 1983); [1977] J.P.L. 116, 397 and 675; [1978] J.P.L. 568 and 785; [1979] J.P.L. 47, 188 and 786; [1980] J.P.L. 469; [1983] J.P.L. 449 and 826; and [1984] J.P.L. 451. See too *Selected Enforcement and Allied Appeals*, pp. 11, 12, 21 and 29.

[97] *Garland* v *Minister of Housing and Local Government* (1968) 20 P. & C.R. 93; and *Kerrier District Council* v *Secretary of State for the Environment* (1980) 41 P. & C.R. 284.

[98] (1980) 41 P. & C.R. 284.

[99] *Copeland Borough Council* v *Secretary of State for the Environment* (1976) 31 P. & C.R. 403; *Royal Borough of Kensington and Chelsea* v *Secretary of State for the Environment and Mia Carla Ltd.* [1981] J.P.L. 50; and *Choudry* v *Secretary of State for the Environment* [1983] J.P.L. 231.

[1] [1981] J.P.L. 50.

[2] [1964] 1 Q.B. 178.

Borough Council v *Secretary of State for the Environment*[3] it was held that where the Secretary of State considered that an enforcement notice contained an unsuitable description of the use of premises he was entitled, and indeed bound,[4] to attempt to obtain accuracy in the notice by substituting a more suitable description in the notice, provided that no injustice would thereby be done to either party; in this case the Secretary of State had erred in concluding that an inappropriate allegation of change of use to guest-house (rather than 'hostel' or some such similar description) was a material error which he could not correct.

It appears that any correction which has the effect of enlarging the scope of the enforcement notice will generally be regarded as material and beyond the powers of the minister. For example, in *T.L.G. Building Materials* v *Secretary of State for the Environment*,[5] Donaldson L.J. commented that it seemed to him that it was 'beyond a mere formality to call upon somebody to stop using some land for the storage of building materials and to amend it to the much wider concept of prohibiting use as a builders merchants yard . . . [A]ny wider condemnation—if that was the right word—in an enforcement notice must be material, except in somewhat exceptional circumstances.' In the same case Hodgson J. said that it was 'only in the most unusual circumstances that one could say that the correction of a notice that altered the planning unit to which the enforcement notice was directed was not material'. Similarly, the English minister has held that it would be beyond his powers to correct a plan attached to an enforcement notice so as to extend the area covered by the notice.[6]

The decision in *Morris* v *Secretary of State for the Environment*[7] would seem to provide an illustration of the 'somewhat exceptional circumstances' referred to by Donaldson L.J. in *T.L.G. Building Materials* when a 'wider condemnation' will not be regarded as material. The enforcement notice alleged as the breach of control the use of premises for the sale, repair and respraying of motor vehicles. The notice required the discontinuance of the use of the site for repairing and respraying vehicles and the removal of the vehicles. Through an oversight it omitted to proscribe the sale of vehicles. The court held that the notice could be corrected to include the sale of vehicles. No injustice would be caused as the omission was a pure error and it was obvious that it should have been there from the start. Similarly, in *Sanders* v *Secretary of State for the Environment*[8] the Divisional Court held that a notice could be corrected so as to proscribe the use of land for the repair of boilers in addition to the storing and cutting up of scrap metal. The

---

3   (1975) 30 P. & C.R. 19. See also *Patel* v *Betts* [1978] J.P.L. 109; and *Bevan* v *Secretary of State for Wales* (1969) 211 E.G. 1245.
4   See also on this point Ackner J. in *London Borough of Hounslow* v *Secretary of State for the Environment* [1981] J.P.L. 510. See too *Wealden District Council* v *Secretary of State for the Environment* [1983] J.P.L. 234; and *Bath City Council* v *Secretary of State for the Environment* (1983) 47 P. & C.R. 663.
5   (1980) 41 P. & C.R. 243.
6   [1971] J.P.L. 348; see too [1974] J.P.L. 734; [1975] J.P.L. 166; and [1976] J.P.L. 710.
7   (1975) 31 P. & C.R. 216.
8   [1981] J.P.L. 593.

additional use had been in issue in the appeal against the enforcement notice and could not be carried on independently of the other proscribed activities; together they formed a composite mixed use of the land. The correction would not, therefore, cause injustice.

Whilst, subject to the exceptions described, any correction which has the effect of enlarging the scope of the notice is likely to be regarded as material, a reduction in the scope of the notice will usually be within the minister's powers.[9] Thus, for example, the minister has been prepared to correct a notice which referred to a larger area than was actually used for the purpose enforced against.[10] The court will return a notice to the minister for correction if there is a risk that it may prohibit a lawful use.[11]

It would seem that a reduction in the scope of a notice may be achieved either by way of correction under s.85(4)(a) or by way of variation of the notice under s.85(5), provided that the variation is in favour of the appellant.[12] The proviso is important because, although these powers overlap to a considerable extent,[13] they do not entirely coincide. In *Morris* v *Secretary of State for the Environment*[14] it was argued that the scope of the notice could not be enlarged so as to prohibit the sale of motor vehicles as this would not be a variation 'in favour of the appellant'. The court held that the enlargement had been effected by way of a correction of the notice so that the question of advantage to the appellant did not arise. In the circumstances of the case the correction did not cause injustice.

Challenging validity of Secretary of State's decision

The validity of any decision[15] of the Secretary of State on an appeal to him on any of the grounds in s.85(1) may not, except as provided in s.233 of the 1972 Act, be questioned in any legal proceedings whatsoever (s.231[16]). Under s.233 any person who is aggrieved by such a decision and who desires to

---

9   See *London Borough of Camden* v *Secretary of State for the Environment* [1979] J.P.L. 311; and *Burner* v *Secretary of State for the Environment* [1983] J.P.L. 459.

10   [1974] J.P.L. 159; see too [1974] J.P.L. 248 and 426.

11   *Mansi* v *Elstree R.D.C.* (1964) 16 P. & C.R. 153; *Newport* v *Secretary of State for the Environment* (1980) 40 P. & C.R. 261; *Trevors Warehouses Ltd.* v *Secretary of State for the Environment* (1972) 23 P. & C.R. 215; and *Day and Mid-Warwickshire Motors Ltd.* v *Secretary of State for the Environment* (1979) 78 L.G.R. 27.

12   See, for example, *Cleaver* v *Secretary of State for the Environment* [1981] J.P.L. 38; *Perkins* v *Secretary of State for the Environment* [1981] J.P.L. 755; and appeal decision reported in [1980] J.P.L. 618.

13   See, for example, *Dunton Park Caravan Site Ltd.* v *Secretary of State for the Environment* [1981] J.P.L. 511.

14   (1975) 31 P. & C.R. 216.

15   If the Secretary of State declines to proceed because he believes no proper notice of appeal has been given, that is a final determination for the purposes of application to the court—see *Button* v *Jenkins* [1975] 3 All E.R. 585; *Chalgray* v *Secretary of State for the Environment* (1976) 33 P. & C.R. 10; and *Wain* v *Secretary of State for the Environment* (1978) 39 P. & C.R. 82. See, however, *Co-operative Retail Services Ltd.* v *Secretary of State for the Environment* [1980] 1 W.L.R. 271.

16   As amended by s.47 of the 1982 Act.

question the validity of the Secretary of State's action on the grounds that the action is not within the powers of the 1972 Act or that any of the relevant statutory requirements have not been complied with, may within six weeks of the decision make application to the Court of Session (see chapter 21).

Challenge of enforcement notice in court

Subject to what is said below about the important statutory provisions, especially s.85(10) of the 1972 Act, which seek to restrict recourse to the courts, the recipient of an enforcement notice which is *ultra vires* may be able to challenge it directly in the Court of Session on ordinary administrative law principles,[17] or might take the risk of simply ignoring the notice, raising the question of *vires* as a defence to proceedings for non-compliance with the notice. However, even if the recipient of an enforcement notice is satisfied that the notice is a nullity, as an enforcement notice 'runs with the land' (see p. 339 below), he may consider it desirable to get a formal pronouncement from the court so as to remove any doubts which might arise in the future. As Lord Denning remarked in *Lovelock* v *Minister of Transport*:[18] 'The plain fact is that, even if such a decision as this is "void" or a "nullity", it remains in being unless and until some steps are taken before the courts to have it declared void.'

The right to challenge an enforcement notice in the courts on ordinary administrative law principles is restricted by s.85(10) of the 1972 Act which provides[19] that: 'The validity of an enforcement notice shall not, except by way of appeal [to the Secretary of State] under this section be questioned in any proceedings whatsoever on any of the grounds specified in paragraphs (b) to (e)' of s.85(1). The purpose of this preclusive clause would therefore seem to be that if it is considered that the planning authority are in error in alleging that the activities in question constitute a breach of control or that a breach of control has taken place, or are in error in describing the breach of control, on questions of immunity from enforcement action or in the service of the notice,[20] the only way in which the mistake may be challenged is by way of an appeal to the Secretary of State under s.85; if no appeal is lodged then the opportunity to challenge such errors is in general lost for good. In *Miller-Mead* v *Minister of Housing and Local Government*[21] Lord Denning explained the legislation's effect in the following terms:

---

[17] This might take the form of an action for declarator and reduction (see *Moss' Empires* v *Assessor for Glasgow* 1917 S.C. (H.L.) 1; *Hamilton* v *Roxburgh County Council* 1970 S.C. 248; 1971 S.L.T. 2; and *London and Clydeside Estates Ltd.* v *Aberdeen District Council* 1980 S.C. (H.L.) 1; 1980 S.L.T. 81) or of suspension and interdict (see *McDaid* v *Clydebank District Council* 1984 S.L.T. 162).
[18] (1980) 40 P. & C.R. 336. See too *London and Clydeside Estates Ltd.* v *Aberdeen District Council* 1980 S.C. (H.L.) 1; 1980 S.L.T. 81.
[19] Subject to the exception mentioned in s.85(11) (below).
[20] See, however, *McDaid* v *Clydebank District Council* 1984 S.L.T. 162 (below).
[21] [1963] 2 Q.B. 196.

'You used previously to be able to raise any of these matters before the courts. But by reason of s.33(8) of the Act of 1960 [the terms of which were very similar to those of s.85(10) of the 1972 Act] you can no longer do so. You cannot raise it by an action for a declaration. You cannot raise it by appeal to the justices. Nor by waiting until there is an attempt to enforce it by criminal proceedings. You can only raise it by an appeal to the Minister. And even if you succeed in your appeal, the Minister can at the most quash it. He cannot declare it to be a nullity or hold it to be void from the beginning. In this way the legislature has disposed of the suggestion that an enforcement notice is a "nullity" on any such ground.'

However, Lord Denning's exposition of the law and a number of other decisions on the effect of the preclusive clause must, so far as Scotland is concerned, now be read in the light of the important decision in *McDaid* v *Clydebank District Council* (below).

In *Pirie* v *Bauld*[22] the Sheriff considered unsound the suggestion that the word 'proceedings' in s.85(10) was not intended to include criminal proceedings under s.86 of the 1972 Act. He declared that 'if the legislature had intended to exclude criminal proceedings from the provisions of the subsection they would have said so clearly and would not have used the phrase "any proceedings whatsoever" '; he considered that 'the matter is put beyond any possible doubt by s.85(11) which provides an exception to the preceding subsection in relation to criminal proceedings brought under s.86 against a particular class of offender.'

In *Jeary* v *Chailey Rural District Council*[23] the Court of Appeal held that the similarly-worded preclusive clause in the Town and Country Planning Act 1962 could not be construed as directed only to groundless challenges of enforcement notices but had to be read as directed also to preventing the assertion of vested rights; even if the appellant in this case had, as he alleged, a vested right to use the premises in question for the purpose which the enforcement notice alleged was in breach of planning control, he was still precluded by the statutory provision from questioning the validity of the notice in the courts.

In *Davy* v *Spelthorne Borough Council*[24] Lord Fraser said that the word 'validity' as used in s.243(1)(a) of the Town and Country Planning Act 1971[25] was not to be understood in its strict legal sense but was to be taken as meaning 'enforceability', so that an action questioning an enforcement notice, even indirectly, on any of the specified grounds would be caught by

---

[22]   1975 S.L.T. (Sh.Ct.) 6. See also *McNaughton* v *Peter McIntyre (Clyde) Ltd.*, High Court of Justiciary, 21st March 1978 (unreported, but see 1981 S.P.L.P. 15); and *R.* v *Smith (Thomas George)* (1984) 48 P. & C.R. 392.
[23]   (1973) 26 P. & C.R. 280.
[24]   [1984] A.C. 262.
[25]   Which is, however, rather wider in its scope than s.85(10) of the 1972 Act.

the preclusive clause.[26] In that case Lord Wilberforce said that there may be some warrant for not giving the preclusive clause a restricted meaning and it has been held in both Scotland and England that in certain circumstances the preclusive clause may act as a bar to proceedings begun *before* the service of an enforcement notice.[27]

In *James Barrie (Sand and Gravel) Ltd.* v *Lanark District Council*[28] the planning authority had resolved to take enforcement action, including the service of a stop notice[29] in respect of allegedly unauthorised sand and gravel workings. The pursuers argued that, as they had been in breach of planning control for more than four years, their activities were immune from enforcement action and that any enforcement notice and related stop notice would therefore be invalid. The pursuers realised that an appeal to the Secretary of State against an enforcement notice on ground (c) of s.85(1) of the 1972 Act would have the effect of suspending the operation of the notice until the matter was determined. However, the service of a stop notice would have the effect of bringing their activities to an immediate halt. The pursuers accordingly raised an action for declarator that their activities did not constitute a breach of planning control and for interdict to prevent the planning authority serving a stop notice. Lord Cowie held that in view of the provisions of s.85(10) of the 1972 Act it was not competent to question the validity of an anticipated enforcement notice in such proceedings on the ground specified in s.85(1)(c) and that was effectively what the pursuers were attempting to do.

However, the decision of the First Division of the Court of Session in *McDaid* v *Clydebank District Council*[30] indicates that s.85(10) is not effective as a bar to all challenges to the validity of an enforcement notice on grounds which might be thought to come within the ambit of paragraphs (b) to (e) of s.85(1). In *McDaid* enforcement notices were served on the occupier of land but not on the owners. Although s.85(1)(e) provides that it is a ground of appeal to the Secretary of State that an enforcement notice has not been served as required by the 1972 Act, the First Division held, firstly, that the court's jurisdiction was not excluded by s.85(10) in a case where, for reasons beyond the control of a person seeking to challenge the enforcement notice, the appeal procedure provided by the legislation could not be used, and, secondly, in respect that the enforcement notices had not been properly served, that they were nullities.

---

[26] In this case the House of Lords doubted whether a claim for damages for negligence involved a challenge of the validity of an enforcement notice but held that even if it did, the plaintiff's assertion that he had acquiesced in an enforcement notice because of the planning authority's negligent advice was not a ground covered by s.243(1)(a).

[27] See *James Barrie (Sand and Gravel) Ltd.* v *Lanark District Council* 1979 S.L.T. 14; and *Square Meals Frozen Foods Ltd.* v *Dunstable Corporation* [1974] 1 W.L.R. 59 (which was referred to without disapproval by Lord Wilberforce in *Davy* (above)).

[28] Above.

[29] On the competency of interdict in connection with stop notices, see *Central Regional Council* v *Clackmannan District Council* 1983 S.L.T. 666; and *Earl Car Sales (Edinburgh) Ltd.* v *City of Edinburgh District Council* 1984 S.L.T. 8, considered at p. 346 below.

[30] 1984 S.L.T. 162.

It could scarcely have been the intention of Parliament, said Lord Cameron, 'that a failure in duty by the planning authority in the matter of service of notice should have the bizarre consequence of depriving a person with an interest as owner, lessee or occupier of any right to challenge the validity of such a notice, which because of the failure in duty he never received, and of which he had no knowledge during the period provided for lodging an appeal, and the effect of which may well be to cause him as owner material and serious loss.' In the court's view, s.85(10) only applied to enforcement notices in the terms and form prescribed by the Act. Here there were no such notices and the preclusive clause could not therefore apply.

The decision in *McDaid* leaves considerable uncertainty as to the scope of s.85(10). The broader of the grounds of the court's decision can be read as implying that the preclusive clause is not to apply to an enforcement notice which is *ultra vires* because of a failure to satisfy the requirements of s.84; in that event an enforcement notice might be vulnerable to challenge years after it had purportedly taken effect.

Section 85(10) is not to apply where criminal proceedings are brought under s.86 of the 1972 Act in respect of non-compliance with an enforcement notice against a person who:

(*a*) has held an interest in the land since before the enforcement notice was served; and
(*b*) did not have the enforcement notice served on him; and
(*c*) satisfies the court that:
    (i)   he did not know and could not reasonably have been expected to know that the enforcement notice had been served; and
    (ii) his interests have been substantially prejudiced by the failure to serve the notice on him (s.85(11)).

While, as mentioned above, it is specifically provided that the validity of an enforcement notice is not, except by way of appeal to the Secretary of State under s.85 of the 1972 Act, to be questioned in any proceedings whatsoever on any of the five grounds specified in paragraphs (b) to (e) of s.85(1), no specific provision is made in relation to challenge of the validity of a notice on the grounds specified in paragraphs (a), (f) and (g) of that subsection.[31] This failure to account for grounds (a), (f) and (g)[32] means that it may, as Alder says,[33] seem 'superficially attractive to assume that these matters can be challenged in other proceedings'. In *Smith* v *King*[34] the Divisional Court held (Lord Parker C.J. dissenting) that in a prosecution

---

[31] Specific provision is, however, made by ss.231 and 233 of the 1972 Act, as amended by s.47 of the 1982 Act, in relation to challenge of the validity of any decision of the *Secretary of State* on an appeal to him under any of the grounds in s.85(1) (see p. 332 above).

[32] In England and Wales these grounds are now included among those on which challenge of an enforcement notice is precluded by s.243(1) of the Town and Country Planning Act 1971.

[33] J. Alder, 'Challenging Enforcement Notices' [1978] J.P.L. 160.

[34] (1969) 21 P. & C.R. 560; followed in *Hutchison* v *Firetto* [1973] J.P.L. 314; and *Redbridge London Borough Council* v *Perry* (1976) 33 P. & C.R. 176.

before justices the validity of an enforcement notice was open to challenge on grounds (f) and (g) and that in this case it had therefore been open to the justices to consider whether, in terms of ground (g), the period allowed for compliance with an enforcement notice fell short 'of what should reasonably be allowed'. Ashworth J. stated that 'any enforcement notice, to be valid, must allow a reasonable period for the execution of the work'. Lord Parker, who dissented, said that grounds (b) to (e) 'clearly go to the validity of the enforcement notice'; if the minister 'finds that the facts are such as to bring the appellants into (b), (c), (d) or (e), he quashes the notice'. Of ground (a)—that planning permission ought to be granted for the development in question—Lord Parker said: 'The one thing which is agreed in this case is that that is a matter entirely for the Minister'; ground (a) could never be raised as a ground for challenging the validity of an enforcement notice. As regards ground (f)—that the requirements of the enforcement notice exceed what is necessary—and ground (g)—that the period specified in the enforcement notice falls short of what should reasonably be allowed—he thought it perfectly clear that these grounds did not raise matters on which the minister could quash an enforcement notice. The minister is, said Lord Parker, 'given powers to vary: if he thinks that the requirements for restoring the land are excessive, he can vary the enforcement notice; if he thinks that the period specified by the local planning authority is insufficient, he can vary and increase the period. But these are not grounds for quashing the notice; they do not go to validity.' 'It seems to me', he said, 'that grounds (a), (f) and (g) were not included [in the preclusive clause] on the very simple ground that they do not go to the validity of the enforcement notice.'

The decision in *Smith* v *King* has been the subject of considerable criticism;[35] and in *Rochdale Metropolitan Borough Council* v *Simmonds*[36] the Divisional Court went some way towards clarifying the scope of the justices' powers in dealing with a challenge to an enforcement notice as a defence to a prosecution for non-compliance. The enforcement notice in question required the dismantling of a fence which had been constructed without planning permission. The fence exceeded the height permitted under the relevant general development order. The justices held that the notice, by requiring the respondents totally to remove the fence rather than just lowering it to the maximum permitted height, exceeded what was necessary to remedy the breach of planning control and was therefore invalid. In other words, they accepted the challenge to the notice on ground (f)—that the requirements of the notice exceeded what was necessary to remedy the breach of control. The Divisional Court, when the matter came before them on appeal, held that the notice could not be challenged before the justices on that ground. Webster J. said that: 'Although the clear inference from section 243(1)(a) [of the Town and Country Planning Act 1971, corresponding to s.85(10) of the 1972 Act] is that an enforcement notice can be questioned

---

[35] See, for example, George Dobry Q.C., *Review of the Development Control System* (H.M.S.O., 1975), para. 12.21.
[36] (1980) 40 P. & C.R. 432.

before the justices, as well as before the Secretary of State, on (*inter alia*) ground (f), it is an equally clear inference that the only question that can be raised before the justices is as to the validity of the notice. *Smith* v *King* cannot, in our judgment, be relied on as an authority for the proposition that the justices can consider a ground of appeal under the Act on its merits.' He continued: 'In specifying [in the enforcement notice] the steps required to be taken, the appellants were not exceeding their powers and are not for any reason to be taken as having misdirected themselves in law. Nor, if the question were material, would that requirement be perverse: that is to say, the steps required to be taken cannot be said to be steps that no reasonable planning authority, acting reasonably and properly directing itself as to the law, would require to be taken.' As a result of this decision, the scope for challenging an enforcement notice on ground (f), and presumably also on ground (g), by way of a defence to a prosecution would seem to be strictly limited.

Whatever doubts may exist as to the extent to which s.85(10) (above) bars recourse to the courts, it is clear that it does not prohibit challenge of the *vires* of a notice on grounds other than those specified in the subsection.[37]

A complicating factor here is that in England, largely as a result of the influential decision of the Court of Appeal in *Miller-Mead* v *Minister of Housing and Local Government*[38] there has been a tendency to draw a sharp distinction between notices which are nullities as being bad on their face and notices which are invalid for other reasons;[39] in the latter case the notice stands, says Grant, 'until it is quashed by the Secretary of State or the court'.[40] However, rigid classifications of this sort are not now followed in administrative law generally[41] and the decision in *McDaid* (above) suggests that the Scottish courts may not be prepared to make distinctions of this type in relation to enforcement notices.

It is suggested that an enforcement notice will be *ultra vires* in the following circumstances:

(a) A notice which fails to specify some essential statutory requirement will be *ultra vires*. If, for example, the notice fails to specify the breach of control, the steps required to remedy the breach, the date on which the notice is to take effect or the period for compliance,[42] or if there has been a failure to serve the notice on one of the parties specified by the legislation,[43]

[37]   See *Davy* v *Spelthorne Borough Council* [1984] A.C. 262, per Lord Fraser of Tullybelton; and *Jeary* v *Chailey R.D.C.* (1973) 26 P. & C.R. 280, per Orr L.J.

[38]   [1963] 2 Q.B. 196.

[39]   See M. Grant, *Urban Planning Law*, pp. 402–409.

[40]   ibid., p. 408.

[41]   See, in particular, *London and Clydeside Estates Ltd.* v *Aberdeen District Council* 1980 S.C. (H.L.) 1; 1980 S.L.T. 81, in which Lord Hailsham stated that 'in the field of the rapidly developing jurisprudence of administrative law' the courts will not consider themselves bound 'to fit the facts of a particular case and a developing chain of events into rigid legal categories or to stretch or cramp them on a bed of Procrustes invented by lawyers for the purposes of convenient exposition'.

[42]   See *Miller-Mead* v *Minister of Housing and Local Government* [1963] 2 Q.B. 196.

[43]   See *McDaid* v *Clydebank District Council* 1984 S.L.T. 162.

the notice will be *ultra vires*. Although a mere technical error will not have the effect of nullifying a notice,[44] failure to comply with the statutory requirements as to identification of the land and as to provision of reasons and a statement of the rights of appeal might do so.[45] It will not, it seems, render a notice *ultra vires* that it proceeds on a false basis of fact and that there has in reality been no breach of planning control;[46] a planning authority may serve an enforcement notice where it *appears* to them that there has been a breach of planning control and, in the words of Upjohn L.J.,[47] 'a *prima facie* case only need be shown to satisfy the prerequisites of a valid notice'.

(*b*) An enforcement notice which is uncertain in the sense that it does not fairly tell the recipient what he has to do will be *ultra vires* (see p. 296 above).

(*c*) An enforcement notice may also be *ultra vires* on the ground that the planning authority have in some way misused their discretionary powers. The validity of a notice might, for example, be challenged on the grounds that in deciding to serve the notice the authority had failed to take account of some relevant factor[48] or that the notice was vitiated by fraud or had been served without the authority's sanction.[49]

D. CONSEQUENCES OF ENFORCEMENT NOTICE

Enforcement notice to have effect against subsequent development

Prior to the 1969 Act, compliance with an enforcement notice had the effect of discharging the notice so that if, for example, a use of land was discontinued in compliance with an enforcement notice, no offence was committed by a subsequent resumption of that use; all that the planning authority could do was serve a fresh enforcement notice.

Section 89(1) of the 1972 Act now provides that compliance with an enforcement notice, whether in respect of the demolition or alteration of any building or works or the discontinuance of any use of land or in respect of any other requirement contained in the notice, does not discharge the notice. Any provision of an enforcement notice requiring a use of land to be discontinued is to operate as a requirement that it shall be discontinued permanently to the extent that it is in contravention of Part III of the 1972 Act and accordingly any resumption of the use at any time after its discontinuance is to that extent in contravention of the enforcement notice (s.89(2)). If development is carried out on land by reinstating or restoring

---

[44] See *Patel* v *Betts* [1978] J.P.L. 109.
[45] See *London and Clydeside Estates Ltd.* v *Aberdeen District Council* 1980 S.C. (H.L.) 1; 1980 S.L.T. 81.
[46] See *Jeary* v *Chailey R.D.C.* (1973) 26 P. & C.R. 280; and *Miller-Mead* (above).
[47] In *Miller-Mead* (above).
[48] See, for example, *Flashman* v *London Borough of Camden* (1980) 130 New L.J. 885 (in which the Court of Appeal distinguished *Square Meals Frozen Foods Ltd.* v *Dunstable Corporation* [1974] 1 W.L.R. 59).
[49] See *Davy* v *Spelthorne Borough Council* [1984] A.C. 262, per Lord Fraser; and *Scarborough Borough Council* v *Adams* (1983) 47 P. & C.R. 133, per Watkins L.J.

buildings or works which have been demolished or altered in compliance with an enforcement notice, the notice, even though its terms may not be apt for the purpose, is deemed to apply in relation to the reinstated or restored building or works as it applied in relation to the building or works before they were demolished or altered[50] (s.89(3)). Any person who, without the grant of planning permission, carries out development by way of reinstating or restoring buildings or works which have been demolished or altered in accordance with an enforcement notice is guilty of an offence and is liable on summary conviction to a fine not exceeding £1,000 (s.89(4)). Presumably the planning authority may also enter upon the land and carry out works under s.88 of the 1972 Act (below).

Effect of subsequent planning permission

For the avoidance of doubt, s.89A of the 1972 Act[51] now provides that, notwithstanding the provisions of s.89(1) to (3), an enforcement notice will cease to have effect[52] to the extent that its terms are inconsistent with the terms of any planning permission granted, or deemed to have been granted, subsequent to the service of the notice. This provision may cause difficulties for the planning authority; if, for example, after service of an enforcement notice they grant planning permission subject to conditions but the developer does not comply with the conditions, the authority will have to issue a fresh enforcement notice.[53]

Alteration of development to comply with enforcement notice

Where a development is altered in accordance with an enforcement notice which specifies, as an alternative to complete restoration of the land, steps required to be taken to bring the land to a condition acceptable to the planning authority, then planning permission is deemed to have been granted for that development.[54] The Secretary of State has suggested that planning authorities should notify recipients of the enforcement notice of the fact that planning permission is deemed to have been granted when they are satisfied that the required steps have been completed.[55] The fact that deemed permission has been granted should be entered in the register of enforcement notices.

Reversion to 'lawful' use after service of enforcement notice

Where an enforcement notice has been served in respect of any development of land, planning permission is not required for the use of that land for

---

[50] In *Broxbourne Borough Council* v *Small* [1980] C.L.Y. 2638 it was held that where a barn which was the subject of enforcement action was replaced by a smaller Nissen hut used for the same purpose, that was a replacement or restoration of the barn.
[51] Inserted by the 1982 Act, s.48 and Schedule 2, para. 25.
[52] The notice is not, however, rendered a nullity—see *R. v Secretary of State for the Environment, ex p. Three Rivers District Council* [1983] J.P.L. 730.
[53] See *London Borough of Havering* v *Secretary of State for the Environment* [1983] J.P.L. 240.
[54] 1972 Act, s.84(7A) (inserted by the 1982 Act, s.48 and Schedule 2, para. 19(c)).
[55] See S.D.D. Circular 6/1984.

the purpose for which (in accordance with the provisions of Part III of the 1972 Act) 'it could lawfully have been used if that development had not been carried out' (s.20(9)).[56]

Non-compliance with an enforcement notice

The possible consequences of failure to comply with the requirements of an effective enforcement notice depend upon the nature of the requirements which have not been complied with. The legislation makes a distinction in this respect between the carrying on of a use of land in contravention of an enforcement notice (s.86) and a failure to carry out steps (other than the discontinuance of a use of land) required to be taken by the notice (s.88). The distinction is not entirely clear cut; breach of a condition or limitation concerned with a use of land or with the carrying out of operations seems to come within the ambit of both s.86 and s.88, as do unauthorised mining operations. Further, unauthorised building or engineering operations may also involve a change in the use of land.

Offences

Section 86 creates two types of offence.[57] The first limb of the section provides that where an enforcement notice requires the discontinuance of a use of land or compliance with conditions or limitations relating to a use of land or to the carrying out of operations thereon, then any person[58] who, without a grant of planning permission, uses the land or causes or permits it to be used, or carries out those operations or causes or permits them to be carried out, in contravention of the notice is guilty of an offence. The penalty on summary conviction is a fine not exceeding £2,000.[59] For a conviction on indictment no maximum fine is prescribed. In *Hodgetts* v *Chiltern District Council*[60] the House of Lords held that this initial offence, though it may take place over a period, is a single offence and not a series of offences committed each day that non-compliance prior to conviction continues.

The second limb of s.86 creates a 'further offence' of continuing the use after conviction; this offence can only be committed by someone who has already been convicted of the initial offence. A person convicted of this offence is liable on summary conviction to a fine not exceeding £100 for each day on which the offence continues. On conviction on indictment of this further offence no maximum fine is prescribed. The offence created by the

---

[56] See p. 168 above.
[57] See *Hodgetts* v *Chiltern District Council* [1983] A.C. 120, per Lord Roskill (dealing with the corresponding provision in the Town and Country Planning Act 1971).
[58] Occupiers, squatters and even trespassers may be guilty of an offence, regardless of their status, if they act in breach of the terms of a notice—see *Scarborough Borough Council* v *Adams* (1983) 47 P. & C.R. 133.
[59] See Increase of Criminal Penalties, etc. (Scotland) Order 1984.
[60] [1983] A.C. 120.

second limb of s.86 is a continuing one.[61]

It may be that *mens rea* is not necessary for the commission of an offence under s.86 of the 1972 Act. In *Stevens* v *Bromley London Borough Council*[62] two members of the Court of Appeal apparently considered that *mens rea* was not required for the commission of an offence under the corresponding English provision; Edmund Davies L.J. said that the effect of the provision is that 'provided an enforcement notice is validly served on someone, *any* person who thereafter uses the land in a manner contravening it is *ipso facto* rendered guilty of a criminal offence, regardless of whether or not he has himself been served and even regardless of whether he has knowledge that a notice has been served at all.' However, in *South Cambridge District Council* v *L.F.W. Stokes*[63] Forbes J. appeared to accept that *mens rea* was a necessary ingredient for the commission of an offence but held that there was an obligation on a person to take all proper care to inform himself of any facts which would make his conduct lawful or unlawful. In *Pirie* v *Bauld*[64] the Sheriff held that the accused lacked the *mens rea* necessary for the commission of the offence of non-compliance with an enforcement notice in that they believed that they had appealed to the minister against the enforcement notices in question. The Sheriff did not, however, find it necessary to decide the case solely on that ground; he was satisfied that a letter sent by one of the accused to the Secretary of State had to be construed as an appeal against the notice under s.85 and that as the effect of such an appeal is to suspend the operation of an enforcement notice until the final determination of the appeal, the prosecution for failure to comply with the notice necessarily failed.

Where the owner of land is not himself in occupation of that land it would seem that he runs the risk of prosecution under this provision only if he does something 'which can be said to amount to a using of the land for the unauthorised purpose, or causing or permitting it to be so used'—see *Johnston* v *Secretary of State for the Environment.*[65] The Divisional Court held in that case that an offence was committed only if a person was in a position to discontinue the unlawful use and, notwithstanding the notice, either continued to use the land in defiance of it or caused or permitted some other person to do so. In *Ragsdale* v *Creswick*[66] the Divisional Court held that the failure of a landowner to take legal proceedings to evict a trespasser on his land who had been acting in breach of an enforcement notice might amount to a failure to take reasonable steps to secure compliance with the

---

[61] See *St. Albans District Council* v *Norman Harper Autosales Ltd.* (1977) 35 P. & C.R. 70. See also *R.* v *Chertsey Justices, ex p. Franks* [1961] 2 Q.B. 152; and *Tandridge District Council* v *Powers* (1982) 80 L.G.R. 453 (which turned on the interpretation of s.89(1) and (4) of the English Act of 1971). See too s.331 of the Criminal Procedure (Scotland) Act 1975.
[62] [1972] Ch. 400. See too *Maidstone Borough Council* v *Mortimer* [1980] 3 All E.R. 552 (knowledge of existence of tree preservation order).
[63] [1981] J.P.L. 594.
[64] 1975 S.L.T. (Sh.Ct.) 6.
[65] (1974) 28 P. & C.R. 424. See too *Test Valley Investments Ltd.* v *Tanner* (1963) 15 P. & C.R. 279; *Bromsgrove District Council* v *Carthy* (1975) 30 P. & C.R. 34; and *London Borough of Redbridge* v *Perry* (1976) 75 L.G.R. 90.
[66] (1984) 271 E.G. 1268.

notice. Much would depend, it was said, on the nature, cost and prospect of success of the proceedings and also upon the prospect of the planning authority securing the cessation of the offending use by the use of criminal sanctions.

In criminal proceedings the validity of an enforcement notice may not be questioned on any of the grounds specified in paragraphs (b) to (e) of s.85(1) of the 1972 Act[67] except in the very limited circumstances mentioned in s.85(11).[68]

Execution of works by planning authority

It would seem that no criminal offence is committed if the failure to comply with an enforcement notice is not of such a kind as is specified in s.86; no criminal offence would seem to be committed, for example, by a failure to comply with a notice requiring removal of a building erected without planning permission. The only remedy in such a case is provided by s.88 of the 1972 Act which states that where any steps required by an enforcement notice to be taken (*other than the discontinuance of a use of land*) have not been taken, the planning authority may enter on the land and take those steps.

The planning authority need not carry out all the steps required by the enforcement notice; they are entitled to take such of those steps as they consider appropriate.[69] There seems no reason why direct action should not be taken to secure the removal of items associated with an unauthorised use of land, provided the enforcement notice specifically requires such removal. For example, although s.88 cannot be used to secure the discontinuance of an unauthorised use of land as a caravan site, it seems that s.88 would support the taking of direct action to remove unauthorised caravans.[70]

The planning authority are entitled to recover from the person who is at that time the owner or lessee of the land àny expenses reasonably incurred in carrying out the necessary work, including appropriate administrative expenses (s.88(1) and (1A)[71]). If that person, having been entitled to appeal to the Secretary of State, failed to make such an appeal, he is not entitled in proceedings under s.88(1) to dispute the validity of action taken in accordance with the notice by the planning authority.

In *Macdonald* v *Glasgow Corporation*[72] the Sheriff-Principal said:

---

[67] 1972 Act, s.85(10); see p. 333 above. And see *Pirie* v *Bauld* 1975 S.L.T. (Sh.Ct.) 6; and *McNaughton* v *Peter McIntyre (Clyde) Ltd.*, High Court of Justiciary, 21st March 1978 (unreported, but see 1981 S.P.L.P. 15).

[68] See p. 336 above.

[69] See *Arcam Demolition and Construction Co. Ltd.* v *Worcestershire County Council* [1964] 1 W.L.R. 661.

[70] See the comments of the reporter in *SPADS* No. A4926 (P/ENA/SA/45, 9th December 1983).

[71] Section 88(1A) was added by the 1982 Act, s.48 and Schedule 2, para. 23.

[72] 1960 S.L.T. (Sh.Ct.) 21.

'It appears to me that there cannot be the slightest dubiety that . . . the person upon whom the enforcement notice is properly served is responsible for the removal of not only what he has done without planning permission but what had been done by his predecessors, and that he has only the doubtful remedy of a civil claim for the appropriate proportional repayment due in respect of the operations of each successive predecessor.'

That 'doubtful remedy' is contained in subsection (2) of s.88 which provides that any expenses incurred by the owner, lessee or occupier of any land for the purpose of complying with an enforcement notice and any sums paid by the owner or lessee under s.88(1) in respect of expenses incurred by the planning authority in taking steps required by the notice are recoverable from the person by whom the breach of planning control was committed.

A planning authority taking steps under s.88(1) may sell any materials removed by them from the land unless they are claimed by the owner within three days of removal. The authority may deduct any expenses recoverable by them from the owner from the proceeds of the sale and pay him the balance, if any (s.88(4)[73]).

E. STOP NOTICES AND INTERDICT

Stop notices

As mentioned above, an enforcement notice does not take effect until any appeal against the notice has been finally determined or withdrawn (s.85(3)). A lengthy period can therefore elapse between service of an enforcement notice and the time when the recipient of the notice needs to comply with it. If allegedly unauthorised operations continue during that period, proper consideration of the merits of an enforcement notice can be prejudiced; it is one thing to tell a developer to remove the foundations of an unauthorised building, but quite a different matter to tell him to pull down a completed building.

Furthermore, the alleged breach of control may cause serious planning problems, for example of a polluting or hazardous nature. Planning authorities have, therefore, been given power to serve what is known as a 'stop notice'. As the name suggests, the effect of the notice is to prohibit the carrying out of the alleged breach of control until such time as any appeal against the enforcement notice has been finally determined or withdrawn.

Section 87(1) of the 1972 Act provides that where a planning authority have served an enforcement notice in respect of any land, they may at any time before the enforcement notice takes effect serve a stop notice for the purpose of prohibiting the carrying out or continuing of *any* activity[74] or part

[73] Added by the 1982 Act, s.48 and Schedule 2, para. 23.
[74] The scope of stop notices was considerably extended by the Town and Country Planning (Scotland) Act 1977. The term 'activity' is not defined in the legislation but clearly includes operations, uses of land and development in breach of a condition or limitation attached to a planning permission.

of any activity which either is alleged in the enforcement notice to constitute or involve a breach of planning control, or is so closely associated therewith as to constitute substantially the same activity. It is clear from the wording of the subsection that a stop notice need not prohibit the whole of an activity alleged to be in breach of planning control; the planning authority could, for example, restrict the operation of a stop notice to particular aspects of the unauthorised activity or to a particular part of the planning unit on which the unauthorised activity is being carried on.

There are two sorts of activities which a stop notice cannot prohibit. First, a stop notice may not prevent the taking of any steps necessary for compliance with an enforcement notice (s.87(2)(a)). Secondly, it is provided that a stop notice may not prohibit any person from continuing to use any building or other land, or any caravan situated upon the land to which the relevant enforcement notice relates, as his permanent residence, 'whether as owner, occupier, tenant, patient, guest or otherwise' (s.87(2)(b)).

A stop notice, as its name suggests, is an instrument of negative control. As was pointed out in *Pirie* v *Bauld*,[75] the notice 'does not oblige the person on whom it is served to remedy the breach of planning control alleged in the enforcement notice'. Whilst it can prohibit the carrying on of an activity alleged in the enforcement notice to constitute a breach of planning control, it cannot require the carrying out of positive conditions, notwithstanding that the failure to implement the condition constitutes a breach of planning control. Furthermore, if it purports to prohibit the carrying on of an activity which is not a matter alleged in the enforcement notice to constitute a breach of planning control then the stop notice will be invalid.[76]

A stop notice must refer to and have enclosed with it a copy of the relevant enforcement notice (s.87(1)). It seems that where a stop notice incorporates the terms of the enforcement notice then any deficiency of particularity in the stop notice may be cured by reference to the enforcement notice.[77]

A stop notice may be served by the planning authority on any person who appears to them to have an interest in the land or to be engaged in activities which constitute or involve the breach of planning control alleged in the enforcement notice (s.87(6)). The notice must specify the date, not less than 3 or more than 28 days from the first date on which it is served (on whatever person), on which it is to come into effect (s.87(3)). The planning authority may, after service of a stop notice on any particular person or persons, publicise the notice by displaying on the land a site notice drawing attention to the stop notice[78] (s.87(7)); such action has the effect of bringing within the scope of the prohibition in the stop notice persons who have not been served with the stop notice.

---

[75] 1975 S.L.T. (Sh.Ct.) 6.
[76] *Clwyd County Council* v *Secretary of State for Wales* [1982] J.P.L. 696.
[77] *Bristol Stadium Ltd.* v *Brown* [1980] J.P.L. 107.
[78] A person duly authorised in writing by the planning authority has power to enter on land in order to display a site notice or to ascertain whether a stop notice is being complied with (see 1972 Act, s.265 (as amended by s.5(3) of the 1977 Act); see too 1972 Act s.266).

If any person causes or permits any activity in contravention of a stop notice which has effect for the time being and which has been served on him or which has been publicised under s.87(7) (above), he is guilty of an offence (s.87(8)(b)).[79] It is a defence in any proceedings under that provision that the stop notice was not served on the accused and that he had no reasonable cause to believe that the activity was prohibited by a stop notice (s.87(8)(c)).

There is no right of appeal against a stop notice. Unless previously withdrawn by the planning authority,[80] a stop notice stands or falls with the enforcement notice to which it relates; a stop notice ceases to have effect when the enforcement notice to which it refers takes effect or is quashed or withdrawn (s.87(4)). Where the enforcement notice is so varied that it no longer relates to an activity prohibited by the stop notice, the stop notice ceases to have effect in relation to that activity (s.87(5)).

Although there is no right of appeal against a stop notice, there is nothing to prevent a person seeking judicial review of the planning authority's action in deciding to serve a stop notice on the ground that the authority would be acting outwith their powers.[81] In *Central Regional Council* v *Clackmannan District Council*,[82] the First Division of the Court of Session recalled an interim interdict preventing service of a stop notice on the ground that there was no averment by the petitioners that the planning authority would be acting *ultra vires*. It was merely averred that the matter alleged in the enforcement notice did not constitute a breach of control. This was a point to be settled on appeal to the Secretary of State and not by the court (see 1972 Act, s.85(1)(b) and (10)). The court therefore had no power to prohibit the exercise by the planning authority of their legal right to serve a stop notice. It was quite irrelevant to plead that as a result of the service of such a notice, the petitioners would suffer loss or damage. A similar decision was reached by the First Division in *Earl Car Sales (Edinburgh) Ltd.* v *City of Edinburgh District Council*.[83] In that case the petitioners' only averment in support of their contention that a stop notice was *ultra vires* was a statement that their use of land for the storage of motor vehicles was not an 'activity' within the meaning of s.87(1). The court was unable to accept that contention and held that the petitioners' pleadings were clearly irrelevant on the question of *vires*.

These decisions suggest that the approach adopted in *Marine Associates Ltd.* v *City of Aberdeen District Council*,[84] in which interim interdict against the enforcement of a stop notice was granted on the balance of convenience, was misconceived.

---

[79]   The maximum penalty for non-compliance with a stop notice was increased to £2,000 by the Increase of Criminal Penalties, etc. (Scotland) Order 1984, while the maximum fine for a continuing contravention was raised from £50 to £100 per day by the 1982 Act.
[80]   The procedure to be followed on withdrawal of a stop notice is set out in s.87(10).
[81]   *Scott Markets Ltd.* v *London Borough of Waltham Forest* (1979) 77 L.G.R. 565.
[82]   1983 S.L.T. 666. See also *James Barrie (Sand and Gravel) Ltd.* v *Lanark District Council* 1979 S.L.T. 14.
[83]   1984 S.L.T. 8.
[84]   1978 S.L.T. (Notes) 41.

On prosecution for failure to comply with a stop notice, the validity of the notice is open to challenge.[85] A prosecution may also be defended on the ground that the enforcement notice to which the stop notice relates is a nullity.[86] It is specifically provided that a stop notice shall not be invalid because the enforcement notice to which it relates was not served as required by s.84(5) of the 1972 Act, if it is shown that the planning authority took all reasonably practicable steps to effect proper service (s.87(9)).

Details of stop notices are to be entered in the register which planning authorities are required to keep (see p. 310 above).

Compensation for loss due to stop notice

Section 166[87] of the 1972 Act provides that where a stop notice ceases to have effect the planning authority will in some circumstances have to pay compensation in respect of any loss or damage 'directly attributable to the prohibition contained in the notice' (see s.166(1)). Subsections (2) and (3) of s.166 detail the precise circumstances in which compensation will be payable for loss due to a stop notice. Broadly speaking, a compensation claim will arise where the stop notice is itself withdrawn independently of the enforcement notice to which it refers, or where the enforcement notice is withdrawn by the planning authority otherwise than in consequence of a grant by them of planning permission, or where the enforcement notice is varied so that the breach ceases to include the activity prohibited by the stop notice, or where the enforcement notice is shown, in effect, to be legally invalid (see s.166(2), (3)), that is to say, if it is quashed on any of the grounds mentioned in s.85(1)(b), (c), (d) or (e) (see p. 323 above). As difficult questions of law may arise on an appeal under s.85(1)(b)[88] and as the facts to support an appeal on s.85(1)(c) or (d) may be outwith the knowledge of the planning authority, this compensation provision may have a deterrent effect on the use of stop notices.

If, however, the planning authority decide to grant planning permission and for that reason withdraw the enforcement notice, or if, on appeal, the Secretary of State decides on the planning merits to grant planning permission for the development to which the enforcement notice relates and for that reason quashes the enforcement notice, compensation will not be payable for loss resulting from service of a stop notice.

A claim for compensation[89] under s.166 may only be made by a person who had an interest (whether as owner or occupier or otherwise) in the land in question at the time when the notice was first served; it is not necessary to the making of a claim that the stop notice should have been served on the

---

[85] *R. v Jenner* [1983] 1 W.L.R. 873.

[86] *Bristol Stadium Ltd. v Brown* [1980] J.P.L. 107.

[87] As amended by s.5(2) of the Town and Country Planning (Scotland) Act 1977.

[88] See, for example, *Malvern Hills District Council v Secretary of State for the Environment* [1982] 46 P. & C.R. 58.

[89] As to the time limit for making a claim see the Town and Country Planning (General) (Scotland) Regulations 1976, reg. 4.

claimant. The loss or damage in respect of which compensation is payable may include a sum payable in respect of a breach of contract caused by the taking of action necessary to comply with the stop notice (s.166(5)). In the assessment of any compensation under s.166 there is to be taken into account any failure on the part of the claimant to comply with the provisions of s.270[90] of the 1972 Act (relating to the powers of authorities to require information as to interests in land and as to the purpose for which land is being used) to the extent that such failure has contributed to the circumstances in which the enforcement notice was withdrawn or varied or quashed, or the stop notice withdrawn (s.166(6)[91]).

Compensation for loss 'directly attributable' to the prohibition in a stop notice which delayed completion of a house was found to be payable in *Sample (Warkworth) Ltd.* v *Alnwick District Council.*[92] The Lands Tribunal held that compensation was payable in respect of the idle time of the builders' labour force and the cost of work needed to rectify deterioration resulting from the delay. The tribunal also awarded compensation in respect of loss of interest on the purchase price of the house from October 1981, the estimated date of completion, to March 1982, the date of actual completion, even though the planning authority had permitted building work to restart in December 1981 and argued that interest should only be payable up to that time; in the tribunal's view the fact that there was likely to be a delay in completing the house, which could be aggravated by the holiday period and the onset of severe weather, was sufficiently contemporaneous in following the prohibition in the stop notice that causation was not broken. The builders were also held entitled to be reimbursed for a payment they had made in respect of the cost of temporary accommodation for the purchasers of the house since it avoided the possible loss of the sale or an action which might have involved greater loss. Compensation was claimed in respect of the costs of the builders' appeal against the enforcement notice, the builders arguing that although planning permission had been granted in December 1981, the enforcement notice and stop notice had not been withdrawn and they were therefore forced to proceed with the appeal in order to qualify for compensation for loss due to the stop notice. The Lands Tribunal held, however, that the costs of the appeal were not 'directly attributable' to the stop notice, the remedy for recovering these costs being exerciseable at the time of the appeal decision itself. The tribunal expressed the view that the words 'directly attributable' as used in the legislation were not to be qualified by the concept of reasonable foreseeability.

The compensation provisions make no mention of the situation where the enforcement notice to which a stop notice relates is held to be a nullity. In such circumstances, presumably the stop notice will also be a nullity but it is not clear whether a person who complies with the stop notice would be entitled to compensation.[93]

---

[90]   Amended by s.5(4) of the Town and Country Planning (Scotland) Act 1977.
[91]   Inserted by s.5(2)(d) of the 1977 Act.
[92]   (1984) 48 P. & C.R. 474.
[93]   See J. Alder, *Development Control*, p. 155; and M. Grant, *Urban Planning Law*, p. 425.

Interdict and the enforcement of planning control

There is considerable uncertainty about whether a planning authority may resort to a civil action for interdict to supplement the statutory procedures and penalties available for the enforcement of planning control.[94] The principal objection to the use of interdict in such cases was summarised by the Lord Chancellor, Lord Herschell, in *Institute of Patent Agents* v *Lockwood*[95] in this way:

'The mode of procedure and the amount of the penalty are often regarded by the legislature as of the utmost importance where they are creating a new offence, and the law would, I believe, contrary to their intention, be most seriously modified if it were held that the party committing a breach of that which for the first time is made an offence were to subject himself by so doing to proceedings of this description which might result in a committal to prison.'

The Scottish courts have therefore been reluctant to sanction resort to the common law process of interdict for the purpose of enforcing regulations where statute makes clear provision for penalties for a breach of control.

In *Magistrates of Buckhaven and Methil* v *Wemyss Coal Co.*[96] the First Division of the Court of Session held that an action for interdict by the Magistrates was incompetent in respect of an unlawful discharge of refuse onto the foreshore. The discharge was an offence under s.381 of the Burgh Police (Scotland) Act 1892 for which penalties were prescribed. The court held that the Magistrates had no title to vindicate any right over the foreshore by way of interdict. Lord President Clyde was also prepared to hold that a public body could not resort to the common law process of interdict for the purpose of enforcing a statute where penalties were prescribed. His Lordship said:

'the law is . . . that when a statutory system of public regulation is fenced in with penalties, the body charged with its administration must be content with the infliction of the statutory penalties upon offenders as the mode of enforcing its administration and is debarred from using common law remedies such as the process of interdict.'

Lord Sands concurred with this view but reserved his opinion on whether, 'if a person found it profitable wilfully and persistently to defy a statute passed by the Legislature in the public interest', an action for interdict might be

---

[94] See G. Jamieson, *Enforcing Planning Control: the Competency of Interdict* (Scottish Planning Law and Practice Occasional Paper, 1983); and W. Kilgour, 'Interdict and the Enforcement of Planning Control', in T. Ramsay and E. Young (eds.), *Enforcement of Planning Control: Law and Practice* (University of Strathclyde, 1980).

[95] (1894) 21 R. (H.L.) 61.

[96] 1932 S.C. 201. See also *Reid* v *Mini-Cabs* 1966 S.C. 137; 1966 S.L.T. 166.

competent. Lord Morrison did not find it necessary to decide this 'important question'.

A number of decisions of the English courts establish that local authorities there may, in certain circumstances, seek an injunction to supplement prescribed statutory penalties.[97] It was formerly necessary to invoke the assistance of the Attorney-General by way of a relator action; as Buckley J. said in *Attorney-General* v *Ashborne Recreation Ground Co.*:[98] 'The Attorney-General suing in respect of the invasion of public rights has at least as large a right to invoke the protection of the Court as a private owner suing in respect of his rights.' Thus in *Attorney-General* v *Bastow*[99] an injunction was issued to restrain the defendant from using land as a caravan site, the defendant having been repeatedly prosecuted for so using his land in contravention of the terms of an enforcement notice. Devlin J. stated:

'When Parliament makes provision which enables local authorities to exercise powers over the use of land, that provision is plainly made with the object of conferring a right upon the public because Parliament considers that the public is entitled not to have the land used in ways which may be considered to be unhealthy or offensive . . . [T]here is the creation of a public right and the Attorney-General is therefore entitled to come to this court to have it enforced.'

Section 222 of the Local Government Act 1972 now allows local authorities in England and Wales to institute civil proceedings in their own name where they consider it expedient to do so for the promotion or protection of the interests of the inhabitants of their area.[1] Thus in *Westminster City Council* v *Jones*[2] the local planning authority successfully sought an interlocutory injunction in its own name under s.222 restraining the defendant from using premises as an amusement arcade. The use of the premises for that purpose was in breach of planning control, an enforcement notice had been served together with a stop notice, and a summons had been issued for failure to comply with the stop notice and was to be heard shortly. Whitford J. considered that the use of s.222 was not confined to cases where there was an emergency or where the penalties imposed for an offence had proved totally inadequate. In his view it was not always necessary for a local authority to exhaust all statutory remedies before they could obtain an injunction; the important factor justifying that remedy in this case was that there had been a plain, deliberate and flagrant flouting of the law. In *Stoke-on-Trent City Council* v *B. & Q. (Retail) Ltd.*[3] the House of Lords held

---

[97]   See, for example, *Attorney-General* v *Ashborne Recreation Ground Co.* [1903] 1 Ch. 101; *Attorney-General* v *Sharp* [1931] 1 Ch. 121; *Attorney-General* v *Bastow* [1957] 1 Q.B. 514; *Attorney-General* v *Smith* [1958] 2 Q.B. 173.
[98]   [1903] 1 Ch. 101.
[99]   [1957] 1 Q.B. 514.
[1]   See, in particular, *Stoke-on-Trent City Council* v *B. & Q. (Retail) Ltd.* [1984] A.C. 754.
[2]   [1981] J.P.L. 750.
[3]   [1984] A.C. 754.

a local authority entitled to seek an injunction to restrain unlawful Sunday trading but their Lordships expressed the view that an injunction should only be granted in such a case if something more than a mere infringement of the law could be shown—for example, that the party against whom the injunction was sought would not be deterred by a fine.

Scottish Law Commission Memorandum No. 14, *Remedies in Administrative Law*, comments that it may be the lack of any direct equivalent to the English relator action which explains the relatively infrequent use of interdict in Scots law to provide an effective sanction against unlawful conduct which statutory penalties are ineffective to prevent.[4] If this is the case, then it would seem that s.189(1) of the Local Government (Scotland) Act 1973 provides a solution. The wording of the section is very similar to that of s.222 of the English Act and allows a local authority to institute any legal proceedings which they consider expedient for the promotion or protection of the interests of the inhabitants of their area or of part of their area. However, although s.189(1) of the 1973 Act would seem to overcome any difficulties as regards title and interest to sue, there remains the objection, voiced in *Lockwood* and *Magistrates of Buckhaven and Methil*, that inderdict is not available where provision is made for a statutory penalty.

In *City of Dundee District Council* v *Peddie*[5] a planning authority sought to interdict the defenders from erecting a dwelling-house because the required planning permission had not been obtained. The Sheriff (J. W. B. Christie) held that the planning authority, as a statutory body exercising statutory powers, could only exercise their powers in accordance with the statute. This accorded, in the Sheriff's view, with the principles enunciated by the Lord President in *Magistrates of Buckhaven and Methil* (above). The Sheriff said:

'The planning Acts provide their own system of enforcement and, in my judgment, the pursuers are restricted to the use of that system. I was informed on behalf of the pursuers that there were certain difficulties in proceeding under the planning Acts but this reinforces the defenders' argument as it does not seem to me to be right to seek to avoid difficulties in the statutory procedure by resorting to a common law remedy.'

It should be said that in this case, not only had the statutory procedures not been exhausted, they had not even been started.

On the other hand, in *Hamilton District Council* v *Alexander Moffat & Son (Demolition) Ltd.*[6] the Sheriff (I. A. Macmillan) was prepared to continue interdict *ad interim* to prevent demolition operations which were *ex facie* in breach of planning control. It is perhaps significant that the Sheriff found that there was no suitable alternative statutory procedure available to the planning authority and he therefore considered interdict appropriate.

---

[4]   See para. 8.6.
[5]   Sheriff Court, Dundee, 27th June 1983 (unreported, but see 1984 S.P.L.P. 21).
[6]   Sheriff Court, Hamilton, 16th February 1984 (unreported, but see 1984 S.P.L.P. 76).

The assertion that interdict is never available where provision is made for a statutory penalty perhaps goes, in Professor J. D. B. Mitchell's words,[7] 'beyond the present state of the authorities', but the position remains very uncertain.

[7] *Constitutional Law* (W. Green & Son, 2nd ed., 1968), p. 239.

CHAPTER 14

ADVERSE PLANNING DECISIONS: COMPENSATION

A. INTRODUCTION

'[I]t is quite clear', said Lord Reid in *Westminster Bank Ltd.* v *Minister of Housing and Local Government*,[1] 'that when planning permission is refused the general rule is that the unsuccessful applicant does not receive any compensation.' There are, as we shall see, three limited exceptions to this rule; these are discussed below.

The general rule, which applies as much to the imposition of conditions as to a refusal of permission, would seem to be in line with the way in which public controls over the use and management of land have developed over the years. During the last one hundred and fifty years owners of property have been compelled to an increasing extent, without compensation, to comply with certain requirements regarding their property, all imposed ostensibly in the public interest. 'Ownership of land', observed the Uthwatt Committee in 1942, 'involves duties to the community as well as rights in the individual owner. It may involve complete surrender of the land to the State or it may involve submission to a limitation of rights of user of the land without surrender of ownership or possession being required.'[2] The question is at what stage are the rights of the individual owner so circumscribed by the requirements of the public interest that compensation should follow?

The conventional approach has been to draw a line between the complete surrender of land and a mere limitation of the landowner's freedom to use his land as he pleases. There is a line of cases which supports the judicial presumption that an intention to take away the property of a subject without giving him a legal right to compensation for its loss is not to be imputed to the legislature unless that intention is expressed in unequivocal terms.[3] On the other hand, a mere limitation on use would seem to give rise to no such

---

[1]   [1971] A.C. 508.
[2]   *Report of the Expert Committee on Compensation and Betterment* (Cmnd. 6386, 1942), para. 32.
[3]   *Burmah Oil Company (Burma Trading) Ltd.* v *Lord Advocate* 1963 S.C. 410; 1964 S.C. (H.L.) 117; *Tiverton and North Devon Railway Co.* v *Loosemore* [1884] 9 App. Cas. 480; *Cannon Brewery Co. Ltd.* v *Gas, Light and Coke Co.* [1904] A.C. 331; *Colonial Sugar Refining Co. Ltd.* v *Melbourne Harbour Trust Commissioners* [1927] A.C. 343; and *Bond* v *Nottingham Corporation* [1940] Ch. 429.

presumption.[4] 'A mere negative prohibition', said Wright J. in *France Fenwick & Co.* v *The King*,[5] 'though it involves interference with an owner's enjoyment of property, does not, I think, merely because it is obeyed, carry with it at common law any right to compensation.' In the absence, therefore, of any specific provision in the legislation, the position is that, subject to the three exceptions discussed below, there is no entitlement to compensation for any loss resulting from an adverse decision on a planning application.

However, simple though the distinction between expropriation and limitation may seem in theory, in practice the effect on a landowner of a limitation may be every bit as severe as an expropriation. The Uthwatt Committee conceded: 'It will always be a matter of difficulty to draw the line with any satisfactory logic, i.e., to determine the point at which the accepted obligations of neighbourliness or citizenship are exceeded and an expropriation is suffered—particularly as the standard of obligation will vary with the political theory of the day.'[6]

The 1972 Act recognises that planning proposals and decisions made in the public interest can have an effect on a landowner similar to expropriation. Part IX of the Act contains provisions which enable a landowner to require a public body to purchase his interest in certain circumstances—a sort of inverse expropriation. These provisions are discussed in detail in chapters 15 and 18.

However, the provisions in Part IX of the 1972 Act only come into operation in narrowly defined circumstances. There may be occasions when obligations imposed by planning authorities on developers through the development control process do not bring these provisions into operation, yet might fairly be described as expropriation without compensation. In *Hall & Co. Ltd.* v *Shoreham-by-Sea Urban District Council*,[7] for example, the local planning authority granted planning permission for industrial development subject to a condition that the developers 'shall construct an ancillary road over the entire frontage of the site at their own expense and as and when required by the local planning authority, and shall give right of passage over it to and from such ancillary roads as may be constructed on adjoining land'. The Court of Appeal held the condition to be so unreasonable as to be *ultra vires*. Willmer L.J. observed: 'I can certainly find no clear and unambiguous words in the Town and Country Planning Act 1947 authorising the defendants in effect to take away the plaintiffs' rights of property without compensation by the imposition of conditions such as those sought to be imposed.' And in *R.* v *Hillingdon London Borough Council, ex parte Royco Homes Ltd.*,[8] where planning permission for residential development was granted subject to conditions that the houses built should be occupied by people on the local authority's waiting list, with security of tenure for ten

---

[4]   *Belfast Corporation* v *O. D. Cars Ltd.* [1960] A.C. 490; and *Westminster Bank Ltd.* v *Minister of Housing and Local Government* [1971] A.C. 508.
[5]   [1927] 1 K.B. 458.
[6]   Cmnd. 6386 (1942), para. 35.
[7]   [1964] 1 W.L.R. 240.
[8]   [1974] Q.B. 720.

years, Lord Widgery C.J. described the conditions as 'a fundamental departure from the rights of ownership and so unreasonable that no planning authority, appreciating its duty and properly applying itself to the facts, could have imposed them'. In cases such as these, where the proper scope of planning powers is in issue, the applicant's remedy lies, not in a claim for compensation, but in having the obligation struck out on appeal to the Secretary of State or by way of recourse to the courts. The scope of planning control is discussed in detail in chapters 9, 10 and 11.

Where there are available to an authority alternative statutory powers of control over development, one providing for payment of compensation and the other not, the authority are not obliged to adopt the procedure which provides for payment of compensation.[9] Thus in *Westminster Bank Ltd.* v *Minister of Housing and Local Government*[10] the House of Lords held that a planning authority were entitled to refuse an application for planning permission on the ground that the land would be required for road-widening, notwithstanding that the authority could have achieved their objective by the alternative method of prescribing an improvement line under the highways legislation, a course of action which would have meant the immediate payment of compensation. Lord Reid expressed the view that an authority would be entitled to employ their planning powers in preference to some alternative power even if their sole reason for so doing was a desire to avoid payment of compensation.

B. THE EXCEPTIONS TO THE GENERAL RULE

We mentioned above that there are three limited exceptions to the general rule that no compensation is payable for an adverse decision on an application for planning permission for the development of land. These exceptions concern:

(*a*) an adverse decision in respect of certain categories of development not constituting 'new development';

(*b*) an adverse decision on an application consequent on the modification or withdrawal of a planning permission granted by development order;

(*c*) an adverse decision on an application for 'new development' on land in respect of which there exists an unexpended balance of established development value.

The first two exceptions are discussed in detail in chapter 16 which deals with control of the existing use of land; in this chapter, we confine ourselves to a brief outline of the relevant statutory provisions. It is, however, appropriate to deal with the third exception in full in this chapter.

---

[9]   *Westminster Bank Ltd.* v *Minister of Housing and Local Government* [1971] A.C. 508. See too *Stringer* v *Minister of Housing and Local Government* [1970] 1 W.L.R. 1281; and *Hoveringham Gravels Ltd.* v *Secretary of State for the Environment* [1975] Q.B. 754.
[10]   Above.

Development not constituting 'new development'

The categories of development which do not constitute 'new development'[11] are defined in Parts I and II of Schedule 6 to the 1972 Act. They are commonly referred to as 'existing use development' because they comprise relatively minor activities closely related to the existing use of the land.

Section 158 of the 1972 Act deals with the position where an adverse decision is made by the Secretary of State on an application for planning permission for any of the classes of existing use development specified in Part II of Schedule 6. If, as a result of the decision, it can be shown that the value of a person's interest in the land is less than it would have been if permission had been granted, or been granted unconditionally, the planning authority must compensate that person for the difference in value.

The modification or withdrawal of planning permission granted by development order

Section 21 of the 1972 Act empowers the Secretary of State to grant planning permission for development by way of development order. Article 3 of the Town and Country Planning (General Development) (Scotland) Order 1981, for example, grants planning permission for the twenty two categories of development listed in Schedule 1 to the order. A planning permission granted by development order may, however, be withdrawn or modified as a result of the revocation or amendment of the order or by the issuing of a direction under powers contained in the order (for example, a direction under Article 4 of the general development order). The effect is to require any proposed development caught by the revocation, amendment or direction to be the subject of a formal application to the planning authority for planning permission in the normal way.

In the event of the refusal of such an application or the imposition of conditions other than those which would originally have been imposed by the development order, ss.153 and 154 of the 1972 Act provide for the payment of compensation. Compensation will be paid by the planning authority to any person with an interest in the land who can show that he has incurred abortive expenditure or has otherwise sustained loss or damage as a direct result of the revocation, amendment or direction.

The unexpended balance of established development value

The third exception to the general rule that no compensation is payable in respect of an adverse decision on an application for planning permission can be explained, as a JUSTICE report *Compensation for Compulsory Acquisition and Remedies for Planning Restrictions* (1969) commented, 'historically but not logically'. Although little now remains of the complex scheme for the control of land values contained in the Town and Country Planning (Scotland) Act 1947, in order to explain this third exception it is necessary to make brief mention of certain aspects of that scheme.

---

[11] 'New development' is simply a reference to any development other than those categories specified in Parts I and II of Schedule 6 to the 1972 Act (1972 Act, s.19(5)).

Proceeding on the basis that 'development value'—broadly, the value which land may have over and above its 'existing use' value because of the possibility that it may be put to some more profitable use—is created by the efforts of the community as a whole, the 1947 Act provided, in effect, for the expropriation by the state of the prospective development value of all land. To achieve this objective, it was laid down that when development was carried out under planning permission the developer was to pay a 'development charge' equal to the amount by which the value of the land was estimated to have increased as a result of the grant of permission. As development value was thus secured to the state it was logical to provide, as the 1947 Act did, that where planning permission was refused or was granted subject to conditions, with the result that the prospective development value of land could not be fully realised, there would generally be no entitlement to compensation in respect of the adverse decision.

In recognition of the hardship which might have resulted in some cases if no payment were made in respect of the loss to individual owners of the development value of their land, there was established, for Britain as a whole, a global fund of £300 million against which claims for loss of development value might be made under Part V of the 1947 Act. It was intended that payment of established claims would be made on a once and for all basis in 1953, but before any such disbursement took place the scheme of the 1947 Act for the control of land values was largely dismantled by the Town and Country Planning Act 1953 and the Town and Country Planning (Scotland) Act 1954.

The abolition of development charge by the 1953 Act meant that development value was in effect restored to landowners; the landowner who obtains planning permission presently enjoys, subject to possible fiscal liabilities, any gain which accrues as a result of that permission. Landowners who are unable, because of planning restrictions, to realise the full development value of their land are, however, seldom entitled to compensation. Parliament was, as Davies says,[12] unwilling to see such owners 'totally deprived of compensation . . . and yet at the same time could not face the logical consequence of awarding full compensation in lieu of lost development value'; as the same writer states, a 'kind of "Alice-in-Wonderland" compromise was worked out' in that it was decided that claims on the £300 million fund made and accepted under the 1947 Act, 'although truly redundant now that development charges were abolished, should be applied to this new situation. To have asked for one thing was now to be made the qualification for getting something different.' The 1954 Act provided that from 1st January 1955 compensation might be payable by central government on a refusal or conditional grant of planning permission for 'new development', that is, development falling outside the categories of 'existing use' development specified in the Third Schedule to the 1947 Act;[13] the right to the once and for all payment out of the global fund was replaced, in effect, by a right to compensation if and when loss of development value

[12] *Law of Compulsory Purchase and Compensation* (Butterworths, 4th ed., 1984),p. 294.
[13] See now 1972 Act, Schedule 6.

actually occurred. Payment of compensation for restrictions upon 'new development' was, however, made conditional upon a claim on the £300 million fund for loss of prospective development value having been made under the 1947 Act. On 1st January 1955 any such claim established under the 1947 Act was (with the addition, in lieu of interest, of one seventh of the amount of the established claim, but under deduction of any payment already made) converted into what is termed the 'original unexpended balance of established development value', attached to and running with the land in respect of which the claim was made.

Compensation is now payable under Part VII of the 1972 Act (re-enacting provisions originally contained in the 1954 Act) in respect of a planning decision restricting 'new development' only if there is attached to the land in question an unexpended balance of established development value. If, therefore, no claim was established on the £300 million fund at the appropriate time, compensation will not now be payable in respect of such a decision. The amount of any compensation payable for restrictions on 'new development' may not exceed the unexpended balance of established development value; since that balance derives from claims made on the basis of market values prevailing in 1947 and is unaffected by factors such as development plan zoning, any compensation now payable is likely to be much less than the actual loss of development value.[14] It may also be observed that payment of compensation in respect of a decision restricting 'new development' is by no means automatic—even where an unexpended balance attaches to the land in question the right to claim compensation is restricted in a number of important ways. The provisions of Part VII of the 1972 Act, dealing with compensation for restrictions on 'new development', are considered in section C of this chapter.

C. COMPENSATION FOR PLANNING DECISIONS
   RESTRICTING NEW DEVELOPMENT

Where planning permission for the carrying out of 'new development' is refused or is granted subject to conditions, compensation may be payable under Part VII of the 1972 Act. 'New development' means 'any development other than development of a class specified in Part I or Part II of Schedule 6' to the 1972 Act (1972 Act, s.19(5)). It is not essential to the making of a claim that the adverse planning decision should have been the subject of an appeal to the Secretary of State.

Unexpended balance of established development value
Payment of compensation under Part VII of the 1972 Act is entirely dependent on there being an unexpended balance of established development value attaching to the land. Brief mention has been made above of the way in which the original unexpended balance derives from claims made

---

[14]   See, for example, *Avis* v *Minister of Housing and Local Government* (1959) 11 P. & C.R. 26.

under Part V of the 1947 Act (see ss.124 to 128 of the 1972 Act); if no such claim was made no balance can now be established.

The original balance may be reduced or become wholly expended in a number of ways. If compensation becomes payable under Part VII of the 1972 Act in respect of depreciation in the value of an interest in land by virtue of a planning decision, the balance is reduced by the amount of that compensation (s.129). If new development on land is permitted and the owner is thus able to realise some of the development value of the land, the unexpended balance is reduced by the value of that new development as at the time when the unexpended balance has to be calculated (s.130). The unexpended balance of established value attaching to any land may also be reduced or extinguished by acquisition of the land under compulsory powers (s.131), by the payment in certain circumstances of compensation for severance or injurious affection (s.132) and by payment in some circumstances of compensation in respect of the revocation or modification of planning permission (s.156). Where necessary, the unexpended balance will be apportioned (s.133).

On application made by any person, the Secretary of State must issue a certificate stating whether particular land had an original unexpended balance; if it did, the certificate must (a) give a general statement of what was taken by the Central Land Board to be the state of the land on 1st July 1948 and (b) specify the amount of that original balance (s.134(1)). Such a certificate *may*, if the Secretary of State thinks fit, include additional information with respect to acts or events in consequence of which a deduction is required to be made from the original unexpended balance (s.134(2)). A prospective purchaser of land may have to make his own calculations as to what deductions fall to be made from the original balance. If the issue of a certificate under s.134 involves a new apportionment, only a person who is for the time being entitled to an interest in the land in question may apply for a certificate (s.134(4)). Notice of the proposed apportionment must be given to persons who will be affected and an opportunity provided for the making of objections (s.134(4)). Any dispute may be referred to the Lands Tribunal for Scotland (s.134(5)). After service of a notice to treat, an authority possessing compulsory purchase powers may obtain a certificate showing the *unexpended* balance attaching to the land in question; notice of any proposed deduction from the original balance must be given to affected parties (see s.134(3)–(5)).

Right to compensation

To succeed with a claim for compensation under Part VII, a claimant has to show that he is entitled to an interest in land, the value of which has been depreciated by an adverse planning decision (s.135). A favourable decision may, however, be treated as subject to a notional condition (and may, therefore, be treated as an 'adverse' decision) if the Secretary of State certifies that he is satisfied that particular buildings or works were included in the application only because the applicant had reason to believe that without their inclusion permission for the development to which the application relates would not have been granted (s.139). It is not incumbent upon a person whose application for permission to develop is refused to prove affirmatively that if permission had been granted, development would in fact have followed.[15]

Excluded cases

The 1972 Act contains a number of provisions which have the effect of excluding payment of compensation under Part VII even though there is an unexpended balance of established development value attached to the land in question.

An important exclusion is made by s.136(1) which states that compensation is not payable in respect of the refusal of planning permission for any development 'which consists of or includes the making of any material change in the use of any buildings or other land'. Despite the wide terms of this subsection, assurances were given in Parliament that in a case where development consisted of, say, building operations but also involved a material change in the use of land only the change of use would be excluded from compensation.

In *Overland* v *Minister of Housing and Local Government*[16] where an outline application for industrial development had been refused by the planning authority, the minister came to the conclusion that compensation in respect of that refusal was excluded on the ground that the development consisted of or included a material change in the use of land. The Lands Tribunal held, however, that since an outline application can only be made in respect of operations, the refusal in this case amounted to a refusal of permission to erect industrial buildings and that the payment of compensation was not therefore excluded by the statute.

Compensation is not payable in respect of the imposition of any condition relating to (*a*) the number or disposition of buildings on any land; (*b*) the dimensions, design, structure or external appearance of any building or the materials to be used in its construction; (*c*) the manner in which any land is to be laid out, including the provision of facilities for the parking, loading or fuelling of vehicles; (*d*) the use of any buildings or other land; or (*e*) the location or design of any means of access to a road or the materials to be used in the construction of any such means of access ('means of access to a road' does not, for this purpose, include a service road); or in respect of any conditions subject to which planning permission is granted for the winning and working of minerals (s.136(2)).

No compensation is payable in respect of a refusal of permission where one of the reasons for refusal is that development of the kind proposed is premature having regard to either or both of the following matters: (*a*) the stages by which development is to be carried out, as indicated in the development plan; and (*b*) any existing deficiency in water supplies or sewerage services, and the period within which any such deficiency may

---

[15] See *Overland* v *Minister of Housing and Local Government* (1957) 8 P. & C.R. 389.
[16] Above.

reasonably be expected to be made good (s.136(4)). As regards a refusal based on (*a*) above this subsection ceases to apply seven years after the date of the first refusal on this ground.[17]

Section 136(1) excludes payment of compensation in respect of any decision on an application for consent to the display of advertisements. Compensation is not payable in respect of the imposition of conditions relating to the duration of planning permission (s.136(3)) nor is it payable in respect of a refusal of permission where one of the reasons for refusal is that the land is unsuitable for the proposed development on account of its liability to flooding or subsidence (s.136(5)).

Planning permission granted subject to a condition prohibiting development on a specified part of land to which an application relates is, for the purposes of s.136, to be treated as a decision refusing permission with respect to that part (s.136(6)).

Under s.137 no compensation is payable under Part VII of the 1972 Act in respect of a refusal of planning permission if, notwithstanding that refusal, there is in force immediately prior to the Secretary of State giving notice of his decision on the claim, a grant of planning permission or an undertaking by the Secretary of State to grant permission for 'any development of a residential, commercial or industrial character, being development which consists wholly or mainly of the construction of houses, flats, shop or office premises, or industrial buildings (including warehouses), or any combination thereof'.

Section 138(1) provides that where an interest in land has been compulsorily acquired by or sold to an authority possessing compulsory purchase powers (other than statutory undertakers and the National Coal Board) no compensation is payable to the authority, or to any person deriving title from them after 1st July 1948, in respect of a planning decision made after service of the notice to treat or after the making of the contract of sale. There are also exclusions in respect of land appropriated by a local authority for a purpose for which the authority could have been authorised to acquire the land compulsorily and in respect of operational land of statutory undertakers and certain land of the National Coal Board (s.138(2), (3)).

Where a claim for compensation under Part VII has been made, the Secretary of State is entitled under s.35 of the 1972 Act to review the planning decision which has given rise to the claim. Where there has been no appeal against the planning authority's decision, the Secretary of State may give a direction substituting for that authority's decision a decision more favourable to the applicant[18] (s.35(2)). Even if there has been an appeal the Secretary of State is entitled in any case to give a direction granting permission for development other than that to which the application related (irrespective of whether or not the claimant wishes to carry out such

---

[17]   1972 Act, s.136(4), amended by the Local Government and Planning (Scotland) Act 1982, Schedule 2, para. 32.

[18]   As to the meaning of the phrase 'decision more favourable to the applicant', see s.35(4).

development) (s.35(3)). Before making a direction under s.35 the Secretary of State must give notice of the proposal to the planning authority and to the claimant and must afford to each of them an opportunity of appearing before and being heard by a person appointed by the Secretary of State for the purpose (s.36). Where the Secretary of State gives a direction under s.35, the claim for compensation then has effect as if it had been made in respect of the modified or substituted decision (s.144). The giving of such a direction may, of course, mean that compensation will not in fact be payable.

Measure of compensation

Where compensation is payable under Part VII of the 1972 Act the amount of the compensation is to be either the amount by which the value of the claimant's interest is depreciated by the planning decision or the amount of the unexpended balance of established development value, whichever of these two amounts is the lesser (s.141). 'Depreciation' must be calculated in accordance with the provisions of s.142 and 'value' is to be calculated in accordance with rules (2) to (4) of the rules set out in s.12 of the Land Compensation (Scotland) Act 1963. Where compensation is payable in respect of two or more interests in land and the aggregate amount of compensation payable would exceed the unexpended balance, then that balance will be allocated between those interests in proportion to the depreciation of the value of each interest (s.141(3)). The balance will be allocated between those interests in respect of which a claim has been made and a late claimant might therefore find that no balance remained. Section 141 also makes provision for determination of the amount of compensation where an unexpended balance attaches to only a part of the land to which the decision relates or where a depreciated interest subsists in only a part of that land.

Claims for and payment of compensation

A claim for compensation under Part VII of the 1972 Act must be made within six months of the adverse planning decision or such longer period as the Secretary of State may allow (s.143(1)–(3)) and is to be made on a form issued by the Secretary of State (Town and Country Planning (Compensation) (Scotland) Regulations 1954, reg. 3). A claimant may be required to furnish certain supporting material (1954 Regulations, reg. 4). Where the Secretary of State considers that the claim is not justified, he will so notify the claimant, giving him an opportunity to withdraw the claim (s.143(4)). In any case where the claim is not withdrawn, the Secretary of State may, under s.35 of the 1972 Act, review the decision which gave rise to the claim (see p.361 above). The Secretary of State must, unless the claim is withdrawn, give notice of the claim to every other person appearing to him to have an interest in the land (s.143(4)) and must then 'cause such investigations to be made and such steps to be taken as he may deem requisite to enable him to determine the claim' (1954 Regulations, reg. 6(1)). Notice of the Secretary of State's determination, stating the compensation payable and the amount of the unexpended balance, must be given to the claimant and, if the determination includes an apportionment, to any other person whose interest in the land is substantially affected by the apportionment (1954 Regulations, reg. 6). Any dispute as to the determination or an apportionment included therein may be referred to the Lands Tribunal for Scotland (1954 Regulations, reg. 7).

Compensation under Part VII of the 1972 Act is paid by the Secretary of State (s.146). Where the compensation payable exceeds £20 the Secretary of State shall, if it appears practicable, apportion the compensation between different parts of the land to which the claim relates according to the way in which those different parts of the land appear to be differently affected by the planning decision (s.147(1), (2)). A notice that compensation exceeding £20 has become payable (a 'compensation notice') must be recorded by the Secretary of State in the Register of Sasines or the Land Register, as appropriate, and a copy of the notice must be sent to the planning authority (s.147(4)).

Provision is made by the Town and Country Planning (Diversion of Payments) (Scotland) Regulations 1955 for cases where compensation is payable in respect of an interest in land which is subject to a heritable security, a feu-duty, a ground annual or a trust.

Repayment of compensation

In certain circumstances compensation paid in respect of a planning decision restricting new development may have to be repaid. No person is to carry out new development of certain specified types on land in respect of which a compensation notice has been recorded until such amount of the compensation as is recoverable under s.148 of the 1972 Act has been repaid or secured to the satisfaction of the Secretary of State (s.148(1)). Such repayment may therefore have to be made by someone other than the person who received the compensation.

Repayment of compensation may be required where it is proposed to carry out any new development:

(*a*) of a residential, commercial or industrial character, consisting wholly or mainly of the construction of houses, flats, shop or office premises or industrial buildings (including warehouses) or any combination thereof;

(*b*) which consists in the winning or working of minerals;

(*c*) 'to which, having regard to the probable value of the development, it is in the opinion of the Secretary of State reasonable' that the provisions as to repayment should apply (s.148(2)).

The repayment provisions will not apply where, on application made to him, the Secretary of State certifies that, having regard to the probable value of the development, it would not be reasonable to require repayment (s.148(3)) and the Secretary of State may remit the whole or part of any compensation recoverable if he is satisfied that the development in question is not likely to be carried out unless he does so (s.149(2)).

Minerals

Certain of the provisions of Part VII of the 1972 Act are modified in their application to minerals by the Town and Country Planning (Minerals) (Scotland) Regulations 1971.

Conclusion

The unexpended balance of established development value has little practical significance today. Most of the land which had development potential in 1948 will either have been developed long since and the development value realised; alternatively, it will, for whatever planning reasons, have remained undeveloped and compensation will have been paid. Either way, the balance of established development value will have been extinguished. For those relatively few cases where an unexpended balance remains, the compensation, based as it is on 1948 development values, will be unlikely to reflect the development value foregone as a result of an adverse planning decision today.

The real anomaly in this area of law, as the JUSTICE report (above) observed, in 1969, 'is not that many people receive no compensation, but that a few people receive some in the shape of the "unexpended balance of established development value" attached to their land'. The report continued: 'We believe that the community has now accepted that there should in general be no payment of compensation for such restrictions.' Its conclusion was that the right to claim compensation should be redeemed over a fixed and limited period of time. There has, however, been no indication that the government is minded to resolve the anomaly.

CHAPTER 15
ADVERSE PLANNING DECISIONS: PURCHASE NOTICES

In certain restricted circumstances the owner or lessee of land in respect of which an adverse planning decision[1] or order has been made may be able to compel the planning authority (or some other authority) to acquire his interest in the land. This 'inverse compulsory purchase' procedure is set in motion by service on the planning authority of a purchase notice. The object of the purchase notice procedure is simply to enable a landowner who, in the public interest, is denied the opportunity to put land to any potentially useful purpose to rid himself of the land.

Conditions for service of purchase notice following an adverse planning decision

Section 169 of the 1972 Act provides that where, on an application for planning permission to develop land, permission is refused or is granted subject to conditions, then if any owner or lessee claims:

(*a*) that the land has become incapable of reasonably beneficial use in its existing state; and

(*b*) in a case where planning permission was granted subject to conditions, that the land cannot be rendered capable of reasonably beneficial use by the carrying out of the permitted development in accordance with those conditions;[2] and

(*c*) in any case, that the land cannot be rendered capable of reasonably beneficial use by the carrying out of any other development for which planning permission has been granted or for which the planning authority or Secretary of State has undertaken to grant planning permission,

he may serve on the planning authority[3] in whose area the land is situated a

---

[1] i.e., a refusal or conditional grant of planning permission. Where land is affected by adverse planning *proposals*, it may be possible, by service of a blight notice, to compel the appropriate authority to acquire the land—see chapter 18.

[2] For the purpose of s.169 conditions under ss.38 and 39 of the 1972 Act, limiting the duration of planning permission, are to be ignored (s.169(4)).

[3] Generally the purchase notice will be served on the district or general planning authority but where the adverse decision has been made by a regional planning authority under the powers contained in s.179 of the Local Government (Scotland) Act 1973, as amended, then the notice should be served on that authority (Local Government and Planning (Scotland) Act 1982, s.48 and Schedule 2, para. 33).

purchase notice, i.e. a notice requiring the authority to purchase his interest in the land.

Where, through the failure of the planning authority to issue a decision within the period specified in the General Development Order, there is a 'deemed' refusal of planning permission, that refusal cannot form the basis for service of a purchase notice;[4] appeal against the deemed refusal will first have to be made to the Secretary of State.

Difficult questions can arise over the interpretation of s.169 and, in particular, in relation to the need to show that the land has become incapable of reasonably beneficial use in its existing state. The equivalent English provision[5] has been the subject of considerable judicial scrutiny.

In *Smart & Courtenay Dale Ltd.* v *Dover R.D.C.*[6] the (English) Lands Tribunal took the view that wherever the words 'the land' are used in the purchase notice provisions, they denote the whole of the land which was the subject of the planning decision; the tribunal held that a purchase notice served by claimants who did not own the whole of the land which had been the subject of an adverse planning decision was on that account invalid. D.H.S. Circular 74/1959 states, however, that the Secretary of State takes the view that 'a notice which relates to a part of the land covered by the planning decision can be accepted as valid where the purchase notice land was severed by the planning decision from the land which was the subject of the application (e.g. where permission is granted for a part of the land and refused for the remainder—the purchase notice land).' That circular declares that a purchase notice will also be acceptable 'where land covered by the planning decision comprises parcels of land in different ownerships, and the owners of those parcels combine to serve a single purchase notice relating to their separate interests, if the notice as served relates to the whole of the land covered by the planning decision'.

In *Purbeck District Council* v *Secretary of State for the Environment*[7] the planning authority argued that the use by Parliament of the words 'has become' indicated that there should be an identifiable change of circumstances which led to the existing situation. Accordingly, it was argued, an area of marshland, which had always been marshland, could not be described as land which 'had become' incapable of reasonably beneficial use. Woolf J. rejected this argument. The section had to be looked at from the point of view of the situation which arose on an adverse decision. Unless the application for planning permission resulted in an adverse decision the section could not apply. If the decision was favourable, it could not be said that the land had become incapable of reasonably beneficial use. It was in this sense that the adverse decision on a planning application could lead to a situation where land could be said to have become incapable of reasonably

---

[4] See ministerial decision noted in [1950] J.P.L. 794.
[5] Section 180 of the Town and Country Planning Act 1971.
[6] (1971) 23 P. & C.R. 408; see too ministerial decisions noted in [1978] J.P.L. 195; and [1980] J.P.L. 193. See, however, ministerial decision noted in [1976] J.P.L. 647.
[7] (1982) 80 L.G.R. 545.

beneficial use.[8] It is not therefore incumbent upon the server of a purchase notice to show that there is a causal connection between the adverse planning decision occasioning the notice and the fact that the land is incapable of reasonably beneficial use.[9]

Incapable of reasonably beneficial use

The phrase which has caused the greatest difficulty is 'incapable of reasonably beneficial use'.[10] The question to be considered in every case is not merely whether the land is of less use or value to the owner in its present state than it would have been if he had been able to develop the land and realise its development potential, but whether, as a matter of fact and degree, the land in its existing state (taking account of any existing permissions and any undertakings to grant permission) is incapable of reasonably beneficial use. As Lord Parker C.J. said in *R. v Minister of Housing and Local Government, ex parte Chichester R.D.C.*:[11] 'I suppose that in every case where land is worth developing and permission to develop is refused, the existing use of the land will be of less beneficial use, it will be less useful to the owner, than if it were developed. The test is whether it has become incapable of reasonably beneficial use in its existing state.'

D.H.S. Circular 74/1959[12] provides some illustrations of the application of this test. The circular states: 'In considering what capacity for use the land has, relevant factors are the physical state of the land, its size, shape and surroundings, and the general pattern of uses in the area. A use of relatively low value may be reasonably beneficial if such a use is common for similar land in the neighbourhood;[13] and a small area of land may in some circumstances be capable of reasonably beneficial use in conjunction with a wider area.'[14] In an English circular[15] it was said that although profit may be a useful test in certain circumstances, 'the absence of profit is not necessarily material; the notion of reasonably beneficial use is not specifically identifiable with profit.' For example, in appropriate circumstances use as garden ground may be a reasonably beneficial use (whether independently or in conjunction with adjoining land).[16]

In *Adams & Wade Ltd. v Minister of Housing and Local Government*[17] Widgery J. held that 'beneficial use' must mean a use which could benefit the owner or prospective owner of the land and the fact that land in its existing

---

[8]   See too ministerial decision noted in [1970] J.P.L. 276.
[9]   See *Hoddesdon U.D.C. v Secretary of State for the Environment* (1971) 115 S.J. 187. See too ministerial decision noted in [1959] J.P.L. 897.
[10] See W. A. Leach, 'Reasonably Beneficial Use' [1977] J.P.L. 283.
[11] [1960] 1 W.L.R. 587. See too *General Estates Co. Ltd. v Minister of Housing and Local Government* (1965) 194 E.G. 201.
[12] See Appendix II, para. 4. See too ministerial decision noted in [1976] J.P.L. 649.
[13] See, for example, ministerial decision noted in [1977] J.P.L. 256.
[14] See ministerial decision noted in [1982] J.P.L. 257.
[15] M.H.L.G. Circular 26/1969.
[16] See, for example, ministerial decision noted in [1980] J.P.L. 194.
[17] (1965) 18 P. & C.R. 60.

state conferred some benefit on the public at large was no bar to service of a purchase notice. However, if for some reason an owner is unwilling to put land to what could be a beneficial use and there is a demand for the land for that use then it seems that a purchase notice will not succeed.[18]

Not only must the purchase notice relate to the whole of the land which was the subject of the planning decision,[19] but it seems that the whole of the land must be shown to be incapable of reasonably beneficial use. In *Wain* v *Secretary of State for the Environment*[20] a purchase notice was served in respect of some 37 acres of land, half of which was covered by grass and thorn bushes and some dilapidated buildings and was described as gently undulating, and half of which was covered with a mixture of grass, weed and reed, with concrete protrusions and containing a reed-covered pond. After an inquiry, the inspector concluded that the gently undulating land could be used for grazing and hay in the spring and summer months and that, if the buildings were made good—which could be done without planning permission—the land could be put to a reasonably beneficial use. He concluded, however, that the outlay required to reclaim the other land would not be justified by the likely return and that that part of the 37 acres was incapable of beneficial use. The Secretary of State refused to confirm the notice, holding that the owner of the land had to show that the whole of the land which was the subject of the planning decision was incapable of reasonably beneficial use. The Court of Appeal upheld his decision. Lord Denning commented that it seemed to him that: ' . . . the true interpretation was that the owner could not claim the right to have the council purchase his land compulsorily except when all the land had become incapable of reasonably beneficial use. If part of the land was capable of reasonably beneficial use, then he could not insist on a compulsory purchase.'[21] There would, however, seem to be nothing to prevent a landowner in this situation from applying for planning permission to develop that part of the land which is incapable of beneficial use and then serving a purchase notice in the event of an adverse decision.

Where land is rendered incapable of reasonably beneficial use as a result of a breach of planning control by the landowner, then it appears that the landowner will not be able to take advantage of the breach by serving a purchase notice. In *Purbeck District Council* v *Secretary of State for the Environment*[22] permission had been granted for the use of land, previously used for clay extraction operations, as a rubbish tip subject to controls designed to secure the reinstatement of the site in a satisfactory form. As a result of what appeared to be total disregard of these controls by the owner's tenant, the land had become incapable of reasonably beneficial use. Woolf J. interpreted the purchase notice provisions as 'excluding a situation where

---

[18]   See ministerial decision noted in [1982] J.P.L. 257.
[19]   *Smart & Courtenay Dale Ltd.* v *Dover R.D.C.* (1971) 23 P. & C.R. 408.
[20]   (1981) 44 P. & C.R. 289.
[21]   See too ministerial decision noted in [1976] J.P.L. 649.
[22]   (1982) 80 L.G.R. 545.

the land had become incapable of beneficial use because of unlawful activities on the land', i.e., activities being carried on in breach of planning control.

The English minister takes the view that in considering whether land has become incapable of reasonably beneficial use in its 'existing state', there can be taken into account alterations and improvements which could be carried out without the need for planning permission:[23] he therefore refused to confirm a purchase notice relating to land which had become semi-derelict and incapable, without improvement, of reasonably beneficial use for agriculture but which could, with normal husbandry and improvement of security, have been made suitable for grazing purposes.[24]

Although D.H.S. Circular 74/1959 states that only planning permissions granted (or deemed to be granted) or undertakings given before the service of the purchase notice can be taken into account by the Secretary of State for the purposes of determining whether the land in question has become incapable of reasonably beneficial use, in considering what action he should take on a purchase notice under s.172 of the 1972 Act (below) the minister has to consider whether the conditions specified in s.169(1)(a) to (c) (above) 'are fulfilled'; the Secretary of State for the Environment now takes the view that this means whether the conditions are fulfilled at the time of his decision and that this necessitates taking into account, *inter alia*, any relevant planning permission, whether granted before or after service of the purchase notice.[25] The relevant time for considering whether land has become incapable of reasonably beneficial use is therefore not the date of service of the purchase notice but the time the minister considers it.

In determining any question as to what is or would be a reasonably beneficial use of land, no account is to be taken of any prospective use of the land which would involve the carrying out of 'new development'[26] (s.169(2)); it may be relevant to consider whether land is denied any prospective usefulness by lack of permission for development specified in the Sixth Schedule[27] to the 1972 Act but the fact that the land could be rendered capable of more beneficial use by Sixth Schedule development is not conclusive evidence that it is incapable of reasonably beneficial use in its existing state.[28]

---

[23]   The Secretary of State for the Environment takes the view that account cannot be taken of works for which planning permission would be required—see [1978] J.P.L. 195 and 197.

[24]   See [1976] J.P.L. 189. Cf. appeal decisions noted in [1982] J.P.L. 792; and [1984] J.P.L. 817.

[25]   See appeal decisions noted in [1981] J.P.L. 762; and [1984] J.P.L. 817.

[26]   i.e., development outside the classes of 'existing use' development specified in the Sixth Schedule to the 1972 Act—see chapter 16. For the purposes of any determination under s.169(2), the Sixth Schedule is modified (see s.169(3)). In addition, for the purposes of any such determination no account is to be taken of any prospective use of the land which would contravene the condition set out in Schedule 16 to the 1972 Act (s.169(2)) (see p. 391 below).

[27]   See chapter 16.

[28]   *Brookdene Investments Ltd.* v *Minister of Housing and Local Government* (1970) 21 P. & C.R. 545 (but see doubts expressed by Fisher J. at p. 550); see too ministerial decisions noted in [1978] J.P.L. 483; and [1982] J.P.L. 259; also D.H.S. Circular 74/1959.

Procedure

There is no prescribed form of purchase notice but a model form is appended to D.H.S. Circular 74/1959. A purchase notice must be served within twelve months of the adverse decision; it is to be served on the planning authority in whose district the land is situated[29] (s.169(1), and Town and Country Planning (General) (Scotland) Regulations 1976, reg. 4(2)). The Secretary of State has power to extend the period for service (reg. 4(2)), but the planning authority do not.

The planning authority should, within three months of service of a purchase notice, themselves serve notice on the owner or lessee by whom the purchase notice was served. If the planning authority are willing to comply with the notice, or if another body has agreed to comply with it in their place, the counter-notice will so state; on the service of such a counter-notice, stating that the planning authority or another authority are prepared to purchase the land, the appropriate authority are deemed to be authorised to acquire compulsorily the relevant interest in accordance with the provisions of Part VI of the 1972 Act, and to have served a notice to treat[30] in respect thereof[31] (s.170(1), (2)). In such cases no reference to the Secretary of State is required. If the planning authority are not willing to comply with the purchase notice and have not found any other body willing to comply with it, the counter-notice must so state and should be accompanied by a statement of the planning authority's reasons for not complying with the notice (s.170(1)(c)); since a purchase notice cannot, in such a case, become effective unless it is confirmed by the Secretary of State, the planning authority must transmit to the minister a copy of the purchase notice and their statement of reasons (s.170(3)).

If the authority fail to serve a counter-notice within the three month period, the notice is deemed to be confirmed at the expiration of that period (s.170(4)).

Action by Secretary of State

Where a purchase notice is transmitted to the Secretary of State, he may take one of the several courses of action specified in s.172 of the 1972 Act. If he is satisfied that the conditions specified in s.169(1)(a) to (c) (above) are fulfilled, he may confirm the notice; in so doing he may substitute for the planning authority on whom the notice was served some other authority[32] (s.172(1), (4)). Where the notice is confirmed, the relevant authority are deemed to be authorised to acquire compulsorily the relevant interest and to

---

[29]   See note 3 above.

[30]   Which cannot be withdrawn under the power conferred by s.39 of the Land Compensation (Scotland) Act 1963 (1972 Act, s.197).

[31]   Sections 49 and 50 of the Land Compensation (Scotland) Act 1973, relating to severance of agricultural land, have effect in relation to a case where notice to treat is deemed to have been served by virtue of the purchase notice provisions.

[32]   A different authority may only be substituted if the Secretary of State first offers a hearing to that authority—see *Ealing Borough Council* v *Minister of Housing and Local Government* [1952] Ch.856.

have served in respect thereof a notice to treat (which cannot be withdrawn under the power conferred by s.39 of the Land Compensation (Scotland) Act 1963) (see 1972 Act, ss.175(1) and 197).

In lieu of confirming the notice the minister may grant planning permission for the development in respect of which permission was refused, or, where permission was granted subject to conditions, may revoke or amend those conditions so far as seems necessary to render the land capable of reasonably beneficial use (s.172(2)). Alternatively, if satisfied that the land, or part of it, could be rendered capable of reasonably beneficial use within a reasonable time by the carrying out of any other development for which planning permission ought to be granted, the Secretary of State may, in lieu of confirming the purchase notice, or in lieu of confirming it so far as relates to that part of the land, direct that planning permission for that development shall be granted (s.172(3)).[33] If the Secretary of State considers that the conditions specified in s.169(1)(a) to (c) (above) are not fulfilled, he will refuse to confirm the notice; by virtue of s.173 he may also refuse to confirm a notice served in respect of land which has a restricted use by virtue of a previous planning permission (below).

Before taking any action with respect to a purchase notice, the Secretary of State must give notice of his proposed action to the parties concerned, any one of whom then has the right to require that the parties be afforded the opportunity of a hearing before a representative of the minister (s.171(1)–(3)); after such a hearing the Secretary of State is entitled to deviate from the course of action originally proposed without giving the parties the opportunity of a further hearing (s.171(4)).

If the Secretary of State has not, within six months of transmission to him of the purchase notice, confirmed the notice or taken such action as is mentioned in s.172(2) or (3) (i.e. has neither made a more beneficial planning decision nor directed that permission for some other development be granted) and has not notified the server of the notice that he does not propose to confirm the notice, then the notice is deemed to be confirmed (s.175(2), (3)). Somewhat oddly, provided the minister gives notice within the time limit that he does not propose to confirm, he then has unlimited time to come to his decision.[34]

The validity of the Secretary of State's decision on a purchase notice may be challenged under s.233 of the 1972 Act but not otherwise (s.231) (see chapter 21).

Land with restricted use by virtue of previous planning permission

Section 173 of the 1972 Act is designed to deal with the type of situation which arose in *Adams & Wade Ltd.* v *Minister of Housing and Local Government*.[35] In that case planning permission for housing development

---

[33] For illustrations of the exercise of this power see ministerial decisions noted in [1976] J.P.L. 649; and [1982] J.P.L. 792.

[34] See *Sheppard* v *Secretary of State for the Environment* (1975) 233 E.G. 1167.

[35] (1965) 18 P. & C.R. 60.

had been granted subject to a condition that a strip of land be reserved as amenity land. After the houses were built application was made for permission to develop the amenity land and on the refusal of permission the owners served a purchase notice. It was argued for the minister that the owner of a piece of land which was, as a whole, capable of reasonably beneficial use could not sever the land and serve a purchase notice in respect of a part which was, in isolation, incapable of reasonably beneficial use. Widgery J. rejected that argument and quashed the minister's decision not to confirm the purchase notice.

Section 173 of the 1972 Act relates to land which has, by virtue of a previous planning permission, a restricted use. Land is to be treated as having a restricted use by virtue of a previous planning permission if it is part of a larger area in respect of which permission was previously granted and either it is an express condition of that planning permission or the planning application contemplated (expressly or by necessary implication) that that part of the land should 'remain undeveloped or be preserved or laid out in a particular way as amenity land in relation to the remainder' (s.173(2)). In the view of the English minister the word 'undeveloped', as used in this provision, stands by itself and is not connected with the words 'as amenity land in relation to the remainder'.[36] This view seems to be borne out by the concluding words of subsection (3) of s.173 (below). It has been held[37] that land only has a 'restricted use by virtue of a previous planning permission' if the restriction in question is one which is capable of enforcement.

On a refusal or conditional grant of permission, and the consequent service of a purchase notice, in respect of land which has a restricted use by virtue of a previous planning permission, the Secretary of State, even though satisfied that the land has become incapable of reasonably beneficial use in its existing state, is not obliged to confirm the notice if it appears to him that the land ought, in accordance with the previous planning permission, to remain undeveloped or, as the case may be, remain or be preserved or laid out as amenity land in relation to the remainder of the larger area for which that permission was granted (s.173(3)). This subsection is permissive only and even though the circumstances of a particular case may satisfy the conditions of s.173, the minister is not obliged to refuse to confirm the purchase notice.[38]

In *Plymouth City Corporation v Secretary of State for the Environment*[39] it was held that these provisions only apply where the whole of the land which was the subject of the purchase notice, and not merely part of it, has a restricted use by virtue of a previous planning permission.

Where a grant of outline permission is followed by approval of detailed plans, it is the outline consent which constitutes the planning permission;[40] it would seem that the provisions of s.173 can only apply in relation to a

---

[36]   See [1974] J.P.L. 158.
[37]   *Sheppard v Secretary of State for the Environment* (1975) 233 E.G. 1167.
[38]   See, for example, ministerial decisions noted in [1974] J.P.L. 158; and [1983] J.P.L. 753.
[39]   [1972] 1 W.L.R. 1347; see too ministerial decision noted in [1978] J.P.L. 394.
[40]   See p. 189 above.

planning permission and can have no application in relation to a decision consisting of a mere approval of details.[41]

Compensation

If a purchase notice is accepted or confirmed, compensation is assessed on the normal compulsory purchase basis.[42] The fact that the land in question has been shown to be incapable of reasonably beneficial use in its existing state does not mean that the measure of compensation for the land will necessarily be limited to the value attributable to its existing use. Much will depend on the reason for the adverse decision. For example, planning permission may have been refused because the land is required for a scheme of public works. It may be possible to show that were it not for the scheme the land would have development potential and that that potential should be taken into account in assessing compensation under the provisions of the Land Compensation (Scotland) Act 1963.

Where the Secretary of State, in lieu of confirming a purchase notice, directs that planning permission ought to be granted for some alternative development, it is possible that the 'permitted development value' of the land (in effect, the value of the land calculated with regard to that alternative permission but assuming that no other planning permission would be granted—see s.176(5)) may be less than the land's 'existing use value' (in effect, its value on the assumption that permission would be granted for development of any class specified in the Sixth Schedule[43]—see s.176(5)); if that is shown to be the case the planning authority are bound to pay compensation of any amount equal to the difference between the two values (see s.176(2)–(5)).

Other cases in which a purchase notice may be served

It is not only a refusal or conditional grant of planning permission that may form the basis for service of a purchase notice; certain other types of adverse planning decision or order may entitle an owner or lessee of land to serve a purchase notice.[44] In particular, where planning permission is revoked or modified (see p. 380) or where an order is made requiring discontinuance of an authorised use or imposing conditions on the continuance of such a use or requiring the alteration or removal of authorised buildings or works (see p.376), an owner or lessee may be able to serve a purchase notice; the procedure outlined above is applied, with certain modifications, to such a case (see ss.177 and 178). Section 179 of, and Schedule 17 to, the 1972 Act make similar provision for the service in certain circumstances of a listed building purchase notice in a case where listed building consent is refused, granted subject to conditions, revoked or modified (see chapter 19).

[41] See ministerial decisions noted in [1974] J.P.L. 38; and [1983] J.P.L. 753.
[42] As to the appropriate date by reference to which compensation is to be assessed see *W. & S. (Long Eaton) Ltd.* v *Derbyshire C.C.* (1975) 31 P. & C.R. 99. See also *Toogood* v *Bristol Corporation* (1973) 26 P. & C.R. 132. There is a duty on the planning authority to negotiate in all good faith for the purchase of the property; in *Bremer* v *Haringey London Borough Council, The Times,* 12th May 1983, damages were awarded against a planning authority for breach of that duty.
[43] See p. 388.
[44] See 1972 Act, ss.177–180.

CHAPTER 16

CONTROL OF THE EXISTING USE OF LAND

A. INTRODUCTION

The general effect of the comprehensive scheme of planning control introduced in 1947 was to regulate the carrying out of new development on land but to leave the landowner with the right to carry on the existing use. 'The system of planning control, then *and now*', says Davies,[1] 'rests on the assumption that the existing use of land—and the value of that use—is the owner's; but the prospect of developing the land—and the value of that prospect—is the community's.'

However, there will be occasions when a planning authority wish to exert control over the existing use of land, perhaps because of a change in planning policy or because of a change in the character of an area. The 1972 Act makes provision for such control but, as it derogates from the right to carry on the existing use of land, the general rule is that such control may only be exercised on payment of compensation. The purpose of this chapter is to examine these controls and the circumstances in which compensation is payable.

There will also be occasions where the value of the existing use of land is adversely affected, not so much by the exercise of direct control, but as a consequence of the carrying through of planning proposals in the locality—for example, the construction of a new road. In certain circumstances, a person with an interest in land which is adversely affected in this way will be able to obtain compensation or, in some cases, to require a public authority to purchase his interest. These circumstances are beyond the scope of this chapter and are discussed in detail in chapter 18.

For the purposes of this chapter we treat the 'existing use' of land as comprising:

(1) activities currently being carried on in conformity with a grant of planning permission, or which are unauthorised but have become immune from enforcement action, or which were instituted prior to the planning legislation coming into force;

(2) other development for which planning permission has been granted either in response to an application or by way of development order but

---

[1]   Keith Davies, *Law of Compulsory Purchase and Compensation* (Butterworths, 4th ed., 1984), p.271.

which has not yet been carried out; and

(3) certain classes of development specified in Schedule 6 to the 1972 Act which are so closely related to the existing use of the land that they are effectively treated as forming part of the existing use (generally referred to as 'existing use development').

The controls over these categories of existing use are considered in turn below.

The general rule, as we have already indicated, is that the exercise of control over the existing use of land is subject to the payment of compensation. However, as Grant observes;[2] 'Local authorities have rarely been in a position to buy environmental improvements by using the powers of direct intervention.' The result is that the formal controls which we describe below have been little used in practice[3] and the regulation of the existing use of land has been largely opportunistic. Planning authorities may well take the opportunity presented by the submission of an application for planning permission for new development either to negotiate some restriction on the existing use through agreement (see chapter 12) or to impose a restriction on the existing use by way of condition on the grant of planning permission for the new development (see chapter 10).

Not surprisingly, the use of conditions for this purpose has been the source of some controversy. Such action could be said to circumvent the general scheme of the legislation that compensation should be paid for restrictions imposed on the existing use of land. In *British Airports Authority* v *Secretary of State for Scotland*[4] counsel for one of the appellants argued, *inter alia*, that the imposition of a condition which restricted the existing use of land was an abuse of the power to impose conditions conferred by s.27(1) of the 1972 Act, and cited a number of authorities in support of this proposition. This argument was rejected by the First Division of the Court of Session. Lord President Emslie stated:

'I have examined [all of the authorities cited] and am clearly of the opinion that they do not establish the particular proposition for which they were cited, namely that the powers of s.27(1) may never be used to restrict, without compensation, existing rights of use of land under the control of an applicant for planning permission. There is, in my opinion, no such general principle to be discovered from a construction of the 1972 Act.'

His Lordship added: 'It may be, however, that where a condition is shown to have been imposed on a grant of planning permission with the ulterior motive of avoiding payment of compensation for discontinuance of existing

2   Malcolm Grant, *Urban Planning Law*, p. 646.
3   With a view to encouraging planning authorities to make wider use of these controls, certain modifications have been made by the Town and Country Planning (Minerals) Act 1981 to the application of the general rule to mineral operations (see chapter 19).
4   1979 S.C. 200; 1979 S.L.T. 197. See too p. 241 above.

use of land which would arise if s.49 powers were used it would be seen to be unreasonable and therefore *ultra vires*.' But so long as a condition serves a planning purpose, is fairly and reasonably related to the subject matter of the application and is not unreasonable, it would seem to be open to a planning authority to impose restrictions on the existing use of land in this way.

B. CONTROL OF EXISTING USES, BUILDINGS AND WORKS

For various reasons a planning authority may wish to modify or prohibit some authorised use of land or may wish to secure the removal or alteration of some authorised building—the authority may, for example, have changed their policy and may now desire the removal of some building for which planning permission was previously granted,[5] or they may wish to remove development which was originally unauthorised but in respect of which enforcement action is now time-barred, or they may wish to put an end to a use which was instituted in an unsuitable location prior to the planning legislation coming into force.

Extent of powers

Section 49 of the 1972 Act empowers a planning authority to make an order:

(*a*) requiring that any use[6] of land should be discontinued[7] or imposing conditions on the continuance of a use of land; or

(*b*) requiring that specified steps be taken for the alteration or removal of any building or works.

The provisions of s.49 were substantially extended in their application to mineral workings by the Town and Country Planning (Minerals) Act 1981 and new sections 49 B–G are discussed in full in chapter 19.

An order under s.49 may be made in any case where such action appears to the planning authority to be expedient in the interests of the proper planning of their area (including the interests of amenity), regard being had to the development plan and to any other material considerations (s.49(1)).

In a case in which the validity of an order made under the corresponding English provision was challenged, Roskill J. held that the powers conferred by the section—i.e.,

---

[5]   If a planning permission has not been implemented it may be revoked or modified under s.42 of the 1972 Act (see below).

[6]   In *Parkes* v *Secretary of State for the Environment* [1978] 1 W.L.R. 1308 it was held that land used for the sorting, processing and disposal of scrap materials was a 'use' of land which could be the subject of a discontinuance order.

[7]   An order can be made effecting a partial discontinuance of use—see [1973] J.P.L. 181.

(*a*) to require discontinuance of a use or to impose conditions on the continuance of a use, or

(*b*) to require alteration or removal of any buildings or works—were alternative and it was not the case that the planning authority could only use power (*b*) in a case where power (*a*) would not suffice.[8]

In the same case Roskill J. also had to consider the meaning of the word 'amenity' as used in this provision. In confirming an order requiring the removal of a building the minister had accepted his inspector's conclusion that although the building did not in its present condition detract from amenity, it would be advisable, since the building was unsuitable for residential use, to remove it now rather than let it fall slowly into a ruinous condition. It was argued that 'amenity' as used in the section must mean amenity as at the time of making the order and that the minister had exceeded his powers in having regard to future amenity. It was held that there was no reason to limit 'amenity' as used in the section to present amenity, Roskill J. declaring: 'I see no reason why the whole concept does not include all amenities, past, present and, in particular, future.' However, in a case where he considered that the existing uses of a site were not sufficiently objectionable to warrant the confirmation of a disconti- nuance order, the Secretary of State for the Environment declared (in 1972) that in considering such an order the minister 'is concerned with the way in which the land is being used at present and that in deciding whether or not to confirm the order it is not open to him to anticipate possible intensification of existing uses at some time in the future'.[9]

Procedure

An order under s.49 cannot take effect unless it is confirmed by the Secretary of State (s.49(4)). On confirming an order the minister may make such modifications as he considers expedient.[10] The English minister has, however, expressed the view that on submission of an order requiring discontinuance of a use, it is not open to him to modify the order in such a way as to make it an order imposing conditions on the continuance of that use; such orders are, in his opinion, 'different in kind and effect'.[11]

Where a district planning authority propose to make an order under s.49 they must give notice of the proposals to their regional planning authority and that authority may make representations or objections to the Secretary of State.[12] It will normally be a district or general planning authority who make an order under s.49, but where a regional planning authority are of

---

[8] *Re Lamplugh* (1967) 19 P. & C.R. 125; *sub. nom. Re Watch House, Boswinger* (1967) 66 L.G.R. 6.
[9] See [1973] J.P.L. 57.
[10] The Secretary of State has no specific power to correct defects in an order but in *Miller* v *Weymouth and Melcombe Regis Corporation* (1974) 27 P. & C.R. 468 the court exercised its discretion not to quash a discontinuance order which contained an obvious clerical error.
[11] See [1974] J.P.L. 607.
[12] Local Government (Scotland) Act 1973, s.181(1).

opinion that a structure plan approved by the Secretary of State would be materially prejudiced if an order under s.49 were not made, they may themselves make such an order.[13]

On submission of an order[14] to the Secretary of State the authority must serve notice on the owner, lessee and occupier of the land and on any other person who in their opinion will be affected by the order; any person on whom the notice is served has the right to demand a hearing before a person appointed by the Secretary of State for the purpose (s.49(5)). On confirmation of an order the planning authority must serve a copy on the owner, lessee and occupier of the land (s.49(6)). In *K. & B. Metals Ltd.* v *Birmingham City Council*[15] Sir Douglas Frank Q.C. expressed the view that since it is specifically provided that a discontinuance order shall not take effect until it is confirmed by the minister (see s.49(4)), 'there is no order as such until it is confirmed'.[16]

An order under s.49 may grant planning permission for any development of the affected land (s.49(2)). Where the requirements of an order made under s.49 will involve the displacement of persons residing in any premises, it is the duty of the planning authority, insofar as there is no other suitable residential accommodation available on reasonable terms, to secure the provision of such accommodation in advance of displacement (s.49(7)). The validity of an order made under s.49 may be questioned under s.233 of the 1972 Act but such an order is otherwise unchallengeable (s.231).[17]

Compensation

An order under s.49 will frequently result in the making of a claim for compensation. If, on a claim made in writing to the planning authority, it is shown that any person has suffered damage in consequence of such an order by depreciation in the value of an interest in the land in question to which he is entitled, or by being disturbed in his enjoyment of the land, the authority are to pay compensation to that person in respect of such damage (s.159(1), (2))[18] In *K. & B. Metals Ltd.* v *Birmingham City Council*[19] the Lands Tribunal held (distinguishing *Blow* v *Norfolk County Council*[20]) that the appropriate date for assessment of compensation on a discontinuance order is the date of confirmation of the order by the minister.

In *Blow* v *Norfolk County Council*[21] the Court of Appeal held that in

---

13 Local Government (Scotland) Act 1973, s.181(2).
14 There is no prescribed form for such an order.
15 (1976) 33 P. & C.R. 135 (L.T.).
16 Contrast, however, the decision of the Court of Session in *Caledonian Terminal Investments Ltd.* v *Edinburgh Corporation* 1970 S.C. 271; 1970 S.L.T. 362 (which concerned a modification order under s.42 of the 1972 Act—see p. 382 below).
17 On recourse to the courts, see chapter 21.
18 New sections 159A and 159B have been added to the 1972 Act by s.30 of the Town and Country Planning (Minerals) Act 1981. For a discussion of their effect see chapter 19.
19 (1976) 33 P. & C.R. 135.
20 [1967] 1 W.L.R. 1280.
21 Above. For an example of a case where a discontinuance order resulted in no depreciation, see *Evans* v *Dorset County Council* (1980) 256 E.G. 503.

assessing the compensation payable in respect of a discontinuance order the Lands Tribunal was entitled to take into account the risks that would influence a prospective purchaser's mind in relation to the price he might pay for the land—in this instance the doubts he would have had as to the extent of 'existing use' rights over the land in question. In *Harrison* v *Gloucester County Council*[22] account was taken, in assessing compensation, of the fact that planning permission for the development in question had only a short time to run and that it could be assumed that the permission would not have been renewed after its expiry.

Compensation payable under s.159 may include any expenses reasonably incurred in carrying out any works in compliance with the order (s.159(3)) but compensation will be reduced by the value of any materials removed for the purpose of complying with the order (s.159(4)). A claim for compensation under s.159 is to be made within six months of the making of the order or such longer period as the Secretary of State may allow (see Town and Country Planning (General) (Scotland) Regulations 1976, reg. 4).

Where a purchase notice takes effect in consequence of an order made under s.49 (below), compensation under s.159 is not payable (s.178(4)).

There is no provision for the repayment of compensation paid by the planning authority under s.159.

Purchase notice

If the effect of an order under s.49 is such as to render the land incapable of reasonably beneficial use, a purchase notice may be served under s.178 of the 1972 Act (see chapter 15).

Enforcement

Any person who fails to comply with an order requiring the discontinuance of a use of land or imposing conditions on the continuance of a use is liable on summary conviction or on conviction on indictment to a fine (1972 Act, s.100(1)).

From a date to be specified, s.28 of the Town and Country Planning (Minerals) Act 1981 will substitute a new s.100 in the 1972 Act. The new section provides that it shall be a defence for a person charged with an offence to prove that he took all reasonable measures and exercised all due diligence to avoid commission of the offence by himself or by any person under his control. The new section also makes provision regarding the procedure to be followed in the event of a person charged with an offence under this section alleging that the commission of the offence was due to the act or default of another person or due to reliance on information supplied by another person.

Where any steps for the alteration or removal of any buildings or works are required to be taken by an order under s.49 but have not been taken within the period specified in the order,[23] the planning authority may enter

[22] (1953) 4 P. & C.R. 99.
[23] The new s.100(4) refers also to 'such extended period as the planning authority may allow'.

on the land and may themselves take those steps (1972 Act, s.100(2)). At present, the authority have no power to recover any expenses incurred in carrying out such works. However, the new s.100 will allow an authority to recover any expenses reasonably incurred from the person who is then the owner of the land. An authority will also be able to sell any materials removed by them from the land, unless the materials are claimed by the owner within three days of their removal. Where an authority sell such materials, they will pay over the proceeds to the owner after first deducting any expenses recoverable by them from the owner.

C. RESTRICTIONS ON DEVELOPMENT WHICH HAS BEEN GRANTED PLANNING PERMISSION BUT WHICH HAS YET TO BE IMPLEMENTED

Circumstances may arise in which a planning authority have a change of heart as regards development for which they have granted planning permission. Sections 42 and 43 of the 1972 Act confer on planning authorities powers to revoke or modify a planning permission granted in response to an application under Part III of the Act. A planning authority may also wish on occasion to prevent advantage being taken of planning permission granted by way of a development order (see chapter 7). Where planning permission has been granted by development order, the order may itself enable a planning authority to direct that the permission will not apply either in relation to development in a particular area or in relation to any particular development (1972 Act, s.21(5)(b)). In particular, Article 4 of the Town and Country Planning (General Development) (Scotland) Order 1981 ('the G.D.O.') empowers a planning authority to issue such a direction in respect of any of the categories of development granted permission by Article 3 of and Schedule 1 to the Order.

As a result of an amendment introduced by the Local Government and Planning (Scotland) Act 1982,[24] s.31 of the 1972 Act now enables a planning authority, at the request of the applicant or of a person acting with his consent, simply to vary any planning permission granted by them without further formality if it appears that the variation sought is not material. This avoids the necessity for a formal modification or the submission of a fresh application where minor variations are proposed.

The procedures governing revocation or modification orders and withdrawal of permission granted by a development order are now considered in turn.

1. *Revocation or modification orders*

Extent of powers. Section 42 of the 1972 Act empowers a planning authority to make an order revoking or modifying, to such extent as they consider expedient, any permission to develop land granted on an application made

[24] See s.46.

under Part III of the 1972 Act;[25] the authority may make such an order in any case where it appears to them, having regard to the development plan and to any other material considerations, that it is expedient to do so. The power conferred by s.42 does not extend to a permission granted by a development order.[26]

An order revoking or modifying planning permission can only be made so long as the planning permission has not been fully implemented.[27] Section 42(4) provides that the power to revoke or modify may be exercised:

(a) where the permission relates to the carrying out of building or other operations, at any time before those operations have been completed; or

(b) where the permission relates to a change of the use of any land, at any time before the change has taken place.

It is also provided that revocation or modification of permission for the carrying out of building or other operations shall not affect so much of those operations as has been carried out before the date on which the order was confirmed.

It would seem from the decision of the Court of Session in *Caledonian Terminal Investments Ltd.* v *Edinburgh Corporation*[28] that for the purposes of this section a change of use does not 'take place' until the land in question is actually put to the new use. In that case planning permission was granted for change of use from dwelling-house to professional office. On 3rd April 1967 work began on internal alterations necessary to make the premises suitable for the new use; on 22nd June 1967 the planning authority approved an order modifying the planning permission; the alterations were completed on 5th July 1967; and the premises were opened for business as an insurance office on 10th July 1967. Rejecting the argument that the change of use took place on the date when the alterations began, the Second Division held that the change of use took place after 22nd June 1967 (i.e., after the date on which the modification order was approved by the authority). The Lord Justice-Clerk (Lord Grant) and Lord Wheatley considered that the change of use did not take place until the date on which the premises actually opened for business.

Procedure. An order revoking or modifying permission[29] will normally be made by a district or general planning authority. Where a district planning authority propose to make such an order they must give notice of the proposals to their regional planning authority and that authority may make

---

[25] Section 25 of the Town and Country Planning (Minerals) Act 1981, has added subsections (5) and (6) to s.42 of the 1972 Act. For a discussion of their effect see chapter 19.
[26] As to withdrawal of such permission see below.
[27] The planning authority have, however, power under s.49 to make an order requiring discontinuance of an authorised use or requiring alteration or removal of authorised buildings or works—see above.
[28] 1970 S.C. 271; 1970 S.L.T. 362.
[29] There is no prescribed form for such an order.

representations or objections to the Secretary of State (Local Government (Scotland) Act 1973, s.181(1)). Where, after consultation with the district planning authority concerned, a regional planning authority are of opinion that a structure plan approved by the Secretary of State would be materially prejudiced if an order under s.42 were not made, they may themselves make such an order (1973 Act, s.181(2)).

Except in the circumstances mentioned below, a revocation or modification order made by a planning authority does not take effect unless it is confirmed by the Secretary of State (s.42(2)). On submitting an order to the Secretary of State for confirmation, the authority must serve notice on the owner, lessee and occupier of the land affected and also on 'any other person who in their opinion will be affected by the order' (s.42(3)). Any person served with such a notice has the right to demand a hearing before a person appointed by the Secretary of State for the purpose (s.42(3)). In confirming such an order the Secretary of State is entitled to modify it (s.42(2)).

In *Caledonian Terminal Investments Ltd.* v *Edinburgh Corporation*[30] the modification order was not confirmed by the Secretary of State until some considerable time after the change of use had taken place. As is mentioned above, the power to revoke or modify planning permission can only be exercised prior to a change of use taking place (s.42(4)) and the appellants' main argument was that the power to revoke or modify is not 'exercised' until the order is confirmed by the minister; the modification order in this case was, they argued, *ultra vires* in that the power had not been exercised until after the change of use took place. The court held that the power was exercised on the date the planning authority made the order; the power had therefore been exercised prior to the change of use taking place and the order was valid. Both the Lord Justice-Clerk and Lord Wheatley stressed the practical difficulties that would result from any other conclusion. It may be mentioned, however, that Lord Walker, though he contented himself with expressing 'a doubt rather than a dissent', found 'great difficulty in understanding how the making of the order by the planning authority could ever amount to an exercise of the power to revoke or modify'. The planning authority's order has, he said, 'no effect unless it is confirmed by the Secretary of State'.

The Secretary of State may himself make a revocation or modification order[31] (1972 Act s.260[32]).

The validity of an order revoking or modifying planning permission may be questioned under s.233 of the 1972 Act but not otherwise (s.231) (see chapter 21).

---

[30] Above. Contrast, however, *K. & B. Metals Ltd.* (above); and *Iveagh* v *Minister of Housing and Local Government* [1964] 1 Q.B. 395 (in which the Court of Appeal held that the word 'made' in relation to a building preservation order meant 'effectively made' and since such an order had no effective operation until it was confirmed by the minister, the order was made on the date it was confirmed).

[31] Only in a very exceptional case is the Secretary of State likely to intervene in this way. A notable example of such intervention was the minister's revocation in 1973 of permission granted by Argyll County Council for a caravan park on the island of Seil.

[32] As amended by the Local Government (Scotland) Act 1973, Sched. 29.

Compensation. Where planning permission is revoked or modified by an order made under s.42 of the 1972 Act, then if it is shown that 'a person interested in the land':

(*a*) has incurred expenditure in carrying out work which is rendered abortive by the revocation or modification;[33] or

(*b*) has otherwise sustained loss or damage which is directly attributable to the revocation or modification,[34]

the planning authority must pay to that person compensation in respect of that expenditure, loss or damage (s.153(1)).[35]

The meaning of the phrase 'a person interested in the land' was considered by the Court of Appeal in *Pennine Raceway Ltd.* v *Kirklees Metropolitan Borough Council.*[36] The claimant company had entered into an agreement with a landowner under the terms of which the company, in return for a pecuniary consideration, had been given the sole rights to promote motor car and motor cycle events on an airfield. On the basis of this agreement, the company subsequently erected safety barriers, cleared and surfaced an area of land for pits and for competitors' car parking and created a banking for spectators. Following the withdrawl of their planning permission, the company claimed compensation for abortive expenditure. The planning authority resisted the claim on the ground that the company was not 'a person interested in the land'. The interest, argued the authority, had to be in the nature of a proprietary interest; the claimants merely had a licence. The Court of Appeal rejected this argument. Eveleigh L.J. said that this was a statute which controlled use of and operations on land; it was not a conveyancing statute and the phrase should be interpreted without regard to technical terms. In the court's view, a person who, like the claimants, had an enforceable right as against the owner to use the land in the way which had now been prohibited was 'a person interested in the land' within the meaning of the section.

Any expenditure incurred in the preparation of plans for the purposes of any work, or upon other similar preparatory matters may be included under head (*a*) above (s.153(2)); subject to that provision, no compensation is payable in respect of any work carried out before the grant of the permission which has been revoked or modified or in respect of any loss or damage

[33] See *Holmes* v *Bradfield R.D.C.* [1949] 2 K.B. 1; and *Southern Olympia (Syndicate) Ltd.* v *West Sussex County Council* (1952) 3 P. & C.R. 60.

[34] As to the circumstances in which loss or damage may be treated as 'directly attributable' to revocation action see *Hobbs (Quarries) Ltd.* v *Somerset County Council* (1975) 30 P. & C.R. 286; and *Cawoods Aggregates (South Eastern) Ltd.* v *Southwark London Borough* (1982) 264 E.G. 1087 (both concerned with loss of anticipated profits); but compare *Halford* v *Oxfordshire County Council* (1952) 2 P. & C.R. 358. See too *Burlin* v *Manchester City Council* (1976) 32 P. & C.R. 115 (L.T.); and *Pennine Raceway Ltd.* v *Kirklees Metropolitan Council*, Lands Tribunal, 22nd March 1984 (unreported, but see (1984) 134 New L.J. 969).

[35] A new section 153A was added to the 1972 Act by s.29 of the Town and Country Planning (Minerals) Act 1981. For a discussion of its effect see chapter 19.

[36] [1983] Q.B. 382.

(except loss or damage consisting of depreciation in the value of an interest in the land) arising out of anything done or omitted to be done prior to the grant of that permission (s.153(3)). Under head (b) will be included depreciation in the value of any interest in the land resulting from the revocation or modification of permission; the claimant will therefore be entitled to the difference between the value of the interest prior to the making of the order and its value thereafter.[37] Compensation for revocation or modification of planning permission is not dependent on there being attached to the land an unexpended balance of established development value (see chapter 14).

In calculating the amount of any depreciation in the value of an interest in land, it is to be assumed that planning permission would be granted for development of any class specified in Schedule 6[38] to the 1972 Act (s.153(4)).[39] This provision apparently excludes the making of any other assumptions as to the grant of planning permission; in assessing the post-revocation value of land it can be assumed that Schedule 6 development would be permitted but no other assumptions as to the grant of planning permission can be made.[40]

The fact that permission for Sixth Schedule development is to be assumed might cause a problem when it is permission to carry out such development that is revoked or modified. As A. E. Telling points out,[41] if, in such a case, a claim for compensation is disputed, the only remedy would seem to be to re-apply for the permission which has been revoked or modified and on refusal of that application to make a claim for compensation under s.158 (see p. 391 below).

A claim for compensation under s.153 should be served on the planning authority within six months of the date of the decision in respect of which the claim is made, but the Secretary of State has power to extend the period in any particular case (see Town and Country Planning (General) (Scotland) Regulations 1976, reg. 4). For this purpose 'the date of the decision' is presumably the date on which the order is made.

Where compensation becomes payable under s.153 and includes a sum exceeding £20 in respect of depreciation, the planning authority must, if practicable, apportion the amount between different parts of the land according to the way in which those parts are differently affected by the order in consequence of which the compensation is payable (s.155(1)–(4)).

---

[37] But see *Pennine Raceway Ltd.* v *Kirklees Metropolitan Council*, Lands Tribunal, 22nd March 1984 (unreported, but see (1984) 134 New L.J. 969). In *Loromah Estates Ltd.* v *London Borough of Haringey* (1978) 38 P. & C.R. 234 the Lands Tribunal held that a principle analogous to the principle established in *Pointe Gourde Quarrying and Transport Co.* v *Sub-Intendent of Crown Lands* [1947] A.C. 565 applied to such cases, so that any depreciation in the value of the land having the benefit of the revoked permission, attributable to the revocation order or its confirmation, ought to be left out of account in the assessment of compensation.

[38] The classes of development specified in Schedule 6 are summarised at p. 388 below.

[39] For this purpose Schedule 6 is modified by the provisions of s.263 of the 1972 Act.

[40] See *Burlin* v *Manchester City Council* (1976) 32 P. & C.R. 115 (L.T.).

[41] *Planning Law and Procedure* (Butterworths, 6th ed., 1982), p. 287.

In a case where the compensation for depreciation exceeds £20 the planning authority must cause notice of that fact to be recorded in the Register of Sasines or the Land Register, as appropriate, and must send a copy of the notice to the Secretary of State (s.155(5)): such compensation may have to be repaid (not necessarily by the person by whom it was received) if 'new development' of one of the types specified in s.148 (see p. 363 above) is subsequently carried out (s.157). For this purpose the meaning of the expression 'new development' is widened to some extent (see s.157(4)).

Provision is made for the making in certain circumstances of a contribution by the Secretary of State towards the compensation payable by a planning authority under s.153. Such a contribution may be made where the circumstances of the case are such that the Secretary of State would have been liable to pay compensation under Part VII of the 1972 Act[42] if the permission revoked or modified had originally been refused, or, as the case may be, granted as so modified (s.156(1)). The Secretary of State can only make such a contribution if there is attached to the land an unexpended balance of established development value and the amount of any such contribution may not exceed that balance (s.156(2)). Any contribution so made by the Secretary of State will, of course, reduce the unexpended balance and in any case where the Secretary of State proposes to make a contribution, notice must therefore be given to any person with an interest in the land to which the proposal relates or with an interest which is substantially affected by an apportionment included in the proposal and also to any person who appears to be substantially affected by the reduction or extinguishment of the unexpended balance (see Town and Country Planning (Compensation) (Scotland) Regulations 1954, reg. 9). Any such person may object to the proposal and, if dissatisfied with the Secretary of State's determination, may refer the dispute to the Lands Tribunal for Scotland (1954 Regulations, reg. 10).

Purchase notice. If the effect of a revocation or modification order is to render the land incapable of reasonably beneficial use, an owner or lessee may be able to serve a purchase notice (see chapter 15). Where such a notice is served, any compensation payable by virtue of s.153 in respect of expenditure incurred in carrying out any work on the land is to be deducted from any compensation payable in respect of the acquisition of an interest in that land in pursuance of the purchase notice (ss.176(1) and 177(2)).

Unopposed revocation or modification. Where the planning authority have made an order under s.42, and the owner, lessee and occupier of the land and all persons who, in the authority's opinion, will be affected by the order have notified the authority in writing that they do not object to the order, then the authority may follow the procedure set out in s.43[43] of the 1972 Act and regulation 7 of the Town and Country Planning (General) (Scotland)

---

[42] Part VII of the 1972 Act is outlined in chapter 14.
[43] As amended by the Local Government (Scotland) Act 1973, Sched. 23, para. 18.

Regulations 1976; this may result in the order taking effect without confirmation by the Secretary of State.

The authority must advertise the making of such an order; the notice is to specify the period within which any person affected by the order may give notice to the Secretary of State that he wishes to be heard and the date on which, if no such notice is given to the minister, the order may take effect (s.43(2)). A notice containing similar information must be served on the affected parties (s.43(3)). A copy of the advertisement must be sent to the Secretary of State (s.43(4)). If no person gives notice to the Secretary of State that he wishes to be heard and the minister does not direct that the order be submitted to him, the order takes effect on the date specified by the authority (s.43(5)).

There is excluded from the operation of s.43 any order revoking or modifying a planning permission granted or deemed to have been granted by the Secretary of State under Parts III, IV or V of the 1972 Act (e.g., a permission granted on appeal to the minister) and any order modifying a condition to which a planning permission is subject by virtue of s.38 or s.39 of the 1972 Act (i.e., a condition limiting the duration of planning permission) (s.43(6)); any such order will always require confirmation.

2. *Withdrawal of permission granted by development order*

If the Secretary of State or a general or district planning authority is satisfied that it is expedient that development falling within any of the classes of 'permitted development' specified in Schedule 1 to the G.D.O. (see p. 172 above) should not be carried out in any particular area, or that any particular development of any of those classes should not be carried out, unless permission is granted on an application in that behalf, the minister or the planning authority may, under Article 4 of the G.D.O., direct that permission granted by the G.D.O. is not to apply to:

(*a*) all or any development of all or any of those classes in any particular area specified in the direction;[44] or

(*b*) any particular development, specified in the direction, falling within any of those classes.

In this way the minister or the planning authority can exercise planning control over development which would otherwise be automatically permitted.

A direction by a planning authority under Article 4 requires the approval of the Secretary of State unless it relates only to a listed building or a building notified to the authority by the Secretary of State as a building of special architectural or historic interest (Art. 4(2)).

---

[44] For an example of an Article 4 direction made by the Secretary of State see the Town and Country Planning (Restriction of Permitted Development) (National Scenic Areas) (Scotland) Direction 1980 (appended to S.D.D. Circular 20/1980).

Notice of any direction given under head (*a*) above (i.e. a direction specifying a particular area) must be published in one or more newspapers circulating in the area and in the Edinburgh Gazette; such a direction comes into force on the date on which the notice is first published (Art. 4(3)). It is not necessary in such a case that notice be served on any owner or occupier of land.[45]

Notice of any direction given under head (*b*) above (i.e. a direction specifying a particular development) must, however, be served by the planning authority on the owner and occupier of the land affected; such a direction comes into force on the date of service on the occupier, or, if there is no occupier, on the owner (Art. 4(4)).

An Article 4 direction can have no effect in a case where permission granted by the G.D.O. was acted upon prior to the direction coming into force.[46]

Where, following the coming into force of a direction under Article 4, application is made for planning permission in respect of development of the type specified in the direction and such permission is refused, or is granted subject to conditions other than those imposed in relation to such development by the G.D.O., compensation may be payable.[47] Section 154 of the 1972 Act states that in any such case the compensation provisions of s.153 shall apply as if the planning permission granted by the development order had been granted by the planning authority under Part III of the Act and had subsequently been revoked or modified by an order under s.42 of the Act.

From time to time the Secretary of State may decide to vary the terms of the G.D.O. (1972 Act, s.273(3)). The effect of a variation may be similar to that of an Article 4 direction. It may bring under the direct control of the planning authority development—which hitherto has been permitted under Article 3 of and Schedule 1 to the Order. For example, the effect of the Town and Country Planning (General Development) (Scotland) Amendment Order 1983 was to remove 'permitted development' status from certain categories of building, plant and machinery, or structures or erections in the nature of plant or machinery used for any purpose which involves the manufacture, processing, keeping or use of hazardous substances (as there defined). If an application for planning permission for such development is subsequently refused or is granted subject to more onerous conditions than would have been the case under the G.D.O., the provisions of ss.153 and 154 come into operation in the same way as for an Article 4 direction (1972 Act, s.154(1) and (2)).[48] Planning authorities may,

---

[45] See *Spedeworth* v *Secretary of State for the Environment* (1972) 71 L.G.R. 123.

[46] *Cole* v *Somerset County Council* [1957] 1 Q.B. 23.

[47] See, for example, *Fry* v *Essex County Council* (1958) 11 P. & C.R. 21; and *Pennine Raceway Ltd.* v *Kirklees Metropolitan Council*, Lands Tribunal, 22nd March 1984 (unreported, but see (1984) 134 New L.J. 969).

[48] Note, however, the Town and Country Planning (Compensation) Bill presently before Parliament. The object of the Bill is to limit the right to compensation for the refusal or conditional grant of planning permission for development following withdrawal of permission by the amendment or revocation of a development order.

therefore, find themselves faced with claims for compensation as a result of variations to the terms of the G.D.O. made by the Secretary of State.

D. EXISTING USE DEVELOPMENT

Schedule 6 to the 1972 Act sets out nine categories of development which are described as 'development not constituting new development'. These categories of development are closely related to the existing use of the land and are commonly referred to as 'existing use development'. They are nonetheless 'development' within the meaning of s.19(1) of the 1972 Act and planning permission is therefore required, either by way of specific grant or by way of a development order, before any such activity can be carried out (1972 Act, s.20(1)). The significance of Schedule 6 is that the value of 'existing use development' is treated in effect as if it belonged to the landowner[49] so that, with the exception of the two categories of development set out in Part I of the Sixth Schedule (see p.389 below), any restrictions on the realisation of this value may only be imposed on payment of compensation.

The explanation for the existence of these categories of development derives from the financial provisions of the 1947 Act (see p.356 above). As a concession to landowners, the Third Schedule to the 1947 Act listed certain categories of development linked to the existing use of land which were treated as falling within the existing use of land. The result was that a grant of planning permission for such development did not give rise to any liability to development charge; furthermore, if planning permission was refused or was granted subject to conditions, compensation generally had to be paid by the planning authority. Although the financial provisions of the 1947 Act have long since been repealed, subsequent legislation has continued to treat the value of existing use development as belonging to the landowner. The categories of existing use development have remained in substantially similar form and are now set out in Schedule 6 to the 1972 Act.

Schedule 6

The classes of development specified in Schedule 6 are broadly as follows:

---

[49]   For this reason s.23(3) of the Land Compensation (Scotland) Act 1963 provides that it is to be assumed, for the purpose of assessing compensation in respect of any compulsory acquisition, that planning permission would be granted for development of any class specified in Schedule 6 to the 1972 Act. The provisions of the Sixth Schedule must also be taken into account in connection with claims for compensation on revocation or modification of planning permission (see p. 384 above). Compensation may be payable under Part VII of the 1972 Act in respect of restrictions on 'new development'; as mentioned above, 'new development' consists of any development other than development of a class specified in Part I or Part II of Schedule 6 (1972 Act, s.19(5)). For certain purposes the provisions of Schedule 6 must, as mentioned below, be read with the modifications contained in s.263 of, and Schedule 16 to, the 1972 Act.

Part I

1. The rebuilding, as often as may be desired, of any building in existence on 1st July 1948, or destroyed or demolished between 7th January 1937 and 1st July 1948, or in existence at a material date, provided that the cubic content[50] of the original building is not exceeded by more than one tenth or, in the case of a dwelling-house, by more than one tenth or 1750 cubic feet, whichever is the greater.

2. The use as two or more separate dwelling-houses of any building used at a material date as a single dwelling-house.

Part II

3. The enlargement, improvement or other alteration,[51] as often as may be desired, of any such building as is mentioned in paragraph 1 or of any building substituted for such a building by the carrying out of any such operations as are mentioned in that paragraph, provided that the cubic content[52] of the original building is not exceeded by more than one tenth or, in the case of a dwelling-house, by more than one tenth or 1750 cubic feet, whichever is the greater. 'Enlargement' includes the erection of an additional building within the curtilage of, and to be used in connection with, the original building (Schedule 6, para. 12).[53]

4. The carrying out, on land which was used for agriculture or forestry at a material date, of any building or other operations required for that use, but excluding the erection, enlargement, improvement or alteration of dwelling-houses or of buildings used for the purposes of market gardens, nursery grounds or timber yards or for other purposes not connected with

---

[50] As ascertained by external measurement (Sched. 6, para. 10).

[51] In *National Provincial Bank Ltd.* v *Portsmouth Corporation* (1959) 11 P. & C.R. 6 the Court of Appeal held that an application for planning permission, though expressed to be for 'the enlargement, improvement and alteration' of premises, was in substance an application to rebuild the premises and therefore fell within paragraph 1 of the Schedule. In *Peaktop Properties (Hampstead) Ltd.* v *Camden London Borough Council* (1983) 82 L.G.R. 101, the Court of Appeal held that a proposal to build further residential flats by way of the construction of an additional storey on each of two existing blocks of flats should be treated as existing use development (as an enlargement) and not new development. In *Growngrand Ltd.* v *Kensington and Chelsea Royal Borough* (1984) 272 E.G. 676 the Lands Tribunal held that a proposal to construct a two-storey dwelling-house in a garden area held together with existing residential property and to be joined to the existing property by an unroofed pergola was not to be treated as an enlargement, improvement or alteration to the existing property. The link was merely cosmetic and the proposed dwelling would be an additional building.

[52] See note 50 above.

[53] In *Growngrand Ltd.* v *Kensington and Chelsea Royal Borough* (1984) 272 E.G. 676 the Lands Tribunal concluded that the phrase 'in connection with' in the corresponding provision of the English Act of 1971 (Sched. 8, para. 11) is likely to mean 'ancillary or complementary to'. A new two-storey dwelling to be erected on garden ground held together with existing residential property would not, on the facts of the case, be erected within the curtilage of the existing property and would in no sense be used in connection with the existing property.

general farming operations[54] or with the cultivation or felling of trees.

5. The winning and working, on land held or occupied with land used for the purposes of agriculture, of minerals reasonably required for the purposes of that use.

6. The winning and working of peat by any person for the domestic requirements of that person.

7. A change of use of a building or other land from one purpose to another purpose falling within the same general class specified in the Town and Country Planning (Use Classes for Third Schedule Purposes) (Scotland) Order 1948.[55]

8. Where part of a building or land was, at a material date, used for a particular purpose, the use for the same purpose of an additional part of the building or land not exceeding one tenth of the cubic content of the part of the building used for that purpose on 1st July 1948 or on the day thereafter when the building began to be so used, or, as the case may be, one tenth of the area of the land so used on that day.

9. The deposit of waste materials or refuse in connection with the working of minerals, on any land used for that purpose at a material date so far as may be reasonably required in connection with the working of those minerals.

It may be noted that certain paragraphs of Schedule 6 employ the expression 'at a material date'; this means either 1st July 1948 or the date by reference to which the Schedule has to be applied (Schedule 6, para. 13). For the purposes of s.158 of the 1972 Act, which provides for payment of compensation in respect of a planning decision restricting development of a class specified in Part II of Schedule 6 (below), the 'material date' would appear to be the date of the planning decision giving rise to the claim for compensation.

It should be mentioned that for some purposes Schedule 6 is subject to certain modifications originally introduced by the Town and Country Planning Act 1963. These modifications, which have the effect of reducing the scope of the Schedule, were introduced for two reasons. First, it was considered that the reference in paragraphs 1 and 3 to an increase in cubic content of one tenth on the rebuilding or alteration of a building was over-generous, in that an increase of one tenth in cubic content might result, through use of modern building methods, in an increase in floor space of anything up to 40 per cent and it was on the value of that lost floor space that compensation might have to be assessed. Secondly, a planning authority might grant planning permission for development which, in their view, utilised the site to the full, and yet find that refusal of a subsequent

---

[54] In *Moxey* v *Hertford Rural District Council* (1973) 27 P. & C.R. 274 the Lands Tribunal held that a broiler house was not a building connected with general farming operations. And see generally the discussion in *Jones* v *Stockport Metropolitan Borough Council* (1983) 269 E.G. 408 of the somewhat different wording of class VI of Schedule 1 to the English G.D.O.

[55] The provisions now contained in the Sixth Schedule to the 1972 Act were originally contained in the Third Schedule to the 1947 Act.

application to enlarge the building made them liable to pay compensation. It is therefore provided[56] that in any case where compensation is to be assessed on the assumption that planning permission would be granted for Schedule 6 development, it is to be assumed as regards development of any class specified in paragraph 1 or paragraph 3 that such permission would be granted subject to certain limitations on increase in gross floor space; in the case of buildings erected after 1st July 1948 (the date when the 1947 Act came into operation) the tolerances in paragraphs 3 and 8 are not to apply.

Compensation for restrictions on Sixth Schedule development

Where, on an application for planning permission to carry out development of any class specified in *Part II* of Schedule 6 to the 1972 Act, the Secretary of State refuses permission or grants it subject to conditions, any person whose interest in land is depreciated in value as a result of the decision is entitled to claim compensation from the planning authority (s.158(1),(2)). The decision must be that of the Secretary of State, either on appeal or on reference of the application to him for determination.

A claim for compensation under s.158 must be served on the planning authority within six months of the date of the adverse decision, unless the Secretary of State agrees to an extension of time in any particular case (Town and Country Planning (General) (Scotland) Regulations 1976, reg. 4).

Where payable, compensation under s.158 is to be an amount equal to the difference between the value of the interest in land following upon the adverse decision and the value that interest would have had if permission had been granted, or had been granted unconditionally, as the case may be (s.158(2)). It cannot always be assumed that the value of an interest in land would necessarily have been higher if planning permission for Sixth Schedule development had been granted, or had been granted unconditionally, as the case may be.[57]

In determining whether, and to what extent, the value of an interest in land has been depreciated as a result of such a decision, it is to be assumed that any subsequent application for 'the like planning permission would be determined in the same way', but if, in the case of a refusal of planning permission, the Secretary of State undertook to grant planning permission for some other development of the land, regard must be had to that undertaking (s.158(3)). In granting planning permission subject to conditions for regulating the design or external appearance of buildings or the size or height of buildings, the Secretary of State may, 'if it appears to him to be reasonable to do so having regard to the local circumstances', direct that those conditions are to be wholly or partially disregarded in assessing compensation (s.158(4)).

---

[56] See 1972 Act, s.263 and Sched. 16; see too s.158 (below) and the decision of the Court of Appeal in *Peaktop Properties (Hampstead) Ltd.* v *Camden London Borough Council* (1983) 82 L.G.R. 101.

[57] See *A. L. Salisbury Ltd.* v *York Corporation* (1960) 11 P. & C.R. 421.

It is only a decision restricting development of a class specified in Part II of the Sixth Schedule that can give rise to a claim for compensation under s.158. For the purposes of s.158 the scope of Part II of the Sixth Schedule has, for the reasons mentioned above, been materially reduced. In determining for the purposes of s.158 whether and to what extent the value of an interest in land has been depreciated, no account is to be taken of any prospective use which would contravene the condition set out in Schedule 16 to the 1972 Act (s.158(3)(c)); that condition is applicable to development specified in paragraph 3 of the Sixth Schedule (enlargement, improvement or other alteration of a building, subject to certain limits as regards increase in the cubic content of the building). The effect of this provision is that in relation to development within paragraph 3 there must be assumed a further condition to the effect that where the building to be altered is the original building,[58] the gross floor space used for any purpose in the altered building may not exceed by more than 10 per cent the gross floor space used for that purpose in the original building, and that where the building to be altered is not the original building no such increase may take place.

In *Peaktop Properties (Hampstead) Ltd.* v *Camden London Borough Council*[59] an application for permission to add an extra storey (of eleven new flats) to each of two blocks of flats was refused. The new flats would have increased the original gross volume of the blocks by less than 10 per cent. The owners claimed compensation in respect of the refusal. The Court of Appeal held that the fact that the proposed development involved the construction of new flats rather than the enlargement of existing flats did not defeat the claim for compensation. However, the proposal would have added 11.49 per cent gross floor space to each of the original blocks of flats and would therefore have breached the '10 per cent additional floor space' rule.[60] The Court held that no account could be taken of any of the prospective use in determining the extent of depreciation resulting from the refusal of planning permission for the enlargement and that no compensation was payable. It seems clear, however, that in such circumstances if the claimant simply redesigned the enlargement so that the additional floor space did not exceed the 10 per cent limitation, the refusal of an application for such development would give rise to a compensation entitlement.[61]

For the purposes of s.158, paragraph 3 of the Sixth Schedule is to be construed as not extending to works involving any increase in the cubic content of a building erected after the appointed day (1st July 1948),

---

[58] 'Original building' means, broadly, a building existing on 1st July 1948, or existing before that date but destroyed or demolished after 7th January 1937, or erected for the first time after 1st July 1948 but not including a building rebuilt after 1st July 1948.

[59] (1983) 82 L.G.R. 101.

[60] See Town and Country Planning Act 1971, s.169(3)(c) and Schedule 18, para. 1.

[61] See, however, the Town and Country Planning (Compensation) Bill, the object of which is to provide that compensation will no longer be payable for the refusal or conditional grant of permission for applications made on or after 24th January 1985 which relate to the addition of new flats to a block which was in existence on 1st July 1948, or which involve an increase of more than one tenth in the cubic content of any dwelling in such a building.

whether original to the site or resulting from rebuilding operations (s.158(6)(a)).

Section 158(6)(b) provides that paragraph 7 of the Sixth Schedule is not to apply to a building erected after 1st July 1948. This reference to paragraph 7 would appear to be a misprint; as originally enacted in the Town and Country Planning Act 1963 the reference was to paragraph 8.[62]

It would seem that compensation paid under s.158 in respect of a decision restricting Sixth Schedule development cannot be reclaimed by the planning authority even if the decision which originally gave rise to the compensation payment is subsequently reversed.

Purchase notice

Compensation is not payable in respect of a planning decision restricting development of a class specified in Part I of the Sixth Schedule to the 1972 Act. It is not clear why this should be so although Davies suggests[63] that if a refusal to allow the rebuilding of a building (para. 1, Part I of the Sixth Schedule) had qualified for compensation in the period after the Second World War, it would have imposed a very heavy burden on planning authorities. If, however, an adverse decision on an application for permission to carry out development within Part I renders the land in question incapable of reasonably beneficial use, a purchase notice might be served on the planning authority (see chapter 15). If such a purchase notice succeeds it will be assumed, in assessing compensation, that planning permission for development of any class specified in Schedule 6 would have been permitted.[64] Otherwise, however, there is no remedy for a decision restricting development falling within Part I of the Sixth Schedule.

---

[62] See 1963 Act, s.2(1), (3); and compare 1972 Act, s.263.
[63] Keith Davies, *Law of Compulsory Purchase and Compensation* (4th ed.), p. 319.
[64] See note 49 above. And see *Sorrell* v *Maidstone R.D.C.* (1961) 13 P. & C.R. 57; and *Walton-on-Thames Charities Trustees* v *Walton and Weybridge U.D.C.* (1970) 21 P. & C.R. 411.

CHAPTER 17
POSITIVE PLANNING

Introduction

Planning authorities are sometimes viewed as little more than regulatory agencies whose task it is to resist development which does not conform to the development plan. This is hardly surprising, as for most people, whether as applicants or objectors, the development control process is their point of contact with the planning system. Yet planning authorities are enabling as well as controlling agencies. They are endowed with wide powers to encourage, assist and undertake development. These are generally referred to as 'positive planning' powers in contrast with development control powers which are seen as essentially 'negative'.[1] 'The essence of positive planning, as we understand it', said the Pilcher Report, 'is that every planning authority should have the power to see that desirable development should happen rather than to have to wait and react to initiatives from others.'[2]

Development plans are intended to have a promotional as well as a controlling influence on development. These plans are to give guidance to prospective developers and 'should identify the needs and opportunities for development with a view to attracting, stimulating and releasing enterprise in the community'.[3] An important function of the plans is to co-ordinate the planning and provision of infrastructure essential for the development of land. The plans may operate as a trigger for further action by the planning authority. The designation, for example, of an action area is intended to signal the start of a programme of development, redevelopment or improvement in an area requiring comprehensive treatment. Furthermore, development plan allocations may be linked to other initiatives such as industrial promotion, undertaken by the same local authority in a different capacity.

---

[1] See, for example, the White Paper *Land* (Cmnd. 5730, 1974). The development control process is generally described as 'negative' because it responds rather than initiates, although the term is sometimes used pejoratively. The Pilcher Report said of the process that 'the value of the control, the positive contribution which it has made to the urban environment in the last thirty years, and the extent to which the pattern and character of commercial development have thereby been constrained should not be underestimated.' *(First Report of the Advisory Group on Commercial Property Development,* H.M.S.O., 1976).

[2] The Pilcher Report (above), para. 3.10.

[3] S.D.D. Circular 32/1983.

More specific promotional powers include the making of revocation and discontinuance orders to clear the way for more desirable forms of development (see chapter 16); the stopping up or diversion of roads, affected by development (see chapter 11); entering into planning agreements to overcome obstacles to development (see chapter 12); and the acquisition of land in connection with development and for other planning purposes (ss. 102 and 109 of the 1972 Act).

The Property Advisory Group singled out two functions in particular as likely to be important aids to the promotion of development during this decade: 'The main role of local authorities in development during the 1980s will be in co-ordinating the provision of infrastructure and assembling land where the private sector cannot or will not do so.'[4] These two functions are now considered in turn.

Co-ordinating the provision of infrastructure

The term 'infrastructure' is not a statutory one but is generally taken to refer to the services required to support the development of land; it will, for example, include main roads, means of drainage, water supply, public open space, schools and buildings for community use.

Restrictions on public expenditure constrain public authorities in the extent to which they can meet demands for the provision of those supporting services for which they are responsible. Careful co-ordination of the planning and provision of these services is necessary and this is an area in which the development plan can play an important role. The ability of various public bodies to commit resources to infrastructure provision will be a material factor in the allocation of land for development in the plans. Development plans are influenced by and will exert an influence upon the capital programmes of the public bodies responsible for the provision of infrastructure. If development plans are to provide clear guidance to potential developers, planning authorities must, as the Secretary of State has stressed, pay close regard to the resources available for plan implementation. It seems likely that the co-ordinating role of development plans will assume increasing importance in the years ahead. 'The co-ordinated planning and provision of all these services to new development and redevelopment areas becomes even more necessary', commented the Property Advisory Group, 'as restraints on all public expenditure become more severe.'[5]

In very broad terms it may be said that while developers seeking planning permission can in appropriate cases be required to provide services such as private car parking, private drains, estate roads and private open space needed to serve the development in question, the cost of providing services which will be enjoyed as of right by the public at large

---

4   *Structure and Activity of the Development Industry* (H.M.S.O., 1980). The Property Advisory Group was set up in 1978 by the Secretary of State for the Environment as a standing successor to the Pilcher Committee.

5   *Structure and Activity of the Development Industry* (above).

cannot be *imposed* on a private developer. Conditions seeking, for example, to impose upon a developer the burden of providing a distributor road, public open space or public car parking have been struck down by the courts and by the Secretary of State on appeal.[6]

However, in the absence of any indication that supporting services will be provided by the public sector, a developer may in practice have to take part or all of the burden upon himself if the development is to proceed. While this sort of burden cannot be imposed on a developer, there is considerable scope for varying the conventional distribution of costs between the public and private sectors by way of agreement (see chapter 12).

Land assembly

The need for power to acquire land in the public interest has long been accepted; the scope of the power has, however, been the subject of ideological differences between the main political parties. There has been, as Grant observes, a clear difference of opinion about 'the *function,* and consequently the extent, of the intervention'.[7] The Conservative Party see the public acquisition of land as a means to an end; the Labour Party have tended to view the public ownership of land as a desirable end in itself. This divergence of view is reflected in the attempt by the last Labour government to bring development land into public ownership through the Community Land Act 1975 and the subsequent repeal of that Act in 1980 by the succeeding Conservative government (see chapter 1).

The present position is that planning authorities have enabling powers to acquire land in connection with development and for other planning purposes. These are set out in Part VI of the 1972 Act, as amended.[8] These powers are, to employ our earlier phraseology, 'a means to an end', the end being broadly the proper planning of the area, including the implementation of the policies and proposals in the development plan. The Local Government (Scotland) Act 1973 gives local authorities other, more general, powers to acquire land for the discharge of any of their functions;[9] more specific powers to acquire land for particular functions such as housing, education, roads and so on, are to be found in the legislation governing these functions.

---

[6]   See, for example, *Hall & Co. Ltd.* v *Shoreham-by-Sea U.D.C.* [1964] 1 W.L.R. 240; *R.* v *Hillingdon London Borough Council, ex parte Royco Homes Ltd.* [1974] Q.B. 720; *M. J. Shanley Ltd. (In Liquidation)* v *Secretary of State for the Environment* [1982] J.P.L. 380; *Westminster Renslade Ltd.* v *Secretary of State for the Environment* (1983) 48 P.&C.R. 255; and see appeal decisions noted at [1967] J.P.L. 493; [1974] J.P.L. 106; [1975] J.P.L. 620; [1980] J.P.L. 841; and [1982] J.P.L. 463; and see, generally, S.D.D. Circular 22/1984.

[7]   *Urban Planning Law,* p.500.

[8]   By the Local Government, Planning and Land Act 1980, s.92(4). Note also the power in s.237 of the 1972 Act for the Secretary of State to make regulations providing for the payment to local authorities of grants to support land assembly for specified purposes (see the Town and Country Planning (Grants) (Scotland) Regulations 1968, as amended by the Town and Country Planning (Grants) (Scotland) Amendment Regulations 1983).

[9]   See ss. 70 and 71.

The need for planning authorities to have wide powers to acquire land for planning purposes was recognised by the Uthwatt Committee: The Committee declared:

'For the urgent task of reconstructing war-damaged areas and the almost equally urgent task of securing the redevelopment of obsolete and unsatisfactory areas . . . it is essential to invest the planning authority with the power to cut through the tangle of separate ownerships and boundary lines and make the whole of the land in the area immediately available for comprehensive re-planning as a single unit. We therefore recommend that for the purpose of securing necessary redevelopment the planning authority should be given the power to purchase the whole of such areas.'[10]

This recommendation was given effect in the Town and Country Planning (Scotland) Act 1945[11] and subsequently in the Town and Country Planning (Scotland) Act 1947.[12] The power was widely employed in dealing with areas of war damage and later in the promotion of town centre redevelopment schemes. The subsequent principal Acts in 1969[13] and 1972 re-enacted the power to acquire land although in different forms.[14] Though the recession has had an effect on the level of public acquisition, the Property Advisory Group concluded, as we mentioned earlier, that planning authorities could provide useful support for the development industry by operating as 'land assemblers where the private sector will not or cannot undertake the task for a desirable scheme'.[15]

The remainder of this chapter is given over to consideration of the nature of the powers of land assembly in Part VI of the 1972 Act, the procedures governing their use and the ways in which local authorities may deal with land they have acquired.

1. Compulsory acquisition of land

Section 102(1) of the 1972 Act, as amended by s.92(4) of the Local Government, Planning and Land Act 1980, enables regional, islands and district councils to acquire land compulsorily for planning purposes. Although local authorities may prefer in many cases to proceed by way of

[10] *Final Report of the Expert Committee on Compensation and Betterment* (Cmnd. 6386, 1942), para. 145.
[11] Town and Country Planning (Scotland) Act 1945, Part I.
[12] Town and Country Planning (Scotland) Act 1947, Part III.
[13] Town and Country Planning (Scotland) Act 1969, Part IV.
[14] Prior to 1969, the power to acquire land compulsorily was conferred for the purpose of comprehensive development and was tied to a designation in the development plan. The 1969 Act dispensed with the need for a development plan designation and slightly extended the purposes for which land could be compulsorily acquired. These powers were repeated in the 1972 Act. An amendment introduced by s.92 of the Local Government, Planning and Land Act 1980 has now broadened still further the purposes for which land may be compulsorily acquired under the 1972 Act.
[15] *Structure and Activity of the Development Industry* (above).

negotiation and agreement (see below), recourse to compulsory acquisition may be necessary where a landowner refuses to negotiate, where a large number of interests in land are to be acquired, or where a local authority wish to take advantage of the procedure for expediting the vesting of land in themselves so as to meet a particular timetable.[16]

Local authorities may acquire by compulsory purchase land in their area:

(i) which is suitable for and is required in order to secure the carrying out of one or more of the following activities, namely, development, redevelopment, and improvements; or

(ii) which is required for a purpose which it is necessary to achieve in the interests of the proper planning of an area in which the land is situated (1972 Act, s.102(1)).[17]

Any such proposal for the compulsory acquisition of land is subject to confirmation by the Secretary of State.

In considering whether land is 'suitable' for development, redevelopment or improvement, the local authority (and the Secretary of State when confirming a proposal) must have regard to a number of factors. These are:

(i) the provisions of the development plan, so far as material:

(ii) whether planning permission for any development on the land is in force; and

(iii) any other consideration which would be material for the purpose of determining an application for planning permission for development on the land (1972 Act, s.102(1A)).

In other words, a proposal to acquire land compulsorily for planning purposes must rest upon sound planning considerations[18] and the onus will be upon the local authority to make the case for acquisition.[19] However, the reference to land being 'required' in connection with development or for other planning purposes does not mean that the acquisition of the land must be shown to be essential; it would appear to be sufficient that the local authority consider the acquisition to be desirable to achieve the proper planning of the area.[20]

Supplementary powers of compulsory acquisition are conferred in respect of (i) adjoining land which is required in order to carry out works designed to facilitate the development or use of the land required for planning purposes—for example, the construction of an access; and (ii)

---

[16] See Town and Country Planning (Scotland) Act 1972, s.278 and Schedule 24.

[17] The 'proper planning of an area' might, for example, require the acquisition of land so as to maintain its existing use or to facilitate the development of other land.

[18] For the meaning of this phrase see the discussion in Chapter 9.

[19] *Coleen Properties Ltd.* v *Minister of Housing and Local Government* [1971] 1 W.L.R. 433.

[20] *Errington* v *Metropolitan District Railway Co. Ltd.* [1882] 19 Ch.D.559; and *Company Developments (Property) Ltd.* v *Secretary of State for the Environment* [1978] J.P.L. 107.

land required to be given in exchange for the land acquired for planning purposes where the latter forms part of a common or open space (1972 Act, s.102(1B)).

Section 102 of the 1972 Act refers to the compulsory acquisition of 'land'. 'Land' is defined in s.275 of the Act as including any interest in land and any servitude or right in or over land. It would seem, however, that such interests, servitudes or rights must be in existence at the time of the compulsory acquisition; the power conferred by s.102 does not extend to the compulsory creation and acquisition of new rights over land. Such a power must be conferred in specific terms.[21] Expropriation cannot take place by implication.[22]

The procedural provisions of the Acquisition of Land (Authorisation Procedure) (Scotland) Act 1947 are applied to the compulsory acquisition of land under the 1972 Act (1972 Act, s.102(4)). These provide for the making of a compulsory purchase order, the giving of notice, the submission of the order to the Secretary of State for confirmation, and the consideration of objections and, where appropriate, the holding of a public inquiry before reaching a decision on the order. The Secretary of State may, however, disregard any objection to the compulsory purchase order which, in his opinion, amounts in substance to an objection to the provisions of the development plan defining the proposed use of the subject land or any other land (1972 Act, s.121(1)).

Although the compulsory acquisition of land for planning purposes will be undertaken by the local authority, the activity or purpose for which it has been acquired may be undertaken or achieved by someone else (1972 Act, s.102(1C)). Thus, a planning authority may undertake land assembly with a view to the subsequent disposal of the land to a developer for development.

Section 103 of the 1972 Act enables the Secretary of State to acquire compulsorily any land necessary for the public service. By contrast with s.102, the section expressly empowers the minister to acquire a servitude or other right over land by the grant of a new right. The appropriate procedural provisions of the Acquisition of Land (Authorisation Procedure) (Scotland) Act 1947 are applied to an exercise of power under s.103.

2. Acquisition of land by agreement

Section 109 of the 1972 Act confers wide powers on planning authorities to acquire land for planning purposes by agreement. A planning authority may acquire land by agreement for any purposes for which they may be authorised to acquire land compulsorily (1972 Act, s.109(1)(a)). The power would seem to be available in respect of any land and not just land within their area.

---

[21] See, for example, s.103(2) of the 1972 Act.
[22] *Sovmots Investments Ltd.* v *Secretary of State for the Environment* [1977] Q.B. 411; and [1979] A.C. 144.

Planning authorities may also acquire any building appearing to them to be of special architectural or historic interest (it need not be listed) (1972 Act, s.109(1)(b)). Furthermore, they may acquire any land comprising, or contiguous or adjacent to, such a building which is required for preserving the building or its amenities, for affording access to it or for its proper control or management (1972 Act, s.109(1)(c)).

While the power contained in s.109 of the 1972 Act may only be exercised in respect of land required for planning purposes, it is not necessary that the land should be required immediately for these purposes. Such land may be purchased by agreement (but not compulsorily) in advance of the authority's requirements and used for the purpose of any of the authority's functions in the interim.[23]

3. *Appropriation of land*

Land acquired by a local authority and held for a particular purpose may be appropriated for the purpose of any other function of the authority.[24] Thus, land acquired compulsorily or by agreement and held for some other function for which it is no longer required may be appropriated (i.e., transferred) for planning purposes.

The consent of the Secretary of State is required for the appropriation of land held for use as allotments;[25] and where the land to be appropriated consists of common or open space (but not allotments), the local authority must first give public notice of their intention by way of advertisement in a local newspaper for two consecutive weeks and must consider any representations.[26]

4. *Development*

Often, land will be acquired for planning purposes by planning authorities with a view to its subsequent disposal to the private sector for development (see below). However, planning authorities themselves have wide powers to undertake the development of land held for planning purposes. Section 114(1) of the 1972 Act provides that planning authorities may erect, construct or carry out any building or work on such land providing the building or work is not or could not be authorised under any alternative enactment.[27] They may also repair, maintain and insure any such buildings or works or generally deal with them in the proper course of management (1972 Act, s.114(5)).

---

[23] Local Government (Scotland) Act 1973, s.70(2).
[24] Local Government (Scotland) Act 1973, s.73(1).
[25] Local Government (Scotland) Act 1973, s.73(2) and (3).
[26] Town and Country Planning (Scotland) Act 1959, s.24, as amended by the Local Government (Miscellaneous Provisions) (Scotland) Act 1981, s.25 and Schedule 2, para. 9.
[27] Section 1 of the Local Government (Development and Finance) (Scotland) Act 1964 states that nothing in that section is to prevent the exercise by a local authority of power to develop land under the planning legislation.

A planning authority must provide suitable alternative accommodation for a residential occupier who is being displaced as a result of the redevelopment of premises which have been acquired or appropriated for planning purposes. The obligation to rehouse such a person exists only in so far as there is no other residential accommodation suitable to his requirements available on reasonable terms (1972 Act, s.120(1)).

Immunity is conferred upon planning authorities and upon persons deriving title from them from any action for interference with servitudes or other rights in erecting, constructing, carrying out or maintaining any such building or work, provided it is done in accordance with any planning permission (1972 Act, s.117(1)). Any such interference may, however, give rise to a claim for compensation under s.61 of the Lands Clauses Consolidation (Scotland) Act 1845 or under s.6 of the Railways Clauses Consolidation (Scotland) Act 1845 (1972 Act, s.117(3)). The immunity does not extend to certain rights vested in or belonging to statutory undertakers for the purpose of carrying on their undertakings (1972 Act, s.108(2)).

Sections 118 and 119 of the 1972 Act deal respectively with the use of land comprising churches or burial grounds and the use of land comprising open space where such categories of land have been acquired for planning purposes.

5. *Disposal*

Planning authorities have considerable flexibility as to the manner of disposal of land held for planning purposes. Section 113(1) of the 1972 Act provides that the authority may dispose of such land to such person, in such manner and subject to such conditions, as may appear to them to be expedient to secure the use and development of the land in accordance with the planning objectives of the area. Disposal may be by way of sale, excambion or lease, or by way of the creation of any servitude, right or privilege, or in any other manner except by way of appropriation, gift or the creation of a heritable security (1972 Act, s.275(1)).[28]

The wide terms in which the power is conferred leave the planning authority free to choose whether the planning objectives of the area are best served by disposal of the land before or after development or whether some form of partnership between the public and private sectors is appropriate.[29] Arrangements for disposal may be tied in with a loan from the local authority under s.7 of the Local Government (Development and Finance) (Scotland) Act 1964 or in designated districts, under the Inner Urban Areas Act 1978.

[28] S.D.D. *Planning Advice Note 26* 'Disposal of Land and the Use of the Developer's Brief' (1981) comments that the repeal of the Community Land Act 1975 has changed the emphasis of the disposal of land from leasing to direct sale.

[29] For a discussion of the different types of partnership arrangements between the public and private sectors see *Report of the Working Party on Local Authority/Private Enterprise Partnership Schemes* (H.M.S.O. 1972); *Structure and Activity of the Development Industry* (above); S.D.D. *Planning Advice Note 26;* and generally, M. Grant, *Urban Planning Law*, pp. 522-528.

The Secretary of State's consent is not required prior to disposal but land is not to be disposed of otherwise than at the best price or on the best terms that can reasonably be obtained (1972 Act, s.113(3)). The wording of the subsection is such that the price or terms of disposal may reflect any difficulties inherent in the development of the site and any restrictions which the planning authority wish to impose on its use and development. It must be doubtful, though, whether it would allow, for example, the sale of a house at less than its market value. The Secretary of State has no power to relax the requirement to obtain the best price or the best terms.[30]

However, where land has been acquired for development, redevelopment or improvement, any person who was living or working on the land before the work took place, and who wishes to obtain accommodation on the land, must, so far as practicable, be given an opportunity to obtain accommodation suitable to his reasonable requirements (1972 Act, s.113(6)).[31] The terms on which such accommodation is to be provided must be settled with due regard to the price at which any land was initially acquired from such a person. Although this subsection appears at first sight to impose a constraint on a planning authority's freedom of disposal, the qualifications which have been built into it are such that any constraint is likely to be minimal. As Grant says of the corresponding provision in the English legislation, '. . . the section imposes no duty to offer new accommodation at a low rent, and the small shopkeepers typically displaced by redevelopment schemes can seldom afford the high rents demanded for the new facilities.'[32] And the phrase 'with due regard to the price at which any land was initially acquired' was considered by Paull J. in *A. Crabtree and Co.* v *Minister of Housing and Local Government*[33] to be 'really a relic from the time when land was often acquired by a planning authority on terms other than its market value and [to] have no real application, except in very exceptional circumstances, to a case where the person dispossessed is entitled, as he is now, to obtain the full market value of such land.'

While planning authorities have considerable freedom regarding the disposal of land held for planning purposes, any person who considers that a refusal by the authority to dispose of land to him or to agree terms for its disposal to him constitutes unfair discrimination or is otherwise oppressive, may make representations to the Secretary of State. The minister will notify the authority of any such representations and will consider their response and may cause an inquiry to be held before deciding what to do.

---

[30]   The effect of s.74(2) of the Local Government (Scotland) Act 1973, which enables a local authority with the consent of the Secretary of State to dispose of land for a consideration less than the best that can reasonably be obtained, is excluded in respect of land held for planning purposes by s.113(8) of the 1972 Act.

[31]   There is no obligation on the authority to offer such accommodation prior to displacement—see *Glasgow Corporation* v *Arbuckle Smith and Co.* 1968 S.L.T. (Sh. Ct.) 69.

[32]   *Urban Planning Law*, p. 516.

[33]   (1965) 17 P.&C.R. 232.

If the representations seem to be well-founded and the minister considers that disposal to that person will secure the use and development of the land in accordance with the planning objectives of the area, he may issue directions for the disposal of the land to that person (1972 Act, s.113(5)).

Part X of the Local Government, Planning and Land Act 1980, which provides for the compilation of a register of the land holdings of public authorities and for the issuing of directions by central government for the disposal of such land, does not apply to Scotland.

6. *Buildings of special architectural and historic interest.*

Sections 104 to 107 of the 1972 Act contain specific powers relating to the compulsory acquisition of listed buildings in need of repair. These powers are described in chapter 19.

Section 115 of the Act requires planning authorities, when exercising their powers of appropriation, development and disposal of land under Part VI, to have regard to the desirability of preserving[34] listed buildings and other features of special architectural or historic interest.

Where a planning authority have acquired a listed building in need of repair (1972 Act, s.104(1)) or any other building appearing to them to be of special architectural or historic interest (listed or otherwise) (1972 Act, s.109(1)(b)), they may make such arrangements as to its management, use or disposal as they consider appropriate for its preservation (1972 Act, s.116(1)).

[34] 'Preserving' in relation to a building means preserving it either in its existing state or subject only to such alterations or extensions as can be carried out without serious detriment to its character (1972 Act, s.115(3)).

CHAPTER 18

PLANNING BLIGHT AND INJURIOUS AFFECTION

A. INTRODUCTION

'Planning blight' has been described as 'the depressing effect on existing property of proposals which imply public acquisition and disturbance of the existing use' of the property.[1] The announcement, for example, of the line of a proposed road may well mean that land in the path of that road becomes either completely unsaleable in the open market or saleable only at a price lower than it would otherwise have fetched. Although the proposals in question may not be due to be implemented for some considerable time and although the proposals may not in the meantime have any effect on the use to which the affected land is put, the marketability of land which is likely to be acquired for some public purpose may well be affected immediately.

One solution to the landowner's difficulty is to wait and see what happens. Either the scheme will be dropped or the land will ultimately be acquired for the purpose in question. In the latter event, the price to be paid by the public authority will be the sum the land would have realised on a sale in the open market by a willing seller.[2] This means that any depreciation in value resulting from the compulsory acquisition, or the shadow of compulsory acquisition, will be ignored in determining the price; such depreciation is not a market factor.

However, several years commonly elapse between the first indiction that land is required for a scheme of public works and either the eventual demise of the scheme or the acquisition of the land by the public authority. The landowner may not be able to wait that long.

For example, a businessman may find it difficult to make any sensible decisions about future levels of investment in the climate of uncertainty created by the proposed scheme; the best interests of the business may dictate an early move to an area free from uncertainty. A householder may be required to move elsewhere in the ordinary course of his employment and have to place his house on the market immediately. In such cases, since the marketability of the property will be adversely affected, perhaps seriously,

---

[1]   *The Future of Development Plans* (H.M.S.O., 1965).
[2]   Land Compensation (Scotland) Act 1963, ss.12(2) and 16.

by the proposed scheme, hardship might well result.[3]

Statute alleviates the hardship caused in some, but by no means all, cases of planning blight. Certain owner-occupiers of 'blighted' land are entitled, in fairly closely-defined circumstances, to serve on the appropriate authority (in effect, the public body by which the land is liable to be acquired in terms of the blighting proposals) a blight notice requiring that authority to acquire the land. Where a blight notice takes effect, the authority concerned must acquire the property immediately, instead of perhaps waiting until they are ready to proceed with the scheme in question, and must do so at a price which ignores the effect of the blighting proposals.

So far we have used the term 'blight' in the narrow sense of the depressing effect on the value of land resulting from a proposal which implies the eventual public acquisition of the land. It is only where 'blight' in this sense exists that a blight notice may be served under the planning legislation; blight notices and their consequences are considered more fully below. However, the term 'blight' is commonly used in the much wider sense of the depressing effect which the construction and use of a scheme of works may have on the value of surrounding land. In this sense, 'blight' is synonymous with 'injurious affection' or 'worsenment'. The most obvious example of this sort of blight is depreciation resulting from schemes of public works such as the building of a major new road. The noise, vibration and dust from traffic using the road will not only be a source of disturbance to people living nearby but is also likely to have an adverse effect on the value of their property.

Such disturbance is not, of course, limited to public works. Private sector development such as the construction and use of industrial premises or the opening of a fish and chip shop may seriously disturb neighbours and reduce the value of their property. Indeed, underlying many objections to planning applications is concern about the effect which the proposal will have on the value of neighbouring land.

At common law, activities which seriously disturb a person in the enjoyment of land may be restrained as a nuisance. Such activities are considered to be an infringement of a person's right to the comfortable enjoyment of heritable property.[4] '[I]f any person', said Lord President Cooper in *Watt* v *Jamieson*,[5] 'so uses his property as to occasion serious disturbance or substantial inconvenience to his neighbour or material damage to his neighbour's property, it is in the general case irrelevant as a defence for the defender to plead merely that he was making a normal and familiar use of his own property. The balance in all such cases has to be held

---

[3] There is thus, as the Skeffington Committee said: 'a conflict between, on the one hand, the desirability of giving full publicity at an early stage to proposals the planning authority are considering, so as to stimulate informed public discussion and, on the other hand, the need to avoid causing hardship to individuals by the casting of blight over land or property that may not be required for many years or, indeed, at all'. (*People and Planning. The Report of the Committee on Public Participation in Planning*) (H.M.S.O., 1969).

[4] Bell, *Principles*, para. 974.

[5] 1954 S.C. 56; 1954 S.L.T. 56.

between the freedom of a proprietor to use his property as he pleases and the duty on a proprietor not to inflict material loss or inconvenience on adjoining proprietors or adjoining property; and in every case the answer depends on considerations of fact and degree.' The law therefore provides a remedy for blight caused by private sector development; it may be restrained as a nuisance by an action for interdict at the suit of the disturbed neighbour. It should be noted, however, that the key to the remedy is not depreciation in the value of the property (although this will often result) but infringement of the right to comfortable enjoyment of the property. The distinction is important in as much as the courts do not recognise as part of that right a right to a view or a right to privacy although the loss of either may have an adverse effect on value.[6]

What of public sector development? To what extent are major public works such as roads, railways, airports, town centre redevelopment schemes, sewage works and so on open to restraint at the suit of a neighbour who may suffer disturbance and depreciation in the value of his property in consequence of such development? It would seem that the plea of 'public interest' is not, of itself, a sufficient answer to an action for nuisance.[7] It has, however, long been established that where an activity is authorised by statute, whether expressly or by implication, then the person or body carrying on the activity will be immune from an action for nuisance.[8] The Act authorising the activity does not usually confer an express immunity; rather it is the inevitable consequence of the authorisation.[9]

Where a person or body carrying out a scheme of public works has statutory immunity from an action for nuisance, it seems reasonable to expect that Parliament will make some provision to alleviate the hardship caused by this form of blight. This expectation has been partly fulfilled by the legislature. It is not possible, as with an action for nuisance, to stop the scheme of works; instead, legislation provides for the payment of compensation in respect of some, but by no means all, cases of this sort of blight—what we refer to in this chapter as 'injurious affection'. Only an outline of the law on injurious affection is provided here; more detailed treatments are to be found in works dealing specifically with compulsory purchase and compensation.

---

[6]   *Caledonian Railway Co.* v *Walker's Trustees* (1881)8R.405, per Lord Curriehill; *Caledonian Railway Co.* v *Ogilvy* (1856) 2 Macq. 229; *Nisbet Hamilton* v *Northern Lighthouses Commissioners* (1886) 13 R. 710; and *Re Penny and South Eastern Railway Co.* (1857) 7 E. & B. 660.

[7]   *Duke of Buccleuch* v *Cowan* (1866) 5 M. 214.

[8]   *Hammersmith and City Railway Co.* v *Brand* (1869) L.R. 4 H.L. 171; *City of Glasgow Union Railway Co.* v *Hunter* (1870) 8 M. (H.L.) 156; *Lord Blantyre and Others* v *Clyde Navigation Trustees* (1871) 9 M. (H.L.) 6; and *Muir* v *Caledonian Railway Co.* (1890) 17 R. 1020.

[9]   *Hammersmith and City Railway Co.* v *Brand* (1869) L.R. 4 H.L. 171; and *Allen* v *Gulf Oil Refining Co.* [1981] A.C. 101. Immunity is only conferred in respect of damage which is the inevitable consequence of operating the works authorised by statute.

B. PLANNING BLIGHT

An owner of land the value of which is adversely affected by a proposal which implies its public acquisition may, in certain circumstances, serve a blight notice on the public authority responsible for the proposals giving rise to the blight; a blight notice requires that authority to acquire the land. If the notice takes effect, the authority must acquire the land at a price which ignores the effects of the blighting proposal.

A blight notice is to be distinguished from a purchase notice. The purchase notice procedure may be employed to compel the planning authority to acquire land which, following the making of an adverse planning decision, has become incapable of reasonably beneficial use in its existing state (see chapter 15). The statutory provisions on planning blight, on the other hand, are concerned with the situation where adverse *proposals* have affected the *marketability* of land even though the land remains perfectly capable in the meantime of beneficial use.

Proposals giving rise to obligation to purchase

It is only if land falls clearly within one of the 'specified descriptions' of land set out in s.181(1) of the 1972 Act, as amended and extended by the Land Compensation (Scotland) Act 1973[10] that a blight notice can succeed. The specified descriptions are complex and diverse; their common feature is that they all involve proposals which imply that land is likely to be acquired in the future by a body possessing powers of compulsory purchase. Statute lays down in relation to each of the specified descriptions of land the stage which the proposals must have reached before land comes within that description; only when that stage has been reached can a blight notice be served. It may be noted that in some cases a blight notice can be served before the proposals in question have been finally approved.

The specified descriptions of land are broadly as follows:[11]

(*a*) Land indicated in a structure plan as land which may be required for the purposes of any functions of a government department, a local authority, statutory undertakers or the National Coal Board, or as land which may be included in an action area;[12] this provision applies if land is earmarked in this way in a structure plan which has come into force, or in a structure plan which has been submitted to the Secretary of State, or in proposals for alterations to a structure plan which have been submitted to the Secretary of State, or in modifications proposed to be made by the minister to any such plan or proposals (1972 Act, s.181(1)(a); L.C.(S.)A.

---

[10] References in this chapter to the L.C.(S.)A. 1973 are references to that Act.

[11] The two specified descriptions added by ss.22(6) and 23(8) of the Community Land Act 1975 were repealed by s.101(1) of, and para. 2 of Schedule 17 to, the Local Government, Planning and Land Act 1980.

[12] On the meaning of the phrase 'may be included in an action area', see *Nowell (Executor)* v *Kirkburton U.D.C.* (1970) 21 P. & C.R. 832.

1973, s.64(1)), but the provision does not apply to land in an area for which there is in force a local plan allocating or defining land for the purposes of any such functions (1972 Act, s.181(2)).

(*b*) Land allocated or defined in a local plan for the purposes of any such functions as are mentioned in para. (*a*) above; this provision applies where a local plan is in force, or where copies of a local plan have been made available for inspection prior to adoption or approval, or where proposals for alterations to a local plan have been made available for inspection, or where modifications to such a plan or proposals have been proposed by the planning authority or the Secretary of State[13] (1972 Act, s.181(1)(b); L.C.(S.)A. 1973, s.64(2)).

Until a relevant local plan comes into operation in any area, land allocated for certain purposes in an 'old style' development plan, or in proposals for alterations or modifications to such a plan, is included within the specified descriptions (s.38(1)(b) of the Town and Country Planning (Scotland) Act 1959, as incorporated in s.181 of the 1972 Act by para. 49 of Sched. 22 to the 1972 Act; L.C.(S.)A. 1973, s.64(3)).

(*c*) Land indicated in a development plan as required for road construction or alteration (1972 Act, s.181(1)(c)).

(*d*) Land authorised by a special enactment (as defined in s.196(a)) to be compulsorily acquired (1972 Act, s.181(1)(d)).

(*e*) Land included in a proposed or operative order or scheme for the construction or alteration of a trunk or special road under certain provisions of the Roads (Scotland) Act 1984 (1972 Act, s.181(1)(e), as substituted by s.156(1) of and Schedule 9 to the Roads (Scotland) Act 1984; L.C.(S.)A. 1973, s.65, as amended by s.156(1) of and Schedule 9 to the Roads (Scotland) Act 1984) and land required for the purpose of mitigating the adverse effect which the existence or use of a new or improved road may have on its surroundings (L.C.(S.)A. 1973, s.70(1)).

(*f*) Land shown on plans approved by a resolution of a local roads authority[14] as required for road construction or improvement or for the mitigation of the adverse effect of a new or improved road (1972 Act, s.181(1)(f), as amended by s.156(1) of and Schedule 9 to the Roads (Scotland) Act 1984; L.C.(S.)A. 1973, s.70(2)).

(*g*) Land in respect of which a compulsory purchase order is in force but in respect of which notice to treat has not yet been served, and land in respect of which a compulsory purchase order has been submitted for confirmation to, or prepared in draft by, a minister (1972 Act, s.181(1)(g); L.C.(S.)A. 1973, s.66). Similar provision is made in respect of land affected by a

[13]   For a discussion of the way in which planning blight may arise from a local plan see A. Walker, 'Recommendations in Local Plans: Can They Create Planning Blight?' 1983 S.P.L.P. 41.

[14]   A plan prepared by a department of the authority but not formally approved by resolution of the authority will not suffice, even though prospective purchasers of property included in the plan have been told that it will be required in the future—see *Fogg* v *Birkenhead County Borough Council* (1971) 22 P. & C.R. 208; *Page* v *Borough of Gillingham* (1970) 21 P. & C.R. 973; and *Flanagan* v *Long Eaton U.D.C.* (1974) 299 E.G. 620.

compulsory purchase order providing for the acquisition of a right in or over that land (1972 Act, s.181(1)(i);[15] L.C.(S.)A. 1973, s.66).

(*h*) Land identified by the Secretary of State in a written notice to the planning authority as the site of a proposed trunk or special road or as land proposed to be acquired for the mitigation of the adverse effects of such a road (1972 Act, s.181(1)(h); L.C.(S.)A. 1973, s.70(2)).

(*i*) Land indicated in a plan (other than a development plan) approved by a resolution of the planning authority as land which may be required for the purposes of a government department, a local authority or statutory undertakers or land in respect of which the planning authority have resolved, or have been directed by the Secretary of State, to take action in order to safeguard the land for development for such purposes[16] (L.C.(S.)A. 1973, s.67).

(*j*) Land included in a draft or operative order designating a new town site (L.C.(S.)A. 1973, s.68).

(*k*) Land within a housing action area and land surrounded by or adjoining a housing action area (L.C.(S.)A. 1973, s.69[17]).

(*l*) Land within an area which is intended to be, or has been, designated as an urban development area (see Local Government, Planning and Land Act 1980, s.147).

Where the statutory provisions refer to land which is 'indicated' in a plan as being required for certain purposes, it would seem that a diagrammatic indication will suffice, provided, of course, that the proposals and the plan in which they appear are such as to satisfy the statutory requirements. In *Bowling* v *Leeds County Borough Council*[18] the Lands Tribunal held that land was 'indicated' as required for highway purposes even though the indication in the plan was diagrammatic only; in the view of the tribunal the word 'indicated' is 'a word of simple meaning which does not import any requirements of a resolution by the council or programming by it or allocation of money by it'.

Only if land falls squarely within one of the specified descriptions can the statutory requirements as to service of a blight notice be fulfilled. In *Bolton Corporation* v *Owen*,[19] for example, a development plan provided that a

---

[15] Added by L.C.(S.)A. 1973, s.71(2).
[16] In *Hill* v *Department of the Environment* [1976] N.I. 43 McGonigal L.J. expressed the view that since the statutory provisions on blight are clearly designed to assist the owner of blighted property, a benevolent construction should be given to the similar (and potentially somewhat ambiguous) provisions appearing in the legislation applying in Northern Ireland.
[17] As amended by the Housing (Scotland) Act 1974.
[18] (1974) 27 P. & C.R. 531. See too *Mercer* v *Manchester Corporation* (1964) 15 P. & C.R. 321; *Williams* v *Cheadle and Gatley U.D.C.* (1965) 17 P. & C.R. 153; and *Smith* v *Somerset County Council* (1966) 17 P. & C.R. 162.
[19] [1962] 1 Q.B. 470; followed in *Ellick* v *Sedgemoor District Council* (1976) 32 P. & C.R. 134 (L.T.). See too *Bone* v *Staines U.D.C.* (1964) 15 P. & C.R. 450; *Allen and Allen* v *Marple U.D.C.* (1972) 23 P. & C.R. 368; *Broderick* v *Erewash Borough Council* (1976) 34 P. & C.R. 214; *Comley and Comley* v *Kent County Council* (1977) 34 P. & C.R. 218; and *Wyse* v *Newcastle-under-Lyme Borough Council*, Lands Tribunal, 3rd September 1979 (unreported, but see (1979) 129 New L.J. 1263).

particular area was to be cleared and redeveloped for residential purposes. The owner-occupier of a dwelling-house situated in the area, having failed to find a purchaser for the house, served a blight notice on the local authority, claiming that the land came within one of the specified descriptions of land, being, he claimed, 'land allocated by a development plan for the purposes of any functions of a . . . local authority'. The Court of Appeal held, reversing the decision of the Lands Tribunal, that the claimant had not discharged the onus of showing that the land fell within that category; the statutory provisions require that land should be directly allocated for the functions of a local authority and in this case it was not directly so allocated since the development plan did not specifically state that the clearance and redevelopment was to be carried out by the local authority. The court considered that the tribunal had erred in speculating upon the probability or otherwise of the redevelopment being carried out by the local authority rather than by private enterprise and in drawing the inference that the area could, 'as a matter of practical politics', only be redeveloped by a local authority acting under statutory powers.

Discretionary acquisition

Despite the provisions of the Land Compensation (Scotland) Act 1973, which extended the specified descriptions and which enabled an owner-occupier to serve a blight notice at an earlier stage than was previously the case, there may still occur cases of planning blight which cause hardship but which do not fall within any of the statutory categories. Local authorities have been asked to deal sympathetically with cases not covered by the statutory blight provisions (e.g. cases where blight is caused by non-statutory proposals) and to endeavour, by means of their powers to acquire land in advance of requirements, to alleviate hardship resulting from local authority proposals which are reasonably certain to go ahead.[20]

Interests qualifying for protection

The right to serve a blight notice is restricted, broadly speaking, to those owners or lessees who might be expected to suffer greatest hardship as a result of planning blight.

Where the whole or part of a hereditament[21] or of an agricultural unit[22] is comprised in land of any of the specified descriptions, a blight notice may be served by a person who claims that he is entitled to such an interest in that hereditament or unit as qualifies for protection under the statute (1972 Act, s.182(1)). The interests which qualify for protection are broadly as follows:

---

[20] See D.H.S. Circular 66/1959; S.D.D. Circular 89/1971; S.D.D. Memorandum 85/1973; and S.D.D. Circular 42/1976.

[21] i.e., the aggregate of the lands and heritages which form the subject of a single entry in the valuation roll—see 1972 Act, s.196(1)–(4). See too *Ley and Ley* v *Kent County Council* (1976) 31 P. & C.R. 439.

[22] As to the meaning of 'agricultural unit' see 1972 Act, s.196(1).

(1) in the case of a hereditament:
  (a) the interest of a resident owner-occuper (1972 Act, s.181(3), (4)(b));
  (b) the interest of a (non-resident) owner-occupier of a hereditament the rateable value of which does not exceed a prescribed amount—presently £12,000[23] (1972 Act, ss.181(3), (4)(a); 196(1));
(2) in the case of an agricultural unit, the interest of an owner-occupier (1972 Act, s.181(3), (5)).

For the purposes of the provisions on planning blight the phrases 'owner-occupier' and 'resident owner-occupier' bear the somewhat specialised meanings given them by s.192 of the 1972 Act; it may be observed in particular that in order to qualify as an owner-occupier or resident owner-occupier certain conditions as to period of occupation must be satisfied, and that 'owner-occupier' does not bear the same meaning when used in relation to a hereditament as it does when used in relation to an agricultural unit—occupation of an agricultural unit must be of the whole unit, whereas occupation of a hereditament need only be of a 'substantial part' (1972 Act, s.192). Where the owner of a house had left it empty but had stored certain articles in outbuildings, it was held by the Court of Appeal that he could not be said to be an 'owner-occupier' for the purposes of the blight provisions.[24]

The interests qualifying for protection under the statutory provisions on planning blight include the interest of a crofter in his croft or a cottar in his subject;[25] also included is the interest of a lessee under a lease with at least three years to run at the date of service of a blight notice[26] (see 1972 Act, s.192(4)[27]).

In certain circumstances a heritable creditor has power to serve a blight notice (1972 Act, s.190). Where a claimant dies after serving a blight notice, the person who has succeeded to his interest in the hereditament or agricultural unit may carry on the proceedings (1972 Act, s.189), and in certain circumstances the personal representative of a person who at the time of his death was entitled to an interest which would have qualified for protection may serve a blight notice (L.C.(S.)A. 1973, s.73). Section 193 of the 1972 Act makes special provision for partnerships.

---

[23] See the Town and Country Planning (Limit of Annual Value) (Scotland) Order 1985 (which came into operation on 1st April 1985).
[24] *Minister of Transport* v *Holland* (1962) 14 P. & C.R. 259; followed in *Segal* v *Manchester Corporation* (1966) 18 P. & C.R. 112. See too *Sparkes* v *Secretary of State for Wales* (1974) 27 P. & C.R. 545; and *Holmes* v *Knowsley Borough Council* (1977) 35 P. & C.R. 119.
[25] See s.11 of the Crofting Reform (Scotland) Act 1976 and the amendments made by Schedule 1 of that Act to the provisions of the 1972 Act and the L.C.(S.)A. 1973.
[26] In *Empire Motors (Swansea) Ltd.* v *Swansea City Council* (1972) 24 P. & C.R. 377 it was held that where lessees had two years and nine months of their lease to run, the fact that they had an option to renew the lease did not turn that interest into a qualifying one.
[27] As amended by the Crofting Reform (Scotland) Act 1976.

Injury to interest in land

It is for the person serving a blight notice, the claimant, to establish that the blighting proposals have resulted in injury to his interest in the land in question.

The claimant must show that he has made reasonable endeavours to sell his interest but that in consequence of the fact that the land or a part of it was, or was likely to be, comprised in land of any of the specified descriptions, he has been unable to sell that interest except at a price substantially lower than that for which it might reasonably have been expected to sell if no part of the land were or were likely to be, included in such proposals (1972 Act, s.182(1)(c), (d); L.C.(S.)A. 1973, s.72). It is thus now possible, in contrast to the position prior to the Land Compensation (Scotland) Act 1973, to satisfy the statutory requirements even though the attempts to sell the land were made before the land actually came within one of the specified descriptions.[28]

The onus[29] is upon the claimant to show that his inability to sell the land at a reasonable price is due to the blighting proposals and that the reduction in value resulting from the blighting proposals is substantial. In *Malcolm Campbell* v *Glasgow Corporation*[30] a blight notice was served in respect of a shop affected by road-widening proposals, the owner-occupiers of the shop claiming that they had been unable to dispose of it at a reasonable price. The authority on whom the notice was served attributed the claimants' failure to sell the shop to a number of factors, including the proximity of a new shopping arcade, an excess of older shops left vacant in the area and traffic restrictions in the vicinity of the shop. The Lands Tribunal for Scotland declined to adopt 'the simple view' that as the claimants had been unable to obtain any offer at all for the shop and since at the very least there was bound to be some element of prejudice attributable to the road-widening proposals, that was enough to entitle the tribunal to declare the notice valid.

The tribunal held that although some element of loss might well be attributable to the road-widening proposals, the claimants had not discharged the onus of proving that it was the road proposals rather than the other adverse factors which had caused a substantial erosion in the value of the shop, nor had they established to the tribunal's satisfaction (a) the price for which the shop might reasonably have been expected to sell if no part had been included in the road proposals and (b) that the only price obtainable was substantially lower; to establish that, it would have been necessary in the circumstances of this case for the claimants to disentangle the effect of the road-widening proposals from the effect of the other adverse factors and that they had failed to do. In this case the tribunal also stated that they did not think that 'simply to invite offers for a property previously advertised for sale at £8,250' sufficiently indicated such willingness on the part of the sellers

---

[28]   See Land Compensation Act 1973, Schedule 2; and L.C.(S.)A. 1973, s.72.
[29]   On onus of proof in relation to blight notices see p. 415 below.
[30]   1972 S.L.T. (Lands Tr.) 8; compare *Bowling* v *Leeds County Borough Council* (1974) 27 P. & C.R. 531; and *Stubbs* v *West Hartlepool Corporation* (1961) 12 P. & C.R. 365.

to reduce their price as to justify the contention by the claimants that they could obtain no price at all for the shop.

What constitutes 'reasonable endeavours to sell' property is a question which will depend on the circumstances of the particular case.[31] In one case, for example, an Official Arbiter concluded that although the claimant had not made every conceivable contact in her endeavours to sell, and had not advertised in every available medium, her endeavours met the requirement of the Act as 'reasonable endeavours'.[32] In another case, where all property which came onto the market in a particular area of Dundee was purchased only by the University and where there were no sales except to the University, an Arbiter concluded that, in the particular circumstances, an offer to the University was a reasonable endeavour to sell.[33] In *Lade and Lade* v *Brighton Corporation*[34] the (English) Lands Tribunal, though they accepted that in most cases the normal procedure would be to advertise the property in the press and to circulate particulars, held in the somewhat special circumstances of the case that, as it was likely that only visiting dealers would have been interested in the antique shop in question, the statutory requirement had been satisfied by the placing of a notice in the shop window and the notification of visiting traders. Nothing short of putting the land on the market will satisfy the statutory provisions; professional advice to the effect that it would be pointless and a waste of time and money to endeavour to sell the land will not suffice.[35]

Service of blight notice

A blight notice should be in one of the three forms prescribed in Schedule 1 to the Town and Country Planning (General) (Scotland) Regulations 1976 (see reg. 3), and should be served on the 'appropriate authority', broadly speaking the government department, local authority or other body by whom, in terms of the blighting proposals, the land is liable to be acquired (see 1972 Act, ss.182(1), 194(1); L.C.(S.)A. 1973, s.68(3)). Any question as to which of two or more authorities is the 'appropriate authority' is determined by the Secretary of State (1972 Act, s.194(2)). A blight notice must relate to the whole of the claimant's interest in the hereditament or

---

[31] The question whether claimants had made 'reasonable endeavours to sell' their interest had to be considered in the decision of an Official Arbiter, Ref. No. 5/1962; and in *Trustees of St John's Church, Galashiels* v *Borders Regional Council* 1976 S.L.T. (Lands Tr.) 39. See too *Stubbs* v *West Hartlepool Corporation* (1961) 12 P. & C.R. 365; *Bowling* v *Leeds County Borough Council* (1974) 27 P. & C.R. 531; *Louisville Investments Ltd.* v *Basingstoke District Council* (1976) 32 P. & C.R. 419; *Glodwick Mutual Institute and Social Club* v *Oldham Metropolitan Borough Council* [1979] R.V.R. 197; and *Mancini* v *Coventry City Council* (1982) 44 P. & C.R. 114 (in which the claimants' endeavours to sell were not accepted as reasonable in that they had informed those who responded to advertisements that the property was subject to a compulsory purchase order but had failed to inform them that the authority had indicated that acquisition would not proceed).

[32] Ref. No. 1/1969.

[33] Ref. No. 3/1969.

[34] (1971) 22 P. & C.R. 427.

[35] See *Perkins* v *West Wiltshire District Council* (1975) 31 P. & C.R. 427.

agricultural unit in question (1972 Act, s.182(2)). The blight notice has to state the specified description of land into which it is claimed that the blighted land falls. Care should be taken to ensure that the correct head is detailed as the Lands Tribunal has no power to allow amendment.[36]

A blight notice may be withdrawn by the claimant within the period set out in s.187 of the 1972 Act.

Counter-notice

Within two months of service of a blight notice the appropriate authority may serve on the claimant a counter-notice,[37] objecting to the blight notice (1972 Act, s.183(1)). Under s.183(2)[38] of the 1972 Act objection may be made by the appropriate authority on one or more of the following grounds: (a) that no part of the land comes within any of the specified descriptions (see p. 407 above); or (b) that unless compelled to do so by virtue of the blight provisions, they do not intend to acquire any part of the hereditament or, in the case of an agricultural unit, any part of the affected area (i.e., so much of the unit as falls within any of the specified descriptions—1972 Act, s.196(1));[39] or (c) that they intend to acquire only a part[40] of the hereditament or affected area; or (d) that in the case of land falling within paragraph (a) or (c), but not paragraph (e), (f) or (h) of s.181(1), the appropriate authority do not propose to acquire any part of the hereditament or, as the case may be, any part of the affected area, during the period of fifteen years (or such longer period as they may specify) from the date of the counter-notice;[41] or (e) that the claimant was not on the date of service of the blight notice entitled to an interest in the land; or (f) that the claimant's interest is not one qualifying for protection (see p. 410 above); or (g) that the statutory provisions relating to endeavours to sell the interest and relating to injury to the claimant's interest (see p. 412 above) are not fulfilled.[42]

---

[36]   See *Bryant & Bryant* v *City of Bristol* (1969) 20 P. & C.R. 742. It may, however, be possible to start afresh with a notice specifying the correct head.

[37]   A counter-notice should be in the form prescribed in Schedule 1 to the Town and Country Planning (General) (Scotland) Regulations 1976.

[38]   As amended by the L.C.(S.)A. 1973, s.71(3).

[39]   See, for example, *McDermott* v *Department of Transport* (1984) 48 P. & C.R. 351.

[40]   In such a case it may be possible for the claimant to employ the compulsory purchase rules on severance in order to compel the authority to acquire the whole of the hereditament or the whole of the affected area—see p. 417 below.

[41]   The Local Government, Planning and Land Act 1980 (s.92(7) and (8)) restores the original wording of paragraph (d) as regards counter-notices served on or after 13th November 1980. Between 1st September 1976 and 13th November 1980 the Community Land Act 1975 (s.58(2) and Schedule 10, para. 7(3)) reduced the period to ten years and broadened the application of paragraph (d).

[42]   This ground of objection allows a counter to both s.182(1)(c)—that the claimant has made reasonable endeavours to sell his interest—and s.182(1)(d)—that it has not been possible to sell except at an unduly low price. It would seem that an authority which objects on the ground that one of these conditions is not satisfied cannot put to the Lands Tribunal arguments supporting an objection to the other condition—see *Trustees of St John's Church, Galashiels* v *Borders Regional Council* 1976 S.L.T. (Lands Tr.) 39.

Grounds (b) and (c) above cannot be employed where the blight notice was served in respect of land affected by a housing action area resolution (L.C.(S.)A. 1973, s.69(2)). An authority may not make objection on ground (d) if objection could be made on the grounds specified in paragraph (b) above (1972 Act, s.183(3)); if, therefore, the authority do not intend to acquire the land at all, the 'fifteen year' ground of objection is not to be employed.

Special provision is made as to the grounds on which objection may be made to a blight notice served by a heritable creditor or by the personal representative of a deceased person.

Where a successful objection is made on grounds (b), (c) or (d) above—i.e., where the authority disclaim an intention to acquire—existing powers of compulsory acquisition cease to have effect (1972 Act, s.188).

Regional, islands and district councils are empowered to make advances to enable any person to acquire a hereditament or agricultural unit in respect of which a counter-notice employing the 'fifteen year' ground of objection has been served, provided that in the case of a hereditament the rateable value does not exceed the amount prescribed for the purposes of s.181(4)(a) (above)—presently £12,000 (1972 Act, s.243).

Reference of objection to Lands Tribunal for Scotland

Within two months of service of a counter-notice the claimant may require that the objection be referred to the Lands Tribunal for Scotland (1972 Act, s.184(1)). On such a reference the tribunal is to consider the matters set out in the blight notice and the grounds of objection specified in the counter-notice. The onus of showing to the satisfaction of the tribunal that the objection is not well-founded lies upon the claimant[43] except that where the authority have disclaimed an intention to acquire—i.e., where objection has been made on grounds (b), (c) or (d) above—the burden of proof lies upon the authority (1972 Act, s.184(2), (3)).[44]

In *Mancini* v *Coventry City Council*[45] the Court of Appeal held that the material date as at which the tribunal has to determine whether an objection is or is not well-founded is the date when the objection was made, i.e., the date of the counter-notice; an event which occurs after the date of service of the counter-notice—for example, the withdrawal of the compulsory purchase order which gave rise to the blight—will not, it seems, affect the situation.

It would seem that an objection on the ground that the authority do not intend to acquire the land may not be effective unless the authority take some formal step to remove the blight. In *Sabey and Sabey* v *Hartlepool*

---

[43] See, for example, *Malcolm Campbell* v *Glasgow Corporation* 1972 S.L.T. (Lands Tr.) 8 (above); and *Trustees of St John's Church, Galashiels* v *Borders Regional Council* 1976 S.L.T. (Lands Tr.) 39.

[44] See, for example, *Trustees of St John's Church, Galashiels* (above).

[45] (1983) 270 E.G. 419. See too *Louisville Investments Ltd.* v *Basingstoke District Council* (1976) 32 P. & C.R. 419; and *Cedar Holdings Ltd.* v *Walsall Metropolitan Borough Council* (1979) 38 P. & C.R. 715.

County Borough Council[46] the (English) Lands Tribunal stated that 'in placing the onus on a local authority to show that an objection of this kind is well-founded, Parliament must have intended the Lands Tribunal to look at all the facts of the case and to dismiss the objection unless satisfied that an effective protection against "blight" is provided'. In this case the tribunal found that, in the absence of amendment of the development plan, the simple statement in the counter-notice that the authority did not intend to acquire any part of the land did little to dispel the blight; for that reason the tribunal refused to uphold the objection. The tribunal has, however, no residual discretion to consider hardship.[47]

The Lands Tribunal for Scotland has no jurisdiction to hear the objections of an authority who have not served a counter-notice within the statutory period, or to deal with any objection not stated in the counter-notice.[48] In *Ibbotson* v *Tayside Regional Council*[49] a blight notice was served on the Regional Council, alleging that a house had been blighted by proposals for a new road. The council responded by way of a letter stating that since the road in question was a trunk road, the appropriate authority was the Secretary of State; they did not, however, serve a counter-notice. When the claimant referred to the Lands Tribunal for Scotland a claim for compensation in respect of the alleged acquisition of the house by the Regional Council, the council sought to challenge the competency of the reference. The tribunal held that the validity of a blight notice could only be raised before the tribunal following the service of a counter-notice and that their jurisdiction was confined to considering matters set out in a blight notice and counter-notice.[50] The tribunal pointed out that a reference to the Secretary of State under s.194 of the 1972 Act, to have him decide upon the 'appropriate authority', has the effect of postponing the operation of a blight notice.[51]

Effect of a valid blight notice

If no counter-notice is served or if a counter-notice is withdrawn or is not upheld by the Lands Tribunal for Scotland, the appropriate authority are

---

[46] (1970) 21 P. & C.R. 448. See too *Duke of Wellington Social Club* v *Blyth Borough Council* (1964) 15 P. & C.R. 212; *Rawson* v *Ministry of Health* (1966) 17 P. & C.R. 239; *Louisville Investments Ltd.* v *Basingstoke District Council* (1976) 32 P. & C.R. 419; and *McKinnon Campbell* v *Greater Manchester Council* (1976) 33 P. & C.R. 110. Cf. *Mancini* v *Coventry City Council* (above).

[47] See *Mancini* v *Coventry City Council* (above).

[48] See *Church of Scotland General Trustees* v *Helensburgh Town Council* 1973 S.L.T. (Lands Tr.) 21; and *Ibbotson* v *Tayside Regional Council* 1978 S.L.T. (Lands Tr.) 25; following *Essex C.C.* v *Essex Incorporated Congregational Church Union* [1963] A.C. 808. See too *Trustees of St John's Church, Galashiels* v *Borders Regional Council* 1976 S.L.T. (Lands Tr.) 39; and *Lockers Estates (Holdings) Ltd.* v *Oadby U.D.C.* (1970) 21 P. & C.R. 836. In certain circumstances, however, the authority are empowered to serve a fresh counter-notice specifying different grounds of objection (see L.C.(S.)A. 1973, ss.64(6) and 65(3)).

[49] 1978 S.L.T. (Lands Tr.) 25.

[50] It may be, however, that the *vires* of a blight notice could be challenged in the Court of Session.

[51] Presumably the Regional Council could have served a counter-notice objecting to the blight notice on the ground that they did not intend to acquire any of the land.

deemed to be authorised[52] to acquire compulsorily the claimant's interest in the hereditament or, in the case of an agricultural unit, the interest of the claimant in so far as it subsists in the affected area, and to have served a notice to treat in respect thereof (1972 Act, s.185(1)). This constructive notice to treat cannot be withdrawn by the authority under the power conferred by s.39 of the Land Compensation (Scotland) Act 1963 (1972 Act, s.197); where, however, the blight notice itself is withdrawn, any deemed notice to treat is thereupon deemed to be withdrawn (1972 Act, s.187(1)).

It may be observed that in the case of an agricultural unit, only the 'affected area' will normally be acquired,[53] though it is the unsaleability of the unit as a whole that must be established.

Where the authority have objected on the ground that they intend to acquire part of the land only, and their objection is accepted by the claimant or is upheld by the Lands Tribunal, the authority are deemed to have served notice to treat in respect of that part only (1972 Act, s.185(3)).

Severance of land

In a case where the authority object to a blight notice on the ground that they only require to take part of the land, the right of the claimant under ordinary compulsory purchase principles to require the acquiring authority in certain circumstances to take the whole of the land[54] is preserved by s.191 of the 1972 Act.[55] The claimant will thus sometimes be able to compel the authority to acquire the whole of the hereditament or, in the case of an agricultural unit, the whole of the affected area, even though the authority only require part of the hereditament or affected area.[56]

Section 74 of the Land Compensation (Scotland) Act 1973 provides that the owner-occupier of an agricultural unit may include in a blight notice a claim that the 'unaffected area' (i.e. that part of the unit not falling within any of the specified descriptions of land) is not reasonably capable of being farmed, either by itself or in conjunction with 'other relevant land',[57] as a separate agricultural unit. Where such a claim succeeds, the authority are required to purchase the claimant's interest in the whole unit (see L.C.(S.)A. 1973, ss.75 and 76).

---

[52] Under the 'appropriate enactment'—see 1972 Act, s.195, as modified by L.C.(S.)A. 1973, Part V.

[53] See, however, L.C.(S.)A. 1973, s.74.

[54] See p. 420 below.

[55] In *Hurley* v *Cheshire County Council* (1975) 31 P. & C.R. 433 the Lands Tribunal inclined to the view that where an authority objected to a blight notice relating to a house and garden on the ground that they proposed to take only a part of the garden for road purposes, the onus lay upon the authority to satisfy the tribunal that the piece of garden ground could be taken without seriously affecting the amenity or convenience of the house. As to the difficulties which may face a claimant who wishes to compel an authority to take the whole rather than part of property see *Lake* v *Cheshire County Council* (1976) 32 P. & C.R. 143.

[56] In *Hill* v *Department of the Environment* [1976] N.I. 43 the Court of Appeal in Northern Ireland accepted that a temporary loss in market value could amount to material detriment and thus enable a landowner to require the appropriate authority to acquire the whole of his land.

[57] As to the meaning of this phrase, see L.C.(S.)A. 1973, s.74(2).

Compensation

Where a blight notice takes effect, compensation for the land acquired will be assessed on the normal compulsory purchase basis;[58] any depreciation attributable to the prospect of compulsory purchase is therefore to be disregarded, so that the depressing effect of the blighting proposals must be ignored (see Land Compensation (Scotland) Act 1963, s.16). Where acquisition takes place in consequence of a blight notice there is, however, no entitlement to a home loss or farm loss payment (L.C.(S.)A. 1973, ss.27(5) and 31(6)).

C. INJURIOUS AFFECTION

In this part of this chapter we are concerned not with the land to be acquired for a scheme of public works, but with neighbouring land the enjoyment of which is adversely affected by the carrying out of the scheme. Subject to one exception (mentioned below) Parliament has not provided a full remedy in such cases but has sought to alleviate hardship by providing for the payment of compensation in some, but by no means all, cases of injurious affection.

The statutory provisions are complex and may conveniently be considered under four separate headings: land held together with land acquired for the scheme; notices of objection to severance; other neighbouring land adversely affected by the *construction* of the works; and other neighbouring land adversely affected by the *use* of the works.

1. *Land held together with land acquired for the scheme*

Section 61 of the Lands Clauses Consolidation (Scotland) Act 1845 provides that in assessing compensation for the compulsory purchase of land regard is to be had not only to the value of the land to be taken 'but also to the damage, if any, to be sustained by the owner of the lands by reason of the severing of the lands taken from the other lands of such owner, or otherwise injuriously affecting such land'.[59] Both severance and other injurious affection may arise where part only of a parcel of land is compulsorily acquired. Our concern in this chapter is with 'other injurious affection'. Severance refers to the physical damage caused to land remaining with the owner by severing the part required for the scheme; other injurious affection refers to the depreciation in the value of the retained land caused by the scheme for which the part was acquired. For example, if part of a person's land is acquired for the construction of a major road, he is entitled to claim compensation for the adverse effects (the 'other injurious affection') which

---

[58]   Certain special rules on compensation are, however, preserved for the two types of case specified in s.186 of the 1972 Act.

[59]   Section 114 of the 1845 Act makes provision for the payment of compensation for other injurious affection to persons having no greater interest in land than as tenants for a year or from year to year.

the construction and use of the road will have on his remaining land.[60]

The remaining land must, however, have been held together with the land acquired. In other words, the pieces of land must have been 'so near to each other and so situated that the possession and control of each gives an enhanced value to all of them'.[61] This requirement may be illustrated by the decision in *Nisbet Hamilton* v *Northern Lighthouses Commissioners*.[62] The Commissioners compulsorily acquired a small island in the Firth of Forth on which to construct a lighthouse. The island formed part of an estate but was located one mile from the mainland and one and a half miles from the main house on the estate. The landowner's claim included an item for damage to the amenity of the main house which would occur if a foghorn was erected on the island. The court held there was no direct link between the land taken and the land alleged to be injuriously affected. They were not 'held together' for the purpose of s.61.

Curiously, it would seem that the scope of a claim for compensation under s.61 for injurious affection may be wider than the scope of an action for nuisance. Although the list of activities which may be recognised by the law as a nuisance is open-ended, there are, as we have indicated already, some activities which in the ordinary sense of the word could be said to disturb a person in the enjoyment of his property and which may depress the value of the property but which will not be regarded as a nuisance. Loss of profits, loss of a pleasant view and loss of privacy are examples.[63] In these cases there is said to be *damnum sine injuria*. The test would appear to be whether the damage is material rather than sentimental or trivial. The dividing line is very much a matter of fact and degree to be determined on the circumstances of each case.

In contrast, the test for compensation for injurious affection under s.61 would appear to be *damnum* alone. The authority for this proposition derives from the decision of the House of Lords in the English case of *Duke of Buccleuch* v *Metropolitan Board of Works*.[64] The claimant leased a house and gardens fronting onto the River Thames together with a causeway jutting out into the river. The Board of Works, who were in process of constructing the Victoria Embankment on the foreshore of the river, acquired and removed the causeway. The embankment was to be used as a

---

[60] Section 41 of the Land Compensation (Scotland) Act 1973 provides that compensation for injurious affection shall be assessed by reference to the whole of the works and not only the part situated on the land compulsorily acquired from the claimant. This overcomes the difficulty encountered by the claimants in *City of Glasgow Union Railway* v *Hunter* (1870) 8 M. (H.L.) 156; and *Edwards* v *Minister of Transport* [1964] 2 Q.B. 134.

[61] *Cowper Essex* v *Acton Local Board* (1889) 14 App. Cas. 153, per Lord Watson at p. 167.

[62] (1886) 13 R. 710. See also *City of Glasgow Union Railway Co.* v *Hunter* (1870) 8 M. (H.L.) 156.

[63] *Caledonian Railway Co.* v *Walker's Trustees* (1881) 8 R. 405, per Lord Curriehill; *Caledonian Railway Co.* v *Ogilvy* (1856) 2 Macq. 229; *Nisbet Hamilton* v *Northern Lighthouses Commissioners* (1886) 13 R. 710; and *Re Penny and South Eastern Railway Co.* (1857) 7 E. & B. 660.

[64] (1872) L.R. 5 H.L. 418. See also *City of Glasgow Union Railway Co.* v *Hunter* (1870) 8 M. (H.L.) 156, per Lord Chancellor Hatherley.

public highway, thus cutting off the claimant's direct access to the river. Compensation was clearly due to the claimant for the taking of the causeway and for the injury to the house as a result of its being denied access to the river. The question at issue was whether the claimant was entitled to compensation for depreciation caused to his property by the conversion of the land between it and the river into a highway and its use by the public. The majority of the House of Lords had no difficulty in concluding that compensation was due under the English equivalent of s.61 of the 1845 Act for any depreciation in the value of the land retained resulting from the exercise of the powers of the acquiring authority, including the depreciating effects of loss of privacy and amenity.

It would seem, therefore, that a landowner, part of whose land has been taken for the scheme, is well placed as a result of the interpretation of this part of s.61 to recover compensation for all damage resulting from other injurious affection.

2. Notices of objection to severance

Where, in the exercise of compulsory powers, an acquiring authority propose to take part only of a parcel of land, the adverse effects of the authority's scheme on the land to be left with the landowner may in some cases be very severe. In such circumstances the landowner may feel that it would be preferable from his point of view for the acquiring authority to take the whole of his land (at its full market value) rather than that he should be left with part, even though he will be compensated for the land taken and for injurious affection. In such a case statute allows the landowner to serve on the acquiring authority what is generally referred to as a 'notice of objection to severance'.[65]

The broad effect of serving such a notice is to give the acquiring authority a choice. They may decide to proceed no further with the acquisition of any part of the land in question; or they may agree to acquire the lot; or they may persist with their intention to take part only, in which case the notice will be referred to the Lands Tribunal for Scotland for a decision.

The notice of objection to severance, as its name implies, is concerned principally with severance, i.e., the physical damage caused to the remaining land by severing the part. The detailed provisions governing such notices are, therefore, outside the scope of this book.

However, an amendment introduced by the Land Compensation (Scotland) Act 1973 indicates that in some cases the injurious effects of the public works for which the land is to be taken may have a material bearing on the outcome of a notice. The test which the Lands Tribunal for Scotland will apply to a notice of objection to severance directed at a house, building or factory is whether the part can be taken without material detriment or damage to the remainder; and for a park or garden belonging to a house the

[65] See Acquisition of Land (Authorisation Procedure) (Scotland) Act 1947, s.1 and Schedule 2, para. 4; Town and Country Planning (Scotland) Act 1972, s.278 and Schedule 24, paras. 19–29; and L.C.(S.)A. 1973, ss.49–53.

test is whether the part can be taken without seriously affecting the amenity or convenience of the house.[66] Section 54 of the Land Compensation (Scotland) Act 1973 provides that in applying these tests the tribunal is to take into account not only the effects of severance, but also the use to be made of the part to be acquired, and if the part is being acquired for a scheme of public works extending to other land, then the tribunal is to have regard to the effect of the whole of the use to be made of the other land.

Where this provision operates, the notice of objection to severance goes further than the compensation provisions of s.61 of the 1845 Act. It provides a full remedy for the landowner in that he can compel the acquiring authority to purchase, at a price which ignores the effects of blight, land which is seriously blighted by their scheme.

3. *Other neighbouring land adversely affected by the construction of the works*

Earlier in this chapter it was suggested that where bodies carrying out schemes of public works have statutory immunity from an action for nuisance, it is reasonable to expect that Parliament will make provision for compensation in lieu. Section 61 of the Lands Clauses Consolidation (Scotland) Act 1845 makes such provision for a landowner who has had part of his land taken for a scheme. However, the injurious effects of a scheme do not discriminate between those who have had land taken and those who have not. Consideration is now given to the position of the landowner who has had no land taken for the scheme.

Sections 6 and 16 of the Railways Clauses Consolidation (Scotland) Act 1845[67] provide for the payment of compensation to a person whose land is injuriously affected by the *construction* of public works, whether or not a part of his land has been acquired for the scheme. For example, the construction of the works may obstruct access to the property resulting in depreciation in its value (irrespective of the use to which the property is put). However, in *Hammersmith and City Railway Co.* v *Brand*,[68] the House of Lords held, on a literal construction of the legislation, that identical provisions in the English Railways Clauses Act of the same year were not to be construed as providing for the payment of compensation for depreciation resulting from the *use* of the public works. And in *City of Glasgow Union Railway Co.* v *Hunter*[69] in the following year the House of Lords held that no

---

[66] Acquisition of Land (Authorisation Procedure) (Scotland) Act 1947, s.1 and Schedule 2, para. 4; and Town and Country Planning (Scotland) Act 1972, s.278 and Schedule 24, para. 26. The correct way to judge the matter in such a case is to consider whether that part of the property remaining after part has been taken is less useful or less valuable in some significant degree compared with the position obtaining prior to acquisition—see *McMillan* v *Strathclyde Regional Council* 1984 S.L.T. (Lands Tr.) 25.

[67] As applied by the Acquisition of Land (Authorisation Procedure) (Scotland) Act 1947, s.1(3) and Schedule 2.

[68] (1869) L.R. 4 H.L. 171.

[69] (1870) 8 M. (H.L.) 156.

provision allowing for the payment of compensation for depreciation resulting from the *use* of public works was to be found in the Lands Clauses Consolidation (Scotland) Act of 1845.

The facts in *Brand* illustrate well the distinction between depreciation resulting from the *construction* and from the *use* of works. A railway was constructed to run alongside the plaintiff's land although none of her land was acquired. The plaintiff claimed against the railway company *inter alia* for the depreciation in the value of her property resulting from the vibration caused by the passage of trains using the railway. After detailed examination of the relevant provisions in the English Lands Clauses and Railways Clauses Acts of 1845 the House of Lords concluded that the Lands Clauses Act did not assist a claimant from whom no land was taken and that the right to compensation in the Railways Clauses Act was limited to injury done by the *construction* of the railway and did not extend to depreciation resulting from its *use*. 'It is not', said Lord Chelmsford, 'that the Legislature has excluded compensation for injury arising as the necessary consequence of using the railway, but that it has not, as far as I can discover, given any right to claim compensation for this species of injury.' The claim by Mrs. Brand accordingly failed.

Although, as we shall see, provision was eventually made in the Land Compensation (Scotland) Act 1973 for the payment of compensation for injurious affection resulting from the *use* of public works, that provision operates concurrently with ss.6 and 16 of the Railways Clauses Consolidation (Scotland) Act (as applied by the Acquisition of Land (Authorisation Procedure) (Scotland) Act 1947). It is upon the Railways Clauses Act that a claim for compensation for blight or injurious affection resulting from the construction of the works must be founded where no part of the land has been acquired for the scheme.

There are two further limitations on the right to compensation under the Railways Clauses Act. First of all, the claimant must be able to show that were it not for the statutory authority for the works there would have been a right of action at common law. The authority for this proposition is to be found in the decision of the House of Lords in *Caledonian Railway Co.* v *Ogilvy*.[70] The inference which the House drew from the legislation was that Parliament intended to confer on landowners a right to compensation co-extensive with the right of action which had been removed by statute; there was nothing to suggest that there had been any intention to improve the position of such people. This contrasts with the rather more generous approach taken by the House in *Buccleuch* as regards injurious affection to land held together with land acquired for the scheme.

Secondly, the claimant must show that the damage is to land or to an interest in land.[71] In *Ogilvy*, for example, compensation was claimed for depreciation resulting from the inconvenience, interruption and delay

---

[70] (1856) 2 Macq. 229.
[71] See *Caledonian Railway Co.* v *Ogilvy* (1856) 2 Macq. 229; *Caledonian Railway Co.* v *Walker's Trustees* (1882) 9 R. (H.L.) 19; *Ricket* v *Metropolitan Railway Co.* (1867) L.R. 2 H.L. 175; and *Metropolitan Board of Works* v *McCarthy* (1874) L.R. 7 H.L. 243.

caused by the placing of a level crossing on a public road some 50 to 60 yards from the entrance to the claimant's property. The House of Lords, however, considered that the injury was no different in kind from that which would be suffered by all users of the highway in question, although it might be different in degree. It was, in other words, a personal inconvenience rather than an injury to property; in the words of the Lord Chancellor (Lord Cranworth): 'all attempts at arguing that this is a damage to the estate is a mere play upon words. It is no damage at all to the estate, except that the owner of that estate would oftener have a right of action from time to time than any other person, inasmuch as he would traverse the spot oftener than other people would traverse it.' The claim accordingly failed.

The decision in *Ogilvy* may be contrasted with that in *Caledonian Railway Co.* v *Walker's Trustees*.[72] The trustees owned property comprising in part a factory and in part dwellings with a frontage to Canal Street in Glasgow. That street provided direct and almost level access to Eglinton Street, some 90 yards away, and one of the main thoroughfares in the city. Canal Street was permanently blocked by works carried out by the railway company and an alternative circuitous route to Eglinton Street was substituted involving a steep gradient. A second access to Eglinton Street via a public road at the rear of the property was also rendered very much less convenient. A claim by the trustees under s.6 of the Railways Clauses Consolidation (Scotland) Act 1845 in respect of diminution in the value of their property resulting from the construction of the works was upheld by the House of Lords. Much of the value of the property, irrespective of any particular use which could be made of it, was dependent upon the existence of the access. The diminution in that value as a result of the closing of the access was sufficient to satisfy the second limitation.

4. *Other neighbouring land adversely affected by the use of the works*

In view of the distinction which the courts made between 'construction' and 'use', compensation for blight or injurious affection to land unconnected with land taken for the scheme could fall substantially short of the compensation obtainable under s.61 of the Lands Clauses Consolidation (Scotland) Act 1845. This distinction was brought very forcefully to the notice of the public during the era of the construction of urban motorways. The bringing into use of roads such as Westway in London and the Monklands Motorway in Glasgow resulted in many householders being injuriously affected by a substantial volume of traffic passing close to their houses at all times of the day and night. As this damage was being caused by the use of the road and not by its construction, it was damage for which no compensation could be claimed. Similar problems resulted from the enlargement of airports. The problem was neatly summarised by JUSTICE in 1969:

---

[72] (1882) 9 R. (H.L.) 19.

'We believe it to be a sad commentary on the present law that an owner of land in an area through which a motorway is to be constructed should prefer that the motorway takes the whole of his property rather than go near it.'[73]

The extent of public dissatisfaction coupled with the publication in 1972 of the report of the Urban Motorways Committee[74] led to the issuing in October 1972 of the White Paper *Development and Compensation—Putting People First*.[75] In the White Paper the government recognised this area of hardship and committed itself to a new statutory right to compensation. This right is set out in Part I of the Land Compensation (Scotland) Act 1973. In addition, Part II of the 1973 Act confers upon public bodies certain powers to mitigate the injurious effect of public works. With one exception,[76] the Act does not alter the position as regards compensation for injurious affection resulting from the construction of public works. Instead, it provides an additional right to compensation for damage resulting from the use of new public works for certain people from whom no land is taken and who are barred from bringing an action at common law for nuisance.[77] The following is a summary of the provisions.

A claim may be made under Part I of the Land Compensation (Scotland) Act 1973 in respect of depreciation resulting from one or more of the following physical factors caused by the use of the public works: noise, vibration, smell, fumes, smoke, artificial lighting, and a discharge on to the land of any solid or liquid substance[78] (s.1(1) and (2)). The source of the physical factors must be situated on or in the public works in question except that physical factors caused by aircraft arriving at or departing from an aerodrome are to be treated as caused by the use of the aerodrome whether or not the aircraft is within the boundaries of the aerodrome (s.1(5)). Loss of privacy, loss of a view and general loss of amenity are not included in the prescribed factors[79] so that the right to compensation for this form of injurious affection is less generous than that in s.61 of the Lands Clauses Consolidation (Scotland) Act 1845.

[73] *Compensation for Compulsory Acquisition and Remedies for Planning Restrictions* (Stevens, 1969) and *Supplemental Report* (1972).
[74] *New Roads in Towns. Report by the Urban Motorways Committee* (H.M.S.O., 1971).
[75] Cmnd. 5124 (1972).
[76] Section 61 provides that the word 'construction' in s.6 of the Railways Clauses Act is to include a reference to the 'execution of works in connection therewith'.
[77] A claim under the Land Compensation (Scotland) Act 1973 is in effect a substitute for an action for nuisance at common law and can therefore only be made where there is statutory immunity from an action for nuisance. If a claim under the 1973 Act is resisted by an authority on the ground that no statutory immunity exists as regards use of the works, the authority are not entitled to rely on any such immunity in an action for nuisance caused by the physical factors covered by the 1973 Act.
[78] The Act does not require that the injury should be of a permanent nature—see *Shepherd and Shepherd* v *Lancashire County Council* (1976) 33 P. & C.R. 296.
[79] Depreciation resulting from the mere proximity of a refuse tip will therefore not give rise to a claim (see *Shepherd and Shepherd* v *Lancashire County Council* (1976) 33 P. & C.R. 296), nor will depreciation resulting from increased danger or apprehension of danger from traffic (see *Hickmott* v *Dorset County Council* (1975) 30 P. & C.R. 237).

The public works, the use of which may give rise to a claim, comprise any road, any aerodrome, and any other works or land provided or used in the exercise of statutory powers (s.1(3)). Depreciation resulting from alterations to the carriageway of an existing road,[80] from runway or apron alterations at an aerodrome, from reconstruction, extension or alterations of other public works, or from a change of use in respect of any public works other than a road or aerodrome may also give rise to a claim (s.9(1), (2) and (3)). Excluded from the list is depreciation resulting from a traffic regulation order or from an intensification in the use of existing public works. For example, the opening of a new major road may substantially increase the volume of traffic on an existing road which now feeds into the new road; the properties adjoining the existing road may suffer depreciation in value as a result but such depreciation will not give rise to a claim under Part I of the 1973 Act.

The claimant must have a qualifying interest and must have acquired it before the 'relevant date';[81] this is the date on which the public works in question first come into use[82] (ss.1(1) and (9), 2(1) and 9(2)). The qualifying interests are similar, although not identical, to the interests which qualify for protection under the blight notice provisions. They are:

(i)   the owner of a dwelling;
(ii) the owner-occupier of an agricultural unit;
(iii) the owner-occupier of a hereditament the annual value of which does not exceed a prescribed amount—presently £12,000[83] (s.2(1), (2) and (3)).

The definition of the terms 'owner's interest'[84] and 'owner-occupier' bear somewhat specialised meanings (see s.2(4) and (5)). An owner's interest includes that of a lessee with at least three years of his lease still to run (s.2(4)(a)). Where the owner's interest in a dwelling carries the right of occupation then the owner must be in occupation to qualify (s.2(2)(b)). Investment owners (other than of dwellings) and owner-occupiers of substantial business premises will not qualify.

A period of twelve months must normally elapse after the relevant date

---

[80] For the purposes of this provision an alteration to a carriageway comprises an alteration (otherwise than by resurfacing) to its location, width or level or the construction of an additional carriageway (see s.9(5)).

[81] There is an exception for an interest acquired by inheritance from a person who acquired that interest before the relevant date (s.11). For the position of certain categories of restricted interests in land see s.10.

[82] As to the date on which works are first used see *Davies* v *Mid-Glamorgan County Council* (1979) 38 P. & C.R. 727; and *Shepherd and Shepherd* v *Lancashire County Council* (1976) 33 P. & C.R. 296.

[83] Town and Country Planning (Limit of Annual Value) (Scotland) Order 1985 (which came into operation on 1st April 1985).

[84] The meaning of this phrase was considered in *Inglis* v *British Airports Authority* 1978 S.L.T. (Lands Tr.) 30.

before a claim can be made (the 'first claim day')[85] (L.C.(S.)A. 1973, s.3(2) as amended by the Local Government, Planning and Land Act 1980, s.112(2)). This allows time for the use of the public works to build up to something like its normal level so that a realistic assessment can be made of any depreciation in the value of neighbouring property. Claims may be submitted to the responsible authority at any time during the five years following the first claim day.[86]

Compensation is assessed on the basis of the depreciating effect of the level of use of the works as at the first claim day but account may be taken of any intensification of use which may then be reasonably expected (s.4(2)). The assessment is based on rules (2) to (4) of s.12 of the Land Compensation (Scotland) Act 1963 (L.C.(S.)A. 1973, s.4(4)(b)) by reference to prices ruling on the first claim day (s.4(1)). The only planning assumption that may be made in valuing the land which is the subject of the claim is that planning permission would be granted for the categories of development set out in Schedule 6 to the 1972 Act[87] (L.C.(S.)A. 1973, s.5(1), (2) and (4)). Otherwise it is to be assumed that planning permission would not be granted for development (see s.5(3)). Where there is a right to insulation works (below), that benefit will be taken into account for compensation purposes, as will the benefit of remedial works carried out by the authority (s.4(3)). Any appreciation in the value of the land, or of other adjoining land to which the claimant is entitled in the same capacity, which is attributable to the existence or use of the public works is to be set off against any compensation (s.6(1)). No payment will be made on a claim unless the amount of compensation exceeds £50. Interest is due on the compensation from the date of claim until the date of payment (s.16). Any question of disputed compensation is to be referred to and determined by the Lands Tribunal for Scotland (s.14).[88]

Part II of the Land Compensation (Scotland) Act 1973 contains provisions enabling public authorities to mitigate the injurious effects of their schemes. Section 18 empowers the Secretary of State to make regulations imposing a duty or conferring a power on the responsible authorities to insulate buildings against noise or to make grants available for this purpose. Regulations have been made under this power requiring roads authorities in specified circumstances to instal or to make grants in aid of the installation of noise insulation in residential property adversely affected by a road scheme.[89]

---

[85] A claim can, however, be made during the twelve month period by an owner who has made a contract for disposing of the land, provided that the claim is made before the land is disposed of; compensation is not payable before the first claim day (s.3(3)). As to the effect of this provision see *Inglis* v *British Airports Authority* 1978 S.L.T. (Lands Tr.) 30.

[86] Section 113 of the Local Government, Planning and Land Act 1980 safeguards certain claims for compensation for depreciation which were out of time when the 1980 Act was passed.

[87] The categories of development specified in Schedule 6 are outlined in chapter 16.

[88] As to the method of assessing such claims see *Inglis* v *British Airports Authority (No. 2)* 1979 S.L.T. (Lands Tr.) 10; and *Stuart* v *British Airports Authority* 1983 S.L.T. (Lands Tr.) 42.

[89] The Noise Insulation (Scotland) Regulations 1975.

Roads authorities are given wide powers to carry out works—for example, the planting of trees and shrubs and the laying out of grassed areas—designed to mitigate the adverse effects of a road scheme, and to acquire land by agreement or compulsorily for this purpose (ss.20(1) and 21). Furthermore, they may arrange for the provision of mitigating works by means of agreements entered into with owners of land in the vicinity of the road (s.22).

Where works for the construction or improvement of a road render the continued occupation of a dwelling impracticable, the roads authority may meet the reasonable expenses of obtaining suitable alternative accommodation until the works are completed (s.26). If the enjoyment of land is seriously affected by the construction, improvement, or use of a road the authority may acquire the land by agreement if the interest of the vendor is one which would qualify for protection under the blight notice provisions (s.20(2)).

Similar powers are given to other authorities carrying out public works with the exception of the power to acquire land compulsorily for the provision of mitigating works and the power to enter into agreements (ss.24(1) and (2), 25 and 26).

D. CONCLUSION

Two general points may be drawn from this discussion of the statutory provisions dealing with blight and injurious affection. First of all it would appear that successive governments have been careful to avoid imposing too great a burden on those promoting schemes of public works. Any broadening of the application of the statutory provisions dealing with planning blight or injurious affection might prejudice the carrying out of much-needed schemes. The legislation therefore attempts to achieve a balance between the need for public sector schemes and the alleviation of the most obvious cases of hardship resulting from such schemes. A consequence of this balancing act is, however, that some cases of undoubted hardship will not be alleviated.[90]

The second point is that the legislation concerned with the alleviation of hardship due to blight, and this comment applies particularly to that concerned with injurious affection, has developed in a piecemeal way. The result is legislation which is unnecessarily complicated and, at times, discriminatory. For example, it is difficult to justify the distinction which the statutory provisions make for compensation purposes between a claimant

[90] However, in one case where an individual had sustained interference with the enjoyment of her land and had suffered 'intolerable stress' as a result of aircraft and motorway noise, an application to the European Commission of Human Rights was held admissible and the case was settled on the basis of an *ex gratia* payment by the Government—see *Arrondelle* v *Government of the United Kingdom* (Application No. 7889/77, 13th May 1982); and see A. C. Evans and P. Q. Watchman, 'The European Convention on Human Rights and Fundamental Freedoms: A New Dimension to Planning Law?' 1981 S.P.L.P. 65; A. C. Evans, 'The Arrondelle Case' 1983 S.P.L.P. 44; and [1982] J.P.L. 770.

who has had part of his land acquired for a scheme and one who has not. The taking of land is not a pre-requisite for injury, yet a person who has had land taken may well receive more in compensation than a person who has not. Nor does there seem to be much justification for continuing the laboured and complicated distinction between injurious affection caused by the construction of the works and that resulting from their use. There would seem to be a strong argument for rationalising these provisions and drawing them together in a separate code.

CHAPTER 19
SPECIAL CONTROLS

A. INTRODUCTION

The discussion so far has largely centred on the general control exercised by planning authorities over the use and development of land under Part III of the 1972 Act. There are, however, numerous other controls exercised by public authorities over the use of land. In some cases it is necessary to comply with these other controls before a planning application can be submitted. For example, s.36 of the Petroleum and Submarine Pipe-lines Act 1975 provides that an application for planning permission for works for the construction or alteration of a refinery or for the adaptation of other types of plant as a refinery is to be of no effect unless the application is accompanied either by a 'refinery authorisation' issued by the Secretary of State for Energy or by a certificate from the applicant stating that an authorisation is not required because the works are within the statutory exemption limits. Similarly, the Health Services Act 1976, as amended, provides that an application for planning permission for the construction or alteration of premises to be used for certain hospital purposes outside the National Health Service, or for the conversion of premises for such purposes, is to be of no effect unless it is accompanied by an authorisation issued by the Secretary of State for Social Services. In other cases planning permission must be obtained before approval or consent can be sought under other legislation. In terms of s.23 of the Licensing (Scotland) Act 1976, for example, an application for a new liquor licence (other than an off-sale licence) is not to be entertained by the licensing board unless the application is accompanied by a certificate from the planning authority that the applicant has obtained planning permission for the premises in question or that permission is not required. Similarly, a caravan site licence may only be issued under Part I of the Caravan Sites and Control of Development Act 1960 if the applicant is entitled to the benefit of a planning permission for the use of the land as a caravan site granted otherwise than by a development order, and every application for a development licence under the terms of the Petroleum (Production) (Landward Areas) Regulations 1984 must be accompanied by a grant of planning permission for the programme of development in question.

With many controls, no sequence is prescribed and practical considerations will dictate the order in which the necessary approvals are sought. Obtaining a building warrant under the Building (Scotland) Acts 1959 and

1970 is an example. It is impossible in a book such as this to deal with these other controls.

However, the planning legislation itself has made provision for a number of special controls, the object of which for the most part is, as with general planning control, the protection and improvement of the physical environment. These special controls are directed at advertisements, trees, buildings of special architectural or historic interest, conservation areas, waste land and minerals. In addition, the Secretary of State has power in the 1972 Act to subject industrial development to special control although this control is not currently in operation. Any discussion of the planning legislation would be incomplete without coverage of these matters and they are, accordingly, dealt with in this chapter.

The need to provide for special regimes of control rests on a number of considerations. In some cases, general planning control may be ineffective because the activity—for example, the felling of a tree, internal works to a listed building or the demolition of a building in a conservation area—does not constitute development. Some of the activities present problems which are not shared by other forms of development; the display of advertisements and mineral operations are examples. In other cases the additional control allows special emphasis to be given to certain matters such as the protection of the nation's supply of interesting buildings or the preservation of the character of attractive groups of buildings.

Although the object of most of the special controls is the protection and improvement of the environment, the way in which they achieve that object differs. Although there are some similarities, the general nature of the controls and the means by which they are tied into the development control process reflect their different characteristics. The control of waste land, for example is primarily a remedial process; the controls over important trees and buildings, on the other hand, are essentially preventive in nature. Listed building control is designed to give additional emphasis to certain features and therefore operates as an addition to normal planning control; advertisement control, on the other hand, is designed to cope with the special problems of displaying advertisements and operates as a substitute for normal planning control; whilst control over trees is concerned with an activity which is not development at all and is, therefore, an entirely separate process.

These special controls are now considered in turn.

B. BUILDINGS OF SPECIAL ARCHITECTURAL OR HISTORIC INTEREST

General

Under the 1947 Act planning authorities were empowered to make building preservation orders in respect of buildings of special architectural or historic interest. A building in respect of which a building preservation order had been made (and confirmed by the Secretary of State) could not be demolished or altered without the consent of the planning authority. In order to provide guidance to planning authorities in the performance of their duties in relation to buildings of special architectural or historic interest the Secretary of State was empowered to compile lists of such buildings. Notice of any proposal to execute works for the demolition of a listed building or for the alteration or extension of such a building in a manner which would seriously affect its character had to be given to the planning authority in order that they might consider making a building preservation order.

As a result of changes made by the 1969 Act the present law[1] on buildings of special architectural or historic interest is fundamentally different from the earlier law. Provision is still made for the compilation or approval by the Secretary of State of lists of buildings of special interest but such 'listing' is now of much greater significance than formerly; under the present law the mere listing of a building means that it thereupon becomes an offence, unless consent has first been obtained, to demolish the building or to alter or extend it in any manner which would affect its character.

The restrictions which follow from the listing of a building may in some circumstances reduce the value of the building. For example, in *Amalgamated Investment and Property Co. Ltd.* v *John Walker and Sons*[2] a warehouse was added to the statutory list some two days after a contract had been signed for its purchase for the purposes of redevelopment. The Court of Appeal rejected an action by the purchaser for recission of the contract. Every purchaser, said the court, should be regarded as being aware of the inherent risk that a building may be listed.

To alleviate the sort of problem that arose in *John Walker* from what is generally referred to as 'spot listing', the Local Government, Planning and Land Act 1980 introduced in England and Wales an immunity certificate procedure.[3] Where an application for planning permission has been made or planning permission has been granted for development involving the alteration, extension or demolition of a building, an individual may ask the Secretary of State to issue a certificate that he does not propose to list the building. The effect of such a certificate is to preclude the minister from listing the building for a period of five years, thus allowing the development to proceed. No such procedure has been introduced in Scotland.

Unfortunate as the effects of the listing procedure may be for a purchaser in the sort of situation that occurred in *John Walker*, there is another side to this particular coin. The demolition of the Firestone factory in Brentford in 1980 before a decision could be made as to whether or not to add the building

---

[1]   Now mostly contained in the 1972 Act (as amended by the Town and Country Amenities Act 1974 and by the Local Government and Planning (Scotland) Act 1982) and the Town and Country Planning (Listed Buildings and Buildings in Conservation Areas) (Scotland) Regulations 1975 (as amended by the Town and Country Planning (Listed Buildings and Buildings in Conservation Areas) (Scotland) Amendment Regulations 1977). Throughout the present section of this chapter these regulations are referred to as 'the Listed Buildings Regulations'.

[2]   [1977] 1 W.L.R. 164.

[3]   Section 90 and Schedule 15, para. 5. See also D.o.E. Circular 72/1981.

to the statutory list (it apparently had a fine Art Deco central facade)
focused attention on what the *Journal of Planning and Environment Law*
referred to as 'the achilles heel of the listing process'. 'Faced with the likely
prospect of listing reducing the value of the property affected, any
professional adviser', commented the *Journal*, 'must surely advise his client
as to what the law is[4]—and leave considerations of morality to his client.'[5]

To avoid this sort of difficulty, planning authorities are empowered to
serve a building preservation notice, to give immediate, if temporary,
protection to an unlisted building of special architectural or historic interest
which is threatened with demolition or alteration in such a way as to affect its
character[6] (see p. 437 below). During the period that the notice is in force,
the building is subject to normal listed building controls including the need
to obtain consent for the demolition or alteration of the building. However,
the procedure is not a complete answer to the difficulty. It will only be
effective if the planning authority are alert to the prospect of demolition.
Furthermore, the authority may have to compensate any person having an
interest in the building for any loss resulting from the serving of the notice if
the building is not subsequently added to the statutory list by the Secretary
of State;[7] the prospect of a claim for compensation may deter an authority
from using the procedure.

A booklet published by the Scottish Development Department, *Scotland's Listed Buildings—a Guide to their Protection*, is obtainable free of
charge from local authorities. More detailed guidance on law and policy on
buildings and areas of special architectural or historic interest is to be found
in the Scottish Development Department's *Memorandum on Listed Buildings and Conservation Areas*, which was issued to planning authorities with
S.D.D. Circular 4/1976.[8]

Listing of buildings

Section 52 of the 1972 Act provides that the Secretary of State is to compile
lists of buildings of special architectural or historic interest or to approve,
with or without modifications, lists compiled by other persons, and may
amend any list so compiled or approved.[9]

---

[4] In practice, the demolition of a building is not usually treated as development and need not,
therefore, be the subject of a planning application (see p. 123).

[5] [1980] J.P.L. 712, current topic.

[6] 1972 Act, s.56.

[7] 1972 Act, s.162.

[8] See too Roger W. Suddards, *Listed Buildings: The Law and Practice* (Sweet and Maxwell,
1982), which discusses law and practice in England and Wales; Scottish Civic Trust and
Scottish Development Department, *New Uses for Older Buildings in Scotland—A Manual
of Practical Encouragement* (H.M.S.O., 1981); and 'Listing and Listed Building Control', a
consultation paper issued by the Historic Buildings Division of the Scottish Development
Department in November 1984.

[9] For an account of the listing process see Janey Tucker, 'Historic Buildings—the List' 1982
S.P.L.P. 30. The Historic Buildings Council for Scotland in their Report for 1982–1983
(H.M.S.O., 1984) stated that they were concerned at the slow progress of the re-survey of
old and unsatisfactory lists of buildings of special architectural and historic interest. See too
consultation paper 'Listing and Listed Building Control' (S.D.D., 1984).

In considering whether a building ought to be listed, the Secretary of State may take into account not only the building itself but also 'any respect in which its exterior contributes to the architectural or historic interest of any group of buildings of which it forms part' (s.52(2)). He may also take into account 'the desirability of preserving, on the grounds of its architectural or historic interest, any feature of the building consisting of a man-made object or structure fixed to the building or forming part of the land and comprised within the curtilage of the building' (s.52(2)); any such object or structure is, for the purposes of the legislation on listed buildings, to be treated as part of the building (s.52(7)). Outbuildings and fixtures of interest will therefore be subject to the same controls as the listed building itself. The definition of 'building' for the purposes of this provision is thus somewhat wider than that contained in s.275 of the 1972 Act.

This may be illustrated by the decision of the Court of Appeal in *Attorney-General* v *Calderdale Borough Council*[10] which turned on the scope of the identical provision in the English legislation.[11] The case concerned a terrace of 15 four-storey mill-workers' dwellings linked by a bridge to a mill. The mill was listed. Until 1973 the mill and the terrace were in the same ownership. In 1973 the terrace but not the mill passed into the ownership of the Calderdale Borough Council. The council proposed to demolish the terrace. The Attorney-General, acting at the relation of local residents who wished to preserve the terrace, argued, *inter alia*, that the terrace was either a structure fixed to the mill or a structure forming part of the land and comprised within the curtilage of the mill[12] and thus fell to be treated as a part of the listed building so that the Secretary of State's consent would be required before demolition of the terrace could take place. Stephenson L.J., giving the court's judgment, adopted a broad approach to the construction of the subsection. A building had to be considered in its setting as well as with any features of special architectural or historic interest which it possessed.[13] 'The setting of a building', he observed, 'might consist of much more than man-made objects or structures, but there might be objects or structures which would not naturally or certainly be regarded as part of a building or features of it, but which nevertheless were so closely related to it that they enhanced it aesthetically and their removal would adversely affect it . . . [I]f the building itself was to be preserved so also should these objects and structures be.' On that approach, he concluded that the terrace was a structure fixed to the mill within the meaning of the subsection.

He also concluded that, notwithstanding the division of ownership, the terrace had not been taken out of the curtilage by the changes which had taken place. The parties were agreed that three factors had to be taken into account in determining whether a structure was within the curtilage of a

---

[10] [1983] J.P.L. 310.
[11] Town and Country Planning Act 1971, s.54(9).
[12] It would seem that the two limbs of the subsection are not mutually exclusive (Stephenson L.J. in *Calderdale*).
[13] See the amendment to s.54(3) of the 1972 Act introduced by the Local Government and Planning (Scotland) Act 1982, s.48 and Schedule 2, para. 15(a)(ii).

listed building. These were (1) the physical layout of the listed building and the structure; (2) their ownership past and present; and (3) their use or function, past and present. The terrace, in Stephenson L.J.'s view, 'remained so closely related physically or geographically to the mill as to constitute with it a single unit and to be comprised within its curtilage' in the sense in which those words are used in this subsection.[14]

After preparation or amendment of any list the Secretary of State is to deposit with regional, general and district planning authorities and with local housing authorities a copy of so much of the list as relates to that authority's district (s.52(4)). Every such authority is to keep available for public inspection copies of so much of any such list as relates to buildings within their area and the Secretary of State is to keep available for inspection copies of all lists compiled, approved or made by him (s.52(6)). Lists are no longer recorded in the Register of Sasines.[15]

Though informal notification of the listing of a building will be given to the owner by the Scottish Development Department, formal notification of the inclusion of any building in a list, or of the exclusion therefrom of any building, is the duty of the planning authority[16] in whose area the building is situated (see 1972 Act, s.52(5); and Listed Buildings Regulations, reg. 12). Such notification is to be given to the owner, lessee and occupier of the building.[17]

There is no direct statutory right of objection to the listing of a building[18] (though if representations against such action are made, the listing will presumably be reconsidered by the Secretary of State) but on a refusal or conditional grant of listed building consent, appeal can be made on the ground that the building is not of special interest and ought to be removed from the list (see p. 441 below).

Any building which, immediately prior to 3rd August 1970, was subject to a building preservation order but was not then listed, is deemed to be a listed building; after consultation with the parties involved the Secretary of State may direct that this provision is not to apply to a particular building (s.52(8), (9)).

According to the booklet *Scotland's Listed Buildings*:

'Most buildings of the early 19th century and earlier whose interesting character remains substantially unimpaired are included [in the list]. Later buildings must be of definite character and quality to qualify.

14 See too *SPADS* No. A3353 (P/PPA/SH/21, HJM/A/SH/3, 12th June 1980) and note in 1981 S.P.L.P. 26. It should be noted, as Stephenson L.J. observed, that adopting a broad approach to the construction of this subsection does not prevent demolition or alteration of a structure; it merely requires consent to it.
15 See D. Hogarth, 'Listing and Property Transactions' 1983 S.P.L.P. 61.
16 i.e., the general or district planning authority.
17 It has been suggested that failure to notify an owner will not relieve him of liability for an offence under the listed building provisions (see [1980] J.P.L. 778, Practical Point).
18 S.D.D. consultation paper 'Listing and Listed Building Control' (1984) suggests that it would be possible to introduce a non-statutory right of appeal for owners against listing but that the case for a formal right of appeal against listing has not been made.

Special regard is paid to: (1) planned streets, villages or burghs; (2) works of well-known architects; (3) buildings associated with famous people or events; (4) good examples of buildings connected with social and industrial history and the development of communications.'[19]

The principles which govern the selection of buildings for listing are set out in greater detail in the S.D.D. Memorandum.

Buildings which are considered by the Secretary of State to be of special architectural or historic interest are divided for administrative purposes into three categories—A, B and C—according to their merit. These categories have no statutory significance. Many of the buildings considered to be of category 'C' quality are not in fact listed buildings—i.e., they are not included in the statutory list—but the Scottish Development Department is carrying out a review of these properties with a view to assessing their worthiness for inclusion in the statutory list. As at October 1984 there were 33,506 items on this statutory list, of which 2,242 were in category A, 23,125 in category B and 8,139 in category C.[20] More than 3,500 items were included in category C (non-statutory) and had still to be assessed for possible inclusion in the statutory list.

Effect of listing

The main effect of the listing of a building is that under s.53(1) of the 1972 Act any person who executes or causes to be executed any works for the demolition of the building or for its alteration or extension in any manner which would affect its character as a building of special architectural or historic interest is guilty of an offence unless written consent for the execution of such works (known as 'listed building consent') has been granted by the planning authority or by the Secretary of State.

A person guilty of an offence under s.53 is liable to a fine or imprisonment or both. In imposing a fine on a person convicted on indictment the court is to have regard to any financial benefit accruing to the offender in consequence of the offence (s.53(5)).

In proceedings for an offence under s.53 it is a defence to prove that the works were urgently necessary in the interests of safety or health,[21] or for the preservation of the building, and that written notice of the need for the works was given to the planning authority as soon as reasonably practicable (s.53(6)).

Under s.55 of the 1972 Act it is an offence for any person who, but for the section, would be acting within his legal rights, to commit or permit any act intended to cause damage to a listed building unless that action is taken in the course of works authorised by a specific consent under the Act.

As is indicated in the following section of this chapter, certain buildings are excluded from the operation of ss.53 and 55.

---

[19] S.D.D. consultation paper 'Listing and Listed Building Control' (1984) adds that special regard is also paid to landmarks.
[20] S.D.D. consultation paper 'Listing and Listed Building Control' (1984).
[21] See appeal decision reported in [1981] J.P.L. 835.

Ecclesiastical buildings and ancient monuments

There would seem to be no restriction on the type of building which can be listed. There are, however, two types of building which, though they may be listed, are not subject to the control over demolition, alteration or extension which normally follows upon the listing of a building. These are: (i) ecclesiastical buildings[22] for the time being used for ecclesiastical purposes (or which would be so used but for works for their demolition, alteration or extension) but excluding any building used or available for use by a minister of religion as a residence from which to perform the duties of his office; and (ii) buildings included in the schedule of monuments compiled and maintained under s.1 of the Ancient Monuments and Archaeological Areas Act 1979 (ss. 54(1), 55(1)).

It would seem, however, that listed building consent will be required in respect of the total demolition of a listed ecclesiastical building. In *Attorney-General (on the relation of Bedfordshire County Council)* v *Trustees of the Howard United Reformed Church, Bedford*[23] the House of Lords held that the words 'for the time being used for ecclesiastical purposes' referred to the time when the works were being carried out; at the time of its demolition a church cannot be said to be so used. Nor could it be said in this case that the ecclesiastical building in question would be used for ecclesiastical purposes 'but for the works' since the real reason why the building would have ceased to be so used was the decision of the owners to demolish it and not the carrying out of the demolition works. Only if an ecclesiastical building was being partially demolished and the works would not prevent the rest of the building being used once more for ecclesiastical purposes after the works had been completed could it be said that the building was not being used for ecclesiastical purposes because of demolition works.

Crown property

Although buildings which are Crown property may be listed, the statutory controls over listed buildings do not apply, subject to what is said below, to the Crown's interest in any such building (see s.253); a tenant of a listed building in Crown ownership would, however, require listed building consent for the demolition, alteration or extension of the building. Furthermore, in order to obtain the benefit of development value on a disposal of Crown land, listed building consent may now be obtained by the Crown in respect of such land but the consent will apply only to work carried out after the land has ceased to be Crown land.[24]

---

[22] As regards the exemption of ecclesiastical buildings see S.D.D. consultation paper 'Ecclesiastical Exemption from Listed Building Control in Scotland' (December 1984). On the meaning of the term 'ecclesiastical building' see *Attorney-General (on the relation of Bedfordshire C.C.)* v *Trustees of the Howard United Reformed Church, Bedford* [1976] A.C. 363.

[23] Above.

[24] See Town and Country Planning Act 1984, s.1; and the Town and Country Planning (Crown Land Applications) (Scotland) Regulations 1984.

Although government departments do not require listed building consent they will consult the appropriate planning authority whenever they propose to demolish a listed building or to alter or extend it in a way which would affect its character; the planning authority will publicise the proposals and if objections to the proposals are not withdrawn, any dispute will be determined by the Secretary of State after giving the parties an opportunity to express their views (see S.D.D. Circular 21/1984 and the Memorandum which accompanied it).

Building preservation notices

If it appears to the planning authority that a particular building in their area is of special architectural or historic interest but is not listed and is in danger of being demolished or of being altered in such a manner as would affect its character, the authority may employ the powers conferred upon them by s.56 of the 1972 Act to issue a building preservation notice[25] and thus place a temporary standstill on operations affecting the building. While a building preservation notice is in force with respect to a building the provisions of the 1972 Act[26] apply to the building as if it were listed (s.56(4)).

A building preservation notice must normally be served on the owner, lessee and occupier of the building and comes into force as soon as it is served (s.56(1), (3)). Where, however, it appears to the planning authority to be urgent that a building preservation notice should come into force, they may, instead of serving the notice in the normal way, simply affix the notice conspicuously to some object on the building; such action is to be treated as service of the notice (s.56(6)). After service of the notice the planning authority will ask the Secretary of State to consider listing the building. The notice remains in force for six months or until such earlier date as the Secretary of State lists the building or informs the authority of his intention not to list it (s.56(3)). There is no direct right of appeal against a building preservation notice but during the period that such a notice is in force application may be made for listed building consent and an appeal can be lodged against a refusal or conditional grant of such consent (below).

If the Secretary of State notifies the planning authority that he does not intend to list a building which was the subject of a building preservation notice,[27] the authority may not serve another such notice in respect of that building during the next twelve months (s.56(5)). A decision by the Secretary of State not to list the building may result in the planning authority having to pay compensation in respect of any loss or damage directly attributable to the effect of the building preservation notice (including any

---

[25] A building preservation notice cannot be served in respect of an 'excepted building', i.e., an ecclesiastical building which is for the time being used for ecclesiastical purposes or a building which is protected under the Ancient Monuments legislation (s.56(2)).

[26] Other than s.55, dealing with acts causing or likely to cause damage to listed buildings.

[27] The S.D.D. consultation paper 'Listing and Listed Building Control' (1984) states that the Department's Historic Buildings Inspectorate are very willing to provide informal advice as to whether or not a building is listable.

438 SCOTTISH PLANNING LAW AND PROCEDURE

sum payable in respect of a breach of contract due to the notice) to any person who had an interest in the building at the time the building preservation notice was served (see 1972 Act, s.162; and Listed Buildings Regulations, reg. 8).

When is listed building consent required?

Listed building consent is necessary where it is proposed to demolish a listed building[28] or to alter or extend such a building in a manner which would affect (in any way) its character as a building of special architectural or historic interest (s.53(1), (2)).[29] Listed building consent may therefore be necessary in respect of relatively minor works such as painting the front door of a listed building. Consent will be required for internal alterations which do not in any way affect the external appearance of the building but which affect the building's character in some way.

There may well be cases in which there is doubt as to whether proposed alterations will have an effect on the building's character and whether therefore listed building consent is required. There is no machinery for obtaining a formal determination of that question prior to the execution of works. Informal guidance on the range of features likely to contribute 'character' to buildings is given in Appendix 1 to the S.D.D. *Memorandum on Listed Buildings and Conservation Areas*.

Making and determination of application for listed building consent

The need for listed building consent is quite distinct from the requirement in an appropriate case to obtain planning permission.[30]

The procedure for making an application for listed building consent, set out in Schedule 10 to the 1972 Act and regulations 4 to 6 of the Listed Buildings Regulations,[31] is very similar to that governing an application for planning permission. Application for listed building consent is to be made to the planning authority in whose area the building is situated; it is to be made on a form issued by the planning authority and is to be accompanied by a plan sufficient to identify the building and by such other plans as are necessary to describe the proposed works. It would seem to be in the best

---

[28] 'Building' is defined in s.275(1) of the 1972 Act to include any part of a building, so that demolition of part of a building requires listed building consent.

[29] The Secretary of State for the Environment has expressed the view that the erection of a free-standing building within the curtilage of a listed building is not an extension—see [1984] J.P.L. 55. However, it would seem that, once erected, such a building becomes subject to listed building control. In a consultation paper issued on 31st July 1984, the S.D.D. suggested that this anomaly should be remedied by removing such buildings from listed building control unless they are listed in their own right. As to alteration affecting the character of a listed building, see [1984] J.P.L. 899.

[30] It is no longer possible for a grant of planning permission to operate also as listed building consent (s.66(2) of and Part 1 of Schedule 4 to the Local Government and Planning (Scotland) Act 1982, repealing s.54(2) of the 1972 Act).

[31] Regulation 6 was amended by the Town and Country Planning (Listed Buildings and Buildings in Conservation Areas) (Scotland) Amendment Regulations 1977.

interests of applicants to submit 'before' and 'after' plans; their absence may lead to enquiries and consequent delays (see para. 2.16 of the S.D.D. *Memorandum on Listed Buildings and Conservation Areas*). If the applicant is not himself the owner of the building, he must give notice in the prescribed form to all those persons who, at the beginning of the period of 21 days ending with the date of the application, were owners of any part of the land to which the application relates.

Every application for listed building consent must be publicised by the planning authority by means of (1) an advertisement in the Edinburgh Gazette and in a local newspaper; and (2) a notice displayed on or near the building in question for a period of at least 7 days. The application and all plans and documents are to be available for public inspection during the period specified in regulation 5 of the Listed Buildings Regulations.

The Secretary of State has directed that notification of any application for consent to demolish a listed building is to be given by the planning authority to the Royal Commission on the Ancient and Historical Monuments of Scotland (see para. 2.14 of the S.D.D. *Memorandum on Listed Buildings and Conservation Areas*).[32]

The planning authority are not to decide an application for listed building consent before the expiry of the period during which the application is available for public inspection; in determining the application the authority must take into account any representations received by them during that period (see reg. 5). The authority are also to take account of any representations made by an owner of any part of the land to which the application relates (reg. 6(3)).

In considering whether to grant listed building consent the planning authority or the Secretary of State, as the case may be, must have special regard to the desirability of preserving the building or its setting or any features of special architectural or historic interest which it possesses (s.54(3)[33]). Guidance as to the factors which planning authorities should take into account in operating listed building control is contained in the S.D.D. *Memorandum on Listed Buildings and Conservation Areas*; as regards applications for consent for demolition of a listed building the Memorandum states that 'the presumption should be in favour of preservation except where a strong case can be made out for a grant of permission to demolish . . . '[34] The Memorandum also declares that applications for the demolition of listed buildings 'should not . . . normally be considered in isolation from proposals for the after-use of the site'.

---

[32]   Note that works for the extension of a listed building may also involve the partial demolition of the building, thus requiring notification (see *R.* v *North Hertfordshire District Council, ex parte Sullivan* [1981] J.P.L. 752).

[33]   As amended by the Local Government and Planning (Scotland) Act 1982, s.48 and Schedule 2, para. 15(a)(ii).

[34]   See on this the appeal decisions noted at [1976] J.P.L. 706; [1978] J.P.L. 273 and 638; [1979] J.P.L. 255 and 496; [1981] J.P.L. 72, 304 and 306; and [1984] J.P.L. 363 and 679; and generally, P. H. Morgan and S. M. Nott, 'Listed Buildings—Planning Law and Planning Reality' [1980] J.P.L. 715. See too *Kent Messenger Ltd.* v *Secretary of State for the Environment* (1976) 241 E.G. 25.

If, having considered an application for listed building consent, the planning authority are disposed to grant consent they must notify the Secretary of State of that fact (see 1972 Act, Schedule 10, para. 5; and G.D.O., Art. 14). The purpose of this notification is to enable the Secretary of State to consider whether to 'call in' the application for decision by himself. If, after 28 days, or such longer period as the Secretary of State may in any particular case direct, the minister has not directed that the application be referred to him, or if the Secretary of State informs the authority that he does not intend to call in the application, the authority may then proceed to grant consent. Before determining an application which he has called in, the Secretary of State must, if either the applicant or the planning authority so desire, afford to each of them an opportunity of being heard by a person appointed for the purpose by the minister.

Listed building consent may be granted subject to conditions, including conditions as to:

(a) the preservation of particular features either as part of the building or after severance from it;

(b) the making good of any damage caused by the permitted works; and

(c) the reconstruction of the building (or part of it) after the execution of any works, with the use of original materials so far as practicable (s.54(4)[35]).

Where the consent is for the demolition of a listed building, the planning authority may impose a condition that no demolition shall take place until one or both of the following requirements have been met:

(a) an agreement regulating the development of the site of the listed building has been made and recorded under s.50 of the 1972 Act; and

(b) the planning authority are satisfied that contracts have been placed either for the redevelopment of the site or for its conversion to open space in accordance with a current planning permission.[36]

If, in the execution of works, there is a failure to comply with any condition attached to a grant of listed building consent, an offence is committed (s.53(4)). A failure to comply with a condition may also lead to listed building enforcement action.

Listed building consents granted on or after 1st November 1982 are to be subject to a condition that the works will commence within a specified period. If no period is specified by the planning authority in the consent, the

[35]   As amended by the Local Government and Planning (Scotland) Act 1982, s.48 and Schedule 2, para. 15(b). In a consultation paper issued on 31st July 1984 the S.D.D. suggested that planning authorities should be given express authority to impose a condition on a listed building consent requiring the later approval of the finer points of detail of the work to be carried out. It was also suggested that provision should be made for applications for the removal or variation of conditions attached to listed building consents.

[36]   Section 54(5) of the 1972 Act, substituted by the Local Government and Planning (Scotland) Act 1982, s.48 and Schedule 2, para 15(c). See, by way of example, the decision noted at [1984] J.P.L. 121.

period will be five years from the date of the grant.[37]

The date of the granting or refusal of a listed building application is the date the decision notice bears.[38]

Consent for demolition

Where listed building consent has been granted for the demolition of a listed building, the work is authorised only after the successful applicant has given notice of the proposed demolition to the Royal Commission on the Ancient and Historical Monuments of Scotland and thereafter the Commission have either been afforded access to the building for recording purposes for a period of at least three months or have stated in writing that they have completed their record or that they do not wish to record the building (s.53(2)(b)). Failure to observe this provision is an offence.

Application of listed building control to planning authorities

Where the planning authority themselves require listed building consent the application must be publicised in the ordinary way and is determined by the Secretary of State (see 1972 Act, s.257 (as substituted by s.7(2) of the Town and Country Amenities Act 1974); and Listed Buildings Regulations, reg. 11).

Appeal against refusal or conditional grant of listed building consent

If listed building consent is refused by the planning authority or is granted subject to conditions, or if the authority fail to give notice of their decision within two months, the applicant may appeal to the Secretary of State (see paras. 7 and 8 of Sched. 10 to the 1972 Act; and regs. 6 and 7 of the Listed Buildings Regulations). It is specifically provided that an appellant may include as one of the grounds of his appeal a claim that the building is not of special architectural or historic interest and ought to be removed from the list. If the parties to an appeal agree to dispense with an inquiry,[39] the appeal may, if the Secretary of State concurs, be decided on the basis of written submissions (see p. 487 below).

Enforcement of listed building control

Where unauthorised works have been carried out on a listed building, the

---

[37] 1972 Act, s.54A (inserted by the Local Government and Planning (Scotland) Act 1982, s.48 and Schedule 2, para. 16). The significance of 1st November 1982 is that it was the date on which this provision was brought into effect by the Local Government and Planning (Scotland) Act 1982 (Commencement No. 2) Order 1982. In the absence of any condition to the contrary, listed building consents granted prior to 1st January 1980 are deemed to be subject to a condition that the works shall commence within a period of 3 years from 1st November 1982; for consents issued between 1st January 1980 and 1st November 1982 the period is 5 years from 1st November 1982 (1972 Act, s.54A(3) and (4)).

[38] Section 54B of the 1972 Act (inserted by the Local Government and Planning (Scotland) Act 1982, s.48 and Schedule 2, para. 16).

[39] The arrangements for any such inquiry will be governed by the Town and Country Planning (Inquiries Procedure) (Scotland) Rules 1980.

planning authority may serve a 'listed building enforcement notice'.[40] The statutory provisions on enforcement of control over listed buildings, contained in ss.92 to 96 of the 1972 Act, are similar to the provisions for the enforcement of ordinary planning control (see chapter 13). The notice must specify either the steps required to restore the building to its former state or the steps required to bring the building to the state it would have been in if the terms and conditions of the listed building consent had been complied with. As a third alternative, the notice may, if complete restoration is not reasonably practicable or is undesirable having regard to the desirability of preserving the character of the building or its features of architectural or historic interest, specify the steps required to alleviate to the satisfaction of the planning authority the effects of the works carried out without listed building consent.[41] The notice must also specify the period within which the steps are to be taken (1972 Act, s.92(1)(b) and (c) and (1A)[42]).

A stop notice cannot be issued in connection with listed building enforcement action, presumably because the criminal offences created by the Act in relation to unauthorised works on listed buildings render such notices unnecessary.

Among the grounds (set out in s.93(1)) on which appeal may be made against a listed building enforcement notice are the following: (1) that the building is not of special architectural or historic interest; (2) that s.53 has not been contravened (i.e., that the works in question have not affected the character of the building); (3) that the works were urgently necessary in the interests of safety or health, or for the preservation of the building; and (4) that the steps required by the notice would not serve the purpose of restoring the character of the building to its former state.[43]

Revocation or modification of listed building consent

The statutory provisions on revocation or modification of listed building consent, set out in Part II of Schedule 10 to the 1972 Act,[44] are similar to those governing revocation or modification of planning permission (see chapter 16). Compensation may be claimed in respect of abortive expendi-

---

[40] The enforcement procedures and the criminal sanctions are not mutually exclusive but in some circumstances—for example, where a listed building is demolished without consent—the remedial character of the enforcement process will be of no avail.

[41] As to the operation of the somewhat differently worded provision in s.96(1)(b)(ii) of the Town and Country Planning Act 1971, see *Bath City Council* v *Secretary of State for the Environment* (1983) 47 P. & C.R. 663. Where steps to alleviate the effects of the works have been taken to the satisfaction of the authority, listed building consent is deemed to have been granted for the works in question (1972 Act, s.92(2A)).

[42] As amended by the Local Government and Planning (Scotland) Act 1982, s.48 and Schedule 2, para. 26. As to the Secretary of State's powers on appeal see *Bath City Council* (above).

[43] See too the three additional grounds added to s.93(1) of the 1972 Act by the Local Government and Planning (Scotland) Act 1982, s.48 and Schedule 2, para. 27(a)(ii).

[44] As amended by the Local Government and Planning (Scotland) Act 1982, s.66(2) and Schedule 4, Part 1.

ture and other loss or damage directly attributable to the making of a revocation or modification order (see 1972 Act, s.161; and Listed Buildings Regulations, reg. 8).

Compensation for refusal or conditional grant of listed building consent

Compensation is not payable in respect of the mere listing of a building. Nor is it payable in respect of a refusal of listed building consent to demolish a listed building.[45] Where an application for the alteration or extension of a listed building has been refused, or has been granted subject to conditions, compensation may be payable by the planning authority under s.160 of the 1972 Act. A claim for compensation under s.160 will only succeed if it can be shown:

(*a*) that the decision in question was made by the Secretary of State (either on appeal or on the reference of an application to him); and

(*b*) that the works in question either do not constitute development or, if they do constitute development, that permission for such works is granted by a development order (so that if the building had not been listed no express grant of permission would have been necessary); and

(*c*) that the value of the claimant's interest in the land is less than it would have been if listed building consent had been granted, or had been granted unconditionally, as the case may be.

Compensation is not payable on a refusal or conditional grant of listed building consent in respect of a building subject to a building preservation notice unless and until the building is listed; a claim may, however, be lodged prior to listing (s.162(2)).

Listed building purchase notice

On a refusal or conditional grant of listed building consent, or on the revocation or modification of such consent, an owner or lessee of the land may, if he considers that the land has become incapable of reasonably beneficial use, serve on the planning authority a listed building purchase notice (see 1972 Act, s.179 and Sched. 17). The statutory provisions on listed building purchase notices are broadly similar to those governing ordinary purchase notices (as to which see chapter 15).

Urgent works for preservation of unoccupied listed buildings

There is no obligation upon the owner of a listed building to maintain it in good condition.[46] However, s.97[47] of the 1972 Act enables the Secretary of

---

[45] It may be possible to serve a purchase notice in such a case.

[46] However, there seems to be no reason why a planning authority should not take action under s.63 of the 1972 Act (see p. 468 below) in respect of a listed building which constitutes a serious injury to amenity.

[47] As substituted by s.5(2) of the Town and Country Amenities Act 1974. See also s.87 of the Civic Government (Scotland) Act 1982 and the supporting enforcement powers.

State or the appropriate planning authority, on giving not less than 7 days notice to the owner of an unoccupied listed building, to take any steps urgently required for the preservation of the building.[48] The purpose of the requirement to give notice is to allow the owner an opportunity to make representations to the authority. In order that the owner may do this, the notice must adequately explain what works are proposed, although in judging the question of adequacy it must be borne in mind that this is an emergency procedure.[49]

The expenses of any works executed by the Secretary of State or by a planning authority under s.97 may be recovered from the owner of the building.[50] The owner is, however, entitled to represent to the Secretary of State that the amount claimed is unreasonable, or that recovery of the expenses would cause him hardship, or that some or all of the works were unnecessary for the building's preservation; following any such representations the amount to be recovered will be determined by the minister.

Compulsory acquisition of listed building in need of repair

Although there is no obligation upon the owner of a listed building to maintain it in good condition, either the planning authority or the Secretary of State may be authorised to acquire compulsorily any listed building[51] which is not being properly preserved (s.104 of the 1972 Act). The Secretary of State is only to make or confirm a compulsory purchase order for the acquisition of such a listed building if he is satisfied that it is expedient to preserve the building (s.104(4)).

As a preliminary to compulsory purchase proceedings under s.104 there must be served on the owner of the building a repairs notice specifying the works considered reasonably necessary for the preservation of the building (s.105). Notice of the making of the compulsory purchase order may not be served earlier than two months after service of the repairs notice (s.105(1)). If the repairs are carried out the authority will presumably not proceed with the acquisition. In any case, any person with an interest in the building may, within 28 days of the making of a compulsory purchase order under s.104, make application to the Sheriff, who will, if satisfied that reasonable steps

---

[48] 'Excepted buildings' as defined in s.56(2) of the 1972 Act (i.e., certain ecclesiastical buildings and ancient monuments) are excluded from this provision. As to the duty to consider the exercise of this power, see *R. v Stroud District Council, ex parte Goodenough* (1980) 43 P. & C.R. 59. In a consultation paper issued on 31st July 1984 the S.D.D. suggested that provision should be made for enabling a s.97 notice to be served in respect of the unoccupied part of a partially occupied building.

[49] See *R. v Secretary of State for the Environment, ex parte Hampshire County Council* (1981) 44 P. & C.R. 343; *R. v Camden London Borough Council, ex parte Comyn Ching and Co. (London) Ltd.* (1983) 47 P. & C.R. 417; and appeal decision noted in [1978] J.P.L. 637.

[50] It would seem that the provision cannot make the owner liable for continuing costs (*Hampshire County Council*, above).

[51] Other than an ecclesiastical building in use as such or an ancient monument. As a possible alternative to compulsory acquisition, see s.87 of the Civic Government (Scotland) Act 1982 and the supporting enforcement powers.

have been taken for preserving the building, make an order prohibiting further proceedings on the compulsory purchase order (s.104(6)).

Where the planning authority or the Secretary of State is satisfied that a listed building has been deliberately allowed to fall into disrepair for the purpose of justifying its demolition and the development or redevelopment of the site (or any adjoining site), there may be included in a compulsory purchase order under s.104 a direction for minimum compensation payable for the building (below). There is a right of appeal to the Sheriff against such a direction (s.107(5)).

Compensation on compulsory acquisition of listed building

Provision as to the compensation payable on compulsory acquisition of a listed building is made by s.106 of the 1972 Act, as amended by s.6 of the Town and Country Amenities Act 1974. In assessing such compensation it can be assumed that listed building consent would be granted for any works for the alteration or extension of the building. It can also be assumed that consent would be granted for the building's demolition for the purpose of 'existing use' development of the classes specified in Schedule 6 to the 1972 Act (see p. 388). It is not otherwise to be automatically assumed that listed building consent for demolition would be granted; this means that the compensation payable may well not reflect the value of the site for redevelopment. It will still be possible, however, to take account of the prospects of consent for demolition being granted.

In assessing compensation for a listed building acquired under a compulsory purchase order which contains a direction for minimum compensation (above), it is to be assumed that planning permission or listed building consent would be granted for development or works necessary for restoring the building to, and maintaining it in, a proper state of repair, but that permission or consent would not otherwise be granted at all (s.107(4)).

Grants and loans

Local authorities may contribute towards the cost of repair and maintenance of a building of architectural or historic interest[52] (see Local Authorities (Historic Buildings) Act 1962, as applied to Scotland by s.5 of the Civic Amenities Act 1967; and Town and Country Planning (Scotland) Act 1969, s.58). Under the Historic Buildings and Ancient Monuments Act 1953 (as amended by s.4 of the Civic Amenities Act 1967) the Secretary of State may make grants for the repair or maintenance of buildings of outstanding architectural or historic interest.[53] In certain circumstances, grants and loans may also be available from the National Heritage Memorial Fund.[54]

---

[52] The building need not be listed.

[53] In their Report for 1981–1982, the Historic Buildings Council for Scotland stated that, in view of the limited allocation of funds for grant aid, priority under all grant schemes would be given to immediately essential repairs which would significantly prolong the life of the building; see, too, the Report for 1982–83.

[54] See 1981 S.P.L.P. 12.

The relation between listed building control and other controls

We mentioned earlier that the need for listed building consent is quite distinct from the requirement in an appropriate case to obtain planning permission.[55] Nonetheless, the effect of a proposed development on a listed building and its setting is a matter which will be of concern in the exercise of normal development control powers. This is reflected in the statutory requirement for the planning authority to publicise a planning application which in their opinion will affect the setting of a listed building (see p. 98 above). Furthermore, in considering whether to grant planning permission for development which affects a listed building or its setting, the planning authority must have special regard to the desirability of preserving the building or its setting or any features of special architectural or historic interest which it possesses (see p. 439 above).

Difficult questions may arise over the relation between listed building control and other controls under, for example, the building, housing or environmental health legislation. The general position appears to be that as these separate codes each have their own distinct purpose, compliance with one does not remove an obligation to comply with another unless this is expressly stated.[56] Section 53(6) of the 1972 Act comes close to such an express statement. Although it does not remove the obligation to comply with listed building control, it does, as we indicated earlier, provide a defence to a prosecution for a breach of listed building control where the works are proved to have been urgently necessary in the interests of safety or health, or for the preservation of the building.

Section 54C of the 1972 Act[57] also has some bearing on the relation between listed building and other controls although it contains no express statement removing the obligation to comply with listed building control. It provides that where a local authority (1) have under any enactment served a notice requiring any person to show cause why a listed building should not conform to the building regulations; or (2) have under any enactment served a notice or made an order requiring the demolition of a listed building or the carrying out of works affecting such a building; or (3) propose (whether under any enactment or otherwise) to carry out emergency works or demolitions affecting such a building, they must forthwith give written notification to the planning authority. Exceptionally, where delay in giving such notification might prejudice public safety, it will be sufficient if such notification (which may in these circumstances initially be oral) is given as soon as may be practicable before commencement of the demolition or works. The object of the provision would seem to be to alert the planning

---

[55] Although the display of outdoor advertisements is controlled under the Town and Country Planning (Control of Advertisements) (Scotland) Regulations 1984, consent under the regulations does not relieve the intending advertiser of the need to comply with listed building control if the advertisement is to be displayed on a listed building in such a manner as to affect its character (see reg. 34 and S.D.D. Circular 10/1984, para. 36).

[56] See s.274 of the 1972 Act. See also, by way of example, s.17(2) of the Building (Scotland) Act 1959.

[57] Inserted by the Local Government and Planning (Scotland) Act 1982, s.42.

authority to the intended operations in good time to enable them to decide how to exercise their powers under the listed building provisions and in particular, whether to exercise their powers to make a grant in aid of repairs, to serve a repairs notice or to carry out urgent repairs themselves where the building is unoccupied.[58]

Although the general position appears to be that compliance with one code of legislation does not remove an obligation to comply with another, it seems that the courts may, in exceptional circumstances, be willing to accord one code precedence over another where the two codes have produced an impasse. In *Glasgow District Council* v *Secretary of State for Scotland*[59] a building warrant was issued for the partial demolition of a building which had been identified by the building authority as in an unsafe condition. Planning permission for the work was, however, refused because of the adverse effect it would have on the future development of the site and on visual amenity. In view of the impasse between planning and building control, the matter could only be resolved by giving precedence to one code. Common sense suggested that public safety should prevail over planning principle. The Court of Session, construing the planning legislation so as to avoid absurdity, concluded that work carried out in the interests of public safety under compulsion from the building authority was exempt from the requirement to obtain planning permission. Whilst it is possible to visualise a similar conflict between listed building control and other controls, it is probable that the statutory defence in s.53(6) of the 1972 Act referred to above would render intervention by the courts unnecessary.

C. CONSERVATION AREAS

Designation of conservation areas

Under s.262[60] of the 1972 Act every planning authority must from time to time determine which parts of their district are areas of special architectural or historic interest, the character or appearance of which it is desirable to preserve or enhance; they are to designate such areas as conservation areas. Designation of a conservation area does not require the approval of the Secretary of State but notice of any such designation (and of the variation or cancellation of any designation) must be given to the minister[61] (s.262(6)). Notice of any such designation, variation or cancellation, with particulars of its effect, is to be published in the Edinburgh Gazette and in at least one local newspaper (s.262(7)). Owners and occupiers of property in the area do not

---

[58] As to the duty to consider the exercise of these powers see *R.* v *Stroud District Council, ex parte Goodenough* (1980) 43 P. & C.R. 59.

[59] 1980 S.C. 150; 1982 S.L.T. 28.

[60] As substituted by s.2(1) of the Town and Country Amenities Act 1974.

[61] As at 1st August 1984, 470 designations had been notified to the minister.

have to be individually notified of action under s.262, nor do they have any right of appeal against such action.[62]

The Secretary of State can himself designate any area as a conservation area (s.262(4)).

The main effects of the designation of an area as a conservation area are outlined below.

Preservation and enhancement of conservation area

Designation of a conservation area should, in the words of the S.D.D. *Memorandum on Listed Buildings and Conservation Areas*,[63] 'only be a preliminary to action to preserve or enhance its character and appearance'.

There is imposed on the planning authority and any other appropriate body a general duty to pay special attention to the desirability of preserving or enhancing the character or appearance of a conservation area whenever they are exercising functions under the 1972 Act or under Part 1 of the Historic Buildings and Ancient Monuments Act 1953 or under the Local Authorities (Historic Buildings) Act 1962 (1972 Act, s.262(8)).

More particularly, under s.262B[64] of the 1972 Act it is the duty of the planning authority to formulate and to publish, from time to time, proposals for the preservation and enhancement of any conservation area in their district. These proposals are to be submitted to a public meeting in the area to which they relate and the planning authority are to have regard to any views expressed by persons attending the meeting.

Development affecting conservation area

One of the objects of the statutory provisions on conservation areas is to stimulate public interest in the preservation or enhancement of the amenity of such areas. In furtherance of this objective it is provided that publicity must be given by the planning authority to any application for planning permission for development which would, in the opinion of the authority, affect the character or appearance of a conservation area (1972 Act, s.25—see p. 198 above). In considering any such application the planning authority must take into account any representations relating to the application (see p. 205 above). The S.D.D. *Memorandum on Listed Buildings and Conservation Areas* suggests that planning authorities should always ask for detailed plans of proposed development within a conservation area rather than grant permission in outline form (see para. 3.30).

Control of demolition in conservation area

Demolition of unlisted buildings in conservation areas is brought under

---

[62]   The S.D.D. consultation paper 'Listing and Listed Building Control' (1984) recommends that planning authorities should consider including proposals for new or extended conservation areas in their local plans.

[63]   Issued to planning authorities with S.D.D. Circular 4/1976. See generally on the subject of conservation areas C. Mynors, 'Conservation Areas: Protecting the Familiar and Cherished Local Scene' [1984] J.P.L. 144 and 235.

[64]   Added by s.2(1) of the Town and Country Amenities Act 1974.

control by s.262A[65] of the 1972 Act. The effect of that section is to apply (with exceptions and modifications[66]) certain of the statutory provisions on listed buildings to buildings in a conservation area. A building[67] to which the provisions of s.262A apply (see below) must not be demolished unless listed building consent[68] has first been obtained.[69] An application for such consent is to be made separately from any application for planning permission.[70] If the planning authority are disposed to grant consent for demolition of a building in a conservation area they must, as with ordinary applications for listed building consent (see p.440 above), notify the Secretary of State. Any consent will be of limited duration.[71]

The S.D.D. *Memorandum on Listed Buildings and Conservation Areas* declares (para. 3.25) that where it is clear that demolition of a building in a conservation area will be followed by redevelopment of the site, 'consent to demolish should in general be given only where there are acceptable and detailed plans for that redevelopment'. In *Richmond upon Thames London Borough Council* v *Secretary of State for the Environment*[72] it was held that in considering an application for consent to demolish a building in a conservation area, the planning authority or the Secretary of State may legitimately take account of the merits of any proposed redevelopment of the site.

These statutory controls on demolition apply to all buildings in conservation areas other than:

(*a*) listed buildings (which are already subject to the statutory controls outlined above);

(*b*) 'excepted buildings' within the meaning of s.56(2) of the 1972 Act (i.e., certain ecclesiastical buildings and ancient monuments)[73]; and

(*c*) buildings excluded from the operation of s.262A by direction of the Secretary of State under s.262A(4).

In pursuance of his powers under s.262A(4) the Secretary of State has

---

[65] Added by s.2(1) of the Town and Country Amenities Act 1974.
[66] See reg. 13 of, and Schedule 6 to, the Town and Country Planning (Listed Buildings and Buildings in Conservation Areas) (Scotland) Regulations 1975.
[67] Since the word 'building' is defined in s.275(1) of the 1972 Act as including 'any part of a building', it would seem that partial demolition of a building in a conservation area will be subject to the statutory controls.
[68] The statutory provisions on listed building consent are outlined above (see, in particular, p. 438).
[69] The provisions of s.54C of the 1972 Act dealing with the intimation of notices and orders requiring, amongst other things, the demolition of listed buildings, are applied to the demolition of unlisted buildings in conservation areas (see Local Government and Planning (Scotland) Act 1982, s.48 and Schedule 2, para. 38(b); and generally p. 446 above).
[70] See the Local Government and Planning (Scotland) Act 1982, s.66(2) and Schedule 4.
[71] See s.54A of the 1972 Act, as applied by s.262A(8) (as amended by the Local Government and Planning (Scotland) Act 1982, s.48 and Schedule 2, para. 38(b)).
[72] (1978) 37 P. & C.R. 151; see also *Westminster City Council* v *Secretary of State for the Environment, The Times*, 24th March 1984.
[73] See p. 436 above.

directed[74] that s.262A is not to apply to the following descriptions of buildings:

(i) buildings with a capacity not exceeding 115 cubic metres (4000 cubic feet);

(ii) any building within the curtilage of a dwellinghouse and erected in pursuance of the permission granted by Article 3 of the Town and Country Planning (General Development) (Scotland) Order 1981 as coming within any of the descriptions of development in Class 1 of Schedule 1 to that Order;

(iii) gates, fences, walls or other means of enclosure erected in pursuance of the permission granted by Article 3 of the G.D.O. as coming within the description of development in Class II of Schedule 1 to that Order;

(iv) temporary buildings erected in pursuance of the permission granted by Article 3 of the G.D.O. as coming within the description of development in Class IV(1) of Schedule 1 to that Order;

(v) agricultural buildings erected in pursuance of the permission granted by Article 3 of the G.D.O. as coming within the description of development in Class V(1) of Schedule 1 to that Order;

(vi) industrial buildings erected in pursuance of the permission granted by Article 3 of the G.D.O. as coming within the description of development in Class VII(1) of Schedule 1 to that Order;

(vii) any building required to be demolished by virtue of a discontinuance order made under s.49 of the 1972 Act;

(viii) any building required to be demolished by virtue of any provision of an agreement made under s.50 of the 1972 Act;

(ix) any building in respect of which the requirements of any effective enforcement notice served under s.84 or s.92 of the 1972 Act require its demolition, in whole or in part, however expressed;

(x) any building required to be demolished by virtue of a condition of a planning permission granted under s.26 of the 1972 Act;

(xi) any building included in an operative clearance order or compulsory purchase order made under Part III of the Housing (Scotland) Act 1966, when the order was made prior to the designation of the conservation area;

(xii) any building which is the subject of a demolition order under Part II of the Housing (Scotland) Act 1966, when the order was made prior to the designation of the conservation area;

(xiii) any building included in an operative compulsory purchase order made under Part I of the Housing (Scotland) Act 1969 which is to be demolished in pursuance of a housing treatment area resolution under s.4 of that Act, when the order was made prior to the designation of the conservation area;

(xiv) any building included in an operative compulsory purchase order made under Part II of the Housing (Scotland) Act 1974 which is to be demolished in pursuance of a final housing action area resolution under s.20

[74] See S.D.D. Circular 28/1980.

of that Act, when the order was made prior to the designation of the conservation area.

The Crown and conservation area consent

In order to permit the Crown to obtain the benefit of development value on a disposal of Crown land, 'conservation area consent' may be obtained by the appropriate Crown body in respect of the demolition of Crown buildings in a conservation area.[75] Such a consent applies only to work carried out after the land has ceased to be Crown land.

Urgent works for preservation of unoccupied buildings

If the Secretary of State is satisfied, in the case of an unlisted unoccupied building in a conservation area, that it is important to preserve the building for the purpose of maintaining the character or appearance of the conservation area, he may direct that s.97[76] of the 1972 Act is to apply to that building (s.97(1)–(3)). Any works urgently necessary for the preservation of the building may then be carried out by the planning authority or the Secretary of State (see p. 443 above).

Protection of trees in conservation areas

Special provision is made by the 1972 Act for the preservation of trees in a conservation area (see p. 467 below).

Control of advertisements in conservation areas

Under s.61(3)[77] of the 1972 Act the Secretary of State is empowered, in making regulations for the control of advertisements, to make special provision concerning the control of advertisements in conservation areas. Regulations making such special provision have not yet been made.

Financial assistance for conservation areas

Under s.10 of the Town and Country Planning (Amendment) Act 1972 the Secretary of State may give financial assistance by way of grant or loan towards expenditure incurred in the preservation or enhancement of the character of a conservation area of outstanding architectural or historic interest.[78]

---

[75] See Town and Country Planning Act 1984, s.1; and the Town and Country Planning (Crown Land Applications) (Scotland) Regulations 1984.

[76] As substituted by s.5(2) of the Town and Country Amenities Act 1974.

[77] As substituted by s.3(2) of the Town and Country Amenities Act 1974. See S.D.D. Circular 10/1984 as to the designation of a conservation area as an area of special control for advertisements.

[78] As at 1st August 1984, 141 conservation areas had been classified as outstanding. On the question of financial assistance see S.D.D. consultation paper 'Listing and Listed Building Control' (1984)

D. CONTROL OF ADVERTISEMENTS

Because of widespread concern in the late 1940s about the effects of uncontrolled advertising, outdoor advertisements[79] have been subjected to a complex and largely self-contained code of control. This code is currently contained in the Town and Country Planning (Control of Advertisements) (Scotland) Regulations 1984.[80] The central provision of the 1984 Regulations is regulation 5 which declares that no advertisement may be displayed without consent granted in that behalf by the planning authority or the Secretary of State or deemed to be granted by virtue of the regulations themselves.

The display of an advertisement may, of course, involve development—an operation such as the erection of an advertisement hoarding would, for example, constitute development and s.19(4) of the 1972 Act specifically provides that the use for the display of advertisements of any external part of a building not normally used for that purpose is to be treated as involving a material change of use—but planning permission is deemed to be granted in respect of any advertisement which is displayed in accordance with the regulations and in such a case no application for planning permission is necessary (see 1972 Act, s.62).

Extent of control

The word 'advertisement' is given a very wide definition in the 1984 Regulations and includes a hoarding or tethered balloon as well as the actual advertising material placed thereon (see reg. 2(1)).[81] The word 'site' in relation to an advertisement means any land or building (other than an advertisement as defined in the 1984 Regulations) on which an advertisement is displayed.[82] An express grant of consent under the regulations permits the use of the site in question for the display of any advertisement in the manner authorised by the consent, whether by the erection of a structure on the site or otherwise (reg. 4(4)).

The scope of the advertisement regulations is wide. They apply to all advertisements except:

(*a*) an advertisement displayed within a building, unless the advertisement is displayed so as to be visible from outside that building and is either:

---

[79]   Certain advertisements displayed within a building are also subject to control—see Town and Country Planning (Control of Advertisements) (Scotland) Regulations 1984, reg. 3(1)(a) and (2), although some of these advertisements will have the benefit of the deemed consent provisions (below).

[80]   Made under ss. 61, 101, 165 and 273 of the 1972 Act. See also S.D.D. Circular 10/1984. Regulation 33(2) provides that any consents, notices, etc. given or made under the previous Regulations will continue in force as though made under the new Regulations.

[81]   See also 1972 Act, s.275.

[82]   But see reg. 3(4) as regards the definition of 'site' for the purposes of the display in certain circumstances of an advertisement on, or consisting of, a tethered balloon.

(i) illuminated, or

(ii) displayed within a building used principally for the display of advertisements, or

(iii) an advertisement any part of which is within 1 metre of any external door or window (reg. 3(1)(a) and (2));

(b) an advertisement displayed on a vehicle or vessel normally employed as a moving vehicle or vessel. The exception will not, however, apply during any period when such a vehicle or vessel is being used primarily for the display of advertisements (reg. 3(1)(b));

(c) an advertisement incorporated in, and forming part of the fabric of, a building (and not merely affixed to or painted on a building), other than a building used principally for advertisements or a hoarding or similar structure (reg. 3(1)(c));

(d) an advertisement displayed on 'enclosed land'[83] and not readily visible from outside the enclosure or from any part of such enclosure over which there is a public right of way or access (reg. 3(1)(d));

(e) an advertisement displayed on or consisting of a tethered balloon flown at a height of more than 60 metres above ground level[84] (reg. 3(1)(e));

(f) an advertisement displayed on or consisting of a balloon tethered to a site[85] which is not within an area of special control, a conservation area or an area designated by the Secretary of State[86] for the purpose of conserving the natural beauty and amenity of the countryside, provided:

(i) no more than one such advertisement is displayed on the site at any one time and,

(ii) the site is not used for the display of such advertisements on more than 10 days in any calendar year (reg. 3(3) and (4));

(g) an advertisement displayed on an article for sale or on the package or container in which an article is sold, or displayed on the pump, dispenser or other container from which an article, gas or liquid is sold, provided such advertisement:

(i) refers wholly to the article, gas or liquid, and

(ii) is not illuminated, and

(iii) does not exceed 0.1 square metre in area (reg. 3(1)(f)).

---

[83] As defined in reg. 2(1).

[84] Including the height of any building to which it is moored. See also reg. 2(3). Advertising by way of tethered balloon had previously been unlawful so that no provision was made in earlier Advertisement Control Regulations. Following the relaxation contained in the Civil Aviation (Aerial Advertising) (Captive Balloons) Regulations 1984 provision has now been made tying this type of advertising into the general framework of advertisement control. Advertisement by tethered balloon at a height exceeding 60 metres above ground level and 'free flight' advertising remain outside the scope of the Advertisement Control Regulations.

[85] As defined for the purposes of reg. 3(3) in reg. 3(4). See also reg. 2(3) and S.D.D. Circular 10/1984, para. 10.

[86] By way of direction under reg. 3(3). In exercise of this power the Secretary of State has made the Town and Country Planning (Control of Tethered Balloon Advertisements in National Scenic Areas) (Scotland) Direction 1984 (see S.D.D. Circular 10/1984, Annex B); this removes the benefit of exemption from control in respect of sites in National Scenic Areas (see p. 184 above).

Subject to these exceptions, no advertisement is to be displayed unless it has express consent granted under the regulations or unless consent is deemed to be granted by the regulations themselves.

Deemed consent: the specified classes

The six classes of advertisement specified in Schedule 4 to the Regulations fall within the scope of the Regulations but may be displayed without express consent[87] from the planning authority because consent is deemed to be granted by virtue of reg. 10. The six classes are as follows:

Class I. Functional advertisements of local authorities, community councils, statutory undertakers and public transport undertakers.

Class II. Miscellaneous advertisements relating to the land on which they are displayed, e.g. direction signs, business nameplates and hotel signs.

Class III. Certain advertisements of a temporary nature, e.g. notices relating to the sale of land or the sale of goods or livestock, signs relating to the carrying out of building work by contractors, announcements of local events and advertisements on hoardings enclosing land designated in the development plan primarily for commerial, industrial or business purposes and on which building operations are taking place.

Class IV. Advertisements displayed on business premises[88] with reference to all or any of the following matters: the business carried on, the goods sold[89] or services provided, and the name and qualification of the person carrying on the business or manufacturing or supplying the goods or services on the premises. Also included are advertisements displayed on the forecourt of business premises wholly with reference to the matters specified above.

Class V. Certain advertisements displayed within any building and not exempted from control by reg. 3(2).

Class VI. Illuminated advertisements displayed on business premises wholly with reference to all or any of the following matters: the business carried on, the goods sold and services provided, and the name or names and qualifications of the person or persons carrying on the business or providing the goods or services on the premises.

---

[87] If, however, application is made for express consent in respect of any advertisement falling within one of the classes specified in Schedule 4, then on determination of that application the provisions of reg. 10 (whereby advertisements may be displayed without express consent) cease to apply to that advertisement (see reg. 10(2) and (3)).

[88] The term 'business premises' is defined in reg. 2(1). On the interpretation of the term see *Dominant Sites Ltd.* v *Berkshire C.C.* (1955) 6 P. & C.R. 10; *Cooper* v *Bailey* (1956) 6 P. & C.R. 261; and *Jones* v *Merioneth C.C.* (1968) 20 P. & C.R. 106. Certain dicta in *Heron Service Stations Ltd.* v *Coupe* [1973] 1 W.L.R. 502 may also be relevant, although the case concerned the somewhat different definition of 'business premises' in the English regulations of 1969.

[89] On the scope of this phrase see *Arthur Maiden Ltd.* v *Lanark County Council (No. 1)* [1958] J.P.L. 417 (Sh.Ct.).

In most of the above cases the advertisement must not exceed a specified surface area, must not contain letters or figures[90] exceeding a specified height, must not be placed more than a specified height above the ground and must not (with the exception of Class VI) be illuminated. In addition to any conditions mentioned in Schedule 4, any advertisement falling within the above six classes is subject to the five standard conditions specified in Parts I and II of Schedule 1 (reg. 6 below) and may be the subject of discontinuance action by the planning authority (reg. 14 below). The Secretary of State has power, in response to representations made to him by the planning authority, to exclude the application of reg. 10 in any particular case or in a particular area (reg. 11).

Deemed consent: other advertisements

The following types of advertisement may also be displayed without express consent:

(1) Where a site was being used for the display of advertisements on 16th August 1948 the site may continue to be so used without express consent (reg. 13(1)). Certain specified conditions[91] must, however, be observed (reg. 13(3)) in addition to the standard conditions prescribed in Schedule 1. These sites may be the subject of discontinuance action by the planning authority (below).

(2) The display of election notices, statutory advertisements and traffic signs may be undertaken without express consent (see reg. 12). Certain specified conditions must, however, be observed (reg. 12(2)) in addition to the standard conditions prescribed in Schedule 1.[92]

(3) Consent is in certain circumstances deemed to be granted for the continued display of advertisements for which express consent has expired (see reg. 19 below).

Discontinuance action for advertisements displayed with deemed consent

The 1984 Regulations introduced a discontinuance procedure to replace the more cumbersome challenge procedure provided under the Town and Country Planning (Control of Advertisements) (Scotland) Regulations 1961.[93]

Regulation 14 provides that the planning authority may serve a notice requiring the discontinuance of the display of an advertisement displayed

---

[90] The previous Regulations referred to 'letters, figures, symbols, emblems or devices'. As to the scope of that phrase see *Arthur Maiden Ltd.* v *Lanark County Council (No. 1)* [1958] J.P.L. 417; and *McDonald* v *Howard Cook Advertising Ltd.* [1972] 1 W.L.R. 90.

[91] There must not, for example, be any substantial alteration in the manner of use of the site. That limitation was considered in *Arthur Maiden Ltd.* v *Lanark County Council (No. 2)* [1958] J.P.L. 422 (Sh.Ct.). See also *Arthur Maiden Ltd.* v *Royal Burgh of Kirkcaldy*, Sheriff Court, Kirkcaldy, 18th November 1965 (unreported, but see comment at 1980 S.P.L.P. 22); and *Mills and Allen* v *City of Glasgow District Council* 1980 S.L.T. (Sh.Ct.) 85.

[92] But see the exceptions noted in reg. 6.

[93] See S.D.D. Circular 10/1984, paras. 11–14.

with deemed consent[94] or the discontinuance of the use of a site for the display of such an advertisement. The authority may only invoke the procedure if they consider it 'expedient to do so to remedy a substantial injury to the amenity of the locality or a danger to members of the public' (reg. 14(1)). The notice must be served on the person displaying the advertisement and on the owner, lessee and occupier of the land on which it is displayed.

The discontinuance notice must specify the advertisement or site to which it relates, the period within which the display or use is to be discontinued and must contain a statement of the authority's reasons for serving the notice. The notice must also specify the period (not being less than 28 days after service) at the end of which it will take effect; however, if within that period an appeal is lodged with the Secretary of State, the notice will be of no effect pending the determination or withdrawal of the appeal (see below for a description of the appeal process).

Principles of control

Where express consent is required for the display of advertisements the powers conferred by the 1984 Regulations with respect to the grant or refusal of consent (and with respect to the revocation or modification of such consent—see regs. 22 and 23 below) are exercisable *only* in the interests of amenity or public safety (1972 Act, s.61(1); 1984 Regulations, reg. 4(1)). 'A planning authority cannot therefore', states S.D.D. Circular 10/1984, 'concern themselves with the content or subject matter of an advertisement,[95] nor can they consider whether there is a need for any particular advertisement. Express consent cannot be refused because the planning authority consider the advertisement to be unnecessary or offensive to public morals. Each application for express consent must be considered on its own merits.'[96] Regulation 4(2) requires planning authorities in exercising their powers to have regard to certain particular aspects of amenity and public safety; the provision is, however, expressed to be 'without prejudice to their power to have regard to any other material factor'.

Procedure for obtaining express consent

The procedure for obtaining express consent for the display of an advertisement is very similar to that for obtaining planning permission—see regs. 15 to 17. The appropriate fee must accompany the application.[97] The planning authority may grant consent subject to the standard conditions specified in Part I of Schedule 1 to the Regulations (below) and to such additional conditions as they think fit, or may refuse consent (see reg. 17).

---

[94] This power does not extend to election notices, statutory notices and traffic signs (see reg. 14(1)).
[95] See also 1972 Act, s.61(8).
[96] Para. 18.
[97] See the Town and Country Planning (Fees for Applications and Deemed Applications) (Scotland) Regulations 1983, reg. 9.

Every grant of express consent must be for a fixed period (see reg. 18). This will be five years unless the planning authority specify a longer or shorter period in the consent. Where a shorter period is specified, the authority must, unless the application was for such shorter period, state in writing their reasons for doing so.

Within the six months preceding the expiry of an express consent, application may be made for renewal of the consent (reg. 18(5)). After expiry of an express consent, however, the advertisement may continue to be displayed unless the consent was granted subject to a condition requiring removal of the advertisement at the expiry of the period specified in the consent or unless renewal of consent has been refused (reg. 19(1)). An advertisement which continues to be displayed with such deemed consent may be the subject of discontinuance action by the authority (see reg. 14 above).

An express consent for the display of an advertisement may be revoked or modified in the interests of amenity or public safety, subject to a possible claim for compensation (see regs. 22 and 23).

Appeal to the Secretary of State

An appeal may be made to the Secretary of State against the refusal by a planning authority to grant express consent; against the grant of express consent subject to conditions; against a deemed refusal arising from the non-determination of an application for express consent; and against a discontinuance notice. Regulation 21 prescribes the procedure for making such an appeal.[98]

Written notice of appeal, stating the grounds on which the appeal is based, is to be given to the Secretary of State within six months from the receipt of notification of the planning authority's decision or within six months of the end of the period within which the decision should have been given. An appeal against a discontinuance notice must be submitted within twenty-eight days of the service of the notice. The appellant must furnish to the Secretary of State within twenty-eight days from giving notice of appeal copies of the documents specified in reg. 21(3). The planning authority, for their part, are required to submit a statement in writing of their observations on the appeal together with two sets of photographs of the site and its surroundings within twenty eight days from the date when the Secretary of State advises them of the appeal (reg. 21(4); and S.D.D. Circular 10/1984, para. 30).

Before determining an appeal, the Secretary of State will, if either the appellant or the planning authority so desire, afford each of them an opportunity of appearing before and being heard by a person appointed by the minister. The Secretary of State expects, however, that appeals will normally be determined on the basis of written submissions supplemented by photographs.[99]

---

[98]   See also S.D.D. Circular 10/1984, paras. 27–35.
[99]   S.D.D. Circular 10/1984, para. 28.

Standard conditions

The five standard conditions to which reference has been made above are contained in Schedule 1 to the 1984 Regulations. Save as otherwise provided in the regulations, the first four standard conditions, set out in Part I of Schedule 1, apply to all consents granted by or under the regulations (see reg. 6). These conditions provide (1) that all advertisements must be kept clean and tidy; (2) that hoardings etc. must be maintained in a safe condition; (3) that when an advertisement is required to be removed under the regulations, the removal shall be carried out to the reasonable satisfaction of the planning authority; and (4) that before an advertisement is displayed on land the permission of the owner of that land or other person entitled to grant permission is to be obtained.[1]

The fifth of the standard conditions, set out in Part II of Schedule 1, provides that an advertisement must not obscure any road, rail or air traffic signal or aid to navigation and must not render hazardous the use of any road, railway, waterway or airfield. Since these matters will have been taken into account by the planning authority in granting any express consent, this condition applies only to advertisements displayed with deemed consent or with consent granted under reg. 27 (below).

Advertisements relating to travelling circuses and fairs

Regulation 27 provides that consent may be granted, subject to the standard conditions and also to the conditions set out in regulation 27(2), for the temporary display on unspecified sites of posters, etc. relating to the visit of a travelling circus or fair.

Enforcement and offences

Regulation 24 of the 1984 Regulations makes provision for the service by the planning authority of an enforcement notice in any case where it appears that an advertisement has been displayed without consent required in that behalf or that any conditions have not been complied with.[2] Such a notice should be served on the owner, lessee and occupier of the land and also on any person known to the authority to be displaying the advertisement.[3]

An enforcement notice must specify the advertisement which is alleged to have been displayed without consent or the matters in respect of which it is alleged that there has been a failure to comply with any condition. The notice must also specify the steps required to be taken; it may, in addition,

---

[1] For advice on the problem of 'fly posting' see S.D.D. Circular 10/1984, para. 37.

[2] In a case where an advertisement is displayed otherwise than in accordance with the regulations, and the display of that advertisement involves development, there is nothing to prevent the planning authority serving an enforcement notice under s.84 of the 1972 Act alleging a breach of planning control instead of serving a notice under the 1984 Regulations alleging display of an advertisement without consent. For examples of the use of 'ordinary' enforcement powers in relation to advertisements see *SPADS* Nos. A2059 (P/ENA/GLW/71, 7th April 1976); and A2133 (P/ENA/GLW/70, 8th July 1976).

[3] As to the circumstances in which a person is to be taken as displaying an advertisement see reg. 2(2).

specify steps to be taken within a given period which would render the display of advertisements acceptable to the planning authority.

The notice will take effect on a date to be specified in the notice which will normally be twenty-eight days from the date of the latest service of the notice, but in cases of extreme urgency may be seven days (reg. 24(4)).

Appeal against an enforcement notice lies to the Secretary of State (reg. 25(1)).[4] An appeal may be lodged in writing, before the notice takes effect, on any of the grounds specified in regulation 25(1)(a)–(d) and operates to suspend the notice pending final determination or withdrawal of the appeal. Before reaching a decision on an appeal, the Secretary of State must, if either the planning authority or the appellant so desire, afford to each of them an opportunity of appearing before and being heard by a person appointed by him for that purpose.

If steps required by an enforcement notice to be taken (other than the discontinuance of a use) are not taken within the period specified in the notice, the planning authority may enter on the land and take those steps themselves (see reg. 26).

Whether or not an enforcement notice has been served, the display of an advertisement in contravention of the provisions of the 1984 Regulations is an offence and a person guilty of such an offence is liable on summary conviction to a fine and to a daily penalty in the case of a continuing offence (see 1972 Act, s.101(2); and 1984 Regulations, reg. 7).[5] For the purposes of these provisions, and without prejudice to their generality, a person is deemed to display an advertisement if the advertisement is displayed on land of which he is the owner or occupier or if the advertisement gives publicity to his goods, trade, business or other concerns; such a person is not, however, to be guilty of an offence if he proves that the advertisement was displayed without his knowledge or consent (see 1972 Act, s.101(3)).

Compensation

Only in two sets of circumstances is compensation payable by the planning authority in connection with advertisement control. First, compensation may be payable on revocation or modification of any express consent for the display of an advertisement (see regs. 22 and 23). Secondly, where any person, for the purpose of complying with any of the regulations, carries out works for the removal of an advertisement which was being displayed on 16th August 1948 or for the discontinuance of the use of a site used for the display of advertisements on that date, he will be entitled to his reasonable expenses from the planning authority (1972 Act, s.165; and 1984 Regulations, reg. 30).

[4]   This replaces the provision in the 1961 Regulations which stipulated an appeal to the sheriff who exercised more limited powers than those now available to the Secretary of State.
[5]   See the Criminal Procedure (Scotland) Act 1975, ss. 289F and 289G (as inserted by the Criminal Justice Act 1982, s.54); also the Local Government and Planning (Scotland) Act 1982, Schedule 2, para. 31. It is a defence to show that the advertisement was displayed without the accused's knowledge (s.101(3) of the 1972 Act); and see *John* v *Reveille Newspapers Ltd.* (1955) 5 P. & C.R. 95. On the matter of continuing offences see *Royal Borough of Kensington and Chelsea* v *Elmton Ltd.* (1978) 245 E.G. 1011.

Areas of special control

Rural areas or areas other than rural areas which appear to the Secretary of State to require special protection on grounds of amenity[6] may be defined as areas of special control. An order defining an area of special control is made by the planning authority; it requires the approval of the Secretary of State (see reg. 8). The procedure for defining an area of special control is set out in Schedule 2 to the 1984 Regulations.

The effect of such an order is to restrict very considerably the types of advertisement which may be displayed in the area (see reg. 9).

Under s.61(3) of the 1972 Act[7] regulations may make special provision with respect to the display of advertisements in conservation areas; no such regulations have yet been made.

Advertisements on listed buildings

Where an advertisement is to be displayed on a listed building and is such as to affect the character of the building, listed building consent will be necessary not only for an advertisement which requires express consent under the 1984 Regulations but also for an advertisement that may be displayed with deemed consent (see p. 438 above).

Controlling advertisements through conditions on planning permissions

The impact of advertisements in an area may be a matter which a planning authority will wish to take into account in the exercise of their normal development control powers. The question arises whether the general power to impose conditions contained in s.26(1) of the 1972 Act may be used to control matters which are the subject of more specific legislation. As a matter of law this would seem in principle to be an appropriate use of a condition.[8] However, the Secretary of State, presumably as a matter of policy, appears to take the view that the more specific control in the Advertisement Control Regulations should be used in preference to conditions and he has, on a number of occasions, exercised his power on appeal to discharge conditions imposed on planning permissions restricting or regulating the display of advertisements.[9]

E. TREE PRESERVATION

Trees make an important contribution to the quality of the landscape. 'Trees', observed a circular issued by the Secretaries of State for the Environment and for Wales, 'enhance the quality of the countryside,

---

[6] See reg. 8(4); also S.D.D. Circular 10/1984, paras. 22 and 23.

[7] As amended by s.3 of the Town and Country Amenities Act 1974.

[8] See *Westminster Bank Ltd.* v *Minister of Housing and Local Government* [1971] A.C. 508. Contrast appeal decision by the Secretary of State for the Environment noted at [1982] J.P.L. 733.

[9] See appeal decisions P/PPA/TB/2; P/PPA/HF/45; P/ADA/HF/4; and P/PPA/CC/83 (discussed at 1983 S.P.L.P. 55 and 88; also correspondence at 1983 S.P.L.P. 91 and 1984 S.P.L.P. 30). See too the appeal decision noted at [1982] J.P.L. 733.

provide a habitat for wildlife and soften and add character to built up areas.'[10] In recent years, a number of factors, such as dutch elm disease and changes in agricultural and forestry practices, have resulted in some loss of quality and variety in the landscape. 'If the tree stock is to be maintained for the future', continued the circular, 'the protection and regeneration of our tree cover, and especially the planting of new trees, is essential.' These comments would seem to be relevant to much of Scotland.

The 1972 Act recognises the importance of trees by requiring planning authorities to make appropriate provision for the planting and preservation of trees (s.57). Although the felling, lopping or destruction of a tree does not constitute development for the purposes of the planning legislation, there are two ways in which an authority may discharge this requirement. First of all, the authority may, in granting planning permission for any development, impose conditions relating to the preservation or planting of trees (ss. 26, 27 and 57). Secondly, the planning authority may make a tree preservation order (ss. 57 and 58).

The term 'tree' is nowhere defined in the Act. However, D.o.E. Circular 36/78 makes a distinction, for the purposes of tree preservation orders, between trees on the one hand and bushes, shrubs and hedges on the other.[11] In *Kent County Council* v *Batchelor*[12] Lord Denning M.R. said that a tree in a woodland 'ought to be something over seven or eight inches in diameter', but this measure was not followed by Phillips J. in *Bullock* v *Secretary of State for the Environment*.[13] Speaking of the corresponding provisions in the English legislation, he said it seemed to him 'that anything that ordinarily one would call a tree is a "tree" within this group of sections in the Act of 1971. It seems to me that, if it were not so, it would be difficult to apply section 59 [corresponding to s.57 of the 1972 Act] which relates to the imposition of conditions for the planting of trees, which in the nature of things are quite likely to be saplings, or section 62 [corresponding to s.60 of the 1972 Act], which makes provision for the replacement of trees, which again in the nature of things are likely to be replaced by saplings.'[14]

Conditions

Section 57(a) of the 1972 Act imposes a duty on planning authorities to ensure, whenever appropriate, that in granting planning permission for any development, adequate provision is made, by the imposition of conditions, for the preservation or planting of trees. Such conditions are widely employed by planning authorities. No advice has yet been issued by the S.D.D. on the use of such conditions but model conditions have been

[10] Department of the Environment Circular 36/78, 'Trees and Forestry', para. 2.
[11] Memorandum annexed to Circular 36/78, para. 44.
[12] (1976) 33 P. & C.R. 185.
[13] (1980) 40 P. & C.R. 246.
[14] See also appeal decision noted at [1979] J.P.L. 483. The Town and Country Planning (Tree Preservation Order and Trees in Conservation Areas) (Scotland) Regulations 1975, reg. 11, exempt trees of less than a prescribed diameter from certain of the controls over trees in conservation areas.

published by the Department of the Environment.[15] Establishing a tree screen for a development will take time, perhaps several years. Conditions may require not just the planting of trees but their maintenance during the first few years and the replacement of any trees that die. However, the D.o.E. circular states that it is not reasonable to use conditions to secure the permanent preservation of trees.[16] If this is needed then recourse should be made to tree preservation orders.

Tree preservation order

If a planning authority consider that 'in the interests of amenity' provision should be made for the preservation of any trees or woodlands in their area, they may make a tree preservation order (s.58(1)). Furthermore, s.57(b) requires a planning authority in connection with a grant of planning permission to make such tree preservation orders as may be necessary either to support a tree planting and preservation condition or otherwise.

It would seem that a planning authority are limited to considerations of amenity in making such orders. This is a notoriously difficult term to define but—D.o.E. Circular 36/78 suggests that: 'Trees may be worthy of preservation for their intrinsic beauty or for their contribution to the landscape; or because they serve to screen an eyesore or future development; the value of trees may be enhanced by their scarcity; and the value of a group of trees or woodland may be collective only.'[17]

Provision may be made by a tree preservation order:

(*a*) for prohibiting the cutting down, topping, lopping, uprooting, wilful damage or wilful destruction of trees except with the consent of the planning authority and for enabling that authority to give their consent subject to conditions (s.58(1)(a), as amended by s.11(1) of the Town and Country Amenities Act 1974);

(*b*) for securing the replanting of any part of a woodland area which is felled in the course of forestry operations permitted by or under the order (s.58(1)(b)); and

(*c*) for applying in relation to any consent under the order the provisions of the 1972 Act relating to planning permission, applications for such permission, appeals to the Secretary of State, purchase notices, etc. (s.58(1)(c); and s.180(1)).

The order may also provide for payment of compensation in respect of loss or damage resulting from a refusal or conditional grant of any consent required under the order (s.163) (below).

Nothing in a tree preservation order is to prohibit the uprooting, felling or lopping of any tree if (a) such action is urgently necessary in the interests of safety, or (b) such action is necessary for the prevention or abatement of a nuisance (provided that written notice of the proposed operations is given to

15 Memorandum annexed to D.o.E. Circular 36/78, Appendix 4.
16 ibid, para 75. See also Department of the Environment Circular 1/85, para. 40.
17 Memorandum annexed to D.o.E. Circular 36/78, para. 40.

the planning authority immediately the necessity arises), or (c) such action is carried out in compliance with any statutory obligation (s.58(6);[18] see too the Second Schedule to the form of tree preservation order set out in the Town and Country Planning (Tree Preservation Order and Trees in Conservation Areas) (Scotland) Regulations 1975 (below)).

In certain circumstances a tree preservation order may only be made if the Forestry Commissioners consent to its making (see s.58(7)). Under s.253(2) of the 1972 Act a tree preservation order can be made in respect of Crown land if a private interest exists in the land and the 'appropriate authority' consents. Under s.2 of the Town and Country Planning Act 1984 planning authorities are empowered to make tree preservation orders in respect of Crown land in which there exists no interest other than that of the Crown if the planning authority consider it expedient to do so in order to preserve trees or woodlands on the land in the event of the land ceasing to be Crown land or becoming subject to a private interest. The consent of the 'appropriate authority' is required and such an order does not take effect until the land ceases to be Crown land or becomes subject to a private interest.

Procedure for making a tree preservation order

The detailed procedure for the making of a tree preservation order is to be found in the Town and Country Planning (Tree Preservation Order and Trees in Conservation Areas) (Scotland) Regulations 1975 as amended by Regulations in 1981 and 1984.[19] The order is to be substantially in the form set out in the Schedule to the 1975 Regulations and is to include a map defining the position of the trees, groups of trees or woodlands to which it relates (reg. 4). The planning authority must advertise the making of the order and a copy of the order and map must be placed on deposit for inspection in at least one place convenient to the locality. In *Vale of Glamorgan Borough Council* v *Palmer and Bowles*[20] the Divisional Court held that the corresponding provision in the English Regulations was to be interpreted as meaning that a copy of the order and map was to remain deposited for inspection for so long as the order was in force, that the provision was mandatory and not merely directory and that a failure to comply with the provision consequently invalidated an order; 'unless [orders] are so deposited', said Webster J., 'members of the public will be unable to find out what trees in any area are affected by a tree preservation order.'

The planning authority must also serve a copy of the order and the accompanying map on the owners, lessees and occupiers of the land affected

---

[18]   As amended by the Town and Country Amenities Act 1974, s.11(2).
[19]   The Town and Country Planning (Tree Preservation Order and Trees in Conservation Areas) (Scotland) Amendment Regulations 1981; and the Town and Country Planning (Tree Preservation Order and Trees in Conservation Areas) (Scotland) Amendment Regulations 1984. As to the making of tree preservation orders in respect of Crown land, see the Town and Country Planning Act 1984, s.2.
[20]   (1982) 81 L.G.R. 679.

and on any person known to them to be entitled to work by surface working any minerals in the land or to fell any of the trees affected by the order (reg. 5). A period of 28 days is allowed for the making of objections and representations to the planning authority (reg. 7[21]).

Subject to the provisions of s.59 of the 1972 Act (see below), a tree preservation order will not take effect until it is confirmed by the planning authority (s.58(4)[22]). Before deciding whether to confirm the order, the authority must take into consideration any objections and representations duly made. There is no obligation to afford objectors the opportunity of a hearing but, if a hearing is arranged, the authority must have regard to the report of the hearing (reg. 8). If the authority decide to confirm the order they may make such modifications as they consider expedient (s.58)4)).

After confirmation, a tree preservation order must be recorded by the planning authority in the Register of Sasines or in the Land Register, as appropriate (s.58(4)).

Provisional tree preservation orders

Normally a tree preservation order does not take effect until it is confirmed by the planning authority (s.58(4)). Since the trees in question might well be destroyed before confirmation, the 1972 Act provides that the planning authority may include in a tree preservation order a direction that the order should take effect provisionally on such date as is specified in the order; in such a case the order continues in force by virtue of s.59 until the expiry of a period of six months from the date the order was made or until the date on which the order is confirmed, whichever occurs first (s.59(1)–(3);[23] 1975 Regulations, reg. 5).

Consents under tree preservation order

The felling or lopping etc. of trees which are subject to a tree preservation order will normally require the consent of the planning authority; if such consent is refused or is granted subject to conditions there is a right of appeal to the Secretary of State (see Art. 8 of, and Third Schedule to, the prescribed form of tree preservation order). Before determining an appeal the Secretary of State is obliged to afford to the appellant and the planning authority an opportunity of appearing before and being heard by a person appointed by him for the purpose; the Secretary of State has, however, drawn attention to the desirability of making greater use of the procedure for deciding suitable appeals on the basis of the parties' written submissions rather than by a public local inquiry (see S.D.D. Circular 87/1975, Appendix III).

---

[21]   As amended by the Town and Country Planning (Tree Preservation Order and Trees in Conservation Areas) (Scotland) Amendment Regulations 1981.

[22]   As amended by the Local Government (Miscellaneous Provisions) (Scotland) Act 1981, s.25 and Schedule 2, para. 22(1). Prior to this amendment, opposed orders required confirmation by the Secretary of State.

[23]   As amended by the Local Government (Miscellaneous Provisions) (Scotland) Act 1981, s.25 and Schedule 2, para. 23(1).

In a letter published in the *Journal of Planning and Environment Law*, a spokesman for the Department of Environment and Transport indicated that, as the Secretary of State no longer had jurisdiction over the confirmation of tree preservation orders, he would now be exceeding his jurisdiction if, in relation to an appeal against refusal of consent, he took account of the merit of an order at the time it was made.[24] It is reasonable to suppose that a similar view would be taken by the Secretary of State for Scotland.

In certain circumstances the control exercised by the planning authority will interact with the general control over the felling of trees exercised by the Forestry Commission. Under the Forestry Act 1967 a licence issued by the Forestry Commissioners is generally required before trees may be felled.[25] A licence is not, however, necessary in respect of the felling of trees growing in an orchard, garden, churchyard or public open space; nor is a licence needed where felling is immediately necessary for the purpose of carrying out development authorised under the planning legislation (1967 Act, s.9(2)(b), (4)(d)).[26] Where a licence is required in respect of trees which are subject to a tree preservation order, application should be made to the Conservator of Forests for a licence (see 1967 Act, s.15) and application for consent need not be made to the planning authority since the licence, if granted, operates as consent under the tree preservation order. If in such a case it is proposed to grant a licence, the planning authority must be so informed; if the authority object to the grant of a licence the application is referred to the Secretary of State.

Replacement of trees

Where a tree (other than a tree forming part of a woodland) which is the subject of a tree preservation order is removed, uprooted or destroyed in contravention of the order or is removed, uprooted, destroyed or dies at a time when its uprooting or felling is authorised only because it is urgently necessary in the interests of safety, it is the duty of the owner of the land to replace the tree in question with another tree of appropriate size and species as soon as he reasonably can (s.60(1)[27]). On application by the owner of the land the planning authority may dispense with this requirement. The tree preservation order applies to the replacement tree (s.60(2)).

In granting consent under a tree preservation order the planning authority may, of course, impose a condition as to replanting or replacement of trees; such a condition is, however, only to be imposed on a consent relating to a woodland in the circumstances set out in Article 5 of the prescribed form of tree preservation order. Article 7 of the prescribed form sets out the circumstances in which the planning authority may give a replanting direction in the case of woodlands.

---

[24]   [1981] J.P.L. 899.
[25]   See the Forestry (Felling of Trees) Regulations 1979.
[26]   See also the Forestry (Exceptions from Restriction of Felling) Regulations 1979 and the Forestry (Exceptions from Restriction of Felling) (Amendment) Regulations 1981.
[27]   As amended by the Town and Country Amenities Act 1974, s.11(2).

Offences and enforcement

A breach of a tree preservation order cannot normally be remedied; the damage to a tree cannot be undone. The sanctions supporting the tree preservation order provisions are, therefore, penal rather than remedial[28] although, as we mentioned above, an owner of land may, in certain circumstances be required to replace a tree.

The penal provisions differentiate between actions which result in the destruction of a tree and actions which cause damage falling short of destruction. The former are dealt with by s.98(1) of the 1972 Act[29] which prescribes penalties on conviction for contravening a tree preservation order by cutting down, uprooting or wilfully destroying a tree or wilfully damaging, topping or lopping a tree in such a manner as to be likely to destroy it. A person wilfully destroys a tree if he intentionally inflicts on it an injury so radical that in all the circumstances any reasonably competent forester would decide that it ought to be felled.[30] It would seem that the offence is absolute; knowledge of the existence of an order is not a necessary ingredient.[31]

Section 98(2) of the 1972 Act[32] prescribes lesser penalties for conviction for other offences relating to trees subject to tree preservation orders including causing damage to a tree short of destruction. Section 98(3)[33] makes provision for continuing offences.

Where it appears to the planning authority that the provisions of s.60 of the 1972 Act relating to the replacement of trees (above), or any conditions attached to a consent under a tree preservation order which require the replacement of trees, have not been complied with, they may, within two years from the date when the failure came to their knowledge, serve on the owner of the land a notice requiring him within a specified period to plant a tree or trees of specified size and species (s.99(1)). There is a right of appeal to the Secretary of State against such a notice on the grounds specified in

---

[28]   In England, local planning authorities have been able to obtain an injunction to support a tree preservation order (see *Kent County Council* v *Batchelor (No. 2)* [1979] 1 W.L.R. 213; *Attorney-General* v *Melville Construction Co. Ltd.* (1968) 20 P. & C.R. 131). It must be doubtful whether the corresponding remedy of interdict would be available in Scotland (see the discussion of interdict and the enforcement of planning control at p. 349 above).

[29]   A new s.98(1) was substituted by s.11(3) of the Town and Country Amenities Act 1974.

[30]   See *Barnet London Borough Council* v *Eastern Electricity Board* [1973] 1 W.L.R. 430.

[31]   *Maidstone Borough Council* v *Mortimer* [1980] 3 All E.R. 552. The order must, however, have been placed on deposit for inspection so that the public are able to find out what trees in the area are protected—*Vale of Glamorgan Borough Council* v *Palmer and Bowles* (1982) 81 L.G.R. 679.

[32]   As amended by the Town and Country Amenities Act 1974, s.11(4) and (5) and subsequently by the Criminal Procedure (Scotland) Act 1975, ss. 289F, 289G (inserted by the Criminal Justice Act 1982, s.54). It is not altogether clear whether the offence of causing or permitting the destruction of a tree in contravention of a tree preservation order is caught by s.98(1) or (2) of the 1972 Act. If the latter is the case then it attracts a lesser penalty than actual destruction of the tree. For a discussion of this area see C. Crawford and P. Schofield, 'A Weak Branch of the Law on Trees?' [1981] J.P.L. 316.

[33]   As amended by the Local Government and Planning (Scotland) Act 1982, Schedule 2, para. 29.

s.99(3) of the 1972 Act. If the notice is not complied with, the planning authority may carry out the required planting themselves and recover their reasonable expenses from the person who is for the time being the owner or lessee of the land (see s.99(5)).

Compensation

The mere making of a tree preservation order will not give rise to any claim for compensation. It is only when consent for the felling etc. of trees is refused or is granted subject to conditions that such a claim may be made (see 1972 Act, s.163; and Arts. 9 to 12 of the prescribed form of tree preservation order).[34] Compensation will not normally be payable if, on refusing consent or granting consent subject to conditions, the planning authority certify that they are satisfied either that the refusal or condition is in the interests of good forestry or, in the case of trees other than trees comprised in woodlands, that the trees have an outstanding or special amenity value. Such a certificate may, however, be the subject of an appeal to the Secretary of State.

Where a replanting requirement is imposed in respect of a woodland area, compensation may be payable by the planning authority for loss or damage resulting from the requirement if the Forestry Commissioners decide not to make any advance under s.4 of the Forestry Act 1967 in respect of the replanting on the ground that the requirement frustrates the use of the woodland area for commercial purposes in accordance with good forestry practice (s.164).

Trees in conservation areas

Section 59A[35] of the 1972 Act provides that any person who cuts down, tops, lops, uproots, wilfully damages or wilfully destroys any tree in a conservation area is guilty of an offence unless he has first given the planning authority six weeks notice of his intention. The purpose of this provision is to give the planning authority an opportunity to consider the making of a tree preservation order. If the planning authority consent to the proposed works or if the six week period expires without the authority taking action, the proposed works may be carried out. If no specific consent has been given, a further notice will have to be given if the work is not carried out within two years from the service of the original notice.

The provisions of s.59A are not to apply to a tree which is subject to a tree preservation order. Nor do they apply in the circumstances specified in regulation 11 of the Town and Country Planning (Tree Preservation Order and Trees in Conservation Areas) (Scotland) Regulations 1975.

A person guilty of an offence under s.59A is liable to the penalties applicable in relation to a contravention of a tree preservation order[36]

---

[34] On the general principles applicable to assessment of compensation following such a decision see *Bollans* v *Surrey County Council* (1968) 20 P. & C.R. 745; see too *Cardigan Timber Co.* v *Cardiganshire C.C.* (1957) 9 P. & C.R. 158.

[35] Section 59A was added by the Town and Country Amenities Act 1974.

[36] See 1972 Act, s.98(4) (added by the Town and Country Amenities Act 1974, s.11(6)).

(above). Where a tree to which s.59A applies is removed, uprooted or destroyed in contravention of s.59A the owner of the land becomes liable to plant another tree of appropriate size and species.

F. WASTE LAND

If it appears to the planning authority that the amenity of any part of their district, or any adjoining district, is seriously injured by reason of the ruinous or dilapidated condition of any building[37] in their district or by the derelict, waste or neglected condition of any other land in their district, the authority may serve on the owner, lessee and occupier of the building or land a notice under s.63 of the 1972 Act, referred to as a 'waste land notice'.[38] The notice must specify the steps to be taken for abating the injury and the period of time within which the steps must be taken. Service is to be effected by serving a copy of the notice. The notice will take effect, subject to the lodging of an appeal, on a specified date not less than twenty eight days after the latest service.

The scope for action in respect of buildings would appear to be fairly wide.[39] So long as serious injury to amenity is caused, the building's condition need be no worse than 'dilapidated'.[40]

The second limb of s.63 (derelict, waste or neglected land) would seem to be concerned with land which is unfit for use or which has been given insufficient attention or which has been abandoned or left to fall into an unsightly state. The principal characteristic would appear to be the element of neglect. It seems that action under s.63 is competent even though the site in question is not visible to passers-by; it suffices to show that the amenity of the site itself is seriously injured.[41]

The fact that land is being put to active business use does not preclude action under s.63 provided something in the nature of neglect can be shown. In *Britt* v *Buckinghamshire County Council*,[42] which concerned the rather differently-worded provision in the English legislation, the Court of Appeal held that if the condition of land was such as to bring it within the scope of the statutory provisions, then a waste land notice was justified, regardless of

---

[37] Other than an ancient monument (s.63(2) of the 1972 Act).

[38] Section 63 of the 1972 Act as substituted by the Local Government and Planning (Scotland) Act 1982, s.48 and Schedule 2, para. 17. In a consultation paper issued on 31st July 1984 the S.D.D. suggested that the provisions of s.63 should be clarified with a view to making them easier to use.

[39] See, generally, E. Young, 'Waste Land Notices: the Scope for Action' 1981 S.P.L.P. 52, an article examining the scope of s.63 of the 1972 Act in its form prior to amendment by the Local Government and Planning (Scotland) Act 1982.

[40] See *SPADS* No. A3191 (P/WEN/TA/1, 15th November 1979). It would seem, however, that a building which is merely incomplete is neither ruinous nor dilapidated (*SPADS* No. A2988 (P/WEN/HH/2, 15th May 1979)).

[41] See *SPADS* Nos. A3409 (P/WEN/SJ/1, 26th August 1980); and A4083 (P/WEN/GA/1, 30th March 1982).

[42] [1964] 1 Q.B. 77.

whether the condition resulted from activity or inactivity.[43] However, it is not sufficient, it would seem, that premises are merely untidy.[44]

The Secretary of State would appear to be of the view that a waste land notice may also be directed at objects left upon land. He has quite often upheld notices served in respect of land on which scrap material, debris, rubbish, etc. has been deposited.[45]

A person on whom a waste land notice is served, or any other person having an interest in the land in question, may appeal in writing to the Secretary of State on one of the stipulated grounds.[46] The appeal must be lodged before the date on which the notice is to take effect. The lodging of an appeal suspends the operation of the notice until such time as the appeal is determined or withdrawn. The process is similar to that for appealing against an enforcement notice served under s.84 of the 1972 Act; indeed, the provisions of subsections (2A)–(2D) of s.85 are applied to waste land appeals (s.63(3)).

No penalty is laid down in respect of a failure to comply with a notice under s.63, but if the steps required by the notice (other than the discontinuance of a use) are not taken within the period specified in the notice, the planning authority may themselves take the necessary steps and are entitled to recover their expenses from the person who is then the owner or lessee of the land (s.63(3), applying s.88 of the 1972 Act).[47]

A planning authority must maintain a register of waste land notices together with enforcement and stop notices, in the manner prescribed[48] and the register must be available for inspection by the public at all reasonable hours (s.87A of the 1972 Act[49]).

G. MINERALS

Mineral operations,[50] as we indicated earlier,[51] constitute development as defined in s.19(1) of the 1972 Act and are subject, therefore, to planning control. However, it has long been recognised that mineral operations

---

[43] This decision was referred to with approval by Lord Fraser in *Stevenson* v *Midlothian District Council* 1983 S.L.T. 433 (H.L.). See also *SPADS* Nos. A3208 (P/WEN/HF/1, 14th December 1979); and A3557 (P/WEN/HH/5, 23rd December 1980).

[44] *Lawrie* v *Edinburgh Corporation* 1953 S.L.T. (Sh.Ct.) 17.

[45] See, for example, *SPADS* Nos. A3191, A3208, A3409 and A3557 (above); and A3192 (P/WEN/LC/2, 16th November 1979). Some support for this view may also be obtained from the comments of Sheriff Middleton in *Lawrie*, above.

[46] See s.63A(1)(a)–(e) of the 1972 Act.

[47] As amended by the Local Government and Planning (Scotland) Act 1982, s.48 and Schedule 2, para. 23(b).

[48] See the Town and Country Planning (Enforcement of Control) (Scotland) Regulations 1984, reg. 7.

[49] Added by the Local Government and Planning (Scotland) Act 1982, s.44.

[50] For the definition of 'mining operations', see s.19(3A) of the 1972 Act; 'development consisting of the winning and working of minerals' and 'mineral-working deposit' are defined in s.251(1A); and 'minerals' is defined in s.275(1).

[51] See page 122.

S

possess certain characteristics which are not shared by other types of development. Building and engineering operations, observed the Stevens Committee in their report *Planning Control over Mineral Working*,[52] are essentially interludes between two successive uses of land; they fit the land for a desired new use which can begin as soon as the operation ends. Mining operations, on the other hand, are an end in themselves; they may continue for many years, often intermittently; they do not fit the land for a desired use; indeed, they are essentially destructive and may render the land unfit for any other use. Furthermore, minerals can only be worked where they exist.

The 1972 Act takes some account of these characteristics by empowering the Secretary of State to make regulations adapting and modifying certain of its provisions in relation to development consisting of mineral operations.[53] Certain adaptations and modifications are currently made by the Town and Country Planning (Minerals) (Scotland) Regulations 1971.[54]

Fuller recognition of these characteristics and their effect followed the publication of the report of the Stevens Committee in 1976[55] and resulted in the Town and Country Planning (Minerals) Act 1981 which made a number of important amendments to the 1972 Act.[56]

The Regulations and the amendments made by the 1981 Act are now considered in turn.

I. *Town and Country Planning (Minerals) (Scotland) Regulations 1971*

The 1971 Regulations provide that for certain purposes mining operations are to be treated as if they constituted a 'use' of land rather than 'operations' (reg. 4). For example, the carrying out of mining operations may be treated as a use of land for the purposes of s.84 of the 1972 Act, with the result that an enforcement notice can require the discontinuance of mining operations; mining operations are also to be treated as a use for the purposes of s.86 of the 1972 Act, so that where, by virtue of an enforcement notice, mineral development is required to be discontinued and that notice is not complied with, an offence is committed (see reg. 4).

As with 'operations' of other sorts, where mining operations are carried out without planning permission an enforcement notice may be served only within four years of the carrying out of the unauthorised development; it was, however, held by the Court of Appeal in *Thomas David (Porthcawl) Ltd.* v *Penybont R.D.C.*[57] that 'each cut by the bulldozer' in the course of

---

[52] H.M.S.O., 1976, chapter 3.
[53] 1972 Act, s.251(1).
[54] Made under powers contained in earlier legislation, now superseded by s.251(1) of the 1972 Act, and see amendments made by the Town and Country Planning (Minerals) (Scotland) Regulations 1982.
[55] See S.D.D. Circular 49/1978 'Report of the Committee on Planning Control over Mineral Workings'.
[56] Further legislation and advice is expected—see S.D.D. Circular 5/1982, Explanatory Memorandum, para. 2.
[57] [1972] 1 W.L.R. 1526.

mining operations constitutes a separate act of development, so that an enforcement notice can restrain any future unauthorised working and can require reinstatement of land on which unauthorised mining operations took place in the preceding four years. Where there is non-compliance with any condition or limitation attached to a grant of planning permission for mining operations, an enforcement notice may be served at any time within four years after the non-compliance has come to the knowledge of the planning authority (reg. 5).

Under regulation 7 every planning permission for mining operations granted before 8th December 1969 was, if the development was not begun before the beginning of 1969, deemed to have been granted subject to a condition that the development had to be begun before 8th December 1979. As regards planning permission for mining operations granted on or after 8th December 1969, however, the regulations do not modify the statute and s.38(1) of the 1972 Act provides that any such permission is, unless the planning authority specify otherwise, deemed to have been granted subject to a condition that the development must be begun within five years. S.D.D. Circular 65/1971 states that in considering what time limit to specify for the commencement of mining operations planning authorities 'will wish to have regard to the length of time for which the mineral operator must plan his production and decide his investment in plant. A period of substantially more than 10 years may well be justified.' The circular stresses the mineral industry's need for long-term planning. Section 38(1) must now be read subject to the terms of s.38(3)(bb).[58] This excludes from the operation of subsection (1) planning permission for the winning and working of minerals which is granted subject to a condition that the development to which it relates must be begun within a specified time after completion of other mineral development which is already being carried out by the applicant. 'In this way', states S.D.D. Circular 5/1982, 'the certainty of development is sustained, but the flexibility needed by operators acquiring mineral-bearing land as it comes onto the market and by planning authorities anxious to safeguard such land is improved.'[59]

II. *Town and Country Planning (Minerals) Act 1981*

The Act implements in modified form some of the recommendations of the Stevens Committee. Stevens recognised that, in view of the length of time during which mineral operations continue, conditions imposed at the outset of the process to protect the environment may be rendered less relevant and effective in time by changing circumstances. The Act introduced a series of amendments to the 1972 Act which are designed to tackle this problem.

Duration of mineral permissions. First of all, s.41A of the 1972 Act[60] provides that mineral permissions, both existing and new, are to have a defined life so that future generations will have an opportunity to review the

---

[58] Introduced by the Town and Country Planning (Minerals) Act 1981, s.23.
[59] See Explanatory Memorandum, para. 22.
[60] Added by the Town and Country Planning (Minerals) Act 1981, s.24.

position. Unless otherwise stated, the term will be sixty years from 22nd February 1982[61] or the date of the permission, whichever is the later.

Duty to review mineral operations. Secondly, s.251A of the 1972 Act[62] imposes a new duty on district and general planning authorities to review mineral operations at such intervals as they see fit with a view to making any changes in the terms of the planning permission which circumstances may require. Such changes will be made by using the existing powers contained in ss. 42 and 49 of the 1972 Act to modify planning permission or to require that a use be discontinued or that buildings or works be removed or altered. For the purposes of s.49, the winning and working of minerals is to be treated as a use of land (s.49(1A) of the 1972 Act[63]) and an order made under that section may provide for alteration or removal of any plant or machinery used for the winning and working of minerals (s.49(1B)[64]).

The powers contained in ss. 42 and 49 are infrequently used at the present time because of the obligation on planning authorities to compensate for all loss (see p. 378 and p. 383) including, for example, the depreciation in the value of land resulting from their action. However, the 1972 Act, as amended, will provide planning authorities with an incentive to use these powers following a review of mineral operations by enabling the Secretary of State to make regulations modifying the compensation provisions in certain circumstances (s.167A of the 1972 Act[65]).

The modifications will operate where certain requirements, referred to as 'mineral compensation requirements', are satisfied. These requirements are complex. Section 153A of the 1972 Act[66] states, for example, that the compensation provisions for modification orders contained in s.153 (see p. 383) will take effect subject to any such modifications where the following requirements are satisfied:

1. the order modifies planning permission for development consisting of the winning and working of minerals (s.153A(2)(a));
2. the order does *not* restrict:

    (*a*) the period, within which mineral operations are to be commenced;
    (*b*) the size of the area to be used for the winning and working of minerals;
    (*c*) the depth of the operations;
    (*d*) the rate of extraction;

---

[61] The date upon which this provision was brought into effect (Town and Country Planning (Minerals) Act 1981 (Commencement No. 1) Order 1982).

[62] Added by the Town and Country Planning (Minerals) Act 1981, s.20. This section has yet to be brought into force.

[63] See n.62 above.

[64] See n.62 above.

[65] Added by the Town and Country Planning (Minerals) Act 1981, s.31. This section has yet to be brought into force.

[66] Added by the Town and Country Planning (Minerals) Act 1981, s.29. This section has yet to be brought into force.

(e) the total quantity of minerals to be extracted; or

(f) the duration of the mineral operations;[67]

3. the order does *not* modify or replace a restriction of the sort referred to in 2. above imposed either by way of condition on the grant of planning permission or by way of an earlier relevant order[68] (s.153A(2)(b));

4. the planning authority carried out consultations prior to the making of the order with:

(a) all persons having an interest in the land or the minerals (ss. 153A(2)(c) and 167B(1)(a));

(b) the appropriate regional planning authority (ss. 153A(2)(c) and 167B(1)(b) and (3)).[69]

5. the permission which is being modified was granted at least five years before the date of the order; or the order imposes what is known as an 'aftercare condition' (see p. 475 below) on a planning permission granted prior to 22nd February 1982[70] (s.153A(2)(d) and (3));

6. the order is made more than five years after any previous relevant order (s.153A(4)).[71]

Sections 159A and 159B of the 1972 Act[72] specify the mineral compensation requirements which must be satisfied before modified compensation provisions apply to a discontinuance order made under s.49 or to a prohibition order (s.49A), a suspension order or a supplementary suspension order (s.49B) (see below).

Regulations modifying the compensation provisions have yet to be made and the impact of the amendments introduced by the 1981 Act will depend very much on the form which these take. The Act, however, lays down a framework for assessing the reduced level of compensation.[73] A threshold is to be set below which no compensation will be paid. The mineral operator

---

[67] See ss. 153A(2)(b)(i) and 167C(1) and (2) of the 1972 Act, added by the Town and Country Planning (Minerals) Act 1981, ss. 29 and 31.

[68] A 'relevant order' is a reference to a revocation or modification order under s.42 of the 1972 Act, a discontinuance order under s.49 or a prohibition order under s.49A (s.167C(3)).

[69] If, exceptionally, the order-making authority is a regional planning authority, consultations must take place with the district planning authority or authorities in whose area or areas the land is situated (s.167B(3)(b)).

[70] The date upon which section 27A of the 1972 Act which provides for the imposition of aftercare conditions was brought into effect (Town and Country Planning (Minerals) Act 1981 (Commencement No. 1) Order 1982).

[71] Orders may be made more frequently but will not have the advantage of the modified compensation provisions. For the definition of 'relevant order' see s.167C(3) of the 1972 Act.

[72] Added by the Town and Country Planning (Minerals) Act 1981, s.30.

[73] See also the consultation paper 'Proposals to Amend the Law Relating to Planning Control Over Mineral Working: Compensation Aspects', issued by the Department of the Environment in September 1980.

will receive in compensation the excess over the threshold. Section 167A(4)–(6) of the 1972 Act[74] sets out the formula for determining the threshold. It is to be 10 per cent of 'the appropriate sum' although a minimum sum will be prescribed. 'The appropriate sum' will represent the product of the annual value of the right to work the minerals and a multiplier based on the life expectancy of the workings.

Prohibition and suspension orders. Thirdly, the 1981 Act recognises the environmental problems that can arise from the intermittent nature of mineral operations and which may become apparent during a review. To cope with such problems, district and general planning authorities are given power to make two new sorts of order.[75]

Section 49A of the 1972 Act[76] provides that where no development has been carried out to any substantial extent at a site for a period of at least two years and it appears that the resumption of development is unlikely, the planning authority may by order prohibit the resumption of development and require specific steps to be taken to tidy up the site.[77] Such an order will not take effect unless it is confirmed by the Secretary of State. On submission of the order for confirmation, the authority must also serve notice of the making of the order on the owner or occupier of the land and on any person likely to be affected by the making of the order. Any such person may, within a specified period, require to be heard by a person appointed by the Secretary of State before a decision is made on the order. In the event of the order being confirmed, the planning permission to which it relates will cease to have effect.

Section 49B of the 1972 Act[78] provides that where no development has been carried out to any substantial extent at a site for a period of at least twelve months but it appears that a resumption of development is likely, the planning authority may by order require specified steps to be taken for preserving the environment. The order will specify a period for compliance commencing with the date on which it takes effect; different periods may be specified for different steps. A suspension order requires confirmation by the Secretary of State, and notification and the right to a hearing apply as for a prohibition order.

The object of the suspension order is not to inhibit a resumption of work but to safeguard the environment in the interim. Work may be resumed after giving notice to the planning authority and once development has

---

[74] Added by the Town and Country Planning (Minerals) Act 1981, s.31.

[75] Regional planning authorities already have power to make modification and discontinuance orders to protect an approved structure plan. Section 49G of the 1972 Act gives them similar powers to make these two new orders.

[76] Added by the Town and Country Planning (Minerals) Act 1981, s.27. This section has yet to be brought into force.

[77] Where appropriate, the order may include an aftercare condition (s.49A(4)); see p. 475 for an explanation of this type of condition.

[78] Added by the Town and Country Planning (Minerals) Act 1981, s.27. This section has yet to be brought into force.

recommenced to a substantial extent[79] the authority must revoke the order. Application may be made to the Secretary of State to revoke the order should the authority fail to do so.

At any time when a suspension order is in operation, the planning authority may by way of supplementary suspension order direct that steps should be carried out in addition to or in substitution for those required to be taken by the suspension order or by any supplementary suspension order or that the suspension order should cease to have effect. The procedure for the making and confirmation of a supplementary suspension order is the same as for a suspension order (except that no confirmation is required where the order merely revokes a previous order and specifies no further steps to be taken).

Prohibition, suspension and supplementary suspension orders will not take effect until registered in the Land Register of Scotland or the Register of Sasines, as appropriate (s.49D of the 1972 Act[80]).

Suspension orders and supplementary suspension orders must be reviewed as provided in s.49E of the 1972 Act to see whether their provisions need supplementing or whether an order prohibiting resumption of work should be made.

Penalties are prescribed for contravention of a prohibition, suspension or supplementary suspension order and planning authorities are given power to enter the land, take the steps specified in the order and recover the costs (s.100 of the 1972 Act[81]).

The compensation provisions of s.159 of the 1972 Act are applied to prohibition, suspension and supplementary suspension orders (s.159A of the 1972 Act) but where the appropriate mineral compensation requirements are satisfied, the modified compensation provisions will operate (ss. 159B and 167A of the 1972 Act[82]).

Aftercare conditions. Fourthly, s.27A of the 1972 Act[83] enables planning authorities in certain circumstances to impose what are referred to as 'aftercare' conditions on grants of planning permission for mineral operations. Where permission for mineral operations is granted subject to a restoration condition requiring, for example, the replacement of sub-soil and top-soil on the completion of works, then an aftercare condition may also be imposed.[84] This will require the land to be planted, cultivated,

---

[79] This provision would seem to be designed to ensure that mineral operators do not get round a suspension order by making a token start.

[80] Added by the Town and Country Planning (Minerals) Act 1981, s.27.

[81] Substituted by the Town and Country Planning (Minerals) Act 1981, s.28.

[82] Added by the Town and Country Planning (Minerals) Act 1981, ss. 30 and 31.

[83] Added by the Town and Country Planning (Minerals) Act 1981, s.22, and brought into effect on 22nd February 1982 (Town and Country Planning (Minerals) Act 1981 (Commencement No. 1) Order 1982); see also S.D.D. Circular 5/1982.

[84] Existing permissions may have a restoration condition and an aftercare condition imposed by way of order under ss. 42, 49 or 49A of the 1972 Act subject to the payment of compensation, although the compensation may be reduced if the appropriate mineral compensation requirements are satisfied.

fertilised, watered, drained or otherwise treated on completion of the restoration condition for a period of up to five years (or such other maximum period as may be prescribed) so as to make it suitable for use for agriculture, forestry or amenity. The condition may itself detail the steps to be taken or may simply provide for the submission and implementation of an aftercare scheme to be approved by the planning authority.[85] Examples of aftercare conditions are set out in Appendices II and III of the Explanatory Memorandum attached to S.D.D. Circular 5/1982.

Consultations with the Department of Agriculture and Fisheries for Scotland are encouraged over the imposition of an aftercare condition specifying agriculture as the after-use and are required with the Forestry Commission where the after-use is to be forestry.[86]

Where the previous use of the land was for agriculture and the use specified in an aftercare condition is for agriculture, then the land will be considered to have been made suitable for that use when its physical characteristics are restored, so far as practicable, to what they were when the land was previously so used (1972 Act, s.27A(9)). Otherwise, the standard of suitability for use for agriculture or forestry is that the land should be 'reasonably fit for that use' (1972 Act, s.27A(10) and (11)). For amenity use the land is brought to the required standard when it is suitable for sustaining trees, shrubs and plants (1972 Act, s.27A(12)). A person with an interest in land which is the subject of an aftercare condition may apply for a certificate from the planning authority that the condition has been complied with (1972 Act, s.27A(17)).

Miscellaneous amendments. (1) Because of widespread concern about the harmful effects of working mineral waste tips and doubts about whether and when such works constitute 'development' and thus fall within the scope of planning control, a new subsection has been added to s.19 of the 1972 Act to clarify the position. Section 19(3A)[87] provides that 'mining operations' are to include:

(*a*) the removal of material of any description

    (i)   from a mineral-working deposit;[88]
    (ii) from a deposit of pulverised fuel ash or other furnace ash or clinker; or
    (iii) from a deposit of iron, steel or other metallic slags; and

---

[85] Any dispute over the scheme may be the subject of appeal to the Secretary of State (s.33(1)(c) of the 1972 Act, substituted by the Local Government and Planning (Scotland) Act 1982, s.48 and Schedule 2, para. 11(a)).

[86] See s.27A(13)–(16) of the 1972 Act (added by the Town and Country Planning (Minerals) Act 1981, s.22); also S.D.D. Circular 5/1982.

[87] Added by the Town and Country Planning (Minerals) Act 1981, s.19(1). This section has yet to be brought into force.

[88] For the definition of 'mineral working deposit' see s.251(1A) of the 1972 Act (added by the Town and Country Planning (Minerals) Act 1981, ss. 19(2) and 35).

(*b*) the extraction of minerals from a disused railway embankment.

(2) Owners of mineral rights in land are now to be notified of an application for the winning and working of minerals in the same way as the owners of the land (s.24(1A) of the 1972 Act[89]). This implements a recommendation of the Stevens Committee that a person who has an interest in minerals in land should be aware of proposals to work other minerals in the land since this could affect his current or potential operations.

(3) In the case of an application for planning permission for underground mining where the applicant is not also the owner of all the land, the applicant's obligation to give notice of the application now extends only to persons whose names and addresses are known to him as being owners of the land to which the application relates (1972 Act, s.24(1)(cc)[90]). This amendment overcomes difficulties encountered in complying with the somewhat stricter obligation imposed by s.24(1)(b) of the 1972 Act where mining operations are likely to extend under a very large area of land. An applicant taking advantage of s.24(1)(cc) must, however, post a site notice and may be required by the planning authority to post additional notices (1972 Act, s.24(2A) and (2B)[91]).

H. INDUSTRIAL DEVELOPMENT CERTIFICATES

Sections 64–70 of the 1972 Act make provision for the exercise of a special form of control over industrial development. Section 65(1) provides that an application for planning permission to develop land by

(*a*) the erection thereon of an industrial building of any class prescribed by regulations; or
(*b*) a change of use whereby premises, not being an industrial building of one of the prescribed classes, will become such an industrial building,

is to be of no effect unless it is accompanied by an industrial development certificate issued by the Secretary of State certifying that the development in question can be carried out consistently with the proper distribution of industry. This control, comments the *Encylopaedia of Planning Law and Practice*[92], 'provides the basis for a nationally administered policy for the regional distribution of industry, and its purpose is to persuade industry to

---

[89] Added by the Town and Country Planning (Minerals) Act 1981, s.21. This provision was brought into effect on 22nd February 1982 (Town and Country Planning (Minerals) Act 1981 (Commencement No. 1) Order 1982). It does not apply to a person entitled to an interest in oil, gas, coal, gold or silver.
[90] Added by the Town and Country Planning (Minerals) Act 1981, s.21(1).
[91] Added by the Town and Country Planning (Minerals) Act 1981, s.21(4).
[92] Sweet and Maxwell, para. 2–1036.

locate or relocate in the regions whose economic development the Government wishes to promote.'

Originally, all classes of industrial development were prescribed for the purposes of s.65(1).[93] However, as a result of the Town and Country Planning (Industrial Development Certificates) (Prescribed Classes of Building) Regulations 1981 no classes are now prescribed and no industrial development certificate is currently required for any building. This would appear to reflect the somewhat limited success of the policy for the regional distribution of industry. However, ss. 64–70 of the 1972 Act remain in force and, in case further classes of industrial building are prescribed in future, we draw attention to the scope of the provisions.

The provisions extend to an application under s.29 of the 1972 Act for permission to retain or continue the use of an industrial building (s.65(2)) and also cover the extension of a building if the extension, taken by itself, would be an industrial building of one of the prescribed classes (s.65(4)). An industrial development certificate can never be required in respect of the change of use of a building from one industrial purpose to another, even though the change of use is such as to require planning permission.

The statutory requirements on industrial development certificates are not to apply where the industrial floor space to be created does not exceed the exemption limit specified in s.66 of the 1972 Act.[94] Nor are they to apply in respect of industrial development in such areas as may be prescribed by regulations.[95]

I. OFFICE DEVELOPMENT PERMITS

Sections 76–83 of the 1972 Act which refer to office development permits were brought into effect for a temporary period only (s.83(1) of the 1972 Act). The provisions have ceased to have effect and are to be treated as if they had been repealed by another Act (s.83(4) of the 1972 Act).

---

[93] Town and Country Planning (Erection of Industrial Buildings) (Scotland) Regulations 1966.

[94] As varied from time to time by order made by the Secretary of State under s.67 of the 1972 Act. See Town and Country Planning (Industrial Development Certificates: Exemptions) Order 1979.

[95] See, for example, Town and Country Planning (Industrial Development Certificate) Regulations 1979.

CHAPTER 20
APPEAL AND OBJECTION PROCEDURES

A. GENERAL

As is indicated at many points throughout this book, the planning
legislation confers wide discretionary powers upon planning authorities.
These powers include, for example, the making of decisions on applications for planning permission, listed building consent and consent under
the advertisement regulations, the initiation of enforcement action and the
making of revocation, discontinuance and compulsory purchase orders.
Inevitably, the exercise of these powers is a fertile source of conflict
between planning authorities and the individuals or bodies most directly
affected by a decision or order. It has long been recognised that if the
discretionary nature of planning processes are to retain general
acceptance, some means of resolving conflict, a sort of pressure valve, is
required. The 1972 Act provides such mechanisms by enabling persons
aggrieved[1] by the exercise of many of the powers possessed by planning
authorities to appeal or object to the Secretary of State.[2] A right of appeal
generally arises as a consequence of an adverse decision by a planning
authority on a proposal (such as an application for planning permission)
submitted by an individual or body, while a right to object generally arises
in response to a proposal (such as the making of a compulsory purchase
order) initiated by a planning authority. The object of this chapter is to
describe the main features of the procedures followed in connection with
appeals and objections.[3]

Characteristically, appeal and objection procedures have two complementary purposes—on the one hand, say Wraith and Lamb,[4] 'to give relief

---

[1]   Members of the public at large are not aggrieved persons for these purposes. Whilst they
may have an opportunity to make representations in the course of appeal and objection
procedures, they cannot initiate the process. Planning control is intended to regulate
development in the public interest—not, generally, to confer new rights on members of
the public.

[2]   Objections to a local plan are, however, normally made to and determined by the
plan-making authority (see chapter 5); and objections to a tree preservation order are
made to and determined by the order-making authority (see chapter 19).

[3]   For general discussion of appeal and objection procedures see R. E. Wraith and G. B.
Lamb, *Public Inquiries as an Instrument of Government* (George Allen & Unwin, 1971);
G. Ganz, *Administrative Procedures* (Sweet and Maxwell, 1974); and C. Harlow and R.
Rawlings, *Law and Administration* (Weidenfield and Nicolson, 1984).

[4]   *Public Inquiries as an Instrument of Government.*

to anyone who may consider himself aggrieved and on the other hand to assist a Minister[5] to come to the best possible administrative decision'.[6] Appeals and objections are dealt with in a variety of ways. In some cases a public inquiry will be held prior to the making of the decision on an appeal or objection, while in other cases the appeal or objection will be determined on the basis of the parties' written submissions. In some cases the decision is made by the Secretary of State, while in others decision-making powers have been delegated to persons appointed by the Secretary of State for the purpose.

The decision which follows proceedings in connection with an appeal or objection is typically of an administrative or executive nature. Although there can arise under the planning legislation cases in which policy considerations will strictly play no part,[7] and although there are, superficially at least, certain similarities between judicial proceedings and those appeal and objection procedures which involve the holding of a public inquiry, in general it may be said that proceedings in connection with an appeal or objection under the planning legislation are but part of a process leading to the making of an administrative decision, a decision which may be based, whatever the weight of evidence presented, on the decision-making body's conception of the requirements of planning policy and the public interest.[8] In the words of Lord Justice-Clerk Thomson:

'there can be no objection to the Secretary of State in the course of his administrative function, which necessarily involves questions of policy, preferring one view to another or ignoring all the views and preferring his own, or those of his own advisers. The report [of the inquiry], though it is the result of a *quasi-lis* is for the Secretary of State only one of the elements which he has to consider in exercising his function. The Secretary of State is not a judge but an administrator and in his administrative capacity he is answerable not to the Courts but to Parliament.'[9]

---

[5] The decision on many appeals under the planning legislation is now made by 'appointed persons' (see below) and on some objections is made by the planning authority (see note 2 above).

[6] For judicial pronouncements on the purposes and essential characteristics of public inquiries see *Bushell* v *Secretary of State for the Environment* [1981] A.C. 75, and *Binney and Anscomb* v *Secretaries of State for Environment and Transport* [1984] J.P.L. 871.

[7] As, for example, where the Secretary of State has to determine an appeal on the question whether particular proposals require planning permission.

[8] While a minister or other person or body responsible for making a planning decision is, of course, entitled to have a general policy on planning matters, the effect of that policy must not be such as to prevent the decision-maker fairly judging all the issues relevant to each individual case—see, for example, *Stringer* v *Minister of Housing and Local Government* [1970] 1 W.L.R. 1281; *H. Lavender and Son Ltd.* v *Minister of Housing and Local Government* [1970] 1 W.L.R. 1231; and *R.* v *Secretary of State for the Environment, ex p. Reinisch* (1971) 22 P.&C.R. 1022.

[9] *General Poster and Publicity Co. Ltd.* v *Secretary of State for Scotland* 1960 S.C. 266; 1961 S.L.T. 62.

Procedural parameters

The Secretary of State and the parties involved have a certain amount of discretion as to the procedure to be adopted in the consideration of appeals and objections. Typically, the 1972 Act provides that before determining an appeal or objection the Secretary of State shall afford the appellant or objector and the planning authority, if either so desires, an opportunity of appearing before and being heard by a person appointed by him for the purpose. Where advantage is taken of this opportunity, the Secretary of State will, in the vast majority of cases, convene a public inquiry in preference to a private hearing.[10] The parties may be content to have the case dealt with without their being heard but the minister may on his own initiative decide that the issues arising in a particular case are such that a public inquiry should be held.

We suggested above that the decision which follows upon an appeal or objection should generally be regarded as being of an administrative nature, in which the decision-maker is free to consider the evidence led against the background of national or local policy.[11] The person responsible for conducting the relevant proceedings and (if different) the person making the decision which follows is not, however, free to act entirely as he pleases. Certain legal requirements (below) have to be observed and administrative guidance on procedures, designed to ensure fairness and efficiency, has also been issued. The most important such guidance is contained in circulars and memoranda issued by the Scottish Development Department; in order to complete the procedural picture these are referred to at appropriate points in this chapter.

As for the legal rules governing procedures, these are not to be found in primary legislation. The 1972 Act is virtually silent on the matter. What we do have, however, are rules which derive from two other sources. One source is delegated legislation made, not under the 1972 Act, but under the Tribunals and Inquiries Act 1971.[12] The other source lies in the judge-made rules of the common law and, in particular, the principles of natural justice.[13] Within the limits imposed by these legal rules there remains some room for procedural manoeuvre at the discretion of the person conducting the proceedings relating to an appeal or objection.

10   Section 267 of the 1972 Act provides that the Secretary of State 'may cause a local inquiry to be held for the purposes of the exercise of any of his functions under any of the provisions of this Act'.

11   See, for example, *General Poster and Publicity Co. Ltd.* v *Secretary of State for Scotland* 1960 S.C. 266; 1961 S.L.T. 62; *Peter Holmes and Son* v *Secretary of State for Scotland* 1965 S.C. 1; 1965 S.L.T. 41; *B. Johnson and Co. (Builders) Ltd.* v *Minister of Health* [1947] 2 All E.R. 395; *Darlassis* v *Minister of Education* (1954) 4 P.&C.R. 281; *Essex County Council* v *Minister of Housing and Local Government* (1967) 18 P.&C.R. 531; and *Bushell* v *Secretary of State for the Environment* [1981] A.C. 75.

12   See the Town and Country Planning (Inquiries Procedure) (Scotland) Rules 1980; and the Town and Country Planning Appeals (Determination by Appointed Person) (Inquiries Procedure) (Scotland) Rules 1980. See also the Compulsory Purchase by Public Authorities (Inquiries Procedure) (Scotland) Rules 1976.

13   Statute may, however, exclude the operation of the rules of natural justice—see, for example, s.12(4)(e) of the 1972 Act (exclusion of right to a hearing).

It was, in part, the widely felt concern that appeal and objection procedures which involved the holding of public inquiries were insufficiently regulated in the interests of fairness and openness that led to the appointment of the Committee on Administrative Tribunals and Enquiries nearly thirty years ago. That Committee's report[14] (the Franks Report) had a considerable effect on procedures involving public inquiries. Some of the Report's recommendations were implemented by administrative measures. Others were given effect by the Tribunals and Inquiries Act 1958 (now replaced by the Tribunals and Inquiries Act 1971). The 1958 Act made provision for the establishment of the Council on Tribunals, with a Scottish Committee; one of the main functions of the Council is to consider and report on administrative procedures involving the holding of a statutory inquiry[15] (see now 1971 Act, s.1(1)(c)). There is a right to demand reasons for any decision taken after the holding of a statutory inquiry or hearing, or for any decision taken in a case in which a person concerned could have insisted on a hearing (see 1971 Act, s.12). The Lord Advocate is empowered to make rules regulating the procedure to be followed in connection with statutory inquiries or hearings in Scotland[16] (see 1971 Act, s.11). Procedures in connection with many types of inquiry held under the planning legislation are regulated by the Town and Country Planning (Inquiries Procedure) (Scotland) Rules 1980 and the Town and Country Planning Appeals (Determination by Appointed Person) (Inquiries Procedure) (Scotland) Rules 1980.[17] The requirements of these rules are considered in section C of this chapter. A failure to comply with the rules can lead to the decision in question being challenged under s.233 of the 1972 Act. The Court of Session is empowered to quash a decision if satisfied that the interests of the applicant have been substantially prejudiced by a failure to comply with the rules (see chapter 21). There have been very many such challenges, and rulings by the Court of Session and by the English High Court in equivalent proceedings have contributed to a fuller understanding of the statutory rules themselves.

When called upon to review the validity of decisions made following upon appeals and objections, the courts have not, however, confined themselves to the content of the express statutory rules. They have also been prepared to infer from the general statutory context the need to

[14] Cmnd. 218, 1957.

[15] References to a 'statutory inquiry' include not only references to an inquiry held in pursuance of a statutory *duty* but also to any inquiry which is held in exercise of a statutory *power* and which is designated by order made under the Tribunals and Inquiries Act; the Tribunals and Inquiries (Discretionary Inquiries) Order 1975 designates, *inter alia,* any inquiry held under s.267 of the Town and Country Planning (Scotland) Act 1972.

[16] This rule-making power was transferred from the Secretary of State to the Lord Advocate by the Transfer of Functions (Secretary of State and Lord Advocate) Order 1972.

[17] See also the Compulsory Purchase by Public Authorities (Inquiries Procedure) (Scotland) Rules 1976. In many respects the statutory procedure rules go further than the requirements of natural justice but compliance with the statutory rules does not mean there must *ipso facto* have been compliance with the rules of natural justice.

observe the common law standards of fair play—the rules of natural justice—although, with the emergence of detailed statutory codes these standards are of less significance for most sorts of planning inquiry. The courts are not, of course, free to infer the existence of rules inconsistent with those laid down under the authority of Parliament; where statutory rules are applicable the rules of natural justice can only apply in so far as they are not inconsistent with the statutory provisions and there is a heavy burden on someone seeking to establish a breach of natural justice in respect of procedures at a public inquiry governed by statutory rules.[18]

The phrase 'natural justice' carries overtones of the procedures followed in the law courts but in recent times the courts have tended simply to declare that appeal and objection procedures must be 'fair'[19] or that the parties must be given 'a fair crack of the whip'.[20] In *Lithgow* v *Secretary of State for Scotland*[21] the nature of the duty which the common law imposes on the person or body making a decision after an inquiry was described by Lord Dunpark in the following terms: 'Even if there is a set statutory procedure it is not enough for [the decision-maker] to comply with it; he must exercise all his powers fairly in relation to those who object to their exercise. He must always give all parties the opportunity of adequately stating their case.'[22] The procedure must also, it seems, be fair to all those (including the general public) who have an interest in the decision, 'whether they have been represented at the inquiry or not'.[23] The same principles apply where a decision on an appeal or objection is made without the holding of a public inquiry.

In the context of appeal and objection procedures the main importance of the common law concept of fairness lies in the requirement that a party be given a fair opportunity to put his case and to answer all significant points adverse to that case.[24] If, for example, an inquiry reporter or the minister proposes to take into account any factual information which he has obtained from one of the parties after the close of an inquiry or which has come into his possession in some other way, fairness demands that he disclose that information and give the parties an opportunity to comment

[18]   See, for example, *Ackerman* v *Secretary of State for the Environment* (1980) 257 E.G. 1037.
[19]   See, for example, *Bushell* v *Secretary of State for the Environment* [1981] A.C. 75.
[20]   See, for example, *Fairmount Investments Ltd.* v *Secretary of State for the Environment* [1976] 1 W.L.R. 1255.
[21]   1973 S.C. 1; 1973 S.L.T. 81.
[22]   Drawing on the decisions in *Errington* v *Minister of Health* [1935] 1 K.B. 249; and *Stafford* v *Minister of Health* [1946] K.B. 621.
[23]   See *Bushell* (above), per Lord Diplock.
[24]   It is also a principle of natural justice that there must be no reasonable suspicion of bias on the part of the decision-maker. In *Halifax Building Society* v *Secretary of State for the Environment* [1983] J.P.L. 816 a decision was quashed because the inquiry inspector appeared hostile to the appellants and seemed reluctant to pay attention to their case. See too *Furmston* v *Secretary of State for the Environment* [1983] J.P.L. 49.

upon the new information.[25]

The concept of natural justice or fairness is not a precise one—what fairness demands in any particular case may depend on the nature of the subject matter and is to be judged in the light of practical realities as to the way in which administrative decisions are reached. However, it may be said that in general the courts will be concerned with the broad question of whether fair procedures have been followed and will not concern themselves with the observance of technicalities appropriate to a private issue decided by a judge;[26] while the courts will, for example, insist on an inquiry being fairly and impartially conducted, they will not insist that formal rules of evidence be applied at an inquiry.[27] As was said in *George* v *Secretary of State for the Environment*,[28] there is no such thing as a 'technical' breach of natural justice; the court will not grant relief unless 'a reasonable person . . . viewing the matter objectively and knowing all the facts which are known to the court, [would] consider that there was a risk that the procedure adopted . . . has resulted in injustice or unfairness.'[29] If, for example, the decision-maker receives further representations from one party after the close of an inquiry but gives the other party no opportunity to comment, there is no unfairness if such an opportunity could not possibly have advanced that party's case.[30]

Measures to improve appeal procedures

In recent times the number of appeals lodged every year under the planning legislation has continued at a high level. The Secretary of State has accordingly taken a number of steps in an effort to ensure that appeal procedures function speedily and efficiently but without breaching the Franks Committee's principles of openness, fairness and impartiality (S.D.D. Circular 14/1975) and 'without prejudice to the fundamental principles of fairness, thoroughness and consistency' (S.D.D. Circular 26/1984). The number of instances every year in which proposals are initiated by planning authorities is limited and, by comparison with appeals, relatively few objections are lodged with the Secretary of State; no corresponding changes have been considered necessary to maintain the efficiency of objection procedures.

S.D.D. Circulars 14/1975 and 26/1984 contain the principal administra-

---

[25]   See, for example, *Hamilton* v *Secretary of State for Scotland* 1972 S.C. 72; 1972 S.L.T. 233; *Hibernian Property Co. Ltd.* v *Secretary of State for the Environment* (1973) 27 P.&C.R. 197; and *Fairmount Investments Ltd.* v *Secretary of State for the Environment* [1976] 1 W.L.R. 1255. There is, however, no obligation to allow the parties to comment on matters of policy—see, for example, *Lithgow* (above) and *Darlassis* v *Minister of Education* (1954) 4 P.&C.R. 281; as these cases show 'fact' and 'policy' are not always easily distinguished.

[26]   See, for example, *Lake District Special Planning Board* v *Secretary of State for the Environment* (1975) 236 E.G. 417.

[27]   See p.501 (below).

[28]   (1979) 38 P.&C.R. 609.

[29]   *Lake District Special Planning Board* (above), per Kerr J.

[30]   See, for example, *George* (above).

tive guidance on appeal procedures.[31] Both seek to ensure that decisions are arrived at as speedily and efficiently as possible and that parties are put to as little expense as possible. In addition to the general procedural guidance which these circulars contain, and which is referred to in sections B and C below, three innovations have been made in recent years which have had an impact upon appeal procedures.

In the first place, the establishment of the Scottish Office Inquiry Reporters' Unit has produced a staff of mainly full-time reporters to replace the former reliance upon the part-time services of advocates and others. This appears to have resulted in a significant speeding up of the decision-making process.

Secondly, since 1976 power to make decisions on certain appeals has been delegated to 'appointed persons'[32] (in practice reporters from the Scottish Office Inquiry Reporters' Unit). Until 1976 it could generally be said to be characteristic of public inquiries that they were ordered by a minister and preceded the making of a ministerial decision. The duty of the reporter, the person appointed to hold the inquiry (in England less helpfully known as an inspector), was restricted to the making of a report and recommendations to the minister who instructed the inquiry. Inquiries of this 'traditional' type are still important under the planning legislation but recent years have witnessed a revolution in inquiry practice. The decision in very many appeals now falls to be made not by the Secretary of State but by the reporter himself.

When this process began in 1976,[33] approximately 30 per cent of all appeals were delegated to appointed persons for decision in order to 'simplify and accelerate the disposal of prescribed classes of planning appeals'.[34] The process of delegation was extended in 1978[35] and again in 1980[36] in order to 'widen still further the benefits of quicker decisions on planning appeals which are possible as a result of delegation'.[37] The result is that the making of the decision on almost all appeals under the planning legislation has now been delegated to appointed persons.[38] The only appeals which are not delegated now are (a) those concerned with listed buildings; (b) certain appeals involving development by statutory undertakers where the decision has to be made by the Secretary of State for

[31] See also S.D.D. Circulars 25/1966 and 47/1980.
[32] See s.279 of and Schedule 7 to the 1972 Act.
[33] By virtue of the Town and Country Planning (Determination of Appeals by Appointed Persons) (Prescribed Classes) (Scotland) Regulations 1976.
[34] S.D.D. Circular 20/1976. And see, generally, C. M. Brand, 'Measures to Expedite Disposal of Planning Appeals' 1979 S.L.T. (News) 99.
[35] See the Town and Country Planning (Determination of Appeals by Appointed Persons) (Prescribed Classes) (Scotland) Regulations 1978.
[36] See the Town and Country Planning (Determination of Appeals by Appointed Persons) (Prescribed Classes) (Scotland) Regulations 1980.
[37] S.D.D. Circular 47/1980.
[38] The decision on appeals under the following statutory provisions have now been delegated to appointed persons: ss.33, 34, 51, 63, 85, 91 and 99 of the 1972 Act and s.179 of the Local Government (Scotland) Act 1973.

Scotland and another minister; (c) advertisement appeals; and (d) appeals involving certificates of appropriate alternative development. The Secretary of State retains the power to recall any delegated case for his own decision[39] but the minister has indicated that this power will only be used in a very small number of exceptional cases.[40]

Schedule 7 to the 1972 Act provides that in a case where an appeal is to be determined by an appointed person, the appellant and the planning authority are to be afforded the opportunity of a hearing by the appointed person; such a hearing may take the form of a public inquiry (and will normally do so). If neither party wishes to be heard, the appeal may, unless the appointed person or the Secretary of State decides otherwise, be determined on the basis of written submissions. In the determination of an appeal, the appointed person has the powers and duties conferred by paragraph 2(1) of Schedule 7 to the 1972 Act.

Thirdly, considerable encouragement is being given to both appellants and planning authorities to adopt the written submissions procedure for disposing of appeals.[41] Although, as we mentioned earlier, the appellant and the planning authority have a right to be heard in connection with an appeal, an inquiry is by no means essential and in many cases the issues can be quite adequately dealt with by means of the written submissions procedure.

The basic concept of the written submissions procedure is a single exchange of written statements by the parties to an appeal.[42] The procedure has advantages for an appellant in terms of a speedier determination of the appeal and less expense. However, where a proposal raises complex or contentious issues and evidence may need to be tested by cross-examination, a public inquiry will be more appropriate. Furthermore, as Brand suggests,[43] the price to the appellant of expediting a planning appeal through use of the written submissions procedure may be some reduction in the scope for challenge in the courts of the decision on the appeal; this would seem to be an inevitable result of using a simplified procedure.

S.D.D. Circular 26/1984 states that the written submissions procedure is already used in some 64 per cent of planning appeals and could be used in a greater number of cases, 'to the benefit of all concerned with the appeals system'. Planning authorities could, says the circular, 'profitably give the written submissions procedure their first serious consideration, opting for an inquiry only where it is essential'.

These three innovations are of considerable significance in practice in that they affect a high proportion of appeals. They are not, however, concerned with mechanisms for the resolution of disputes relating to major

---

[39]   See 1972 Act, Schedule 7, para. 3.
[40]   S.D.D. Circular 47/1980.
[41]   See S.D.D. Circular 26/1984; also S.D.D. Circular 47/1980.
[42]   S.D.D. Memorandum 27/1984 sets out an administrative code for planning appeals handled by written submissions.
[43]   C. M. Brand, 'Measures to Expedite Disposal of Planning Appeals' 1979 S.L.T. (News) 99.

and complex development proposals and raising, perhaps, issues of national significance. Major proposals of this kind are in general subject to the same decision-making processes as the more run of the mill cases.[44] The number of such major proposals is, of course, small but a good deal of concern has been expressed about the efficiency, fairness and legitimacy of decision-making in such cases and the capacity of ordinary procedures to handle the very largest development proposals. This is the subject of brief consideration in section D of this chapter.

The procedures for dealing with appeals by way of written submissions are outlined in section B, while the biggest part of the chapter, section C, is devoted to consideration of the large amount of law relating to public inquiries.

B. WRITTEN SUBMISSIONS

There are no formal rules governing the written submissions procedure but S.D.D. Memorandum 27/1984 sets out an administrative code of practice together with a target timetable. The code is directed principally at appeals under ss.33 and 34 of the 1972 Act but the minister has indicated that its provisions also apply in general terms to other appeals which may be adequately dealt with in writing—for example, some appeals against enforcement notices. The code will also be generally followed when the Secretary of State 'calls in' a planning application for his own determination and a public inquiry is not to be held.

The procedure for lodging appeals under ss.33 and 34 of the 1972 Act has already been described (see chapter 11)[45] and is the same whether matters are to proceed by written submissions or public inquiry. The detailed procedure is set out in Article 16 of the Town and Country Planning (General Development) (Scotland) Order 1981. Notice of appeal under s.33 or s.34 is to be sent within the prescribed period[46] to the Secretary of State on a standard form obtainable from the Scottish Development Department. A copy of the planning application, all relevant plans, the decision notice and any related correspondence must accompany the notice. Notice of appeal must be given to owners and to any agricultural tenants and also to neighbours. The standard form of appeal

---

[44] Some major development proposals are subject to objection procedures under legislation other than the planning Acts. For example, a proposal to construct a trunk or special road on a particular line does not require a formal grant of planning permission but there is a statutory objection procedure under the Roads (Scotland) Act 1984; and the construction of a nuclear power station requires the approval of the Secretary of State for Energy under the Electric Lighting Act 1909 and the Electricity Act 1957.

[45] The procedure for lodging an appeal against an enforcement notice is described in chapter 13.

[46] For appeals under ss.33 and 34 of the 1972 Act the period is six months from the date of the decision or from the expiry of the time allowed for the giving of notice of the planning authority's decision or within such longer period as the Secretary of State may at any time allow.

asks the appellant to state whether he wishes to proceed by way of written submissions or public inquiry.

On receipt of a valid appeal, the Secretary of State informs the planning authority and sends them a copy of the notice of appeal, together with copies of other relevant documentation.[47] The planning authority are requested to complete and return a standard form of questionnaire[48] within fourteen days; this will indicate, among other things, whether the authority are agreeable to the appeal being dealt with by written submissions.

Where both parties have indicated their willingness to dispense with a public inquiry, the Secretary of State will normally agree to the written submissions procedure unless this is considered inappropriate because of the scale or complexity of the proposed development, the possibility of a serious dispute as to the facts, or the existence of considerable third party interests. As soon as the method of dealing with an appeal has been decided, the parties will be notified. Initial agreement on written submissions does not prevent the appellant, the planning authority or the Secretary of State (or the appointed person where appropriate) from deciding to opt instead for a public inquiry at any time before a decision is reached.

The Secretary of State will consider whether to advertise receipt of an appeal in the local press. Any advertisement will state that the minister proposes to decide the appeal on the basis of written submissions, describe the site and the development proposal and say where the grounds of appeal are available for inspection. Any representations should be made to the Secretary of State within fourteen days.

The planning authority have a statutory period of two months from the date of notification of an appeal in which to provide their statement of observations.[49] Annex 3 to S.D.D. Memorandum 27/1984 gives guidance on the recommended format for such statements.[50] If the observations are not submitted within the prescribed period, the Secretary of State may proceed to determine the appeal.[51] The appellant will have a further two weeks within which to comment on the planning authority's statement. The code of practice suggests that supplementary comments by the planning authority and final comments by the appellant will not normally be called for unless new material facts have been introduced. Repeated exchanges of representations, says S.D.D. Circular 26/1984, are rarely helpful. Third parties will be expected to work within similar time limits.

---

[47]   When the appeal is against the decision of a district planning authority, the Secretary of State must serve a copy of the notice of appeal on the regional planning authority (G.D.O., Art. 16(5)) so that they may decide whether to take part in the appeal proceedings. Similar provision is made for notification of the appropriate district authority where the appeal is against a decision made by the regional planning authority (G.D.O., Art. 16(8)).

[48]   For a copy of this see S.D.D. Memorandum 27/1984, Appendix 1.

[49]   G.D.O., Art. 16(4).

[50]   See also paragraph 8 of the Memorandum and S.D.D. Circular 26/1984.

[51]   G.D.O., Art. 16(7).

Once the planning authority's statement of observations has been received, the appellant and the planning authority will be informed whether the appeal is to be decided by an appointed person or by the Secretary of State after taking account of a site report by a reporter. Arrangements will then be put in hand for the site inspection. The parties will be asked whether they wish to accompany the appointed person or reporter. S.D.D. Circular 26/1984 points out that as no discussion of the merits of an appeal is allowed at a site inspection it is often unnecessary for an appointed person or reporter to be accompanied.[52] Generally, the aim will be to hold the site inspection between the third and sixth week after submission of the planning authority's statement of observations; this should allow time for any comments which the appellant may have on the authority's statement to reach the appointed person or the reporter before the inspection takes place.

Thereafter, if the decision on an appeal has been delegated to an appointed person, he will issue a reasoned decision letter some weeks after the site inspection. If the appeal is being decided by the Secretary of State, the reporter will submit his site report to the minister who will in due course issue a reasoned decision letter.[53] The letter and the report will be sent to the appellant and the planning authority and to third parties who have submitted written representations.

Although the written submissions procedure is not governed by statutory rules, the rules of natural justice will have to be observed in the conduct of the appeal. The decision is therefore liable to be quashed if the Secretary of State or the appointed person takes account of relevant factual information without giving the parties an opportunity to comment on that information.[54]

The Secretary of State has no power to award expenses in the case of appeals dealt with by written submissions.[55] These will, accordingly, be borne by the parties themselves.

---

[52] In practice, an appointed person or reporter will always be accompanied when entering enclosed premises.

[53] See s.12(1) of the Tribunals and Inquiries Act 1971 (applied to decisions made by appointed persons by para. 7(1) of Schedule 7 to the 1972 Act). Section 12(1) of the 1971 Act only requires that reasons be given if they are requested on or before notification of the decision but in practice they are provided automatically. Reasons must meet the standards discussed at p.511 below.

[54] See, for example, *Granada Theatres Ltd.* v *Secretary of State for the Environment* [1976] J.P.L. 96; *Wontner Smith and Co.* v *Secretary of State for the Environment* [1977] J.P.L. 103; and *Ellinas* v *Secretary of State for the Environment* [1977] J.P.L. 249.

[55] In July 1984 the S.D.D. issued a consultation paper which proposed that the minister should be empowered to award expenses in connection with planning appeals dealt with under the written submissions procedure and that appointed persons should be empowered to determine applications for an award of expenses in delegated cases.

C. PUBLIC INQUIRIES[56]

The public inquiry presents the planning process at its highest profile. It is the institution which, for the public at large, creates the image of planning they know best—the making of a major decision on a controversial development after public and hotly-contested debate. In truth, of course, the reality of most planning inquiries is very different—with lower stakes, less prominence and less controversy.

As already indicated, the main rules governing procedures at most types of inquiry held under the planning legislation are those made under the Tribunals and Inquiries Act 1971 and much of this section is concerned with consideration of these rules and their interpretation by the courts. There are, on the one hand, the Town and Country Planning (Inquiries Procedure) (Scotland) Rules 1980 (the 'Inquiries Procedure Rules' or 'I.P.R.') which apply to those inquiries which culminate in the presentation to the Secretary of State of a report on the inquiry. The Secretary of State then decides. These rules apply to all inquires ordered by the Secretary of State for the purpose of any planning application which the minister has 'called in' for decision by himself rather than by the planning authority (see p.202 above) and to any appeal (other than those mentioned below which are delegated to an appointed person) made to the Secretary of State under the 1972 Act, under any regulations made under that Act and under s.179(4) of the Local Government (Scotland) Act 1973[57] (I.P.R., r.2). Relatively few inquiries are held under these rules but those that are tend to be the more important ones and those most likely to be the subject of legal challenge. These inquiries are, therefore, considered below in more detail than might seem to be justified by their numbers.

On the other hand there are the Town and Country Planning Appeals (Determination by Appointed Person) (Inquiries Procedure) (Scotland) Rules 1980 (the 'Delegated Appeals Rules' or 'D.A.R.') which apply to these inquiries which culminate in the making of a final decision not by the Secretary of State but by the reporter[58] himself. The delegated classes are defined in the rules and include, subject to certain exceptions, appeals under ss.33 and 34 of the 1972 Act (i.e., appeals against planning authorities' decisions on planning applications or applications for approval of reserved matters and appeals in default of a planning decision), appeals against s.51 determinations, appeals against enforcement notices and waste land notices, and appeals against established use certificates.[59]

---

[56]   In addition to the works mentioned at note 3 (p.479 above), see Anthony Barker and Mary Couper, 'The Art of Quasi-Judicial Administration: The Planning Appeal and Inquiry Systems in England' (1984) 6 Urban Law and Policy 363.

[57]   As substituted by the Local Government and Planning (Scotland) Act 1982, s.69(2) and Schedule 3, para. 24.

[58]   Technically the reporter in such cases is the 'appointed person' but in this chapter the term 'reporter' is frequently used to embrace both 'reporters' and 'appointed persons'.

[59]   See D.A.R., r.2 and Schedule; and the Town and Country Planning (Determination of Appeals by Appointed Persons) (Prescribed Classes) (Scotland) Regulations 1980.

The procedures under the two sets of rules are very similar but references to both sets are included as appropriate. They both apply, with modifications, to appeals dealt with by a hearing rather than by an inquiry but do not apply to any appeal dealt with by way of written submissions (I.P.R., r.2; D.A.R., r.2).

There are several types of inquiry held under the planning legislation which are not governed by procedural rules.[60] These include, for example, inquiries into objections to revocation and discontinuance orders (see chapter 16) and inquiries convened by planning authorities to hear objections to local plans (see chapter 5). In relation to structure plans, the conventional type of public inquiry into objections has been abandoned altogether in favour of an examination in public of those strategic issues which the Secretary of State considers ought to be examined (see chapter 5).

The conduct of examinations in public and local plan inquiries is governed by codes of practice issued by the Scottish Development Department (see chapter 5). Guidance as regards the conduct of other inquiries held under the planning legislation, whether regulated by procedure rules or not, is to be found in the Memorandum accompanying S.D.D. Circular 14/1975 and in S.D.D. Circular 26/1984. Although this guidance has, of course, no binding effect, reporters will be able, by use of their wide powers to regulate procedure at an inquiry and their power to recommend an award of expenses against a party considered to have disrupted the proceedings, to ensure that most of the provisions of S.D.D. Circular 26/1984 and of the code of guidance contained in S.D.D. Memorandum 14/1975 are in practice observed by the parties to an inquiry. The recommended procedures are, of course, to be followed at any particular inquiry only in so far as they are consistent with any enactment or any statutory or common law[61] rules which may be applicable. The guidance would seem, however, to accord with the Inquiries Procedure Rules and the Delegated Appeals Rules and in relation to inquiries governed by the Rules much of the advice can be taken as supplementing the rules. Certain of the provisions of S.D.D. Memorandum 14/1975 and of S.D.D. Circular 26/1984 are outlined below.

Where the Inquiries Procedure Rules or the Delegated Appeals Rules apply, they begin to operate from the stage when the planning authority are notified by the Secretary of State of his intention to hold an inquiry. It is from that time that the rules, augmented by the administrative guidance from the Secretary of State, provide that special procedural mix which characterises the public local inquiry. It is not a completely comprehensive code and much is left to the reporter's discretion. Emphasis in this section

---

[60] Inquiries into objections to compulsory purchase orders promoted under Part VI of the 1972 Act are governed by the Compulsory Purchase by Public Authorities (Inquiries Procedure) (Scotland) Rules 1976.

[61] In certain respects the rules of natural justice impose upon the decision-making body obligations similar to those laid down in the Inquiries Procedure Rules and the Delegated Appeals Rules.

is placed inevitably upon those parts of the procedure which are more fully regulated and those, in particular, which have attracted litigation in which decisions consequent upon inquiries have been challenged in the courts. Because challenge to the ultimate legal validity of decisions is frequently founded on procedural error and because inquiries produce such a wealth of publicly-accessible procedural activity, they are a rich vein for aggrieved developers and others to exploit.

Although the courts have on a number of occasions warned against subjecting inquiry reports and decisions to microscopic examinations,[62] partly as a result of the opportunities for review provided by the procedure rules and partly, it seems as a result of an increased readiness on the part of the judiciary to intervene, the courts have in recent years often been prepared to scrutinise inquiry procedures, reports and decisions fairly closely, exercising what Alder describes[63] as 'a degree of control more detailed than in any other area of judicial review'. This chapter does no more than mention a small proportion of the very large number of decisions on inquiries made by the English courts. The effect of the procedure rules and of the courts' decisions in this field has clearly been to reduce the discretion of the decision-maker; the extent to which this has happened and the question whether such a development is necessarily beneficial are matters on which views can differ markedly.

This concern for procedural justice by parties to inquiries and, through them, the courts, coupled with the concern that they share with the Secretary of State for a certain level of speed and efficiency in decision-making, is what produces the central features of the procedural rules. It is they which are supposed to ensure that appropriate persons and bodies have access to an inquiry and that others are, or may be, excluded; that some persons admitted are given a greater role than others; that appropriate issues are brought before the inquiry and tested in public examination whilst others, including much of central government policy, are excluded; that there is a generally adversarial structure but moderated by an inquisitorial role for the reporter; and that the overall style is sufficiently formal to ensure an adequate marshalling of opposing arguments to test the validity of propositions asserted but without the high degree of formality associated with judicial rules of evidence and procedure. The tension between the demands of justice and efficiency through structure and formality on the one hand, and flexibility and informality on the other is nowhere better illustrated than in the study of the inquiry rules.

A significant amount of space in this section is devoted to pre-inquiry procedures, to the rules according to which evidence is gathered in and to the principles governing procedure at inquiries. Consideration of these matters is important because it is essential to any general description of the combination of formality and, in comparison with courts of law, informality which characterises local inquiry proceedings. It is also

---

[62]   See, for example, *London and Clydeside Properties Ltd.* v *City of Aberdeen District Council* 1984 S.L.T. 50.
[63]   *Development Control*, p.174.

important, however, as a preface to discussion of the contents of reports on inquiries and the decisions based on them. When the legal validity of these decisions is challenged, it is frequently on the basis that an unfair procedure has been followed, evidence admitted or excluded unfairly, or the principles of natural justice not observed.

We turn now to discussion of the law relating to public inquiries and, in the interests of clarity of presentation but at some cost to analytical coherence, a broadly chronological approach based on the order of events at an inquiry is adopted.

1. PRE-INQUIRY PROCEDURES

(a) *Statutory rules*

Preliminary information. On being notified by the Secretary of State of his intention to proceed with consideration of an appeal or a 'called in' application and of the names and addresses of all 'section 26 parties' who have made representations to the Secretary of State, the planning authority must (a) inform the appellant or applicant of the names and addresses of all section 26 parties and (b) inform the Secretary of State of any such persons who have made representations to the planning authority (I.P.R., r.4(1); D.A.R., r.4(1). 'Section 26 parties' are persons falling within certain specified categories who have made representations on the appeal or application (see r.3(1) of both sets of rules).

Where the Secretary of State has given a direction restricting the grant of permission for the development to which the application or appeal relates or where a government department or local authority or development corporation have expressed the view that the application should not be granted, or should be granted only subject to conditions, the planning authority must inform the Secretary of State or the appropriate department or authority that the direction or expression of view is relevant to the application. In such circumstances the Secretary of State or department or authority is then to furnish to the planning authority a written statement of the reasons for the direction or expression of view (see r.4(2) of both sets of rules).

Notification of inquiry. The Secretary of State or appointed person must give at least 28 days notice[64] of the date, time and place of the inquiry to (1) the appellant or applicant; (2) the planning authority; and (3) all

---

[64] The appellant and the planning authority can agree to a shorter period of notice.

section 26 parties[65] (I.P.R., r.5(1); D.A.R., r.6(1)). In a non-delegated case notice must also be given to any other person who has lodged objections in relation to any matter in question at the inquiry (see I.P.R., r.5(1); and 1972 Act, s.267(3)).

The Secretary of State or appointed person may require the planning authority to take steps to publicise the inquiry including the publication of notices in newspapers and the posting of notices in conspicuous places near the site (I.P.R., r.5(2); D.A.R., r.6(2)).

Statements to be served prior to inquiry. In the case of an inquiry into a 'called in' application the Secretary of State is required, not later than 28 days before the date of the inquiry, to serve on the applicant, the planning authority and the section 26 parties copies of a written statement of the reasons for the call in and of any matters which seem to him to be likely to be relevant to his consideration of the application (I.P.R., r.6(1)). In such a case the planning authority must, not later than 14 days before the inquiry, serve on the applicant, the section 26 parties and the Secretary of State a written statement containing the observations which the authority propose to put forward at the inquiry (I.P.R., r.6(2)).

In the case of an inquiry into an appeal the authority's statement of observations must be submitted not later than 28 days before the date of the inquiry (I.P.R., r.6(2); D.A.R., r.7(1)). The planning authority's statement must include a copy of any relevant direction given by the Secretary of State and any reasons for it (I.P.R., r.6(3); D.A.R., r.7(2)). The statement must also include any written expression of view made by a government department, local authority or development corporation on which the planning authority propose to rely in their submission at the inquiry. They must in any case include any expression of view by any such body that the application should be granted (I.P.R., r.6(4); D.A.R., r.7(3)).

In *Davies* v *Secretary of State for Wales*[66] there was a failure to serve a written statement on the appellant but since there was no evidence to show that the failure had caused the appellant substantial prejudice, an application to quash the Secretary of State's decision failed.

The planning authority's statement must be accompanied by a list of any documents (including maps and plans) which the authority propose to refer

---

[65]   In *Co-operative Retail Services Ltd.* v *Secretary of State for the Environment* [1980] 1 W.L.R. 271 the Court of Appeal held that there was no statutory jurisdiction to quash a decision of the Secretary of State to refuse to postpone the start of an inquiry. There was, in any event, no evidence that the minister's refusal had resulted in a breach of the rules of natural justice, having regard to the wide discretion of the inspector to adjourn an inquiry if he thought it necessary in the interests of justice—see p.500 below. See too *Ostreicher* v *Secretary of State for the Environment* [1978] 1 W.L.R. 810. However, in *R.* v *Secretary of State for the Environment, ex parte Mistral Investments* [1984] J.P.L. 516 it was held that in deciding, at the request of the local planning authority, to postpone the holding of a public inquiry, the minister had acted contrary to natural justice in that he had failed to consult the appellants.

[66]   (1977) 33 P.&C.R. 330.

to or put in evidence at the inquiry,[67] together with a notice stating the time and place at which the documents may be inspected by the appellant or applicant and all s.26 parties. The planning authority must afford such parties a reasonable opportunity to inspect and, where practicable, to take copies of the documents[68] (I.P.R., r.6(6); D.A.R., r.7(5)). Interested parties must also be given an opportunity to inspect and, where practicable, take copies of the written statements and other documents (I.P.R., r.6(7); D.A.R., r.7(6)).

If required to do so by the Secretary of State or the appointed person, the applicant or appellant must serve on the planning authority, all s.26 parties and on the Secretary of State or appointed person a written statement of the observations which he proposes to put forward at the inquiry (I.P.R., r.6(8); D.A.R., r.7(7)).

The rules require the disclosure of a considerable amount of information. However, neither the procedure rules nor the principles of natural justice require the disclosure of information (such as the contents of correspondence between a planning authority and the Secretary of State) which has come into the possession of the decision-maker prior to the lodging of the appeal or objection.[69] Nor, it seems, is the decision-maker required to make advance disclosure of 'policy' issues.[70]

Attendance of departmental and local authority witnesses. Both sets of rules provide that in specified circumstances a party to an inquiry can require a representative of the Secretary of State or a government department or a local authority to attend the inquiry as a witness (I.P.R., rules 8 and 9; D.A.R., rules 9 and 10).

(b) *S.D.D. advice*

It is principally towards the stage prior to a public inquiry that the S.D.D.'s guidance is directed. The aim is to ensure the most efficient conduct of the inquiry itself but it is assumed that this aim may be best achieved by preparations made beforehand. In the first place, the fixing of an early date for the inquiry is encouraged. The Inquiry Reporters' Unit, which has the initial responsibility for setting dates, is to agree to deferment only where this is clearly justified (S.D.D. Circular 26/1984). Public bodies are asked to provide a full statement of their reasons for the action or decision giving rise to the inquiry. Objectors or appellants are usually under an obligation to state their grounds of objection or appeal and where any such statement appears inadequate to allow proper preparation for an inquiry, the

---

[67] The rules give the reporter discretion to allow the introduction of new evidence at the inquiry—see p.500 below.

[68] See *Performance Cars* v *Secretary of State for the Environment* (1977) 34 P.&C.R. 92 in which the Court of Appeal held that there had been a breach of the corresponding requirement in the English rules.

[69] See *B. Johnson & Co. (Builders) Ltd.* v *Minister of Health* [1947] 2 All E.R. 395.

[70] See dicta in *H. Lavender & Son Ltd.* v *Minister of Housing and Local Government* [1970] 1 W.L.R. 1231; and *Kent County Council* v *Secretary of State for the Environment* (1976) 33 P.&C.R. 70.

Secretary of State or the reporter will attempt to secure amplification in prior correspondence. In order that the actual inquiry can be kept as short, simple and inexpensive as possible, S.D.D. Memorandum 14/1975 recommends that in all but the most straightforward inquiries the reporter should arrange for the advance circulation among the parties of (i) the written statements of their cases or objections; (ii) the precognitions of any persons to be called as witnesses; (iii) any documents to be founded on; and (iv) the written statement of any policy, whether local or national, which may be relevant. In the view of the Secretary of State the use, for tactical advantage, of 'surprise' evidence is strongly to be deprecated; the withholding of important documentary evidence until the last minute or failure to comply with a request by the reporter to submit written material may, if it causes disruption or adjournment of the inquiry, lead to an award of expenses against the party at fault. An objector who intends to refer to an alternative site should notify the reporter and the Secretary of State as early as possible.

On the authority's side, they are urged in S.D.D. Circular 26/1984 to offer views on conditions which they would wish to see attached if, contrary to their objections, a planning appeal is allowed. The circular states that any fear that their case may be prejudiced is unfounded. The Secretary of State or reporter will, on the contrary, attach great importance, in the interests of achieving the best possible result, to an authority's reasoned views on possible conditions. Both these and the views of the appellant in response would be open to comment or discussion at the inquiry.[71]

The reporter will consider whether to hold a procedural meeting prior to the inquiry. He may well feel that such a meeting is unnecessary if the inquiry is likely to be short and fairly straightforward. The main purposes of such a meeting will be 'to identify the issues, to define the areas of agreement and disagreement between the parties and to determine the likely programme of the inquiry'. Written evidence on agreed matters may then be taken as read and cross-examination on such matters will not normally be allowed. The reporter will also 'try to establish whether areas of disagreement are on minor matters which can be settled by an exchange of correspondence before the inquiry begins or whether they are of such major importance as to justify examination and cross-examination at the inquiry'. A procedural meeting will be advertised and may be held in public.

2. PROCEDURE AT INQUIRY

Appearances at the inquiry. The persons entitled under the rules to appear at, and participate in, an inquiry are: the appellant or applicant; the planning authority; where a direction has been given by the Secretary of State restricting the grant of planning permission, a representative of the Secretary of State; a representative of any government department which

---

[71]   The circular also urges the copying of material between the parties themselves rather than leaving it all to the S.D.D. and the Inquiry Reporters' Unit.

has expressed a written view included in the planning authority's observations; any local authority; a new town development corporation in whose area the land in question is situated; all section 26 parties; any other person on whom the Secretary of State has required notification to be served and (in a non-delegated case) any person to whom notification has been given under s.267(3) of the 1972 Act (I.P.R., r.7; D.A.R., r.8).

That is the list of persons entitled to appear at an inquiry. It is a list which ensures that not only the persons most directly concerned (the appellant or applicant and the planning authority) are involved but also some others who may be regarded as interested 'third parties'. This extension is clearly important as a means of achieving, where necessary, a broad coverage of issues from different perspectives. It ensures a degree of participation in the inquiry process. The statutory list of interested 'third parties' is not, however, comprehensive. It does not open up the inquiry to the public as a whole. This purpose is, however, normally achieved through the exercise of the reporter's discretion. He may permit any other person to appear at the inquiry and it is, in practice, very rare for a reporter to refuse a request to appear. The public inquiry has thus come to be viewed by some as a vehicle for 'public participation' in the planning process.

A local authority or development corporation may be represented by any officer or by counsel or solicitor; any other person may appear on his own behalf or be represented by counsel, solicitor or any other person (I.P.R., r.7(3); D.A.R., r.8(3)).

Paragraphs 22 and 23 of S.D.D. Memorandum 14/1975 set out the procedure which should normally be followed at the opening of an inquiry by those who wish to appear. If any person entitled to appear at an inquiry fails to do so, the reporter or appointed person has discretion to proceed with the inquiry[72] (I.P.R., r.10(8); D.A.R., r.11(8)).

The inquiry. At the inquiry stage proper,[73] S.D.D. Memorandum 14/1975 states that, subject to the fundamental principles of openness, fairness and impartiality, the main emphasis should be on informality, with the avoidance so far as possible of formal procedures and terminology. This is particularly important to help and encourage those who wish to give evidence or to make statements at an inquiry but are not professionally represented. The procedure rules themselves state that, except as otherwise provided, the procedure to be followed at an inquiry is at the

---

[72]   See *Ackerman* v *Secretary of State for the Environment* [1979] J.P.L. 616 (in the circumstances of the case no breach of natural justice in holding inquiry in absence of a party). See too the comments of Lord Denning M.R. in *Ostreicher* v *Secretary of State for the Environment* [1978] 1 W.L.R. 810.

[73]   Although in Scotland, there is no formal rule (cf. Planning Inquiries (Attendance of Public) Act 1982, applicable to England and Wales), inquiries are public in the sense that oral evidence is given in public and documentary evidence is available for inspection. The reporter is entitled, however, to exclude from the inquiry a person who disrupts the proceedings; see the comments of Roskill L.J. in *Lovelock* v *Secretary of State for Transport* (1979) 39 P.&C.R. 468.

discretion of the reporter (I.P.R., r.10(1); D.A.R., r.11(1)). At the commencement of the inquiry the reporter must, however, state the procedure which, subject to consideration of any submission by the parties, he proposes to adopt (I.P.R., r.10(2); D.A.R., r.11(2)).

The appellant or applicant is to be heard first unless the reporter, with the consent of the appellant or applicant, decides otherwise. Other persons entitled or permitted to appear are to be heard in such order as the reporter decides and any closing statements are normally to be made in the same order as that in which the parties were heard; at the discretion of the reporter, the applicant or appellant may be afforded the right to reply to closing statements by the other parties (I.P.R., r.10(3); D.A.R., r.11(3)).

The applicant or appellant, the planning authority and the section 26 parties are entitled to call evidence, to cross-examine persons giving evidence[74] and to make closing statements but any other person appearing at the inquiry may do so only to the extent permitted by the reporter (I.P.R., r.10(4); D.A.R., r.11(4)). The reporter has, in the words of Diplock L. J.,[75] 'a wide discretion to exclude irrelevancies and to curb repetition, to control the procedure and to decide how material probative of relevant fact or opinion shall be adduced'.

Although the rules do not confer upon all parties a right to cross-examine witnesses, it may be that a refusal to permit cross-examination by a party without such an express right will in some circumstances amount to a breach of the rules of natural justice. In *Nicholson* v *Secretary of State for Energy*[76] Sir Douglas Frank held that the rules of natural justice conferred on an objector a right to cross-examine witnesses, provided his questions were directed to evidence contrary to his case and were not repetitive, irrelevant or directed to a purpose contrary to the relevant legislation. But in *Bushell* v *Secretary of State for the Environment*[77] the House of Lords held that although the procedure at an inquiry has to be fair to all concerned, the question of what is fair, including whether cross-examination should be allowed, will depend on the subject-matter of the

---

[74]   Where a planning officer had given evidence on the considerations which led to the planning authority's decision but was reluctant, when asked in cross-examination, to express his personal opinion, the English minister expressed the view that the inspector had acted properly in not pressing the witness to divulge his own views—see [1968] J.P.L. 708. In *Accountancy Tuition Centre* v *Secretary of State for the Environment* [1977] J.P.L. 792 Sir Douglas Frank said, however, that such an attitude on the part of a witness was to be deplored for it was not for a witness to decide what questions he should or should not answer. See too [1979] J.P.L. 257. A Practice Advice Note, 'Planning Officers as Witnesses at Inquiries', produced by the Royal Town Planning Institute and published in *The Planner* of May 1979, deals with the position of a planning officer called as a witness in a case where his professional opinion is not in conformity with the decision of the authority by which he is employed or with the view of a superior officer.

[75]   *Wednesbury Corporation* v *Minister of Housing and Local Government (No. 2)* [1966] 2 Q.B. 275.

[76]   (1978) 76 L.G.R. 693. See, however, *T. A. Miller Ltd.* v *Minister of Housing and Local Government* [1968] 1 W.L.R. 992 (below).

[77]   [1981] A.C. 75. See too *Harris* v *Secretary of State for Scotland,* Court of Session, 14th February 1980 (unreported, but see 1980 S.P.L.P. 18).

particular inquiry and is to be judged in the light of practical realities as to the way in which adminstrative decisions are made; the refusal of an inspector at a motorway inquiry[78] to permit cross-examination of departmental witnesses on issues which their Lordships considered to involve government policy was held in the circumstances of that case not to be unfair.

In its reference to 'government policy' the *Bushell* case raises a more general issue about the scope of local inquiries. There are certain matters which are outwith the remit of an ordinary inquiry. In the first place, where a representative of a government department gives evidence at an inquiry, the reporter must disallow any question to that representative which, in his opinion, is directed to the merits of government policy (I.P.R., r.8(4); D.A.R., r.9(4)). Given the general purpose of a public inquiry, this is not, in principle, surprising. The Secretary of State is not holding an inquiry to subject his government's policy to scrutiny but in order to enable him or his delegate to decide a local issue in the light of any relevant policy. The place for challenging government policy, it is argued, is in Parliament and not in a public hall in Portree. The same position is maintained when, following an inquiry, the decision on an appeal or application is made on the basis of government policy which has not been mentioned at the inquiry. The views of the parties on the policy are presumed to be irrelevant and no injustice can, therefore, arise from a failure to discuss it at the inquiry (see p.509 below). In the majority of small planning inquiries the exclusion from debate of government policy is of little consequence. It is in some large inquiries, however, that, whatever the constitutional justification for leaving the scrutiny of the policies of ministers to Parliament, the merits of such policies are so central to the issues before the inquiry that they can be ignored only at the expense of public frustration (see section D below). It may be particularly frustrating for objectors where a very broad view is taken of what actually constitutes government policy. In the *Bushell* case, it was surprising to have the House of Lords hold that the traffic forecasts upon which a proposal to build a road was based were a part of government policy and, therefore, not subject to investigation at a local inquiry.[79]

Secondly, the reporter's discretion to admit any evidence, written or oral, is subject to a general exclusion of evidence which would be 'contrary to the public interest'. Such evidence must not be allowed (I.P.R., r.10(6); D.A.R., r.11(6)). In *Wordie Property Co. Ltd.* v *Secretary of State for Scotland*[80] there had been a refusal on the part of a reporter to require the disclosure by prospective developers of the estimated profitability of their proposed development. The First Division of the Court of Session took the

---

[78] Procedure at the inquiry was not governed by statutory rules.

[79] This is to be contrasted with the approach of Lord Denning M.R. in the Court of Appeal ((1979) 39 P.&C.R. 341) and the dissenting opinion of Lord Edmund Davies in the House of Lords ([1981] A.C. 75 at pp.114-115.) See also *Kent County Council* v *Secretary of State for the Environment* (1976) 33 P.&C.R. 70 (ministerial statement in House of Commons as to need for oil refineries a matter of government policy); and S.D.D. Memorandum 14/1975, para. 40.

[80] 1984 S.L.T. 345.

view that since the information was clearly of a confidential nature, and was not required for a proper assessment of the risk that the development might not be completed, it could not be said that the public interest required disclosure of the information.

Subject to its being disclosed at the inquiry, the reporter is entitled to take account of any written representation or statement received by him prior to the inquiry from any person, but he must circulate any such document in advance where he considers this to be practicable (I.P.R., r.10(9); D.A.R., r.11(9)).

The reporter may also allow the planning authority or the appellant or applicant to add to the observations contained in any statement served under the rules or to add to any list of documents which accompanied such a statement, 'so far as may be necessary for the purpose of determining the questions in controversy between the parties',[81] but he must (by adjourning the inquiry if necessary) allow the appellant or applicant or planning authority, as the case may be, and all section 26 parties an adequate opportunity of considering any such fresh observations or documents (I.P.R., r.10(7); D.A.R., r.11(7)). In *Performance Cars Ltd.* v *Secretary of State for the Environment*[82] the Court of Appeal held that an extended lunch break did not give the appellants an adequate opportunity to consider documents which had been handed to them by the planning authority just as the inquiry was about to begin. There had therefore been a breach of the procedure rules and of the rules of natural justice.

The reporter or appointed person may make a recommendation to the Secretary of State as to payment of any additional expenses occasioned by an adjournment resulting from the submission of additional observations or documents. The reporter has a general discretion to adjourn the inquiry (I.P.R., r.10(10); D.A.R., r.11(10)). This power he can exercise whenever he thinks it necessary in the interests of justice to any party.[83] In *Gill & Co. (London) Ltd.* v *Secretary of State for the Environment*[84] the inspector conducting an inquiry was asked to grant an adjournment because of the illness of the main witness for one of the parties. Although the other main party did not oppose the request the inspector refused it. His decision was held to contravene the rules of natural justice.

The reporter has wide (though rarely used) powers to compel the attendance of witnesses and the production of documents.[85] He may examine witnesses on oath and may accept in lieu of evidence on oath by any person a statement in writing by that person (1972 Act, s.267(5)). As S.D.D. Memorandum 14/1975 makes clear, the reporter may himself ask

---

[81]   In *Behrman* v *Secretary of State for the Environment* [1979] J.P.L. 677 the view was expressed that it was not incumbent upon the inspector conducting an inquiry to constantly check every document to see whether it was included in the list; the onus was on the parties themselves to be vigilant.

[82]   (1977) 34 P.&C.R. 92.

[83]   See *Co-operative Retail Services Ltd.* v *Secretary of State for the Environment* [1980] 1 W.L.R. 271.

[84]   [1978] J.P.L. 373.

[85]   See 1972 Act, s.267(4) and Schedule 7, para. 5.

questions of parties or witnesses on matters he considers relevant to the inquiry. He may wish to clarify a point or to ensure that any evidence given is properly examined or to bring out matters which might not otherwise be raised. However, the reporter is under no general obligation to seek out material facts or to go routing around to ascertain whether there are any policy documents to which he has not been referred.[86] On occasion the reporter may have to adopt an inquisitorial role in order to safeguard the discretion of the Secretary of State to deal with a planning application as if it had been made to him in the first place[87] and there may be cases where the reporter might properly take it upon himself to correct a failure on the part of a planning authority to refer to a relevant policy.[88]

Although the person appointed to conduct an inquiry will generally give a good deal of assistance to a party who is not professionally represented, it is not part of his duty to act as advocate for such a party.[89]

Evidence. Just as the procedures governing who can give evidence are less rigidly controlled than in a court, so also are the rules of evidence themselves. There is no obligation for evidence to be given on oath and there is no rule against the admission of hearsay evidence. In *T. A. Miller Ltd.* v *Minister of Housing and Local Government*[90] the Court of Appeal rejected the argument that a letter which had been written by a person not present at an inquiry into an enforcement notice appeal, and which was contradicted by witnesses giving evidence (in this instance on oath) at the inquiry, ought not to have been admitted or relied upon by the inspector who conducted the inquiry because it was hearsay and could not be tested by cross-examination. Lord Denning M. R. said: 'Most of the evidence here was on oath, but that is no reason why hearsay should not be admitted where it can fairly be regarded as reliable. Tribunals are entitled to act on any material which is logically probative, even though it is not evidence in a court of law.' In this case natural justice had been satisfied by giving the appellants a fair opportunity to comment on the letter and to contradict it. However, in *French Kier Developments Ltd.* v *Secretary of State for the Environment*[91] Willis J. said that 'some limit must surely be imposed in fairness to an appellant on the scope of so-called evidence which by no stretch of the imagination can be said to have the slightest evidential value'.

Where hearsay evidence is admitted, it is a matter of judgment as to how much weight it should be accorded.[92]

86   See *Rhodes* v *Minister of Housing and Local Government* [1963] 1 W.L.R. 208; and *London Borough of Greenwich* v *Secretary of State for the Environment* [1981] J.P.L. 809. See, however, p.513 below.
87   See 1972 Act, s.33(3).
88   See *London Borough of Greenwich* (above).
89   See *Snow* v *Secretary of State for the Environment* (1976) 33 P.&C.R. 81. Paragraph 20 of S.D.D. Memorandum 14/1975 suggests that assistance is best given by the conduct of proceedings in an informal manner.
90   [1968] 1 W.L.R. 992; see too *Knights Motors* v *Secretary of State for the Environment* [1984] J.P.L. 584.
91   [1977] 1 All E.R. 296.
92   See *Collis Radio* v *Secretary of State for the Environment* (1975) 29 P.&C.R. 390.

T

Site inspection. A personal visit to the site which is the subject matter of the inquiry will not always be particularly helpful to the reporter but the rules do permit him to make an unaccompanied inspection of the appeal site before, during or after the inquiry without notifying his intention to the parties (I.P.R., r.11; D.A.R., r.12). Furthermore, he may, and, if so requested by the appellant or applicant or by the planning authority, he must, inspect the site in the company of such of the parties as wish to accompany him. (See also S.D.D. Memorandum 14/1975, paras. 35 and 36).

In so far as the site inspection does no more than assist the reporter to form a clearer understanding of the evidence given at the inquiry or to test the validity of statements made at the inquiry, it can properly be taken into account without any need to afford the parties an opportunity for comment.[93] If, however, in the course of the site inspection the reporter or appointed person obtains information which was not considered at the inquiry, and there is a real risk that one of the parties might thereby be prejudiced, then, unless the parties are told of the fresh information and given an opportunity to present argument and, if need be, evidence upon the matter, the proceedings may be in breach of the rules of natural justice.[94]

3. PROCEDURE FROM CLOSE OF INQUIRY TO DECISION

Up to the stage at which the inquiry itself closes, the procedures in non-delegated and delegated cases run very much in parallel. The objective to that point is the same—to ensure that relevant evidence and arguments are brought to the attention of the reporter in a manner which is both efficient and fair. Thereafter, however, the procedures diverge sharply to reflect the difference in the decision-making process. In the case of a non-delegated appeal or application, attention is focused upon the report of the inquiry—how it is prepared and what it should contain; the possibility of the admission of further evidence thereafter; and the Secretary of State's decision. Delegated cases are, unsurprisingly, procedurally more simple since the step from inquiry to decision by the appointed person is more direct. In what follows, the procedure in non-delegated cases is described first.

---

[93]   See *Winchester City Council* v *Secretary of State for the Environment* (1978) 36 P.&C.R. 455; affirmed (1979) 39 P.&C.R. 1; and *Coleen Properties* v *Minister of Housing and Local Government* [1971] 1 W.L.R. 433, per Sachs L.J.

[94]   See *Hibernian Property Co. Ltd.* v *Secretary of State for the Environment* (1973) 27 P.&C.R. 197 (in which the inspector in the course of the site inspection put to the occupiers of houses which were the subject of the inquiry proceedings questions as to their views on the proposals for the houses); *Fairmount Investments Ltd.* v *Secretary of State for the Environment* [1976] 1 W.L.R. 1255 (in which the inspector concluded from what he saw on the site inspection that the foundations of the houses which were the subject of the inquiry proceedings were inadequate though no such suggestion had been made at the inquiry); and *Wontner Smith & Co. Ltd.* v *Secretary of State for the Environment* [1977] J.P.L. 103.

Non-delegated case: the report. Where the decision is to be made by the Secretary of State, the reporter who conducted the inquiry will have to prepare a report on the inquiry for submission to the minister. In accordance with the recommendations of the Franks Committee, the Inquiries Procedure Rules require that the report be prepared in two parts.[95]

The rules provide that after the close of the inquiry the reporter is to prepare the first part of his report which is to include his findings of fact (r.12(1)). He must, if so required by any of the parties, provide every party to the inquiry with a copy of part I of the report and must consider any comments received from the parties within 14 days of his furnishing them with part I. While the reporter is not, of course, in any way bound to give effect to the views of the parties, he may, in the light of comments received from any party and after consulting all the other parties,[96] amend part I (r.12(1)(c)). Without the consent of the parties the reporter is not, however, to introduce into the report any matter which was not raised at the inquiry.

The reporter then prepares the second part of his report, which is to include any necessary reasoning and his recommendations if any, or his reasons for not making any recommendation (r.12(2)). Both parts of the report are then submitted to the Secretary of State.

The division of the report into two parts sounds as though it should lead both to the fairness between the parties which is intended to flow from the consultation on the findings of fact and also to a procedure which is simple to operate. In particular, the differentiation between the 'facts' in part I and the 'reasoning and recommendations' in part II seems, in this context, to be sensible and comprehensible. In practice, however, this distinction, along with questions of the sufficiency of findings of fact, have been the cause of some confusion and, because of the opportunity for procedural challenge which this presents, of litigation.

In the important case of *Paterson* v *Secretary of State for Scotland*[97] Lord Cameron stated:

> 'It is, in my opinion, of the first importance, that in matters which so closely affect the rights and interests of the subject, the procedure laid down by the rules should be strictly adhered to, more especially in that part of the procedure which is designed to afford an opportunity to one of the parties to consider and make comments on the draft findings of fact which the reporter proposes to make, after his consideration of the evidence which he has heard, or upon the omission of other findings which the party may consider relevant and important to a proper decision of the appeal. The only proper place

---

[95] Similar provision is made as regards inquiries not regulated by statutory rules by S.D.D. Memorandum 14/1975 (see paras. 42-49).

[96] See *Hamilton* v *Roxburgh County Council* 1970 S.C. 248; 1971 S.L.T. 2, in which the Lord President and Lord Cameron were of the opinion that a reporter had not carried out the consultation required by the rules regulating compulsory purchase inquiries (which are in this respect virtually indentical to the planning inquiries rules).

[97] 1971 S.C. 1; 1971 S.L.T. (Notes) 2.

therefore, for findings of fact, is and must be, in Part I of the report. If there are no findings of fact in that part, or if, what are in reality findings of fact, especially findings which are neither matters of admission nor proof, on which a conclusion and recommendation are based, should appear in Part II of the report and are therefore not available for scrutiny and comment by the parties, this, in my opinion, constitutes a fundamental departure from the required procedure.

'If, as here, the majority of what are findings of fact are contained in Part II of the report, they are in the first place not "findings of fact" at all within the meaning of the rules, and in the second place are therefore not findings on which the reporter is entitled to base his recommendations or the Secretary of State entitled to found his decision.'

In that case the Court of Session quashed the Secretary of State's decision on the ground that the reporter had, by making no proper findings of fact in part I of his report, failed to comply with the procedural rules. The court took the same action in *J. & A. Kirkpatrick* v *Lord Advocate*[98] because of a similar failure on the part of the reporter to comply with the rules.

In *London and Clydeside Properties Ltd.* v *City of Aberdeen District Council*[99] the Second Division seem to have taken a somewhat less strict view of the reporter's obligations in the preparation of part I of a report. Distinguishing *Kirkpatrick* and *Paterson,* which Lord Wheatley described as 'extreme cases', the court held that although the reporter concerned should have made fuller and more particular findings, nevertheless his findings were sufficient to enable the Secretary of State to discharge his duty to decide the appeal. Lord Wheatley said that he did not consider that 'the court should be scrutinising the report as if it were a conveyancing document or treating the procedure as requiring absolute rigid compliance'. In the same case Lord Robertson said that in his opinion it would be extravagant 'to suggest that the reporter must traverse every matter mentioned at the inquiry and make a finding upon it . . . To place such a duty upon the reporter . . . would make his task impossible.' Lord Robertson went on to acknowledge that there could be difficulty in deciding what are 'strictly facts' and therefore appropriate to part I of a report, and 'what are more simply expressions of opinion or speculations by planners or other experts', which are not.[1] In the case before him he was satisfied that questions concerning *inter alia* the agricultural potential of a site and the effect of a proposed development on amenity did not involve issues of fact but were 'essentially matters of opinion and speculation, discussion and negotiation for the future'.

---

[98] 1967 S.C. 165; 1967 S.L.T. (Notes) 27.
[99] 1984 S.L.T. 50; and see comment in 1983 S.P.L.P. 49.
[1] See the decisions mentioned at p.508-p.509 below and the comment on *Wordie Property Co. Ltd.* v *Secretary of State for Scotland* 1984 S.L.T. 345 in 1983 S.P.L.P. 75.

Shortly after the *London and Clydeside* case came the decision of the First Division in *Wordie Property Co. Ltd.* v *Secretary of State for Scotland.*[2] This was another case turning in part upon what constitutes a finding of fact requiring to be included in part I of a report. It was argued, on the one hand, that facts (in this case involving future requirements for shopping floorspace) were to be sharply distinguished from opinions and judgments; facts are matters to be established by direct evidence with precision but do not require the application of further reasoning. On the other hand, it was urged that for the purposes of the inquiry procedure rules facts must, in appropriate cases, include those turning upon an expression of opinion and the employment by the reporter of a reasoning process to find the answer.

It was this latter approach that the court accepted. Lord President Emslie stated[3] that 'reading rule 10(1) [now r.12(1)] as a whole the broad distinction is between findings-in-fact, including inferences of fact, and expressions of opinion, reasoning, and value-judgments on planning merits . . . [W]hen one can clearly identify a question, which can and must be answered, as a question of fact, the answer to that question, no matter how it is arrived at, must go into part I.' In the opinion of Lord Cameron (drawing support from the judgment of Lord Denning M.R. in *Coleen Properties* v *Minister of Housing and Local Government*[4] the distinction to be drawn was between inferences *of* fact (which might certainly include a judgment on, for example, conflicting expert opinion) and inferences *from* facts (which might be among the conclusions and recommendations deriving from the findings of fact and thus appropriate for inclusion in part II of a report).

Whatever the conceptual clarity of this distinction, it is widely acknowledged that, for the reporter himself, there may be quite severe practical difficulties in applying it in the preparation of a report. It was this concern which led the S.D.D. in September 1983 to issue a consultation paper on the procedure rules in which the principal suggestion was that the rules should be amended to remove the need for a report in two parts. Not only would the problems already discussed be removed but time and administrative effort would also be saved. In England and Wales, where the rules have never required the circulation of a separate part I of a report, this has not been the subject of strong criticism. The proposal did not, however, draw support and the rules requiring a divided report in Scotland continue to operate. It therefore remains useful advice to a party to an inquiry to avail himself of his right to see a draft of part I of the report;[5] if he considers that a significant error or omission has been made he will have an opportunity to draw the matter to the reporter's attention.

---

2   1984 S.L.T. 345.
3   Citing the judgment of Lord Denning in *Lord Luke of Pavenham* v *Minister of Housing and Local Government* [1968] 1 Q.B. 172 (see p.508 below).
4   [1971] 1 W.L.R. 433.
5   And see the comments of Lord Wheatley in *London and Clydeside Properties* (above), distinguishing the view of Lord Cameron in *Paterson* v *Secretary of State for Scotland* 1971 S.C. 1; 1971 S.L.T. (Notes) 2.

In *J. & A. Kirkpatrick* v *Lord Advocate*[6] Lord President Clyde said that it was not possible to tell from the inquiry report at issue in that case 'what parts of the evidence [the reporter] accepted as true or indeed whether he accepted any of it'. 'The whole factual foundation upon which any such report must be based', said his Lordship, 'is completely absent. This is a fatal defect in the report for it not only involves a failure to comply with the explicit terms of the rules, but it produces a report in the air without any basis of proved facts behind it.' In both *Wordie Property Co. Ltd.* v *Secretary of State for Scotland*[7] and *Wilson* v *Secretary of State for Scotland*[8] the Court of Session held that the findings in fact in part I of the inquiry report were inadequate to provide a basis for the reporter's recommendations (and consequently for the minister's decision); the result was that the decision in each case had to be quashed.[9] It is clear that the reporter's conclusions must not be based on some factual issue not raised by the parties or on factual evidence which he has discovered on his own initiative, unless he first gives the parties an opportunity to deal with the matter.[10]

Although in *London and Clydeside Properties Ltd.* v *City of Aberdeen District Council*[11] it was held that it is primarily for the reporter to determine which issues are basic and require to be the subject of findings of fact[12] (any other approach would, said Lord Wheatley, turn the findings 'into a full-blown judgment' and that was not the purpose of the rules), the reporter must, it seems, make findings on all fundamental disputed issues[13] and if a matter of real importance has been misunderstood or if the report contains a factual error such as might have affected the decision,[14] the decision may be quashed. There is a duty on the reporter to place the

---

[6]   1967 S.C. 165; 1967 S.L.T. (Notes) 27.
[7]   1984 S.L.T. 345.
[8]   Court of Session, 9th May 1978 (unreported, but see 1981 S.P.L.P. 16). Contrast *J. Smart & Co. (Contractors) Ltd.* v *Secretary of State for Scotland*, Court of Session, 19th December 1980 (unreported, but see 1981 S.P.L.P. 75).
[9]   See too, for example, *Ladbroke (Rentals) Ltd.* v *Secretary of State for the Environment* [1981] J.P.L. 427; and *Banks Horticultural Products* v *Secretary of State for the Environment* [1980] J.P.L. 33.
[10]   See, for example, *Charlton Sand & Ballast Co.* v *Minister of Housing and Local Government* (1964) 190 E.G. 965; *H. Sabey & Co. Ltd.* v *Secretary of State for the Environment* [1978] 1 All E.R. 586; and *D. E. Hudson* v *Secretary of State for the Environment* [1984] J.P.L. 258.
[11]   1984 S.L.T. 50. See too *Paterson* v *Secretary of State for Scotland* 1971 S.C. 1; 1971 S.L.T. (Notes) 2.
[12]   See too *J. Smart & Co. (Contractors) Ltd.* v *Secretary of State for Scotland*, Court of Session, 19th December 1980 (unreported, but see 1981 S.P.L.P. 75); *Continental Sprays Ltd.* v *Minister of Housing and Local Government* (1968) 19 P.&C.R. 774; and *William Boyer & Sons Ltd.* v *Minister of Housing and Local Government* (1968) 19 P.&C.R. 176.
[13]   See, for example, *London and Clydeside Properties Ltd.* v *City of Aberdeen District Council* 1984 S.L.T. 50; *Forkhurst Ltd.* v *Secretary of State for the Environment* [1982] J.P.L. 448; and *Hewlett* v *Secretary of State for the Environment* [1981] J.P.L. 187.
[14]   See, for example, *Hollis* v *Secretary of State for the Environment* (1982) 47 P.&C.R. 351; and *East Hampshire District Council* v *Secretary of State for the Environment* [1978] J.P.L. 182; affirmed [1979] J.P.L. 553.

parties' cases fairly before the Secretary of State.[15] In general a reporter cannot be faulted for failing to deal with an issue not put to him at the inquiry.[16]

The reporter is, however, entitled to make use of his own knowledge, experience and common sense and is not bound to accept the evidence of experts or others, even if uncontradicted.[17] He does not, for example, require expert evidence in order to enable him to come to a conclusion on matters of judgment or opinion such as questions of aesthetic taste[18] and he is entitled to make value judgments on technical issues falling within his qualifications and experience.[19] 'It is', said Lord Widgery C.J. in *Wholesale Mail Order Supplies Ltd.* v *Secretary of State for the Environment*[20] 'a complete misconception to take the view that matters of professional opinion, in planning in particular, require the sort of factual support in evidence which is required in proving the existence of a criminal case.'

Non-delegated case: new evidence after inquiry. Rule 12(3) of the Inquiries Procedure Rules is in the following terms:

'Where the Secretary of State—

(a) differs from the reporter on a finding of fact, or
(b) after the close of the inquiry proposes to take into consideration any new evidence (including expert opinion on a matter of fact) or any new issue of fact (not being a matter of government policy) which was not raised at the inquiry,

and by reason thereof[21] is disposed to disagree with a recommendation made by the reporter, he shall not come to a decision which is at

---

[15] See, for example, *Preston Borough Council* v *Secretary of State for the Environment* [1978] J.P.L. 548; and *Calflane Ltd.* v *Secretary of State for the Environment* [1981] J.P.L. 879.

[16] See, for example, *Newbury District Council* v *Secretary of State for the Environment* [1983] J.P.L. 381; and *Mason* v *Secretary of State for the Environment* [1984] J.P.L. 332; but see p.513 below.

[17] See, for example, *Fairmount Investments Ltd.* v *Secretary of State for the Environment* [1976] 1 W.L.R. 1255, per Lord Russell of Killowen; *J. Smart & Co. (Contractors) Ltd.* v *Secretary of State for Scotland,* Court of Session, 19th December 1980 (unreported, but see 1981 S.P.L.P. 75); *Barratt Developments (Scotland) Ltd.* v *Secretary of State for Scotland,* Court of Session, 17th December 1982 (unreported, but see 1983 S.P.L.P. 50); and *Kentucky Fried Chicken (G.B.) Ltd.* v *Secretary of State for the Environment* (1977) 245 E.G. 839.

[18] See *Winchester City Council* v *Secretary of State for the Environment* (1979) 39 P.&C.R. 1.

[19] See *Westminster Renslade Ltd.* v *Secretary of State for the Environment* (1983) 48 P.&C.R. 255.

[20] (1975) 237 E.G. 185.

[21] If the minister is not influenced by a piece of new evidence he has received, rule 12(3) would not, it seems, operate—see *Lake District Special Planning Board* v *Secretary of State for the Environment* (1975) 236 E.G. 417.

variance with any such recommendation without first notifying the applicant, the planning authority and all section 26 parties who appeared at the inquiry[22] of his disagreement and the reasons for it and affording them an opportunity of making representations thereon in writing within 21 days or (if the Secretary of State has received new evidence or taken into consideration any new issue of fact not being a matter of government policy) of asking within 21 days for the re-opening of the inquiry.'

If asked to do so in accordance with rule 12(3), the Secretary of State must re-open the inquiry and may do so in any other case if he thinks fit (rule 12(4)).

The application of rule 12(3) can give rise to substantial difficulties in practice. The courts have tended to take a pragmatic approach to the rule; it was, said Ormrod L. J. in *Camden London Borough Council* v *Secretary of State for the Environment*,[23] 'made in order to assist practical people to come to practical conclusions and to be fair; and it should be so construed'.

The first branch of rule 12(3) applies only where the Secretary of State differs from the reporter on a 'finding of fact'. A mere difference on a matter of planning judgment does not render the decision vulnerable to attack under the rules. It may therefore be necessary to draw a distinction between, on the one hand, a finding of fact[24] by the reporter and, on the other hand, an expression of opinion by him on the planning merits.[25] The many cases in which this question has had to be considered by the courts show that distinctions of this kind can be very difficult to draw.

In *Lord Luke of Pavenham* v *Minister of Housing and Local Government*,[26] for example, an inquiry report included the statement that the appeal site was defined by a fine-looking wall and formed part of a long-established group of buildings contributing to the attractive character of the area. The Court of Appeal concluded that that was a finding of fact. On the other hand, the report also stated that a well-designed house on the site would not harm the charm of the setting and would not create a precedent. That, the court held, was a mere statement of opinion on the planning merits. The minister was therefore entitled to issue a decision disagreeing with his inspector on the second point without having to give the parties an opportunity to comment.

In *Wordie Property Co. Ltd.* v *Secretary of State for Scotland*[27] (see p.505 above) the First Division of the Court of Session took the view that the

---

22 The minister is not obliged to notify third parties. As a matter of practice, however, the Secretary of State will, it seems, seek to inform them of any consultation under rule 12 when it concerns issues in which they are interested.

23 (1975) 235 E.G. 375.

24 Including, it seems, an inference *of* fact—see *Wordie Property Co. Ltd.* v *Secretary of State for Scotland* 1984 S.L.T. 345 (p.505 above).

25 Including, it seems, inferences *from* facts and matters of judgment—see *J. Smart & Co. (Contractors) Ltd.* v *Secretary of State for Scotland*, Court of Session, 19th December 1980 (unreported, but see 1981 S.P.L.P. 75).

26 [1968] 1 Q.B. 172.

27 1984 S.L.T. 345.

amount of shopping space that would be required within Aberdeen in the future was a matter of fact but that the *type* of shopping space required was a matter of 'planning judgment only'.

It is difficult to draw from the judgments in *Luke* and *Wordie* any clear rules for distinguishing findings of fact from expressions of opinion on planning merits and it may be impossible to prescribe any exhaustive guidelines.[28] In *Pyrford Properties Ltd.* v *Secretary of State for the Environment,*[29] however, Sir Douglas Frank suggested that a finding on an existing state of affairs, not being a finding dependent upon aesthetic taste or other subjective opinion, must be a finding of fact, whereas an expression of subjective opinion on the potential consequences of a proposed development would be an expression on planning merits. While this test would not seem to be capable of providing a solution in every case, it may often be of assistance.

The second branch of rule 12(3) may also leave room for doubts. It may not be easy to say whether material received by the minister constitutes 'new evidence'.[30] In *French Kier Developments Ltd.* v *Secretary of State for the Environment*[31] Willis J. held that where an inspector had disregarded a report which had merely been mentioned at an inquiry, for the Secretary of State to attach any weight to the report amounted to taking 'new evidence' into consideration.

As with 'findings of fact', it can be difficult to decide whether a particular matter should be treated as a 'new issue of fact'.[32] Whether a matter can sensibly and fairly be said to be an 'issue of fact' is, as Willis J. said in *Camden London Borough Council* v *Secretary of State for the Environment,*[33] very much a matter of impression to be gathered not only from the actual words used but also from the context in which they appear.

Matters of 'government policy' do not have to be disclosed under rule 12(3).[34] In this context 'policy' is, as Lord Diplock said in *Bushell* v *Secretary of State for the Environment,*[35] 'a protean word', and the majority decision of the House of Lords in that case demonstrates how difficult it

---

[28] See, for example, *Hamilton* v *Roxburgh County Council* 1970 S.C. 248; 1971 S.L.T. 2; *London and Clydeside Properties Ltd.* v *City of Aberdeen District Council* 1984 S.L.T. 50; *Coleen Properties* v *Minister of Housing and Local Government* [1971] 1 W.L.R. 433; *Vale Estates (Acton) Ltd.* v *Secretary of State for the Environment* (1970) 69 L.G.R. 543; and *Pollock* v *Secretary of State for the Environment* (1979) 40 P.&C.R. 94.

[29] (1977) 36 P.&C.R. 28.

[30] See, for example, *Hamilton* v *Roxburgh County Council* 1970 S.C. 248; 1971 S.L.T. 2. See too *Fairmount Investments Ltd.* v *Secretary of State for the Environment* [1976] 1 W.L.R. 1255; *Bushell* v *Secretary of State for the Environment* [1981] A.C. 75; and *Rea* v *Minister of Transport* (1982) 48 P.&C.R. 239.

[31] [1977] 1 All E.R. 296.

[32] See, for example, *Vale Estates (Acton) Ltd.* (above) (mere aesthetic judgment not an issue of fact).

[33] (1975) 235 E.G. 375.

[34] This includes the policy of another minister. See for example, *Darlassis* v *Minister of Education* (1954) 4 P.&C.R. 281; and *Kent County Council* v *Secretary of State for the Environment* (1976) 33 P.&C.R. 70. Contrast, however, *H. Lavender & Son Ltd.* v *Minister of Housing and Local Government* [1970] 1 W.L.R. 1231.

[35] [1981] A.C. 75.

can be to distinguish between 'fact' and 'policy'.[36] In *Bushell* it was held that particular methods of traffic forecasting employed to determine motorway construction priorities were policy issues. This might be thought to be stretching the word 'policy' to its very limits.[37].

It may be noted that it is only where the Secretary of State is disposed to disagree with a recommendation made by the reporter that the obligations imposed on him by rule 12(3) come into operation. If no recommendation has been made,[38] or if the Secretary of State agrees with the reporter's recommendation, the rules do not oblige the minister to give the parties an opportunity to comment on new findings or fresh evidence. If, however, the minister fails to give the parties a chance to comment on such fresh findings or evidence, his action may well be successfully challenged as contrary to natural justice.[39]

In parallel with the statutory procedural rules, it seems clear that the principles of natural justice impose on the Secretary of State similar obligations. In *Lithgow* v *Secretary of State for Scotland*[40] Lord Dunpark stated that the Secretary of State is 'not entitled to obtain relevant and material factual information from one of the parties without giving opposing parties an opportunity to answer this. Failure in this respect is so great an infringement of the right of every person with a legal interest to a fair hearing that it invalidates the decision.' A breach of natural justice may also occur if the decision-maker takes account of relevant information obtained from a source other than one of the parties or bases his decision on some matter which was not in issue at the inquiry.[41] The decision-maker is, however, free to take account of and to attach such weight as he thinks fit to matters of policy, whether or not these have been canvassed at the inquiry and whether or not the parties have had an opportunity to comment.[42]

In relation to those inquiries not governed by statutory rules the procedure which the Secretary of State will follow where he receives new evidence or takes into consideration any new issue of fact and is, as a result, disposed to disagree with a recommendation made by the reporter, is set out in paragraph 50 of S.D.D. Memorandum 14/1975. That paragraph is broadly similar in its terms to rule 12(3) of the Inquiries

---

[36]   See too *Lithgow* v *Secretary of State for Scotland* 1973 S.C. 1; 1973 S.L.T. 81 (matter of policy that extra cost of alternative route for road outweighed loss of agricultural land).

[37]   On the exclusion of consideration of the merits of 'government policy' at the inquiry itself, see p.499 above.

[38]   See *Westminster Bank Ltd.* v *Minister of Housing and Local Government* [1971] A.C. 508, per Lord Reid.

[39]   See *Hambledon and Chiddingfold Parish Councils* v *Secretary of State for the Environment* [1976] J.P.L. 502.

[40]   1973 S.C. 1; 1973 S.L.T. 81.

[41]   See, for example, the cases cited in note 94 (p.502 above); but contrast *Harris* v *Secretary of State for Scotland*, Court of Session, 14th February 1980 (unreported, but see 1980 S.P.L.P. 18); and *Pople* v *Secretary of State for Scotland*, Court of Session, 23rd September 1981 (unreported, but see 1982 S.P.L.P. 16).

[42]   See, for example, *Darlassis* v *Minister of Education* (1954) 4 P.&C.R. 281; and *Bushell* v *Secretary of State for the Environment* [1981] A.C. 75.

Procedure Rules (above). In any case, the rules of natural justice will apply.

Non-delegated case: decision and reasons. Rule 13 of the Inquiries Procedure Rules requires the Secretary of State to give notice of his decision, with reasons,[43] to the appellant or applicant, the section 26 parties and the planning authority, and to any other party who appeared at the inquiry and asked to be notified of the decision. This rule also provides that any such person who has not received a copy of the inquiry report may obtain one on request.

In *Wordie Property Co. Ltd.* v *Secretary of State for Scotland*[44] Lord Grieve said that 'in framing a decision letter a minister is given a wide discretion and the words he uses will not be construed like a conveyancing document . . .' However, the courts have generally been concerned to impose high standards as regards the nature and extent of reasons given for a decision. In *Wordie Property Co.* (above) the First Division of the Court of Session held that the reasons set out in the minister's decision letter on a planning appeal did not reach the appropriate standard of clarity. In order to comply with his duty under the rules the minister must, said the Lord President (Lord Emslie), 'give proper and adequate reasons for his decision', i.e., reasons which 'deal with the substantial questions in an intelligible way' and which 'leave the informed reader and the court in no real and substantial doubt as to what the reasons for [the decision] were and what were the material considerations which were taken into account in reaching it'.[45] In this case Lord Emslie considered it 'most unfortunate' that the Secretary of State did not in his decision letter expressly state whether or not he accepted the reporter's findings in fact or his conclusions; his Lordship was, however, prepared to accept that it could be inferred from the decision letter that the minister did not disagree with the reporter's findings and had had regard to these matters. In the court's view, however, the decision letter in this case failed in a number of respects to satisfy the tests of adequacy and intelligibility mentioned above. The letter stated that the 'principal reasons' for the decision were based on certain points in the inquiry report. However, it was nowhere made clear what those 'principal reasons' or the points on which they were based actually were. Further, in the court's view the rules required the minister to give *all* his reasons, not just his principal reasons; the reader could not tell

---

[43]   Apart from the rules, s.12 of the Tribunals and Inquiries Act 1971 requires that reasons be given (if asked) for any decision taken after the holding of a statutory inquiry.

[44]   1984 S.L.T. 345.

[45]   Lord Emslie found support for this view in the decisions in *Re Poyser and Mills' Arbitration* [1964] 2 Q.B. 467; *Givaudan* v *Minister of Housing and Local Government* [1967] 1 W.L.R. 250; and *Albyn Properties Ltd.* v *Knox* 1977 S.C. 109; 1977 S.L.T. 41. See too *French Kier Developments Ltd.* v *Secretary of State for the Environment* [1977] 1 All E.R. 296; *Accountancy Tuition Centre* v *Secretary of State for the Environment* [1977] J.P.L. 792; and *Niarchos (London) Ltd.* v *Secretary of State for the Environment* (1977) 35 P.&C.R. 259.

from the decision letter whether the unidentified reasons were such as a reasonable minister was entitled to employ.

In the English courts it has been a frequent ground of challenge that there has been a failure to comply with the statutory requirement to provide a reasoned decision letter. Decisions have, for example, been quashed on the grounds that the letter conveying the decision did not deal adequately with the main issues;[46] or that it omitted to refer to an important recommendation in the inquiry report;[47] or that it did not make clear whether the minister had had regard to an important consideration;[48] or that it did not make clear the reasons for preferring one view to another;[49] or that it contained contradictory reasons;[50] or that it was simply insufficiently detailed to explain or justify the decision.[51]

The decision letter must make clear any reason for disagreeing with the reporter and since there is more scope for misunderstanding in such a case, more comprehensive reasons may be required in such circumstances than where the minister is merely agreeing with the reporter.[52] The Secretary of State is entitled simply to adopt the reporter's reasoning and recommendations[53] but it is not enough that the reasons can only be arrived at by some complex exercise involving cross-reference from one set of documents to another.[54] However, mere surplusage which does not detract from the rest of the letter will not vitiate the decision.[55] Provided that there is evidence before him to justify such action and provided the parties have had an opportunity to deal with relevant issues, the Secretary of State is entitled to come to a decision in accordance with the recommendation in the inquiry report but for different or additional reasons.[56]

It is primarily for the parties to an inquiry to put forward any issues they wish to be considered. In general, no complaint can be made if the Secretary of State fails to take account of some factor or argument not

[46]   See, for example, *French Kier Developments Ltd.* v *Secretary of State for the Environment (No. 2)* [1977] J.P.L. 311; and *London Borough of Camden* v *Secretary of State for the Environment* [1980] J.P.L. 31.
[47]   See, for example, *Kent Messenger Ltd.* v *Secretary of State for the Environment* (1977) 241 E.G. 25.
[48]   See, for example, *Ynystawe, Ynyforgan and Glais Gipsy Site Action Group* v *Secretary of State for Wales* [1981] J.P.L. 874.
[49]   See, for example, *Seddon Properties Ltd.* v *Secretary of State for the Environment* (1978) 248 E.G. 951.
[50]   See, for example, *Knights Motors* v *Secretary of State for the Environment* [1984] J.P.L. 584.
[51]   See, for example, *Banks Horticultural Products Ltd.* v *Secretary of State for the Environment* (1979) 252 E.G. 811; and *Thornville Properties Ltd.* v *Secretary of State for the Environment* [1981] J.P.L. 116.
[52]   See *London Borough of Greenwich* v *Secretary of State for the Environment* [1981] J.P.L. 808.
[53]   *London Welsh Association* v *Secretary of State for the Environment* [1980] J.P.L. 745.
[54]   See *Sheffield City Council* v *Secretary of State for the Environment* (1979) 251 E.G. 165, per Drake J.
[55]   See *French Kier Developments Ltd.* v *Secretary of State for the Environment* [1977] 1 All E.R. 296, per Willis J.
[56]   See *Tempo Discount Warehouses* v *London Borough of Enfield* [1979] J.P.L. 97.

raised expressly or by implication at the inquiry;[57] the minister is not, for example, bound to consider whether a particular condition can be devised which would overcome a particular planning objection and allow planning permission to be granted rather than refused.[58] If, however, a particular issue has been raised at the inquiry the minister will have to consider it;[59] where, for example, a particular condition has been canvassed but the minister considers it unsuitable, he may be under an obligation to consider whether the same object could be achieved by a differently-worded condition.[60] Further, the Secretary of State is presumed to have at his disposal all the information available to his department and may therefore have to call his own attention to any such relevant information.[61]

It appears to be the case that once a decision letter has been issued, any mistake or clerical error it may contain cannot subsequently be corrected.[62] After the issue of the letter the minister is *functus officio*. An obvious silly mistake or clerical error in the letter will not, however, vitiate the decision, so long as the error is not such as to mislead the recipient.[63]

The obligation to provide reasons for a decision may, of course, provide an aggrieved party with ammunition with which to attack the decision. The purpose of the statutory requirements is, said Lord Denning in *Earl of Iveagh* v *Minister of Housing and Local Government*,[64] 'to enable the parties and the courts to see what matters [the minister] has taken into consideration and what view he has reached on points of fact and law that arise'; the reasons may demonstrate, for example, that an irrelevant consideration was taken into account in arriving at the decision.

Delegated case: inquiry to decision. Post-inquiry procedure for an appeal delegated for decision to an appointed person is designed to be simpler. There is no separate report on the inquiry. Instead, the appointed person normally moves directly to the notification of the parties of his decision and reasons (D.A.R., r.14). If, however, he proposes to take into account any new evidence or any new issue of fact, he must first notify the parties and give them an opportunity of making representations or of asking for the re-opening of the inquiry (D.A.R., r.13(1), which is very similar in its

---

57   See, for example, *Chris Fashionware (West End) Ltd.* v *Secretary of State for the Environment* [1980] J.P.L. 678.
58   See *Marie Finlay* v *Secretary of State for the Environment* [1983] J.P.L. 802. If the minister has it in mind to take such action, the rules of natural justice may require that he give the parties an opportunity to comment—see *L. R. Jillings* v *Secretary of State for the Environment* [1984] J.P.L. 32.
59   See *Tierney* v *Secretary of State for the Environment* [1983] J.P.L. 799.
60   See *Robert Hitchins Builders Ltd.* v *Secretary of State for the Environment* [1979] J.P.L. 534.
61   See *Prest* v *Secretary of State for Wales* (1983) 81 L.G.R. 193; and *Hollis* v *Secretary of State for the Environment* (1982) 47 P.&C.R. 351.
62   See dicta in *Miller* v *Weymouth and Melcombe Regis Corporation* (1974) 27 P.&C.R. 468; *Gosling* v *Secretary of State for the Environment* (1975) 234 E.G. 531; and *Preston Borough Council* v *Secretary of State for the Environment* [1978] J.P.L. 547.
63   See, for example, *Hope* v *Secretary of State for the Environment* [1979] J.P.L. 104.
64   [1964] 1 Q.B. 395.

terms to r.12(3) of the Inquiries Procedure Rules (see p.507 above)). Like the Secretary of State, he may apply aspects of government policy to his findings and the other 'new evidence' principles and problems also apply.[65]

Although there have been indications that in a delegated case reasons somewhat less comprehensive than are required in a non-delegated case (above) may suffice,[66] the principles governing their nature and extent are broadly similar to those applicable to non-delegated appeals.[67] The decision letter must set out the main issues and the factual basis for the appointed person's conclusions and must be sufficiently detailed to let the parties know what conclusions the appointed person reached on the principal issues of controversy and why he has reached those conclusions.[68]

4. AWARD OF EXPENSES

The Secretary of State is empowered to make orders as to the expenses incurred by him in relation to a local inquiry and as to the expenses incurred by the parties to the inquiry and as to the parties by whom such expenses shall be paid (1972 Act, s.267(7)). An order requiring any party to pay expenses may be enforced in the same manner as a recorded decree arbitral (s.267(8)). These provisions are applied to inquiries into delegated appeals (see 1972 Act, Sched. 7, para. 5). There is, however, no power to make an order as to expenses in relation to a case dealt with at a hearing or by written submissions.[69]

The Secretary of State's policy on the award of expenses is set out in S.D.D. Circular 25/1966. The circular makes clear that it is only in very limited circumstances that an award of expenses will be made. Broadly speaking, where a person has successfully defended his property against action initiated by a public authority—where, for example, a landowner's objections to a compulsory purchase order are upheld following an inquiry and the order is not confirmed—an award of expenses will generally be made. The types of inquiry in which expenses will be awarded to successful objectors include inquiries arising out of orders revoking or modifying planning permission, orders requiring discontinuance of an authorised use

---

[65]   A good recent example is *Barratt Developments (Scotland) Ltd.* v *Secretary of State for Scotland,* Court of Session, 17th December 1982 (unreported, but see 1983 S.P.L.P. 50). See too *Lewis Thirkwell* v *Secretary of State for the Environment* [1978] J.P.L. 844.

[66]   See, for example, *Ellis* v *Secretary of State for the Environment* (1974) 31 P.&C.R. 130; and *London Borough of Greenwich* v *Secretary of State for the Environment* [1981] J.P.L. 808.

[67]   See, for example, *London Borough of Greenwich* (above); *Duffy* v *Secretary of State for the Environment* (1981) 259 E.G. 1081; and *Hope* v *Secretary of State for the Environment* (1975) 31 P.&C.R. 120.

[68]   See *Hope* (above); *D.F.P. (Midlands)* v *Secretary of State for the Environment* [1978] J.P.L. 319; *Bell & Colvill Ltd.* v *Secretary of State for the Environment* [1980] J.P.L. 823; *Hewlett* v *Secretary of State for the Environment* [1981] J.P.L. 187; and *Enticott & Fullite Ltd.* v *Secretary of State for the Environment* [1981] J.P.L. 759.

[69]   See, however, the consultation paper issued by the S.D.D. in July 1984 and mentioned at p.489 above.

or the alteration or removal of authorised buildings or works, and compulsory purchase orders.[70] Where an objector is partly successful at such an inquiry—where, for example, he succeeds in having part of his land excluded from a compulsory purchase order—he will be awarded a proportion of his expenses.

In other cases expenses will normally be awarded only where one party has been guilty of unreasonable behaviour. Even though 'successful', for example, in an appeal against a refusal of planning permission, an appellant will generally not be awarded expenses.

Where an inquiry is adjourned or postponed through the fault of any party (including any 'third party' who has been allowed to appear) the Secretary of State will consider applications from other parties for the extra expenses occasioned by the adjournment or postponement.[71] Otherwise, expenses will normally be awarded only where one party has behaved 'unreasonably, vexatiously or frivolously'. In considering such an allegation the Secretary of State will, states the circular, have regard to the considerations set out in paragraphs 23 to 29 of the report of the Council on Tribunals on the Award of Costs at Statutory Inquiries.[72] That part of the report states that it is reasonable to expect a higher standard of behaviour from planning authorities than from appellants and that it should be regarded as exceptional to award expenses against an objector where the proposal in issue was initiated by a public body. The report declares that the main criterion of unreasonable behaviour is whether one party has been put to unnecessary and unreasonable expense either because the matter should never have come to inquiry or because of the conduct of one of the parties. Paragraphs 27 to 29 state that the minister might, for example, award expenses:

(a) where a previous ministerial decision had made it clear what the decision would be; or
(b) where the planning authority have been unable to support their decision by any substantial evidence; or
(c) where the appeal could have been avoided by discussion or exchange of information which has been refused by one party; or
(d) where the appeal or the authority's decision was obviously prompted by considerations which had little or nothing to do with planning.

The reporter will record any representations made about expenses and in cases where a party produces new evidence at a late stage and causes the disruption or adjournment of the inquiry, the reporter may well make a recommendation as to payment of expenses by that party.[73] S.D.D. Circular 25/1966 states that the making of an application is not a necessary

---

[70] Enforcement notices are not considered to be analogous in character to such orders—see [1979] J.P.L. 788. See too *R. v Secretary of State for the Environment, ex parte Reinisch* (1971) 22 P.&.C.R. 1022.
[71] See too paras. 13 and 14 of S.D.D. Memorandum 14/1975.
[72] Cmnd. 2471, 1964.
[73] See I.P.R., r.10(7); D.A.R., r.11(7); and para. 49 of S.D.D. Memorandum 14/1975.

pre-requisite for an award. The amount of any award will in the first place be left for agreement between the parties. Failing agreement, parties will be asked to agree to final submission of their accounts to the Auditor of the Court of Session who will tax them in manner similar to that in which he taxes judicial accounts in the Court of Session.

D. MAJOR INQUIRIES

The procedures described in section C above apply to all public inquiries into planning appeals and into planning applications called in for a decision by the Secretary of State, whatever the size or complexity of the proposal in question. However, since the 1960s concern has been expressed about the limitations of the planning inquiry as a mechanism for investigating major proposals.[74]

In part, this concern reflects some dissatisfaction with the wider decision-making process within which the public inquiry operates. This is especially true of certain proposals founded on national policy. Where a promoter supports a proposal by reference to national policy, objectors, not surprisingly, may wish to question the merits of that policy. The general position is that the merits of national policy are not in issue at a public inquiry; they are a matter on which the government is, in theory, accountable to Parliament. The difficulty arises in cases where there has been little or no Parliamentary discussion of the underlying policy. In such cases, objectors may seek to use the public inquiry as a vehicle for questioning national policy. The disruption of a number of major road inquiries during the 1970s was, in part, symptomatic of this frustration with the wider decision-making process. Consideration of possible solutions to this difficulty are beyond the scope of this book. We mention the difficulty as one explanation for the concern which has been expressed.

From time to time development proposals raising national policy implications will come forward in what might be described as a policy vacuum. In these circumstances it would seem unavoidable that the investigatory process should consider where the national interest lies. Some of the concern that has been expressed reflects doubts about whether a planning inquiry into what are ostensibly the land use implications of a proposal to develop a particular site can canvass the range of issues that may need to be investigated in order to determine where the national interest lies. The experience of recent years suggests that there may now be less cause for concern on this count. The wide discretion vested in reporters and inspectors concerning the agenda for inquiries is being exercised in such a way as to enable an increasingly broad range of issues to be canvassed, some of which may have only a tenuous connection with land use.

---

[74]   See, for example, G. Ganz, *Administrative Procedures;* D. Pearce, L. Edwards and G. Beuret, *Decision Making for Energy Futures* (Macmillan, 1979); Outer Circle Policy Unit in association with JUSTICE and the Council of Science and Society, *The Big Public Inquiry* (1979); and J. Rowan-Robinson, 'The Big Public Inquiry' (1981) 4 Urban Law and Policy 373.

It is, however, questionable whether the planning inquiry is well suited to give adequate consideration to matters of alternative sites, alternative strategies and alternative technologies. By the time a proposal is submitted to develop a particular site, plans for the development may be well advanced and the opportunity to persuade the developer to give serious consideration to alternatives may have passed.

Perhaps the most serious criticism of the public inquiry as a mechanism for investigating major proposals is directed at the method of investigation. The Town and Country Planning Association summarised this concern when they commented in the context of the Windscale inquiry[75] that 'the very process of the inquiry might be as important for the future of the nuclear energy debate as the issues under discussion'.[76] Although the inquiry procedure combines features of both an inquisitorial and an adversarial process, the method of investigation is essentially adversarial. Whilst the adversarial process has advantages in terms of the thorough testing of evidence, the inquiry is in effect a confrontation between parties who are likely to be more concerned with defending their position than with determining where the public interest lies. With this type of procedure the initiative as regards seeking out and providing the information for the decision-maker rests largely upon those contributing to, rather than upon the person conducting, the inquiry. With major proposals, inequality between the parties in matters of access to information, expertise and funding may result in an unequal contribution to the inquiry. The investigation procedure where a major development proposal is in issue is likely to be viewed, therefore, as neither fair nor comprehensive.[77]

As long ago as 1967 the government acknowledged that where proposals raised wide or novel issues of more than local significance, 'the ordinary public local inquiry is not satisfactory either as a method of permitting the full issues to be thrashed out or as a basis for a decision which can take into account the whole range of practicable alternatives'.[78] The result was the introduction of a new investigatory procedure, the Planning Inquiry Commission (P.I.C.), provision for which is now contained in ss.44 to 47 of the 1972 Act.

The P.I.C. is intended to cater for planning proposals which raise considerations of national or regional importance or which present unfamiliar technical or scientific aspects and which, in either case, merit a special inquiry. The P.I.C. would operate in two stages. Stage one would involve consideration of the general background to a proposal on the lines of a Royal Commission. Stage two would be a site-specific local inquiry (or inquiries) to look at the details of the proposal and objections to it. The Commission would comprise a panel of between three and five members

---

[75] This was an inquiry held in 1977 under s.35 of the Town and Country Planning Act 1971 into a proposal by British Nuclear Fuels Ltd. to construct a thermal oxide reprocessing plant at Windscale in Cumbria.

[76] *Town and Country Planning*, May 1978, p.269.

[77] This difficulty has been alleviated in some cases by the appointment of counsel to the inquiry.

[78] Cmnd. 3333, 1967.

who would have power to initiate research and consider alternative sites.

The P.I.C. has never been used. The reasons for this are a matter for conjecture;[79] it has been suggested, however, that the procedure would be unacceptable because the first stage of the process would pre-empt the decision on the second stage.[80]

In the meantime, there has been no shortage of proposals for alternative procedures for investigating major development proposals.[81] However, recent indications suggest that the present government is thinking in terms of modifications to the conventional public inquiry rather than an alternative procedure for handling such major developments.[82]

---

[79] See L. Edwards and J. Rowan-Robinson, 'Whatever Happened to the Planning Inquiry Commission?' [1980] J.P.L. 307.

[80] See announcement by Mr. Peter Shore, then Secretary of State for the Environment, reprinted in [1978] J.P.L. 731. See also *The Big Public Inquiry* (above).

[81] For discussion of some of these see J. Rowan-Robinson, 'The Big Public Inquiry' (1981) 4 Urban Law and Policy 373.

[82] 'Preparing for Major Inquiries: a Code of Practice', Department of the Environment, June 1984.

CHAPTER 21

CHALLENGE OF PLANS, ORDERS AND PLANNING DECISIONS IN THE COURT OF SESSION

The position regarding recourse to the courts in respect of plans, orders and decisions made under the planning legislation is somewhat complex. The public interest would seem to demand that the validity of plans and the more important types of planning orders and decisions should at some stage become unchallengeable in the courts. Without some cut off point, public or private resources might, for example, be wasted upon development carried out on the strength of a decision subsequently found to have been unlawful. Sections 231 to 233 of the 1972 Act therefore provide that structure plans, local plans and certain types of planning orders and decisions can be challenged on specified grounds in the Court of Session within a short period but are not otherwise to be questioned in any legal proceedings whatsoever. The effect of ss.231 to 233 is considered in section A of this chapter.

Challenge of enforcement notices is discussed in detail in chapter 13 but brief mention of the statutory provisions governing challenge of such notices is made in section B of this chapter.

Section 234 of the 1972 Act, which makes provision for appeal to the Court of Session against determinations under s.51 of the 1972 Act, is considered in section C.

Although ss.231 to 233 (above) govern challenge of many of the more important decisions that can be made under the planning legislation, they do not apply to all decisions or actions that may be taken under the legislation; those decisions not covered by the statutory provisions on challenge are subject to the general supervisory jurisdiction of the Court of Session. The challenge of such decisions is discussed in section D.

A. STATUTORY APPLICATIONS TO QUASH

Section 231 of the 1972 Act states, in effect, that except as provided in the Act the validity of structure plans, local plans and specified types of orders and decisions 'shall not be questioned in any legal proceedings whatsoever'. This ouster of the courts' jurisdiction is, however, linked with provisions under which the validity of any such plan, order or decision may be challenged in the Court of Session[1] within a six week period on the

---

[1]   Application is to be made to the Inner House—see *Rules of the Court of Session*, rule 290.

grounds laid down in ss.232 and 233 of the 1972 Act. Almost identical provisions are to be found in legislation on compulsory purchase, housing and roads, and several of the cases mentioned in this section arose as a result of action taken under such legislation.

While the grounds on which decisions may be challenged under the 1972 Act have been generously interpreted by the courts, the construction of the provisions setting a time limit upon challenge has generally been strict.

The period of six weeks allowed for challenge in the Court of Session has often been stigmatised as unduly short. It has also been frequently argued that ss.231 to 233 are wider in their scope than is necessary; it is, for example, by no means obvious that the right to challenge a tree preservation order needs to be cut off after the expiry of six weeks.

Applications to Court of Session: scope

Structure and local plans, roads orders, etc. Under s.232 of the 1972 Act 'any person aggrieved'[2] by a structure plan or local plan, or by any alteration, repeal or replacement of such a plan, may question its validity in the Court of Session within six weeks of the publication of the first notice of approval of the plan, alteration, repeal or replacement. Application under s.232 may be made on the grounds that the plan, alteration, repeal or replacement is wholly or to any extent outside the powers of Part II of the 1972 Act or that the requirements of Part II of the Act or of any regulations made thereunder have not been complied with in relation to the approval or adoption[3] of the plan or its alteration, repeal or replacement.[4] A failure to comply with the non-statutory Codes of Practice for the examination in public of structure plans and for local plan inquiries (see p.89 and p.103 above) will not on that account alone provide grounds for an application under s.232, though in some circumstances such a failure might involve a breach of the rules of natural justice (in which case the plan might be treated as outwith the powers of the Act (below)).

Section 232 also applies (with appropriate modifications) to challenge of the validity of certain roads orders made under the 1972 Act and to orders under s.224 of the 1972 Act relieving statutory undertakers from undertakings which have become impracticable (see s.232(3)[5]).

The wording of s.232 suggests that it is only when a plan has been approved or adopted that its validity can be questioned. Further, s.231(1) provides that, except as provided in s.232, the validity of a structure plan, a local plan or any alteration, repeal or replacement of any such plan shall not be questioned in any legal proceedings whatsoever, whether before or

---

[2]   The meaning of this expression is considered at p.528 below.

[3]   In *Sand and Gravel Association Ltd.* v *Buckinghamshire County Council* (Court of Appeal, unreported, 14th November 1984) Purchas L. J. pointed out that this provision only applies to procedures relating to 'the approval or adoption of the plan' and may not apply to all the earlier procedures required by Part II of the Act.

[4]   English decisions on applications to quash structure and local plans are discussed in chapter 5 above.

[5]   Inserted by the Local Government and Planning (Scotland) Act 1982, Schedule 2, para. 36; and amended by the Roads (Scotland) Act 1984, Schedule 11.

after the plan, alteration, repeal or replacement has been approved or adopted. Taken together, these provisions would seem to mean that any challenge of the validity of the procedures leading up to adoption or approval of a plan must be postponed until the plan has actually been approved or adopted, and that procedures leading up to adoption or approval of a plan are not subject to challenge at common law. However, the statutory provisions only relate to challenge of the validity of a plan or its alteration, repeal or replacement and it would seem that a decision *not to approve or adopt* a plan might in some circumstances be challengeable on common law grounds[6] (see section D of this chapter).

Other orders and actions. In broadly similar fashion, s.233 of the 1972 Act provides that if any person is aggrieved by any order or action to which the section applies and desires to question the validity of such order or action on the grounds that it is not within the powers of the Act or that any of the 'relevant requirements' have not been complied with, he may, within six weeks from the date on which the order was confirmed or the action taken[7], make application to the Court of Session to have the order or action quashed. The expression 'relevant requirements' means any requirements of the 1972 Act or of the Tribunals and Inquiries Act 1971 (or of any enactment replaced thereby) or of any relevant order, regulations or rules made under those statutes (s.233(7)); a failure to comply with the rules relating to inquiry procedures will therefore provide grounds for an application under s.233.

Among the more important orders to which s.233 applies are orders revoking or modifying planning permission, orders discontinuing or modifying authorised uses, tree preservation orders, orders defining areas of special advertisement control and listed building revocation or modification orders. Section 233 also applies, *inter alia*, to the following decisions of the Secretary of State: decisions on planning appeals under s.33 of the 1972 Act, decisions on applications referred to the minister under s.32, decisions relating to applications for consent under tree preservation orders, decisions relating to consents under the advertisement regulations, decisions on appeals against waste land notices, decisions on appeals against enforcement notices, decisions to confirm or not to confirm purchase notices and decisions on applications for listed building consent referred to the minister (see s.233(3)[8]).

Section 233 therefore applies to many, though not all, of the more important types of order which can be made by the Secretary of State and by planning authorities under the 1972 Act and to many of the decisions or

---

6   See *London Borough of Islington* v *Secretary of State for the Environment* [1980] J.P.L. 739.

7   As to the date when action is 'taken' see *Griffiths* v *Secretary of State for the Environment* [1983] 2 A.C. 51 (see p.533 below).

8   Applying s.231(2) and (3) (as amended by the Local Government and Planning (Scotland) Act 1982, s.47; Schedule 2, para. 35; and Schedule 4, Part I; and (prospectively) by the Town and Country Planning (Minerals) Act 1981).

actions which may be taken by the Secretary of State[9] under the Act. Much local authority decision-making is, however, outwith the scope of s.233, with the result that it will sometimes be possible to challenge such decisions at common law.

In some cases s.233 speaks of decisions 'relating to' an application, while in other cases it speaks of decisions 'on' particular matters. In *Co-operative Retail Services Ltd.* v *Secretary of State for the Environment*[10] it was held that a decision of the Secretary of State 'on an appeal' meant a decision disposing of the appeal and did not include a decision relating to the adjournment of a public inquiry.[11] It seems that a decision not to entertain an appeal cannot be said to be a decision on an appeal.[12] The reference in s.233 to action 'on the part of' the Secretary of State means that action taken by a planning authority (such as a failure to comply with the rules relating to inquiry procedures), even though it occurs in the course of proceedings before the Secretary of State, does not come within the ambit of s.233.[13]

Where, as in the *Co-operative Retail Services* case (above), the court has no jurisdiction to hear an application under the statute, action at common law may be possible. Section 233(4) of the 1972 Act specifically provides that nothing in s.233 is to affect the exercise of any jurisdiction of any court in respect of any refusal or failure on the part of the Secretary of State to take any such action as is mentioned in s.231(3) (i.e., to make a decision of the types mentioned above).

The statutory grounds of challenge

The plans, orders and decisions to which ss.232 and 233 are applicable may be challenged in the Court of Session on one or both of two grounds. Though the wording in the two sections differs somewhat, the grounds on which the validity of a plan, order or decision may be attacked under s.232 or s.233 are essentially similar—(1) that the plan, order or decision in question is outwith the powers of the Act; and (2) that there has been a failure to comply with a relevant statutory requirement (see s.232(1), (2)(b); and s.233(1), (4)(b)).

In *Wordie Property Co. Ltd.* v *Secretary of the State for Scotland*[14] the Lord President (Lord Emslie) said that there could be 'little doubt' as to the scope of the statutory grounds of challenge, the law now being 'well

---

9   The decision of a person appointed by the Secretary of State to determine a planning or enforcement appeal is treated as that of the Secretary of State (1972 Act, Schedule 7, para. 2(4)).

10   [1980] 1 W.L.R. 271.

11   Brandon L.J. expressed doubts as to the correctness of views expressed by Slynn J. in *Chalgray Ltd.* v *Secretary of State for the Environment* (1977) 33 P. & C.R. 10.

12   *Lenlyn Ltd.* v *Secretary of State for the Environment, The Times,* 5th December 1984.

13   See, for example, *Davies* v *Secretary of State for Wales* (1976) 33 P. & C.R. 330; and *Performance Cars Ltd.* v *Secretary of State for the Environment* (1977) 34 P. & C.R. 92. Such proceedings may, however, be tainted by failure to comply with the rules of natural justice.

14   1984 S.L.T. 345.

settled'. Some lingering doubts do, however, remain, mainly as a consequence of divergent views expressed in the House of Lords in *Smith* v *East Elloe Rural District Council*,[15] as to the breadth of the first ground; these views are outlined below. Questions can also arise as to where the dividing line between the two grounds of challenge is to be drawn.

In *Easter Ross Land Use Committee* v *Secretary of State for Scotland*[16] the Lord President (Lord Clyde) expressed the view that the two grounds of challenge are 'quite separate'. The courts have, however, found considerable difficulties 'in seeking to define different spheres for, or to draw a borderline between, on the one hand, situations in which the order is "not within the powers of this Act" and, on the other hand, situations in which a "requirement of this Act has not been complied with".'[17] Although, as indicated below, the courts have not sought to draw fine distinctions between the two grounds, the borderline can sometimes be of significance in that an application made on the second ground—failure to comply with a statutory requirement—will only succeed if the court is satisfied that the applicant's interests have been substantially prejudiced by the failure (see p.527 below). No such condition needs to be satisfied where a plan, order or decision is attacked on the first ground.

Ground (1) appears to be an attempt to encapsulate in statutory form the common law doctrine of *ultra vires* but in *Smith* v *East Elloe Rural District Council*[18] a majority of the House of Lords considered (*obiter*) that this ground of challenge should be given a narrow interpretation. Lord Reid would have excluded from the ambit of the statutory provision any misuse of power, whether *bona fide* or *mala fide*. In his view, this ground of challenge included only violation of express statutory requirements. The importance of this view is that, assuming that the statutory provision ousting the court's jurisdiction after six weeks[19] is effective, those defects which are based on common law presumptions, such as breach of natural justice, unreasonableness or acting from improper motives, would not be subject to the court's supervision. In the same case Lords Morton and Somervell expressed the view that challenge on the ground of *mala fides* was excluded. Viscount Simonds and Lord Radcliffe, on the other hand, were inclined to give the provision a wide construction, Lord Radcliffe stating that in his view the words 'is not empowered' were 'apt to include a challenge not only on the ground of *vires* but also on the ground of bad faith or any other ground which would justify the court in setting aside a purported exercise of statutory power'.

Differing views as to the scope of this ground of challenge are also to be

---

15   [1956] A.C. 736.
16   1970 S.C. 182; 1970 S.L.T. 317. See too *McCowan* v *Secretary of State for Scotland* 1972 S.C. 93; 1972 S.L.T. 163.
17   *Gordondale Investments Ltd.* v *Secretary of State for the Environment* (1971) 23 P. & C.R. 334, per Megaw L. J.
18   [1956] A.C. 736.
19   See p.533 below.

found in Scottish decisions. In *Hamilton* v *Secretary of State for Scotland*[20] Lord Kissen stated that the narrow construction favoured by Lord Reid in the *East Elloe* case was to be preferred; this ground would not, Lord Kissen thought, allow challenge on the ground of failure to observe the rules of natural justice or on grounds of procedural *ultra vires.* Lord Kissen considered that unless one took this narrow view of the first limb of the statutory grounds, the second limb would be superfluous since procedural defects would come under ground (1).[21].

On the other hand, in *Lithgow* v *Secretary of State for Scotland*[22] Lord Dunpark expressed the view that the phrase 'not within the powers of this Act' should receive a broad construction and, though he found that there was no such breach in the case before him, considered the phrase wide enough to allow the court to quash a decision for breach of the rules of natural justice; if, his Lordship said, 'a Minister exercises a statutory power in a manner prohibited by common law, that, in my opinion, is just as much a non-exercise of his statutory powers as the purported exercise of non-existent powers.'[23] As Lord Dunpark pointed out, however, there may be cases where the same facts will 'found two arguments, viz, (i) breach of a statutory requirement and (ii) cumulatively or alternatively, breach of the principles of natural justice' (which would in his view mean that the decision was outwith the statutory powers).

As indicated below, it is the broad view of the first ground of challenge which appears to have prevailed. The second ground of challenge embraces those sorts of failure to comply with legislative requirements which do not fall within the first ground and will therefore include defects (such as failure to give reasons for a decision) which would not render a decision *ultra vires* at common law.

The 'Ashbridge formula'

In recent times the courts in both Scotland and England have adopted a broad approach to the scope of the statutory grounds of challenge and have not generally sought to draw fine distinctions between the two grounds. This development owes much to Lord Denning. In *Webb* v *Minister of Housing and Local Government*[24] he described the judgments in the *East Elloe* case as 'so differing that they give no clear guidance, or at any rate,

---

[20]   1972 S.C. 72; 1972 S.L.T. 233. See too *Peter Holmes & Son* v *Secretary of State for Scotland* 1965 S.C. 1; 1965 S.L.T. 41.

[21]   However, this appears to ignore the fact that not all procedural defects go to jurisdiction so as to render a decision *ultra vires.*

[22]   1973 S.C. 1; 1973 S.L.T. 81.

[23]   In *Fairmount Investments Ltd* v *Secretary of State for the Environment* [1976] 1 W.L.R. 1255 Lord Russell of Killowen expressed the view that breach of the principles of natural justice came within both of the statutory grounds of challenge. See too *Errington* v *Minister of Health* [1935] 1 K.B. 249; *Hibernian Property Co. Ltd.* v *Secretary of State for the Environment* (1973) 27 P. & C.R. 197; *Hamilton* v *Roxburgh County Council* 1970 S.C. 248; 1971 S.L.T. 2; and *George* v *Secretary of State for the Environment* (1979) 38 P. & C.R. 609.

[24]   [1965] 1 W.L.R. 755.

no guidance that binds us' and in *Ashbridge Investments Ltd.* v *Minister of Housing and Local Government*[25] he said of the statutory grounds of challenge:[26]

'The Court can only interfere on the ground that the Minister has gone outside the powers of the Act or that any requirement of the Act has not been complied with. Under this section it seems to me that the court can interfere with the Minister's decision if he has acted on no evidence; or if he has come to a conclusion to which on the evidence he could not reasonably come; or if he has given a wrong interpretation to the words of the statute; or if he has taken into consideration matters which he ought not to have taken into account, or *vice versa*; or has otherwise gone wrong in law. It is identical with the position where the Court has power to interfere with the decision of a lower tribunal which has erred in point of law.'

In addition, of course, the statutory grounds of challenge enable the court to quash a decision on account of failure to comply with a statutory requirement.

Lord Denning accepted that the *'Ashbridge* formula' represents an extension of the scope of the statutory provisions.[27] However, in *R.* v *Secretary of State for the Environment, ex parte Ostler*[28] he said of his statement in *Ashbridge*: '. . .the Minister did not dispute it. It has been repeatedly followed in this Court ever since[29] and never disputed by any Minister. So it is the accepted interpretation.' Assuming that the *'Ashbridge* formula' represents the law, the result is, as Corfield and Carnwath say[30], 'that little, if any, effect is to be given to the actual words of the statutory provision'.

The *'Ashbridge* formula' has been implicitly accepted by the Scottish courts.[31] As well as being open to attack on the ground that there has been a failure to comply with a requirement of the Act or of relevant regulations

[25]   [1965] 1 W.L.R. 1320.
[26]   In this case those contained in the Housing Act 1957.
[27]   See, for example, *The Discipline of Law* (Butterworths, 1979), pp. 106-108.
[28]   [1977] Q.B. 122.
[29]   See, for example, *Re Lamplugh* (1967) 19 P. & C.R. 125; *Coleen Properties* v *Minister of Housing and Local Government* [1971] 1 W.L.R. 433; *Gordondale Investments Ltd.* v *Secretary of State for the Environment* (1971) 23 P. & C.R. 334; *British Dredging (Services) Ltd.* v *Secretary of State for Wales* [1975] 1 W.L.R. 687; *Eckersley* v *Secretary of State for the Environment* (1977) 34 P. & C.R. 124; and *Pyrford Properties Ltd.* v *Secretary of State for the Environment* (1977) 36 P. & C.R. 28. The circumstances in which the court will quash a decision under the statutory grounds were summarised by Forbes J. in *Seddon Properties Ltd.* v *Secretary of State for the Environment* (1978) 42 P. & C.R. 26.
[30]   *Compulsory Acquisition and Compensation* (Butterworths, 1978), p. 55.
[31]   See, in particular, the judgment of the Lord President (Lord Emslie) in *Wordie Property Co. Ltd.* v *Secretary of State for Scotland* 1984 S.L.T. 345.

or rules[32] (including failure to give proper and adequate reasons[33]), a plan, order or decision may competently be challenged on the grounds that in arriving at the decision there has been an error of law, that there has been a failure in natural justice, that a relevant matter has been omitted from consideration, or an irrelevant matter taken into account, that the decision is unreasonable (in the sense of the 'Wednesbury principles'[34]) or that the essential factual basis for the decision is lacking.[35]

In *Edwin H. Bradley and Sons Ltd.* v *Secretary of State for the Environment*[36] Glidewell J. said that in the *Ashbridge* case Lord Denning was enunciating 'exactly the same principles' as those formulated by Lord Greene in the *Wednesbury* case.[37] In the latter case Lord Greene set out the principles, accepted on both sides of the border, on which the courts will exercise their common law powers of supervision over administrative decision-making. It would therefore appear to be the case that the statutory grounds of challenge contained in ss.232 and 233 of the 1972 Act embrace all the grounds on which a public authority's decision may be attacked at common law.[38] And as regards procedural matters, the statutory grounds of challenge appear to be wider than the common law in respect that the statutory grounds permit the court to quash for breach of some non-mandatory procedural requirement.[39] The Court of Session's common law powers of review do not extend to errors of law within jurisdiction;[40] it is not clear whether the statutory grounds of challenge are similarly restricted. In *Wordie Property Co. Ltd.* v *Secretary of State for Scotland*[41] the Lord President (Lord Emslie) appears to have thought so, saying that a decision will be challengeable under the statutory provisions 'if it is based upon a material error of law going to the root of the question for determination'.

---

[32] See, for example, *Kirkpatrick* v *Lord Advocate* 1967 S.C. 165; 1967 S.L.T. (Notes) 27; *Paterson* v *Secretary of State for Scotland* 1971 S.C. 1; 1971 S.L.T. (Notes) 2; and *Wordie Property Co. Ltd.* (above). See too p. 503 above.

[33] See p. 29 above, *Wordie Property Co. Ltd.* (above).

[34] See p. 29 above.

[35] See, for example, *Lithgow* v *Secretary of State for Scotland* 1973 S.C. 1; 1973 S.L.T. 81; *British Airports Authority* v *Secretary of State for Scotland* 1979 S.C. 200; 1979 S.L.T. 197; *Harris* v *Secretary of State for Scotland*, Court of Session, 14th February 1980 (unreported, but see 1980 S.P.L.P. 18); *Glasgow District Council* v *Secretary of State for Scotland* 1980 S.C. 150; 1982 S.L.T. 28; *Grampian Regional Council* v *Secretary of State for Scotland* 1983 S.L.T. 526 (Court of Session); and 1984 S.L.T. 197 (House of Lords); and *Wordie Property Co. Ltd.* v *Secretary of State for Scotland* 1984 S.L.T. 345.

[36] (1982) 47 P. & C.R. 374.

[37] *Associated Provincial Picture Houses Ltd.* v *Wednesbury Corporation* [1948] 1 K.B. 233; see p. 29 above.

[38] See chapter 2.

[39] Subject to the qualification that the applicant will have to satisfy the court that he has been substantially prejudiced by the breach (below).

[40] See *Watt* v *Lord Advocate* 1979 S.C. 120; 1979 S.L.T. 137.

[41] 1984 S.L.T. 345.

Substantial prejudice

So far as the second ground of challenge—failure to comply with a relevant statutory requirement—is concerned, 'exact compliance with the letter of the [legislation] is only indispensable if it has caused "substantial prejudice" ',[42] the court is entitled to disregard a failure to comply with statutory requirements if it considers that the interests of the applicant have not been substantially prejudiced by the failure[43] (see s.232(2)(b); and s.233(4)(b)). (The court's general discretion not to quash is considered at p.531 below).

It is not necessary for the applicant to show that the decision would have been different if the statutory requirements had been complied with; 'the loss of a chance of being better off'[44] will be enough to constitute substantial prejudice. If therefore, the defect is more than a mere technicality, the courts will in general readily accept that the applicant has suffered substantial prejudice.[45] In *McCowan* v *Secretary of State for Scotland,*[46] for example, notice of the making of a compulsory purchase order had not been served on an owner of part of the land which was the subject of the order; the First Division of the Court of Session held that not only had that owner been substantially prejudiced by the failure to comply with the statute but so too had the other owners of the land comprised in the order since they had been deprived of the possible aid of another objector to the order. In *Tameside Metropolitan Borough Council* v *Secretary of State for the Environment*[47] it was held that since the result of allowing a decision of the Secretary of State to stand would be that an eyesore would continue to exist, the planning authority had been substantially prejudiced by a defect in the making of the decision.

In *Wordie Property Co. Ltd* v *Secretary of State for Scotland*[48] the Lord President (Lord Emslie) said that a failure on the part of the minister to give proper and adequate reasons for his decision on a planning application

---

[42] *M'Millan* v *Inverness-shire County Council* 1949 S.C. 77; 1949 S.L.T. 77, per Lord President Cooper.

[43] See, for example, *M'Millan* (above); *Steele* v *Minister of Housing and Local Government* (1956) 6 P. & C.R. 386; *Gordondale Investments Ltd.* v *Secretary of State for the Environment* (1971) 23 P. & C.R. 334; *Miller* v *Weymouth and Melcombe Regis Corporation* (1974) 27 P. & C.R. 468; *Camden London Borough Council* v *Secretary of State for the Environment* (1975) 235 E.G. 375; *Kent County Council* v *Secretary of State for the Environment* (1976) 33 P. & C.R. 70; *London Borough of Greenwich* v *Secretary of State for the Environment* [1981] J.P.L. 809; and *Schleider* v *Secretary of State for the Environment* [1983] J.P.L. 383.

[44] *Hibernian Property Co. Ltd.* v *Secretary of State for the Environment* (1973) 27 P. & C.R. 197, per Browne J.

[45] See, for example, *Paterson* v *Secretary of State for Scotland* 1971 S.C. 1; 1971 S.L.T. (Notes) 2; *McCowan* v *Secretary of State for Scotland* 1972 S.C. 93; 1972 S.L.T. 163; *Darlassis* v *Minister of Education* (1954) 4 P. & C.R. 281; *Hibernian Property Co. Ltd.* (above); *Wilson* v *Secretary of State for the Environment* [1973] 1 W.L.R. 1083; and *McMeechan* v *Secretary of State for the Environment* [1974] J.P.L. 411.

[46] Court of Session, 2nd February 1973 (unreported).

[47] [1984] J.P.L. 180.

[48] 1984 S.L.T. 345.

could not be other than prejudicial to the applicant. In the same case Lord Cameron said: 'Where an applicant has been deprived of the exercise of a right conferred upon him by Parliament, that fact alone would appear to me *prima facie* to indicate that he has suffered substantial prejudice.'[49]

It seems that failure to make early objection to an alleged irregularity may be treated as a factor tending to show that the applicant has not been substantially prejudiced. In *Midlothian District Council* v *Secretary of State for Scotland*[50] it was held that the planning authority had failed to show that they had been substantially prejudiced by the leading, in the course of a public inquiry, of evidence dealing with matters of which no prior notice had been given; the authority had made no objection at the inquiry, had not sought an opportunity to lead further evidence themselves, and there was, in any event, nothing to suggest that further evidence would have made any difference to the decision.

Standing

Only a 'person aggrieved' by a structure plan or local plan or by the alteration, repeal or replacement of such a plan is entitled to make application to the court under s.232 of the 1972 Act. Under s.233 application to quash any order or decision to which that section applies can be made by (a) a 'person aggrieved' by the order or action in question; or (b) an authority 'directly concerned'[51] with the order or action.

The meaning of the expression 'person aggrieved' as used in the 1972 Act[52] does not seem to have been considered by the Scottish courts[53] but Professor A. W. Bradley has suggested[54] that it is probable that the expression would be interpreted 'by reference to general notions of title and interest to sue'. However, as is mentioned below,[55] there is little recent Scottish authority on the question of title and interest to sue in the field of town and country planning (or in public law generally); such authority as there is on the matter suggests that the Scottish courts may not

---

49   See too Lord Cameron's comments on this matter in *Paterson* v *Secretary of State for Scotland* 1971 S.C. 1; 1971 S.L.T. (Notes) 2 (see p.503 above).
50   1980 S.C. 210 (and see comment in 1981 S.P.L.P. 17). See too *Davies* v *Secretary of State for Wales* [1977] J.P.L. 102; and *George* v *Secretary of State for the Environment* (1979) 38 P. & C.R. 609.
51   As to the meaning of this expression see s.233(7).
52   The meaning of the phrase was considered in *Magistrates of Kilsyth* v *Stirling County Council* 1936 S.C. 149 but, as was pointed out by MacDermott L.C.J. in *R. (Nicholl)* v *Recorder of Belfast* [1965] N.I. 7, the scope of the phrase may well vary according to the context in which it is used.
53   In *Easter Ross Land Use Committee* v *Secretary of State for Scotland* 1970 S.C. 182; 1970 S.L.T. 317, *Bearsden Town Council* v *Glasgow Corporation* 1971 S.C. 274; 1971 S.L.T. (Notes) 66, and *Harris* v *Secretary of State for Scotland*, Court of Session, 14th February 1980 (unreported, but see 1980 S.P.L.P. 18) there was in each case an initial denial that the applicant was an 'aggrieved person' but in none of the cases was the point argued.
54   Scottish Law Commission Memorandum No. 14, *Remedies in Administrative Law* (1971), para. 10.5.
55   See p. 540.

be prepared to give a broad interpretation to the phrase 'person aggrieved'. In the English courts there has been a trend towards giving the phrase a wider construction than it received in earlier times but it still seems clear that in this context the word 'aggrieved' cannot simply be treated as a synonym for 'dissatisfied'.

In *Buxton* v *Minister of Housing and Local Government*[56] a landowner who had been permitted to appear at a public inquiry into an appeal against a refusal of planning permission in respect of land adjacent to his and who claimed that the minister's decision to grant permission would injure the amenities and diminish the value of his land, was held not to have any right to question the validity of the minister's decision as he was not, for the purposes of the planning legislation, a 'person aggrieved' by the decision. Salmon J. considered that in the context of the planning legislation a person is 'aggrieved' by a decision only if his legal rights are infringed in some way.

In *Attorney-General of the Gambia* v *N'Jie*[57] Lord Denning expressed his disapproval of this narrow interpretation, saying that the words 'person aggrieved' 'are of wide import and should not be subjected to a restrictive interpretation. They do not include, of course, a mere busybody who is interfering in things which do not concern him; but they do include a person who has a genuine grievance because an order has been made which prejudicially affects his interests.' In *Maurice* v *London County Council*[58] the Court of Appeal considered that a householder, the amenities of whose property would have been injuriously affected by the construction of a tall building nearby, was an aggrieved person for the purpose of the London Building Act.

In *Turner* v *Secretary of State for the Environment*[59] Ackner J. refused to follow the decision in *Buxton* and held that members of an amenity society who had given evidence at a public inquiry into a planning application 'called in' by the Secretary of State were 'aggrieved persons' for the purpose of an application to the High Court under the statutory provisions relating to the challenge of planning decisions. In *Bizony* v *Secretary of State for the Environment*[60] Bridge J. was prepared to assume that a 'third party' who had made representations on a planning appeal dealt with on the basis of written representations was an 'aggrieved person'.

It should perhaps be added that in *Buxton* (above) Salmon J. expressed the view that: '. . . anyone given a statutory right to have his representations considered by the Minister impliedly has the right that the Minister, in considering those representations, shall act within the powers conferred upon him by the statute and should comply with the relevant requirements

56 [1961] 1 Q.B. 278. See too *Simpson* v *Edinburgh Corporation* 1960 S.C. 313; 1961 S.L.T. 17 (see p. 541 below).
57 [1961] A.C. 617. See too *Arsenal Football Club Ltd.* v *Ende* [1979] A.C. 1.
58 [1964] 2 Q.B. 362.
59 (1973) 28 P. & C.R. 123. See too the comments of Glidewell J. in *Hollis* v *Secretary of State for the Environment* (1982) 47 P. & C.R. 351.
60 [1976] J.P.L. 306.

of the statute. If these rights are infringed, then any such person is an aggrieved person within the meaning of . . . the Act.'

In the absence of any Scottish decisions on the matter, one can do little more than speculate as to the scope of the expression 'aggrieved person'. For the purposes of s.233 it is suggested that the phrase will embrace not only persons whose property or legal rights are directly affected by an order or decision to which the section applies but also any person who objected to the order or decision in question or who took part in a public inquiry or in written representations procedures relating to the order or decision. In *Turner* (above) it was said that 'any person who, in the ordinary sense of the word, is aggrieved by the decision . . . should have the right to establish in the courts that the decision is bad in law', and it may be that participation in the decision-making process is not essential before a person who is adversely affected by an order or decision can qualify as an 'aggrieved person'.[61]

As regards challenge of a structure plan or local plan, or the alteration, repeal or replacement of such a plan, it is tentatively suggested that 'aggrieved persons' would include objectors, persons selected to appear at the public examination of a structure plan, persons who appeared at a local plan inquiry, bodies who have to be consulted in the making of a plan, and any person whose property is affected by a plan.[62] It may be that those 'aggrieved' by a structure or local plan might be held to include those who in terms of s.6 or s.10 of the 1972 Act might be expected 'to desire an opportunity of making representations' on the plan, but perhaps only if they did in fact make representations.

Section 232 makes no express provision for challenge of a plan or alteration, etc. by a planning authority, and it is not certain that a planning authority would necessarily qualify as an 'aggrieved person' in relation to action taken by the Secretary of State on the authority's own plan[63] or in relation to a plan made by a different planning authority.

Powers of Court of Session

On an application under either s.232 or s.233 the Court of Session may make an interim order suspending the operation of the plan, or the

---

[61]   As to the possible consequences of the introduction of the statutory procedures for notifying neighbours of the making of a planning application, see C.M. Brand and Brian Thompson, 'Third Parties and Development Control—A Better Deal for Scottish Neighbours?' [1982] J.P.L. 743.

[62]   See *Edwin H. Bradley & Sons Ltd.* v *Secretary of State for the Environment* (1982) 47 P. & C.R. 374; and *Sand and Gravel Association Ltd.* v *Buckinghamshire County Council* [1984] J.P.L. 798. In the former case the applicants were the owners of land affected by a structure plan, had objected to the plan and had taken part in the plan's public examination, while in the latter case the applicants were an association of mineral operators with interests in land affected by a local plan; in neither case was the applicant's standing questioned.

[63]   In *Ealing Corporation* v *Jones* [1959] 1 Q.B. 384 a planning authority were held not to be aggrieved by the quashing by the minister of an enforcement notice served by the authority. (The legislation was subsequently amended.)

alteration, repeal or replacement of a plan,[64] or of the order or action which is the subject of the application until the final determination of the proceedings[65] (s.232(2)(a); s.233(4)(a)). If satisfied that either of the statutory grounds of challenge has been made out, the court may quash the plan, order or action in question (s.232(2)(b); s.233(4)(b)).

The courts have taken the view that the word 'may' as used in these provisions is to be construed in a permissive sense, so that even if the statutory conditions for quashing have been satisfied, the court has a discretion not to take such action. In *Peak Park Joint Planning Board* v *Secretary of State for the Environment*[66] Sir Douglas Frank said that in general the court's discretion not to quash should be exercised only rarely and in unusual circumstances—only, in effect, where the defect is purely technical or there is no possibility of detriment to the applicant.[67] Where, for example, a factor wrongly taken into account or omitted from consideration was insignificant or did not affect the decision, or an error has operated in the applicant's favour, the court may exercise its discretion not to quash the decision in question.[68] If, however, there is any doubt as to whether a defect may have affected the decision, that doubt will operate in favour of the applicant.[69]

On a number of occasions the English courts have stressed that it is only in exceptional circumstances that they will, on a statutory application to quash, admit fresh or extrinsic evidence. They have, however, been prepared to allow such additional evidence (a) to show what material was before the decision-making body; (b) to enable the court to determine whether essential jurisdictional facts were present or essential procedural

---

[64]   The operation of a plan, alteration, repeal or replacement may be suspended either generally or in so far as it affects any property of the applicant.

[65]   This provision does not apply to applications questioning the validity of tree preservation orders, presumably because suspension of such an order might result in the immediate destruction of the trees in question.

[66]   (1979) 39 P. & C.R. 361.

[67]   See too the judgment of Glidewell J. in *London Borough of Richmond upon Thames* v *Secretary of State for the Environment* [1984] J.P.L. 24 (in the exceptional circumstances of which, however, it was held that quashing was unnecessary).

[68]   See *Hanks* v *Minister of Housing and Local Government* [1963] 1 Q.B. 999; *Miller* v *Weymouth and Melcombe Regis Corporation* (1974) 27 P. & C.R. 468; *Gosling* v *Secretary of State for the Environment* (1974) 234 E.G. 531; *Kent County Council* v *Secretary of State for the Environment* (1976) 33 P. & C.R. 70; *Chichester District Council* v *Secretary of State for the Environment* [1981] J.P.L. 591; *Property Investment Holdings Ltd.* v *Secretary of State for the Environment* [1984] J.P.L. 587, and the comments of Lord Justice-Clerk Wheatley and Lord Robertson in *London and Clydeside Properties Ltd.* v *City of Aberdeen District Council* 1984 S.L.T. 50. In *Glasgow District Council* v *Secretary of State for Scotland* 1980 S.C. 150; 1982 S.L.T. 28 it was held that although the reasoning which led the minister to a particular decision was defective, the decision itself was correct and it would therefore be wrong to quash the decision.

[69]   See *Preston Borough Council* v *Secretary of State for the Environment* [1978] J.P.L. 548.

requirements had been followed; and (c) to establish 'misconduct' such as bias on the part of the decision-maker.[70]

Effect of quashing

A structure plan, local plan or any alteration, repeal or replacement of any such plan may be quashed in whole or in part and either generally or in so far as it affects the applicant's property (s.232(2)). The manner in which the legislation is phrased appears to mean that it is the plan or other document that is invalidated and not merely the decision to approve or adopt the plan; the result would appear to be that if a plan is quashed the whole plan-making process must begin afresh.

Section 233 of the 1972 Act is silent as to the effect of quashing an order or decision of a kind to which that section applies. So far as orders are concerned, the affect of quashing is that the procedure for making the order will have to begin afresh.[71] The effect of quashing a decision by the Secretary of State will normally be that the matter is remitted back to him for further consideration in the light of the court's ruling.[72] Often it will not be necessary to make a completely fresh start; if, for example, the Secretary of State's decision on a planning appeal is quashed because of a failure to provide adequate reasons, the minister may have to do no more than issue a fresh decision setting out the reasons clearly, or if there has been a failure to consider some relevant matter at a public inquiry it may be unnecessary for the Secretary of State to do more than give the parties an opportunity to comment on that matter.[73]

In dealing with an application under s.233 the court must generally either quash the decision or order *in toto* or leave it standing; there is, in Lord Cameron's words,[74] 'no power to vary or alter or remodel' the order or decision under review. In *British Airports Authority v Secretary of State for Scotland*[75] the First Division of the Court of Session held that having decided that certain conditions attached to grants of planning permission were *ultra vires*, the court could not (even if they had wished to do so)

---

[70] See, for example, *R. v Secretary of State for the Environment, ex parte Powis* [1981] 1 W.L.R. 584; *Ashbridge Investments Ltd.* v *Minister of Housing and Local Government* [1965] 1 W.L.R. 1320; and *Hollis* v *Secretary of State for the Environment* (1982) 47 P. & C.R. 351. See too *Barratt Developments (Scotland) Ltd.* v *Secretary of State for Scotland*, Court of Session, 17th December 1982 (unreported, but see 1983 S.P.L.P. 50).

[71] See *Whiteacre Estates U.K. Ltd.* v *Secretary of State for the Environment* [1984] J.P.L. 177 (successful challenge of Secretary of State's decision on purchase notice meant that the notice was itself quashed).

[72] See *Hartnell* v *Minister of Housing and Local Government* [1964] 2 Q.B. 510, per Danckwerts L. J.; and [1963] 1 W.L.R. 1141, per Sachs J.; *Price Brothers (Rode Heath) Ltd.* v *Secretary of State for the Environment* (1978) 38 P. & C.R. 579; and *Rogelan Building Group* v *Secretary of State for the Environment* [1981] J.P.L. 506.

[73] In making a fresh decision the Secretary of State is entitled (and indeed bound) to take account of any material considerations which may have arisen since the date of his original decision—see *Price Brothers (Rode Heath)* (above).

[74] *British Airports Authority* v *Secretary of State for Scotland* 1979 S.C. 200; 1979 S.L.T. 197.

[75] Above.

simply excise the invalid conditions; the court's only power was to quash the decisions (i.e., the planning permissions to which the invalid conditions were attached).

However, under s.233(5) the court has power to quash in part a tree preservation order or an order defining an area of special advertisement control.

'Shall not be questioned'

Under ss.232 and 233 of the 1972 Act an application seeking to challenge the validity of a plan or of an order or action of one of the types specified in the sections must be made before the expiry of a fairly short time limit. In the case of a structure plan or local plan, or any alteration, repeal or replacement of such a plan, application must be made to the Court of Session within six weeks from the date of publication of the first notice of the approval or adoption of the plan, alteration, repeal or replacement (s.232(1)). In the case of orders and decisions covered by s.233, application must be made within six weeks from the date when the order was confirmed or the action in question taken (s.233(1)).

Unless challenged in this fashion, the validity of any such plan, order or action 'shall not be questioned in any legal[76] proceedings whatsoever'[77] (s.231(1)[78]).

The shortness of the period allowed for challenge has often been the subject of criticism. In *Smith* v *East Elloe Rural District Council*,[79] for example, Lord Radcliffe described the six week period as 'pitifully inadequate'. Added point is given to that statement by the decision of the House of Lords in *Griffiths* v *Secretary of State for the Environment*[80] in which it was held that action was 'taken' in the sense of the legislation when a letter conveying the Secretary of State's decision was date-stamped and signed, with the result that the six week period began to run from that date and not from the date the letter was received.

In *Smith* v *East Elloe Rural District Council*[81] the House of Lords held that an 'ouster' clause very similar in its terms to s.231 of the 1972 Act precluded any challenge of a compulsory purchase order outwith the six week period even where bad faith in the making of the order was alleged.

---

[76] Since s.231(1) only bars challenge in *legal* proceedings, it may not preclude challenge of the *vires* of a development plan's provisions on appeal to the Secretary of State—see *Westminster City Council* v *Secretary of State for the Environment* [1984] J.P.L. 27, per Mr. David Widdiecombe Q.C., sitting as a deputy High Court judge.

[77] Despite dicta in *Hamilton* v *Roxburgh County Council* 1970 S.C. 248; 1971 S.L.T. 2 suggesting otherwise, it is clear that the effectiveness of exclusion clauses of this type is not affected by the Tribunals and Inquiries Act 1971—see *Hamilton* v *Secretary of State for Scotland* 1972 S.C. 72; 1972 S.L.T. 233; and *Lithgow* v *Secretary of State for Scotland* 1973 S.C. 1; 1973 S.L.T. 81.

[78] As amended by the Local Government and Planning (Scotland) Act 1982, Schedule 4, Part I.

[79] [1956] A.C. 736.

[80] [1983] 2 A.C. 51.

[81] [1956] A.C. 736.

The majority of their Lordships considered that after the expiry of the six weeks the jurisdiction of the courts was completely ousted.

It is, however, somewhat difficult to reconcile the decision in *Smith* with the later decision of the House of Lords in *Anisminic Ltd.* v *Foreign Compensation Commission*[82] in which it was held that an 'ouster' clause providing that a determination of the Commission should 'not be called into question in any court of law' would not serve to protect a determination made without jurisdiction and which was thus a nullity. In this case Lord Reid said that he could not regard *Smith* as 'a very satisfactory case', there having been in that case 'no citation of the authorities on the question whether a clause ousting the jurisdiction of the court applied when nullity was in question'. It is also worthy of note that in *Anisminic* the Court took a very wide view of the circumstances in which a body would be deprived of jurisdiction and its decision therefore rendered a nullity. Lord Reid considered, for example, that a refusal on the part of a decision-making body to consider some matter required to be taken into account or the taking into account of some irrelevant consideration or a failure in the course of a public inquiry to observe the rules of natural justice would render the body's decision a nullity.

In *Hamilton* v *Secretary of State for Scotland*[83] the pursuers argued, on the basis of *Anisminic*, that breaches of the rules of natural justice on the part of the confirming authority rendered a compulsory purchase order a nullity and that the 'ouster' clause would not serve to protect it. Lord Kissen held, however, following *Smith*, that the court's jurisdiction was totally ousted and dismissed the action as incompetent. He distinguished *Anisminic* on the ground that the 'ouster' clause considered in that case was absolute, in the sense that there was no provision whatsoever in the statute for challenging a decision of the Commission, whereas the statutory provision with which he was concerned did make provision (as does the 1972 Act) 'for quashing at least some kinds of null orders'. He was unable to see 'how it can be said, on the basis of *Anisminic*, that, as pursuers' counsel maintained, one kind of nullity can be remedied by the application of said paragraph 15 [the paragraph allowing for the quashing of a compulsory purchase order on grounds of *ultra vires* or failure to comply with a statutory requirement] but all other kinds can be remedied by ordinary legal proceedings in the courts.'

In *R.* v *Secretary of State for the Environment, ex parte Ostler*,[84] another case in which it was sought to challenge the validity of a compulsory purchase order outside the six week period, the Court of Appeal followed *Smith* in preference to *Anisminic*, holding that after the expiry of the time limit, challenge in the courts was absolutely prohibited. In *Ostler* the *Anisminic* decision was distinguished on the grounds that the preclusive

82   [1969] 2 A.C. 147.
83   1972 S.C. 72; 1972 S.L.T. 233. See too *Lithgow* v *Secretary of State for Scotland* 1973 S.C. 1; 1973 S.L.T. 81.
84   [1977] Q.B. 122. See too *Routh* v *Reading Corporation* (1970) 217 E.G. 1337; and *Jeary* v *Chailey Rural District Council* (1973) 26 P. & C.R. 280.

clause at issue in *Anisminic* sought to oust the courts' jurisdiction completely, whereas in *Ostler* the legislation allowed a six week period for challenge;[85] that *Anisminic* concerned a decision by a 'truly judicial body' whereas in *Ostler* the order was 'very much in the nature of an administrative decision'; that in contrast to the position in *Anisminic*, it was not the minister's jurisdiction to make the order that was sought to be impugned in *Ostler;* and that public policy demanded certainty after the expiry of the six week period. All but the last of these reasons may be thought somewhat unsatisfactory and it is perhaps a matter for regret that by refusing leave to appeal in the *Ostler* case the House of Lords passed up the opportunity to put the law beyond doubt.[86]

In *Westminster City Council v Secretary of State for the Environment*[87] Mr. David Widdicombe Q.C., sitting as a deputy High Court judge, held that after the expiry of the six week period, not only was it too late to challenge the validity of a local plan as such, it was also too late to question the validity of an individual policy in the plan; after the expiry of the six weeks it was too late to argue in legal proceedings[88] that a particular policy was *ultra vires* and therefore could not properly be applied in determining a planning application.

So far as Scotland is concerned, some doubt as to the effectiveness of preclusive clauses has resulted from the decision of the First Division of the Court of Session in *McDaid v Clydebank District Council.*[89] In that case (discussed in chapter 13) it was held that s.85(10) of the 1972 Act, which provides that the validity of an enforcement notice 'shall not, except by way of an appeal [to the Secretary of State], be questioned in any proceedings whatsoever' on specified grounds, did not serve to exclude the court's jurisdiction in respect of an enforcement notice which had not been served as required by the Act and was therefore a nullity. The court's reasoning in *McDaid* has been described as 'impeccably that of *Anisminic*, to which the court made approving reference'.[90] Unfortunately, the court made no reference to the decisions in *Smith, Hamilton* or *Ostler*. It may therefore be that the court considered that the absolute ouster contained in s.85(10) is to be distinguished from preclusive provisions such as ss.231 to 233 of the 1972 Act which permit challenge in the Court of Session within a limited period. Thus regarded, the decision in *McDaid* could be reconciled with *Smith, Hamilton* and *Ostler*. *McDaid* could, however, be read as implying that no preclusive clause will serve to protect a nullity.

We think it unlikely that the Court of Session would take such a view of

---

85   However, in *Anisminic* a majority of the House of Lords had denied the significance of this distinction.
86   [1977] 1 W.L.R. 258. The Parliamentary Commissioner for Administration found 'serious shortcomings' in the way the Department of the Environment had handled the road scheme in question.
87   [1984] J.P.L. 27.
88   The statutory provisions, barring only challenge in 'legal proceedings', may not preclude challenge of *vires* in an appeal to the Secretary of State.
89   1984 S.L.T. 162. And see comment by Colin T. Reid in 1984 S.P.L.P. 74.
90   'The Exclusion of Judicial Review' 1984 S.L.T. (News) 297.

McDaid. To do so would be to make ss.231 to 233 of the 1972 Act (and the similar provisions in other statutes) virtually redundant. It seems to us that Lord Kissen's judgment in *Hamilton* (above) is indicative of the right approach[91] and that the wording of the statutory provisions on challenge and the associated ouster leaves no room for the operation of the *Anisminic* principle in relation to ss.231 to 233. The statutory provisions allowing for challenge of decisions within six weeks include within their scope decisions which are beyond the powers of the legislation and are in consequence nullities; the natural reading of the associated ouster clause is therefore to include among the decisions to which it refers decisions which are nullities, with the result that after the expiry of the time limit, the court's jurisdiction to interfere with a decision which is a nullity is excluded.

B. QUESTIONING THE VALIDITY OF ENFORCEMENT NOTICES

The provisions of the 1972 Act on the enforcement of planning control restrict direct access to the courts in respect of enforcement notices and seek to ensure that in the majority of cases a person who wishes to challenge an enforcement notice (on legal or other grounds) will, in the first place at least, have to make use of the statutory machinery for appeal to the Secretary of State. Subject to one exception, s.85(10) of the 1972 Act provides that the validity of an enforcement notice 'shall not, except by way of an appeal [to the Secretary of State] under this section be questioned in any proceedings whatsoever on any of the grounds specified in paragraphs (b) to (e)' of s.85(1). The grounds specified in paragraphs (b) to (e) of s.85(1) encompass many of the grounds on which the *vires* of an enforcement notice might, in the absence of the statutory provisions, be open to direct challenge in the courts. The somewhat complex effects of s.85(10) of the 1972 Act are discussed in chapter 13.

So far as challenge of the Secretary of State's decision on an appeal against an enforcement notice is concerned, the position is more straightforward. Except as provided in s.233 of the 1972 Act, the validity of any decision of the Secretary of State on an appeal against an enforcement notice is not to be questioned in any legal proceedings whatsoever (s.231). The validity of the Secretary of State's decision in such a case is therefore subject to challenge under s.233 of the 1972 Act in the manner considered in section A of this chapter.

C. APPEALS AGAINST SECTION 51 DETERMINATIONS

Section 51 of the 1972 Act provides machinery by means of which any person who proposes to carry out operations on land or to make any change in the use of land can apply for a determination as to whether

[91] See too J. Alder, 'Time Limit Clauses and Judicial Review—*Smith* v *East Elloe* Revisited' (1975) 38 M.L.R. 274.

planning permission would be required (see chapter 6). In the case of a decision of the Secretary of State on a s.51 application 'called in' by him or on an appeal from the decision of a planning authority under s.51, either the person who made the application or the planning authority may, if dissatisfied with the decision in point of law, appeal to the Court of Session[92] (1972 Act, s.234). The reference in s.234 to a decision 'on an application' or 'on an appeal' suggests that it is only the final determination of the Secretary of State that can be the subject of an appeal.[93] Under s.234 the court will be able to correct an error of law that does not go to jurisdiction.

D. NON-STATUTORY CHALLENGE

Those planning decisions and actions which are not subject to the preclusive provisions of the 1972 Act discussed above are subject to the general supervisory jurisdiction of the Court of Session. The principles on which the Court of Session will exercise its powers of review are outlined in chapter 2.[94]

As mentioned above, although the preclusive provisions contained in ss.231 to 233 of the 1972 Act apply to many of the more important decisions and orders made by the Secretary of State under the Act, they do not apply to all decisions made by the minister. While it is not possible to give an exhaustive list, the preclusive provisions do not, for example, apply to decisions relating to the award of expenses incurred in connection with appeals,[95] to decisions relating to costs incurred in carrying out urgent works on listed buildings,[96] to interlocutory decisions made in the course of certain kinds of appeal[97] or to a refusal or failure on the part of the Secretary of State to take action of the types specified in subsection (3) of s.231 of the 1972 Act.[98]

So far as the actions of planning authorities are concerned, challenge of the validity of enforcement notices is restricted to some extent by s.85 (10) of the 1972 Act (see p.333 above) and an exclusive statutory remedy is provided by s.233 in respect of the types of orders specified in subsection (2) of s.231 of the 1972 Act (see section A of this chapter). Much local

[92]   See, for example, *Argyll and Bute District Council* v *Secretary of State for Scotland* 1976 S.C. 248; 1977 S.L.T. 33.

[93]   Cf. *Co-operative Retail Services* v *Secretary of State for the Environment* [1980] 1 W.L.R. 271 (p. 522 above).

[94]   See in particular pp. 28-40.

[95]   See, for example, *R.* v *Secretary of State for the Environment, ex parte Reinisch* (1971) 22 P. & C.R. 1022; and *R.* v *Secretary of State for the Environment, ex parte Three Rivers District Council* [1983] J.P.L. 730.

[96]   See, for example, *R.* v *Secretary of State for the Environment, ex parte Hampshire County Council* (1980) 44 P. & C.R. 343.

[97]   See, for example, *Co-operative Retail Services Ltd.* v *Secretary of State for the Environment* [1980] 1 W.L.R. 271.

[98]   1972 Act, s.231(4); and see, for example, *R.* v *Secretary of State for the Environment, ex parte Percy Bilton Industrial Properties Ltd.* (1975) 31 P. & C.R. 154.

authority decision-making is, however, outwith the scope of the preclusive provisions of the 1972 Act. In *Bovis Homes (Scotland) Ltd.* v *Inverclyde District Council,*[99] for example, the pursuers were granted declarator that the planning authority were bound to determine an application for approval of reserved matters, while in *McDaid* v *Clydebank District Council*[1] the pursuers successfully sought suspension of two enforcement notices and interdict against the planning authority acting on the basis of the notices.

The preclusive provisions of the 1972 Act do not exclude the court's common law supervisory jurisdiction where the interpretation of a document such as a planning permission, rather than its validity, is in issue,[2] nor will they prevent a pursuer seeking declarator that conditions attached to a planning permission are *ultra vires*.[3] Where direct challenge of the validity of a decision is barred by the 1972 Act, it may still be competent for the court to consider whether a decision was within the area of an authority's statutory discretion for the purposes of an action for damages.[4]

Limitations

Even where there is no statutory bar to challenge of the validity of a particular decision, the Court of Session may for various reasons refuse to entertain an action questioning the validity of the decision. Of particular importance in the field of town and country planning is the principle that any statutory remedy must be exhausted before judicial review can be sought.[5] In accordance with that principle the Court of Session might well refuse, for example, to entertain an action by an applicant for planning permission seeking to challenge a refusal or conditional grant of planning permission by a planning authority in that statute provides for appeal to the Secretary of State against such a decision.

In *Bellway Ltd.* v *Strathclyde Regional Council*[6] an action seeking reduction of directions made by the regional planning authority 'calling in' planning applications submitted by the pursuers was dismissed by Lord Brand as premature on the ground that there existed a right of appeal to the Secretary of State on a refusal of planning permission by the regional

99   1982 S.L.T. 473.
1   1984 S.L.T. 162.
2   See, for example, *Edgewarebury Park Investments Ltd.* v *Minister of Housing and Local Government* [1963] 2 Q.B. 408; and *Slough Estates Ltd.* v *Slough Borough Council (No. 2)* [1971] A. C. 958.
3   See, for example, *Fawcett Properties Ltd.* v *Buckingham County Council* [1961] A.C. 636. See, however, what is said below about the exhaustion of statutory remedies.
4   See, for example, *Davy* v *Spelthorne Borough Council* [1984] A.C. 262.
5   See *Caledonian Railway Co.* v *Glasgow Corporation* (1905) 7 F. 1020; and Colin T. Reid, 'Failure to Exhaust Statutory Remedies' 1984 J.R. 185.
6   1979 S.C. 92; 1980 S.L.T. 66; and see comment by Paul Q. Watchman in 1981 S.P.L.P. 43.

planning authority and thereafter to the Court of Session.[7] Lord Brand said that 'the pursuers must exhaust their statutory remedies before resorting to reduction' and that it could not be assumed that any prejudice suffered by the pursuers would not be remedied if the prescribed statutory procedure was followed out.

Much will, however, depend on the court's view of the nature and adequacy of the particular statutory remedy. In *Inverclyde District Council v Inverkip Building Co. Ltd.*,[8] in which the planning authority sought reduction of a planning permission granted by their predecessors, Lord McDonald expressed the view that s.42 of the 1972 Act (which empowers a planning authority to revoke or modify planning permission) did not provide an appropriate alternative to reduction of a planning permission. In *Bovis Homes (Scotland) Ltd.* v *Inverclyde District Council*[9] Lord Wylie was not prepared to accept that the pursuers' failure to take advantage of the statutory right of appeal to the Secretary of State which arose when the planning authority failed to issue notice of their decision on a planning application within the prescribed period rendered incompetent an action seeking to have the planning authority ordained to determine the application. Lord Wylie's judgment does not really explain why in these circumstances the general principle that the availability of a statutory remedy excludes recourse to common law remedies should not be applied.

Although the courts will normally require exhaustion of any statutory remedy, if the court considers that in order to prevent injustice a more immediate remedy is required than would be possible if the statutory procedures were followed through, the court may be prepared to intervene without recourse being had to the normal statutory procedures.[10]

A neighbour or other interested party does not, of course, have any right of appeal against a grant of planning permission and no question of exhaustion of statutory remedies can arise where a 'third party' seeks to challenge such a decision.

Where, as in the case of several of the provisions of the planning legislation, statute declares a particular type of decision to be 'final', this does not have the effect of excluding the court's jurisdiction to review the decision in question.[11] Views expressed by Lord Brand in *Bellway Ltd.* v

[7] This decision can be criticised on the ground that the remedy provided by the legislation relates to the decision on a planning application, whereas it was the regional planning authority's right to 'call in' the particular planning applications that was the subject of the court action.

[8] 1981 S.C. 401; 1982 S.L.T. 401. See too *Hamilton District Council* v *Alexander Moffat & Son (Demolition) Ltd*, Sheriff Court, Hamilton, 16th February 1984 (unreported, but see 1984 S.P.L.P. 76).

[9] 1982 S.L.T. 473; and see comment by Colin T. Reid in 1982 S.P.L.P. 46. See too *London and Clydeside Estates Ltd.* v *Aberdeen District Counil.* 1980 S.C. (H.L.) 1; 1980 S.L.T. 81; and *McDaid* v *Clydebank District Council* 1984 S.L.T. 162.

[10] See, for example, *R.* v *Hillingdon London Borough Council, ex parte Royco Homes Ltd.* [1974] Q.B. 720; and *R.* v *Camden London Borough Council, ex parte Comyn Ching & Co. (London) Ltd.* (1983) 47 P. & C.R. 417. See too *Pyx Granite Co. Ltd.* v *Minister of Housing and Local Government* [1960] A.C. 260.

[11] See, for example, *Watt* v *Lord Advocate* 1979 S.C. 120; 1979 S.L.T. 137.

Strathclyde Regional Council[12] might at first sight seem to run counter to that principle. In that case the pursuers sought reduction of a direction made by the regional planning authority 'calling in' an application for planning permission. The Secretary of State had dismissed an appeal by the district planning authority against the 'call in'. Section 179 (2) of the Local Government (Scotland) Act 1973 declares the decision of the Secretary of State on such an appeal to be 'final'. Lord Brand expressed the opinion that the pursuers' action was incompetent in that the legislation declared the Secretary of State's decision to be 'final' and it was not the minister's decision but the 'call in' by the regional planning authority that was being challenged.

Several of the obligations imposed by the planning legislation are expressed in such broad terms that their enforcement would seem to present substantial practical problems. It is, for example, difficult to envisage circumstances which would enable a court to hold that a planning authority had not fulfilled their duty to take 'such steps as will in their opinion' secure that persons who may be expected to desire an opportunity to make representations on the contents of a structure plan are given an 'adequate' opportunity of doing so (see 1972 Act, s.6(1)). On the other hand, the mere fact that a power or duty is expressed in subjective terms such as 'if the Secretary of State is satisfied'[13] does not necessarily mean that the court will be prepared to allow the administrative authority to be final arbiter of its own powers; it may be necessary for the authority to satisfy the court that there is a proper basis for the action taken.[14]

Title and interest to sue

Not every person who claims to have been adversely affected by administrative action is accorded the right of access to the courts. In *D. & J. Nicol* v *Dundee Harbour Trustees*[15] Lord Dunedin said:

> 'By the law of Scotland a litigant and in particular a pursuer must always qualify title and interest . . . I think it may fairly be said that for a person to have such a title he must be a party (using that word in the widest sense) to some legal relation which gives him some right which the person against whom he raises the action either infringes or denies.'

Where it is proposed to challenge a decision under the planning legislation the only Scottish decisions on the matter suggest that it may be

---

12   1979 S.C. 92; 1980 S.L.T. 66.
13   See, for example, 1972 Act, s.6(4).
14   See *Secretary of State for Education and Science* v *Tameside Metropolitan Borough Council* [1977] A. C. 1014. Contrast, however, *Peter Holmes & Son* v *Secretary of State for Scotland* 1965 S.C. 1; 1965 S.L.T. 41 in which the Lord Justice-Clerk (Lord Grant) said that the use of such a phrase meant that it was for the minister 'to decide whether he is "satisfied", not for us to say whether on the facts and evidence before him he was entitled to be satisfied'.
15   1915 S.C. (H.L.) 7.

difficult for anyone other than the person against whom the decision was made or a person with an interest in the land to which the decision relates to satisfy the court that he has title and interest to sue in respect of the decision in question.

In *Simpson* v *Edinburgh Corporation*[16] the owner of a house in a city square who sought to have certain planning permissions granted in respect of other land in the square declared *ultra vires* was held not to have title to sue. The Lord Ordinary (Lord Guest) said:

'From the preamble to the Act of 1947, it is apparent that it is a public code for planning the development and use of land in Scotland. It is not intended primarily for the protection or benefit of individual proprietors . . . In the general case, there are no provisions for notice to neighbours before or after planning permission is granted; the neighbour is given no *locus* at the hearing of the application for planning permission, nor is he given any right of appeal against a grant of permission.'

Lord Guest expressed the view that in considering whether an individual has title to sue: 'The whole Act and the circumstances in which it was passed must be considered. It is not only the section imposing the particular duty which must be considered.' His Lordship was satisfied, having regard to the scope and purpose of the planning legislation that 'it was not intended by Parliament that a separate right of action should be conferred on an interested neighbour' to enforce the provisions of the legislation. In order to have a title to sue, a neighbour would, in Lord Guest's view, have to show that some legal right conferred on him by the legislation had been contravened. He contrasted the case before him with the situation in *Black* v *Tennent*[17] in which neighbouring proprietors were held to have title to reduce an invalid grant of a public house licence. In that case the pursuers' title was sustained, said Lord Guest, 'on the ground that they had a statutory right to object to the grant of the certificate and had in fact unsuccessfully objected'; in the case before him, however, the pursuer had 'no right under the [planning] Act to object to the grant of planning permission'.

In *Bellway Ltd.* v *Strathclyde Regional Council*[18] a similarly restrictive approach to the question of title and interest to sue was adopted by Lord Brand. In that case Bellway challenged the validity of directions made by the regional planning authority 'calling in' applications for planning permission made by the company. Lord Brand thought it clear from the relevant statutory provisions that Bellway had no title or interest to challenge the validity of the directions, at this stage of the proceedings at

[16]   1960 S.C. 313; 1961 S.L.T. 17. See too *Gregory* v *Camden London Borough Council* [1966] 1 W.L.R. 899; and the cases cited at p. 528 above on the meaning of 'aggrieved person'.

[17]   (1899) 1 F. 423.

[18]   1979 S.C. 92; 1980 S.L.T. 66; and see comment by Paul Q. Watchman in 1981 S.P.L.P. 43.

least, notwithstanding that the company's applications for permission were the subject of the directions and that the effect of the directions might well be to delay determination of the applications. Lord Brand pointed out that the district planning authority were entitled to appeal to the Secretary of State against the 'call in' directions and that in determining such an appeal the minister was not required to consult or hear anyone other than the planning authorities. Bellway would ultimately be able, if planning permission was refused, or granted subject to conditions, to appeal to the Secretary of State and in determining such an appeal the minister, with his power to deal with the matter *de novo*, would be able to correct any antecedent irregularity or invalidity.

In neither *Simpson* nor *Bellway* could the pursuer be described as a mere busybody seeking to interfere with a decision which did not affect his interests. Both decisions turned on the court's view that it was not part of the scheme of the legislation to confer a right of action upon persons such as the pursuers. The circumstances of *Bellway* can be regarded as somewhat special and in the period since *Simpson* was decided planning procedures have been amended in important respects. Provision has been made for increased public involvement in the making of development plans and a right to make representations on applications for planning permission has been conferred on neighbours and others; it can no longer be said that a planning application concerns only the applicant and the planning authority. It is therefore difficult to know how much authority the decision in *Simpson* retains. In particular, neighbours' rights to make representations on planning applications would appear to put them in a position similar to that of the neighbouring proprietors who were held in *Black* v *Tennent* to have title and interest to sue.[19]

To depart from the restrictive view taken in *Simpson* would be to bring Scots law on standing into line with the more liberal position which has been reached in England and Wales and in Northern Ireland[20] without the benefit of the neighbour notification procedures which now operate in Scotland and which would seem to justify a change in judicial policy.[21]

---

[19]   See C. M. Brand and Brian Thompson, 'Third Parties and Development Control—A Better Deal for Scottish Neighbours?' [1982] J.P.L. 743; and C. M. Brand, 'Neighbour Notification: Existing Problems and the Litigious Future' 1982 S.P.L.P. 72.

[20]   See, for example, *Covent Garden Community Association Ltd.* v *Greater London Council* [1981] J.P.L. 183 *(locus standi* accorded to local amenity group); *R.* v *Stroud District Council, ex parte Goodenough* (1980) 43 P. & C.R. 59 (individuals held to have standing because of their connection with an area affected by planning proposals and their membership of a local action group); and *R. (Bryson)* v *Ministry of Development for Northern Ireland* [1967] N.I. 180 (occupier of house held to have standing because a proposed development would interfere with the amenities of his residence).

[21]   That the matter is almost wholly one of the judicial policy is perhaps illustrated by the liberal approach to the question of title and interest to sue taken by Lord Ross in *Wilson* v *Independent Broadcasting Authority* 1979 S.C. 351; 1979 S.L.T. 279.

APPENDIX 1
PLANNING AUTHORITIES IN SCOTLAND

Regional Planning Authorities	*District Planning Authorities*
Central	Clackmannan, Falkirk, and Stirling
Fife	Dunfermline, Kirkcaldy, and North East Fife
Grampian	City of Aberdeen, Banff and Buchan, Gordon, Kincardine and Deeside, and Moray
Lothian	East Lothian, City of Edinburgh, Midlothian, and West Lothian
Tayside	Angus, City of Dundee, Perth, and Kinross
Strathclyde	Argyll and Bute, Bearsden and Milngavie, Clydebank, Clydesdale, Cumbernauld and Kilsyth, Cumnock and Doon Valley, Cunninghame, Dumbarton, Eastwood, East Kilbride, City of Glasgow, Hamilton, Inverclyde, Kilmarnock and Loudoun, Kyle and Carrick, Monklands, Motherwell, Renfrew, and Strathkelvin

General Planning Authorities

Regions
Borders
Dumfries and
  Galloway
Highland

District councils within these regions have no statutory planning functions

Islands areas
Orkney
Shetland
Western Isles

APPENDIX 2
SCALE OF FEES FOR PLANNING APPLICATIONS

Outline applications

For one dwellinghouse	£47
For alterations etc. to existing dwelling-house	£24 per dwellinghouse. Maximum £47
Other	£47 per 0.1 ha. (or part thereof) of site area. Maximum £1,175 for sites of 2.5 ha. or more

Full planning applications and reserved matters

Alterations etc. to existing dwellings	£24 per dwellinghouse. Maximum £47
Erection of dwellings	£47 per dwellinghouse created. Maximum £2,350 (50 dwellinghouses)
Erection of buildings other than dwellings, plant and machinery	Works not creating more than 40 sq.m. of additional floor space—£24
	More than 40 sq.m. but not more than 75 sq.m. of additional floor space—£47
	Each additional 75 sq.m. (or part thereof)—£47. Maximum £2,350 (for 3,750 sq.m. or more)
Erection, alteration or replacement of plant and machinery	£47 per 0.1 ha. (or part thereof) of site area. Maximum £2,350 (for site of 5 ha. or more)
Approval of reserved matters where flat rate (below) does not apply	A fee based on floor space/numbers of dwellinghouses involved
Reserved matters where applicant's earlier reserved matters applications have incurred total fees equalling that for a full application for entire scheme	£47
Winning, working or storage of minerals etc. (other than peat) and waste disposal	£24 per 0.1 ha. (or part thereof) of site area. Maximum £3,600 (for site of 15 ha. or more)
Winning and working of peat	£24 per ha. (or part thereof) of site area. Maximum of £360 for 15 ha. or more
Car parks, service roads or other accesses	£24 (existing uses only)

Other operations on land	£24 per 0.1 ha. (or part thereof) of site area. Maximum £240 (for site of 1 ha. or more)
For non-compliance with conditions	£47
Change of use to and sub-division of dwellings	£47 per additional dwelling created. Maximum £2,350
Other changes of use except waste or minerals	£47
Advertisements	£24

Concessionary fees and exemptions

Works to improve a disabled person's access to a public building, or to improve his access, safety, health or comfort at his dwellinghouse	No fee
Applications (including advertisement applications) by community councils	Half the normal fee
Applications required because of the removal of permitted development rights by a condition or by an Article 4 direction	No fee
Playing fields (for sports clubs etc.)	£47
Revised or fresh application for development or advertisements of the same character or description within 12 months of refusal, or of the making of the earlier application if withdrawn, or within 12 months of expiry of the statutory 8 weeks period where the applicant has appealed to the Secretary of State on the grounds of non-determination	No fee
Revised or fresh application for development of the same character or description within 12 months of receiving permission	No fee
Duplicate applications made by the same applicant within 28 days	Normal fee for the first application and a quarter fee for the second
Alternative schemes	Highest of the fees applicable for each option and a sum equal to half the rest
Development crossing planning authority boundaries, requiring several applications	Only one fee, paid to the authority having the larger site but calculated for whole scheme, and subject to special ceiling

(Source: S.D.D. Circular 33/1983)

APPENDIX 3
PLANNING CIRCULARS

There are listed below the main departmental circulars relating to town and country planning in Scotland (as at 31st March 1985).

D.H.S. Circular No	Description
75/1951	Town and Country Planning (Technical Sites) (Scotland) Direction 1951
41/1958	Overspill and Town Development (Part II of the Housing and Town Development (Scotland) Act 1957)
66/1959	Town and Country Planning (Scotland) Act 1959 (Paras. 1 to 17 and 22 to 30 no longer relevant)
74/1959	Town and Country Planning (Scotland) Acts 1947-1959: Purchase Notices. (Advice still valid although provisions of 1947 and 1959 Acts have been incorporated into 1972 Act)
40/1960	Green Belts and New Houses in the Country
S.D.D. Circular No	
2/1962	Development Plans: Areas of Great Landscape Value; and Tourist Development Proposals
27/1965	Petrol Filling Stations—Siting
25/1966	Award of Expenses at Statutory Inquiries. (See too circular 14/1975)
15/1968	Local Government (Scotland) Act 1966—Grants to Local Authorities in Respect of Comprehensive Redevelopment and Public Open Space
41/1968	Planning Control of Radio Masts
49/1971	Publicity for Planning Proposals. (See too circular 59/1974)
65/1971	Town and Country Planning (Minerals) (Scotland) Regulations 1971

89/1971	Planning Blight
17/1972	Central Register of Air Photography of Scotland
92/1972	Disused Railway Lines in the Countryside
94/1972	Town and Country Planning (Scotland) Act 1972—Introductory Circular
116/1972	General Information System for Planning
23/1973	Planning and Noise
25/1973	Post Office Operational Land
68/1973	Town and Country Planning (Use Classes) (Scotland) Order 1973
84/1973	Land Compensation (Scotland) Act 1973
51/1974	Development Affecting Fishery Interests
59/1974	Publicity for Planning Proposals (See too circular 49/1971)
61/1974	North Sea Oil and Gas: Coastal Planning Guidelines
71/1974	Forest Policy: Consultation with Planning Authorities
14/1975	Public Inquiry Procedures
77/1975	Development of Agricultural Land—Consultations with DAFS Lands Staff etc
79/1975	Offshore · Petroleum Development (Scotland) Act 1975—Reinstatement of Land (ss.8 and 9 of 1975 Act)
87/1975	Town and Country Amenities Act 1974. Tree Preservation Orders and Trees in Conservation Areas. (Amended by circular 7/1984)
89/1975	Special Financial Assistance for Oil-Related Infrastructure Provided by Local Authorities
103/1975	Town and Country Planning (National Coal Board) (Scotland) Regulations 1975
126/1975	Town and Country Planning (Listed Buildings and Buildings in Conservation Areas) (Scotland) Regulations 1975
4/1976	Listed Buildings and Conservation. (Amended by circular 28/1980)

8/1976	National Land Use Classification
13/1976	Petroleum and Submarine Pipe-lines Act 1975—Refinery Controls
42/1976	Compulsory Purchase Procedures
63/1976	Compulsory Purchase by Public Authorities (Inquiries Procedure) (Scotland) Rules 1976
74/1976	Town and Country Planning (General) (Scotland) Regulations 1976
16/1977	Town and Country Planning (Scotland) Act 1977. (Paras. 1.1 to 1.5 cancelled by circular 32/1983)
19/1977	National Planning Guidelines: Petro-chemical Developments; Large Industrial Sites and Rural Conservation. (Amended by circular 20/1980)
26/1977	Town Development Grants Towards Cost of Amenity Buildings and Works
42/1977	Code of Practice for Local Plan Inquiries and Hearings
43/1977	Code of Practice for Examination in Public of Structure Plans
51/1977	National Planning Guidelines: Aggregates
56/1977	Nature Conservation and Planning
38/1978	Consultation with the Royal Fine Art Commission for Scotland
46/1978	Report of the Advisory Committee on Aggregates: Government Response
49/1978	Report of the Committee on Planning Control over Mineral Working: Government Response
53/1978	Theatres Trust (Scotland) Act 1978
65/1978	National Planning Guidelines on the Location of Major Shopping Developments
38/1979	Disposal of Surplus Land
20/1980	Development Control in National Scenic Areas
28/1980	Town and Country Planning (Scotland) Act 1972. Exemption from Listed Building Control

39/1980	Development in the Vicinity of British Gas Installations—Notification Procedures. Commercial Pipelines: Planning Advice and Notification Procedures
46/1980	Local Government, Planning and Land Act 1980
47/1980	Town and Country Planning (Determination of Appeals by Appointed Persons) (Prescribed Classes) (Scotland) Regulations 1980. Town and Country Planning (Inquiries Procedure) (Scotland) Rules 1980. Town and Country Planning Appeals (Determination by Appointed Person) (Inquiries Procedure) (Scotland) Rules 1980.
24/1981	Development Control. (Partially replaced by circular 6/1984)
29/1981	Provision of Public Buildings: Consideration of the Needs of the Disabled
31/1981	Town and Country Planning (Tree Preservation Order and Trees in Conservation Areas) (Scotland) Amendment Regulations 1981
5/1982	Town and Country Planning (Minerals) Act 1981
16/1982	Safeguarding of Aerodromes, Technical Sites and Explosive Storage Areas. Town and Country Planning (Aerodromes) (Scotland) Direction 1982
29/1982	Local Government and Planning (Scotland) Act 1982: Planning Provisions
7/1983	Town and Country Planning (Grants) (Scotland) Amendment Regulations 1983
21/1983	Private House Building. Land Supply: Joint Venture Schemes
32/1983	Structure and Local Plans
33/1983	Town and Country Planning (Fees for Applications and Deemed Applications) (Scotland) Regulations 1983
4/1984	Opencast Coal Mining
6/1984	Local Government and Planning (Scotland) Act 1982
7/1984	Forestry. A—Consultations with Local Authorities; B—Town and Country Planning (Tree Preservation Order and Trees in Conservation Areas) (Scotland) Amendment Regulations 1984
9/1984	Planning Controls Over Hazardous Development

10/1984	Town and Country Planning (Control of Advertisements) (Scotland) Regulations 1984
21/1984	Crown Land and Crown Development
22/1984	Town and Country Planning (Scotland) Act 1972. Section 50 Agreements
26/1984	Town and Country Planning (Scotland) Act 1972. Planning Appeals
10/1985	Town and Country Planning (Limit of Annual Value) (Scotland) Order 1985. Home Loss Payments (Scotland) Order 1985

S.E.P.D. Circular No

| 1978/2 | Industrial Strategy: Contribution of the Local Authorities |

Scottish Office Finance Division Circular No

| 16/1981 | Local Government (Miscellaneous Provisions) (Scotland) Act 1981 |

Note: This list is derived in Part from the S.D.D. List of Department Circulars and Memoranda, Acts and Statutory Instruments current on 31st December 1982.

APPENDIX 4
DIRECTIONS

Listed below are the main directions of general application made under the town and country planning legislation in Scotland:

Town and Country Planning (Technical Sites) (Scotland) Direction 1951 (issued with D.H.S. Circular 75/1951).

Direction requiring planning authorities to notify the Royal Commission on the Ancient and Historical Monuments of Scotland of any application for consent to demolish a listed building (see para. 9 of S.D.D. Memorandum 74/1970 and para. 2.14 of the S.D.D. *Memorandum on Listed Buildings and Conservation Areas* issued with S.D.D. Circular 4/1976).

Town and Country Planning (Restriction of Permitted Development) (National Scenic Areas) (Scotland) Direction 1980 (issued with S.D.D. Circular 20/1980).

Town and Country Planning (Notification of Applications) (Scotland) Direction 1980 (issued with S.D.D. Circular 20/1980).

Direction under s.262A of the Town and Country Planning (Scotland) Act 1972 exempting certain buildings in conservation areas from listed building control (see S.D.D. Circular 28/1980).

Town and Country Planning (Development Contrary to Development Plans) (Scotland) Direction 1981 (issued with S.D.D. Circular 24/1981).

Town and Country Planning (Notification of Applications) (Scotland) Direction 1981 (issued with S.D.D. Circular 24/1981).

Town and Country Planning (Aerodromes) (Scotland) Direction 1982 (issued with S.D.D. Circular 16/1982).

Town and Country Planning (Development Contrary to Development Plans) (Scotland) (Amendment) Direction 1984 (issued with S.D.D. Circular 6/1984).

Town and Country Planning (Notification of Applications) (Scotland) (Amendment) Direction 1984 (issued with S.D.D. Circular 6/1984).

Town and Country Planning (Planning Applications—Weekly Lists) (Scotland) Direction 1984 (issued with S.D.D. Circular 6/1984).

Town and Country Planning (Notification of Applications) (Scotland) (Amendment) (No. 2) Direction 1984 (issued with S.D.D. Circular 9/1984).

Town and Country Planning (Control of Tethered Balloon Advertisements in National Scenic Areas) (Scotland) Direction 1984 (issued with S.D.D. Circular 10/1984).

INDEX

Acquisition of land

agreement to acquire, 399
blight. *See* 'Blight notice'
compulsory purchase powers, 397-399
compulsory purchase procedures, 399
development of land acquired, 400
disposal of land acquired, 399, 401-403
listed buildings in need of repair, 403, 444-445
planning purposes, for, 396-397, 398
purchase notice. *See* 'Purchase notice'

Action area. *See* 'Development plans'

Advertisements

amenity, 456, 457, 460
appeals—
    enforcement notice, 459
    refusal etc. of consent, 457
application for consent, 456-457
areas of special control, 460
building—
    forming part of, 453
    within, 452-453, 454
business premises, on, 454
circuses and fairs, 458
compensation, 459
consent to display—
    application for, procedure, 456-457
    deemed, 452, 454-455
    express, 452, 456-457
    revocation or modification, 457
conservation area, in, 451, 460
definition, 452
discontinuance, power to require, 455-456, 457
display—
    after expiry of express consent, 455
    development, as, 163, 452
enclosed land, on, 453
enforcement of control, 458-459
existing, 455
fees, 456
illuminated, 453, 454, 455
offences, 459

planning permission deemed to be granted, 171, 452
principles of control, 67, 228, 456
public safety, 456, 457
scope of control, 452-454
specified classes deemed to have consent, 454-455
standard conditions, 455, 456, 458
statutory, 455
temporary, 454
tethered balloons, 452, 453
vehicles, on or in, 453
vessels, on or in, 453

'Aggrieved person'. *See* 'Statutory application to quash'

Agreement

fettering powers and duties, 277, 285-287
development control, link with, 284-285
material consideration, 226
parties, 279-281
planning gain, 278-279
purpose of, 245-246, 276-277, 396
restricting or regulating the development or use of land, 281-283
variation and termination, 287-288

Agriculture

agricultural buildings and uses, permitted development, 179-181
agricultural land, meaning, 155
agricultural tenant—
    notice of appeal, 266, 487
    notification of planning application to, 193-194
agricultural unit—
    blight. *See* 'Blight notice'
    meaning, 410 n
definition, 155, 180
development ranking for compensation, 389-390
use of land for, does not involve development, 154, 155

553

Amenity

advertisements, 456, 457, 460
conservation area, 447-448
material consideration, 215
tree preservation, 462
waste land, 468

Ancient monuments, 436

Appeals. *See also* 'Public inquiries'

advertisements—
 enforcement notice, 459
 refusal, etc. of consent, 457
approval required under a development
 order, refusal or conditional grant of,
 266-268
administrative guidance on, 481, 484-485,
 487, 488, 489, 491, 495-496, 497, 510
appointed persons, determination by—
 delegated classes, 490
 powers and duties, 486, 489, 496, 497,
 498, 500, 501, 513-514
bulletins of selected decisions, 268
'call in' by regional planning authority,
 against, 203-204
consent, agreement or approval required
 by condition, refusal or conditional grant
 of, 266-268
Court of Session, to. *See* 'Court of
 Session', 'statutory application to quash'
 and 'judicial review'
determination that development involved,
 against, 166
enforcement notice, against, 322-332
established use certificate, against refusal
 of, 319-320
expenses, 489, 491, 500, 514-516
failure to determine planning application,
 260, 266-268, 487-489
function of, 479-480, 499
hearing to determine, 481, 491
listed buildings—
 minimum compensation direction, 445
 refusal, etc. of consent, 441
natural justice, rules of, 481, 483-484, 489,
 510-511
nature of decision, 480, 481
planning permission, refusal or conditional
 grant of, 266-268, 487-489
 decision of regional planning authority,
  267
 determination by appointed person, 267,
  489, 513-514
 determination by Secretary of State, 267,
  489, 511-513
 notification of owners and agricultural
  tenants, 266, 487
 procedure, 266-267, 487-489, 493 *et seq.*

reference to Planning Inquiry Commission, 268, 517-518
procedural rules, 481, 482, 490, 491
public inquiry to determine. *See* 'Public
 Inquiries'
Sheriff, to. *See* 'Sheriff'
Scottish Planning Appeal Decisions
 (SPADS), 60 *n,* 268
tree preservation order, under, 464,
 466-467
waste land, notice requiring abatement of
 injury, 469
written submissions, 204, 486, 487-489

Appointed person. *See* 'Appeals'

'Bad neighbour' development, 197-198

Betterment

recovery of, 11-13
Uthwatt Committee, 11

Betterment levy, 12

Blight. *See also* 'Blight notice'

causes of, 404-406
discretionary acquisition, 410
nuisance, action for, 405-406, 419

Blight notice

agricultural unit, 410-411
 affected area, 417
 severance of, 417
annual value, limit of, 411
'appropriate authority', 413
'appropriate enactment', 417 *n*
compensation, 418
counter-notice, 414
effect of, 405, 407, 416-417
efforts to sell land, 412
form of, 413
hereditament, 410-411
injury to interests in land, 412-413
interest qualifying for protection, 410-411
notice to treat, deemed, 417
objection—
 grounds of, 414-415
 onus of proof, 415
 reference to Lands Tribunal for Scotland, 415
owner-occupier, 411
persons entitled to serve, 410-411
proposals giving rise to obligation to
 purchase, 407-410
purchase notice, distinguished from, 407
resident owner-occupier, 411
service of, 413-414

severance, 417
specified descriptions of land, 407-410
withdrawal of, 417

Building

agricultural. *See* 'Agriculture'
alteration—
  not amounting to development, 119, 120
  compensation, 388-389
definition, 118, 119
demolition, 121, 123-125, 435, 436, 438,
  441
demolition in conservation area, 448-451
extension below ground, 119, 120
industrial. *See* 'Industry'
internal works not development, 119, 176
operations, 118-121. *See also* 'Development'
order requiring alteration or discontinuance. *See* 'Discontinuance order'
part of, 118, 121
special architectural or historic interest.
  See 'Listed buildings'
structure, whether constitutes, 118
temporary, 178-179

Building operations, 181-121. *And see*
  'Development'

Building preservation notice, 432, 437-438.
  And see 'Listed buildings'

Caravan

dwelling-house, within curtilage of, 154
'permitted development', 182, 183
planning permission as prerequisite for site
  licence, 429

Circulars, 60, 63, 67-69, 221-222, 546-550

Commissioner for local administration, 53,
  55-57

Community councils, 48, 56

Community land scheme

objectives of, 13
White Paper *Land,* 11, 13

Compensation

Act of 1947, under, 11, 357-358
Acts of 1909 and 1932, under, 11
Acts of 1953 and 1954, under, 12, 357-358
acquisition of land, 404
advertisements, 459
authorised development, restriction of,
  378-379

blight notice, 418
building preservation notice, 437-438
community land scheme, under, 13
development value—
  compensation for loss of, 11-13, 357-364
  transfer to State under 1947 Act, 11-12,
    357
discontinuance order, 378-379
established development value—
  original unexpended balance, 358, 359
  reduction or extinguishment, 359
  unexpended balance, 358-359, 360, 362,
    364, 385
injurious affection. *See* 'Injurious affection'
interference with servitude, 401
listed buildings. *See* 'Listed buildings'
notice of payment, 363, 385
permitted development, restriction of, 356
planning permission—
  refusal or conditional grant of, 353-364
  revocation or modification of, 383-385
purchase notice, following, 354, 373
restrictions on development other than
  'new', for, 356, 391-393
restrictions on mineral operations. *See*
  'Minerals'
restrictions on 'new' development, for,
  355, 358-364
  amount, 362
  excluded in certain cases, 360-361
  payable by Secretary of State, 363, 385
  procedure, 362-363
  repayment, 363
stop notice, loss due to, 347
tree preservation order, under, 467
use, discontinuance of, 378-379
Uthwatt Committee, 11

Completion notice, 265-266

Conditions. *See* 'Planning Permission'

Conservation area

advertisements in, 451, 460
demolition in, 448-451
designation of, 447-448
development affecting, 199, 448
effects of designation, 448-451
financial assistance, 451
trees in, 451, 467-468
works urgently required, 451

Court of Session

appeal against s.51 determination, 536-537
application to quash under 1972 Act. *See*
  'Statutory application to quash'

inherent power of review. *See* 'Judicial Review'

exclusion of jurisdiction, 25, 533-536, 537-538

Crown

application for planning permission and other consents, 169-171, 191-192, 436-437, 451

development by, 169

enforcement action in respect of Crown land, 309-310

Notice of Proposed Development, 170

Delegation

appointed persons, to, 485-486, 490

local authority officers, to, 35-39, 49

ostensible authority, doctrine of, 34-39

Demolition

conservation area, in, 448-449

listed building, of, 435, 436, 438, 441

whether development, 121, 123-125

Development

advertisements, display of, 163, 452

agreements for regulating, 281-283

agricultural or forestry use does not involve, 154-155

'bad neighbour', 197-198

beginning of, 264

building. *See* 'Building'

building operations, 118-121

change of use, as, 116, 125 *et seq.*, 178. *See also* 'Use'

'Crown', by, 169-171

definition, 116 *et seq.*

demolition, 121, 123-125

deposit of refuse, 162, 163

determination as to whether proposals constitute, 163-166

development plan, contrary to, 199, 208-210

dwelling-house—
    curtilage, within, 174-177
    multiple occupation, 136, 137, 161, 162
    use as two or more separate dwellings, 132, 161, 162
    use of curtilage not development, 152-154

engineering operations, 121, 122

government departments, by, 168-171

industrial. *See* 'Industry'

local authorities, by, 171, 273

material change of use—
    abandonment of use, 142, 143, 270
    ancillary use, 129, 130, 147-151

character of use as test, 135-137

discontinuance of use not development, 141, 142

extinguishment of use, 144-147

general purpose remaining the same, 135-137

intensification, 139, 140

'materiality', 125, 133-139

material from a planning point of view as test, 137-139

multiple uses, 147-152

planning unit, relevance of, 117, 126-127

planning unit, identification of, 127-133

primary use, 125, 147-151

resumption of abandoned use, 142-143

time when change occurs, 140, 141

mining operations, 122-123, 469, 476-477. *And see* 'Minerals'

'new'. *See* 'Compensation'

operations, 118-125, 177-178

'operations' and 'use' distinguished, 116, 117

'other operations', 123

'permitted', 172-174. *And see* 'Planning permission'

planning authorities, by, 171, 182, 273

planning permission for. *See* 'Planning permission'

rebuilding works, 120

road improvements, etc. excluded, 122

unauthorised. *See* 'Enforcement notice'

Use Classes Order, 50, 60, 61, 155-161

Development Charge, 12, 357

Development Gains Tax, 12

Development Land Tax, 13

Development order, 51, 171

General Development Order, 172-184, 380, 386-388

planning permission, under. *See* 'Planning permission'

special development order, 6, 62, 63, 172, 184

Development plans

action area, 86, 87, 96, 394

comprehensive development area, 76, 77

compulsory acquisition, and, 77

development contrary to, 199, 208-210

draft development plans, effect of, 114, 210-211

effect of, 73, 74, 207-208

land blighted by, 407-408, 410

local plan, 75, 76, 79, 94-107
    action area, 96

adoption, 105
alteration and repeal, 106, 107
authorities responsible for, 95
'call in' by Secretary of State, 105
consideration of objections, 102-104
consultation with specified bodies, 101, 102
date of taking effect, 106
form and content, 96-100
map, 96, 99, 100
objections to, 102-104
obligation to prepare for whole district, 95, 96, 100
'old style' plan, replacing, 78, 79
plan period, 99
preparation in advance of approved structure plan, 100
preparation of, 100-102
public consultation, 101
public inquiry, 102-104, 491
public inquiry, Code of Practice for, 103, 491
purposes of, 94, 95
regional planning authority, preparation by, 95
regional planning authority's consent to preparation, 100, 101
register, 107
structure plan, must conform to, 94, 101, 102, 105
subject plans, 96
survey, 100
types of, 96
validity, 97, 98, 106, 520-521, 528-530
written statement, 96-99
'new style', 75, 79 et seq., 107-109. (See also under local plan and structure plan)
commencement of new system, 76
meaning, 79
'old style' plans, replacing, 78, 79
hopes for new system 107-109
'old style', 74-75, 76-79
amendment of, 77
conflict with structure plan, 78
criticisms of, 74, 75
form and content of, 76, 77
replacement, 78, 79
public participation—
adequacy of, 82, 87, 88, 101, 102
local and structure plans, in, 81-83, 101
report, 'People and Planning', 82
purpose of, 72, 80, 94, 207, 394
regional report. See 'Regional report'
register of structure and local plans, 79, 94, 107
structure plan, 75, 76, 79, 80-94, 107-109
action area, 86, 87
alteration, 93, 94
approval by Secretary of State, 81, 92, 93
authorities responsible for, 80
consideration by Secretary of State, 87-92
consultation with specified bodies, 81
date of taking effect, 93
diagrams, 83, 86
examination in public, 89-92, 491
form and content, 83-86
local plans must conform to, 94, 101, 102, 105
objections, 88-92
objections, consideration by Secretary of State, 89
'old style' plan, conflict with, 78
plan period, 86
policies and proposals, 84
preparation, 81-83
public consultation, 81-83
purposes of, 72, 80
register, 79, 94
submission to Secretary of State, 81, 87
survey, 80, 81
validity of, 93, 520-521, 528-530
written statement, 83-86
transition to new system, 78, 79

Development value. See 'Compensation'

Directions
made by Secretary of State, 551-552

Discontinuance order
compensation, 378-379
enforcement of, 379-380
extent of powers, 376-377
mineral operations. See 'Minerals'
procedure, 377-378
purchase notice, 373, 379
regional planning authority, made by, 377-378
validity of, 378, 521 et seq.

District planning authority. See 'Planning authorities'

Dwelling-house
curtilage—
development within, 174-177
meaning of, 152
use of not development, 152-154
enlargement, etc. of, 175-177
meaning of, 153, 174 n
multiple occupation, 136, 137, 161
use as single dwelling-house and 'four year' rule, 313-314
use as two or more dwellings, 132, 161, 162

Ecclesiastical buildings, 436

Enforcement notice
advertisements, 458-459
appeal against
    correction, power of, 301, 302, 328-332
    determination by appointed person, 326,
        327, 485-486, 513-514
    determination of, 326-328
    grounds of appeal, 294-295, 306-307,
        321, 322-324
    procedure, 324-326
    public inquiry. See 'Public inquiries'
    Secretary of State's powers, 327-328
breach of planning control, 290, 298-302
certificate of established use. See
    'Established use'
compliance, period for, 306-307
conditions, breach of, 173, 290, 298, 313,
    314-315
contents of, 295
continuing effect of, 339-340
criminal proceedings, 336, 341-343
date on which notice takes effect, 306
'four year' rule, 310-314, 315, 323, 470-471
information, requirement to provide, 292
interdict. See 'Interdict'
limitation, 301
listed buildings, 441-442
matters alleged to constitute a breach of
    control, 298-302
mineral development, 308-309, 311-312,
    470
non-compliance, consequences of, 341-344
    execution of works by planning
        authority, 343-344
offences, 292, 341-343
'planning unit', 307-309
power to serve, 290-292
reasons for, 309
restricting established rights, 304-306, 324
reversion to 'lawful use', 340-341
service—
    failure to serve on persons with an
        interest in the land, 294-295, 324
    persons to be served, 292-294
    time limits for, 310-315
steps required by, 297, 202-306, 312
stop notice. See 'Stop notice'
subsequent grant of planning permission,
    effects of, 340
validity, 294, 297-298, 303, 307, 321,
    328-332, 333-339, 536
    restrictions on challenge in courts, 294,
        321, 333-338, 343, 536
withdrawal, 295

Engineering operations. See 'Development'

Enterprise zones
effects of designation, 6, 60, 62, 184, 272

Entry
right of, 292

Environmental assessment, 52, 53

Established use
certification of, 315-320
    effect, 315, 316
    fees, 320
    procedure, 317-320

European Economic Community, 52, 53

Examination in public of structure plan.
See 'Development plans'

Fees for applications, 199-200, 320, 325,
    544-545

Fences
permitted development, 178

Forestry
buildings and works permitted develop-
    ment, 181
felling licences, 465
tree preservation. See 'Trees'
use of land for, not development, 154, 155.
    And see 'Trees'

Franks Committee
report of, 482, 484, 503

Garage
erection within curtilage of dwelling,
    175-176

General Development Order, 172-184, 380,
    386-388

General planning authority. See 'Planning
    authorities'

Government department
blight notice, where land allocated for
    purposes of, 407, 409
development by, 168-171, 191-192
listed buildings, alterations of, 436-437

Hazardous substances, 10, 60, 156, 173, 201

Hearings, 481, 491. And see 'Public
    inquiries'

Highway. See 'Road'

Housing action area
land blighted by, 409

Industry

industrial building—
  defined, 158, 159
  permitted development, 178, 181-182
  Use Classes Order, 158, 159
industrial development—
  notification of applications to Secretary
    of State, 201
  permitted development, 181-182
industrial   development   certificates,
  477-478
oil refineries, construction or extension of,
  429
oil-related development, notification of
  Secretary of State, 201

Infrastructure

provision of, 220-221, 243-244, 245,
  395-396
role of development plans, 394-395

Injurious affection

land held together with land acquired for
  scheme, 418-420
neighbouring land affected by construction
  of public works, 421-423
neighbouring land affected by use of public
  works, 422, 423-427
notice of objection to severance, 420-421

Inquiry. *See* 'Public inquiries'

Interdict

enforcing planning control, 335, 346,
  349-352

Judicial review. *See* 'Court of Session' and
  'Statutory application to quash'

abuse of discretion, 28, 29-32, 251-254
decisions, severance of, 27
error of law, 26
exclusion of jurisdiction, 25, 539-540
exhaustion of alternative remedies, 25,
  538-539
impact on planning system, 40-42, 537-538
inherent power of review, 22
natural justice, 28, 39-40
personal bar, 34-39
petition for, 28
principles of, 24-28
procedural irregularity, 28, 32-34
  mandatory or directory requirements,
    32-34
remedies, 28
title and interest to sue, 24, 25, 540-542
void or voidable, 27, 28

Land

acquisition. *See* 'Acquisition of land'
entry on, 292
incapable of reasonably beneficial use,
  366-369
meaning, 399

Listed buildings

alteration of, 435, 438
ancient monuments, 436
building preservation notice, 432, 437-438
building preservation order, 431
compensation—
  building preservation notice, loss due to,
    437-438
  compulsory acquisition, on, 445
  minimum compensation direction, 445
  refusal, etc. of listed building consent,
    443
compulsory acquisition, 403, 444
Crown land, 169, 436-437
demolition, 435, 436, 438, 441
development affecting setting of, 199, 446
ecclesiastical buildings, 436
effect of listing, 431, 435
enforcement of control, 441-442
grants and loans, 445
listed building consent—
  appeal against refusal or conditional
    grant, 441
  application for, 438
  necessity for, 438
  procedure, 438-441
  revocation or modification, 442-443
listing', 431, 432-435
offences, 431, 435
planning authorities, application of control
  to, 441
puchase notice, 373, 443
relation with other controls, 438, 446-447
repairs notice, 444-445
special architectural interest, 434-435
'spot listing', 431
works urgently required, 435, 443-444

Local authorities. *See* 'Planning authorities'
blight, where land allocated for purposes
  of, 407, 409
delegation of powers to committees and
  officials, 35-39, 49
development by, 171, 273
distribution of functions, 44, 45
internal functioning, 48-50
pattern of authorities following local
  government reorganisation, 43, 44

Local inquiry. *See* 'Public inquiries'

Local plan. *See* 'Development plans'

Maladministration

by government department, 53, 54
by local authority, 55-57
meaning of, 54, 57 *n*

Material change of use. *See* 'Development'

Material considerations

advertisement control, 456
alternative sites, 224-225
amenity, 215
application for listed building consent, 439
application for planning permission, 212 *et seq.*
circulars, etc., 221-222
comfort and convenience of occupants, 225-226
compatability with other uses, 215-216
definition, 212-214
economic and financial considerations, 218-221
existing rights and planning history, 222-223
need, 224
personal circumstances and attributes, 225
precedent, 217
private interests, 216
retaining the existing use, 216-217
safety, 218
social considerations, 223-224

Minerals

aftercare conditions, 232, 475-476
compensation, 364, 472-474
definition, 122, 476-477
development, working constitutes, 122-123, 469
development by mineral undertakers permitted under G.D.O., 182
mineral waste tips, working of, 122, 476-477
mineral operations, 122-123, 469-477
adaptations of 1972 Act, 471-477
compensation, 472-474
discontinuance, 376, 470
duration of permission, 232, 266, 471-472
duty to review, 472-474
enforcement action, 470
prohibition order, 474-475
suspension order, 474-475
time for commencement, 471

Mining operations. *See* 'Development' and 'Minerals'

Modification of planning permission. *See* 'Revocation or modification of planning permission'

National planning guidelines

benefits of, 66, 67
current guidelines, 66
objectives of, 64

Natural justice

application to quash planning decisions, 28, 39-40, 481, 483-484, 489, 510-511
public inquiries, 40, 481, 483-484, 510-511
written submissions, 40, 481, 483-484, 489

Neighbour notification, 195-197, 266, 487

New towns

land blighted by designation order, 409
special development orders, 62, 184

Non-statutory policy statements, 73, 97, 211

draft development plans, 114, 210-211
supplementary development guidance, 113, 114
validity of, 97, 112-115

Objection procedures. *See* 'Appeals'

Office

office development permits, 478
Use Classes Order, 157

Oil-related development. *See* 'Industry'

Outdoor advertisement. *See* 'Advertisements'

Outline planning permission. *See* 'Planning permission'

Painting

exterior of building, 178

Parliamentary Commissioner for Administration, 53, 54

Peat

working, permitted development, 182

Personal bar. *See* 'Judicial review'

Pipelines, 70, 171, 173

construction of, 171

Planning advice notes, 69-71
current advice notes, 71

Planning and other controls
relation between, 26, 27, 227-230, 355

Planning authorities
procedural irregularity; whether decision
  binding, 34-39
delegation to officials, 35-39, 49
development by, 171, 182, 199, 273
discharge of functions, 45, 48-50
district planning authority, 45, 543
  functions, 45, 46, 47
extent of jurisdiction, 47, 48
general planning authority, 45, 543
  functions, 45
negligence, 21
personal bar, 34-39
powers and duties, 45-47
powers to require information, 187, 292
regional planning authority, 45, 543
  functions, 45, 46

Planning blight. *See* 'Blight notice'

Planning Inquiry Commission
constitution, 517-518
local inquiry, 517
procedure on reference to, 517-518
reference to, 268

Planning permission
abandonment of, 270
application for—
  acknowledgement, 200
  'bad neighbour' development, 197-198
  'call in' by Secretary of State, 202
  certificates, 193-194, 196, 200
  conservation area, affecting, 199, 448
  consultations by planning authority,
    204-205
  determination   whether   required,
    164-166
  development contrary to development
    plan, 199, 208-210
  development plan, provisions of, 207-210
  directions as to dealing with, 209
  duty to determine, 260
  fee, 199-200
  form of, 187, 188, 190
  listed building, affecting the setting of,
    199, 446
  'material considerations', 205, 206, 212
    et seq.
  matters   relevant   to   determination,
    205-206

  notification of neighbours, 195-197
  notification of owners and agricultural
    tenants, 193-194
  notification of owners of mineral rights,
    193, 477
  notification   of   Secretary   of   State,
    201-202, 208-209
  outline, 186-187, 188-189
  press advertisement, 197, 198
  publicity,   when   required,   194-195,
    197-199
  representations on, 194, 195, 199, 205,
    206
  reserved matters, 188, 189-191
  retrospective permission, 187, 257
  variation of application, 187-188, 191
'call in' by regional authority, 202-204, 209
conditions—
  application for consent under, 188, 192
  aftercare, 232, 475-476
  breach of, 173, 290, 298, 313, 314-315
  commencement of development, 232,
    261-265
  factors beyond the applicant's control,
    238-241, 245
  financial   and   other   requirements,
    243-246
  limited period permission, 232, 256
  must not be unreasonable, 238-246, 396
  must relate to development permitted,
    235-238
  must relate to planning considerations,
    233-235
  necessity, 247
  occupancy restrictions, 234-235
  'permitted   development',   excluding,
    172, 173
  power to impose, 231-233
  reasons for, 261
  reserved matters, 188, 189-191, 257-258
  restricting 'existing use' rights, 241-243,
    375, 391
  severance of invalid, 248-250
  suspensive, 239-240
  tests for, 233 *et seq.*
  tree preservation, 232, 461-462
  uncertainty, 246
  Use Classes Order, restricting, 242
decision of planning authority—
  departing from the terms of the applica-
    tion, 254-255
  generally, 259-261
  notice of, 259
  time limits for giving, 259-260
deemed refusal of, 260
deemed to be granted, 171, 452
development orders, under, 171-184
  Article 4 direction, 183-184, 356, 386-387

conditions and limitations on, 172, 173
    variation of terms of, 183, 387-388
    standard conditions, 173, 174
discretion, exercise of, 206, 207, 251-254,
    284-285
effect of, 256-257, 268-271
enterprise zones, 6, 62, 184, 272
hazardous substances, 156, 173
health care facilities, authorisation for, 429
industrial development certificate, 477-478
interpretation of, 271-272
'lawful use', 168
local authorities, development by. *See*
    'Local authorities' and 'Planning
    authorities'
modification of. *See* 'Revocation or
    modification of planning permission'
necessity for, 116
not required, 167, 168
outline, 257-259
    time limits on, 258-259, 262-265
personal, 256
planning authority, development by. *See*
    'Planning authorities'
refinery authorisation, necessity for, 429
refusal or conditional grant of—
    appeal against. *See* 'Appeals'
    compensation. *See* 'Compensation'
    purchase notice. *See* 'Purchase notice'
renewal of time-limited, 265
reserved matters, 257-259, 263-265
revocation of. *See* 'Revocation or modifica-
    tion of planning permission'
statutory undertakers, development by,
    171
temporary, 256
time limits upon, 200, 256, 261-265
    appeal against, 264
    compensation, 265
    completion notice, 265-266
variation of, 192, 380

Planning unit

enforcement notices and, 307-309
identification of, 127-133
relevance of, 117, 126, 127

Public inquiries. *See* 'Appeals'

adjournment, 500, 515
administrative guidance, 481, 484-485, 491,
    495-496, 497, 510
advertisements, 457, 459
appearances at, 496-497
appointed person—
    delegated classes of appeals, 490
    duties of, 486, 489, 496, 513-514
    powers of, 486, 496, 497, 498, 500, 501
award of expenses, 491, 500, 514-516

cross-examination, 498-499
decision following, 480, 481, 511-513, 514
evidence at, 501
Franks Report, 482, 484, 503
function of, 479-480, 499
government departments, representatives
    of, 495, 496-497
government policy, 495, 499, 516
hearing, 481, 491
judicial safeguards, 481, 492
local plans, 491
    Code of Practice, 491
natural justice, rules of, 481, 483-484,
    510-511
new evidence after inquiry, 507-511, 513,
    514
notice of, 493-494
notification of decision, 511-513, 514
Planning Inquiry Commission, 268,
    517-518
power to dispense with, 486, 488
procedural rules, 481, 482, 490, 491
procedural meetings, 496
procedure—
    after inquiry, 502-504
    at inquiry, 496-502
    prior to inquiry, 493-496
re-opening, 508, 513
report, 503
reporter, 485
    duties of, 485, 489, 496, 503-507
    powers of, 496, 497, 498, 500, 501
    Secretary of State disagreeing with,
        507-511
site inspection, 502
statements to be served prior to inquiry,
    493, 494-495, 496

Public participation. *See* 'Development
plans'

Purchase notice

acceptance of, 370
blight notice, distinguished from, 407
compensation, 373, 379, 393
discontinuance order, 373, 379
form of, 370
grounds for serving, 365, 373
incapable of reasonably beneficial use,
    366-369
listed buildings, 373, 443
procedure, 370
refusal, etc. of planning permission, on,
    354, 365, 371-372, 393
refusal to purchase, reasons, 370
revocation or modification of planning
    permission, 373, 385

Secretary of State—
confirmation by, 370-371, 372
reference to, 370
refusal to confirm, 371, 372
service of, 370
validity, challenge of, 371, 521 *et seq.*

Refuse

deposit of, as development, 162, 163

Regional planning authority. *See* 'Planning authorities'

Regional report

effect of, 110, 111
local plan, and, 101
preparation, 109, 110
purposes of, 109
Secretary of State—
directions, 110, 111
observations, 110

Register

enforcement notices, stop notices and waste land notices, 310, 340, 347, 469
established use certificates, 320
land holdings, of, 403
Notices of Proposed Development, 170
orders under s.18(7) of 1972 Act, of, 78
planning applications, 261
structure and local plans, of, 79, 94, 107

Reporter. *See* 'Public inquiries'

Revocation or modification of planning permission

compensation, 383-385
development order, changes to, 183-184, 380, 386-388
extent of power, 380-381
procedure, 381-382
purchase notice, 373, 385
regional planning authority, by, 382
unopposed, 385
validity of order, 382, 521 *et seq.*
variation of planning permission, 380

Road

formation of access to, 122
land blighted by proposals, 408, 409
stopping up and diversion of, 274-275

Scottish Development Department, 51

national planning guidelines, 64-67
planning advice notes, 69-71
planning circulars, 67-69, 546-550

Secretary of State for Scotland, 50-52

directions made by, 551-552
national planning policy, development of, 58 *et seq. And see* 'Circulars, National planning guidelines, planning advice notes' and 'Town planning legislation'

Sheriff

appeal to, minimum compensation direction, 445
application on listed buildings compulsory purchase order, 444-445
general supervisory jurisdiction, lack of, 22

Shop

division of, 132
'permitted development', 178
Use Classes Order, 157

Simplified planning zones, 6, 61, 63

Sixth Schedule development

classes of, 388-391
compensation for restrictions on, 356, 384, 391-393

Statutory application to quash. *See* 'Court of Session' and 'Judicial review'

'aggrieved person', 528-530
breach of procedural rules, 482
decision of Secretary of State—
enforcement appeal, on, 521
established use certificate, on, 320
planning and related appeals, on, 268, 521
purchase notice, on, 371, 521
discontinuance order, 378, 521
exclusion of courts' jurisdiction, 519-520, 533-536
grounds of challenge, 522-528
'Ashbridge' formula, 524-526
outwith statutory powers, 522-526
statutory requirements, non-compliance with, 521, 522-523, 524-528
substantial prejudice, 527-528
local plan, 106, 520-521
order revoking or modifying planning permission, 382, 521
powers of Court of Session, 530-532
quashing, effect of, 27, 532-533
structure plan, 93, 520-521
time limits upon application, 519-520, 533-536
tree preservation order, 521, 531 *n*

Statutory undertakers

blight notice, where land allocated for purposes of, 407, 409
development by, 171, 274
works not classed as development, 122

Stop notice

compensation for loss due to, 347
contravention of, 346
effect of, 344, 345
power to serve, 344-345
procedure, 345
withdrawal, 347

Structure plan. *See* 'Development plans'

Town planning legislation

English and Welsh legislation, differences, 4, 18, 19
historical development of, 8-11
implementation of policy, 62, 63
objectives of, 1-3
principal features of, 13 *et seq.*
reliance on in preference to other legislation, 26, 27, 227-230, 355
sub-delegated legislation, 63

Trees

conditions as to, 232, 461-462
conservation area, in, 451, 467-468
felling licence, 465
felling of, not development, 461
replacement of, 462, 465, 466-467, 468
tree preservation orders—
appeal under, 464, 466-467
compensation, 462, 467
confirmation, 464
consents under, 464-465
Crown land, 463
enforcement, 466-467
form of, 463
objections to, 464
offences, 466
power to make, 461, 462
procedure for making, 463
provisional, 464
scope of, 462-463
validity, 521 *et seq.*

Ultra vires. *See* 'Court of Session', 'Judicial review' and 'Statutory application to quash'

Use

abandonment of, 142, 143, 270
ancillary, 129, 130, 147-151
agricultural. *See* 'Agriculture'

deposit of refuse, 162, 163
discontinuance of, not development, 141, 142
discontinuance order. *See* 'Discontinuance order'
established. *See* 'Established use'
'existing use' rights—
abandonment of, 142, 143, 270
conditions restricting, 241-243, 375
extinguishment, 144-147, 374
material consideration, 222-223
industrial. *See* 'Industry'
intensification of, 139, 140
'lawful', 168
material change of. *See* 'Development'
multiple uses, 147-152
occasional use, 167, 178-179
'operations' distinguished from, 116, 117
primary, 125, 147-151
resumption of former, 142
seasonal or periodic, 143, 144
temporary, 178-179
time when change occurs, 140, 141

Use classes order, 51, 60, 61, 155-161

change within not development, 155-161
condition restricting operation of, 160, 161, 242
incidental use, 160
intensification of use, and, 156
planning unit, 159, 160

Uthwatt Committee, 2

compensation and betterment, on, 11

Validity of planning decisions, challenge of.
See 'Court of Session', 'Judicial review' and 'Statutory application to quash'

Walls

permitted development, 178

Waste land

appeal, 469
buildings, ruinous or dilapidated, 468
land, derelict, waste or neglected, 468-469
register, 469